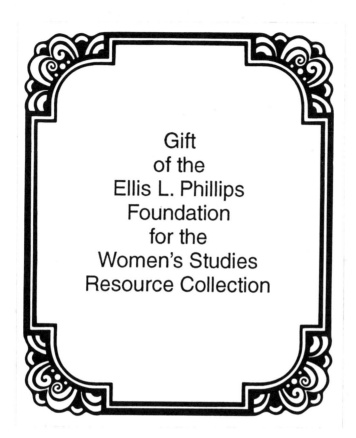

United States Government Documents on Women, 1800–1990

United States Government Documents on Women, 1800–1990

A Comprehensive Bibliography

Volume I: Social Issues

MARY ELLEN HULS

Bibliographies and Indexes in Women's Studies,
Number 17

Greenwood Press
Westport, Connecticut • London

Z
7964
.U49
H85
1993
v. 1
C.1

2685479

Library of Congress Cataloging-in-Publication Data

Huls, Mary Ellen.
 United States government documents on women, 1800-1990 : a
comprehensive bibliography / Mary Ellen Huls.
  p.   cm.—(Bibliographies and indexes in women's studies,
ISSN 0742-6941 ; no. 17)
 Includes bibliographical references and index.
 Contents: v. 1. Social issues.
  1. Women—United States—History—Sources—Bibliography.
  2. Women—United States—Social conditions—Sources—Bibliography.
  3. Women—Employment—United States—History—Sources—Bibliography.
 I. Title. II. Series.
 Z7964.U49H85   1993
 [HQ1410]
 016.3054—dc20   92-38990

ISBN 0-313-29016-4 (alk. paper : set)
ISBN 0-313-26712-X (alk. paper: vol. 1)
ISBN 0-313-28157-2 (alk. paper : vol. 2)

British Library Cataloguing in Publication Data is available.

Library of Congress Catalog Card Number: 92-38990
ISBN: 0-313-29016-4 (set)
ISBN: 0-313-26712-X (vol. 1)
ISBN: 0-313-28157-2 (vol. 2)
ISSN: 0742-6941

First published in 1993

Greenwood Press, 88 Post Road West, Westport, CT 06881
An imprint of Greenwood Publishing Group, Inc.

Printed in the United States of America

The paper used in this book complies with the
Permanent Paper Standard issued by the National
Information Standards Organization (Z39.48-1984).

10 9 8 7 6 5 4 3

To the women of my family

Contents

Acknowledgments

Many people contributed to the completion of this volume and deserve credit for their assistance. Without the advice and support of Marilyn Moody and David Tyckoson this project would never have started. To Lorna Petersen, who kept telling me I would finish and it would be worth the effort, I owe my deepest gratitude. Kathy Parsons lent not only her moral support, but her keyboarding skills as well. The support of Iowa State University during the first three years of work was essential. I would also like to thank Janet Kinney and the staff of the College of St. Catherine Library who put up with a very distracted department head during the final year's work. Thanks also go to the documents department staff at the University of Minnesota and the University of Iowa, and to the interlibrary loan and circulation staff at the Iowa State University Library. Many more people deserve recognition for their assistance and support, among them Pam Williams, Tammy Lusher, Ellie Matthews, Lisa Gilbert, Todd Johnston, Deloris Savard, Mary Bye, and the staff of the Center for Legislative Archives.

Introduction

Public documents of the United States government have covered the problems of American women since the early 1800s. They provide factual information on the status of women, and reflect the government's perception of women's role in society. The nearly 7,000 documents described in the two volumes of this bibliography represent most of the published reports of agencies, commissions, and Congress on women or on topics directly affecting women's health and welfare. The bibliography is intended to facilitate identification of government documents on women past and present. In so doing, it also provides some historical perspective on government interest in contemporary issues such as day care, child support, and women's health. Coverage of the bibliography extends from 1800 through 1990. While an effort was made to identify as many 1990 documents as possible, the significant lag time between publication and listing of a document in the *Monthly Catalog of United States Government Publications* precluded the inclusion of documents from 1991.

SCOPE

Documents were identified using the *Monthly Catalog*, *The Cumulative Title Index to United States Public Documents, 1789-1976*, the *CIS US Serial Set Index*, the *CIS US Congressional Committee Hearings Index*, the *CIS Annual*, and the *Checklist of U.S. Public Documents, 1789-1976*. Most of the documents identified were obtainable from nearby regional depository libraries. Approximately four hundred documents which could not be located elsewhere were obtained from the National Archives. The National Archives, Center for Legislative Archives, Record Group 287 is the archival collection of the publications distributed through the Government Printing Office.

The decision to include or exclude a document from the bibliography was based on a number of factors. Documents devoted entirely to women or to a closely-related topic were automatically included regardless of length. In many instances, particularly in the case of congressional hearings, the decision to include a document was based on the portion of the document devoted to women's issues. Hundreds of hearings published in the last twenty years which include some discussion of women as part of a longer hearing were not included. These hearings can be easily identified, however, by using the *CIS Annual*, a detailed index to congressional documents. Among the hearings generally excluded from the bibliography were appropriations hearings. Anyone researching government-sponsored programs should check the appropriations hearings for the responsible agency.

Certain classes of documents were automatically eliminated from the bibliography. Publications issued as ERIC documents were excluded since they are fully abstracted and indexed in *Resources in Education* and its widely available electronic versions. Technical reports and most reprints of journal articles were also eliminated. A few additional documents were dropped after extensive efforts to obtain a copy proved unsuccessful.

ORGANIZATION

The bibliography was initially conceived as one volume of approximately 3,000 entries. When it became obvious that the number of entries would be closer to 7,000, the decision was made to split the bibliography into two volumes. The first volume covers general works and social issues. Among the subjects represented are women's rights, contraception and maternity, health, public assistance, and retirement income. The second volume describes documents related to women in paid employment. Topics covered in volume two include protective labor legislation, affirmative action, federal employment and training programs, vocational counseling, and day care. Persons researching labor issues should consult both volumes, however, since volume one includes the hearings on the Equal Rights Amendment and the general reports on the status of women, many of which discuss labor issues at length.

The documents in each volume are grouped into chapters by subject. A short introduction precedes the bibliographic entries and highlights documents of particular note. Entries within each chapter are arranged first in chronological order and then by issuing agency. Serials are listed at the end of each chapter. Many documents covered more than one topic and could have been included in any of several chapters. In this case the document was listed in the chapter of the predominant topic. Use of the subject index is essential to locate all documents on a topic.

BIBLIOGRAPHIC ENTRIES

To facilitate the arrangement of the bibliography, the governmental body which produced the document is listed as the corporate author for all entries. Personal authors and non-government corporate authors are listed after the title. Information on the number of pages is provided as a convenience to aid in the identification of documents and as a guide in estimating photocopy or interlibrary loan charges. The page numbers do not represent an exact collation. Most entries for agency documents also include a Superintendent of Documents, or SuDoc, number. SuDoc numbers are assigned by the Government Printing Office and are the primary method used to arrange the documents collection in most U.S. depository libraries. Entries for House and Senate reports cite a volume of the *U.S. Serial Set* in lieu of a SuDoc number.

A few documents are cited for which no SuDoc number could be identified. Congressional hearings with no SuDoc number include a number preceded by either Greenwood or CIS. The Greenwood number is a reference number in the microfiche set *U.S. Congressional Committee Hearings on Microfiche*, produced by the CIS Greenwood Press division. Numbers beginning with CIS refer to the microfiche set which accompanies the *CIS Annual*, the *CIS Microfiche Library*.

Abbreviations and initialisms are used throughout the bibliography in order to save space. A separate List of Abbreviations may be found following this Introduction to the Bibliography.

SOME FINAL THOUGHTS

Attempting to provide an overview of nearly two hundred years of government publishing on women within the space of this introduction would be a futile task, but a few general observations are possible. The pre-1900 documents are almost entirely the work of Congress. Although the topics are limited by the legislation under consideration, these documents do provide an interesting glimpse of the congressional view of woman. In particular, the documents on woman suffrage and on military widows' pensions are revealing in their discussions of good women, bad women, and the proper role of woman in society.

By 1920 the Children's Bureau, the Women's Bureau, and the Office of Education were major producers of documents relating to women. World War Two inspired a wealth of publications from a wide variety of agencies. The 1960s and 1970s were notable for the establishment of special commissions and councils on women, from which a number of excellent documents were issued. During their glory years in the 1970s, the Commission on Civil Rights and the Equal Employment Opportunity Commission produced many substantial documents on the issues affecting women's lives.

In the last decade government publishing on women has come nearly full circle. By the late 1980s the documents were again predominantly congressional, supplemented by a steady stream of reports from the Bureau of the Census and from health-related agencies. Only a trickle of publications were coming out of the Women's Bureau, once a prolific producer of substantial reports, and the embattled Commission on Civil Rights had turned its focus away from women's issues.

In spite of the cutbacks, government documents continue to be an important source of information on women. It is my hope that those who use this bibliography to locate past documents on women will be inspired to seek out and include the newer documents in their future research.

List of Abbreviations

Some of the common abbreviations used in the Bibliography, and other shortened notations are listed below.

AA- affirmative action
AB - Aid to the Blind
ACLU - American Civil Liberties Union
ADAMHA - Alcohol, Drug Abuse, and Mental Health Administration
ADC - Aid to Dependent Children
AFDC - Aid to Families with Dependent Children
AID - Agency for International Development
APTD - Aid to the Permanently and Totally Disabled
BLS - Bureau of Labor Statistics
CETA - Comprehensive Employment and Training Act
CFR - Code of Federal Regulations
CIS - Congressional Information Service
Cong. - Congress
CRS - Congressional Research Service
DAR - Daughters of the American Revolution
DBE - Disadvantaged Business Enterprise
DES - Diethylstilbestrol
Doc. - Document
DoD - Department of Defense
EEO - equal employment opportunity
EEOC - Equal Employment Opportunity Commission
ERA - Equal Rights Amendment
Ex - Executive
FAA - Federal Aviation Administration
FCC - Federal Communications Commission
FDA - Food and Drug Administration
FLSA - Fair Labor Standards Act
FWP - Federal Women's Program
GAO - General Accounting Office
GPO - Government Printing Office
GS - General Schedule
GSA - General Services Administration
H. Rept. - House Report
HEW - Department of Health, Education, and Welfare
HHS - Department of Health and Human Services

HRA - Health Resources Administration
IHS - Indian Health Service
ILO - International Labor Organization
IRS - Internal Revenue Service
JEDI -Jobs for Employable Dependent Individuals program
JTPA - Job Training Partnership Act
LDC - lesser developed country
LEAA - Law Enforcement Assistance Administration
MBE - Minority Business Enterprise
MDTA - Manpower Development and Training Act
MOS - Military Occupational Specialty
NCI - National Cancer Institute
NIAAA - National Institute on Alcohol Abuse and Alcoholism
NICHD - National Institute of Child Health and Human Development
NIDA - National Institute on Drug Abuse
NIH - National Institutes of Health
NIMH - National Institute of Mental Health
NIOSH - National Institute of Occupational Safety and Health
NLRB - National Labor Relations Board
NRA - National Recovery Administration
NSF - National Science Foundation
OAA - Old-Age Assistance
OASDHI - Old-Age, Survivors, Disability, and Health Insurance
OASI - Old-Age and Survivors Insurance
OEO - Office of Economic Opportunity
OFCCP - Office of Federal Contract Compliance Programs
OMB - Office of Management and Budget
OPM - Office of Personnel Management
OWI - Office of War Information
PHS - Public Health Service
PHSA - Public Health Services Act
S. Rept. - Senate Report
SBA - Small Business Administration
sess. - session
SMSA - Standard Metropolitan Statistical Area
SSA - Social Security Act
SSI - Supplemental Security Insurance
Title VII - Civil Rights Act of 1964, Title VII
Title IX - Education Amendments of 1972, Title IX
Title X - Public Health Services Act, Title X
Title XX - Social Security Act, Title XX
UN - United Nations
USDA - United States Department of Agriculture
USIA - United States Information Agency
VA - Veterans Administration
WAAC - Women's Army Auxiliary Corps
WAC - Women's Army Corps
WASP - Women's Airforce Service Pilots
WBE - Women's Business Enterprise
WEEA - Women's Educational Equity Act
WG - Wage Grade
WIC - Supplemental Food Program for Women, Infants and Children
WIN - Work Incentive Program
WPA - Works Progress Administration or Works Projects Administration

1

General Works on Women

This general chapter lists publications describing the lives of women in the United States and detailing international efforts to promote the status of women. Some miscellaneous publications are also included here. Several of the documents provide excellent overviews of the issues affecting women at the time they were published. The earliest of these is volume II of a fascinating series of hearings on *Relations between Labor and Capitol* (1). Almost every social issue of 1883 is discussed at some point as witnesses touch on everything from woman suffrage to dress reform. The next comprehensive overview of women in the U.S. doesn't appear until 1954 when a report on American women was issued for the Inter-American Commission on the Status of Women (42). *Spotlight on Women in the United States, 1956-57* (46) provides a good statistical review of women's economic status.

The establishment in 1962 of the President's Commission on the Status of Women resulted in intense scrutiny of the status of American women and the issues affecting their lives. The commission report, *American Women* (56), reviews the commission's findings and presents its recommendations for change. Conferences of the state commissions also provide good overviews of progress and remaining problems from the 1960s point of view (73, 78, 82). A follow-up report to *American Women* was issued in 1968 by the Interdepartmental Committee on the Status of Women and the Citizens Advisory Council on the Status of Women (80). The National Commission on the Observance of International Women's Year issued a number of reports in 1977 and 1978, including *American Women Today and Tomorrow* which reports the results of a survey on women's lives and attitudes (116). In *The Spirit of Houston*, the lengthy report of the National Women's Conference, the enthusiasm of the conference is expressed and the details of the National Plan of Action are presented (133). In 1979 the Senate Labor and Human Resources Committee held hearings on the issues facing women in the 1980s and explored their relevance to federal policies and progress (141-142). Several longitudinal studies of women highlighting marital status, employment histories, activities, and future plans are reported. The first of these studied college graduates of 1945 (57), the second looked at the Class of 1957 (74), and the third, the Longitudinal Survey of Mature Women, began in 1967 (130).

The economic problems of women were the focus of a number of documents beginning in the early 1970s. The effect of sex discrimination and employment patterns on women's economic status are explored in Congressional hearings held between 1974 and 1982 (92, 97, 171), and by the mid-1970s Congress had discovered older women and their problems. Select Committee on Aging reports and hearings are revealing in their discussion of women at midlife and beyond (126, 127, 140, 169, 170). Federal policies and legislation affecting women over 40 are detailed in the Administration on Aging report, *The Direction of Federal Legislation Affecting Women over Forty* (168). The problems of older women continued to be a concern of Congress through the 1980s as evidenced in a 1988 hearing on *The Quality of Life for Older Women: Women Living Alone* (188-189).

International efforts to focus attention on the lives of women are also revealed in U.S. documents starting with the report of the 2d Pan American Scientific Congress (7) held in 1916 and continuing with the reports on the Inter-American Commission of Women (21, 25, 30) issued between 1944 and 1949. The work of the United Nations Commission on the Status of Women figures in documents published in 1959 (50-51). The activities of International Women's Year in 1975 (98) and the United Nations Decade for Women are detailed in congressional and Department of State publications (150, 165, 187). Additional publications on the status of women are listed in Chapter 4, Discrimination and Women's Rights, and documents on women in other countries and on the politics of the U.N. Decade for Women are included in Chapter 21.

1.   U.S. Congress. Senate. Committee on Education and Labor. *Relations between Labor and Capital, Report and Testimony Taken by the Committee, Volume II: Testimony.* 47th Cong., 2d sess., 1883. 1412p. Y4.Ed8/3:L11/2.   Testimony covers a wide array of topics including labor unions, income tax, transportation of good, tariffs, living conditions of workers, and education of workers and children.   Specifically related to women is testimony on the desirability of practical design education for women, wages, woman suffrage, guardianship of children, jail matrons, women in the civil service, trade education, and the problems of working girls.   Women and training in housework, dress reform, and the Women's Christian Temperance Union are also topics of testimony.

2.   U.S. Congress. House. Committee on the Territories. *Marriage in Territory of Utah, Report to Accompany Bill H.R. 6765.* H. Rept. 1351, part 1, 48th Cong., 1st sess., 1884. 4p. Serial 2257.   Report on a bill providing for the registration of all marriages in Utah territory so as to discourage the practice of polygamy.   Reviews the extent of the practice in the Utah territory.

3.   U.S. Congress. House. Committee on the Judiciary. *Polygamy, Report to Accompany H. Res. 176 [to Amend the Constitution to Prohibit Polygamy].* H. Rept. 2568, 49th Cong., 1st sess., 1886. 12p. Serial 2442.   Report reviews the history of the Church of Jesus Christ of Latter Day Saints (Mormon) and examines the right of the federal government to legislate relative to marriage and divorce.

4.   U.S. Congress. House. Committee on the Judiciary. *Polygamy.* 57th Cong., 1st sess., 25 Feb. 1902. 17p. Y4.J89/1:P76.   Hearing on a proposed amendment to the constitution prohibiting polygamy does not specifically address how polygamy affects women although, according to the hearing, the amendment was sought primarily by women's organizations "in defense of womanhood."

5.   Pan American Scientific Congress. *[Program] 2d Pan American Scientific Congress: Women's Auxiliary Conference.* Washington, DC: GPO, 1915. 14p. S5.14/2:14P94/1e.   Topics of sessions and featured speakers are listed in the conference program along with receptions and other related events during the Women's Auxiliary Conference of the 2d Pan American Scientific Congress.   A second edition was also published in 1915, and two Spanish editions were issued.

6.   U.S. Dept. of Agriculture. Office of the Secretary. *Social and Labor Needs of Farm Women.* USDA Report no. 103. Washington, DC: GPO, 1915. 100p. A1.8:103.   The lives of farm women are revealed in excerpts from letters written by farm women and men in response to a request for information on how the USDA could improve its services to women.   Throughout the letters runs a common theme of isolation, backbreaking work,

and the lack of available hired help. Also noted is the need for telephone service and better roads.

7. Pan American Scientific Congress. Women's Auxiliary Conference. *Report on Women's Auxiliary Conference Held in Washington in U.S.A. in Connection with 2d Pan American Scientific Congress, Dec. 28, 1915 - Jan. 7, 1916.* by Mrs. Glen Levin Swiggett. Washington, DC: GPO, 1916. 73p. S5.14/2:14R29. Report describes the women-related topics covered at past Latin America Scientific Congresses and the organization of the Women's Auxiliary Conference of the Second Pan American Scientific Congress. Provides abstracts of papers presented on the patriotism of women, the Latin American woman, changes in the education of U.S. southern women, women in Argentina, libraries, and standards of living. Education and women's work in social progress are common themes.

8. Pan American Scientific Congress. Women's Auxiliary Committee of the United States. *The Women's Auxiliary Committee of the United States of the Second Pan American Scientific Congress.* Washington, DC: The Committee, 1917. 6p. leaflet. S5.14/2:14P94/3e. Summary of the Women's Auxiliary Conference of the Second Pan American Scientific Congress briefly describes the organization of the conference, the resolutions adopted, and the progress made in establishing an International Committee to further the cooperation of women in the American republics.

9. U.S. Women's Bureau. *Home Environment and Employment Opportunities of Women in Coal-Mine Workers' Families.* Bulletin no. 45. Washington, DC: GPO, 1925. 61p. L13.3:45. Study conducted by the Women's Bureau and the Coal Commission looks at the communities and living conditions of coal-mine worker's families with particular emphasis on the lives of wives and daughters. Employment of wives and daughters, and their contributions to the family in terms of money and household duties, are examined.

10. U.S. Children's Bureau. *Welfare of Prisoners' Families in Kentucky.* Publication no. 182. Washington, DC: GPO, 1928. 50p. L5.20:182. Kentucky family case studies reveal family conditions before and during the father's imprisonment. Factors examined include martial status of parents, employment of father and mother prior to incarceration, and source of support for families after incarceration of father.

11. U.S. Congress. Senate. Committee on the Library. *Statute in Honor of the America Mother and Other Patriotic Women of the United States, Report to Accompany S.J. Res. 246.* S. Rept. 1486, 71st Cong., 3d sess., 1931. 1p. Serial 9323.

12. U.S. Extension Service. *Social and Economic Problems of Farm Girl.* by Gertrude L. Warren. Circular no. 159. Washington, DC: The Service, 1931. 33p. A43.5/6:159. Paper presented at the Eastern States Regional Extension Conference, New Brunswick, New Jersey, outlines the effect of a rapidly changing society on the desires and temptations of rural teenage girls. Lack of suitable leisure activities and an unhappy home atmosphere are seen as contributors to rural youth problems. Home extension personnel are viewed as essential in teaching the young wife household economy so that her farmer husband can some day buy a farm. The quality of education available to rural girls, their reasons for leaving school, and their vocational education needs are discussed. The fact that many rural girls will seek work in the city and the need to prepare them for that experience is also examined.

13. U.S. Smithsonian Institution. *The Narrative of a Southern Cheyenne Woman.* Smithsonian Collections vol. 87, no. 5. Washington, DC: The Institution, 1932. 13p. SI1.7:87/5. An account of the life of a Cheyenne woman describes her girlhood and her life as a wife and as a widow. Provides insight into the sexual mores proscribing the behavior of a young Cheyenne woman.

14.   U.S. Women's Bureau. *America Will Be as Strong as Her Women.* Washington, DC: The Bureau, 1938. poster. L13.9:Am3.

15.   U.S. Office of Education. *Gallant American Women [#2], Women and Peace, November 7, 1939.* by Jane Ashman. Washington, DC: The Office, 1939. 20p. FS5.15:2. Script for a radio broadcast highlights women's work for peace from an Iroquois woman in pre-Colonial America to Clara Barton. Stresses women's knowledge of the cost of war learned through personal sacrifice.

16.   U.S. Office of Education. *Gallant American Women #3, Women on the Land, November 14, 1939.* Washington, DC: The Office, 1939. 24p. FS5.15:3. Radio script tells the story of women as pioneers and farmers from the Indians who helped the colonists to those struggling to survive in the dust bowl days in Oklahoma.

17.   U.S. Office of Education. *Gallant American Women #16, [Fashions in Sentiment], February 13, 1940.* by Jane Ashman. Washington, DC: The Office, 1940. 22p. FS15:16. Traditions in selecting a husband are the focus of the vignettes in the sixteenth episode of "Gallant American Women." A list of resources consulted is included.

18.   U.S. Office of Education. *Gallant American Women #21, Women and Fashion, March 19, 1940.* by Jane Ashman. Washington, DC: The Office, 1940. 27p. FS5.15:21. Women as slaves of fashion is the basic theme of this radio script which stresses the ever changing nature of fashionable women's apparel. A list of research materials consulted is appended to the script.

19.   U.S. Office of Education. *Listen! Gallant American Women: Women in the Making of America, Program of Drama and History, Now Broadcast at Night on NBC Blue Network.* Washington, DC: The Office, 1940. 1p. FS5.20:G13.

20.   U.S. Extension Service. *What is the Opportunity for Farm Girl to Obtain a Successful, Happy Family Life on a Farm.* by Eugene Merritt. Circular no. 368. Washington, DC: The Service, 1941. 10p. A43.4:156. Questions which young women should address when considering life as the wife of a farmer are presented to encourage a discussion among young farm women.

21.   U.S. Women's Bureau. *Fourth Meeting of the Inter-American Commission of Women.* Washington, DC: The Bureau, 1944. 4p. L13.2:In8. Summary of the activities and resolutions of the fourth meeting of the Inter-American Commission of Women includes a photograph of the Commission, a list of representatives, and a statement on the future of the Commission by Senora Elena Mederos de Gonzales, the Cuban delegate.

22.   U.S. Children's Bureau. *Significance to Women of the Inter-American Conference on Problems of War and Peace, Mexico City.* by Katherine F. Lenroot. Washington, DC: The Bureau, 1945. 5p. L5.47:In8. Address before the Pan American Committee of Women's Organizations luncheon in honor of women delegates to the conference, held March 26, 1945, expresses hope for international cooperation and highlights the achievements and resolutions of the Mexico City Conference relating to women, children and the family.

23.   U.S. War Manpower Commission. Women's Advisory Committee. *What's Ahead for the Woman Who Earns.* Washington, DC: The Bureau, 1946. 5p. L13.12:W84/4. Speech given at a March 14, 1946 Women's Bureau conference discusses eloquently the position of women, both employees and homemakers, in a postwar world determined to undermine gains made in women's status during WWII.

24. U.S. Women's Bureau. *Report of Frieda S. Miller, Director, Women's Bureau, before Conference of Women's Organizations, March 14, 1946 on United Nations Sessions in London.* Washington, DC: The Bureau, 1946. 12p. L13.12:Un3. Report on the formation of the United Nations notes, among other things, the charge relating to women's rights given to the Commission on Human Rights of the Economic and Social Council and the establishment of a sub-commission on the status of women. Organizations requesting consultative relations with the Economic and Social Council, many of which are women's organizations, are listed.

25. Pan American Union. *Project of Organic Statute of Inter-American Commission of Women, Submitted to 9th International Conference of American States by Resolution of Governing Board of Pan American Union at Meeting of February 4, 1948.* Washington, DC: GPO, 1948. 13p. PA1.44/9:In8/9. Background on the Inter-American Commission of Women accompanies the statute setting the organization and functions of the commission within the Pan American Union.

26. Union Panamericana. *Projecto de Estatuto Organico de la Comision Interamericana de Mujeres, Sometido a la Novena Conferencia Internacional Americana por Acuerdo del Consejo Directivo de la Union Panamericana Tomado en la Sesion del 4 de Fedrero de 1948.* Washington, DC: GPO, 1948. 13p. PA1.44/9:In8/9/spanish. See 25 for abstract.

27. U.S. Women's Bureau. *Social Patterns for Women: The Present and the Prospects.* by Ordway Tead. Washington, DC: The Bureau, 1948. 9p. L13.12:Am3/7. The basic groups of working women and their need to gain recognition is the theme of this speech given at the 1948 Women's Bureau Conference, "The American Woman, Her Changing Role as Worker, Homemaker, Citizen." Tead discusses the limits on women's creativity in the modern home and at work.

28. U.S. Women's Bureau. *Women's Status, Yesterday - Today - Tomorrow: A Chapter in the History of Freedom, 1848-1948.* by C. Mildred Thompson. Washington, DC: The Bureau, 1948. 9p. L13.12:Am3/5. Speech by C. Mildred Thompson, Dean of Vassar College, given at the 1948 Women's Bureau Conference, "The American Women, Her Changing Role as Worker, Homemaker, Citizen," reviews advances in women's status since 1848. Thompson points out the lack of notable women in the sciences and the arts, and notes the pressures on women's lives which contribute to their incomplete achievement. The speech expounds at some length on the path to greater opportunities for women in higher education and on the trend towards a women's curriculum of home economics and child care.

29. U.S. Women's Bureau. *Women in the United States in Jobs, under Law, in Organizations.* Washington, DC: The Bureau, 1949. 4p. L13.2:W84/24. Summary information on the progress of women in employment, political and civil status, and trade unions briefly reviews labor legislation and lists prominent women's organizations.

30. U.S. Inter-American Commission of Women. *Report on the Extraordinary Assembly of the Inter-American Commission of Women, Buenos Aires, Argentina, August 1949.* by Mary M. Cannon. Washington, DC: The Bureau, 1950?. 6p. L13.2:In8/2. Summarizes the organization and resulting resolutions of the Extraordinary Assembly of the Inter-American Commission of Women. Resolutions relate to the legal and political status of women, education, discriminatory clauses in penal codes, and equal pay legislation.

31. U.S. Women's Bureau. *American Women: A Selected Bibliography of Basic Sources of Current and Historic Interest.* Washington, DC: The Bureau, 1950. 13p. L13.2:Am3/950. Briefly annotated list of sources on current and historic information on women as citizens, as workers, and as homemakers. Earlier edition published in 1948.

32.   U.S. Women's Bureau. *Exchange Program for Women Leaders from Germany, Suggestions and Requests to Local Sponsors.* Washington, DC: The Bureau, 1950. 3p. L13.2:W84/28 or L13.2:Ex2. Advice on planning for the visit of women leaders from Germany includes suggestions on activities during local visits. The purpose of the program was to allow women in leadership positions in Germany to observe American democracy in action and to experience the American way of life.

33.   U.S. Women's Bureau. *International Relations, the Distaff Side.* by Mary M. Cannon. Washington, DC: The Bureau, 1950. 9p. L13.12:In85. Speech given before the South Atlantic Regional Conference of the American Association of University Women describes the role of women in exchange programs to introduce German and Japanese women to American democracy. The limited roles of women in official foreign diplomacy in spite of the "natural" peacemaking skills of women are noted.

34.   U.S. Women's Bureau. *Suggestions to Sponsors of German Women Leaders, the Exchange of Persons Program.* Washington, DC: The Bureau, 1950. 4p. L13.2:Ex2/2. Details on the operation of the German women leaders exchange program provides suggestions to local sponsors on housing arrangements, entertainment, and visits to include in the local program. The purpose of the program was to broaden the women's understanding of the American way of life and to foster an appreciation of democracy.

35.   U.S. Federal Communications Commission. *Women and the Future of Broadcasting, Address by Frieda B. Hennock, Commissioner, Federal Communications Commission, before Association of Women in Radio and Television, New York City, N.Y., April 7, 1951.* Washington, DC: The Commission, 1951. 4p. CC1.15:H39/9. Commissioner Hennock encourages women in media to avoid the tendency to underestimate the interests of women, and urges them to provide more intelligent daytime programming.

36.   U.S. Women's Bureau. *Progress of Women in the United States, 1949-1951.* Washington, DC: The Bureau, 1951. 28p. L13.2:P94/949-51. Overview of the progress of women in the U.S. prepared for a report to the Inter-American Commission of Women covers topics of politics, government service, employment, education, economic and civil status, and women in the government's exchange of persons program.

37.   U.S. Women's Bureau. *Happy Time in a Happy Country.* by Rohtraut Schulz-Baesken. Washington, DC: The Bureau, 1952. 6p. L13.2:H21. Observations of Dr. Rohtraut Schulz-Baesken, who appears to have been one of the participants in the German Women Leaders Exchange program, focus on the American lifestyle, the consumerism of all classes, the role of the church, the status of workers, and the political system. Her observations on American husbands, who willingly help in the kitchen, and the attractiveness of housewives and their houses, are particularly interesting.

38.   U.S. Women's Bureau. *Status of Women in the United States, 1952.* Washington, DC: The Bureau, 1952. 15p. L13.2:St2/3. Review of the status of women in the U.S. summarizes women's rights in the areas of voting, elected office, and government service, and their opportunities in the world of paid employment. Women's position in the professions, unions, and international relations is also noted.

39.   U.S. Women's Bureau. *The Status of Women in the United States, 1953.* Bulletin no. 249. Washington, DC: GPO, 1953. 26p. L13.3:249. Summary of the status of women in the U.S. in 1953 looks at women's participation in government and politics, employment trends, opportunities in the professions, related activities of various unions and women's organizations, and recent legislation affecting women.

40. U.S. Office of Vocational Rehabilitation. *Disabled Women Rehabilitated in Fiscal Year 1952.* Rehabilitation Service Series no. 259. Washington, DC: The Office, 1954. 2p. FS13.207:259. Brief statistical overview profiles the personal and employment characteristics of disabled women rehabilitated in 1952.

41. U.S. Soil Conservation Service. *Women and Soil and Water Conservation.* by W.R. Tascher. Washington, DC: The Service, 1954. 9p. A57.25:T18. Talk given at the Women's Section of the Area Meeting of the Soil Conservation Districts, Lafayette, Indiana, reviews the role of women as land owners and community leaders in soil conservation activities. The role of home demonstration clubs in women's conservation activities and some specific programs are highlighted.

42. U.S. Women's Bureau. *Report on Status of Women in the United States, 1954, for Inter-American Commission for Women.* Washington, DC: The Bureau, 1954. 19p. L13.2:W84/33/954. Good overview of the status of women in the U.S. as of 1954 covers political participation, employment trends and opportunities, professional opportunities, labor laws, child care tax deductions, jury service, employment of older women, unions, and women's organizations. Provides a listing of women appointed to policy-making level government positions, reviews the economic status of women workers, and summarizes the status of women in the military.

43. U.S. Women's Bureau. *Conference on the Effective Use of Womanpower, March 10-11, 1955, Horizons for Women, the American Woman's Role.* by Florence Rockwood Kluckholm. Washington, DC: The Bureau, 1955. 9p. L13.2:C76/2/955-4. The contradictory pull of the domestic role of women and the women's rights movement is put into the context of the sociology of women's role as it has developed in America. Particularly stressed is the effect of the concept of businessman as the American ideal and the role of woman a culture bearer, a less-valued position.

44. U.S. Women's Bureau. *Conference on the Effective Use of Womanpower, March 10-11, 1955, Women in Transition, a Social Psychologist's Approach.* by Marie Johoda. Washington, DC: The Bureau, 1955. 2p. L13.2:C76/2/955. Briefly describes the conflicting messages sent women as traditional roles change, but some old values and mores remain.

45. U.S. Marine Corps. *Behind Every Good Man -- You Will Always Find a Good Woman.* Washington, DC: GPO, 1957. [8]p. D214.2:M31. Information for the Marine wife on helping her husband decide to reenlist.

46. U.S. Women's Bureau. *Spotlight on Women in the United States, 1956-57.* Washington, DC: GPO, 1958. 46p. L13.2:W84/35. Synthesis of statistics on women in the U.S. in 1956 and 1957 looks at changes in education, employment, and public service. Women's economic status and investments, and their participation in women's organizations and labor unions, are reviewed. Finally, the report examines changes in women's legal status and notes labor legislation of special interest such as minimum wage laws, equal pay law proposals, and Social Security.

47. U.S. Women's Bureau and U.S. Office of Vocational Rehabilitation. *Help for Handicapped Women.* Women's Bureau Pamphlet no. 5. Washington, DC: GPO, 1958. 52p. L13.19:5. Describes rehabilitation programs for handicapped women to assist them to lead useful lives whether as homemakers or as wage earners. Community resources, ways of easing the financial burden of handicapped conditions, and career opportunities in rehabilitation are reviewed.

48.   U.S. Dept. of Agriculture. *[Address by Secretary of Agriculture Ezra Taft Benson at Annual Awards Luncheon, American Mothers Committee, Inc., New York, N.Y., May 8, 1959].* Washington, DC: The Department, 1959. 15p. A1.40:B44/263. Speech exalts the role of the mother as the most important role for women and warns of the need to protect the home from internal and external threats.

49.   U.S. Post Office Dept. *Talk by Postmaster General Arthur E. Summerfield, before Annual Republican Women's Conference, Washington, DC, April 13, 1959.* Washington, DC: The Office, 1959. 8p. P1.27:Su6/6. Mostly political speech before the 1959 Republican Women's Conference highlights the employment of women in the Postal Service and notes the political issues which affect women, praising the current administration on each point.

50.   U.S. Women's Bureau. *Report of the Conference on the Status of Women around the World.* Washington, DC: The Bureau, 1959. 26p. L13.2:W84/37/959. Report of a conference held March 30, 1959 includes transcripts of panels on the political rights of women, the status of women in private law, the nationality of married women, women's access to education, and women's economic opportunities. Panelists were delegates to the U.N. Commission on the Status of Women and representative of U.S. voluntary organizations.

51.   U.S. Women's Bureau. *The UN Commission on the Status of Women, a Brief Summary of Progress.* Washington, DC: The Bureau, 1959. 9p. L13.2:W84/37/959/supp. Supplement to *Report of the Conference on the Status of Women around the World* (50) summarizes progress made by the UN Commission worldwide in the areas of women's political rights, access to education, legal status, and economic opportunities. Also assesses progress in the areas of equal pay and nationality of married women.

52.   U.S. Post Office Dept. *4-Cent American Women Commemorative Postage Stamp Available at Your Local Post Office, June 3, 1960.* Washington, DC: Postmaster General, 1960. poster. P1.26/2:W84.

53.   U.S. Post Office Dept. *Talk by Postmaster General Arthur E. Summerfield, Dedicating the American Woman Stamp, Washington, D.C., June 2, 1960.* Washington, DC: The Department, 1960. 3p. P1.27:Su6/26. Brief comments on the moral and spiritual contributions of women is followed by an explanation of the design of the American Woman stamp, a tribute to the many roles of women.

54.   U.S. Office of the President. *Full Partnership of Women in Our Democracy.* Washington, DC: GPO, 1962. [8]p. leaflet. Pr35.8:W84/P25. Flyer on the President's Commission on the Status of Women reviews the commission's mandate and provides quotes from commission members on equal opportunity for women.

55.   U.S. Public Health Service. *A Woman's View Point.* Washington, DC: GPO, 1962. 8p. FS2.98:W84. Pamphlet based on a speech given at the National Conference on Air Pollution, Nov. 19, 1958, by Chloe Gifford, president of the General Federation of Women's Clubs urges women to bring their energy to bear on solving the air pollution problem.

56.   U.S. Women's Bureau. *Address before the Annual Convention of Canadian Federation of Business and Professional Women's Clubs, St. Andrew-by-the-Sea, Canada.* by Esther Peterson. Washington, DC: The Bureau, 1962. 11p. L13.12:P44/3. After general comments on promoting the status of women in the U.S., Canada, and the developing countries, Peterson talked briefly about the pending U.S. equal pay bill and at greater length on the President's Commission on the Status of Women. The progress and activities of the commission's committees on women's education, protective labor legislation, tax

laws and social insurance, political and civil rights, new and expanded services, and government contractor employment practices are reviewed.

57. U.S. Women's Bureau. *Fifteen Years after College: A Study of Alumnae of the Class of 1945.* Bulletin no. 283. Washington, DC: GPO, 1962. 26p. L13.3:283. Survey of the women alumnae of the Class of 1945 from four colleges examined their marital and family status and their current and future employment plans. Data was collected on education including undergraduate major and education beyond the four year degree, employment status in 1960, by marital status and employment history, volunteer activities and occupations. The survey looked at future plans and interest in additional job-related training and vocational counseling. Statistics provided include marital and family status, undergraduate major, educational attainment, formal education since college, employment status, employment status and plans of married graduates, years of paid employment since college, most responsible position ever held, and training and education plans and interest by employment status.

58. U.S. President's Commission on the Status of Women. *American Women: Report of the President's Commission on the Status of Women.* Washington, DC: GPO, 1963. 86p. Pr35.8:W84/Am3. Summary report of the findings and recommendations of the Committees on Education, Home and Community, Private Employment, Federal Service, Labor Standards, Social Security, and Political and Civil Rights provides a good overview of the status of women in the U.S. in the early 1960's. Articulates the direction and philosophy of changes put forward by the commission.

59. U.S. President's Commission on the Status of Women. *Four Consultations: Private Employment Opportunities, New Patterns of Volunteer Work, Portrayal of Women by Mass Media, Problems of Negro Women.* Washington, DC: GPO, 1963. 38p. Pr35.8:W84/C76. Short reports highlight commission consultations on issues of employment opportunity in the private sector, volunteer work, the portrayal of women in the mass media, and the problems of black women.

60. U.S. President's Commission on the Status of Women. *Report of Committee on Home and Community to President's Commission of the Status of Women.* Washington, DC: GPO, 1963. 51p. Pr35.8:W84/H75. Recommendations of the committee relating to availability of child care services, homemaker services, and home management advisory services are reported, and the need to elevate the status of household employment is discussed. Other services mentioned in recommendations include family counseling and health services. The role of volunteer services and the question of responsibility for developing and maintaining services are also covered.

61. U.S. Public Health Service. *Woman's View of Air Pollution.* by Chloe Gifford. Washington, DC: GPO, 1963. 8p. FS2.98:W84/963. Reissue with a revised title of *A Woman's View Point* (55).

62. U.S. Dept. of Labor. *Remarks by Secretary of Labor W. Willard Wirtz, at the Equal Pay Conference, Washington, D.C., June 11, 1964.* Washington, DC: The Department, 1964. 4p. L1.13:W74/47. Tongue-in-cheek remarks of Wirtz carry the desire to eliminate sexism in the English language to its extreme. Wirtz justifies his frivolous speech by noting that the battle for equal pay has come to a "satisfactory culmination."

63. U.S. Government Printing Office. *Publications of the President's Commission on the Status of Women Available from the Superintendent of Documents.* Washington, DC: GPO, 1964. leaflet. GP3.22:W84.

64.   U.S. Women's Bureau. *Governor's Commission on the Status of Women.* Leaflet no. 38. Washington, DC: The Bureau, February 1964. leaflet. L13.11:38. Presents basic information on setting up a Governor's Commission on the Status of Women. Revised editions published October 1964 and May 1965.

65.   U.S. Women's Bureau. *New Horizons for North Dakota Women, Report of Conference Held in Bismark, North Dakota, July 17-18, 1964.* Washington, DC: GPO, 1964? 19p. L13.2:N81d. Summary of a conference on the status of women in North Dakota focuses on the past and present civil and political rights of women. Speeches highlight opportunities outside the home for women, the problems of women in poverty, and the problems of working women. Workshops briefly summarized cover topics of North Dakota women and education, community services, volunteer work, employment, and legal rights.

66.   U.S. Women's Bureau. *Report of Statewide Meeting of the Governor's Commission on the Status of Women Held at Hotel Savory, Des Moines, Iowa, November 20-21, 1964.* Washington, DC: The Bureau, 1964? 33p. L13.2:St2/7. Keynote speaker Mary Dublin Keyserling spoke on the President's Commission on the Status of Women and generally on the changing status of women world wide. Reports of the Iowa Commission summarize findings in the areas of employment practices, state labor laws, legal treatment, services for women including child care, and education. The activities of commissions in the Midwest are briefly summarized. Two persons not on the commission speak their views on implementing the commission's report.

67.   U.S. Women's Bureau. *Report of the Arrowhead Regional Conference on the Status of Women in Northern Minnesota, Held at Athletic Club, Duluth, Minn, July 17, 1964.* Washington, DC: The Bureau, 1964? 21p. L13.2:St2/5. Conference speakers describe the economic conditions in northern Minnesota and the characteristics of its women workers. State and federal laws affecting women workers and the role of organized labor in Minnesota are briefly covered. Workshop summaries cover topics of women's employment, education, legal and civil problems, and service needs such as day care. Mary Dublin Keyserling gave the keynote address, discussing the President's Commission on the Status of Women.

68.   U.S. Women's Bureau. *Research and Your Job, Address by Mary Dublin Keyserling, Director of the Women's Bureau, Department of Labor, before the National Federation of Business and Professional Women's Clubs, Inc., Foundation Meeting, Detroit, Michigan, July 18, 1964.* Washington, DC: The Bureau, 1964. 16p. L13.12:K52/2. Speech summarizes women's work patterns, the war on poverty, and the findings of the President's Commission on the Status of Women, and commends the work of the state commissions. The need for research and experimentation to adjust education and employment to meet the needs of mid-life women is noted.

69.   U.S. Women's Bureau. *Challenges Ahead, Address by Mary Dublin Keyserling, Director, Women's Bureau, Department of Labor, July 29, 1965, Conference of Governors' Commissions on the Status of Women, Washington, D.C.* Washington, DC: The Bureau, 1965. 11p. L13.12:K52/11. Highlights the unfinished business in the movement toward equal opportunity for women addressing the areas of education, employment opportunities, income, the need to maintain labor legislation to protect women, and women's participation in politics. In closing, Keyserling urges women to play a role in "building the Great Society."

70.   U.S. Women's Bureau. *Four International Meetings, Notes on Agendas, 1965, United Nations Commission on the Status of Women, Inter-American Commission of Women, International Labor Conference, ILO Panel of Consultants on Problems of Women*

Workers. Washington, DC: The Bureau, 1965. 15p. L13.2:In8/3. Annotated outline of the agendas for the meetings of the UN Commission on the Status of Women, the Inter-American Commission of Women, the International Labor Conference and the ILO Panel of Consultants on Problems of Women Workers. Some detail is provided on the ILO agenda item on the employment of women with family responsibilities.

71.   U.S. Women's Bureau. *[Lets Look Ahead], Address by Assistant Secretary of Labor Esther Peterson before the Professional Panhellenic Association, Chicago, Ill., November 13, 1965.* Washington, DC: The Bureau, 1965. 18p. L13.12:P44/7. Summarizes the problems of poverty in America, and highlights the new government programs to address the problems, and tells women how they can participate in the building of the Great Society. The opportunities which will open to women in government service, education, health and community improvement are noted as is the need for women in policy-making positions, particularly in education. The growing trend for women to return to work after the children reach school age is discussed along with the implications of a dual homemaking-worker role. The low wages paid to women, and its contribution to women's susceptibility to poverty, are briefly touched upon.

72.   U.S. Women's Bureau. *Report of a Conference on Women's Destiny, Choice or Chance? Held at Student Union Building, University of Washington, November 21-22, 1963.* Washington, DC: GPO, 1965. 96p. L13.2:W84/42. Proceedings of a conference on the role women can play in meeting the needs of other women reprints, in part, a speech by Betty Friedan on the new image of woman and the keynote address by Esther Peterson on the need for educated women. Symposiums dealt with the importance of education and the current state of women's civil and political rights. Other sessions dealt with unions, part-time employment, social services, legislation, and career counseling.

73.   U.S. Citizens' Advisory Council on the Status of Women and U.S. Interdepartmental Committee on the Status of Women. *Progress and Prospects: The Report of the Second National Conference of Governors' Commissions on the Status of Women, Washington, D.C., July 28-30, 1965.* Washington, DC: GPO, 1966. 80p. Y3.In8/21:2G74/965. Conference report includes texts of speeches on the status of American women and on the work of the commissions. Workshop reports cover the legal status of women, Title VII, employment, education, vocational guidance, home and community, consumer education, community services, labor standards, income maintenance and women in family life.

74.   U.S. Women's Bureau. *College Women Seven Years after Graduation: Resurvey of Women Graduates, Class of 1957.* Bulletin no. 292. Washington, DC: GPO, 1966. 54p. L13.3:292. Part of a longitudinal study of college women, this survey conducted in 1964 asked the Class of 1957 about continuing education, employment history, family status, and future employment and educational plans. Data from the questionnaire includes age, marital and family status, residence in 1964 compared to residence in 1957-58, undergraduate major, postgraduate education, undergraduate major and employment status, reason for working by marital status, employment status by marital and family status, husband's attitude toward wife's employment, child care arrangements, weekly hours worked, occupational distribution, salaries by major and by occupation, and reasons for leaving the work force.

75.   U.S. Women's Bureau. *International Cooperation Programs Advancing the Status of Women, Reports of U.S. Government Agencies.* Washington, DC: GPO, 1966. 50p. L13.2:In85/2. Describes the role of federal agencies in advancing the status of women internationally. Areas of assistance include home economics extension in foreign countries, educational assistance programs, health programs, public welfare training, and Women's Bureau training programs and technical assistance. Also describes benefits to women from

foreign exchange programs and activities of the Agency for International Development. Finally, the report covers the information programs of the U.S. Information Agency.

76.   U.S. Women's Bureau. *President's Commission on the Status of Women, Why Commission? Functions, Operational Procedures, Ongoing Results.* Washington, DC: The Bureau, 1966. 12p. L13.2:P92. Overview of the President's Commission on the Status of Women includes statements of President Kennedy and of Eleanor Roosevelt, Chairwoman of the commission, on the reasons for its establishment. The organization and work of the commission, its committees, and staff are outlined, and the results of the commission's work are summarized. Progress in civil service employment, employment discrimination legislation, and work with women's organizations are highlighted. The formation of state commissions based on the federal model, and the focus of their actions, are also reviewed.

77.   U.S. Atomic Energy Commission. *Women and the Year 2000: Remarks by Glenn T. Seaborg, Chairman of the U.S. Atomic Energy Commission to the Women's National Democratic Club, Washington, D.C., February 6, 1967.* Washington, DC: The Commission, 1967. 11p. Y3.At7:34Se1/129. Speech theorizes about changes by the year 2000 that will effect women and anticipates robot housekeeping and wider educational opportunities.

78.   U.S. Interdepartmental Committee on the Status of Women and U.S. Citizen's Advisory Council on the Status of Women. *Targets for Action: The Report of the Third National Conference of Commissions on the Status of Women.* Washington, DC: GPO, 1967. 90p. Y3.In8/21:2C76/966. Texts of speeches and summaries of workshops cover topics such as employment opportunities and protective labor legislation, welfare services, day care, family planning, vocational counseling, education and training, status of private household workers, and sex discrimination in the legal system.

79.   U.S. Citizen's Advisory Council on the Status of Women. *Report of the Task Force on Health and Welfare.* Washington, DC: GPO, 1968. 59p. Y3.In8/21:2H34. Broad based report discusses issues of public assistance reform, women in the labor force as it related to family and day care, social services for children and the elderly, and access to health and family planning services. Includes a statement supporting abortion rights and an opposing view.

80.   U.S. Interdepartmental Committee on the Status of Women and U.S. Citizen's Advisory Council on the Status of Women. *American Women 1963-1968: Report of the Interdepartmental Committee on the Status of Women.* Washington, DC: GPO, 1968. 41p. Y3.In8/21:2Am3/963-68. Report on the progress of women between 1963 and 1968 examines the areas of education, home and community, employment, labor standards and legal rights. Comparison is made to the 1963 report *American Women* (58) issued by the President's Commission on the Status of Women.

81.   U.S. Smithsonian Institution. Museum of History and Technology. *Women's Bathing and Swimming Costume in the United States.* United States National Museum Bulletin no. 250, Contributions from the Museum of History and Technology Paper no. 64. Washington, DC: The Smithsonian Institution Press, 1968. 32p. SI3.3:250/paper 64. Illustrated history of the development of the modern swimming suit from the colonial period to the 1960's discusses the role of function, fashion, and social mores in the evolution from the bathing dress to the modern maillot.

82.   U.S. Interdepartmental Committee on the Status of Women and U.S. Citizen's Advisory Council on the Status of Women. *1968: Time for Action, Highlights of the Fourth National Conference of Commissions on the Status of Women.* Washington, DC: GPO,

1969. 97p. Y3.In8/21:2C76/968. Topics of speeches and workshops summarized include day care, employment opportunities, political involvement and leadership positions, and reports from state commissions.

83.   U.S. Dept. of Labor. Library. *Women, Their Social and Economic Status: Selected References.* Washington, DC: The Department, 1970. 41p. L1.34:W84. Bibliography of monographs relating to the social and economic status of women in the U.S. includes publications of federal and state governments and national organizations as well as conference proceedings. Includes notations on holding libraries.

84.   U.S. Women's Bureau. *Report of Consultation of Women's Organizations on Common Goals and Objectives for the Future, Washington, D.C., February 26, 1970.* Washington, DC: The Bureau, 1970. 14p. L13.2:Or3/2. Summary of a Bureau consultation called to form an agenda on women's issues outlines the areas examined by the workgroups. Major recommendations of the workshop sessions relate to child care, education, employment, women at the policy-making level, image of women in media, grassroots organization, and information networks. The bulk of the report is the speech by Elizabeth Duncan Koontz highlighting issues still to be fully addressed if women workers were to have real job opportunities. Women's wages, vocational opportunities, protective labor legislation, sex discrimination in education, and the Equal Rights Amendment are reviewed.

85.   U.S. Citizen's Advisory Council on the Status of Women. *Citizen's Advisory Council Release Task Force Recommendations.* Washington, DC: GPO, 1971. 23p. Y3.In8/21:2C49. Recommendations of the Task Forces of the Citizen's Advisory Council on the Status of Women deal with family law and policy, health and welfare, labor standards, and social insurance and taxes.

86.   U.S. Women's Bureau. *American Women at the Crossroads: Directions for the Future, Report of the Fiftieth Anniversary Conference of the Women's Bureau of the Department of Labor.* Washington, DC: GPO, 1971. 126p. L36.102:Am3. Report highlights the recommendations of numerous workshops, lists all participants, and presents a bibliography on women's social and economic status in the 19th and 20th centuries.

87.   U.S. Women's Bureau. *Changing Patterns of Women's Lives.* Leaflet no. 54. Washington, DC: GPO, 1971. 4p. L36.110:54. Comparison of statistics on women in 1920 and 1970 summarizes changing patterns in women's family and employment status.

88.   U.S. Women's Bureau. *A Guide to Sources of Data on Women and Women Workers for the United States and for Regions, States, and Local Areas.* Washington, DC: GPO, 1972. 15p. L36.108:W84. Charts highlight some of the major statistical sources of information on women and women workers.

89.   U.S. Bureau of the Census. *We the American Women.* Washington, DC: GPO, 1973. 12p. C56.234:4. Basic statistics on population, education, employment, income, and household situation of American women in the earlier 1970s includes some conservative data for earlier years.

90.   U.S. Women's Bureau. *Facts about Women Heads of Households and Heads of Families.* Washington, DC: The Bureau, 1973. 10p. L36.102:H35. Presents summary data on race, age, and marital status of women heads of household, and details race/ethnicity, age, marital status, number of children, educational attainment, residence, employment status, work experience, occupation and income of female heads of families. Looks at the low-income status of female headed families analyzed by race, number of children, and educational attainment.

91.   U.S. Bureau of the Census. *Female Family Heads.* Current Population Reports Series P-23, no. 50. Washington, DC: GPO, 1974. 30p. C56.218:P-23/50. Report of data for 1960 to 1973 on female-headed households by age, race, marital status, education, work experience, occupation, and income also looks at size of families, place of residence, and the gross rent-income ratio.

92.   U.S. Congress. Joint Economic Committee. *Economic Problems of Women, Hearings.* 93d Cong., 1st and 2d sess., 10 July 1973 - 17 June 1974. 4 vol. Y4.Ec7:W84/pt.1-4. Part one of hearings exploring the economic problems of women covers the issues of women's economic role and treatment in the labor force, federal programs to end sex discrimination in employment, and credit and insurance problems. The second part of the hearings covers federal tax laws and women, women under Social Security and private pension plans, sex discrimination in unemployment insurance, veterans programs, and public assistance. Also examined is HEW's role in eliminating sex discrimination. Part three prints statements for the record from commissions, women's organizations, and congresswomen on various aspects of women's economic condition. Part four of the hearings includes testimony on household workers, training programs for women, day care, tax laws, social security, and housing.

93.   U.S. Women's Bureau. *Highlights of Women's Employment and Education.* Washington, DC: The Bureau, 1974. 2p. L36.102:W84/3. Presents basic facts on employment and education of women in 1972-1973.

94.   U.S.Congress. House. Committee on Government Operations. *Providing for a National Women's Conference, Report to Accompany H.R. 9924.* H. Rept. 94-562, 94th Cong., 1st sess., 1975. 6p. Serial 13099-8. Reports a bill directing the National Commission on the Observance of International Women's Year to organize a National Women's Conference.

95.   U.S. Congress. House. Committee on Government Operations. Subcommittee on Government Information and Individual Rights. *National Women's Conference, Hearing on H.R. 8903.* 94th Cong., 1st sess., 30 Sept. 1975. 53p. Y4.G74/7:W84. Discusses the proposed organization and structure of a National Women's Conference to be held in conjunction with the observance of International Women's Year.

96.   U.S. Congress. House. Committee on International Relations. *Sense of Congress with Respect to International Women's Year, Report to Accompany H.Con. Res. 309.* H. Rept. 94-450, 94th Cong., 1st sess., 1975. 6p. Serial 13099-7. Favorable report on H. Con. Res. 309 which expresses the support of Congress for the UN International Women's Year and encourages new programs and attitudes towards the role of women.

97.   U.S. Congress. House. Select Committee on Aging. Subcommittee on Retirement Income and Employment. *Economic Problems of Aging Women, Hearing.* 94th Cong., 1st sess., 15 July 1975. 29p. Y4.Ag4/2:Ec7. Economic problems of older women are discussed highlighting factors of low wages, divorce, and disparate treatment of women under Social Security. The employment patterns of women as they contribute to economic problems in later years and at divorce are reviewed, and legislative action to address these problems are suggested.

98.   U.S. Congress. Senate. Committee on Government Operations. *World Conference of the International Women's Year, Report by Senator Charles H. Percy.* 94th Cong., 1st sess., 8 Sept. 1975. 73p. Y4.G74/6:In8/15. Report describes major activities of the World Conference of the International Women's Year, with emphasis on the efforts of the U.S. Delegation. Guidelines and resolutions passed at the conference, a summary of the World Plan of Action, and a list of United Nations documents related to the conference are included.

99. U.S. National Institute of Mental Health. *Sex Roles: A Research Bibliography.* by Helen S. Astin, et al. Washington, DC: GPO, 1975. 362p. HE20.8113:Se9. Bibliography lists 456 monographs and journal articles on sex differences and sex roles from a wide variety of disciplines. Annotations are substantial and an author and subject index is included.

100. U.S. National Institutes of Health. *Sex-Role Attitude Items and Scales from U.S. Sample Surveys.* by Karen Oppenheim Mason. Rockville, MD: The Institute, 1975. 65p. HE20.8102:Se9. Items which could he used by researchers conducting survey oriented research on sex-role attitudes were drawn from over forty different studies.

101. U.S. Postal Service. *International Women's Year Commemorative Stamp, Issue Date August 26, 1975.* Washington, DC: Postmaster General, 1975. poster. P1.26/2:W84/5.

102. U.S. Women's Bureau. *Commissions on the Status of Women.* Washington, DC: GPO, 1975. 21p. L36.102:St2. Information on the structure, funding and activities of state and local commissions on the status of women includes a list of the active state, municipal and national commissions.

103. U.S. Air Force Academy. Library. *Women and the American Economy.* Special Bibliography Series no. 52. N.p., 1976. 31p. D305.12:52. Lists monographs, periodical articles, and government documents published in the 1960s and 1970s on women and women's employment in the United States.

104. U.S. Army Reserve. *A Word to the Wives of Army Reservists.* Washington, DC: GPO, 1976. 9p. D101.2:R31/34. Tells the wife how serving in the Army Reserve will help her husband's career and suggests things she can do while he is at annual training.

105. U.S. Bureau of the Census. *A Statistical Portrait of Women in the United States.* Current Population Reports Series P-23, no. 58. Washington, DC: GPO, 1976. 90p. C3.186:P-23/58. Statistics on American women covers distribution of the population by age and sex, longevity, mortality and health, residence and migration, marital and family status, fertility, education, labor force participation, occupation and industry, work experience, income and poverty status, voting and public office holding, crime and victimization, and women of color.

106. U.S. Commission on Civil Rights. *Making the Constitution Work for All Americans: A Report of the Proceedings of Regional Civil Rights Conference III Sponsored by the U.S. Commission on Civil Rights in Atlanta, Georgia, April 16-18, 1975.* Washington, DC: GPO, 1976. 135p. CR1.2:C76/8. Civil rights conference for southern states deals primarily with general civil rights issues and practical organizing strategies. Of particular relevance to women is an exchange on the abortion issue and the report of the Women's Caucus.

107. U.S. Congress. House. Committee on Education and Labor. Subcommittee on Equal Opportunities. *Equal Opportunities for Displaced Homemakers Act, Hearing on H.R. 10272.* 94th Cong., 2d sess., 18 Nov. 1976. 74p. Y4.Ed8/1:H75. Hearing on a bill to provide a range of support services for displaced homemakers presents testimony from representatives of women's organizations on the characteristics and problems of displaced homemakers. The need for economic security for homemakers as divorcees and widows is stressed. The failure of CETA programs to address the needs of older women is also noted.

108. U.S. Federal Council on the Aging. *National Policy Concerns for Older Women: Commitment to a Better Life.* Washington, DC: The Council, 1976. 51p. Y3.F31/15:2W84.

Overview of issues affecting older women covers job discrimination, inequitable pension systems, health care, and community services.

109. U.S. National Institute of Mental Health. *How Women See Their Roles, a Change in Attitudes.* Rockville, MD: The Institute, 1976. 5p. HE20.8122/2:W84. Report on women's roles summarizes research reports from a study conducted by Karen Oppenhiem Mason on changing sex role attitudes of women between 1964 and 1973. The study focused on southern white women, northern working women and college educated women.

110. U.S. Women's Bureau. *Department of Labor Activities in Response to IWY '75.* Washington, DC: GPO, 1976. 29p. L36.102:L11. Summarizes the activities of the various subgroups of the Department of Labor in response to International Women's Year. Describes activities of the regional offices relating to women.

111. U.S. Women's Bureau. *Women in the Economy: Full Freedom of Choice.* Washington, DC: GPO, 1976. 47p. L36.102:W84/4. Summary of conference minisessions covers topics of minority concerns, taking advantage of federal funding for projects, changing patterns in education and training, child care and the dual responsibilities of workplace and home, projects to improve women's role in policy making, making EEOC enforcement work, and strategies for improving the position of women in the media. Also includes special sessions on women offenders, economic contributions of homemakers, child care, and private household workers.

112. U.S. Women's Bureau. *Women of Spanish Origin in the United States.* Washington, DC: The Bureau, 1976. 17p. L36.102:Sp2. Statistical profile of women of Spanish origin in the U.S. reports at age, residence, marital and family status, education, labor force participation and income. Provides detailed statistics on type of family, educational attainment, employment status, occupation, work experience of wives and women family heads, labor force participation rates of mothers, and income.

113. U.S. Congress. House. Committee on Education and Labor. Subcommittee on Employment Opportunities. *The Displaced Homemakers Act, Hearing on H.R. 28.* 95th Cong., 1st sess., 14 July 1977. 231p. Y4.Ed8/1:H75/2. Hearing on a bill to create multipurpose service centers for displaced homemakers explores the problems of these women and the extent of the problem nationwide.

114. U.S. Congress. Senate. Committee on Human Resources. Subcommittee on Employment, Poverty, and Migratory Labor. *Displaced Homemakers Act, 1977, Hearings on S. 418.* 95th Cong., 1st sess., 12-13 Sept. 1977. 150p. Y4.H88:D63/977. Testimony on the problems of displaced homemakers highlights the job related problems of women over 40 and the failure of existing agencies and programs to meet their needs. The bill under consideration would provide funds to establish local multiservice centers to address their emotional and job training needs.

115. U.S. National Commission for UNESCO. *Report on Women in America.* International Organization and Conference Series no. 132. Washington, DC: GPO, 1977. 54p. S1.70:132. Overview of the history and current status of women in the U.S. focuses on conditions and legal action relating to education, work, and social welfare.

116. U.S. National Commission on the Observance of International Women's Year. *American Women Today and Tomorrow.* Washington, DC: GPO, 1977. 80p. Y3.W84:2Am3. Results of a survey of American women's lives and attitudes covers education, work patterns, marital status, motherhood, family planning, child care, leisure activities, the image of women in the media, and the women's movement.

117. U.S. National Commission on the Observance of International Women's Year. *International Interdependence.* Washington, DC: GPO, 1977. 51p. Y3.W84:10/9. Guidelines for conducting a workshop to explore international issues relating to the lives of American women includes background information for participants and a list of related films and publications.

118. U.S. National Commission on the Observance of International Women's Year. *Media.* Washington, DC: GPO, 1977. 55p. Y3.W84:10/12. Workshop guide provides guidelines and resources for conducting a workshop on the image and employment of women in the mass media. Fact sheets highlight work already done in the media field to improve the status of women.

119. U.S. National Commission on the Observance of International Women's Year. *Older Women: A Workshop Guide.* Washington, DC: GPO, 1977. 39p. Y3.W84:10/13. Provides fact sheets and lists of publications, films, and speakers for a workshop on the problems of older women.

120. U.S. Women's Bureau. *Women of Puerto Rican Origin in the Continental United States.* Washington, DC: GPO, 1977. 4p. L36.102:P96. Statistical profile of women of Puerto Rican origin in the continental U.S. describes age, marital status, family type, labor force status, occupation, income and poverty status.

121. U.S. Alcohol, Drug Abuse, and Mental Health Administration. *Shattering Sex Role Stereotypes ... Foundations for Growth.* Rockville, MD: The Administration, 1978. folder and 25 sheets. HE20.8002:Se9. Brief descriptions of various aspects of sex role stereotypes describes the psychology of sex roles, sex role adaptability, stereotypes and therapy, and sex roles and mental and behavioral problems such as alcoholism, depression, and rape.

122. U.S. Bureau of Indian Affairs. North American Indian Women's Association. *Special Needs of Handicapped Indian Children and Indian Women's Problems.* Washington, DC: GPO, 1978. 294p. I20.2:H19. Report of information gathered through interviews on problems of Indian women and children covers physical and mental handicaps, child abuse and neglect, physical abuse of women, adolescent parenthood, solo parenthood, unwanted pregnancies and malnutrition.

123. U.S. Commission on Civil Rights. *Hearings Held in Chicago, Illinois.* Washington, DC: GPO, 1977-78. 4 vol. CR1.8:C43/v.1-4. Extensive hearings examine all aspects of women's rights including welfare, pensions, employment opportunities and childcare. Volume one includes general testimony on women's sources of income and volume two focuses specifically on women in clerical occupations. Volumes three and four reprint the exhibits and supporting statistical tables.

124. U.S. Commission on Civil Rights. *Social Indicators of Equality for Minorities and Women.* Washington, DC: The Commission, 1978. 136p. CR1.2:So1/2. Statistics illustrate the progress, or lack of progress, of minorities and women in the areas of education, employment, income, poverty and housing. The report notes the shortcomings of the statistical approach to assessing progress.

125. U.S. Congress. House. *Message from the President of the United States Transmitting a Report on the Status of Administration Actions to Implement the National Plan of Action Development at the National Women's Conference Held in November, 1977.* H. Doc. 95-387, 95th Cong., 2d sess., 1978. 58p. Serial 13211-2. Report summarizes the federal agency reports on legislation and executive actions related to the National Plan of Action of International Women's Year. Women's issues represented include arts and humanities,

business, child care, credit, education, employment, health insurance, rape, reproductive freedom, poverty and other areas. Legislation pending before Congress related to battered women, displaced homemakers, child care, employment and other areas is also noted.

126. U.S. Congress. House. Select Committee on Aging. Subcommittee on Retirement Income and Employment. *Women in Midlife, Security and Fulfillment, Part 1: A Compendium of Papers.* Washington, DC: GPO, 1978. Committee print. 333p. Y4.Ag4/2:W84/2/pt.1. Collection of seventeen papers on the trends and problems of midlife women examines displaced homemakers, recognition of volunteer work, continuing education, work and family responsibilities, financial independence, private pensions, age and sex discrimination, political participation, and prospects for middle-aged women.

127. U.S. Congress. House. Select Committee on Aging. Subcommittee on Retirement Income and Employment. *Women in Midlife, Security and Fulfillment, Part 2: Annotated Bibliography.* Washington, DC: GPO, 1978. Committee print. 181p. Y4.Ag4/2:W84/2/pt.2. Bibliography on midlife women covers issues of financial security, work, education, pensions, volunteer work, displaced homemakers, alternative housing, mental health, and political participation.

128. U.S. Congress. Senate. Committee on Human Resources. Subcommittee on Child and Human Development and U.S. Congress. House. Committee on Education and Labor. Subcommittee on Select Education. *White House Conference on Families, 1978, Joint Hearings.* 95th Cong., 2d sess., 2-3 Feb. 1978. 746p. Y4.H88:F21/2/978. Testimony on the organization of the proposed White House Conference on Families emphasizes changes in family structure and women-related issues of welfare, employment discrimination, and domestic violence.

129. U.S. Dept. of Housing and Urban Development. Office of Policy Development and Research. *How Well Are We Housed? 2. Female-Headed Households.* Washington, DC: GPO, 1978. 19p. HH1.2:H81/59/no.2. Statistical overview of the characteristics of housing for female-headed households examines the portion of income required to obtain adequate housing and analyzes age, race, and household size in relation to inadequate housing for female- and male-headed households.

130. U.S. National Commission for Manpower Policy and U.S. Employment and Training Administration. *Women's Changing Roles at Home and on the Job: Proceedings of a Conference on the National Longitudinal Survey of Mature Women.* Special Report no. 26. Washington, DC: The Commission, 1978. 332p. Y3.M31:9/26. Conference papers highlight the changing roles of women as revealed in a longitudinal survey of women age 30 to 44 which began in 1967. Papers examine work life by race, attitudes toward work, employment and family stability, the economic consequences of divorce, and the relationship between earnings and occupational status for women. Gives statistics on economic welfare of women by race and marital status, length of poverty status by race and marital status, family income by race, and labor force participation by marital status, race, and presence of preschool children.

131. U.S. National Commission on the Observance of International Women's Year. *National Plan of Action Adopted at National Women's Conference, November 18-21, 1977, Houston, Texas.* Washington, DC: GPO, 1978. 32p. Y3.W84:2Ac8. Recommended actions adopted at the National Women's Conference address women's issues such as battered women, child care, credit, education, politics, employment, health, rape, reproductive freedom, and sexual preference.

132. U.S. National Commission on the Observance of International Women's Year. *Plan Nacional de Accion Adoptado en la Conferencia Nacional de la Mujer, 18-21 de*

Noviembre, 1977, Houston, Texas.   Washington, DC: GPO,   1978.   35p.
Y3.W84:2Ac8/spanish.   See 131 for abstract.

133.   U.S. National Commission on the Observance of International Women's Year. *The Spirit of Houston: The First National Women's Conference.* Washington, DC: GPO, 1978. 308p. Y3.W84:1/978. Detailed report describes the first National Women's Conference held in Houston Texas in 1977. Each plank of the National Plan of Action is presented with background information and a summary of activities at the state meetings. Includes a day by day summary of conference activities and excerpts from major speeches. Brief biographies of the commission members are provided.

134.   U.S. National Institute of Mental Health. *Women's Worlds: NIMH Research Projects on Women.* Washington, DC: GPO, 1978. 106p. HE20.8131/2:W84. Overview of NIMH research projects on women highlights studies of sex roles and sex stereotypes, women's work, marriage and divorce, women and depression, living in a woman's body, and women seeking help.

135.   U.S. Office of Education. *Resources in Women's Educational Equity: Non-Print Media and Materials.* Washington, DC: GPO, 1978. 243p. HE19.128:W84/3. List of non-print resources on history of women, equal rights legislation, family and lifestyles, sex roles and stereotypes, women and work, and notable women drawn from the National Center for Educational Media and from the National Instruction Materials Information System databases.

136.   U.S. Women's Bureau. *Commissions, Committees, and Councils on the Status of Women: Chairpersons, Executive Directors, and/or Other Staff.* Washington, DC: GPO, 1978. 8p. L36.102:St2/2. Directory of commissions, committees and councils on the status of women.

137.   U.S. Women's Bureau. *Women's Bureau and Commissions on the Status of Women, Avoiding the Obstacle Course.* Washington, DC: GPO, 1978. 21p. L36.102:Ob7. Guide to setting up state women's bureaus or commissions on the status of women notes common pitfalls.

138.   U.S. Bureau of the Census. *Census Bureau Conference on Issues in Federal Statistical Needs Relating to Women.* Current Population Reports Series P-23, no. 83. Washington, DC: GPO, 1979. 152p. C3.186:P-23/83. Report examines the data needs relating to the status of women and recommends federal data gathering activities. Specific areas reviewed are income, occupation, discrimination, household structure, education and health. Includes discussion of public policy issues and responses from the primary statistical gathering agencies.

139.   U.S. Congress. House. Select Committee on Aging. Subcommittee on Retirement Income and Employment. *Midlife Women, Policy Proposals on Their Problems, a Summary of Papers.* 96th Cong., 1st sess, 1979. Committee print. 21p. Y4.Ag4/2:W84/3. Future retirement security issues are the focus of recommendations for federal action on the problems of midlife women. Areas covered include work, education, displaced homemakers, retirement and pensions, counseling, age discrimination, and housing.

140.   U.S. Congress. House. Select Committee on Aging. Subcommittee on Retirement Income and Employment. *National Policy Proposals Affecting Midlife Women, Hearings.* 96th Cong., 1st sess., 7-8 May 1979. 284p. Y4.Ag4/2:W84/4. Discussion of the problems of midlife women and of ways for federal policy to react to those needs highlights problems of depression, alcoholism and drug dependency. Economic discrimination and pension issues predominate, especially as they relate to divorce. The ability of federal jobs training

and educational assistance programs to meet the needs of displaced homemakers entering the work force or interested in returning to school are reviewed. Also examined are the special problems of foreign service and military service wives. Provides background statistics on the labor force status and earnings of women 40 to 64 by personal characteristics.

141.   U.S. Congress. Senate. Committee on Labor and Human Resources. *The Coming Decade: American Women and Human Resources, Policies and Programs, 1979, Hearings, Part 1.* 96th Cong., 1st sess., 31 Jan.- 1 Feb. 1979.   1458p. Y4.L11/4:W84/pt.1.   Hearing testimony and supporting materials highlight the changing patterns of women's employment, and discusses the implications of the changing patterns for federal policies and programs. Among the topics examined are displaced homemakers, child care, the wage gap, sex stereotypes in vocational counseling, balancing work and home demands, political participation, recognition of the work of housewives, women and poverty, comparable worth, health insurance, ERA, pregnancy leave, and jobs programs. Provides background statistics and reprints *Women in America: A Source Book*, a report compiled by the Congressional Research Service.

142.   U.S. Congress. Senate. Committee on Labor and Human Resources. *The Coming Decade: American Women and Human Resources, Policies and Programs, 1979, Hearings, Part 2.* 96th Cong., 1st sess., 9 Apr. 1979. 287p. Y4.L11/4:W84/pt.2. Second part of hearing on women and federal policy addresses the needs of Hispanic women, domestic violence, women as business owners, economic inequities, women and mental health, day care, and other topics.

143.   U.S. Dept. of State. Bureau of Public Affairs. *Gist: UN Decade for Women, 1976-1985.* Washington, DC: The Bureau, 1979. 2p. S1.128:W84. Brief overview of the U.S. role in and reaction to the U.N. Decade for Women describes the general objectives and accomplishments of the first three years of the decade.

144.   U.S. Employment and Training Administration. *The Socioeconomic Status of Households Headed by Women.* R & D Monograph no. 72. Washington, DC: GPO, 1979. 68p. L37.14:72. Analysis of data obtained from a longitudinal study of women's labor market experience explores the socioeconomic status of households headed by women. In particular the study looks at the effect of marital disruption on employment and income of black families compared to white families.

145.   U.S. National Institute of Education. *Sex Role Socialization and Sex Discrimination: A Bibliography.* Washington, DC: The Institute, 1979. 120p. HE19.213:Se9. Comprehensive bibliography drawn from a variety of disciplines lists published and unpublished books, papers, journal articles, and dissertations on sex role socialization and sex discrimination written between 1960 and 1974, with a select additions for 1975 to 1978.

146.   U.S. Women's Bureau. *Facts about Women Heads of Household and Heads of Families.* Washington, DC: The Bureau, 1979. 9p. L36.102:H34/979. Statistical profile of women heads of households and heads of families provides data on race/ethnicity, age, marital status, number of children, educational attainment, residence, employment status, occupation and income.

147.   U.S. Commission on Civil Rights. Colorado Advisory Committee. *Energy Policy Handbook: Challenges, Alternatives, and Resources.* Washington, DC: GPO, 1980. 16p. CR1.6/2:En2. Presents ways to help women and minorities share in the economic advantages of energy industry development in Colorado. The adverse impact of inflation, particularly energy costs, on women and minorities is discussed.

148. U.S. Commission on Civil Rights. Maine Advisory Committee. *Civil Rights in Maine.* Washington, DC: GPO, 1980. 40p. CR1.2:M28. Panel discussion on civil rights in Maine identifies the major problem areas as public awareness, noncompliance by government at all levels, and lack of resources. Other discussion centers on spouse abuse, rental housing for families, treatment of women in jails and administration of the general assistance program.

149. U.S. Commission on Civil Rights. Texas Advisory Committee. *Texas: The State of Civil Rights.* Washington, DC: GPO, 1980. 71p. CR1.2:T31/4. The status of women and minorities in Texas is examined focusing on education, employment, political participation and the administration of justice.

150. U.S. Congress. House. Committee on Foreign Affairs. *U.N. World Conference of the U.N. Decade for Women, Copenhagen, Denmark, July 14-30, 1980, Report of Congressional Staff Advisors to the U.S. Delegation.* 96th Cong., 2d sess., 1980. 72p. Y4.F76/1:W89/10. Summary of the World Conference of the U.N. Decade for Women outlines the organization and outcome of the conference, lists members of the U.S. delegation, and reprints the "Convention on the elimination of all forms of discrimination" and the text of resolutions sponsored by the U.S. delegation.

151. U.S. Congress. House. Select Committee on Aging. Subcommittee on Retirement Income and Employment. *The Status of Mid-Life Women and Options for Their Future: A Report with Additional Views.* Washington, DC: GPO, 1980. 34p. Y4.Ag4/2:W84/5. Summary of research into the problems faced by mid-life women covers to education and jobs programs, counseling services, social security and private pensions, health, and parent care, and presents policy recommendations.

152. U.S. Dept. of State. *United States Women: Issues and Progress in the UN Decade for Women, 1976-1985.* Washington, DC: GPO, 1980. 46p. S1.70:150. Report on regional conferences sponsored by the government and by non-governmental organizations highlights discussions on health, education, employment and legal rights. Successful local and regional programs addressing special needs of women are noted. Excerpts some of the comments from participant evaluations.

153. U.S. Dept. of Transportation. Research and Special Programs Administration. *Women's Travel Issues: Research Needs and Priorities, Conference Proceedings and Papers.* Washington, DC: GPO, 1980. 792p. TD10.2:W84. Compilation of papers from the Conference on Women's Travel Issues addresses topics such as women's entry into the labor force and related travel needs, gender differences in travel patterns, and transportation planning and women.

154. U.S. National Institutes of Health. *Federal Programs for Minorities, Women, and the Handicapped Excerpted from the Catalog of Federal Domestic Assistance.* Washington, DC: GPO, 1980. 45p. HE20.3002:M66/3. Provides details of federal grants relating to minorities and women, Native Americans, the handicapped, and civil rights.

155. U.S. President's Advisory Committee for Women. *Voices for Women: 1980 Report of the President's Advisory Committee for Women.* Washington, DC: GPO, 1980. 192p. Pr39.8:W84/2/V87/1980. Overview of the major issues in women and health, human services, work and income security, and education is supplemented by reports from women's testimony at hearings held on the topics. Federal initiatives addressing the problems are summarized.

156. U.S. President's Commission for a National Agenda for the Eighties. *Government and the Advancement of Social Justice: Health, Welfare, Education, and Civil Rights in the*

Eighties. Washington, DC: GPO, 1980. 132p. Pr39.8:Ag3/So1. Report on social policy issues for the 1980s includes discussion of health care and welfare.

157.　U.S. White House Conference on Families. *Listening to America's Families, Action for the 80's.* Washington, DC: GPO, 1980. 249p. Y3.W58/22:1/980. Report on the White House Conference on Families details recommendations on economic well-being, status of homemakers, family violence, family education, child care, and government policy.

158.　U.S. White House Conference on Families. *Listening to America's Families, Action for the 80's: A Summary of the Report to the President, Congress and Families of the Nation.* Washington, DC: GPO, 1980. 100p. Y3.W58/22:1/980/sum. See 157 for abstract.

159.　U.S. White House Conference on Families. *National Hearings Summary.* Washington, DC: GPO, 1980? 127p. Y3.W58/22:2N21. Summary of state hearings for the White House Conference on Families touches on issues of families and employment, displaced homemakers, family violence, and child care.

160.　U.S. White House Conference on Families. *Summary of State Reports.* Washington, DC: GPO, 1980. 3 vol. Y3.W58/22:2St2/v.1-3. Recommendations from state reports for the White House Conference on Families center on issues of families and work, family violence, child care, education, sex education, poverty, tax policy, and care for the aged.

161.　U.S. Administration for Children Youth and Families. *Single Parent Families.* Washington, DC: GPO, 1981. 41p. HE23.1002:Si6. Information for single parents on dealing with the economic problems of raising children alone addresses the concerns of single mothers, single fathers, unwed mothers and fathers, budgeting and child care.

162.　U.S. Agency for International Development. Office of Women in Development. *Decade for Women: World Plan of Action.* Washington, DC: The Office, 1981? 20p. S18.55:W84/2. Condensed version of the World Plan of Action for the U.N. Decade for Women describes issues relating to women and nongovernmental and intergovernmental organizations, and lists the goals and activities which government should adopt to improve the situation of women.

163.　U.S. Air Force. *Air Force Conference on Families, 24-26 September 1980.* Washington, DC: GPO, 1981. 110p. D301.2:F21/2. Report of the conference includes sections focusing on the growing number of working spouses, child care and family counseling needs.

164.　U.S. Dept. of Education. *Native American Women: A Bibliography.* Washington, DC: The Department, 1981. 106p. ED1.17:N21.

165.　U.S. Dept. of State. *Report of the United States Delegation to the World Conference of the United Nations Decade for Women's Equality, Development and Peace, July 14-30, Copenhagen, Denmark.* Washington, DC: GPO, 1981. 144p. S1.2:W84/3. Report describes the activities of the United Nations and the U.S. during the first half of the U.N. Decade for Women and reports on the discussion and outcome of the U.N. sponsored conference. The role of the U.S. delegation and the political friction in the attempt to adopt a world plan of action to improve the status of women are reviewed.

166.　U.S. Executive Office of the President. Office of Sarah Weddington, Assistant to the President. *Women, a Documentary of Progress during the Administration of Jimmy Carter, 1977 to 1981.* Washington, DC: The Office, 1981. 271p. PrEx1.2:W84. Overview of the progress of women under the Carter Administration lists major appointments of women to government posts and the bench, and reprints issues of the newsletter *White House News on Women.* The top 600 women in government positions are listed by department or agency, and program initiatives which relate to women are highlighted.

167. U.S. Smithsonian Institution. Research Institute on Immigration and Ethnic Studies. *Female Immigrants to the United States: Caribbean, Latin American, and African Experiences.* Edited by Delores M. Mortimer and Roy S. Bryce-Lapotre. Washington, DC: The Institution, 1981. 488p. SI1.40/2:2. Collection of papers describes trends and experiences of the female immigrants who formed part of the "new immigration" from Caribbean, Latin American, and African countries, and includes a substantial bibliography on women and migration.

168. U.S. Administration on Aging. National Policy Center on Women and Aging. *The Direction of Federal Legislation Affecting Women Over Forty.* Edited by Marilyn R. Block. College Park, MD: National Policy Center on Women and Aging, 1982. 162p. HE23.3002:W84. Summarizes federal policies and legislation affecting women over 40 in the areas of health care, mental health, employment and training, education, income maintenance, housing, transportation, energy, and crime. Also provides statistics on marital status, poverty rates, employment status, medical care expenses, and social security benefits for older women.

169. U.S. Congress. House. Select Committee on Aging. *Problems of Aging Women, Hearing.* 97th Cong., 2d sess., 26 July 1982. Omaha, NE. 157p. Y4.Ag4/2:W84/7. Presents views on issues affecting older women with an emphasis on osteoporosis, health insurance, displaced homemakers, and pensions. Problems of rural older women are outlined as are problems of housing and adult day care. Coverage of Medicare and Medicaid as it relates to older women is also discussed.

170. U.S. Congress. House. Select Committee on Aging. Subcommittee on Retirement Income and Employment. *The Impact of Reagan Economics on Aging Women, Oregon, Hearing.* 97th Cong., 2d sess., 1 Sept. 1982. 65p. Y4.Ag4/2:W84/8. The situation of older women under Reagan Administration economic policies is the focus of four panels which discuss Social Security and income maintenance, health care cuts, community service programs and budget cuts, and the total impact of Reagan budget cuts.

171. U.S. Congress. Joint Economic Committee. *Economic Status of Women, Hearing.* 97th Cong., 2d sess., 3 Feb. 1982. 136p. Y4.Ec7:W84/5. Hearing on the economic status of women focuses on changing social patterns, the wage gap, women caught in the poverty cycle by low wages, and retirement income protection. All of these issues are discussed in relation to federal policy. An excellent overview of trends in women's economic situation in the 1970s is provided. Statistics on employed persons by occupation and sex, women employed in the federal government by GS-level, poverty rate by type of family, and child support payments to mothers by absent fathers are presented.

172. U.S. National Institute of Child Health and Human Development. *Women, a Developmental Perspective.* Washington, DC: GPO, 1982. 411p. HE20.3352:W84. Proceedings of a research conference includes papers on women's health, physical and psychological development, employment, family relationships, sexuality, and childbearing.

173. U.S. Women's Bureau. *Economic Recovery Tax Act: Selected Provisions of Interest to Women.* Washington, DC: GPO, 1982. 4p. L36.102:Ec7/2. Briefly discusses how the Economic Recovery Tax Act of 1981 may affect women in the areas of deductions, child care credit, retirement/savings incentives, estate and gift taxes, and corporate and business taxes.

174.   U.S. Administration on Aging. *Policy Framework Handbook.* by Marilyn R. Block, et al. National Policy Center on Women and Aging Working Paper no. 1. College Park, MD: The Center, 1983. 92p. HE23.3002:W84/2/wk. paper 1. Handbook presents summaries and background data on policy issues affecting older women such as occupational development and earnings, unemployment, volunteerism, retirement income systems, poverty risk, and health care systems. Provides detailed statistics on age structure, life expectancy, marital status, educational attainment, economic status and occupational attainment.

175.   U.S. Bureau of the Census. Center for Demographic Studies. *American Women: Three Decades of Change.* Special Demographic Analysis CDS-80-8. Washington, DC: GPO, 1983. 39p. C3.261:80-8. Review of studies and statistical trends in women's marriage, childbearing, employment, and education from 1950 to 1980 provides an analysis of factors involved and discusses the possible relationship of trends. Provides basic data on childbearing; labor force participation and earned income by sex and occupation; poverty by race and family type; marital status by age and sex; and household headship status of women.

176.   U.S. Commission on Civil Rights. Vermont Advisory Committee. *Stereotyping and You, a Program for Awareness and Action.* Washington, DC: GPO, 1983. leaflet. CR1.2:St4.

177.   U.S. Congress. House. Select Committee on Children, Youth, and Families. *Children, Youth, and Families in the Southwest, Hearing.* 98th Cong., 1st sess., 7 Dec. 1983. Santa Ana, Calif. 261p. Y4.C43/2:C43/9. Hearing presents witnesses describing child welfare issues in the Southwest including teen pregnancy and infant welfare. Lengthy testimony examines child care needs and describes a study of child care needs and usage by University of California student parents. Other hearing topics include children in refugee families, child sexual abuse, domestic violence, and prenatal care.

178.   U.S. Congress. House. Select Committee on Children, Youth, and Families. *Children, Youth, and Families of the Mountain West, Hearing.* 98th Cong., 1st sess., 6 Dec. 1983, Salt Lake City. 288p. Y4.C43/2:C43/8. Among the problems relating to children and families discussed in this hearing are family violence, affordable child care, child support enforcement, and adolescent pregnancy. A housing program, Project PRIDE, for female-headed households is described.

179.   U.S. Congress. House. Select Committee on Children, Youth, and Families. *Supporting a Family: Providing the Basics, Hearing.* 98th Cong., 1st sess., 18 July 1983. 203p. Y4.C43/2:F21/2. The problems of families trying to survive financially in the eighties are discussed by hearing witnesses. The position of women in the labor market and the sources of income for female-headed families are examined, and the effectiveness of the poverty "safety net" is questioned. Housing affordability, particularly for families with children, is a major focus of testimony.

180.   U.S. Dept. of Transportation. *The Impact of Changing Women's Roles on Transportation Needs and Usage.* Washington, DC: The Department, 1983. 116p. TD1.20/8:85-01. Issues addressed in this study of the impact of changing women's roles on their transportation needs and usage include new travel patterns and demands, sex differences in travel patterns, and objective factors affecting women's travel conditions. Factors which influenced women's travel patterns include income, employment, marital status, and children. Most of the data in the report is from a study done in Toronto, Canada.

181.   U.S. Bureau of the Census. *We the American Women.* Washington, DC: GPO, 1984. 15p. C3.2:Am3/6/no.2. Basic statistics on population, education, employment, income, and household type of American women from the 1980 Census.

182. U.S. Congress. House. Select Committee on Children, Youth and Families. *Children, Youth and Families: 1983, A Year End Report on the Activities of the Select Committee on Children, Youth, and Families with Minority and Additional Views.* H. Rept. 98-1179. 98th Cong., 2d sess., 1984. 192p. Serial 13604.

183. U.S. Congress. Senate. Special Committee on Aging. *Women in Our Aging Society, Hearing.* 98th Cong., 2d sess., 8 Oct. 1984. 107p. Y4.Ag4:S.hrg.98-1238. The combined barriers of sex and age discrimination are discussed as they affect the lives of older women. Personal narratives describe the work histories of women and highlight the effect of family responsibilities, pension program rules, and age discrimination on women's ability to maintain an adequate income as they get older. The problems of Medicare payments, health care costs, and methods of health care delivery are also reviewed.

184. U.S. President's Committee on the Employment of the Handicapped. *Disabled Women in America: A Statistical Report Drawn from Census Bureau Data.* Washington, DC: The Committee, 1984? 26p. PrEx1.10:D63/7. Demographic profile of the disabled female population in the U.S. presents data on age, years of school completed, residential and geographic distribution, marital status, employment status by educational attainment, income, and occupational category.

185. U.S. Air Force. Headquarters. *Commander's Spouse Course -- Items of Interest: Personnel.* Washington, DC: The Dept., 1985. looseleaf. D301.35:30-46. Booklet describes the personnel policies of the Air Force for what appears to be a basic orientation course for spouses. Topics covered include recruitment, training and assignment of personnel, and entitlements. Family services, alcohol and drug abuse control, child care, and survivor benefits programs are also reviewed. The role of women in the Air Force and benefits for former spouses are also covered.

186. U.S. Congress. Senate. Special Committee on Aging. *Challenges for Women: Taking Charge, Taking Care, Hearing.* 99th Cong., 1st sess., 18 November 1985. 79p. Y4.Ag4:S.hrg.99-629. Hearing testimony examines the problem of caring for an aging population and the role of women as caregivers. Implications of changing family structures for the care of the elderly are discussed.

187. U.S. Congress. House. Committee on Foreign Affairs. *U.N. Conference to Review and Appraise the U.N. Decade for Women, July 15-26, 1985: Report of Congressional Staff Advisors to the Nairobi Conference.* 99th Cong., 2d sess., Jan. 1986. Committee print. 181p. Y4.F76/1:Un35/78/985. Report on the U.N. Conference to Review and Appraise the U.N. Decade for Women summarizes the conference and the work of the U.S. delegation. The bulk of the report is appendices reprinting correspondence, press releases and conference documents. Included in the appendix is "The Forward-Looking Strategies", a document adopted at the conference defining issues and objectives to continue to address the problems of women worldwide.

188. U.S. Congress. House. Select Committee on Aging. *The Quality of Life for Older Women: Older Women Living Alone, a Report by the Chairman of the Select Committee on Aging.* 100th Cong., 2d sess., 1988. 12p. Committee Print. Y4.Ag4/2:L62/2. Summary of hearings on the economic and medical problems facing older women who live alone reviews topics of poverty and retirement income, health care costs, the lack of mental health research on older women, and housing. Witnesses' analysis of the policy issues and of the causes of poverty among older women are also summarized.

189. U.S. Congress. House. Select Committee on Aging. *Quality of Life for Older Women: Older Women Living Alone, Hearing.* 100th Cong., 2d sess., 27 Sept. 1988. 154p. Y4.Ag4/2:L62/3. Hearing explores the bias against older women in social support

programs. Social Security, Medicare and Medicaid are the target of much of the testimony as witnesses describe the typical situation of older women living alone. Possibilities for changing Social Security and ERISA to avoid a large population of impoverished older women in the future are discussed along with the likelihood that changing labor force patterns alone will address the problem. Specifically noted are the retirement prospects for clerical workers and displaced homemakers.

190. U.S. Congress. House. Select Committee on Children, Youth, and Families. *Children and Families: Key Trends in the 1980's, a Staff Report.* 100th Cong., 2d sess., 1988. 51p. Committee print. Y4.C43/2:C43/22. Statistical snapshot of trends affecting U.S. families highlights working mothers, childcare, health care, and housing, and notes trends in government policies and funding.

191. U.S. Bureau of the Census. *Single Parents and Their Children.* Statistical Brief 3-89. Washington, DC: GPO, 1989. 2p. C3.205/8:3-89. Basic trends in characteristics of single parent families are highlighted noting the problems of single mothers in the areas of education, employment and income.

192. U.S. Bureau of the Census. *Studies in Marriage and the Family: Singleness in America, Single Parents and Their Children, Married-Couple Families with Children.* Current Population Reports Series P-23, no. 162. Washington, DC: GPO, 1989. 38p. C3.186:P-93/162. Three reports on marriage and the family provide a statistical profile of single Americans, single parents, and "traditional" families. Reports on singleness and single parent families provide analysis of statistics by gender.

193. U.S. Congress. House. Committee on the Budget. Task Force on Human Resources. *Funding for Children in Fiscal Year 1990, Hearing.* 101 Cong., 1st sess., 8 March 1989. 137p. Y4.B85/3:101-5-2. Overview of government programs affecting children examines funding and program outcomes within a whole-family context. Child care, prenatal care, the WIC program, and education of at risk students are among the topics discussed.

SERIALS

194. U.S. Government Printing Office. Superintendent of Documents. *Women.* Subject Bibliography no. 111. Washington, DC: GPO, 1977-. irreg. GP3.22/2:111/no. Brief list of documents on women or of interest to women which are available from the Superintendent of Documents.

195. U.S. Interdepartmental Committee on the Status of Women and U.S. Citizens' Advisory Council on the Status of Women. *Report on Progress in [year] on the Status of Women, Annual Report of Interdepartmental Committee and Citizens' Advisory Council on the Status of Women.* Washington, DC: GPO, 1964-1966. annual. Y3.In8/21:1/year. Report describes projects of the federal government and national organizations to improve the status of women and presents information on actions by state commissions on the status of women. Topics of education, employment, labor legislation, political participation, and home and community are covered, and related publications of the federal government and of state commissions are listed. International actions on the status of women are reviewed.

196. U.S. National Commission on the Observance of International Women's Year. Office of Public Information. *Update.* 1977-1978? irreg. Y3.W84:11/no. Newsletter provides updates on commission activities.

197. U.S. Navy Dept. Navy Internal Relations Activity. *Navy Wifeline.* Washington, DC: The Department, 1977. quarterly. D201.25:date. Continued by *Wifeline* (198).

198. U.S. Navy Dept. Navy Internal Relations Activity. *Wifeline.* Washington, DC: The Department, Summer 1977 - Spring 1989. quarterly. D201.25:date. Continues *Navy Wifeline* (197).

199. U.S. Women's Bureau. *Fact Sheet on Changing Patterns of Women's Lives.* Washington, DC: GPO, 1965 -1970. irreg. L13.2:W84/43/970.

2
Notable Women

Throughout the years the achievements of individual women, mostly Americans, were recognized in government documents. Brief reports of congressional committees highlight the accomplishments of women such as Clara Barton, Dorothea Dix, and Mary Ball Washington while discussing the appropriation of funds for monuments and national historic sites. Occasionally federal agencies would issue publications on the lives of famous women. Some of the more unique profiles of American women are found in the scripts for radio programs produced in the late 1930s and early 1940s. Each episode of the series "Gallant American Women" describes the contributions of women to a particular area of endeavor. Women as authors (226) and journalists (227, 229), in the fine arts (230, 232, 236) and athletics (235), and as wives (234) and mothers (228) are featured. The First Ladies are the focus of a number of publications with one of the most interesting being a script for "The World is Yours" radio program. In this episode Dolly Madison tells a little about the lives of the First Ladies during their years at the White House (222).

A number of women artists are featured in glossy publications of the Smithsonian Institution. Among the artists whose works are highlighted are Alice Pike Barney (254), Mary Cassatt (265, 290), Lilly Martin Spencer (276), Maria Martinez (289), and Elizabeth Nourse (307). Publications with African American women as subjects describe the accomplishments of educator Anna J. Cooper (299) and artist Alma Thomas (300). Numerous congressional reports describe the work of Mary McLeod Bethune, educator and founder of the National Council of Negro Women. Other interesting documents on American women include *Manners in the Senate Chambers: 19th Century Women's Views* (294), and a collection of Voice of America interviews with eight notable women including Grace Hopper, Betty Friedan, and Maya Angelou (314). When Congress authorized the design of a new one dollar coin in 1978, one of the issues debated was whether or not to place the likeness of a women on the coin and which woman to honor. The contributions of the major candidates, particularly Susan B. Anthony, are highlighted in the hearings and reports (283-286). Extensive bibliographies listing books and articles on notable American women were published by the Library of Congress between 1931 and 1941 (214, 219, 237-238).

200. U.S. Congress. House. Committee on Public Buildings and Grounds. *Monument to Mary Washington, Report to Accompany Bill H.R. 4135.* H. Rept. 1659, 47th Cong., 1st sess., 1882. 1p. Serial 2070. Reports a bill to fund completion of a monument to Mary Washington, at Fredericksburg, Virginia.

201. U.S. Congress. House. Committee on the Library. *Monument to Mary, the Mother of Washington, Report to Accompany Bill H.R. 1905.* H. Rept. 937, 50th Cong., 1st sess., 1888. 2p. Serial 2600. Favorable report on a bill to allocate funds for the completion of

a monument to Mary Washington at Fredericksburg, Virginia, briefly reviews past legislative action on the issue.

202. U.S. Congress. House. Committee on the Library. *Monument to Mary Washington, Mother of Washington, Report to Accompany Bill S. 1211.* H. Rept. 3102, 50th Cong., 1st sess., 1888. 1p. Serial 2605. Reports a bill to fund completion of the monument.

203. U.S. Congress. Senate. Committee on the Library. *National Dorothea Dix Memorial Association: Letter from the Superintendent of the Government Hospital for the Insane, Transmitting a Memorial of the National Dorothea Dix Memorial Association Praying for an Appropriation for the Building of a Monument to Mark the Birthplace at Hampden, Me., of Miss Dorothea Lynde Dix.* S. Doc. 49, 56th Cong., 2d sess., 1900. 5p. Serial 4033. A short biography of Dorothea Dix and an overview of her work for the insane is included in this petition for funds to erect a monument near her birthplace. Also printed in H. Rept. 2985 (204) and S. Rept. 1772 (205).

204. U.S. Congress. House. Committee on the Library. *Monument to Dorothea Lynde Dix, Report to Accompany H.J. Res. 313.* H. Rept. 2985, 56th Cong., 2d sess., 1901. 6p. Serial 4214. See 203 for abstract.

205. U.S. Congress. Senate. Committee on the Library. *National Dorothea Dix Memorial Association, Report to Accompany S.R. 140.* S. Rept. 1772, 56th Cong., 2d sess., 1901. 6p. Serial 4064. See 203 for abstract.

206. U.S. Congress. Senate. Committee on the Library. *Monument to Dorothea Lynde Dix, Report to Accompany S.R. 30.* S. Rept. 226, 57th Cong., 1st sess., 1902. 6p. Serial 4257. Basically a reprint of S. Rept. 1772, 56th Congress (205).

207. U.S. Congress. House. Committee on the Library. *Monument to Dorothea Lynde Dix, Report to Accompany S.R. 30.* H. Rept. 3877, 57th Cong., 2d sess., 1903. 1p. Serial 4415.

208. U.S. Congress. Senate. Committee on the Library. *Monument to the Memory of Dorothea Lynde Dix, Report to Accompany S.R. 12.* S. Rept. 815, 58th Cong., 2d sess., 1904. 7p. Serial 4572. Report on S.R. 12, to erect a monument to Dorothea Dix reprints earlier House and Senate reports.

209. U.S. Congress. Senate. Committee on the Library. *Monument to the Memory of Dorothea Lynde Dix, Report to Accompany S.R. 1.* S. Rept. 1215, 59th Cong., 1st sess., 1906. 7p. Serial 4904. Report on a joint resolution on the erection of a monument to Dorothea Lynde Dix reprints previous House and Senate reports.

210. U.S. Congress. House. Committee on the Library. *Memorial to Clara Barton, Hearings on H.R. 16606.* 64th Cong., 1st & 2d sess., 24 July 1916, 2 Feb. 1917. 35p. Y4.L61/1:B28. Hearing on a bill to place a table in honor of Clara Barton in the Women's Memorial Building reviews Barton's work for the sick and wounded of the Civil War and with the Red Cross in war and peace.

211. U.S. Congress. House. Committee on the Library. *Memorial to Miss Clara Barton, Adverse Report to Accompany H.R. 16606.* H. Rept. 1512, 64th Cong., 2d sess., 1917. 2p. Serial 7110. Adverse report rejects placing a memorial to Clara Barton in the building being erected as a memorial to the women of the Civil War and to be used as headquarters for the American National Red Cross. Donors to the building project objected to a memorial to an individual in the building.

212.   U.S. Smithsonian Institution. National Museum. *Catalogue of Collection of Busts of Prominent Personages in Bronze and Terra Cotta by Mrs. Nancy Cox-McCormack, on View in South Room of National Gallery, Natural History Building, National Museum, December 16, 1924 - January 16, 1925.* Washington, DC: The Institution, 1924. 4p. SI6.2:C889.

213.   U.S. Commission for the Celebration of the 200th Anniversary of the Birth of George Washington, 1732-1932. *Mother of George Washington, Radio Address by Mrs. John Dickinson Sherman, Washington, D.C., Mothers' Day, May 11, 1930.* Washington, DC: The Commission, 1931. 8p. Y3.W27/2:2M85/931. Speech depicts Mary Bell Washington as a devoted mother guiding and inspiring her son to leadership.

214.   U.S. Library of Congress. Division of Bibliography. *List of References Relating to Notable American Women.* by Florence S. Hellman. Washington, DC: The Library, 1931. 76p. LC2.2:W84. Unannotated bibliography provides 942 references to popular and scholarly works on notable American women arranged by individual with notes on articles within general biographical works.

215.   U.S. Congress. House. Committee on Accounts. *Wreath on Grave of the Mother of Washington, Report to Accompany H. Con. Res. 19.* H. Rept. 416, 72d Cong., 1st sess., 1932. 1p. Serial 9495.

216.   U.S. Post Office Dept. *Susan B. Anthony Commemorative Postage Stamp.* Washington, DC: Postmaster General, 1936. poster. P4.2:An2.

217.   U.S. Dept. of Labor. *Frances Perkins: A Bibliographical List.* Washington, DC: The Department, 1937. 18p. L1.2:P41. Bibliography of works by and about Frances Perkins, Secretary of Labor includes published statements and addresses.

218.   U.S. Dept. of the Interior. Office of Information. *Ladies of the White House.* Answer Me This, Historical Series [radio scripts] no. 4. Washington, DC: The Office, 1937. 13p. I16.58/5:4. Radio quiz describes various first ladies and then asks questions.

219.   U.S. Library of Congress. Division of Bibliography. *List of References Relating to Notable American Women, Supplement to Mimeographed List, 1932.* by Florence S. Hellman. Washington, DC: The Library, 1937. 144p. LC2.2:W84/supp.1. Supplement to *List of Reference Relating to Notable American Women* (214) provides 1693 additional references.

220.   U.S. Office of Education. *Pearl S. Buck.* Washington, DC: The Office, 1937? 4p. I16.65/2:B85. Supplement to the Pearl Buck presentation of the radio series "Treasures Next Door" describes some of the influences on her philosophy and writing.

221.   U.S. Office of Education. *Private Life of Louisa M. Alcott.* Washington, DC: The Office, 1937? 3p. I16.65/2:Al1. Biographical sketch of Louisa May Alcott with a list of sources was published as a supplement to the radio broadcast of *Little Women.*

222.   U.S. Office of Education. *First Ladies Fashions, April 9, 1939.* The World is Yours no. 148. Washington, DC: The Office, 1939. 28p. I16.56/2:148. In this radio script Dolly Madison comes out of her display case in the First Ladies Hall and gossips with the night watchman about the First Ladies while describing their dresses. Short vignettes show scenes from the First Ladies' lives in the White House.

223. U.S. Office of Education. *Gallant American Women, No. 5, Refugee Women, November 28, 1939.* by Jane Ashman. Washington, DC: The Office, 1939. 23p. FS5.15:5. The contributions of women who came to the U.S. as refugees are described in the vignettes of this radio script.

224. U.S. Office of Education. *The World Is Yours, Supplement to First Ladies Fashions, Broadcast, April 23, 1939.* Washington, DC: The Office, 1939. 2p. I16.56/2a:Apr. 23, 1939. Description with illustrations of the Easter dresses of First Ladies Julia Dent Grant, Lucy Webb Hayes, Lucretia R. Garfield, and Mary Arthur McElroy.

225. U.S. Office of Education. *Gallant American Women #12, Women Explorers, January 16, 1940.* by Jane Ashman. Washington, DC: The Office, 1940. 22p. FS5.15:12. Exciting stories of the dangers faced by women as they went out, with their husbands or on their own, to explore the world are told in this radio script.

226. U.S. Office of Education. *Gallant American Women #13, Women of Letters, January 23, 1940.* by Jane Ashman. Washington, DC: The Office, 1940. 24p. FS5.15:13. A special guest on the thirteenth episode of "Gallant American Women" was Pearl Buck, winner of the Nobel Prize for Literature. The contributions of other women to literature are highlighted with vignettes on the writings of Mercy Warren, Anne Bradstreet, and Harriet Beecher Stowe among others.

227. U.S. Office of Education. *Gallant American Women #14, Ladies of the Press, January 30, 1940.* by Jane Ashman. Washington, DC: The Office, 1940. 24p. FS5.15:14. The newspaper women who fought to protect the freedom of the press are honored in short radio sketches telling about their dedication to publishing their opinions.

228. U.S. Office of Education. *Gallant American Women #15, Mothers of Great Americans, February 6, 1940.* by Jane Ashman. Washington, DC: The Office, 1940. 25p. FS5.15:15. Radio script tells the story of Mary Ball Washington, mother of George Washington, and of Nancy Hanks Lincoln, mother of Abraham Lincoln, focusing on their influence on their sons. Includes a list of resources consulted.

229. U.S. Office of Education. *Gallant American Women [#18], Ladies of the Press, February 27, 1940.* by Jane Ashman. Washington, DC: The Office, 1940. 21p. FS5.15:18. From printing anti-British newspapers in Colonial America to writing the women's page of the 1940's newspaper, this radio script tells the story of women as newspaper printers, reporters, and readers. Much of the script is similar to episode no. 14 (227) but the ending is revised.

230. U.S. Office of Education. *Gallant American Women [#19], Women in Opera, March 5, 1940.* by Jane Ashman. Washington, DC: The Office, 1940. 23p. FS5.15:19. Radio script provides brief dialogue depicting the careers of women opera singers and the women who helped support opera in America. The program closes with a word from Dusolina Giannini in support of the Metropolitan Opera Association.

231. U.S. Office of Education. *Gallant American Women #24, Women in Science, April 16, 1940.* by Irve Tunick. Washington, DC: The Office, 1940. 25p. FS5.15:24. Women's achievements in science are touted in this radio script which includes a vignette on Maria Mitchell's discovery of a new comet.

232. U.S. Office of Education. *Gallant American Women #25, Behind the Footlights, April 30 [23], 1940.* by Jane Ashman. Washington, DC: The Office, 1940. 22p. FS5.15:25. The actresses who helped to bring theater to America are the focus of this radio script with

anecdotes on the crude conditions faced by early theater troupes. A list of materials consulted is appended.

233. U.S. Office of Education. *Gallant American Women #27, Women with Wings, May 7, 1940.* by Jane Ashman. Washington, DC: The Office, 1940. 23p. FS5.15:27. Women in aviation, from Katherine Wright, who helped finance her famous brothers, to barnstormer Katherine Stinson, and the more famous Amelia Earhart and Jacqueline Cochran, are depicted in this half-hour radio script in the "Gallant American Women" series.

234. U.S. Office of Education. *Gallant American Women #31, Wives of Great Americans, June 3, 1940.* by Jane Ashman. Washington, DC: The Office, 1940. 22p. FS5.15:31. Lucy Audubon and Josephine Peary are featured in vignettes extolling the role of great women as wives of great men.

235. U.S. Office of Education. *Gallant American Women #32, Women in Sports, June 10, 1940.* by Jane Ashman. Washington, DC: The Office, 1940. 26p. FS5.15:32. From the victorian ideal of the gentle, nonathletic woman to swimmer Gertrude Ederle, the story of women in sports and the idea of sports as democracy are presented in this episode of the "Gallant American Women" radio series.

236. U.S. Office of Education. *Gallant American Women #34, On with the Dance, July 1, 1940.* by Jane Ashman. Washington, DC: The Office, 1940. 30p. FS5.15:34. Last of the radio scripts for the "Gallant American Women" series reveals through vignettes the social importance of dance in America and highlights the contributions of women such as Isadora Duncan, Irene Castle, and Ruth St. Denis.

237. U.S. Library of Congress. Division of Bibliography. *Comprehensive Index to Notable American Women, 1932, 1937, 1941.* by Florence S. Hellman. Washington, DC: The Library, 1941. 28p. LC2.2:W84/ind. Subject index to *List of References Relating to Notable American Women* (204) and its supplements (209,228).

238. U.S. Library of Congress. Division of Bibliography. *List of References Relating to Notable American Women, Supplement to Mimeographed Lists 1932, 1937.* by Florence S. Hellman. Washington, DC: The Library, 1941. 122p. LC2.2:W84/supp.2. Supplement to *List of References Relating to Notable American Women* (204) provides 1559 additional references.

239. U.S. Office of the Coordinator of Inter-American Affairs. *Prominent Women in Latin America.* by Kathleen Tappen and Bernice T. Morris. Washington, DC: The Office, 1944. 22p. Pr32.4602:W84/4. A who's who of Latin American women gives place and date of birth and career highlights. Includes writers, feminists, entertainers, diplomats and other notable women.

240. U.S. Women's Bureau. *Women in the United Nations, April 1942.* by Frances W. Kerr. Washington, DC: The Bureau, 1947. 17p. L13.2:Un3/2. Describes job opportunities for women in the United Nations Secretariat and provides biographical notes on women attending the General Assembly in New York in October 1946 and women members of the Commission on the Status of Women. Also lists women attending the UN Conference in San Francisco, June 1945, and the General Assembly in London, January 1946. U.S. delegates and advisors to the various subgroups of the United Nations are listed.

241. U.S. Congress. House. Committee on Post Office and Civil Service. *Authorizing the Issuance of a Special Series of Stamps Commemorative of Juliette Low, Founder and*

Organizer of Girl Scouting in the United State of America, Report to Accompany H.J. Res. 327. H. Rept. 2174, 80th Cong., 2d sess., 1948. 2p. Serial 11212.

242. U.S. Congress. Senate. Committee on Post Office and Civil Service. *Authorizing the Issuance of a Special Series of Stamps Commemorative of Juliette Low, Founder and Organizer of Girls Scouting in the United States of American, Report to Accompany H.J. Res. 327.* S. Rept. 1681, 80th Cong., 2d sess., 1948. 2p. Serial 11208.

243. U.S. Women's Bureau. *Biographical Notes on Members of the Secretary of Labor's Women's Advisory Committee on Defense Manpower.* Washington, DC: The Bureau, 1951. 4p. L13.2:M31/2.

244. U.S. Smithsonian Institution. *Photographs of First Ladies of the White House.* Information Leaflet Series no. 3. Washington, DC: The Institution, 1952. 1p. SI1.19:3.

245. U.S. Smithsonian Institution. National Museum. *Dresses of the First Ladies of the White House.* by Margaret W. Brown. Washington, DC: The Smithsonian Institution Press, 1952. 149p. SI3.2:D81. Photographs of the dresses of the First Ladies as exhibited in the National Museum are accompanied by one-page biographical sketches. Each dress is described within the context of the fashions of the period.

246. U.S. Women's Bureau. *Biographical Notes on Participants in National Conference on Equal Pay, March 31 - April 1, 1952, Interdepartmental Auditorium, Washington.* Washington, DC: The Bureau, 1952. 6p. L13.2:N21.

247. U.S. Women's Bureau. *Biographical Sketch of Alice K. Leopold, Director, Women's Bureau, U.S. Department of Labor.* Washington, DC: The Bureau, 1953. 2p. L13.2:L55.

248. U.S. Congress. House. Committee on Foreign Affairs. *Inviting Nurse Genevieve de Galard-Terraube to be an Honored Guest of the United States, Report to Accompany H. Con. Res. 236.* H. Rept. 1755, 83rd Cong., 2d sess., 1954. 2p. Serial 11740. Favorable report on a resolution inviting Genevieve de Galard-Terraube, "The Angel of Dien Bien Phen" (Vietnam), to visit the U.S. as an honored guest.

249. U.S. Congress. Senate. Committee on Foreign Relations. *Inviting Nurse Genevieve de Galard-Terraube to be an Honored Guest to the United States, Report to Accompany H. Con. Res. 236.* S. Rept. 1507, 83rd Cong., 2d sess., 1954. 2p. Serial 11729. See 238 for abstract.

250. U.S. Smithsonian Institution. *The First Ladies Hall.* Baltimore, MD: Lord Baltimore Press, 1955. 10p. SI1.2:F51. Illustrated booklet describes the rooms of the First Ladies Hall where dresses of the First Ladies are displayed.

251. U.S. Women's Bureau. *Conference on Effective Use of Woman Power, March 10-11, 1955, Biographical Notes on Speakers.* Washington, DC: The Bureau, 1955. 8p. L13.2:C76/2/955-3.

252. U.S. Congress. *Memorial Services Held in the House of Representatives and the Senate of the United States, Together with Remarks Presented in Eulogy of Vera Daerr Buchanan, Late a Representative from Pennsylvania.* Washington, DC: GPO, 1956. 48p. Y7.1:B851/3. Remarks praise Congresswoman Vera Daerr Buchanan, who was elected to fill the vacancy caused by the death of her husband and reelected to Congress twice.

253. U.S. Smithsonian Institution. National Museum. *Collection of Dresses of First Ladies of the White House in the National Museum.* Information Leaflet Series no. 25. Washington, DC: The Institution, 1956. 1p. SI1.19:25.

254. U.S. Smithsonian Institution. National Collection of Fine Art. *Alice Pike Barney: Portraits in Oil and Pastel.* Washington, DC: The Institution, 1957. 5p. + 98 plates. SI6.2:B26. Collection of black and white reproductions of the oils and pastels of artist Alice Pike Barney provides minimal commentary.

255. U.S. Smithsonian Institution. National Museum. *Bibliography on First Ladies of the White House Represented in Costume Collection of National Museum.* Information Leaflet Series no. 22. Washington, DC: The Smithsonian, 1957. 1p. SI1.19:22.

256. U.S. Smithsonian Institution. National Museum. *Gown of Mrs. Dwight D. Eisenhower as Displayed in the National Museum, Smithsonian Institution.* by Margaret Brown Klapthor. Washington, DC: The Smithsonian, 1958. 5p. S13.2:D84/supp.

257. U.S. Congress. Senate. Committee on Rules and Administration. *Statue of Ester Morris Presented by the State of Wyoming for the National Statutory Hall Collection, Report to Accompany S. Con. Res. 55, S. Con. Res. 56, and S. Con. Res. 57.* S. Rept. 625, 86th Cong., 1st sess., 1959. 4p. Serial 1251. Favorable report on accepting a statue of Ester Morris, leader in the establishment of woman suffrage in Wyoming, includes a short biography of Morris emphasizing her commitment to woman's rights.

258. U.S. Library of Congress. *Willa Cather: Paradox of Success.* by Leon Edel. Washington, DC: GPO, 1960. 17p. LC29.9:Ed2.

259. U.S. Women's Bureau. *Career Highlights of Speakers and Panelists, 40th Anniversary Conference of the Women's Bureau, June 2 and 3, 1960.* Washington, DC: The Bureau, 1960. 14p. L13.2:C18.

260. U.S. Congress. *Memorial Services Held in the House of Representatives and Senate of the United States, Together with Remarks Presented in Eulogy of Edith Nourse Rogers, Late a Representative from Massachusetts.* Washington, DC: GPO, 1961. 92p. Y7.1:R631/2. Remarks eulogize Edith Nourse Rogers who served in Congress for 35 years. Rogers was best known for her support of veterans, and for her role in the establishment of the Women's Army Corps.

261. U.S. Post Office Dept. *5-Cent Eleanor Roosevelt Commemorative Postage Stamp, Available at Your Local Post Office, Oct. 12, 1963.* Washington, DC: GPO, 1963. poster. P1.26/2:R67.

262. U.S. Post Office Dept. *8-Cent Amelia Earhart, Commemorative Air Mail Postage Stamp, Available at Your Local Post Office, July 25, 1963.* Washington, DC: The Department, 1963. poster. P1.26/2:Ea7.

263. U.S. Smithsonian Institution. National Museum. *Gown of Mrs. John F. Kennedy, as Displayed in the National Museum, Smithsonian Institution.* by Margaret Brown Klapthor. Washington, DC: The Smithsonian, 1963. 5p. SI3.2:D81/supp.2.

264. U.S. Post Office Dept. *5-Cent Mary Cassatt American Painting Commemorative Postage Stamp, Available at Your Local Post Office Nov. 18, 1966.* Washington, DC: The Department, 1966. poster. P1.26/2:C27.

265. U.S. Smithsonian Institution and Museum of Graphic Art. *Graphic Art of Mary Cassatt.* Washington, DC: Smithsonian Institution Press, 1967. 112p. SI1.2:C27. Catalog for an exhibition on Mary Cassatt's graphic art provides a brief introduction, a biographical chronology, a selected bibliography, a summary of Cassatt exhibitions featuring prints, and 85 plates of Cassatt's work in soft-ground, drypoint and aquatint.

266. U.S. Post Office Dept. *50-Cent Lucy Stone Regular Postage Stamp Will Be Placed on Sale Aug. 13, 1968, at Dorchester, Mass.* Washington, DC: GPO, 1968. poster. P1.26/2:St7.

267. U.S. Library of Congress. *Louisa May Alcott.* Washington, DC: GPO, 1969. 91p. LC2.2:Al1/2. Annotated and illustrated bibliography describes the works of Louisa May Alcott.

268. U.S. Post Office Dept. *6-Cent Grandma Moses American Folklore Commemorative Postage Stamp Will Be First Placed on Sale at Washington, D.C. on May 1, 1969.* Washington, DC: The Office, 1969. poster. P1.26/2:M85.

269. U.S. Congress. House. Committee on House Administration. *Extending for 4 Years the Existing Authority for the Erection in the District of Columbia of a Memorial to Mary McLeod Bethune, Report to Accompany H.J. Res. 1069.* H. Rept. 91-999, 91st Cong., 2d sess., 1970. 3p. Serial 12884-2. Reports a resolution to extend the time limitation for the National Council of Negro Women to secure funds for the erection of a monument to Mary McLeod Bethune, black educator and founder of the National Council of Negro Women.

270. U.S. Congress. Senate. Committee on Rules and Administration. *Extending for 2 Years the Existing Authority for the Erection in the District of Columbia of a Memorial to Mary McLeod Bethune, Report to Accompany S.J. Res. 111.* S. Rept. 151, 92d Cong., 1st sess., 1971. 4p. Serial 12929-2. Favorable report on granting an extended period of time for the erection of a monument to Mary McLeod Bethune, a prominent black educator. Erection of the memorial on public grounds was a project of the National Council on Negro Women under the authority of House Joint Resolution 502, 86th Congress. Correspondence from the Council and the Department of the Interior detail the amount of work completed.

271. U.S. Postal Service. *Emily Dickinson 8-Cent Stamp, Issue Date Aug. 28, 1971, Amherst, Mass.* Washington, DC: The Service, 1971. poster. P1.26/2:D56.

272. U.S. Library of Congress. *Louise Bogan: A Woman's World.* Washington, DC: GPO, 1972. 81p. LC1.14:Sm6. Collection of essays on the life and work of Louise Bogan, poet and critic, includes a bibliography of her works held by the Library of Congress.

273. U.S. Postal Service. *18-Cent Elizabeth Blackwell Regular Postage Stamp, Issue Date Jan. 23, 1974, Geneva, N.Y.* Washington, DC: The Service, 1973. poster. P1.26/2:B56.

274. U.S. Postal Service. *Willa Cather Commemorative Stamp, American Arts Series, Issue Date Sept. 20, 1973, Red Cloud, Nebr.* Washington, DC: The Service, 1973. poster. P1.26/2:C28.

275. U.S. Smithsonian Institution. Museum of History and Technology. *The First Ladies Hall.* Washington, DC: The Smithsonian Institution Press, 1973. 24p. SI1.2:F51/973. Pictures of the rooms of the First Ladies Hall, which displays dresses worn by the First Ladies, are accompanied by a short description of each dress.

276. U.S. Smithsonian Institution. National Collection of Fine Arts. *Lilly Martin Spencer: The Joys of Sentiment.* Washington, DC: The Smithsonian Institution Press, 1973. 254p.

SI6.2:Sp3. Catalog for an exhibition of the work of Lilly Martin Spencer, American painter active between 1839 and 1902, includes as brief biography, reference list, and 138 illustrations.

277.   U.S. Congress. Senate. Committee on Interior and Insular Affairs. *Clara Barton House National Historic Site, Maryland, Report to Accompany S. 3700.* S. Rept. 93-1020, 93d Cong., 2d sess., 1974. 5p. Serial 13057-5. Report on a bill declaring the Clara Barton House in Glen Echo, Maryland a National Historic Site provides background on the history of the house and its use as Red Cross Headquarters.

278.   U.S. Congress. Senate. Committee on Interior and Insular Affairs. *Providing for the Establishment of the Clara Barton National Historic Site, MD; John Day Fossil Beds National Monument, Oreg.; Knife River Indian Village National Historic Site, N. Dak.; Springfield Armory National Historic Site, Mass.; Tuskegee Institute National Historic Site, N.Y.; and Sewall-Belmont House National Historic Site, Washington D.C.; and for Other Purposes, Report to Accompany H.R. 13157.* S. Rept. 93-1233, 93d Cong., 2d sess., 1974. 25p. Serial 13057-9. Favorable report on designating a number of National Historic Sites, including Clara Barton's House and the Sewall-Belmont House, former headquarters of the National Woman's Party, provides Department of the Interior reports on each site.

279.   U.S. Congress. House. Committee on Post Office and Civil Service. *National Saint Elizabeth Seton Day, Report to Accompany H.J. Res. 597.* H. Rept. 94-458, 94th Cong., 1st sess., 1975. 3p. Serial 13099-7. Reports a resolution commemorating the work of Saint Elizabeth Seton, founder of the Sisters of Charity of St. Joseph and the first natural born American to be canonized.

280.   U.S. Dept. of Health, Education, and Welfare. *Historical Women in Health, Education and Welfare.* Washington, DC: GPO, 1975. 22p. HE1.2:W84. Presents brief historical biographies of women involved in health care, education, and public welfare.

281.   U.S. Federal Aviation Administration. Office of General Aviation. *A Salute to Women in Aerospace.* by Jean Ross Howard. Washington, DC: The Office, 1976? 6p. TD4.25:Ae8/4. Profiles of women in aerospace past and present are reprinted from *Aerospace* magazine.

282.   U.S. Smithsonian Institution. National Air and Space Museum. *Amelia Earhart.* Washington, DC: The Institution, 1976? [5]p. leaflet. SI9.2:Ea7.

283.   U.S. Congress. House. Committee on Banking, Finance, and Urban Affairs. *Susan B. Anthony Dollar Coin Act of 1978, Report Together with Additional and Dissenting Views to Accompany H.R. 12728.* H. Rept. 95-1576, 95th Cong., 2d sess. 1978. 11p. Serial 1576. This favorable report on the creation of a new dollar coin briefly explains the rational for designating the likeness of Susan B. Anthony for the coin's design.

284.   U.S. Congress. House. Committee on Banking, Finance, and Urban Affairs. Subcommittee on Historic Preservation and Coinage. *Proposed Smaller One-Dollar Coin, Hearings on H.R. 12444.* 95th Cong., 2d sess., 17,31 May 1978. 248p. Y4.B22/1:C66/6. Although most of this hearing deals with the size and metal for the proposed one-dollar coin, testimony is also presented supporting the placement of the image of a woman on the coin. The women proposed for the coin include Susan B. Anthony, Harriet Ross Tubman, and Maggie L. Walker.

285.   U.S. Congress. Senate. Committee on Banking, Housing, and Urban Affairs. *Susan B. Anthony Dollar Coin Act of 1978, Hearing on S. 3036.* 95th Cong., 2d sess., 17 July

1978. 191p. Y4.B22/3:An8/2. Hearing on the design of a new dollar coin highlights the debate over the Treasury plan to put the image of liberty on the coin versus congressional and public desire to commemorate a woman, either Susan B. Anthony or Harriet Ross Tubman, on the coin.

286. U.S. Congress. Senate. Committee on Banking, Housing, and Urban Affairs. *The Susan B. Anthony Dollar Coin Act of 1978, Report to Accompany S. 3036.* S. Rept. 95-1120, 95th Cong., 2d sess., 1978. 8p. Serial 13197-10. Committee reasons for designating the likeness of Susan B. Anthony for the new dollar coin are briefly set out in this favorable report on a newly designed dollar coin.

287. U.S. Library of Congress. Archive of Folk Song. *Women and Folk Music: A Selected Bibliography.* Washington, DC: The Library, 1978. 12p. LC1.12/2:W84/2. Bibliography without annotations lists books and articles on women as folk singers and women in folk music.

288. U.S. Smithsonian Institution. *United States Women in Aviation through World War I.* by Claudia M. Oakes. Smithsonian Studies in Air and Space no. 2. Washington, DC: GPO, 1978. 44p. SI1.42:2. Illustrated history features women parachutists, balloonists and airplane pilots in the U.S. through World War I.

289. U.S. Smithsonian Institution. National Collection of Fine Arts. *Maria Martinez: Five Generations of Potters.* by Susan Peterson. Washington, DC: Smithsonian Institution Press, 1978. 48p. SI6.2:M36. Illustrations and descriptions of the Native-American pottery of Maria Montoya Martinez and her family.

290. U.S. Smithsonian Institution. National Collection of Fine Arts. *Mary Cassatt, Pastels and Color Prints.* Washington, DC: Smithsonian Institution Press, 1978. 39p. SI6.2:C27. Exhibition catalog of Mary Cassatt's pastels and color prints includes a brief description of her work and techniques.

291. U.S. Internal Revenue Service. Federal Women's Program. *Women's Work.* Washington, DC: GPO, 1979. leaflet. T22.2:W84/2. Identifies briefly the accomplishments of the women portrayed on the poster "Women's Work, The Rest is Up to You." (292).

292. U.S. Internal Revenue Service. Federal Women's Program. *Women's Work...The Rest Is Up to You.* Washington, DC: GPO, 1979. poster. T22.41:W84. Poster depicts past women leaders. The accomplishments of the women portrayed are summarized by the leaflet *Women's Work* (291).

293. U.S. Congress. House. Committee on House Administration. *Authorizing the Printing of a Collection of Statements Made in Tribute to the Late Mamie Doud Eisenhower, Report to Accompany H. Res. 759.* H. Rept. 96-1421, 96th Cong., 2d sess., 1980. 2p. Serial 13379.

294. U.S. Congress. Senate. Commission on Arts and Humanities. *Manners in the Senate Chambers: 19th Century Women's Views.* Washington, DC: GPO, 1980. 20p. Y4.Ar7:M32. Excerpts from diaries, letters and newspaper columns written by women reveal their views on the manners in the Senate Chamber, describing both the senators and the spectators in the gallery. One page biographies of the authors, Virginia Clay-Clopton, Frances Kemble, Sara Jane Lippincott (pen name Grace Greenwood), Mary Logan, Harriet Martineau, Margaret Bayard Smith, Jane Grey Swisshelm, Frances Trollope, Mary Jane Windle, and Emily Briggs, are provided.

295.   U.S. Congress. Senate. Committee on Foreign Relations. *Nomination of Jeane J. Kirkpatrick, Hearing.* 97th Cong., 1st sess., 15 Jan. 1981. 110p. Y4.F76/2:K63. Nomination hearing on Jeane J. Kirkpatrick to be the U.S. representative to the United Nations reviews her career and reveals her political views. The hearing record also reprints articles by Kirkpatrick on U.S. foreign affairs.

296.   U.S. Congress. Senate. Committee on the Judiciary. *Nomination of Sandra Day O'Connor, Hearings.* 97th Cong., 1st sess., 9-11 Sept. 1981. 414p. Y4.J89/2:J-97-51. Hearing on the nomination of Sandra Day O'Connor to be an Associate Justice of the Supreme Court provides information on her career and her legal philosophy. A considerable amount of the hearing questioning is devoted to the abortion issue and O'Connor's views on the *Roe v. Wade* decision. Also discussed is the unique position she would hold as the first woman on the Supreme Court.

297.   U.S. Congress. Senate. Committee on the Judiciary. *Nomination of Sandra Day O'Connor, Report Together with Additional, Supplemental, and Separate Views to Accompany the Nomination of Sandra Day O'Connor.* S. Exec. Rept. 97-22, 97th Cong., 1st sess., 1981. 8p. Serial 13406. Brief favorable report on the nomination of Sandra Day O'Connor to be a justice on the Supreme Court is accompanied by several statements of individual Senators expressing concern of O'Connor's refusal to answer some questions during confirmation hearings. In particular her refusal to comment on *Roe v. Wade* is cited.

298.   U.S. Dept. of the Interior. National Park Service. *Clara Barton: Clara Barton National Historic Site, Maryland.* National Park Service Handbook no. 110. Washington, DC: GPO, 1981. 78p. I29.9/5:110. Biography of Clara Barton, founder of the American Red Cross, accompanies a description of the Clara Barton National Historic Site and other National Park Service sites associated with Barton.

299.   U.S. Smithsonian Institution. Anacosta Neighborhood Museum. *Anna J. Cooper: A Voice from the South.* by Louise Daniel Hutchinson. Washington, DC: Smithsonian Institution Press, 1981. 208p. SI1.2:C78. Biography of Dr. Anna J. Cooper, notable black educator, examines her life against the background of the times in which she lived. Photographs from the Smithsonian exhibit on Cooper accompany the text.

300.   U.S. Smithsonian Institution. National Museum of American Art. *A Life in Art, Alma Thomas, 1891 - 1978.* by Merry A. Foresta. Washington, DC: Smithsonian Institution Press, 1981. 56p. SI6.2:T36. Biography and exhibition catalog on Alma Thomas, black American artist, reproduces 42 of her works with some color plates.

301.   U.S. White House Historical Association. *The First Ladies.* by Margaret Brown Klapthor. Washington, DC: The Association, 1981. 89p. Y3.H62/4:2F51. Portraits and one page biographies of the First Ladies provide basic background information on their lives and interests.

302.   U.S. Congress. House. Committee on Interior and Insular Affairs. *Designating the Mary McLeod Bethune Council House in Washington, District of Columbia, as a National Historic Site, and for Other Purposes, Report to Accompany H.R. 6091.* H. Rept. 97-668, 97th Cong., 2d sess., 1982. 6p. Serial 13486. Reports, with amendment, a bill declaring the Mary McLeod Bethune Council House in Washington, D.C. a National Historic Site. The report provides a brief biographical statement on Bethune, highlighting her accomplishments as an educator, a political leader, and the founder of the National Council of Negro Women.

303. U.S. Congress. House. Committee on Interior and Insular Affairs. Subcommittee on Public Lands and National Parks. *Public Land Management Policy, Part IX, Hearings on H.R. 5990, H.R. 6033, H.R. 6091.* 97th Cong., 2d sess., 22 Apr.- 20 May 1982. 170p. Y4.In8/14:97-8/pt.9. One of the bills considered, H.R. 6091, would designate the Mary McLeod Bethune Council House as a National Historic Site and would provide site preservation assistance to the National Council of Negro Women. Testimony and submitted materials describe the contributions of Bethune and the importance of designating a site in Washington, D.C. to honor her.

304. U.S. Congress. Senate. Committee on Energy and Natural Resources. *Designating the Mary McLeod Bethune Council House as a National Historic Site, Report to Accompany S. 2436.* S. Rept. 97-534, 97th Cong., 2d sess., 1982. 5p. Serial 13453. Favorable report on declaring the Council House in Washington, D.C. as a National Historic Site. The house was the last residence of Mary McLeod Bethune, educator, political leader and founder of Bethune-Cookman College and the National Council of Negro Women. The Council House is the location of the Mary McLeod Bethune Memorial Museum and the National Archive for Black History.

305. U.S. Congress. Senate. Committee on Energy and Natural Resources. Subcommittee on Public Lands and Reserved Water. *Wolf Trap Farm Park and Mary McLeod Bethune Council House, Hearing on S. 1999, S. 2436.* 97th Cong., 2d sess., 2 July 1982. 79p. Y4.En2:97-111. Witnesses describe the contributions of Mary McLeod Bethune, educator and founder of the National Council of Negro Women, in support of a bill to designate the Mary McLeod Bethune Council House as a National Historic Site. The importance of the National Archives for Black Women's History, located at the Council House, to the study of African-American women is also stressed. The Department of the Interior opposed the bill based on the lack of a study of the historical significance of the property.

306. U.S. Smithsonian Institution. National Museum of American Art. *Berenice Abbott, the 20's and the 30's: A Traveling Exhibition Organized by the International Center of Photography with Support from the National Endowment for the Arts and the Sondra and Charles Gilman, Jr. Foundation.* Washington, DC: Smithsonian Institution Press, 1982. 5p. 15 plates. SI6.2:Ab2. Chronology and short bibliography on Berenice Abbott, American photographer, accompanies reproductions of selected photographs from the 1920s and 30s.

307. U.S. Smithsonian Institution. National Museum of American Art. *Elizabeth Nourse, 1859-1938: A Salon Career.* Washington, DC: Smithsonian Institution Press, 1983. 288p. SI6.2:N85. Catalog of the paintings of American-born artist Elizabeth Nourse includes a substantial bibliography.

308. U.S. Smithsonian Institution. National Museum of American Art. *Elizabeth Nourse, 1859-1938: A Salon Career, Checklist for the Exhibition.* Washington, DC: Smithsonian Institution Press, 1983. 11p. SI6.2:N85/check.

309. U.S. Library of Congress. General Reading Rooms Division. *First Lady: A Bibliography of Selected Material by and about Eleanor Roosevelt.* Washington, DC: GPO, 1984. 46p. LC25.9:R67. Bibliography with short annotations cites works by and about Eleanor Roosevelt.

310. U.S. Congress. House. Committee on Interior and Insular Affairs. *Amending the Act of October 15,1982, Entitled, "An Act to designate the Mary McLeod Bethune Council House in Washington, District of Columbia, as a National Historic Site, and for other Purposes," Report to Accompany H.R. 1391.* H. Rept. 99-312, 99th Cong., 1st sess., 1985. 7p. Serial 13656. Clarifying amendments and authorization of appropriations are the purpose of this

bill amending the act establishing the Mary McLeod Bethune Council House as a National Historic Site.

311.   U.S. Congress. House. Committee on Interior and Insular Affairs. *Authorizing Funds for the Mary McLeod Bethune National Historic Site and Land Conveyances in the State of Maryland, Hearing on H.R. 682, H.R. 1391, H.R. 3003.* 99th Cong., 1st sess., 18 July 1985. 193p. Y4.In8/14:99-69. Discussion of a bill to authorize continued funding of the Bethune Museum and Archives highlights the importance of the site's collections and programs for the study of black women's history. The cooperative agreement between the National Council of Negro Women and the National Park Service regarding the Mary McLeod Bethune Council House is reprinted.

312.   U.S. Congress. Senate. Committee on Energy and Natural Resource. *Mary McLeod Bethune Council House, Report to Accompany S. 1116.* S. Rept. 99-181, 99th Cong., 1st sess., 1985. 9p. Serial 13625. Reports a bill authorizing an additional appropriation for the operation of the Mary McLeod Bethune Council House, home of the Bethune Museum and Archives and former residence of Mary McLeod Bethune, founder of the National Council of Negro Woman. Correspondence from the Secretary of the Interior recommends against passage based on the argument that historic site funds are to be used to mark, interpret, and restore historic sites, and are not intended to pay operating costs.

313.   U.S. Congress. Senate. Committee on Energy and Natural Resources. Subcommittee on Public Lands, Reserved Water, and Resource Conservation. *Miscellaneous Conveyances, Increases in Authorization for Appropriations, and Commemoration of Units in the National Park System, Hearing on S. 1596, H.R. 2776, S. 1116, S.J. Res. 187.* 99th Cong., 1st sess., 10 Oct. 1985. 147p. Y4.En2:S.hrg.99-361. Much of the testimony at this hearing concerns S. 1116, a bill to authorize appropriations for the Bethune Museum and Archives, and stresses the importance of the site for the study of Black Americans and women. The Bethune Council House was the home of Mary McLeod Bethune, founder of the National Council of Negro Women. Opposition to the bill by the National Park Service is based on the use of funds for staff salaries.

314.   U.S. Information Agency. Voice of America. *Voice of America Interviews with Eight American Women of Achievement.* Washington, DC: GPO, 1985. 64p. IA1.2:V87/8. Transcripts of interviews with Grace Hopper, Betty Friedan, Nancy Landon Kassebaum, Mary Calerone, Helen Thomas, Julia Montgomery Walsh, Maya Angelou, and Nancy Clark Reynolds reflect their lives and accomplishments.

315.   U.S. Smithsonian Institution. *United States Women in Aviation, 1930-1939.* by Claudia M. Oakes. Smithsonian Studies in Air and Space no. 6. Washington, DC: Smithsonian Institution Press, 1985. 71p. SI1.42:6. The contribution of women to aviation in the 1930s is illustrated with stories of the women and their achievements. The study highlights the involvement of women in races and stunt work, as well as commercial flying. The publicity work of female pilots is particularly stressed and the role of stewardesses in getting out the message that flying was safe is described. A list of air races in which women participated includes the women's names, the planes they flew, their finish times, and any prize money won.

316.   U.S. Indian Arts and Crafts Board. Sioux Indian Museum and Crafts Center. *Three Women Artists, Hudgens, Sevier, Teters.* Rapid City, SD: The Center, 1987. 4p. I1.84:W84. Brochure promotes the art work of Native American artists Diana B. Hudgens, Jackie Sevier, and Charlene Teters.

317.   U.S. Congress. Senate. Committee on Energy and Natural Resources. *Authorizing a Study of Methods to Commemorate the Nationally Significant Contributions of Georgia O'Keeffe,*

Report to Accompany S. 2750. S. Rept. 100-574, 100th Cong., 2d sess., 1988. 5p. Serial 13867. Reports a bill directing the Department of the Interior to study possible ways to commemorate the work of artist Georgia O'Keeffe, including the establishment of a "landscape museum" in New Mexico.

318. U.S. Congress. House. Committee on Interior and Insular Affairs. *Redesignating a Certain Portion of the George Washington Memorial Parkway as the "Clara Barton Parkway," Report to Accompany H.R. 1310.* H. Rept. 101-285, 101st Cong., 1st sess., 1989. 3p. Report provides brief highlights of the life and contributions of Clara Barton and notes the need to rename part of the George Washington Memorial Parkway.

319. U.S. Congress. Senate. Committee on Energy and Natural Resources. *Redesignating a Certain Portion of the George Washington Memorial Parkway as the "Clara Barton Parkway", Report to Accompany H.R. 1310.* S. Rept. 101-202, 101st Cong., 1st sess., 1989. 4p. See 318 for abstract.

320. U.S. Congress. House. Committee on Education and Labor. Subcommittee on Postsecondary Education. *Hearing on H.R. 3252, the Margaret Walker Alexander National African American Research Center.* 101st Cong., 2d sess., 29 June 1990, Jackson, MS. 81p. Y4.Ed8/1:101-123. Hearing to consider funding the creation of the Margaret Walker Alexander National African American Research Center at Jackson State University in Mississippi includes testimony on the need for the Center. The accomplishments of author and former English professor Dr. Margaret Walker Alexander are highlighted.

321. U.S. Congress. House. Committee on Interior and Insular Affairs. *Authorizing the National Park Service to Acquire and Manage the Mary McLeod Bethune Council House National Historic Site, and for Other Purposes, Report to Accompany H.R. 5084.* H. Rept. 101-636, 101st Cong., 2d sess., 1990. 6p. Brief report details a bill authorizing the purchase and management of the Mary McLeod Bethune Council House National Historic Site. A short background section highlights the accomplishments of Bethune and describes the Bethune Museum and Archives.

322. U.S. Congress. Senate. Committee on Energy and Natural Resources. *Mary McLeod Bethune Council House National Historic Site, Report to Accompany H.R. 5084.* S. Rept. 101-507, 101st Cong., 2d sess., 1990. 6p. Reports a bill authorizing the Department of the Interior to purchase the Mary McLeod Bethune Council House and to manage the house as part of the National Park Service.

323. U.S. Congress. Senate. Committee on Energy and Natural Resources. Subcommittee on Public Lands, National Parks and Forests. *Miscellaneous National Parks Measures, Hearing on S. 2771, S. 2802, S.2809, H.R. 3863, S. 2818, H.R. 4834, H.R. 5084.* 101st Cong., 2d sess., 20 Sept. 1990. 106p. Y4.En2:S.hrg.101-1147. Hearing on miscellaneous national park bills includes brief testimony from the Department of the Interior opposing H.R. 5084, a bill authorizing the acquisition of the Mary McLeod Bethune Council House National Historic Site.

324. U.S. Indian Arts and Crafts Board. Museum of the Plains Indian Crafts Center. *Paintings by Rose Azure Moran, Exhibition, May 27 - June 20, 1990.* Browning, MT: The Center, 1990. 4p. I1.84:P16/2. Brochure reproduces several art works by Native American artist Rose Azure Moran.

325. U.S. Indian Arts and Crafts Board. Sioux Indian Museum and Crafts Center. *Artwork by Tona Thomas.* Rapid City, SD: The Center, 1990. 4p. I1.84:T36. Illustrations and a brief biography highlight the work of Sioux artist Tona Thomas.

3

Women's Organizations

Most of the government's interest in women's organizations has been in relation to the granting of federal charters. The vast majority of these organizations were patriotic in nature, and their membership and activities are briefly described in the House and Senate reports on their incorporation. Other reports provide background on funding for international meetings of the Associated Country Women of the World (381, 384, 385) and the Women's Christian Temperance Union (383, 386, 413, 417). The proceedings of the Third Triennial Conference of the Associated Country Women of the World was printed as a Department of State document (397). One of the groups regularly receiving support through congressional action were the Girl Scouts, whose annual reports have been printed in the U.S. Serial Set since 1950 (507). Another group which often sought government assistance was the Daughters of the American Revolution. Although their requests were generally favorably reported, charges of racial discrimination did appear in a 1947 hearing (415). Between 1890 and 1948 the D.A.R.'s annual reports were also printed in the Serial Set (508).

Some departmental publications suggested activities for women's clubs such as Americanization work with immigrants (421, 362, 371), conservation work (375, 401, 428, 488), work for the disabled (464, 465, 470), and highway safety promotion (473-475, 479). In the early 1950s women's organizations came under the scrutiny of the House Un-American Activities Committee, which issued two reports on the communist backing of women's peace organizations (422, 425). Women's organizations in Ecuador, Paraguay and Peru are briefly described in a 1943 Women's Bureau publication (407). More information on women's organizations in other countries, particularly their potential in lesser developed countries, are described in Chapter 21. Additional documents describing rural women's organizations are found in Chapter 14, Home Economics and Home Demonstration Work.

326. U.S. Congress. Senate. *Memorial of the Officers and Managers of the National Association for the Relief of Destitute Colored Women and Children, Praying Such Action as May Secure Them from Loss in a Law Suit Instituted against Them by Richard S. Cox, and Protect Them in Their Pursuits While Carrying Out the Objectives of the Association.* S. Misc. Doc. 14, 39th Cong., 2d sess., 1867. 2p. Serial 1278. Memorial explains the problems of the National Association for the Relief of Destitute Colored Women and Children in relation to their possession of property confiscated from a rebel soldier during the war and given to them for their use by the Secretary of War.

327. U.S. Congress. Senate. *Annual Report and Petition of the National Association for the Relief of Destitute Colored Women and Children.* S. Misc. Doc. 18, 46th Cong., 2d sess., 1879. 10p. Serial 1890. The fifteenth annual report of the National Association for the

Relief of Destitute Colored Women and Children sets forth their request for funds in the sum of $7,000, reprints their act of incorporation and by-laws, and lists the 1878 officers. The primary focus of the annual report is on the operation of the home for children and aged women in Washington, D.C.

328. U.S. Congress. Senate. Committee on the District of Columbia. *Report to Accompany Bill S. 1859 [Making Appropriation to Erect a New Building for the Use of the National Association for the Relief of Destitute Colored Women and Children of the District of Columbia].* S. Rept. 569, 47th Cong., 1st sess., 1882. 3p. Serial 2006. The new building requested would replace an existing home for aged women and orphans in the District.

329. U.S. Congress. House. *Women's National Press Association, Resolution.* H. Misc. Doc. 378, 49th Cong., 1st sess., 1886. 1p. Serial 2422. Brief resolution to designate a seat in the reporters gallery for the use of the Women's National Press Association.

330. U.S. Congress. House. *Letter from the Commissioner of Agriculture Transmitting a Report of Expenditures and the Results Obtained by the Ladies' Silk Culture Association of California.* H. Misc. Doc. 543, 50th Cong., 1st sess., 1888. 7p. Serial 2570. Annual report for the fiscal year ending June 30, 1888 describes activities encouraging the cultivation of mulberry tress and silk worms.

331. U.S. Congress. House. *Letter from the Commissioner of Agriculture Transmitting the Annual Report of the Women's Silk Culture Association of the United States.* H. Misc. Doc. 103, 50th Cong., 1st sess., 1888. 4p. Serial 2565. Annual report of the Women's Silk Culture Association describes activities to promote the silk industry in the United States. The association received federal appropriations to demonstrate the practicability of home reeling.

332. U.S. Congress. House. *Women's Silk Culture Association: Letter from the Secretary of Agriculture Transmitting Reports upon the Operations of the Women's Silk Culture Association of the United States and of the Ladies Silk Culture Society of California; and upon Experiments Made in the District of Columbia with Silk-Reeling Machinery.* H. Ex. Doc. 110, 51st Cong., 2d sess., 1890. 30p. Serial 2643. Report on activities to promote the silk industry in the U.S. stresses that the feeding of silk worms and selling of cocoons is an industry to which women and children are well suited and thus fulfills a "moral and humanitarian" role. The report includes a list of persons from whom cocoons were purchased including name, town, county, state, weight and value of cocoons for 1888-1889.

333. U.S. Congress. House. *Appropriation for Board of Lady Managers World's Columbian Exposition, Letter from the Secretary of the Treasury.* H. Ex. Doc. 74, 52d Cong., 2d sess., 1892. 3p. Serial 3103. Brief description of expenses and educational activities of the Board of Lady Managers of the World's Columbian Exposition.

334. U.S. Congress. House. *Letter from the Acting Secretary of the Treasury, Transmitting Estimate for Appropriations for the Board of Lady Managers, World's Columbian Exposition, for the Fiscal Year Ending June 30, 1893.* H. Ex. Doc. 157, 52d Cong., 1st sess., 1892. 2p. Serial 2955.

335. U.S. Congress. House. Committee on the Library. *Society of the Colonial Dames of America, Report to Accompany H.R. 1519.* H. Rept. 256, 52d Cong., 1st sess., 1892. 1p. Serial 3042. Reports favorably on a bill to grant a federal charter to a women's patriotic organization established in New York, to be known as the Society of the Colonial Dames of America.

336.   U.S. Congress. Senate. Committee on Public Buildings and Grounds. *Site for Memorial Continental Hall, Report to Accompany S. 3608.* S. Rept. 1463, 54th Cong., 2d sess., 1897. 2p. Serial 3476. Reports on a bill granting land in the District of Columbia to the Daughters of the American Revolution for the purpose of constructing a memorial hall to the founders of the nation and to the past members of the DAR.

337.   U.S. Congress. Senate. Committee on the Library. *Colonial Dames of America, Adverse Report to Accompany S. 3087 and S. 3356.* S. Rept. 1552, 54th Cong., 2d sess., 1897. 55p. Serial 3476. Brief comments by the Committee advise the two organizations claiming rights to the name Colonial Dames of America to settle their differences outside of Congress before the question of a federal charter is considered. The transcripts of the hearing are appended to the report.

338.   U.S. Congress. Senate. Committee on the Library. *Societies of Colonial Dames of America, Hearing on Bill (S. 3087) to Incorporate the National Society of Colonial Dames of America, and Bill (S. 3356) to Incorporate the Society of Colonial Dames of America.* 54th Cong., 2d sess., 13 Feb. 1897. 55p. Y4.L61/3:C71. Hearing considers bills granting charters to the National Society of Colonial Dames of America, a New York society, and the Society of Colonial Dames, chartered under the laws of Pennsylvania. Testimony reviews the history and objectives of each organization. Both society's state their claim to the federal charter and to the right to use the name. Reprinted in full in the Senate report (337).

339.   U.S. Congress. House. Committee on the District of Columbia. *National Congress of Mothers, Report to Accompany H.R. 10341.* H. Rept. 1531, 55th Cong., 2d sess., 8 June 1898. 1p. Serial 3722.

340.   U.S. Congress. House. *Letter from the Secretary of the Treasury, Transmitting an Estimate of Appropriation for Compensation of Women Commissioner to Unveiling of Statue of Lafayette at Paris Exposition.* H. Doc. 614, 56th Cong., 1st sess., 1900. 1p. Serial 3997.

341.   U.S. Congress. House. Committee on Foreign Affairs. *Women's Commissioner at the Exposition in Paris, France, in 1900, Report to Accompany S. R. 55.* H. Rept. 384, 56th Cong., 1st sess., 1900. 1p. Serial 4022.

342.   U.S. Congress. House. Committee on the District of Columbia. *National Society of United States Daughters of Eighteen Hundred and Twelve, Report to Accompany H.R. 8067.* H. Rept. 1019, 56th Cong., 1st sess., 1900. 2p. Serial 4024.

343.   U.S. Congress. Senate. *Statement Submitted by the Subcommittee of the Daughters of the American Revolution on Memorial or Continental Hall to the Senate Committee on Public Buildings and Grounds.* S. Doc. 64, 56th Cong., 1st sess., 1900. 7p. Serial 3848. Report reviews the purpose of the DAR and the justification for a grant of land in the District of Columbia for a building to serve as a monument and museum of the Revolutionary War. Senate Report 1463, 54th Congress (336), is reprinted.

344.   U.S. Congress. Senate. Committee on Public Buildings and Grounds. *Memorial Hall, Daughters of the American Revolution, Report to Accompany S. 2237.* S. Rept. 975, 56th Cong., 1st sess., 1900. 7p. Serial 3890. Favorable report on a bill to allocate land to the DAR for the erection of a monument to the men and women of the Revolutionary War reviews the status of the DAR and the purpose of the proposed building.

345. U.S. Congress. Senate. Committee on the Library. *National Society United States Daughters of Eighteen Hundred and Twelve, Report to Accompany S. 2859.* S. Rept. 611, 56th Cong., 1st sess., 1900. 1p. Serial 3889.

346. U.S. Congress. House. Committee on the District of Columbia. *Exempting from Taxation Certain Property of the Daughters of the American Revolution, Report to Accompany S. 6515.* H. Rept. 3845, 57th Cong., 2d sess., 1903. 2p. Serial 4415.

347. U.S. Congress. Senate. Committee on the District of Columbia. *Exempting from Taxation Certain Property of the Daughters of the American Revolution, Report to Accompany S. 6515.* S. Rept. 2666, 57th Cong., 2d sess., 1903. 2p. Serial 4411.

348. U.S. Congress. House. Committee on the District of Columbia. *General Federation of Women's Clubs, Report to Accompany S. 5583.* H. Rept. 2896, 58th Cong., 2d sess., 1904. 2p. Serial 4584.

349. U.S. Congress. House. Committee on the Library. *The National Society of the Women of the Civil War, Report to Accompany H.R. 20578.* H. Rept. 1169, 62d Cong., 2d sess., 1912. 1p. Serial 6133.

350. U.S. Congress. Senate. Committee on Corporations Organized in the District of Columbia. *Mother's Day Association, Report to Accompany H.R. 16298.* S. Rept. 1040, 63d Cong., 3d sess., 1915. 1p. Serial 6762. Reports favorably on the incorporation of the Mother's Day Association, an organization dedicated to perpetuating the all-national observance of Mother's Day.

351. U.S. Congress. House. Committee on Patents. *Insignia of the Daughter of the American Revolution, Hearings.* 64th Cong., 1st sess., 4 Apr. 1916. 7p. Y4.P27/1:D26. Representatives of the DAR express their desire for a congressional act to prevent commercial enterprises from using their insignia.

352. U.S. Congress. Senate. Committee on Claims. *Women's Board of Domestic Missions, Reformed Church in America, Adverse Report to Accompany S. 5367.* S. Rept. 957, 64th Cong., 2d sess., 1917. 1p. Serial 7108. Adverse report on reimbursement to the Women's Board of Domestic Missions for buildings on the Fort Sill Military Reserve, Oklahoma.

353. U.S. National Park Service. *Women's Part in National Park Development, Address by Mrs. John Dickinson Sherman, Delivered at the National Parks Conference at Washington, D.C., January 2, 1917.* Washington, DC: GPO, 1917. 6p. I29.5/a:W842. Conservation chairman of the General Federation of Women's Clubs talks about the need to preserve the beauty of our scenic areas and urges women's clubs to play a role in designating areas national or state parks.

354. U.S. Congress. House. Committee on Indian Affairs. *Women's Board of Domestic Missions, Report to Accompany H.R. 8202.* H. Rept. 396, 65th Cong., 2d sess., 1918. 7p. Serial 7309. Report includes correspondence supporting reimbursement to the Women's Board of Domestic Missions for their buildings at Fort Sill Military Reserve. The removal of the Apache Indian prisoners to the Mascalero Reservation made the Boards' plant at Fort Sill useless.

355. U.S. Congress. House. Committee on the District of Columbia. *Incorporation of War Mothers of America, Report to Accompany H.R. 13072.* H. Rept. 827, 65th Cong., 2d sess., 1918. 2p. Serial 7208.

356. U.S. Dept. of Agriculture. *Women's Rural Organizations and Their Activities.* by Anne M. Evans. Bulletin no. 719. Washington, DC: GPO, 1918. 15p. A1.3:719. The rural organizations described in this bulletin include chapters of national organizations such as the General Federation of Women's Clubs, the National Women's Christian Temperance Union, the National Farm and Garden Association and the National Congress of Farm Women, as well as local unaffiliated groups. A wide variety of activities of the organizations are described including child welfare education, food preparation, demonstration of labor saving techniques and devices, education in farm management and agricultural marketing, and sponsored community social activities.

357. U.S. Bureau of Education. *The Girl Scouts as an Educational Force.* Bulletin 1919 no. 33. Washington, DC: GPO, 1919. 8p. I16.3:919/33. Overview of the accomplishments required of girls to make each of the three grades of Girl Scouts also provides examples of the war work performed by Girl Scouts.

358. U.S. Congress. House. Committee on the District of Columbia. *Incorporation of War Mothers of America, Report to Accompany H.R. 15608.* H. Rept. 1047, 65th Cong., 3d sess., 1919. 2p. Serial 7455.

359. U.S. Dept. of the Treasury. *Plan for Thrift Work in Women's Organizations.* Washington, D.C.: The Department, 1919. 4p. leaflet. T1.27/32:W84.

360. U.S. Bureau of Education. *Educational Work of the Girls Scouts.* Bulletin 1921 no. 46. Washington, DC: GPO, 1921. 14p. I16.3:921/46. Information on the educational focus of the Girl Scouts reports statistics on the number and subject of badges earned in 1919-20.

361. U.S. Bureau of Naturalization. *Suggestions for Americanization Work among Foreign-born Women.* Washington, DC: GPO, 1921. 12p. L6.2:W84. Detailed outline for organizing educational work with foreign-born women focuses on encouraging these women to contribute to the community. Lesson topics suggested are generally in the areas of homemaking, child welfare, and daily living skills such as getting around the city and purchasing household goods. Examples of accomplishments of successful programs around the country are given.

362. U.S. Bureau of Naturalization. *Suggestions How Women's Organizations May Help in Americanization Work.* Washington, DC: The Bureau, 1921. 3p. L6.2:W84/2. See 361 for abstract.

363. U.S. Congress. House. Committee on Military Affairs. *World Disarmament, Hearings.* 66th Cong., 3rd sess., 11 June 1921. 46p. Y4.M59/1:D63. Hearing organized by the Women's Peace Society features women representing the Society, the Quakers, the American Federation of Labor, the National Women's Trade Union League, and the Women's International League for Peace and Freedom speaking on disarmament and the expense of a large standing army.

364. U.S. Congress. House. Committee on the Judiciary. *Incorporation of the National Federation of Business and Professional Women's Clubs, Hearing on H.R. 26.* 76th Cong., 1st sess., 17 May 1921. 25p. Y4.J89/1:N21/2. The history and purpose of the National Federation of Business and Professional Women's Club is described by witness in this hearing on a federal charter. One line of attack against the charter is the charge by Congressman Tillman that the Federation creates a "sex war" by excluding men.

365. U.S. Congress. House. Committee on the Judiciary. *Amending Charter of General Federation of Women's Clubs, Report to Accompany H.R. 9979.* H. Rept. 592, 67th Cong., 2d sess., 1922. 1p. Serial 7955. Reports a bill to amend the charter of the General

Federation of Women's Clubs to increase their allowable property holdings above the set level of $200,000.

366. U.S. Congress. House. Committee on the Judiciary. *Incorporation of Women's Overseas Service League, Hearing on H.R. 7299.* 67th Cong., 2d sess., 12 Jan. 1922. 20p. Y4.J89/1:W84/11. Hearing on a request for a federal charter for the Women's Overseas League describes the organization, membership and purpose of this organization of women who served in relief work overseas in WWI.

367. U.S. Congress. House. Committee on the Judiciary. *The Women's Overseas Service League, Report to Accompany H.R. 7299.* H. Rept. 715, 67th Cong., 2d sess., 1922. 4p. Serial 7955. The objectives of the Women's Overseas Service League, an organization of women who served overseas in WWI, are reviewed in this favorable report on their incorporation.

368. U.S. Congress. House. Committee on the Territories. *Granting Certain Buildings in Alaska to the Women's Home Missionary Society, Report to Accompany H.J.Res. 249.* H. Rept. 560, 67th Cong., 2d sess., 1922. 2p. Serial 7958. Reports a bill to allow the Women's Home Missionary Society to remove the lumber, doors, and windows of the buildings at Fort Davis, Alaska for the purpose of building a hospital in Nome.

369. U.S. Congress. Senate. Committee on Territories and Insular Possessions. *Granting Certain Buildings in Alaska to the Woman's Home Missionary Society, Report to Accompany H.J.Res. 249.* S. Rept. 583, 67th Cong., 2d sess., 1922. 1p. Serial 7952. See 368 for abstract.

370. U.S. Bureau of Education. *Education Work of the Young Women's Christian Association.* Bulletin 1923 no. 26. Washington, DC: GPO, 1923. 24p. I16.3:923/26. Description of the educational work of the YWCA gives examples of formal classes, clubs and programs geared toward black, foreign born, and Native American women.

371. U.S. Bureau of Naturalization. *How Women's Organizations May Help in Americanization Work.* Washington, DC: The Bureau, 1923. 4p. L6.2:W84/3. Many of the suggestions listed here for women's clubs desiring to help with Americanization relate to providing services to immigrant women and girls in relation to family responsibilities. Other activities suggested include information campaigns, social activities, fund raising, and volunteering as teaching assistants.

372. U.S. Congress. House. Committee on the Judiciary. *To Incorporate the American War Mothers, Report to Accompany H.R. 9095.* H. Rept. 931, 68th Cong., 1st sess., 1924. 1p. Serial 8229.

373. U.S. Congress. House. Committee on the Judiciary and U.S. Congress. Senate. Committee on the Judiciary. *To Incorporate the American War Mothers, Joint Hearing on H.R. 8980 and H.R. 9095.* 68th Cong., 1st sess., 6 May 1924. 12p. Y4.J89/1:Am3/5. Joint hearing is characterized by close questioning on the need for a congressional charter for this service organization composed of mothers of those who served in the war.

374. U.S. Congress. House. Committee on the Judiciary. *Amend the Act Granting a Charter to the General Federation of Women's Clubs, Report to Accompany H.R. 16619.* H. Rept. 1952, 69th Cong., 2d sess., 1927. 1p. Serial 8689. Reports a bill amending the charter of the General Federation of Women's Clubs by changing the objective of the organization to "the betterment of humanity" and changing the limit on allowable assets.

375. U. S. Dept. of Agriculture. *A Forest Program for Women's Organizations.* by Lilian T. Conway. Miscellaneous Circular no. 91. Washington, DC: GPO, 1927. 14p. A1.5/2:91. The first part of this pamphlet was apparently intended for use at women's club meetings as informational/inspirational readings to inspire club members to support forestry. The appeal directly to women comes at the end where we learn that ecology is characteristically feminine.

376. U.S. Congress. House. Committee on Judiciary. *To Incorporate the Ladies of the Grand Army of the Republic, Hearing on H.R. 16553.* 70th Cong., 2d sess., 11 Feb. 1929. 4p. Y4.J89/1:L12. Brief hearing on granting a national charter to the National Society of the Ladies of the Grand Army of the Republic.

377. U.S. National Recovery Administration. *To All N.R.A. Committees: Special Attention, the Leader of Women's Activities, [Circular Letter, August 23, 1933].* Washington, DC: The Administration, 1933. 6p. Y3.N21/8:2W84.

378. U.S. Congress. House. Committee on the Judiciary. *Amend the Charter of the General Federation of Women's Clubs, Report to Accompany S. 2696.* H. Rept. 997, 73d Cong., 2d sess., 1934. 3p. Serial 9775. Bill to change the charter of the General Federation of Women's Clubs primarily allows the establishment of a foundation fund for general expenses.

379. U.S. Congress. Senate. Committee on the Judiciary. *Amend an Act Granting a Charter to the General Federation of Women's Clubs, Report to Accompany S. 2696.* S. Rept. 339, 73d Cong., 2d sess., 1934. 2p. Serial 9769. Committee recommends amending the charter of the Federation to provide for the establishment of a Foundation Fund from whose interest the general expenses would be paid.

380. U.S. Office of the President. *To All N.R.A. Women's Committees [Circular Letter].* by Franklin Delano Roosevelt. Washington, DC: The Office, 1934. 1p. Pr32.2:N213/5. Letter from Roosevelt to N.R.A. Women's Committees thanks them for their work and informs them of the formation of a National Emergency Council which would assume many of the duties of the Women's Committees.

381. U.S. Congress. Senate. Committee on Agriculture and Forestry. *Triennial Meeting of Associated Country Women of the World, Report to Accompany S. 2664.* S. Rept. 797, 74th Cong., 1st sess., 1935. 3p. Serial 9879. Favorable report on a bill to provide $5,000 in support of the Third Triennial Meeting of the Associated Country Women of the World summarizes the history of this international meeting of rural women's organizations.

382. U.S. Congress. Senate. Committee on the Judiciary. *To Incorporate the National Yeoman F, Report to Accompany S. 1687.* S. Rept. 1449, 74th Cong., 1st sess., 1935. 1p. Serial 9880. Reports a bill to incorporate the National Yeoman F, an organization of women who served with the Navy in WWI.

383. U.S. Congress. House. Committee on Foreign Affairs. *Sixteenth Triennial Convention of the World's Woman's Christian Temperance Union, Report to Accompany S. 3950.* H. Rept. 2387, 74th Cong., 2d sess., 1936. 1p. Serial 9993. Report on a $10,000 appropriation for the Sixteenth Triennial Convention of the World WCTU.

384. U.S. Congress. House. Committee on Foreign Affairs. *Third Triennial Meeting of the Associated Country Women of the World, Hearings on S. 2664.* 74th Cong., 2d sess., 3 March 1936. 17p. Y4.F76/1:As7. Hearing on a special appropriation of $5,000 to help the 3rd Triennial Meeting of the Associated Country Women of the World in the U.S. describes the organization and notes ways state farm women's organizations participate.

The agenda for the Triennial Meeting is laid out. Also provides a good overview of women's activities at farmer's markets in the United States.

385. U.S. Congress. House. Committee on Foreign Affairs. *Triennial Meeting of the Associated Country Women of the World, Report to Accompany S. 2664.* H. Rept. 2126, 74th Cong., 2d sess., 1936. 3p. Serial 9992. Favorable report on a bill to provide support for the 3rd Triennial Meeting of the Associated Country Women of the World amends the bill by raising the appropriation from $5,000 to $10,000.

386. U.S. Congress. House. Committee on Foreign Affairs. *World's Women's Christian Temperance Union, Hearing on S. 3950.* 74th Cong., 2d sess., 7 Apr. 1936. 15p. Y4.F76/1:W89/2. Hearing on a request for funding for the Sixteenth Triennial Convention of the World's Women's Christian Temperance Union describes the goals of the WCTU and highlights activities of WCTU chapters in the U.S. in the areas of prostitution, child health, and world peace.

387. U.S. Congress. House. Committee on Naval Affairs. *Directing the Secretary of the Navy to Transmit to the House of Representatives at the Earliest Practicable Moment Certain Information, Adverse Report to Accompany H.Res. 407.* H. Rept. 1931, 74th Cong., 2d sess., 1936. 2p. Serial 9995. Letter from the Secretary of the Navy explains that a section of the Marine Band was scheduled to perform at the Women's Patriotic Conference on National Defense, but that the engagement was canceled due to the political tone set by the conference's lead-off speaker.

388. U.S. Congress. House. Committee on the District of Columbia. *Incorporation of the National Yeoman F, Report to Accompany S. 1687.* H. Rept. 2894, 74th Cong., 2d sess., 1936. 1p. Serial 9994. See 382 for abstract.

389. U.S. Congress. House. Committee on the Judiciary. *To Authorize Certain Payments to the American War Mothers, Inc., Report to Accompany S. 3296.* H. Rept. 2888, 74th Cong., 2d sess., 1936. 8p. Serial 9994. Reports a bill designating that the income from the Recreation Fund, Army, be paid to the American War Mothers, Inc., to spend as they see fit.

390. U.S. Congress. Senate. Committee on Foreign Relations. *World's Woman's Christian Temperance Union, Report to Accompany S. 3950.* S. Rept. 1632, 74th Cong., 2d sess., 1936. 1p. Serial 9988. Favorable report on a bill to provide $10,000 in support of the 16th Triennial Convention of the World's Woman's Chiristian Temperance Union.

391. U.S. Congress. Senate. Committee on Military Affairs. *Designating the Last Sunday in September as "Gold Star Mother's Day", Report to Accompany S.J. Res. 115.* S. Rept. 1981, 74th Cong., 2d sess., 1936. 3p. Serial 9988.

392. U.S. Congress. Senate. Committee on Military Affairs. *To Authorize Certain Payments to the American War Mothers, Inc., Report to Accompany S. 3296.* S. Rept. 1744, 74th Cong., 2d sess., 1936. 6p. Serial 9988. The bill reported provides for the payment of $20,000 a year to the American War Mothers, Inc. from the interest on the Recreation Fund, Army. Letters of support for the action from various veterans organizations are appended as is correspondence from the War Department and the Treasury Department.

393. U.S. Congress. House. Committee on Immigration and Naturalization. *To Permit Temporary Entry into the United States of Alien Participants in Girl Guides and Girl Scouts Silver Jubilee Camp, 1937, Report to Accompany H.R. 7206.* H. Rept. 1038, 75th Cong., 1st sess., 1937. 4p. Serial 10084.

394. U.S. Congress. House. Committee on Military Affairs. *Authorizing Certain Payments to American War Mothers, Inc., et al., Report to Accompany S. 1516.* H. Rept. 1438, 75th Cong., 1st sess., 1937. 7p. Serial 10085. Report on a bill to pay the proceeds from the Recreation Fund, Army, to the American Gold Star Mothers of the World War, the American War Mothers, Inc., the Veterans of Foreign Wars of the US, Inc. and the Disabled American Veterans of the World War, Inc.

395. U.S. Congress. Senate. Committee on Immigration. *Temporary Entry of Alien Participants, Etc., of the World Association of Girl Guides and Girl Scouts Silver Jubilee Camp in the United States, 1937, Report to Accompany S. 2664.* S. Rept. 794, 75th Cong., 1st sess., 1937. 2p. Serial 10077.

396. U.S. Congress. Senate. Committee on Military Affairs. *Authorize Certain Payments to the American War Mothers, Inc., the Veterans of Foreign Wars of the United States, Inc., and the Disabled American Veterans of the World War, Inc., Report to Accompany S. 1516.* S. Rept. 285, 75th Cong., 1st sess., 1937. 6p. Serial 10076. Favorable report on a bill to pay the proceeds from the Recreation Fund, Army in equal parts to the organizations named.

397. U.S. Dept. of State. *The Associated Country Women of the World, Proceedings of the Third Triennial Conference Held at Washington, May 31 - June 11, 1936.* Department of State Conference Series no. 34. Washington, DC: GPO, 1937. 309p. S5.30:34. Part I of the conference proceedings includes a history of the association and a complete list of delegates. Part II briefly describes the business sessions while part III reports on group discussions covering topics of rural life, women and the economic problem, drama, education for country life, health services in rural areas, and library services in rural areas. Part four provides the text of addresses by F.D. Roosevelt, Cordell Hull, Henry A. Wallace, Carrie Chapman Catt, and Eleanor Roosevelt. Part five is comprised of reports from country associations around the world.

398. U.S. Congress. House. Committee on the District of Columbia. *Exempting Property of Young Women's Christian Association from Taxation, Report to Accompany H.R. 10673.* H. Rept. 2421, 75th Cong., 3d sess., 1938. 2p. Serial 10235.

399. U.S. Congress. Senate. Committee on Military Affairs. *Authorizing Certain Payments to the American War Mothers, Inc., Report to Accompany S. 3318.* S. Rept. 1547, 75th Cong., 3d sess., 1938. 6p. Serial 10229. Favorable report on a bill to allocate one third of the Recreation Fund, Army to the American War Mothers, Inc. to spend as they see fit.

400. U.S. Congress. Senate. Committee on the District of Columbia. *Exempting Certain Property of Young Women's Christian Association from Taxation, Report to Accompany S. 4035.* S. Rept. 1903, 75th Cong., 3d sess., 1938. 2p. Serial 10230.

401. U.S. Dept. of Agriculture. *Forestry and Conservation Programs for Utah Women's Clubs.* Washington, DC: The Department, 1938. 95p. A13.2:F76/32.

402. U.S. Congress. Senate. Committee on the Judiciary. *Incorporating the Ladies of the Grand Army of the Republic, Report to Accompany S. 521.* S. Rept. 618, 76th Cong., 1st sess., 1939. 1p. Serial 10294.

403. U.S. Forest Service. *Material of Interest to Women's Organizations.* Washington, DC: The Service, 1939. 5p. A13.2:W84. Lists forestry related publications appropriate for women's club activities.

404. U.S. Office of Education. *Gallant American Women #17, the Women Who Saved Mount Vernon, February 20, 1940.* Washington, DC: The Office, 1940. 23p. FS5.15:17. Radio script pays tribute to women as preservers of history, particularly noting the work of women's organizations in saving historic landmarks such as Mount Vernon.

405. U.S. Congress. House. Committee on the Judiciary. *Amending the Act Incorporating American War Mothers, Report to Accompany H.R. 6401.* H. Rept. 2213, 77th Cong., 2d sess., 1942. 2p. Serial 10663. Favorable report supports amending the charter of the American War Mothers to include mothers of World War II servicemen and women in its membership.

406. U.S. Congress. Senate. Committee on the Judiciary. *Amending the Act Incorporating American War Mothers, Report to Accompany H.R. 6401.* S. Rept. 1587, 77th Cong., 2d sess., 1942. 2p. Serial 10658. Report recommends a bill to change the charter of the American War Mothers by expanding their membership to include mothers of WWII servicemen and women.

407. U.S. Women's Bureau. *Women's Organizations in Ecuador, Paraguay, and Peru.* by Mary M. Cannon. Washington, DC: GPO, 1943. 8p. L13.2:Or3. Description of the activities of some of the major women's organization in Ecuador, Paraguay, and Peru provides insight into the activities of South American women. Some of the organizations highlighted include the Legion Pro-Education Popular and the Ligu di Empleadas Catolicas in Ecuador; the Consejo de Mujerus and Obra de Beneficencia a Domicilio in Paraguay; and the Accion Femenina Peruana, an anti-fascist organization, the Union Cultural Femenina, Accion Catolocas, the Consejo Nacional de Mujerus, the Sociedad Emplendas de Comercio, and Accion Femenina Peruana in Peru. Includes pictures of some organization presidents and members.

408. U.S. Congress. House. Committee on Judiciary. Subcommittee No. 1. *Mothers of World War No. 2 (Incorporation), Hearing on H.R. 3435.* 78th Cong., 2d sess., 25 May 1944. 14p. Y4.J89/1:M85/5. Hearing considers granting a national charter to Mothers of World War II which would then encompass all the "mother groups" seeking congressional charters including Gold Star Mothers, United War Mothers of American, Inc., Army Air Corps Mothers, etc. Activities of the organization include war bond drives, scrap drives, assisting the Red Cross Blood Banks, operating canteens and recreation rooms for service men and women, and sending items to veteran's hospitals. Also describes the planned activities of the organizations in the post-war era.

409. U.S. Congress. Senate. Committee on the District of Columbia. *Dissolution of Women's Christian Association of the District of Columbia and Transfer Its Assets, Report to Accompany S. 2205.* S. Rept. 1307, 78th Cong., 2d sess., 1944. 1p. Serial 10843. Reports a bill to permit the dissolution of the Women's Christian Association of the District of Columbia and to transfer the assets to the YWCA of the District of Columbia.

410. U.S. Congress. House. Committee on the Judiciary. *Incorporating "The Mothers of World War Number Two", Report to Accompany H.R. 2538.* H. Rept. 683, 79th Cong., 1st sess., 1945. 2p. Serial 10933.

411. U.S. Congress. Senate. Committee on the Judiciary. *Providing for the Incorporation of the National Women's Relief Corps, Auxiliary to the Grand Army of the Republic, Report to Accompany S. 1650.* S. Rept. 1826, 79th Cong., 2d sess., 1946. 1p. Serial 11017.

412. U.S. Office of Price Administration. *Speech Delivered by Marriner S. Eccles before the League of Women Voters, Kansas City, May 1, 1946.* Washington, DC: The Office, 1946. 6p. Pr32.4213:Ec2. Speech praises the League of Women Voters for its objective

examination of social issues and goes on to discuss economic stability and the role the League can play in informing the public.

413. U.S. Congress. House. Committee on Foreign Affairs. *Seventeenth Triennial Convention of the World's Women's Christian Temperance Union, Report to Accompany H.R. 1179.* H. Rept. 318, 80th Cong., 1st sess., 1947. 2p. Serial 11119. Favorable report on granting $5,000 in aid to the cost of the 17th Triennial Convention of the World's WCTU cites past precedent for granting such assistance.

414. U.S. Congress. House. Committee on Post Office and Civil Service. *Authorizing the Issuance of a Special Series of Commemorative Stamps in Honor of Gold Star Mothers, Report to Accompany S. 1180.* H. Rept. 985, 80th Cong., 1st sess., 1947. 1p. Serial 11122.

415. U.S. Congress. House. Committee on Public Works. Subcommittee on Public Buildings and Grounds. *Authorize Furnishing Steam from Central Heating Plant to Property of Daughters of the American Revolution, Hearings on H. R. 2086.* 80th Cong., 1st sess., 4 Mar. 1947. 10p. Y4.P96/11:80-1/1. The interesting part of this discussion on a bill to provide heat to Constitution Hall, a DAR property, is a statement opposing the bill because the DAR refused to allow black performers to appear in the Hall.

416. U.S. Congress. Senate. Committee on Civil Service. *Authorizing Issuance of a Series of Commemorative Stamps Honoring Gold Star Mothers, Report to Accompany S. 1180.* S. Rept. 367, 80th Cong., 1st sess., 1947. 2p. Serial 11115.

417. U.S. Congress. Senate. Committee on Foreign Relations. *Sixteenth Triennial Convention of the World's Woman's Christian Temperance Union, Report to Accompany H.R. 1179.* S. Rept. 198, 80th Cong., 1st sess., 1947. 2p. Serial 11115. Report recommends a $5,000 appropriation to help defray the cost of the 17th Triennial Convention of the World's WCTU to be held in the United States in June 1947.

418. U.S. Women's Bureau. *Proposed Program in the United States for Leaders of Women's Organizations of Western and Eastern Hemispheres.* Washington, DC: The Bureau, 1948. 2p. L13.2:L46. To "counteract anti-democratic infiltration," the bureau recommends that women leaders in Latin America and the Eastern Hemisphere countries be invited to visit the United States. While here the women would observe the role of women's organizations in a democracy.

419. U.S. Women's Bureau. *Report of the Women Leaders Program.* Washington, DC: The Bureau, 1949. 34p. L13.2:W84/26. The Women Leaders Program brought five women, three from Mexico, one from Brazil and one from Uruguay to the U.S. to observe the structure and programs of women's organizations. This report outlines the program and provides a summary evaluation of its success. Appendices include statement of the program, brief biographies of the women, their itineraries while in the U.S., and selected press releases.

420. U.S. Congress. House. Committee on House Administration. *Authorizing the Printing of the Annual Report of the Girl Scouts of the United States of American as Separate House Documents, Report to Accompany H.R. 9291.* H. Rept. 2965, 81st Cong., 2d sess., 1950. 2p. Serial 11384.

421. U.S. Congress. House. Committee on the District of Columbia. *Incorporating the Girl Scouts, Report to Accompany H.R. 6670.* H. Rept. 1615, 81st Cong., 2d sess., 1950. 2p. Serial 11378.

422. U.S. Congress. House. Committee on Un-American Activities. *Report on the Congress of American Women, Report Pursuant to H.Res. 5, 79th Congress 1st Session.* H. Rept. 1953, 81st Cong., 2d sess., 1950. 114p. Serial 11380. Also issued as a committee print under SuDoc number Y4.Un1/2:C76. Report on the Congress of American Women and the Women's International Democratic Federation, described as communist front organizations, reveals the motives behind their peace initiatives. Profiles the activities of Rumanian Anna Parker and Americans Muriel Draper, Margaret Undjus Krunbein, Susan Anthony McAvoy, and Nora Stanton Barney. The picture drawn of the Congress of American Women is that of a communist front organization designed to "ensnare idealistically minded but politically gullible women."

423. U.S. Congress. Senate. Committee on the Judiciary. *Incorporating the Girl Scouts, Report to Accompany H.R. 6670.* S. Rept. 1321, 81st Cong., 2d sess., 1950. 2p. Serial 11367.

424. U.S. Congress. House. Committee on House Administration. *Authorizing the Printing of the Annual Reports of the Girl Scouts of the United States of America as Separate House Documents, Report to Accompany H.R. 3020.* H. Rept. 266, 82d Cong., 1st sess., 1951. 1p. Serial 11496.

425. U.S. Congress. House. Committee on Un-American Activities. *Report for the Communist "Peace" Offensive, a Campaign to Disarm and Defeat the United States.* 82d Cong., 1st sess., 1 Apr. 1951. 166p. Y4.Un1/2:C73/23. Report for the House Committee on Un-American Activities labels peace initiatives, such as a ban the A-Bomb campaign, as communist plots to undermine U.S. strength and the military strength of other democracies. Included is a chapter on women's groups and the peace campaign, which discusses the Paris World Peace Conference, the Women's International Democratic Federation, and the Congress of American Women as communist-directed organizations.

426. U.S. Congress. Senate. Committee on the Judiciary. *Protecting Emblems and Badges of the Girl Scouts, Report to Accompany H.R. 3442.* S. Rept. 568, 82d Cong., 1st sess., 1951. 2p. Serial 11488.

427. U.S. Dept. of Treasury. *Address by Secretary Snyder before Business Women's Week Meeting of Business and Professional Women's Clubs of St. Louis, St. Louis, Mo., September 27, 1951.* Washington, D.C.: The Department, 1951. 8p. T1.31:Sn9/20. Speech before the Business and Professional Women's Club of St. Louis mostly talks about the bond drive, stressing the role of outstanding women in selling bonds and in getting community business involved with the payroll savings plan.

428. U. S. Dept. of Agriculture. *How to Plan Forest Show-Me Trip for Club Women.* Washington, DC: The Service, 1952. 4p. A13.2:T73.

429. U.S. Dept. of the Treasury. U.S. Savings Bonds Division. Women's Section. *Madam Chairman-Your Challenge, Your Opportunity.* Washington, DC: GPO, 1952. 2p. leaflet. T66.2:M26. Tells how women's organization can become involved in the savings bond program.

430. U.S. Congress. House. Committee on the District of Columbia. *Amending the Charter of the Girl Scouts of America, Report to Accompany H.R. 6252.* H. Rept. 916, 83d Cong., 1st sess., 1953. 4p. Serial 11667. Report recommends amending the charter of the Girl Scouts in relation to membership on the National Council, meetings of the Council, and annual reports.

431. U.S. Congress. House. Committee on the Judiciary. *Amending the Charter of the American War Mothers, Report to Accompany H.R. 1434.* H. Rept. 336, 83d Cong., 1st

sess., 1953. 2p. Serial 11665. Committee supports amending the federal charter of the American War Mothers in order to expand eligibility for membership to include mothers of servicemen and women of the Korean conflict and subsequent wars.

432.   U.S. Congress. Senate. Committee on the District of Columbia. *Amending the Charter of the Girl Scouts of America, Report to Accompany H.R. 6252.* S. Rept. 790, 83d Cong., 1st sess., 1953. 4p. Serial 11661. Report supports legislation clarifying and amending provisions of the federal charter of the Girl Scouts of America in respect to the membership and meetings of the National Council.

433.   U.S. Congress. Senate. Committee on the Judiciary. *American War Mothers, Report to Accompany H.R. 1434.* S. Rept. 375, 83d Cong., 1st sess., 1953. 2p. Serial 11660. See 431 for abstract.

434.   U.S. Congress. House. Committee on Armed Services. *Authorizing the Secretary of Defense to Lend Certain Army, Navy and Air Force Equipment to the Girl Scouts of America, Report to Accompany H.R. 4218.* H. Rept. 848, 84th Cong., 1st sess, 1955. 2p. Serial 11823. Reports a bill authorizing the Department of Defense to loan equipment to the Girl Scouts of the USA for use during the Girl Scout Senior Roundup Encampment, June and July 1956.

435.   U.S. Congress. Senate. Committee on Armed Services. *Authorizing the Secretary of Defense to Lend Certain Army, Navy, and Air Force Equipment to the Girl Scouts of America, Report to Accompany H.R. 4218.* S. Rept. 1078, 84th Cong., 1st sess., 1955. 2p. Serial 11817. See 434 for abstract.

436.   U.S. Congress. House. Committee on the District of Columbia. *Exempting from Taxation Certain Property of the General Federation of Women's Clubs, Inc., Report to Accompany H.R. 8493.* H. Rept. 1879, 84th Cong., 2d sess., 1956. 1p. Serial 11902.

437.   U.S. Congress. Senate. Committee on the District of Columbia. *Exempting from Taxation Certain Property of the General Federation of Women's Clubs, Inc., Report to Accompany H.R. 8493.* S. Rept. 2244, 84th Cong., 2d sess., 1956. 1p. Serial 11892.

438.   U.S. Congress. Senate. Committee on the District of Columbia. *Exempting from Taxation Certain Property of the National Association of Colored Women's Clubs, Inc., in the District of Columbia, Report to Accompany S. 4044.* S. Rept. 2644, 84th Cong., 2d sess., 1956. 1p. Serial 11893.

439.   U.S. Farmer Cooperative Service. *How Women Help Their Farmer Co-ops.* by Oscar R. LeBeau and John H. Heckman. FCS Circular no. 15. Washington, DC: GPO, 1956. 43p. A89.4:15. Describes how women can play a role in their farm cooperative through evaluating farm and family needs, keeping the family informed, serving on committees, improving marketing, and assisting with legislation efforts. Successful women's programs at five cooperatives are spotlighted.

440.   U.S. Congress. Senate. Committee on the District of Columbia. *Exempting from Taxation Certain Property of the National Association of Colored Women's Clubs, Inc., in the District of Columbia, Report to Accompany S. 105.* S. Rept. 315, 85th Cong., 1st sess., 1957. 1p. Serial 11980.

441.   U.S. Congress. House. Committee on Armed Services. *Loan of Certain Equipment and Use of Certain Lands by Girl Scouts, Report to Accompany S. 2630.* H. Rept. 1987, 85th Cong., 2d sess., 1958. 3p. Serial 12074. Report legislation authorizing the Defense Department to loan equipment to the Girl Scouts for their Senior Roundup Encampment

at Colorado Springs, Colorado, June and July 1959, and to permit the use of certain Air Force land.

442. U.S. Congress. House. Committee on the District of Columbia. *Exempting from Taxation Certain Property of the National Association of Colored Women's Clubs, Inc., in the District of Columbia, Report to Accompany S. 105.* H. Rept. 2140, 85th Cong., 2d sess., 1958. 1p. Serial 12079.

443. U.S. Congress. House. Committee on the District of Columbia. *Exempting from Taxation Certain Property of the National Council of Negro Women, Inc., in the District of Columbia, Report to Accompany S. 2725.* H. Rept. 1559, 85th Cong., 2d sess., 1958. 1p. Serial 12078.

444. U.S. Congress. Senate. Committee on Armed Services. *Authorizing Loan of Certain Equipment and Use of Certain Lands by Girl Scouts, Report to Accompany S. 2630.* S. Rept. 1350, 85th Cong., 2d sess., 1958. 3p. Serial 12061. See 441 for abstract.

445. U.S. Congress. Senate. Committee on the District of Columbia. *Exempting from Taxation Certain Property of the National Council of Negro Women, Inc., in the District of Columbia, Report to Accompany S. 2725.* S. Rept. 1298, 85th Cong., 2d sess., 1958. 1p. Serial 12066.

446. U.S. Congress. Senate. Committee on the Judiciary. *Blue Star Mothers of America, Inc., Report to Accompany S. 1315.* S. Rept. 215, 86th Cong., 1st sess., 1959. 4p. Serial 12154. Favorable report on a federal charter for the Blue Star Mothers of America, Inc., an organization of mothers or stepmothers of men and women who served in the armed services in WWII and the Korean conflict, or who currently serve in the armed forces. The members of the organization perform volunteer work with the Veterans Administration.

447. U.S. Congress. House. Committee on the District of Columbia. *Exempting from Taxation Certain Property of the American Association of University Women, Educational Foundation, Inc., in the District of Columbia, Report to Accompany S. 3415.* H. Rept. 2143, 86th Cong., 2d sess., 1960. 2p. Serial 12248.

448. U.S. Congress. House. Committee on the District of Columbia. *Exempting from Taxation Ceratin Property of the National Woman's Party, Inc., in the District of Columbia, Report to Accompany S. 2306.* H. Rept. 2142, 86th Cong., 2d sess., 1960. 2p. Serial 12248.

449. U.S. Congress. House. Committee on the District of Columbia. *Incorporation of Blue Star Mothers of America, Inc., Report to Accompany S. 1315.* H. Rept. 1344, 86th Cong., 2d sess., 1960. 2p. Serial 12250. See 446 for abstract.

450. U.S. Congress. Senate. Committee on the District of Columbia. *Exempting from Taxation Certain Property of the American Association of University Women, Educational Foundation, Inc., in the District of Columbia, Report to Accompany S. 3415.* S. Rept. 1641, 86th Cong., 2d sess., 1960. 2p. Serial 12236.

451. U.S. Congress. Senate. Committee on the District of Columbia. *Exempting from Taxation Certain Property of the American War Mothers, Inc., Report to Accompany S. 2671.* S. Rept. 1226, 86th Cong., 2d sess., 1960. 2p. Serial 12234.

452.   U.S. Congress. Senate. Committee on the District of Columbia. *Exempting from Taxation Certain Property of the Army Distaff Foundation, Report to Accompany S. 3195.* S. Rept. 1642, 86th Cong., 2d sess., 1960. 3p. Serial 12236.

453.   U.S. Congress. Senate. Committee on the District of Columbia. *Exempting from Taxation Certain Property of the National Woman's Party, Inc., in the District of Columbia, Report to Accompany S. 2306.* S. Rept. 1227, 86th Cong., 2d sess., 1960. 3p. Serial 12234.

454.   U.S. Post Office Dept. *Camp Fire Girls Stamp Ceremony, Remarks by Franklin R. Bruns, Jr., Director, Division of Philately, New York, N.Y., November 1, 1960.* Washington, DC: The Department, 1960. 3p. P1.27:B83. Speech praises the service work of the Camp Fire Girls upon the issuance of a commemorative stamp celebrating their 50th anniversary.

455.   U.S. Post Office Dept. *Commemorative Postage Stamp, 4-Cent Camp Fire Girls, Available at Your Local Post Office Nov. 2, 1960.* Washington, DC: Postmaster General, 1960. poster. P1.26/2:C15.

456.   U.S. Congress. House. Committee on Armed Services. *Authorizing the Secretary of Defense to Assist the Girl Scouts at Their 1962 Encampment, Report to Accompany H.R. 5228.* H. Rept. 737, 87th Cong., 1st sess., 1961. 4p. Serial 12341.

457.   U.S. Congress. House. Committee on the District of Columbia. *Exempting from Taxation Certain Property of the Army Distaff Foundation, Report to Accompany H.R. 2838.* H. Rept. 1152, 87th Cong., 1st sess., 1961. 2p. Serial 12342.

458.   U.S. Congress. Senate. Committee on Armed Services. *Loan of Army, Navy and Air Force Equipment for Use at 1962 Girl Scout Senior Roundup Encampment, Report to Accompany S. 1240.* S. Rept. 661, 87th Cong., 1st sess., 1961. 3p. Serial 12324.

459.   U.S. Congress. House. Committee on the District of Columbia. *Providing for the Incorporation of the National Women's Relief Corps, Auxiliary to the Grand Army of the Republic, Report to Accompany S. 2250.* H. Rept. 2263, 87th Cong., 2d sess., 1962. 2p. Serial 12433.

460.   U.S. Congress. Senate. Committee on the District of Columbia. *Exempting from Taxation Certain Property of the American War Mothers, Inc., Report to Accompany S. 2139.* S. Rept. 1597, 87th Cong., 2d sess., 1962. 2p. Serial 12423.

461.   U.S. Congress. Senate. Committee on the District of Columbia. *Exempting from Taxation Certain Property of the Army Distaff Foundation, Report to Accompany H.R. 2838.* S. Rept. 1349, 87th Cong., 2d sess., 1962. 3p. Serial 12422.

462.   U.S. Congress. Senate. Committee on the District of Columbia. *Providing for the Incorporation of the National Woman's Relief Corps, Auxiliary to the Grand Army of the Republic, Organized 1883, 78 Years Old, Report to Accompany S. 2250.* S. Rept. 1356, 87th Cong., 2d sess., 1962. 4p. Serial 12416. Favorable report on incorporation of the National Woman's Relief Corps briefly describes the organization dedicated to preserving the records and documentation pertaining to the Grand Army of the Republic, and to promoting patriotism and the American principle of representative government.

463.   U.S. Post Office Dept. *4-Cent Girl Scout Commemorative Postage Stamp, Available at Your Local Post Office July 25, 1962.* Washington, DC: Postmaster General, 1962. poster. P1.26/2:G44.

464. U.S. President's Committee on Employment of the Handicapped. Women's Committee. *The Microphone, Women's Committee Idea Exchange.* Washington, DC: The Committee, 1962. 2p. L16.44/6:1. First, and apparently only, issue of a newsletter presenting information on handicapped access publications and suggestions for women's organization activities related to the disabled.

465. U.S. Bureau of Labor Standards. *Operation-Volunteers, Program to Help the Handicapped, Sponsored by Women's Committee of President's Committee on Employment of the Handicapped, Washington, D.C.* Washington, DC: GPO, 1963. [6]p. leaflet. L16.44/2:V88.

466. U.S. Congress. Senate. Committee on the District of Columbia. *Authorizing the Association of the Universalist Women to Consolidate with the Alliance of Unitarian Women, Report to Accompany S. 1227.* S. Rept. 177, 88th Cong., 1st sess., 1963. 3p. Serial 12533.

467. U.S. Congress. House. Committee on Armed Services. *Authorizing the Secretary of Defense to Assist the Girl Scouts at Their 1965 Encampment, Report to Accompany H.R. 9634.* H. Rept. 1513, 88th Cong., 2d sess., 1964. 5p. Serial 12619-3.

468. U.S. Congress. Senate. Committee on Armed Services. *Authorizing the Secretary of Defense to Lend Certain Equipment and Provide Certain Services to the Girl Scouts at Their 1965 Encampment, Report to Accompany H.R. 9634.* S. Rept. 1271, 88th Cong., 2d sess., 1964. 4p. Serial 12616-3.

469. U.S. Dept. of Health, Education, and Welfare. *Women's Role in War on Poverty, Address by Grace L. Hewell, Program Coordinator Officer, Department of Health, Education, and Welfare, Presented at the 11th Annual Founders' Day Luncheon of New York Club of National Association of Negro Business and Professional Women's Clubs, Inc., New York, N.Y., May 17, 1964.* by Grace L. Hewell. Washington, DC: The Department, 1964. 8p. FS1.7:H49/2. Speech describes the characteristics of poverty in the U.S. and stresses the role women can play as catalysts in providing community opportunities to help raise young people out of poverty.

470. U.S. President's Committee on Employment of the Handicapped. Women's Committee. *Ability Calling...A Program Guide for Women's Groups.* Washington, DC: GPO, 1964. 27p. L16.44/2:Ab5/3. Describes programs for bringing handicapped individuals more fully into society noting how women's organizations can participate in these programs.

471. U.S. Welfare Administration. *Woman's Role in Bringing Peace through Understanding.* Washington, DC: The Administration, 1964. 12p. FS14.11:W73/9. Address before the annual convention of the General Federation of Women's Clubs emphasizes the capacity of women for compassion and the contribution women's clubs can make in helping families and individuals rise out of poverty.

472. U.S. Armed Forces Chaplains Board. *Guidelines for Protestant Women of the Chapel.* Washington, D.C.: GPO, 1965. 19p. D1.6/2:P94/5. The activities of the Protestant Women of the Chapel are geared toward other women and include evangelism, stewardship, and teaching. Booklet sets forth guidelines for the organization of Protestant Women of the Chapel chapters.

473. U.S. President's Committee for Traffic Safety. *Drive Right, Adult Driver Improvement Project Guide for Women's Groups.* Washington, DC: GPO, 1965. 16p. C37.7:D83.

474. U.S. President's Committee for Traffic Safety. *Organized Citizen Support, (Highway Safety Action Conferences) Feminine Touch.* Washington, DC: GPO, 1965. 20p. C37.7:Or3/2. Report describes the organization of national and regional conferences to bring women's organizations into traffic safety activities.

475. U.S. President's Committee for Traffic Safety. *Proceedings, Midwestern Regional Conference for Women's National Organizations on Efficient Highway Transportation and Reduction of Traffic Accidents, Sheraton-Blackstone Hotel, Chicago, Illinois, February 16-17, 1965.* Washington, DC: GPO, 1965. 91p. C37.7:W84/2/965. Presents general information on activities of women's organizations in promoting traffic safety.

476. U.S. Post Office Dept. *5-Cent General Federation of Women's Clubs, Commemorative Stamp Available at Your Local Post Office, Sept. 13, 1966.* Washington, DC: GPO, 1966. poster. P1.26/2:W84/2.

477. U.S. Executive Office of the President. Office of Economic Opportunity. *Conference Proceeding, 2d Annual Conference on Women in the War on Poverty, Washington, DC, May 15-17, 1968.* Washington, DC: GPO, 1968. 64p. PrEx10.2:W84/968. Sessions and speakers highlight the problems of poverty in the U.S. emphasizing issues of race and courses of action to alleviate or eliminate the problem. Workshop summaries pinpoint the critical issues in areas of human relations, education, welfare, housing, health and employment, and note actions women as individual and in organizations can take.

478. U.S. Congress. House. Committee on the District of Columbia. *Incorporate Gold Star Wives of America, Report to Accompany H.R. 10677.* H. Rept. 606, 92d Cong., 1st sess., 1971. 5p. Serial 12933. Report recommends incorporation of the Gold Star Wives of America, an organization of war widows which conducts patriotic activities, and which has played a support role in helping Vietnam War widows adjust.

479. U.S. National Highway Traffic Safety Administration. National Association of Women Highway Safety Leaders. *Forum on Traffic Safety Alcohol Countermeasures for Women's National Organizations, January 11-13, 1971.* Washington, DC: GPO, 1971. 35p. TD8.2:Al1/2/971. Conference highlights the problem of drunk driving and the role national women's organizations can play in lessening the drunk driving problem.

480. U.S. Congress. Senate. Committee on the Judiciary. *Girl Scouts of America, Report to Accompany S. Res. 259.* S. Rept. 92-630, 92d Cong., 2d sess., 1972. 2p. Serial 12971-1. Praise for the Girl Scouts and brief history are included in this report on a resolution commemorating the Girl Scouts of America on their 60th anniversary.

481. U.S. Congress. Senate. Committee on the Judiciary. *Amending the Act of February 24, 1925, Incorporating the American War Mothers, Report to Accompany S. 2441.* S. Rept. 93-576, 93d Cong., 1st sess., 1973. 2p. Serial 13017-8. Report recommends amending the charter of the American War Mothers to allow as members the stepmother or adoptive mother of members of the Armed Forces.

482. U.S. Congress. House. Committee on the Judiciary. *Amending the Act of February 24, 1925, Incorporating the American War Mothers, Report to Accompany S. 2441.* H. Rept. 93-933, 93d Cong., 2d sess., 1974. 2p. Serial 13061-2. See 481 for abstract.

483. U.S. Congress. House. Committee on the Judiciary. *Amending the Act Entitled "An Act Granting a Charter to the General Federation of Women's Clubs," Report to Accompany S. 240.* H. Rept. 94-555, 94th Cong., 1st sess., 1975. 5p. Serial 13099-8. Report approves a bill to amend the charter of the General Federation of Women's Clubs by

removing the monetary limit on corporate property holdings and by including it in the list of private corporations required to make an annual report to Congress.

484. U.S. Congress. Senate. Committee on the Judiciary. *General Federation of Women's Clubs, Report to Accompany S. 240.* S. Rept. 94-105, 94th Cong., 1st sess., 1975. 2p. Serial 13096-2. Favorable report on amendment of the Federation charter supports changes related to the value of property which the national organization may own.

485. U.S. Congress. Senate. Committee on the Judiciary. *Amending the Incorporation of the Daughters of the American Revolution, Report to Accompany H.R. 11149.* S. Rept. 94-1249, 94th Cong., 2d sess., 1976. 5p. Serial 13130-10. The bill reported amends the charter of the National Society of the Daughters of the American Revolution by removing the limit on the amount of property which the DAR can own and granting the DAR exclusive right to the use of its name and emblem.

486. U.S. Congress. House. Committee on the Judiciary. *Amending the Federal Charter of the Big Brothers of America to Include Big Sisters International, Inc., and for Other Purposes, Report to Accompany H.R. 7249.* H. Rept. 95-750, 95th Cong., 1st sess., 1977. 11p. Serial 13172-12. Report on amending the charter of Big Brothers of America to recognize their merger with Big Sisters International includes a brief history of both organizations.

487. U.S. Congress. Senate. Committee on the Judiciary. *Big Brothers - Big Sisters of America, Report to Accompany S. 2208.* S. Rept. 95-510, 95th Cong., 1st sess., 1977. 9p. Serial 13168-10. Details of the history of Big Brothers of America and Big Sisters of America are included in the report on a bill to amend the federal charter of Big Brothers of America and to merge the two organizations creating Big Brothers-Big Sisters of America.

488. U.S. Environmental Protection Agency. Office of Public Awareness. *Women and the Environment...Women as Agents of Change.* Washington, DC: The Agency, 1977. 15p. EP1.2:W84. Pamphlet shows how women are affected by and can effect environmental policy. Includes a list of women involved in protecting the environment.

489. U.S. Congress. House. Committee on Armed Services. *Authorizing the Secretary of Defense to Provide Transportation to the Girl Scouts of the United States of America in Connection with International World Friendship Events or Troops on Foreign Soil Meetings, and for Other Purposes, Report to Accompany S. 3373.* H. Rept. 95-1572, 95th Cong., 2d sess., 1978. 5p. Serial 13201-13. The bill reported would grant the Girl Scouts the same use of equipment and transportation service of the Department of Defense as is enjoyed by the Boy Scouts.

490. U.S. Congress. Senate. Committee on the Judiciary. *Federal Charter to Gold Star Wives of America, S. 1179, Hearing.* 96th Cong., 1st sess., 16 Nov. 1979. 34p. Y4.J89/2:96-35. Hearing on granting a federal charter to the Gold Star Wives of America describes the mission, membership, and activities of this organization of widows of men who died in active military service.

491. U.S. Congress. Senate. Committee on the Judiciary. *Granting a Federal Charter to Gold Star Wives of America, Report to Accompany S. 1179.* S. Rept. 96-479, 96th Cong., 1st sess., 1979. 3p. Serial 13249. Report on granting a federal charter to the Gold Star Wives of America briefly describes the organization of widows of servicemen killed in the line of military duty.

492. U.S. Employment and Training Administration. Bureau of Apprenticeship and Training. *Directory for Reaching Minority and Women's Groups.* Washington, DC: GPO, 1979.

301p. L37.102:M66. Directory lists local and state level groups useful in resolving equal employment or civil rights problems. Organizations include business and industrial groups, educational institutions, fraternities and sororities, government offices, religious organizations, mass media outlets, and minority and women's organization.

493.   U.S. Environmental Protection Agency. Office of Public Awareness. *Women/Consumer Calendar of Events 1979-80.* Washington, DC: The Agency, 1979. 6p. EP1.84:979-80. Calendar lists events sponsored by women's or consumer groups ranging from the Garden Club of America to the Society of Women Engineers.

494.   U.S. Congress. House. Committee on the Judiciary. *Gold Star Wives of America, Report to Accompany H.R. 154.* H. Rept. 96-1397, 96th Cong., 2d sess., 1980. 8p. Serial 13379. See 491 for abstract.

495.   U.S. Congress. House. Committee on the Judiciary. Subcommittee on Administrative Law and Governmental Relation. *Gold Star Wives, Hearing on H.R. 154.* 96th Cong., 2d sess., 16 June 1980, 16 June 1980. 112p. Y4.J89/1:96-50. Hearing considers granting a federal charter to the Gold Star Wives of America, an organization of the widows of servicemen killed in the line of military duty. The history and activities of the organization are briefly described.

496.   U.S. Congress. House. Committee on the Judiciary. Subcommittee on Administrative Law and Governmental Relations. *American Gold Star Mothers, Inc., Hearing on H.R. 3811.* 98th Cong., 2d sess., 21 Mar. 1984. 10p. Y4.J89/1:98-40. Very brief hearing reviews support for granting a federal charter to the American Gold Star Mothers, Inc., a service organization whose members are mothers of men and women killed in actions during U.S. wars. The organization promotes patriotism and provides services to veterans and veterans hospitals.

497.   U.S. Congress. House. Committee on the Judiciary. Subcommittee on Administrative Law and Governmental Relations. *Daughters of the Union Veterans of the Civil War 1861-65, Hearing on H.R. 3406.* 98th Cong., 2d sess., 1 Aug. 1984. 10p. Y4.J89/1:98/77. Hearing on a bill to grant a federal charter to the Daughters of the Union Veterans of the Civil War, 1861-1865, Inc. reprints the bill and provides a brief statement on the organization's history and activities. The organization's goal was the promotion of U.S. history with a focus on preserving the memory of the Union soldiers of the Civil War.

498.   U.S. Congress. House. Committee on the Judiciary. Subcommittee on Administrative Law and Governmental Relations. *National Society, Daughters of the American Colonists, Hearing on H.R. 1881.* 98th Cong., 2d sess., 1 Aug. 1984. 90p. Y4.J89/1:98/78. Record of a hearing on a bill to grant a federal charter to the Nation Society Daughters of the American Colonists, an organization dedicated to research on American colonists and patriotism, consists primarily of correspondence from state and local chapters voicing support for the bill.

499.   U.S. Congress. House. Committee on the Judiciary. Subcommittee on Administrative Law and Governmental Relations. *Navy Wives Clubs of America, Hearing on H.R. 2372.* 98th Cong., 2d sess., 1 Aug. 1984. 46p. Y4.J89/1:98/76. The organization and objectives of the Navy Wives Clubs of America are described in this hearing on granting a federal charter to the organization. The organization is primarily a social and service organization for wives and widows of Navy personnel.

500.   U.S. Congress. Senate. Committee on the Judiciary. *American Gold Star Mothers, Inc., Report to Accompany S. 2413.* S. Rept. 98-379, 98th Cong., 1st sess., 1984. 4p. Serial

13557. Reports a bill granting a federal charter to the American Gold Star Mothers, Inc., an organization of mothers of men and women killed in military action founded in 1928.

501. U.S. Dept. of State. *Soviet Fronts, Women and Youth.* Washington, DC: GPO, 1984. 5p. S1.126/3:So8/4. Overview of three "Soviet front" organizations, the World Federation of Democratic Youth, the International Union of Students, and the Women's International Democratic Federation, reviews their history, organization, and activities.

502. U.S. Congress. House. Committee on the Judiciary. *Daughters of Union Veterans of the Civil War 1861-1865, Report to Accompany H.R. 1806.* H. Rept. 99-70, 99th Cong., 1st sess., 1985. 4p. Serial 13645. Reports a bill for the recognition of the Daughters of Union Veterans of the Civil War 1861-1865 by granting it a federal charter. The organization founded in 1885 promotes U.S. history and works to honor the memory of Union Civil War soldiers.

503. U.S. Congress. Senate. Committee on the Judiciary. *Daughters of Union Veterans of the Civil War 1861-1865, Report to Accompany H.R. 1806.* S. Rept. 99-179, 99th Cong., 1st sess., 1985. 5p. Serial 13625. See 502 for abstract.

504. U.S. Congress. House. Committee on the Judiciary. *Amendments to Federal Charter of General Federation of Women's Clubs, Report to Accompany H.R. 4434.* H. Rept. 99-595, 99th Cong., 2d sess., 1986. 5p. Serial 13700. Proposed amendment of the General Federation of Women's Clubs' charter provides a new statement of purpose and clearly defines the organization's tax-exempt status.

505. U.S. Congress. Senate. Committee on the Judiciary. *General Federation of Women's Clubs, Report to Accompany S. 1827.* S. Rept. 99-319, 99th Cong., 2d sess., 1986. 7p. Serial 13675. Report on a bill amending the charter of the General Federation of Women's Clubs to more clearly define its purpose and its tax-exempt status provides a brief history of the organization and highlights some of its past and current projects.

SERIALS

506. District of Columbia. *Annual Report of the Women's Christian Association of the District of Columbia.* Washington, DC: Judd and Detweiler, Printers, 1899 - 1906. annual. DC26.1:year. According to the charter of the Women's Christian Association of the District of Columbia their objectives are to aid the destitute and the unemployed, house the homeless, sympathize with the friendless, reform the fallen, and "bestow such Christian benevolence upon the needy as our means will allow." The annual report reprints the charter and constitution, and lists officers, committees, and members. A brief report of the secretary describes their work with homeless girls and women. Brief financial reports and committee reports are also included. Description based on the report for the year ending June 30, 1900.

507. U.S. Congress. House. *Girl Scouts of the United States of America, Annual Report.* Washington, DC: GPO, 1950 - . annual. Annual report of the Girl Scouts reviews national programs and reports on membership and finances. These reports were issued as House Documents and can be located in the Serial Set.

508. U.S. Smithsonian Institution. *Daughters of the American Revolution, Annual Report.* Washington, DC: The Institution, 1890-1948. annual. SI5.1:year. The act incorporating the society requires that a report shall be made annually to the secretary of the Smithsonian Institution. The first report covers the years 1890 - 1897. These annual reports were also printed as Senate documents and can be located in the Serial Set.

4

Discrimination and Women's Rights

The legal status of women, particularly of married women, has been described in publications since the late 1800s. Although no documents of the time covered the 1848 Women's Rights Convention in Seneca Falls, New York, extensive documentation is found in the National Park Service reports on the Women's Rights National Historical Park (766, 770). The earliest documents on women's rights are primarily House and Senate reports which reflect the process of establishing married women's rights under the Homestead Act. Two of the most unique of the congressional documents are *The Mission of Women* (518), an anti-feminist tirade reprinted from an 1871 issue of the *Southern Review*, and a 1921 hearing on a bill to prohibit women from smoking in public in the District of Columbia (524). The slow process of establishing a woman's right to serve on juries is also documented through hearings and reports on amending the laws of Hawaii and the District of Columbia, and in numerous status reports from the Women's Bureau. A 1937 hearing on allowing women to serve on federal juries stresses the inappropriateness of sequestering women with men and contends that women were too frail to withstand the stress of the courtroom (542).

Numerous publications over the years detail the status of women in federal and state law. First issued in 1938 and periodically revised, *The Legal Status of Women in the United States* series provides state reports with clear, concise summaries of state statutes governing the political and civil rights of women (791-792). Another series of reports issued in the late 1970s detail the legal status of homemakers in each state (655-660, 673-717, 727). The most lengthy discussions of sex discrimination and women's rights are found in the hearings and reports on the Equal Rights Amendment. The same issues of protective labor legislation and the legal protection of wives and children are present from the first hearing in 1925 (526) to the last hearing prior to passage in 1971 (619). Hearings on extending the ratification period focus more on the issue of the constitutionality of the extension than the need for the amendment (721-723). The most extensive hearings on the impact of the ERA were held in 1983 and 1984 when the battle for the amendment was essentially over (750, 759-760, 765).

Specific areas of sex discrimination are addressed in publications from the 1970s and 1980s. The issue of women's access to credit is the subject of Civil Rights Commission reports (645-646, 740) and extensive House hearings (634-636). Insurance industry practices, particularly in relation to disability plans and annuities, are examined in numerous hearings on fair insurance practices legislation (739, 744, 749, 752). In 1984 and 1985 legislation removing gender-based distinctions in the *U.S. Code* was discussed at hearings where witnesses noted the need to retain such distinctions in certain sections of the *Code*, particularly in selective service laws (757, 764, 768). Ratification of the U.N. Convention on the Elimination of All Forms of Discrimination against Women was considered in a 1990 hearing which compared U.S. law against the convention's provisions (780). Other chapters dealing with women's rights and sex discrimination are Chapter

5, Suffrage and Political Participation, Chapter 6, Citizenship and Immigration, Chapter 9, Education, and Chapter 17, Retirement and Survivor Benefits. The issue of discrimination in the work place and in military service is covered more fully in Volume Two.

509. U.S. Congress. House. *A Petition of 22,626 Women of Utah Asking for the Repeal of Certain Laws, the Enactment of Others, and the Admission of the Territory of Utah as a State.* H. Misc. Doc. 42, 44th Cong., 1st sess., 1876. 2p. Serial 1698. Petition requests the repeal of anti-polygamy laws, territorial control of appointment of law officials, and the right to homestead for married women of Utah.

510. U.S. Congress. House. Committee on the Judiciary. *Common Law Marriage, Etc., Report to Accompany Bill H.R. 7594.* H. Rept. 1189, 50th Cong., 1st sess., 1888. 1p. Serial 2601. Adverse report on a bill to regulate the rights of married women in the District of Columbia and in the territories argues that women's property rights are already fully covered by existing laws.

511. U.S. Congress. Senate. Committee on the District of Columbia. *Report to Accompany S. 1659 [To Amend the Laws of the District of Columbia as to Married Women, to Make Parents the Natural Guardians of Their Minor Children, and for Other Purposes].* S. Rept. 836, 54th Cong., 1st sess., 1896. 6p. Serial 3365. Reports on a bill to protect a woman's right to her income and to recognize mothers as guardians of their children. Attached correspondence details the inequities of existing District of Columbia laws and presents numerous objections to the provisions of the proposed law.

512. U.S. Congress. House. Committee on Public Lands. *Settlers on Public Lands, Report to Accompany H.R. 6440.* H. Rept. 779, 56th Cong., 1st sess., 1900. 2p. Serial 4023. Reports favorably on a bill to correct the situation where a single woman making a homestead loses her claim if she marries before the claim is surveyed and recorded. The amended law provides for the retention of the homestead so long as she continues to reside on the land in question.

513. U.S. Congress. Senate. Committee on Public Lands. *Settlers on the Public Lands, Report to Accompany S. 4020.* S. Rept. 1333, 56th Cong., 1st sess., 1900. 2p. Serial 3894. Favorable report on a bill to remedy the situation arising upon the marriage of a female homestead claimant before perfection of her entry.

514. U.S. General Land Office. *Homestead by Married Women, Act of June 6, 1900 - Instructions.* Washington, DC: GPO, 1900. 1p. I21.10:900. Instructions to receivers and registrars of U.S. Land Offices in applying the June 6, 1900 "Act for the relief of settlers on the public lands" which protects an unmarried female settler's right to apply for a homestead entry after her marriage.

515. U.S. Congress. House. *Allotment of Lands to Married Women on Certain Indian Reservations: Letter from the Secretary of the Interior, Transmitting, with a Copy of a Communication from the Commissioner of Indian Affairs, a Draft of a Bill for Allotment of Lands to Married Women on Certain Indian Reservations in North and South Dakota.* H. Doc. 257, 59th Cong., 2d sess., 1906. 3p. Serial 5153. Correspondence explains the problems inherent in the law controlling allotments of grazing lands on the Cheyenne River, Standing Rock, and Pine Ridge reservations which grants allotments to every person except married women. Marriage practices and other factors affecting this issue are discussed.

516. U.S. Congress. Senate. Committee on the District of Columbia. *To Amend the Code of the District of Columbia Relating to Dower, Adverse Report to Accompany S. 2320.* S. Rept. 474, 59th Cong., 1st sess., 1906. 2p. Serial 4904. Adverse report on a bill to

amend the D.C. Code so as to endow the wife in lands held by the husband by equitable or legal title at the time of his death. Corporation Counsel for the Commissioner of the District of Columbia advised that the existing code favored the wife.

517.   U.S. Congress. Senate. Committee on Public Lands. *Right of Homestead Entry to Married Women, Report to Accompany S. 5465.* S. Rept. 480, 62d Cong., 2d sess., 1912. 2p. Serial 6120. Report with substantial amendments on a bill to preserve a woman's right to pursue a homestead entry after marriage. The amendments limit the husband's right to pursue a claim at the same time as his wife.

518.   U.S. Congress. Senate. *The Mission of Woman.* by Albert Taylor Bledsoe. S. Doc. 174, 63d Cong., 1st sess., 1913. 16p. Serial 6537. Reprint of an article which appeared in the October 1871 *Southern Review* expounds on the women's rights movement and the role of women. Basic argument is that equal rights will destroy marriage and lead to a serious drop in the birth rate. Also notes the objection to the word "obey" in the marriage ceremony and the view that women's rights advocates are all destined to be spinsters because no man will marry a strong-minded woman.

519.   U.S. Congress. Senate. Committee on Printing. *The Mission of Woman, Report, S.Res. 171.* S. Rept. 110, 63d Cong., 1st sess., 1913. 1p. Serial 6511. Report on a resolution ordering that Albert Taylor Bledsoe's article "The Mission of Woman" be printed in the *Congressional Record* and as a Senate document.

520.   U.S. Congress. House. Committee on the Public Lands. *Marriage of Homestead Entrymen and Entrywomen, Report to Accompany H.R. 11102.* H. Rept. 247, 63d Cong., 2d sess., 1914. 2p. Serial 6558. Reports a bill allowing both the homestead entryman and the entrywoman to retain their right to patent upon marriage provided that they complied with the law for a year previously.

521.   U.S. Congress. Senate. Committee on Public Lands. *Marriage of Homestead Entrymen with Homestead Entrywomen, Report to Accompany H.R. 11102.* S. Rept. 288, 63d Cong., 2d sess., 1914. 1p. Serial 6552. See 520 for abstract.

522.   U.S. General Land Office. *Act of April 6, 1914 (38 Stat 312) Intermarriage of Homesteaders.* Washington, DC: GPO, 1919. 2p. reprint, amended, 8 Apr. 1919. I21.4:330/2. Regulations on the rights of homestead entrymen and entrywomen in the event of marriage. Neither loses the right to a patent, but the husband is granted the privilege of choosing which entry will be the homestead.

523.   U.S. Congress. House. Committee on Public Lands. *Homestead Credit to Widows, Report to Accompany H.R. 70.* H. Rept. 40, 67th Cong., 1st sess., 1921. 2p. Serial 7920. Bill reported extends to widows of WWI soldiers the right to apply the length of the soldiers' military service to homestead resident requirements.

524.   U.S. Congress. House. Committee on the District of Columbia. *Anticigarette Bill, Hearing on H.R. 7252.* 67th Cong., 1st sess., 27 July 1921. 20p. Y4.D63/1:C48. Hearing on a bill to prohibit women from smoking in public in the District of Columbia. Among the highlights are comments on fashionable girls' schools where young girls learn to smoke and close questioning of witnesses on their views regarding women's voting rights and prohibition. Also includes some interesting observations on the type of woman who smokes and the general decline in the morality of women.

525.   U.S. General Land Office. *Act of April 6, 1914 (38 Stat. 312), As Amended by Act of March 1, 1921 (Public 339), Intermarriage of Homesteaders, [Instructions to] Registers and Receivers.* Circular no. 753. Washington, DC: GPO, 1921. 2p. I21.4:753.

526. U.S. Congress. House. Committee on the Judiciary. *Equal Rights Amendment to the Constitution, Hearing on H.J. Res 75.* 68th Cong., 2d sess., 4-5 Feb. 1925. 91p. Y4.J89/1:Eq2. First hearing on a proposed equal rights amendment describes the legal status of women in the United States and the interpretation of their status by the courts. Opponents support the state-by-state, law-by-law approach to change. Witnesses in support are from the National Woman's Party, those opposed from the League of Women Voters, the Women's Bureau, and labor leaders. Protective labor legislation is a major issue.

527. U.S. Congress. House. Committee on the District of Columbia. *Amend Code of Law for the District of Columbia, Minority Report to Accompany S. 2730.* H. Rept. 1055, part 2, 69th Cong., 1st sess., 1926. 1p. Serial 8533. Minority view offers an amendment to protect married women in some cases under a bill removing restrictions on a married woman's power to make contracts.

528. U.S. Congress. House. Committee on the District of Columbia. *Amending Section 1155 of District of Columbia Code, Report to Accompany S. 2730.* H. Rept. 1055, 69th Cong., 1st sess., 1926. 10p. Serial 8533. Reports on a bill removing a provision in the District code which restricts a married woman's power to make contracts.

529. U.S. Congress. House. Committee on the District of Columbia. *To Amend the Code of Law for the District of Columbia in Relation to the Qualifications of Jurors, Report to Accompany H.R. 5823.* H. Rept. 595, 69th Cong., 1st sess., 1926. 2p. Serial 8532. Reports a bill extending to women citizens of the District of Columbia the privilege of serving on juries and granting them the same rights of exemption.

530. U.S. Congress. Senate. Committee on the District of Columbia. *Amending Section 1155 of an Act Entitled "An Act to Establish a Code of Law for the District of Columbia", Report to Accompany S. 2730.* S. Rept. 370, 69th Cong., 1st sess., 1926. 4p. Serial 8524. Favorable report on a bill to remove a restriction on a married woman's power to make contracts. The limitations on a married woman's ability to run a business caused by the current code are described as is the court's interpretation of the conflicting laws in this area.

531. U.S. Congress. House. Committee on the Territories. *Hawaii, Qualifying Women for Jury Service, Hearings on H.R. 5575.* 70th Cong., 1st sess., 27 Dec. 1927. 2p. Y4.T27/1:H31/33. Very brief hearing on granting women the right to serve on juries in Hawaii consists mostly of the text of the resolution of the Legislature of the Territory of Hawaii and of Section 83 of the Hawaiian Organic Act, and a brief speech by Congressman Houston of Hawaii.

532. U.S. Congress. Senate. Committee on the District of Columbia. *Permitting Women to Serve on Juries in the District of Columbia, Report to Accompany H.R. 5823.* S. Rept. 1514, 69th Cong., 2d sess., 1927. 2p. Serial 8685. See 529 for abstract.

533. U.S. Congress. House. Committee on the Territories. *To Amend the Hawaiian Organic Act, as Amended, Report to Accompany H.R. 5575.* H. Rept. 129, 70th Cong., 1st sess., 1928. 1p. Serial 8835. Reports a bill amending the Hawaiian Organic Act to remove gender as a disqualifying factor for jury service.

534. U.S. Congress. Senate. Committee on the Judiciary. *Equal Rights Amendment, Hearing on S.J. Res. 64.* 70th Cong., 2d sess., 1 Feb. 1929. 79p. Y4.J89/2:Eq2. Testimony highlights inequities toward women in areas of public office, citizenship, marriage and divorce, and property. Testimony centers on the issue of protective labor legislation and other legislation benefiting women's welfare. Disagreement also centers on the best approach to removing inequities.

535.   U.S. Congress. House. Committee on the Territories. *Amend the Hawaiian Organic Act, as Amended, Report to Accompany H.R. 4656.* H. Rept. 494, 71d Cong., 2d sess., 1930. 2p. Serial 9190. Reports a bill giving the Hawaiian Legislature the power to enact a law allowing women to serve on juries. The report includes the resolution of the Hawaiian Legislature and the letter from the governor supporting this measure.

536.   U.S. Congress. Senate. Committee on the Judiciary. Subcommittee on Senate Joint Resolution 52. *Equal Rights, Hearing on S.J. Res. 52.* 71st Cong., 3d sess., 6 Jan. 1931. 103p. Y4.J89/2:Eq2/2. Statements of proponents and opponents of a federal equal rights amendment highlight examples of differing treatment of women under the law but differ on the proper approach to correcting the inequities. Opponents support the law-by-law approach arguing that the amendment would cause confusion and would remove needed protection for industrial women. Includes publications both for and against addressing the arguments of the other sides.

537.   U.S. Congress. Senate. Committee on the Judiciary. *Equal Rights Amendment to the Constitution, Hearing on H.J. Res 197.* 72d Cong., 1st sess., 16 Mar. 1932. 84p. Y4.J89/1:Eq2/2. Proponents of the amendment, primarily from the National Woman's Party, highlight the current inequities in state laws and the conservative opinions of the courts which discriminate against women. Much discussion for and against centers on protective labor legislation and the effect of the proposed amendment. The role unions have or have not played in securing equal job opportunity and pay for women is discussed.

538.   U.S. Congress. Senate. Committee on the Judiciary. Subcommittee on S.J. Res. 1. *Equal Rights for Men and Women, Hearing on S.J. Res. 1.* 93rd Cong., 1st sess., 27 May 1933. 32p. Y4.J89/2:Eq2/3. Testimony in favor of the equal rights amendment focuses on the effects of state protective labor laws on women's ability to secure employment and points out discrepancies in property laws. Many of the statements pro and con focus on the issues of wage and hour laws which apply only to women and on the best way to remove discriminatory laws.

539.   U.S. Congress. House. Committee on Ways and Means. *Community Property Income, Hearing on H.R. 8396.* 73d Cong., 2d sess., 1 May - 13 June 1934. 326p. Y4.W36:In2/7. Lengthy hearing considers the question of taxation in community property states. Proposed legislation required that one tax return be filed by the person who managed the money, property, etc. to eliminate tax avoidance by a husband and wife both filing returns as a partnership. One issue debated is how the law would affect the right of married women with separate business income to file their own return.

540.   U.S. Congress. House. Committee on the District of Columbia. *Amending the Code of Laws for the District of Columbia in Relation to the Qualifications of Jurors, Report to Accompany H.R. 8583.* H. Rept. 1424, 74th Cong., 1st sess., 1935. 1p. Serial 9888. Reports a bill removing the provision in the D.C. Code allowing women the option of declining to serve on a jury.

541.   U.S. Congress. Senate. *A Comparison of the Political and Civil Rights of Men and Women in the United States.* S. Doc. 270, 74th Cong., 2d sess., 1936. 249p. Serial 10016. Detailed examination of the political and civil rights and duties of men and women in the U.S. covers the topics of nationality, political participation, right to work and labor laws, and ability to serve as legal guardian or executrix. Marriage and divorce laws relating to domicile, property, contracts, support, estate, guardianship and support of children, and illegitimate children are examined. Important court cases and the effect of economic conditions are noted.

542. U.S. Congress. House. Committee on the Judiciary. Subcommittee No. 1. *Women Jurors in Federal Courts, Hearing on H.R. 3409.* 75th Cong., 1st sess., 3 Mar. 1937. 37p. Y4.J89/1:W84/13. Hearing on the suitability of women as jurors discusses women's ability to withstand the stress of a trial, the appropriateness of women being shut in a room with men during deliberations, and housing women when jurors are kept overnight. Includes an interesting interchange on whether women would come to different verdicts than men and the moral decline of women since the 19th Amendment. The experience with women jurors in the States is highlighted.

543. U.S. Congress. Senate. Committee on the Judiciary. *Equal Rights Amendment, Report to Accompany S.J.Res. 65.* S. Rept. 1641, 75th Cong., 3d sess., 1938. 1p. Serial 10229. Report on the proposed Equal Rights Amendment indicates that the committee was equally split between those for and against the amendment.

544. U.S. Congress. Senate. Committee on the Judiciary. Subcommittee on S.J. Res. 65. *Equal Rights for Men and Women, Hearing on S.J. Res. 65.* 75th Cong., 3d sess., 7-10 Feb. 1938. 172p. Y4.89/2:Eq2/4. The first two days of hearings present arguments opposing an Equal Rights Amendment based on a loss to women of "rights" such as right to support and protective labor laws and on the claim that the amendment would create legal chaos. Much of the testimony points out the inequities against women in various states but advocates case-by-case change which will come with time. The role of the National Woman's Party in gaining equal rights for women is discussed by several witnesses. Testimony in favor of the ERA advances arguments based on the ineffectiveness of protective labor laws and continuing legal discrimination against married women. The discussion on protective labor laws points to the discriminatory effect of such laws and the economic need of many women to work. Witnesses from the printing trades and transit industry note the negative effect of hours laws on women. The limitations of case-by-case change and the extent of state laws allowing women to serve on juries are discussed.

545. U.S. Congress. Senate. Committee on the Judiciary. Subcommittee on S.J. Res. 65. *Equal Rights for Men and Women, Hearing on S.J. Res. 65, Part 2, Supplemental Statements.* 75th Cong., 3d sess., 7 Mar. 1938. 178-197pp. Y4.J89/2:Eq2/4/pt. 2. Additional statements submitted both for and against ERA.

546. U.S. Office of Education. *Gallant American Women [#1], These Freedoms, October 31, 1939.* by Jane Ashman. Washington, DC: The Office, 1939. 26p. FS5.15:1. The first episode of the "Gallant American Women" radio series depicts the role of women in the fight for civil rights in the U.S., highlighting individual women such as Mary Dyer and Lucretia Mott.

547. U.S. Office of Education. *Gallant American Women #7, Laws and the Woman, December 12, 1939.* by Jane Ashman. Washington, DC: GPO, 1939. 27p. FS5.15:7. Radio script tells the story of the treatment of women under the law with a strong slant toward equal rights for women. Property laws and the rights of married women who work are two of the topics covered. A reference list of sources consulted is appended.

548. U.S. Congress. Senate. *Equal Rights Amendment: Questions and Answers.* by Research Dept., National Woman's Party. S. Doc. 97, 78th Cong., 1st sess., 1943. 16p. Serial 10773. Overview of the Equal Rights Amendment answers questions on the history of congressional action, organizations supporting the amendment, the constitutional amendment approach, the effect of the amendment on "women's" laws and society, court interpretations, and the appropriateness of pushing the measure in wartime.

549.   U.S. Congress. Senate. Committee on the Judiciary. Subcommittee on S.J. Res. 25. *Equal Rights, Report to Accompany S.J. Res. 25.* S. Rept. 267, 78th Cong., 1st sess., 1943. 4p. Serial 10756. Favorable report provides an overview of committee action relative to the wording of the amendment and the issue of state's rights.

550.   U.S. Dept. of Labor. *Comments by Secretary of Labor to Judiciary Committee of House of Representatives on Equal Rights Amendment.* Washington, DC: The Department, 1944. 21p. L1.13:Eq25. Statement by Secretary of Labor Frances Perkins before the House Judiciary Committee expresses opposition to the Equal Rights Amendment on the grounds that women still need the protection of labor laws and family support laws which the amendment would jeopardize. Claims of the amendment's proponents are rejected based on the argument that the amendment would not solve the inequities which exist. Perkins also advances the argument that for the most part the statutory method of eliminating discrimination is working well. The Fourteenth Amendment is also viewed as providing sufficient protection from unreasonable discrimination. Laws which would be affected by the amendment, such as rape, divorce, and property laws, are examined individually for the possible effects of the amendment.

551.   U.S. Women's Bureau. *Legal Status of Women, Analysis of Sex Distinctions, United States of America.* Washington, DC: The Bureau, 1944. 12p. L13.2:W84/9. Summarizes distinctions based on gender in state laws in the areas of public office, jury service, domicile, marriage and divorce, parent and child, family support, business, property ownership, and inheritance.

552.   U.S. Congress. House. Committee on the Judiciary. *Equal-Rights Amendment, Report to Accompany H.J.Res. 49.* H. Rept. 907, 79th Cong., 1st sess., 1945. 6p. Serial 10934. Report on the ERA reviews the committee action on H.J. Res. 49 and similar resolutions and briefly states the committee's response to opposing arguments. Minority views note the areas of discrimination in existing laws and oppose the amendment as leaving women unprotected.

553.   U.S. Congress. House. Committee on the Judiciary. Subcommittee No. 2. *Amend the Constitution Relative to Equal Rights for Men and Women, Statements on H.J. Res. 1, H.J. Res. 5, H.J. Res. 30, H.J. Res. 42, H.J. Res. 49, H.J. Res. 66, H.J. Res. 71, H.J. Res. 80, H.J. Res. 82, and H.J. Res. 96.* 79th Cong., 1st sess., 1945. 154p. Y4.J89/1:C76/15. Statements supporting and opposing the ERA are accompanied by lists of persons, organizations, etc. in each camp. Having determined that they had already heard all of the arguments pro and con, the subcommittee choose to forgo a hearing and have both sides submit written statements. Highlights of statements include a review of equity legislation already enacted in the states, governor's endorsements by state, a summary of pros and cons by the General Federation of Women's Clubs, and a list of state laws which discriminate in favor of women.

554.   U.S. Congress. Senate. Committee on the Judiciary. *Equal Rights Amendment, Hearing on S.J. Res. 61.* 79th Cong., 1st sess., 28 Sept. 1945. 158p. Y4.J89/2:Eq2/5. Hearing on the ERA includes two hours of testimony from each side of the issue. The only real difference between this and earlier hearings on ERA is the added element of the role played by women in WWII. Includes a state-by-state list of laws which would be "jeopardized" by passage of the ERA.

555.   U.S. Women's Bureau. *Don't Buy a Gold Brick.* Washington, DC: The Bureau, 1945. [8]p. leaflet. L13.2:G57. Main points of argument against the Equal Rights Amendment presented are that it would cause confusion in the courts, that state legislation is a better approach, that it would undermine the legal right of a wife to support and alimony, and finally, that it would remove protective labor laws for women.

556. U.S. Women's Bureau. *Legal Status of Women in the United States, Analysis of Sex Distinctions in Political and Civil Laws (Revised)*. Washington, DC: The Bureau, 1945. 12p. L13.2:W84/9/945. See 551 for abstract.

557. U.S. Women's Bureau. *Women's Eligibility for Jury Duty*. Washington, DC: GPO, 1945. [2]p. leaflet. L13.2:J97/945-2.

558. U.S. Women's Bureau. *Women's Status under Political and Civil Laws, Preliminary Summary*. Washington, DC: The Bureau, 1945. 3p. L13.2:W84/15/prelim.

559. U.S. Congress. Senate. *Equal Rights Amendment: Questions and Answers on the Equal Rights Amendment*. by Research Dept., National Woman's Party. S. Doc. 209, 79th Cong., 2d sess., 1946. 20p. Serial 11037. Basic background information supporting the ERA in a question and answer format. Reviews congressional action including introducers of the amendment, political party support and governors' endorsements, and women's organizations supporting the amendment. The effect of the amendment is discussed with particular emphasis on labor laws but also covering military service, divorce, and rape. The U.N. Social and Economic Council report on the status of women is reprinted.

560. U.S. Congress. Senate. Committee on the Judiciary. *Equal Rights Amendment, Individual Views to Accompany S.J.Res. 61*. S. Rept. 1013, part 2, 79th Cong., 2d sess., 1946. 2p. Serial 11014. Opposition to the ERA voices concern over a shift to the federal government of the burden of enforcement and the elimination of protective labor laws.

561. U.S. Congress. Senate. Committee on the Judiciary. *Equal Rights Amendment, Report to Accompany S.J.Res. 61 Together with the Minority Views*. S. Rept. 1013, 79th Cong., 2d sess., 1946. 12p. Serial 11014. Brief favorable report on the ERA is followed by a lengthy minority report opposing the amendment on the grounds that many women's organizations oppose the measure, that enforcement is impracticable, and that it would cause chaos in state laws designed to protect women.

562. U.S. Women's Bureau. *The Legal Status of Women in the United States of America, Trends in Political and Civil Laws 1938-1945*. Washington, DC: The Bureau, 1946. 2p. L13.2:W84/21/938-45.

563. U.S. Women's Bureau. *International Documents on the Status of Women*. Bulletin no. 217. Washington, DC: GPO, 1947. 116p. L13.3:217. Overview of history of work by intergovernmental organizations, particularly the United Nations, on the status of women. Appendix A reproduces international documents concerning the status of women between 1920-1946. Appendix B lists women officials in the League of Nations, and Appendix C charts the status of women suffrage in countries of the world as of fall 1946.

564. U.S. Women's Bureau. *Women's Eligibility for Jury Duty*. Washington, DC: GPO, 1947. [2]p. leaflet. L13.2:J97/945.

565. U.S. Congress. House. Committee on the Judiciary. *Proposing an Amendment to the Constitution of the United States Relative to Equal Rights for Men and Women, Report to Accompany H.J.Res. 397*. H. Rept. 2196, 80th Cong., 2d sess., 1948. 7p. Serial 11212. Report on the ERA reviews support for the amendment and addresses the issue of "protective" laws. Minority views oppose the amendment citing its effect on laws providing support for widows and mothers and protecting women workers.

566. U.S. Congress. House. Committee on the Judiciary. Subcommittee No. 1. *Equal Rights Amendment to the Constitution and Commission on the Legal Status of Women, Hearings*. 80th Cong., 2d sess., 10, 12 Mar. 1948. 218p. Y4.J89/1:C76/16. Hearing considers

numerous resolutions for an ERA and resolutions on establishing a commission on the legal status of women. Testimony for the amendment focuses on discrimination in employee benefits and Social Security, discrimination against married women in business and property ownership, etc. Opposition by pro-ERA witnesses to the establishment of a commission on the legal status of women centers on arguments that such a commission would be used to legitimize existing gender-based distinctions in state laws. Those opposing the ERA but supporting the commission bill base their arguments on a need to maintain legal distinction based on gender to protect the social position and health of women while eliminating only discrimination deemed harmful by the commission.

567.   U.S. Congress. Senate. Committee on the Judiciary. *Proposing an Amendment to the Constitution of the United States Relative to Equal Rights for Men and Women, Report to Accompany S.J.Res. 76.* S. Rept. 1208, 80th Cong., 2d sess., 1948. 2p. Serial 11207. Favorable report on ERA briefly outlines recent congressional action on the amendment.

568.   U.S. Women's Bureau. *The Legal Status of Women in the United States: Reports and Summary for the Territories and Possessions.* Bulletin no. 157-50. Washington, DC: GPO, 1948. 83p. L13.3:157-50. Concise summary for Alaska, Hawaii, Puerto Rico, Canal Zone and Virgin Islands of statutes relating to women in the areas of contracts and property, marriage and divorce, parents and children, and political rights. An addendum for Hawaii was issued in 1956 and separate reports were issued for Hawaii in 1959 and Alaska in 1958.

569.   U.S. Women's Bureau. *The Political and Civil Status of Women in the United States of American, Summary. [Preliminary].* Washington, DC: GPO, 1948. 6p. L13.2:P75/948. Concise summary of the status of women in the U.S. in the areas of voting, jury duty, eligibility for public office and civil service positions, laws of domicile, property laws, marriage and divorce laws, guardianship of children, family support, and power to make contracts.

570.   U.S. Women's Bureau. *Replies to the ECOSOC Questionnaire on the Legal Status and Treatment of Women, Part I, Public Law, Section C, Public Services and Functions.* Washington, DC: The Bureau, 1948. 23p. L13.2:Ec7/part 1/sec. C. Briefly describes the legal status of women in the U.S. in the areas of civil service, military and labor service, and jury service citing state statutes.

571.   U.S. Women's Bureau. *Replies to the ECOSOC Questionnaire on the Legal Status and Treatment of Women, Part I, Public Law, Section E, Civil Liberties.* Washington, DC: The Bureau, 1948. 7p. L13.2:Ec7/pt.1/sec.E. Brief overview of women's rights in the U.S. relative to civil liberties, representation in court, and free choice to marry is in response to a U.N. Economic and Social Council questionnaire.

572.   U.S. Women's Bureau. *Replies to the ECOSOC Questionnaire on the Legal Status and Treatment of Women, Part I, Public Law, Section F, Fiscal Laws.* Washington, DC: The Bureau, 1948. 8p. L13.2:Ec7/pt.1/sec.F. Answers to U.N. Economic and Social Council questionnaire describes U.S. laws governing taxes as they apply to women, including the areas of income tax, inheritance tax, and gift tax. Tax laws which treat women differently from men are noted.

573.   U.S. Women's Bureau. *Reply of United States Government to Questionnaire of United Nations Economic and Social Council on the Legal Status and Treatment of Women.* Washington, DC: The Bureau, 1948. 1p. L13.2:Ec7/ann. Summary of Women's Bureau actions relating to the questionnaire.

574. U.S. Congress. Senate. Committee on the Judiciary. *Equal Rights, Report to Accompany S.J.Res. 25.* S. Rept. 137, 81st Cong., 1st sess., 1949. 1p. Serial 11291. Favorable report on the ERA without comment.

575. U.S. Women's Bureau. *Comments by Secretary of Labor, Frances Perkins, to Judiciary Committee of the House of Representatives on Equal Rights Amendment, 1945.* Washington, DC: The Bureau, 1949. 24p. L13.2:Eq2/4. Statement of Perkins in opposition to the ERA focuses on topics of the elimination of "reasonable" differences in the treatment of women and men under the law, the legal confusion the amendment would cause, elimination of laws to protect the wife and family, and elimination of protective labor legislation for women. Perkins expresses the viewpoint that progress is occurring already to remove unreasonable discrimination against women.

576. U.S. Congress. House. Committee on Public Lands. *Amending Section 83 of the Hawaiian Organic Act to Provide That Women May Serve on Juries in the Territory of Hawaii, Report to Accompany H.R. 176.* H. Rept. 1791, 81st Cong., 2d sess., 1950. 2p. Serial 11379.

577. U.S. Congress. House. Committee on Interior and Insular Affairs. *Amending the Hawaiian Organic Act Relating to Qualifications of Jurors, Report to Accompany H.R. 4798.* H. Rept. 912, 82d Cong., 1st sess., 1951. 2p. Serial 11498.

578. U.S. Congress. Senate. *Equal Rights Amendment: Questions and Answers on the Equal Rights Amendment Prepared by the Research Department of the National Woman's Party.* Edited by Ethel Ernest Murrell. S. Doc. 74, 82d Cong., 1st sess., 1951. 8p. Serial 11511. Information on the ERA is presented as answers to forty questions on the need for the amendment and its effect on marriage and family law and on women in industry.

579. U.S. Congress. Senate. Committee on the Judiciary. *Equal Rights Amendment, Report to Accompany S.J.Res. 3.* S. Rept. 356, 82d Cong., 1st sess., 1951. 1p. Serial 11487. Favorable report without comment on the Equal Rights Amendment.

580. U.S. Women's Bureau. *Legal Status of the American Family.* Washington, DC: GPO, 1951. 27p. L13.2:F21. Summary of family law in the U.S. covers topics of age of consent to marry, common-law marriage, community property, family support and public assistance, nonsupport laws, property rights, powers of contract, custody and control of children, unmarried parents, and dissolution of marriage. Child welfare laws and adoption are also reviewed.

581. U.S. Women's Bureau. *State Laws of Special Value to Women, January 1, 1951.* Washington, DC: The Bureau, 1951. 51p. L13.2:L44/951. One page summaries of state laws affecting women as wives, mothers, widows, and workers. Reviews support, marriage, property, estate and labor laws. Earlier edition published in 1950.

582. U.S. Congress. Senate. Committee on International Affairs. *Amending the Hawaiian Organic Act Relating to Qualifications of Jurors, Report to Accompany H.R. 4798.* S. Rept. 1299, 82d Cong., 2d sess., 1952. 2p. Serial 11566. Favorable report on legislation to amend the Hawaiian Organic Act so as to permit women to serve as jurors.

583. U.S. Congress. Senate. Committee on the Judiciary. *Equal Rights for Men and Women, Report to Accompany S.J.Res. 49.* S. Rept. 221, 83d Cong., 1st sess., 1953. 1p. Serial 11659. Reports the ERA with minimal comment.

584. U.S. Women's Bureau. *Jury Duty for Women.* Leaflet no. 6. Washington, DC: GPO, 1953. leaflet. L13.11:6. Revisions issued as inserts for 1954, 1955 and 1956.

585. U.S. Women's Bureau. *What Are Your Legal Rights? A Checklist on Women's Property - Family - Political Rights.* Leaflet no. 21. Washington, DC: The Bureau, 1955. 5p. L13.11:21. Checklist of questions on legal rights of women which can be answered in the state reports *The Legal Status of Women in the United States of America*, Bulletin 157 nos. 1-50 (755, 756). Slightly revised edition issued in 1956 and reprinted in 1958.

586. U.S. Congress. Senate. Committee on the Judiciary. *Equal Rights for Men and Women, Report to Accompany S.J.Res. 39.* S. Rept. 1991, 84th Cong., 2d sess., 1956. 2p. Serial 11888. Favorable report on the ERA summarizes support for the amendment and notes that the measure has been the topic of hearings and has been favorably reported several times.

587. U.S. Congress. Senate. Committee on the Judiciary. *Equal Rights, Hearings on S.J. Res. 39.* 84th Cong., 2d sess., 11,13 Apr. 1956. 79p. Y4.J89/2:Eq2/6. Hearing on a proposed Equal Rights Amendment covers the issues of military service, community property, and protective labor laws. Focus of the opposition argument is on protective labor legislation.

588. U.S. Congress. Senate. Committee on the Judiciary. *Equal Rights for Men and Women, Report to Accompany S.J. Res. 80.* S. Rept. 1150, 85th Cong., 1st sess., 27 Aug. 1957. 2p. Serial 11979. Favorable report on the ERA briefly reviews the language of the amendment, past congressional action, national organizations supporting the amendment, and the international status of equal rights for women.

589. U.S. Women's Bureau. *Women's New Role on the International Scene, Address by Mrs. Alice K. Leopold, Assistant to Secretary of Labor for Women's Affairs, before the National Order of Women Legislators, Annual Convention, Hartford, Conn., June 7, 1957.* Washington, DC: The Bureau, 1957. 17p. L13.12:L55.3. Overview of the role of women in intergovernmental organizations highlights the progress of those organizations in addressing women's equality of opportunity world wide. The history of the Inter-American Commission of Women and the role of women's organizations in improving the status of women here and abroad are reviewed. The representation of women in government policy-making and diplomatic roles in various countries are listed.

590. U.S. Women's Bureau. *Property and Political Rights of Women, January 1, 1938 - January 1, 1958.* Washington, DC: The Bureau, 1958. 11p. L13.2:P94/3/938-58. Brief comparison of the legal status of women in 1938 and 1958 examines the areas of jury service, eligibility for elective office, domicile of married women, contractual rights of married women, procedures required for a married woman to engage in a separate business, married woman's management and control of her own earnings, family homestead, survivor benefits, responsibility for family support, and guardianship of minor children.

591. U.S. Congress. Senate. Committee on the Judiciary. *Equal Rights for Men and Women, Report to Accompany S.J.Res. 69.* S. Rept. 303, 86th Cong., 1st sess., 1959. 2p. Serial 12150. Favorable report on the ERA reviews the supporting arguments of earlier reports.

592. U.S. Women's Bureau. *Report on 14th Session of the Commission on the Status of Women, Held in Buenos Aires, Argentina, March 28 - April 14, 1960.* by Lorena B. Hahn. Washington, DC: The Bureau, 1960. 7p. L13.2:W84/37/960. Report of the U.S. representative to the U.N. Commission on the Status of Women on the 1960 session reviews action on the topics of political rights, education, equal pay and marriage laws.

593. U.S. Women's Bureau. *Equal Rights Amendment.* Washington, DC: The Bureau, 1961. 9p. L13.2:Eq2/14. Objective report reviews the history of the Equal Rights Amendment and the major arguments of both proponents and opponents. The major players in the

amendment debate are identified. This report was originally compiled in 1950 and revised in 1955 by the Legislative Reference Service of the Library of Congress.

594. U.S. Women's Bureau. *Report on 15th Session of the United Nations Commission on the Status of Women, Held at UN Headquarters, Geneva, Switzerland, March 13-30, 1961.* by Mrs. Charles W. Tillett. Washington, DC: The Bureau, 1961. 5p. L13.2:St2/4. Review of action taken at the 15th session of the U.N. Commission on the Status of Women on political rights, marriage, economic opportunities, and access to education.

595. U.S. Congress. Senate. *Equal Rights Amendment: Questions and Answers Prepared by the Research Department of the National Woman's Party.* Edited by Margery C. Leonard. S. Doc. 164, 87th Cong., 2d sess., 1962. 30p. Serial 12445. Expanded version of S. Doc. 82-74 uses a question and answer format to review the purpose and need for the ERA, the support and history of the proposed amendment, and the current legal status of women in education, political participation, and labor. Addresses objections based on the need to protect women and on the issue of states' rights. The document makes liberal use of quotes supporting the amendment.

596. U.S. Congress. Senate. Committee on Rules and Administration. *Authorizing the Printing of a Revised Edition of Senate Document 74, 87th Congress, Entitled "Equal Rights Amendment - Questions and Answers", Report to Accompany S.Res. 410.* S. Rept. 2256, 87th Cong., 2d sess., 1962. 2p. Serial 12421.

597. U.S. Congress. Senate. Committee on the Judiciary. *Equal Rights for Men and Women, Report to Accompany S.J.Res. 142.* S. Rept. 2192, 87th Cong., 2d sess., 1962. 3p. Serial 12421. The committee favorably reports the ERA briefly reviewing the legislative history of the proposed amendment, the need for the amendment, the reason for rejecting a proposed clause to preserve the "rights, benefits or exemptions" conferred by law upon persons of the female sex, and the organizations supporting the amendment.

598. U.S. President's Commission on the Status of Women. *Report of the Committee on Civil and Political Rights to the President's Commission on the Status of Women.* Washington, DC: GPO, 1963. 83p. Pr35.8:W84/C49. Examination of the participation of women in the political and judicial arena and discussion of existing legal and social barriers. Political office, judicial appointment, political party activity, jury service, and personal and property rights of married women are examined. Reviews the means of achieving greater recognition of the rights of women, including the proposed Equal Rights Amendment, and litigation under the 5th and 14th amendments to the Constitution. Appendix reviews selected court decisions determining the validity of laws which distinguish on the basis of gender.

599. U.S. Congress. Senate. Committee on the Judiciary. *Equal Rights for Men and Women, Report to Accompany S.J. Res. 45.* S. Rept. 1558, 88th Cong., 2d sess., 1964, 3p. Serial 12616-5. Favorable report on the ERA briefly reviews past congressional action and support from state legislatures and governors.

600. U.S. Women's Bureau. *State Laws Governing Emancipation of Minors by Marriage.* Washington, DC: The Bureau, 1964. 6p. L13.2:M666/2. Charts summarize the provisions of state statutes governing the emancipation of minors by marriage noting gender distinctions.

601. U.S. Women's Bureau. *State Laws Governing Emancipation of Minors Permitted by Court Order, January 1, 1964.* Washington, DC: The Bureau, 1964. 3p. L13.2:M666. Summary of state laws governing the removal of "disabilities of minority" by petitioning the court notes differences in the treatment of men and women.

602.   U.S. Women's Bureau. *State Laws Governing Natural Guardianship and Support of Minor Children, January 1, 1964.* Washington, DC: The Bureau, 1964. 4p. L13.2:G93. Chart summarizes the basic provisions of state laws governing natural guardianship of minor children when parents live together and responsibility for support of minor children. A general summary follows the chart noting the general trends in guardianship and support.

603.   U.S. Women's Bureau. *State Laws Governing the Age of Majority, January 1, 1964.* Washington, DC: The Bureau, 1964. 2p. L13.2:M28. Charts summarize state laws, both common law and statutory law, governing age of majority for males and for females.

604.   U.S. Women's Bureau. *State Laws Governing the Right of a Minor, 14 Years of Age or Over, to Nominate Own Guardian, as of January 1, 1964.* Washington, DC: The Bureau, 1964. 5p. L13.2:M666/3. Summary of provisions of state laws giving minors 14 to 21 the right to name their own guardian or the guardian of his or her estate.

605.   U.S. Women's Bureau. *Know Your Rights: What a Working Wife Should Know about Her Legal Rights.* Washington, DC: GPO, 1965. 14p. L13.11:39. Summary of rights of married women regarding property, earnings, and place of residence during marriage, in the event of the husband's death and in the case of divorce.

606.   U.S. Women's Bureau. *Political and Civil Status of Women as of July 15, 1965.* Washington, DC: The Bureau, 1965 12p. L13.2:P75/965. Advanced draft of chapter 8 of the *Handbook on Women Workers* provides an overview of women's status in the US in the areas of citizenship, voting and public office, eligibility for civil service positions, jury service, and domicile. Also covers marriage and divorce laws, guardianship of children, family support laws, power to make contracts, property laws, and inheritance laws. Briefly covers the Uniform Reciprocal Enforcement of Support Act.

607.   U.S. Women's Bureau. *Laws Governing Eligibility of Women for Jury Service.* Washington, DC: The Bureau, 1966. revised edition. 7p. L13.2:J97/3/966-2. Summary of federal and state laws governing women's eligibility for jury service reviews related state legislative actions in 1965-66. Special note is made of child care and/or family care exemptions in state laws.

608.   U.S. Women's Bureau. *Conozca sus Derechos, lo que Una Esposa que Trabaja Debe Saber Sobre sus Derechos.* by Harriet F. Pipel and Minna Post Peyser. Leaflet no. 39-A. Washington, DC: The Bureau, 1967. 20p. L13.11:39-A. Spanish edition of *Know Your Rights* (605).

609.   U.S. Women's Bureau. *Highlights of 1966 State Legislation of Special Interest to Women: Civil and Political Status.* Washington, DC: The Bureau, 1967. 3p. L13.2:L52/4 or L13.2:C49/966. Summary of state laws enacted in 1966 relating to women and jury service, marriage and divorce, family support, and child abuse.

610.   U.S. Women's Bureau. *Marriage Laws as of July 1, 1966.* Washington, DC: The Bureau, 1967? 1p. L13.6/4:966. Summary of the provisions of state marriage laws in chart form. Earlier edition covering laws as of July 1, 1965 published in 1966.

611.   U.S. Citizens Advisory Council on the Status of Women. *Report of the Task Force on Family Law and Policy.* Washington, DC: GPO, 1968. 69p. Y3.In8/21:2F21. General overview of the current laws in the United States dealing with ownership of property during and at the dissolution of marriage, child support and alimony, child custody, inheritance, abortion and birth control. Reviews state marriage and divorce laws and rules of domicile.

612. U.S. Citizens' Advisory Council on the Status of Women. *The Equal Rights Amendment: What It Will and Won't Do.* Washington, DC: The Council, 1970. 4p. Y3.In8/21:2Eq2/5. Summary of the effect of the ERA on divorce, property rights, "protective" labor laws, retirement, and military service.

613. U.S. Citizens' Advisory Council on the Status of Women. *Statement on Bayh Substitute and Ervin Amendments to the Equal Rights Amendment.* Washington, DC: The Council, 1970. 2p. Y3.In8/21:Eq2/3. Lists the reasons for rejecting the proposed Bayh substitute and the Ervin amendment to the ERA, measures allowing the continuation of gender-based differential treatment in cases of a "compelling and overriding public interest" and in military service.

614. U.S. Congress. Senate. Committee on the Judiciary. *Equal Rights 1970, Hearings on S.J.Res. 61 and S.J.Res. 231.* 91st Cong., 2d sess., 9-15 Sept. 1970. 433p. Y4.J89/2:Eq2/6/970-1-2. Hearing on the legal ramifications of the proposed equal rights amendment includes numerous statements opposing the amendment based on issues of the elimination of protective laws, sex restricted restrooms, and military service exemption. Testimony both for and against the amendment focuses on protective labor legislation. Considerable discussion centers on coverage of the 14th Amendment in sex discrimination cases.

615. U.S. Congress. Senate. Committee on the Judiciary. Subcommittee on Constitutional Amendments. *The "Equal Rights" Amendment, Hearings on S.J.Res. 61.* 91st Cong., 2d sess., 5-7 May 1970. 793p. Y4.J89/2:Eq2/6/970. Testimony from a wide array of witnesses highlights the need for and concerns regarding the proposed equal rights amendment. Issues raised include abortion, education discrimination, employment discrimination, protective labor laws, property rights, divorce, jury service, military service, and right to support.

616. U.S. President's Task Force on Women's Rights and Responsibilities. *A Matter of Simple Justice.* Washington, DC: GPO, 1970. 33p. Pr37.8:W84/R29. The report of the Task Force focuses on the need to ensure through legislation the civil rights of women. Major problem areas of sex discrimination in education, employment, and public assistance policy are noted and the need for federal agencies and programs to take women's needs into consideration are stressed. A minority view urges the extension of the provisions of the federal Fair Labor Standards Act, notably minimum wage, to all workers.

617. U.S. Commission on Civil Rights. *Federal Civil Rights Enforcement Effort.* by Geneva E. Adkins, et al. Washington, DC: GPO, 1971. 400p. CR1.2:En2/971. Reviews areas in which federal agencies have civil rights enforcement obligations including employment, housing and public assistance. The only section which speaks directly to sex equity is employment discrimination.

618. U.S. Congress. House. Committee on the Judiciary. *Equal Rights of Men and Women, Report Together with Separate and Minority Views to Accompany H.J.Res. 208.* H. Rept. 92-359, 92d Cong., 1st sess., 1971. 16p. Serial 12932-3. Favorable report on the ERA with amendments to exempt women from compulsory military service and to protect any law which "reasonably promotes the health and safety of the people." The committee statement reviews the need for the amendment and discusses amendments to the original language. Separate views included in the report object to the "health and safety" amendment and the concept of "equality" under the amended and unamended versions as well as the military service question. Additional views also argue that existing legislation is adequate to remove discrimination against women.

619. U.S. Congress. House. Committee on the Judiciary. Subcommittee No. 4. *Equal Rights for Men and Women, 1971, Hearings on H.J. Res. 35, 208 and Related Bills and H.R. 916 and Related Bills.* 92d Cong., 1st sess., 24 Mar. - 5 Apr. 1971. 724p. Y4.J89/1:92-2. Hearing on proposed equal rights amendment and a proposed federal statute to address specific areas of sex discrimination. Testimony highlights general and specific cases of sex discrimination and covers the major arguments for and against an equal rights amendment. Discusses whether women are covered by the 14th amendment and court rulings on sex discrimination cases. The view that the amendment would go too far and allow no distinctions between the sexes is debated. Issues of religious organizations, the military draft, the armed forces, and international implications of failure to approve resolutions guaranteeing equal rights are discussed. Protective labor laws are a point of discussion for both sides. Related court cases are highlighted and sex discrimination in federal employment is specifically addressed. Reprints the documents *A Matter of Simple Justice: The Report of the President's Task Force on Women's Rights and Responsibilities* (616) and the United Nations' "Declaration on the Elimination of Discrimination against Women."

620. U.S. Congress. Senate. Committee on the District of Columbia. *District of Columbia Administration of Estates Act, Report to Accompany H.R. 7931.* S. Rept. 92-321, 92d Cong., 1st sess., 1971. 13p. Serial 12929-3. Reports a bill which, among other things, eliminates discrimination against women in appointment as the administrator of an estate of a person dying intestate.

621. U.S. Congress. Senate. Committee on the Judiciary. Subcommittee on Constitutional Amendments. *Constitutional Amendments Report Pursuant to S.Res. 335.* S. Rept. 92-501, 92d Cong., 1st sess., 1971. 19p. Serial 12931-1. Report on constitutional amendments provides a legislative history of the Equal Rights Amendment.

622. U.S. Citizens' Advisory Council on the Status of Women. *The Proposed Equal Rights Amendment to the United States Constitution: A Memorandum.* Washington, DC: The Council, 1972. 18p. Y3.In8/21:2Eq2. Analysis of women's rights under the Constitution and the effect of the ERA reviews case law relating to women's rights. Earlier edition published in 1970.

623. U.S. Congress. House. *Commission on Civil Rights, Conference Report to Accompany H.R. 12652.* H. Rept. 92-1444, 92 Cong., 2d sess., 1972. 2p. Serial 12974-6. Differences between the House and Senate versions of H.R. 12652, a bill extending the jurisdiction of the Commission on Civil Rights to include discrimination based on sex, mainly related to appropriation levels.

624. U.S. Congress. House. Committee on Education and Labor. Ad Hoc Subcommittee on Discrimination against Women. *Oversight Hearings on Discrimination against Women.* 92 Cong., 2d sess., 26 April - 10 May 1972. 409p. Y4.Ed8/1:W84/4. Hearing examines sex discrimination in HEW's Office of Education and Office of Education Grant and Contract Procedure.

625. U.S. Congress. House. Committee on the Judiciary. *Civil Rights Commission, Report to Accompany H.R. 12652.* H. Rept. 92-946, 92d Cong., 2d sess., 1972. 8p. Serial 12974-1. Reports a bill expanding the jurisdiction of the Civil Rights Commission to include sex discrimination. Correspondence from the EEOC, HEW and Department of Labor supports the inclusion of sex discrimination under the commission's jurisdiction.

626. U.S. Congress. House. Committee on the Judiciary. Subcommittee No. 5. *Civil Rights Commission, Hearings on H.R. 12652.* 92d Cong., 2d sess., 24 Feb. 1972. 46p. Y4.J89/1:92-23. Brief hearing presents testimony supporting the work of the Civil Rights

Commission and specifically describes the need to expand the commission's mandate to include sex discrimination.

627. U.S. Congress. Senate. Committee on the Judiciary. *Equal Rights for Men and Women, Report Together with Individual Views to Accompany S.J.Res. 8, S.J.Res. 9, and H.J.Res. 208.* S. Rept. 92-689, 92d Cong., 2d sess., 1972. 52p. Serial 12971-1. Lengthy report on the ERA expresses a number of views on the need for an ERA, and the desirability of exempting military service and laws for the protection of women from the provisions of the amendment. The arguments pro and con are reviewed as is the legislative history of the amendment and major court cases. The various substitute amendments are also described both in the main report and in the individual views.

628. U.S. Congress. Senate. Committee on the Judiciary. *Women's Rights Day, Report to Accompany S. 13490.* S. Rept. 92-1049, 92d Cong., 2d sess., 1972. 2p. Serial 12971-6.

629. U.S. Congress. Senate. Committee on the Judiciary. Subcommittee on Constitutional Rights. *Civil Rights Commission, Hearing on S. 3121, H.R. 12652.* 92d Cong., 2d sess., 16 June 1972. 56p. Y4.J89/2:C49/10/972. Hearing presents testimony mostly in support of continuing the authorization for the Civil Rights Commission and expanding its authority to include sex discrimination. The opening statement of subcommittee chairman Ervin opposes the commission based on the premise that other agencies exist to enforce anti-discrimination laws and that the proposed expansion to cover sex discrimination would duplicate the work of the Women's Bureau and other agencies. Witnesses testify on the growing body of knowledge on sex discrimination and highlight the need for further studies of civil rights and women.

630. U.S. Congress. Senate. Committee on Banking, Housing and Urban Affairs. *Truth in Lending Act Amendments, Report to Accompany S. 2101 Together with Additional Views.* S. Rept. 93-278, 93d Cong., 1st sess., 28 June 1973. 47p. Serial 13017-4. Title III of the bill reported provides for equal credit opportunity for women. The report describes discriminatory acts by lenders on the basis of sex and marital status.

631. U.S. Congress. Senate. Committee on the Judiciary. Subcommittee on the Constitutional amendments. *Constitutional Amendments, Report Pursuant to S.Res. 256, Section 5, Ninety-Second Congress, Second Session.* S. Rept. 93-450, 93d Cong., 1st sess., 1973. 28p. Serial 13019-1. Summary of action on proposed constitutional amendments includes a report on the legislative history of the Equal Rights Amendment.

632. U.S. Citizens' Advisory Council on the Status of Women. *Interpretation of the Equal Rights Amendment in Accordance with Legislative History.* Washington, DC: The Council, 1974. 15p. Y3.In8/21:2Eq2/4. Excerpts from the legislative history of the ERA answer questions on the effect of the amendment on private business and personal relationships, the right to support, states rights, and military service.

633. U.S. Commission on Civil Rights. *Mortgage Money: Who Gets It?* Clearinghouse Publication no. 48. Washington, DC: GPO, 1974. 36p. CR1.10:48. Study of the availability of mortgages to minorities and women in Hartford, Connecticut found subtle discrimination against minorities and blatant discrimination against women.

634. U.S. Congress. House. Committee on Banking and Currency. Subcommittee on Consumer Affairs. *Credit Discrimination, Part 1, Hearings on H.R. 14856, H.R. 14908.* 93d Cong., 2d sess., 20,21 June 1974. 491p. Y4.B22/1:C86/14/pt.1. Hearing considers two bills amending the Truth in Lending Act to prohibit discrimination on the basis of gender or marital status in the extension of credit. Witnesses discuss the coverage and enforcement of the various proposals and review the problems of women and minorities

in obtaining credit. The policies and practices of lenders are reviewed for discriminatory aspects. A chart summarizes provisions of state credit laws.

635. U.S. Congress. House. Committee on Banking and Currency. Subcommittee on Consumer Affairs. *Credit Discrimination, Part 2, Hearings, Appendix.* 93d Cong., 2d sess., 1974. 493-724pp. Y4.B22/1:C86/14/pt.2. Appendix to hearings on proposed legislation to prohibit sex discrimination in credit transactions includes a report of the National Commissioner of Consumer Finance, "Special Problems of Availability," and a series of Congressional Research Service reports. Topics covered in CRS reports are legal remedies available to women victims of discrimination, the impact of dower and courtesy laws on sex discrimination in credit transactions, and a 50-state study of the effect of interest rate ceiling laws on the ability of women to obtain credit.

636. U.S. Congress. House. Committee on Banking and Currency. Subcommittee on Consumer Affairs. *Credit Discrimination, Part 3, Hearings, Appendix.* 93d Cong., 2d sess., 1974. 725-1301pp. Y4.B22/1:C86/14/pt.3. Final part of the appendix to hearings on the Equal Credit Opportunity Act includes a detailed CRS report, "Women and Credit: a 50-State Study of Laws in the Area of Married Women's Property Rights, Support Laws, Divorce, Exemption, Homestead, Dower and Courtesy for Purposes of Identifying Possible Statutory Origins of Discrimination in the Granting of Credit When Such Treatment Is Based Primarily on Sex or Marital Status." The report reprints the relevant statutes without analysis.

637. U.S. Congress. House. Committee on the Judiciary. *Amending the Act to Incorporate Little League Baseball to Provide That the League Shall be Open to Girls as Well as Boys, Report to Accompany H.R. 8864.* H. Rept. 1409, 93d Cong., 2d sess., 1974. 3p. Serial 13061-9. The history of Little League Baseball and the controversy over the exclusion of girls is briefly reviewed in this favorable report on amending the Little League Baseball charter to permit the participation of girls.

638. U.S. Congress. House. Committee on the Judiciary. *Amending the Act to Incorporate the Naval Sea Cadet Corps to Eliminate Discrimination Based on Sex in the Youth Programs, Report to Accompany H.R. 13054.* H. Rept. 1410, 93d Cong., 2d sess., 1974. 2p. Serial 13061-9. Favorable report on amending the charter of the Naval Sea Cadet Corps to permit the participation of girls.

639. U.S. Congress. Senate. Committee on Interior and Insular Affairs. *Sewall-Belmont House National Historic Site, Report to Accompany S. 3188.* S. Rept. 93-938, 93d Cong., 2d sess., 1974. 5p. Serial 13057-4. Favorable report on making the Sewall-Belmont House, headquarters of the National Woman's Party, a national historic site commemorating the women's rights movement.

640. U.S. Congress. Senate. Committee on Interior and Insular Affairs. Subcommittee on Parks and Recreation. *Sewall-Belmont House National Historic Site, Hearing on S. 3188.* 93d Cong., 2d sess., 31 May 1974. 89p. Y4.In8/13:Se8. Testimony supporting designation of the Sewall-Belmont House, headquarters of the National Woman's Party, as a National Historic Site reviews the history of the women's right's movement in the U.S., emphasizing the role of the National Woman's Party. Also included in the hearing testimony is a description of the formation of the Inter-American Commission of Women, OAS and the NWP's role in its creation.

641. U.S. Congress. Senate. Committee on the Judiciary. *Amending the Act to Incorporate Little League Baseball to Provide That the League Shall be Open to Girls as Well as Boys, Report to Accompany H.R. 8864.* S. Rept. 93-1352, 93d Cong., 2d sess., 1974. 3p. Serial 13057-12. See 637 for abstract.

642. U.S. Congress. Senate. Committee on the Judiciary. *Naval Sea Cadet Corps, Report to Accompany S. 3204.* S. Rept. 93-1191, 93d Cong., 2d sess., 1974. 3p. Serial 13057-9. See 638 for abstract.

643. U.S. Dept. of Health, Education, and Welfare. *The Rights and Responsibilities of Women: Recommendations of the Secretary's Advisory Committee on the Rights and Responsibilities of Women, 1973, 1974.* Washington, DC: GPO, 1974? 103p. HE1.2:W84/2. Report focuses on HEW related topics of women's access to health care, Title IX, Social Security, and career advancement of departmental clerical and secretarial employees.

644. U.S. Secretary of State's Advisory Committee on Private International Law. *Report on United States Response to Questionnaire on the Conflict of Laws in Matrimonial Property Matters: Hague Conference on International Law.* Washington, DC: The Committee, 1974. 23p. S1.130:M42. Technical report summarizes the application of legal principles of property rights under the marriage, divorce, and estate laws in the United States. The likely interpretation by the U.S. courts of the law in specific situations, particularly relating to marital property agreements and capacity of spouse to effect martial property, is described.

645. U.S. Commission on Civil Rights. Kansas Advisory Committee. *The Availability of Credit to Kansas Women.* Washington, DC: The Commission, 1975. 79p. CR1.2:C86/2. An investigation into the problems experienced by Kansas women in obtaining credit found little difficulty for never married women, but major barriers for divorced or widowed women. Specific cases illustrate the problems caused by credit histories in the husband's name only and credit bureau practices.

646. U.S. Commission on Civil Rights. Utah Advisory Committee. *Credit Availability to Women in Utah.* Washington, DC: The Commission, 1975. 116p. CR1.2:C86. Although lenders in Utah espouse a policy of equal credit opportunity, their practices, as revealed in testimony, discriminate against women who apply for credit.

647. U.S. Congress. House. Committee on International Relations. *Interparlementary Union Conference, Colombo, Sri Lanka: Report of the United States Delegation to the Spring Meeting of the Interparlementary Union, Held at Colombo, Sri Lanka, March 31 - April 5, 1975 Pursuant to Law (22 U.S.C. 276, as Amended).* 94th Cong., 1st sess., 1975. Committee print. 37p. Y4.In8/16:In8/975-2. Report on the U.S. delegation to the Spring meeting of the Interparlementary Union primarily covers military issues and apartheid but includes details of resolutions relating to women's rights and endorsing International Women's Year.

648. U.S. Congress. House. Committee on Interstate and Foreign Commerce. Subcommittee on Communications. *Long-Range Financing for Public Broadcasting, Hearings on H.R. 4563.* 94th Cong., 1st sess., 8-22 Apr. 1975. 551p. Y4.In8/4:94-34. Hearing on financing for the Corporation for Public Broadcasting includes criticism of the responsiveness of public broadcasting to the interests of women and minorities. Affirmative action and employment of women and minorities in public broadcasting is also examined.

649. U.S. Dept. of Transportation. Office of Administrative Operations. Library Services Division. *Women's Rights: Selected References.* Bibliographic List no. 9. Washington, DC: The Division, 1975. 64p. TD1.15:9. List of 386 books, documents, and journal articles on women's rights from the DOT Library.

650. U.S. Commission on Civil Rights. *A Guide to Federal Laws and Regulations Prohibiting Sex Discrimination.* Clearinghouse Publication no. 46. Washington, DC: GPO, 1976.

189p. CR1.10:46/976. Explains federal laws and regulations prohibiting sex discrimination in employment, credit, and education. In addition to the coverage of each law or regulation, the complaint/enforcement process is described. A final chapter provides an overview of informational or fact finding agencies such as the Women's Bureau and the Commission on Civil Rights.

651. U.S. Congress. Senate. Committee on the Judiciary. *Constitutional Amendments, Report Pursuant to S.Res. 72, Section 5.* S. Rept. 94-1373, 94th Cong., 2d sess., 1976. 19p. Serial 13132. Report on the status of proposed constitutional amendments includes a legislative history of the ERA and an update on the status of state ratification. The legislative history of a proposed amendment defining life as beginning at conception and protecting such life from abortions is also provided.

652. U.S. Dept. of Housing and Urban Development. Office of Policy Development and Research. *Women in the Mortgage Market: Statistical Methods and Tables for Use in Appraising the Stability of Women's Income.* by Kenton, Inc. Washington, DC: GPO, 1976. 110p. HH1.2:W84/4. Study of the stability of women's income is used to develop statistical methods to project women's expected income during the early years of a mortgage. Looks at the probability of a decline in family income for married women and projected growth in family income based on married women's contribution. Factors such as race and marital status are examined.

653. U.S. Dept. of Housing and Urban Development. Office of the Assistant Secretary for Fair Housing and Equal Opportunity. *Women and Housing: A Report on Sex Discrimination in Five American Cities.* by National Council of Negro Women, Inc. Washington, DC: GPO, 1976. 196p. HH1.2:W84/3. Report of a study of women's experience in seeking housing in cities examined sex-based discrimination in apartment rentals and home ownership. Legal remedies and recommended actions are listed.

654. U.S. Federal Trade Commission. *Equal Credit Opportunity Act.* Washington, DC: The Commission, 1976? 1p. leaflet. FT1.2:C86/4.

655. U.S. National Commission on the Observance of International Women's Year. Homemakers Committee. *The Legal Status of Homemakers in Colorado.* by Joyce S. Steinhardt. Washington, DC: GPO, 1976. 46p. Y3.W84:9/6. See 673 for abstract.

656. U.S. National Commission on the Observance of International Women's Year. Homemakers Committee. *The Legal Status of Homemakers in Iowa.* by Roxanne Barton Conlin. Washington, DC: GPO, 1976. 56p. Y3.W84:9/16. See 673 for abstract.

657. U.S. National Commission on the Observance of International Women's Year. Homemakers Committee. *The Legal Status of Homemakers in Louisiana.* by Sylvia Roberts. Washington, DC: GPO, 1976. 39p. Y3.W84:9/19. See 673 for abstract.

658. U.S. National Commission on the Observance of International Women's Year. Homemakers Committee. *The Legal Status of Homemakers in Missouri.* by Joan M. Krauskopf. Washington, DC: GPO, 1976. 54p. Y3.W84:9/26. See 673 for abstract.

659. U.S. National Commission on the Observance of International Women's Year. Homemakers Committee. *The Legal Status of Homemakers in Montana.* by Rosemary Blachard Zion. Washington, DC: GPO, 1976. 58p. Y3.W84:9/27. See 673 for abstract.

660. U.S. National Commission on the Observance of International Women's Year. Homemakers Committee. *The Legal Status of Homemakers in Nevada.* by Phyllis Halsey Atkins. Washington, DC: GPO, 1976. 49p. Y3.W84:9/29. See 673 for abstract.

661. U.S. Women's Bureau. *State Equal Rights Amendments.* Washington, DC: GPO, 1976. revised. 6p. L36.102:Eq2. Reviews equal rights provisions in the constitutions of the 16 states having such a provision.

662. U.S. Commission on Civil Rights. *The Federal Civil Rights Enforcement Effort, 1974.* Washington, DC: GPO, 1974-1977. 7 vol. CR1.2:En2/2/974/v.1-7. Study describes the structure, mechanisms and procedures utilized by federal departments and agencies in their effort to end discrimination based on race and sex. In most cases the report documents inaction on the part of the departments and agencies reviewed. Complaints received and agency action is documented. Volume 1, "To Regulate in the Public Interest" covers radio, television and common carriers, telecommunications and cable television, under the FCC, the Interstate Commerce Commission, the Civil Aeronautics Board, the Federal Power Commission, and the Securities and Exchange Commission. Volume II, "To Provide...For Fair Housing" covers HUD, Office of the Comptroller of Currency, Federal Deposit Insurance Corporation, Federal Home Loan Bank Board, Federal Reserve System, the Veterans Administration, and the General Services Administration. Volume III, "To Ensure Equal Educational Opportunity" covers HEW, the IRS, and the Veterans Administration and volume IV, "To Provide Fiscal Assistance" covers the Office of Revenue Sharing. The Civil Service Commission, Dept. of Labor, Equal Employment Opportunity Commission, and the Equal Employment Opportunity Coordinating Council are covered in Volume V, "To Eliminate Employment Discrimination." Volume VI "To Extend Federal Financial Assistance" examines nine agencies administering major grant programs. Volume VII "To Preserve, Protect, and Defend the Constitution" covers the White House, the Office of Management and Budget, the Federal Regional Councils and the Federal Executive Boards.

663. U.S. Commission on Civil Rights. *Sex Bias in the U.S. Code.* Washington, DC: GPO, 1977. 230p. CR1.2:Se9. Part one addresses sex bias in the armed forces and Social Security laws, while the second part provides a title-by-title review of sex bias in the *U.S. Code* both in language and interpretation.

664. U.S. Commission on Civil Rights. *The Unfinished Business Twenty Years Later...A Report Submitted to the U.S. Commission on Civil Rights by Its Fifty-One State Advisory Committees.* Washington, DC: GPO, 1977. 221p. CR1.2:Un2. Brief state reports summarize civil rights developments particularly in areas of education, housing, and employment. Many of the reports have a separate section on women.

665. U.S. Congress. Senate. Committee on the Judiciary. *Constitutional Amendments Annual Report 1976.* S. Rept. 95-126, 95th Cong., 1st sess., 1977. 19p. Serial 13170. The legislative history and progress in ratification of the Equal Rights Amendment is a major focus of this annual report on the status of proposed constitutional amendments. Also discussed is committee action on proposed constitutional amendments relating to abortion and some background on the abortion issue since *Roe v. Wade* (410 US 113) and *Doe v. Bolton* (410 US 1970).

666. U.S. Dept. of Housing and Urban Development. *Housing and Community Development: Making It Work for Women: Report of a Conference Held April 5-6, 1976 in Washington, D.C.* Washington, DC: The Department, 1977. 36p. HH1.2:H81/56. Conference report reviews the concerns over sex discrimination in Housing and Urban Development programs as revealed in past Commission on Civil Rights and HUD sponsored investigations. Recommendations for HUD policies and actions relating to marketing, finance, research and evaluation, education and information programs, enforcement, and employment are presented. Session summaries and texts of selected speeches highlight the subtle and blatant discrimination against women in housing.

667.   U.S. National Commission on the Observance of International Women's Year. *Credit: A Workshop Guide*. Washington, DC: GPO, 1977. 28p. Y3.W84:10/3.   Guide   to conducting a workshop on women and credit includes fact sheets on the credit system as it relates to women.

668.   U.S. National Commission on the Observance of International Women's Year. *Equal Rights Amendment: A Workshop Guide*. Washington, DC: GPO, 1977. 19p. Y3.W84:10/6. Guidelines for setting up a workshop on the ERA provides a list of possible speakers and a brief guide to available A/V resources.

669.   U.S. National Commission on the Observance of International Women's Year. *Legal Status of Homemakers: A Workshop Guide*. Washington, DC: GPO, 1977. 21p. Y3.W84:10/10. Outline for a workshop on the legal status of homemakers includes IWY commission recommendations on laws affecting homemakers and a list of A/V materials and resource people for workshops.

670.   U.S. National Commission on the Observance of International Women's Year. *Sexual Preference*. Washington, DC: GPO, 1977. 61p. Y3.W84:10/14. Discussion of lesbian rights as a women's issue accompanies guidelines for conducting a workshop on sexual preference issues. Includes a list or organizations, speakers and audiovisual materials.

671.   U.S. National Commission on the Observance of International Women's Year. *Strategies for Change*. Washington, DC: GPO, 1977. 19p. Y3.W84:10/11.   Guidelines and resources for conducting a workshop to develop strategies for addressing inequities against women.

672.   U.S. National Commission on the Observance of International Women's Year. *"...To Form a More Perfect Union..."*, *Justice for American Women*. Washington, DC: GPO, 1977. 391p. Y3.W84:1/976. Detailed report on progress in the status of American women highlights the inequities which still exist in the treatment of homemakers under inheritance taxes, women's position in the mass media and the arts, and women in politics and power positions. Sex discrimination in education, athletics, and the workplace are described. The added burdens of sex discrimination with age and race discrimination are examined. Issues of reproductive freedom, child care, and welfare are also covered. Finally the role of the commission and its recommendations are reviewed.

673.   U.S. National Commission on the Observance of International Women's Year. Homemakers Committee. *The Legal Status of Homemakers in Alabama*. by Judith Sullivan Crittenden. Washington, DC: GPO, 1977. 49p. Y3.W84:9/1. Review and analysis of state laws relating to rights within marriage, divorce, and widowhood, particularly as they affect homemakers. Examines laws relating to property rights, credit and wife abuse.

674.   U.S. National Commission on the Observance of International Women's Year. Homemakers Committee. *The Legal Status of Homemakers in Alaska*. by Sandra K. Saville. Washington, DC: GPO, 1977. 50p. Y3.W84:9/2. See 673 for abstract.

675.   U.S. National Commission on the Observance of International Women's Year. Homemakers Committee. *The Legal Status of Homemakers in Arizona*. by Heather Sigworth. Washington, DC: GPO, 1977. 45p. Y3.W84:9/3. See 673 for abstract.

676.   U.S. National Commission on the Observance of International Women's Year. Homemakers Committee. *The Legal Status of Homemakers in Arkansas*. by Pamela D. Walker. Washington, DC: GPO, 1977. 52p. Y3.W84:9/4. See 673 for abstract.

677. U.S. National Commission on the Observance of International Women's Year. Homemakers Committee. *The Legal Status of Homemakers in California.* by Blanche C. Bersch. Washington, DC: GPO, 1977. 45p. Y3.W84:9/5. See 673 for abstract.

678. U.S. National Commission on the Observance of International Women's Year. Homemakers Committee. *The Legal Status of Homemakers in Connecticut.* by Ann C. Hill. Washington, DC: GPO, 1977. 68p. Y3.W84:9/7. See 673 for abstract.

679. U.S. National Commission on the Observance of International Women's Year. Homemakers Committee. *The Legal Status of Homemakers in Delaware.* by Susan C. Del Pesco and Marsha Kramarck. Washington, DC: GPO, 1977. 53p. Y3.W84:9/8. See 673 for abstract.

680. U.S. National Commission on the Observance of International Women's Year. Homemakers Committee. *The Legal Status of Homemakers in the District of Columbia.* Washington, DC: GPO, 1977. 48p. Y3.W84:9/9. See 673 for abstract.

681. U.S. National Commission on the Observance of International Women's Year. Homemakers Committee. *The Legal Status of Homemakers in Florida.* by James P. O'Flarity. Washington, DC: GPO, 1977. 51p. Y3.W84:9/10. See 673 for abstract.

682. U.S. National Commission on the Observance of International Women's Year. Homemakers Committee. *The Legal Status of Homemakers in Georgia.* by Lucy S. McGough. Washington, DC: GPO, 1977. 55p. Y3.W84:9/11. See 673 for abstract.

683. U.S. National Commission on the Observance of International Women's Year. Homemakers Committee. *The Legal Status of Homemakers in Hawaii.* by Dorothy N.W. Lamott. Washington, DC: GPO, 1977. 49p. Y3.W84:9/12. See 673 for abstract.

684. U.S. National Commission on the Observance of International Women's Year. Homemakers Committee. *The Legal Status of Homemakers in Idaho.* by Linda J. Cook. Washington, DC: GPO, 1977. 47p. Y3.W84:9/13. See 673 for abstract.

685. U.S. National Commission on the Observance of International Women's Year. Homemakers Committee. *The Legal Status of Homemakers in Illinois.* by Sheribel Rothenberg and Marien Barnes. Washington, DC: GPO, 1977. 47p. Y3.W84:9/14. See 673 for abstract.

686. U.S. National Commission on the Observance of International Women's Year. Homemakers Committee. *The Legal Status of Homemakers in Indiana.* by Linda L. Chezem. Washington, DC: GPO, 1977. 44p. Y3.W84:9/15. See 673 for abstract.

687. U.S. National Commission on the Observance of International Women's Year. Homemakers Committee. *The Legal Status of Homemakers in Kansas.* by Marcia L. Harley and Jane B. Werholtz. Washington, DC: GPO, 1977. 45p. Y3.W84:9/17 See 673 for abstract.

688. U.S. National Commission on the Observance of International Women's Year. Homemakers Committee. *The Legal Status of Homemakers in Kentucky.* by Ellen B. Ewing and Patricia W. Owen. Washington, DC: GPO, 1977. 44p. Y3.W84:9/18. See 673 for abstract.

689. U.S. National Commission on the Observance of International Women's Year. Homemakers Committee. *The Legal Status of Homemakers in Maine.* by Caroline Glassman. Washington, DC: GPO, 1977. 50p. Y3.W84:9/20. See 673 for abstract.

690.   U.S. National Commission on the Observance of International Women's Year. Homemakers Committee. *The Legal Status of Homemakers in Maryland.* by Alice Strohminger, Ann Hoffman and Kathleen O'Farrell Friedman. Washington, DC: GPO, 1977. 55p. Y3.W84:9/21. See 673 for abstract.

691.   U.S. National Commission on the Observance of International Women's Year. Homemakers Committee. *The Legal Status of Homemakers in Massachusetts.* by Roxanne Barton Conlin. Washington, DC: GPO, 1977. 51p. Y3.W84:9/22. See 673 for abstract.

692.   U.S. National Commission on the Observance of International Women's Year. Homemakers Committee. *The Legal Status of Homemakers in Michigan.* by Roxanne Barton Conlin. Washington, DC: GPO, 1977. 49p. Y3.W84:9/23. See Y3.W84:9/23. See 673 for abstract.

693.   U.S. National Commission on the Observance of International Women's Year. Homemakers Committee. *The Legal Status of Homemakers in Minnesota.* by Ellen Dresselhuis. Washington, DC: GPO, 1977. 46p. Y3.W84:9/24. See 673 for abstract.

694.   U.S. National Commission on the Observance of International Women's Year. Homemakers Committee. *The Legal Status of Homemakers in Mississippi.* by Constance Iona Slaughter. Washington, DC: GPO, 1977. 41p. Y3.W84:9/25. See 673 for abstract.

695.   U.S. National Commission on the Observance of International Women's Year. Homemakers Committee. *The Legal Status of Homemakers in Nebraska.* by Sarah Jane Cunningham. Washington, DC: GPO, 1977. 48p. Y3.W84:9/28. See 673 for abstract.

696.   U.S. National Commission on the Observance of International Women's Year. Homemakers Committee. *The Legal Status of Homemakers in New Hampshire.* by Laura Jane Kahn. Washington, DC: GPO, 1977. 44p. Y3.W84:9/30. See 673 for abstract.

697.   U.S. National Commission on the Observance of International Women's Year. Homemakers Committee. *The Legal Status of Homemakers in New Jersey.* by Elizabeth F. Defeis and Mary V. Harear. Washington, DC: GPO, 1977. 42p. Y3.W84:9/31. See 673 for abstract.

698.   U.S. National Commission on the Observance of International Women's Year. Homemakers Committee. *The Legal Status of Homemakers in New Mexico.* by Anne K. Bingaman. Washington, DC: GPO, 1977. 50p. Y3.W84:9/32. See 673 for abstract.

699.   U.S. National Commission on the Observance of International Women's Year. Homemakers Committee. *The Legal Status of Homemakers in New York.* by Janice Goodman. Washington, DC: GPO, 1977. 56p. Y3.W84:9/33. See 673 for abstract.

700.   U.S. National Commission on the Observance of International Women's Year. Homemakers Committee. *The Legal Status of Homemakers in North Carolina.* by Elisabeth S. Petersen and Craig R. Mariger. Washington, DC: GPO, 1977. 65p. Y3.W84:9/34. See 673 for abstract.

701.   U.S. National Commission on the Observance of International Women's Year. Homemakers Committee. *The Legal Status of Homemakers in North Dakota.* by Nancy G. Maxwell. Washington, DC: GPO, 1977. 33p. Y3.W84:9/35. See 673 for abstract.

702.   U.S. National Commission on the Observance of International Women's Year. Homemakers Committee. *The Legal Status of Homemakers in Ohio.* by Elizabeth Boyer. Washington, DC: GPO, 1977. 44p. Y3.W84:9/36. See 673 for abstract.

703. U.S. National Commission on the Observance of International Women's Year. Homemakers Committee. *The Legal Status of Homemakers in Oklahoma.* by Terry A. Pendell. Washington, DC: GPO, 1977. 48p. Y3.W84:9/37. See 673 for abstract.

704. U.S. National Commission on the Observance of International Women's Year. Homemakers Committee. *The Legal Status of Homemakers in Oregon.* by Susan Elizabeth Reese. Washington, DC: GPO, 1977. 54p. Y3.W84:9/38. See 673 for abstract.

705. U.S. National Commission on the Observance of International Women's Year. Homemakers Committee. *The Legal Status of Homemakers in Pennsylvania.* by Linda Backiel and Roxanne Barton Conlin. Washington, DC: GPO, 1977. 52p. Y3.W84:9/39. See 673 for abstract.

706. U.S. National Commission on the Observance of International Women's Year. Homemakers Committee. *The Legal Status of Homemakers in Rhode Island.* by Sheila Cabral Sousa and Mildred White Tracey. Washington, DC: GPO, 1977. 47p. Y3.W84:9/40. See 673 for abstract.

707. U.S. National Commission on the Observance of International Women's Year. Homemakers Committee. *The Legal Status of Homemakers in South Carolina.* by Victoria L. Eslinger and Lucy M. Knowles. Washington, DC: GPO, 1977. 51p. Y3.W84:9/41. See 673 for abstract.

708. U.S. National Commission on the Observance of International Women's Year. Homemakers Committee. *The Legal Status of Homemakers in South Dakota.* by Mary Ellen McEldowney. Washington, DC: GPO, 1977. 47p. Y3.W84:9/42. See 673 for abstract.

709. U.S. National Commission on the Observance of International Women's Year. Homemakers Committee. *The Legal Status of Homemakers in Tennessee.* by Bonnie Cowan. Washington, DC: GPO, 1977. 48p. Y3.W84:9/43. See 673 for abstract.

710. U.S. National Commission on the Observance of International Women's Year. Homemakers Committee. *The Legal Status of Homemakers in Texas.* by Sarah Ragle Weddington. Washington, DC: GPO, 1977. 62p. Y3.W84:9/44. See 673 for abstract.

711. U.S. National Commission on the Observance of International Women's Year. Homemakers Committee. *The Legal Status of Homemakers in Utah.* by Kathryn Collard. Washington, DC: GPO, 1977. 46p. Y3.W84:9/45. See 673 for abstract.

712. U.S. National Commission on the Observance of International Women's Year. Homemakers Committee. *The Legal Status of Homemakers in Vermont.* by Martha Holden. Washington, DC: GPO, 1977. 47p. Y3.W84:9/46. See 673 for abstract.

713. U.S. National Commission on the Observance of International Women's Year. Homemakers Committee. *The Legal Status of Homemakers in Virginia.* by Richard E. Crouch. Washington, DC: GPO, 1977. 64p. Y3.W84:9/47. See 673 for abstract.

714. U.S. National Commission on the Observance of International Women's Year. Homemakers Committee. *The Legal Status of Homemakers in Washington.* by Marilyn D. Sloan. Washington, DC: GPO, 1977. 48p. Y3.W84:9/48. See 673 for abstract.

715. U.S. National Commission on the Observance of International Women's Year. Homemakers Committee. *The Legal Status of Homemakers in West Virginia.* by Marjorie Martorella. Washington, DC: GPO, 1977. 45p. Y3.W84:9/49. See 673 for abstract.

716.   U.S. National Commission on the Observance of International Women's Year. Homemakers Committee. *The Legal Status of Homemakers in Wisconsin.* by Marygold Shire Melli. Washington, DC: GPO, 1977. 52p. Y3.W84:9/50. See 673 for abstract.

717.   U.S. National Commission on the Observance of International Women's Year. Homemakers Committee. *The Legal Status of Homemakers in Wyoming.* by Laurie Brooke Seidenberg. Washington, DC: GPO, 1977. 43p. Y3.W84:9/51. See 673 for abstract.

718.   U.S. Commission on Civil Rights. *Discrimination against Minorities and Women in Pensions and Health, Life, and Disability Insurance.* Washington, DC: GPO, 1978. 2 vol. CR1.2:M66/v.1-2. Consultation conducted by the commission explores sex discrimination in pensions and insurance through expert testimony. Although the primary focus is sex equity, some discussion of age and racial discrimination is included. Statistics are provided comparing female to male insurance claim costs by age, occupation, and experience; women hired and employed by insurance companies by asset rank and region, 1976; and expected births to female workers by age.

719.   U.S. Commission on Civil Rights. *Statement on the Equal Rights Amendment.* Clearinghouse Publication no. 56. Washington, DC: GPO, 1978. 32p. CR1.10:56. Detailed argument in support of the Equal Rights Amendment highlights the limitations of existing law and the prevalence of discriminatory practices.

720.   U.S. Commission on Civil Rights. Nevada Advisory Committee. *Public Forum on Women's Rights and Responsibilities.* Washington, DC: The Commission, 1978. 20p. CR1.2:W84/6. Public forum key note address and panel discussion looks at the history of women's rights and current concepts from a variety of view points.

721.   U.S. Congress. House. Committee on the Judiciary. *Proposed Equal Rights Amendment Extension, Report Together with Concurring, Supplemental, Additional, Individual, Separate, Dissenting, and Minority Views to Accompany H.J.Res. 638.* H. Rept. 95-1405, 95th Cong., 2d sess., 1978. 64p. Serial 13201-10. Favorable report on extending the period for ratification of the ERA includes numerous views on the authority of Congress to extend the ratification period and on the ability of a state to rescind its ratification.

722.   U.S. Congress. House. Committee on the Judiciary. Subcommittee on Civil and Constitutional Rights. *Equal Rights Amendment Extension, Hearings on H.J.Res. 638.* 95th Cong., 1st and 2d sess., 1 Nov. 1977 - 19 May 1978. 378p. Y4.J89/1:95-41. Testimony on extending the period for ratification of the ERA discusses the constitutionality of the extension, the application of state equal rights amendments in specific cases, and the continuing need for a national ERA. Phyllis Schlafly states the case against the ERA.

723.   U.S. Congress. Senate. Committee on the Judiciary. Subcommittee on the Constitution. *Equal Rights Amendment Extension, Hearings on S.J.Res. 134.* 95th Cong., 2d sess., 2-4 Aug. 1978. 764p. Y4.J89/2:Eq2/7. Hearings on extending the time period for ratification of the ERA focus on the constitutionality of the extension. Public testimony for and against the ERA was marked by aggressive questioning of witnesses opposing the extension.

724.   U.S. Congress. Senate. Committee on the Judiciary. Subcommittee on the Constitution. *Subcommittee on the Constitution Annual Report 1977, Report Pursuant to S.Res. 170.* S. Rept. 95-724, 95th Cong., 2d sess., 1978. 71p. Serial 13199. Ratification of the Equal Rights Amendment is one of the topics in this review of 95th Congress action on constitutional amendments. The history of the ERA and the current status of ratification

is reviewed. Also reported on is a proposed amendment protecting the rights of the unborn by restricting abortion.

725. U.S. Dept. of Housing and Urban Development. Office of Assistant Secretary for Fair Housing and Equal Opportunity. *Fair Housing, an American Right/Right for Americans: Summary Report of Conference Proceedings.* Washington, DC: GPO, 1978. 60p. HH1.2:F15/9. Summary of a national conference on volunteer programs in fair housing describes the effectiveness of programs for women and minorities.

726. U.S. Federal Trade Commission. *Women and Credit Histories.* Washington, DC: The Commission, 1978. 7p. FT1.2:W84. Presents a checklist for women on establishing a credit history.

727. U.S. National Commission on the Observance of International Women's Year. Homemakers Committee. *The Legal Status of Homemakers in the Virgin Islands.* by Edith Lucille Bornn. Washington, DC: GPO, 1978. 52p. Y3.W84:9/52. See 673 for abstract.

728. U.S. Congress. House. Committee on the Judiciary. Subcommittee on Civil and Constitutional Rights. *Authorization Request of the Civil Rights Division of the Department of Justice, Hearings, Part 1.* 96th Cong., 1st sess., 14 Mar. 1979. 53p. Y4.J89/1:96/85/pt.1. Authorization hearing on the Civil Rights Division of the Department of Justice briefly describes its activities and planned projects for Fiscal Year 1980. One point of discussion is a planned decrease in funding for the Sex Discrimination Task Force. Includes a financial summary of fiscal year 1979 program expenditures and proposed 1980 expenditures.

729. U.S. Congress. Senate. Committee on the Judiciary. *U.S. Commission on Civil Rights Fiscal Year 1980 Authorization, Report Together with Additional Views to Accompany S. 72.* S. Rept. 96-167, 96th Cong., 1st sess., 1979. 9p. Serial 13240. A brief review of past Civil Rights Commission activities and an overview of proposed areas of investigation support a favorable report on the fiscal year 1980 commission authorization. The additional views of Senator Orrin Hatch attack the commission's support of ERA and its studies of television and textbook sex stereotyping.

730. U.S. Dept. of Housing and Urban Development. *Announcing HUD's Women and Mortgage Credit Project.* Washington, DC: The Department, 1979? [3]p. leaflet. HH1.2:W84/6.

731. U.S. Dept. of Justice. Women's Rights Task Force. *Women's Rights in the United States of America.* Clearinghouse Publication no. 57. Washington, DC: GPO, 1979. 15p. CR1.10:57. Overview of all aspects of women's rights in America includes a summary of major legislation affecting women's issues.

732. U.S. Congress. House. Committee on Interstate and Foreign Commerce. Subcommittee on Consumer Protection and Finance. *Nondiscrimination in Insurance, Hearings on H.R. 100.* 96th Cong., 2d sess., 21,28 August 1980. 425p. Y4.In8/4:96-232. Testimony on legislation to prohibit discrimination in insurance practices based on race, sex, or national origin focuses on the issue of sex-based rates, particularly as they relate to life insurance, disability insurance, and annuities. The principle point of debate is whether sex-based rates are unfairly discriminatory or an essential pricing tool based on sound risk assessment theory. Includes supporting statistics.

733. U.S. Congress. House. Committee on the Judiciary. *Civil Rights Commission Authorization Act of 1980, Report to Accompany H.R. 6888.* H. Rept. 96-969, 96th

Cong., 2d sess., 1980. 7p. Serial 13366. Basic background on the history of the commission's mandate and past activities are included in this report authorizing appropriations for fiscal year 1981.

734. U.S. Congress. House. Committee on the Judiciary. Subcommittee on Civil and Constitutional Rights. *Authorization Request of the Civil Rights Division of the Department of Justice, Hearings, Part 2.* 96th Cong., 2d sess., 7,13 Mar. 1980. 131p. Y4.J98/1:96/85/pt.2. Hearing on the fiscal year 1981 authorization request for the Civil Rights Division of the Department of Justice highlights civil rights enforcement in school desegregation and housing. Specific deficiencies in enforcement of anti-sex discrimination laws relating to housing, credit, and education are singled out. Appendix includes a list of Civil Rights Division sex discrimination cases filed since 1970 noting the status of each case and final decisions where applicable.

735. U.S. Congress. House. Committee on the Judiciary. Subcommittee on Civil and Constitutional Rights. *Authorization Request of the U.S. Commission on Civil Rights, Hearing.* 96th Cong., 2d sess., 28 Mar. 1980. 16p. Y4.J89/1:96/37. Otherwise routine authorization hearing for the U.S. Commission on Civil rights includes an interesting exchange regarding the appropriateness of lobbying efforts by the Virginia State Advisory Committee on behalf of the ERA.

736. U.S. Congress. Senate. *Message from the President of the United States Transmitting the Convention on the Elimination of All Forms of Discrimination against Women, Adopted by the United Nations General Assembly on December 18, 1979, and Signed on Behalf of the United States of America on July 17, 1980.* Sen. Ex. Doc. R., 96th Cong., 2d sess., 1980. 19p. Serial 13319. Report of the State Department on ratification of the UN Convention on the Elimination of All Forms of Discrimination Against Women reviews U.S. law for conformity and possible conflicts with the convention's provisions.

737. U.S. Congress. Senate. Committee on Energy and Natural Resources. Subcommittee on Parks, Recreation, and Renewable Resources. *The National Hostel System Act of 1980; and the Women's Rights National Historic Park in New York, Hearing on S. 2263, S. 3092, H.R. 7105.* 96th Cong., 2d sess., 8 Sept. 1980. 211p. Y4.En2:96-151. The second half of this hearing highlights the lack of preservation of historic buildings in Seneca Falls, New York, the site of the first women's rights convention in the United States. The need to preserve this site and the importance of the Seneca Falls convention to the women's rights movement is discussed.

738. U.S. Congress. Senate. Committee on the Judiciary. *U.S. Commission on Civil Rights Fiscal Year 1981 Authorization, Report Together with Minority Views to Accompany S. 2511, as Amended.* S. Rept. 96-706, 96th Cong., 2d sess., 14 May 1980. 11p. Serial 13323. Report on a bill authorizing funds for the Commission on Civil Rights for fiscal year 1981 summarizes the commissions past year activities and proposed areas of study. The minority view of Senator Orrin Hatch attacks the commission for its supportive position on affirmative action, ERA and sex stereotyping elimination, and its involvement with the abortion controversy.

739. U.S. Congress. Senate. Committee on the Judiciary. Subcommittee on Antitrust, Monopoly and Business Rights. *Nondiscrimination in Insurance Act, S. 2477, Hearing.* 96th Cong., 2d sess., 30 April 1980. 416p. Y4.J89/2:96-80. Hearing considers a bill to prohibit discrimination on the basis of race, color, religion, sex or national origin in the sale or underwriting of any kind of insurance. Testimony focuses on the issue of differentials in life insurance based on sex and whether this constitutes a case of unfair sex discrimination. Also discussed is the treatment of pregnancy under disability plans. The implications of

the *City of Los Angeles v. Manhart* decision, which held against pension contributions for women based on sex differentiated mortality tables, is examined.

740. U.S. Dept. of Housing and Urban Development. Office of Policy Development and Research. *Equal Credit Opportunity: Accessibility to Mortgage Funds by Women and by Minorities.* by Robert Schafer and Helen F. Ladd. Washington, DC: GPO, 1980. 2 vol. HH1.2:C86/4/v.1-2. A study of mortgage application data from California and New York found no evidence of discrimination against women, but did find evidence of discrimination based on minority status.

741. U.S. Commission on Civil Rights. *The Equal Rights Amendment: Guaranteeing Equal Rights for Women under the Constitution.* Clearinghouse Publication no. 68. Washington, DC: GPO, 1981. 29p. CR1.10:68. Problem areas in women's rights which would be addressed by an Equal Rights Amendment to the Constitution include employment and wage discrimination, marital rights, divorce and child support, and pensions. Areas not affected by ERA are reviewed.

742. U.S. Commission on Civil Rights. *U.S. Commission on Civil Rights Report to the President and to Congress.* Washington, DC: The Commission, 1981. 20p. No SuDoc number. The Commission recommendations action for Congress and the President to take in combating discrimination. Many of the recommendations relate to effective enforcement of existing laws. The report also calls for a executive order prohibiting sex discrimination in any federally funded program or activity.

743. U.S. Commission on Civil Rights. Maryland Advisory Committee. *A Civil Rights Agenda for the 1980s.* Washington, DC: GPO, 1981. 48p. CR1.2:C49/6. Report of a conference to identify civil rights issues and to bring civil rights leaders together discusses educational equity, housing, ageism and state government affirmative action.

744. U.S. Congress. House. Committee on Energy and Commerce. Subcommittee on Commerce, Transportation, and Tourism. *Nondiscrimination in Insurance Act of 1981, Hearing on H.R. 100.* 97th Cong., 1st sess., 20 May 1981. 324p. Y4.En2/3:97-22. Hearing focuses on the use of sex and age to determine premiums and benefits in insurance and annuity plans. Witnesses debate whether such practices are discriminatory or simply sound business practices. Specific cases where sex is used to determine rates are highlighted. Statistics on automobile accident rates and motor vehicle violations by sex are included.

745. U.S. Library of Congress. Law Library. *The Law of Marital Property in Czechoslovakia and the Soviet Union.* Washington, DC: The Library, 1981. 49p. LC42.2:M33. Reviews the history and current status of marital property law in Czechoslovakia and the Soviet Union, and provides a short bibliography.

746. U.S. Commission on Civil Rights. *Health Insurance Coverage and Employment Opportunities for Minorities and Women.* Clearinghouse Publication no. 72. Washington, DC: GPO, 1982. 56p. CR1.10:72. Report reviews existing information on the underrepresentation of women and minorities in the insurance industry work force and looks at discrimination in accessibility of health insurance coverage. Provides data by sex, race/ethnicity, and occupation in the insurance industry, and hiring and promotion rates for minorities and women, 1974-80. Also provides data broken down by sex and race/ethnicity on health insurance coverage and employment status, occupation and industry and coverage of family heads by employment status, sex, and race/ethnicity.

747. U.S. Congress. Senate. Committee on Commerce, Science and Transportation. *Fair Insurance Practices Act, Hearing on S. 2204.* 97th Cong., 2d sess., 15 July 1982. 196p.

Y4.C73/7:97-137. Hearing examines the issue of the validity of gender as a determinant of insurance rates. The experience of women under annuity plans and life, health, and auto insurance are reviewed. Supporters of the act view sex-based rates as unfair discrimination while the insurance industry defends the practice as actuarially sound and predicts that unisex rates would be costly to women.

748.   U.S. Commission on Civil Rights. *State of Civil Rights 1957-1983.* Washington, DC: GPO, 1983. 82p. CR1.2:C49/5/957-83. Report reviews the civil rights issues examined by the U.S. Commission on Civil Rights from its inception in 1957 through 1983. Topics of special interest to women include Title IX, EEO, domestic violence and ERA.

749.   U.S. Congress. House. Committee on Energy and Commerce. Subcommittee on Commerce, Transportation and Tourism. *Nondiscrimination in Insurance Act of 1983, Hearings on H.R. 100.* 98th Cong., 1st sess., 22,24 Feb. 1983. 1171p. Y4.En2/3:98-35. Hearings on a bill to prohibit the use of actuarial tables based on race, color, religion, sex or national origin in calculating insurance costs and benefits presents lengthy testimony on how current systems operate and how they may discriminate against women. Pension annuities, disability insurance, and automobile insurance are the primary targets of testimony. The effect of current practices on women, the cost of providing equal retirement annuities, and the increased cost of automobile insurance under the bill, are discussed.

750.   U.S. Congress. House. Committee on the Judiciary. Subcommittee on Civil and Constitutional Rights. *Equal Rights Amendment, Hearings on H.J. Res. 1.* 98th Cong., 1st sess., 13 July - 3 Nov. 1983. 832p. Y4.J89/1:98/115. Wide-ranging testimony on the Equal Rights Amendment reviews the status of women in the United States, with emphasis on the economic effects of sex discrimination. Testimony against the amendment focuses on the conservation faction's desire to limit the scope of the Amendment to allow "reasonable" differences in treatment. The military draft, abortion rights, veterans preference legislation, insurance, retirement benefits, and the feminization of poverty are all discussed in relation to the need for, and effect of, the ERA. Continuing progress in educational equity under Title IX is also a recurring theme. A review of the effect of state equal rights amendments is provided by ERA opponent Phyllis Schlafly.

751.   U.S. Congress. Joint Committee on Taxation. *Description of Bills Relating to Economic Equality in Various Tax, Pension, and Related Federal Laws, Scheduled for a Hearing before the Committee on Ways and Means on October 25-26, 1983.* 98th Cong., 1st sess., 21 Oct. 1983. Committee print. 34p. Y4.T19/4:Ec7/4. Overview of pending bills relating to women's economic equity describes the various proposals and indicates how each would effect existing law. The bills described relate primarily to individual retirement accounts, survivor benefits, income taxes and child care credits, and target jobs programs for displaced homemakers.

752.   U.S. Congress. Senate. Committee on Commerce, Science, and Transportation. *Fair Insurance Practices Act, Hearings on S. 372.* 98th Cong., 1st sess., 12, 25 Apr. 1983. 403p. Y4.C73/7:S.hrg.98-349. Representatives of women's organizations and lobbying groups detail discrimination against women in disability policies and annuity payments, while insurance industry representatives defend their practices as actuarially sound. Testimony points out both the situations where gender-based rates work against women and where they work in women's favor.

753.   U.S. Executive Office of the President. Office of Public Liaison. *President Reagan's 50 State Project, Status of the States: 1982 Year-end Report, a Report.* Washington, DC: GPO, 1983. 140p. Pr40.2:St2. Report describes studies of state statutes for gender bias and legislative action to eliminate discriminatory laws. A few states, such as Ohio,

California, and Georgia, provide detailed lists of state statutes with gender bias, but most reports are short and vague.

754. U.S. Commission on Civil Rights. *A Sheltered Crisis: The State of Fair Housing in the Eighties, Presentations at a Consultation Sponsored by the United States Commission on Civil Rights, Washington, DC, September 26-27, 1983.* Washington, DC: GPO, 1984. 227p. CR1.2:F15/3. Collection of papers on equal access to housing focuses on racial discrimination, but also includes four papers on housing discrimination faced by women with children.

755. U.S. Congress. House. Committee on Interior and Insular Affairs. *Amending Section 16019(d) of Public Laws 96-607 to Permit the Secretary of the Interior to Acquire Title in Fee Simple to McClintock House at 16 East Williams Street, Waterloo, New York, Report to Accompany H.R. 4596.* H. Rept. 98-722, 98th Cong., 2d sess., 1984. 6p. Serial 13590. Favorable report on a bill giving the Secretary of the Interior the authority to obtain title to the McClintock House, site of the drafting of the "Declaration of Sentiments" for the first National Women's Rights Convention. The structures are part of the Women's Rights National Historic Park, which commemorates the Seneca Falls Convention.

756. U.S. Congress. Senate. Committee on Energy and Natural Resources. *Acquisition of McClintock House, Women's Rights National Historic Park, New York, Report to Accompany H.R. 4596.* S. Rept. 98-558, 98th Cong., 2d sess., 1984. 7p. Serial 13561.

757. U.S. Congress. Senate. Committee on the Judiciary. *Sex Discrimination in the United States Code Reform Act of 1983, Report on S. 501 Together with Additional Views.* S. Rept. 98-390, 98th Cong., 2d sess., 1984. 111p. Serial 13557. Background on this bill. which would remove gender-specific language from over 150 provisions of the United States Code, includes a history of efforts to remove sex-bias from the code. The areas affected by the bill and the gender-based statutes exempted are reviewed. Most of the report is a reprint of the affected sections showing proposed changes.

758. U.S. Congress. Senate. Committee on the Judiciary. Subcommittee on the Constitution. *Federal Civil Rights Laws: A Sourcebook.* 98th Cong., 2d sess., 1984. Committee print. 149p. Y4.J89/2:S.prt.98-245. Text of federal civil rights laws and their legislative histories, federal executive orders, and a summary of civil rights Supreme Court decisions provides a complete compilation of federal anti-discrimination efforts in employment and education.

759. U.S. Congress. Senate. Committee on the Judiciary. Subcommittee on the Constitution. *The Impact of the Equal Rights Amendment, Hearing on S.J. Res. 10, Part 1.* 98th Cong., 1st and 2d sess., 26 May 1983 - 23 May 1984. 1032p. Y4.J89/2:S.hrg.98-1259/pt.1. Testimony and supplemental material provide extensive analysis of the impact of the ERA on private education, the military, abortion rights, veterans programs, and homosexual rights. Issues of social security and defining discrimination are discussed.

760. U.S. Congress. Senate. Committee on the Judiciary. Subcommittee on the Constitution. *The Impact of the Equal Rights Amendment, Hearing on S.J.Res. 10, Part 2.* 98th Cong., 1st and 2d sess., 22 June - 19 Sept. 1984. 835p. Y4.J89/2:S.hrg.98-1259/pt.2. Second part of a hearing on the impact of the ERA looks specifically at family law and at possibilities for changing the language to meet major objections to the current wording. The experience under state ERAs and the implications for a federal law are reviewed. Appendix materials present diverse views on the impact of ERA on American life, national defense, employment, abortion, insurance, and religious organizations.

761.   U.S. Social Security Administration. Office of Civil Rights and Equal Opportunity. *August, Women's Equity Day: Anniversary of the Passage of the Women's Suffrage Amendment, August 26, 1920.* Baltimore, MD?: The Office, 1984? poster. HE3.22:W84.

762.   U.S. Congress. House. Committee on Foreign Affairs. *Report of the United States Delegation to the 72d Conference of the Interparlementary Union Held at Geneva Switzerland, September 22-29, 1984.* 98th Cong., 2d sess., 1985. 52p. Y4.F76/1:In8/52/984-2. Action at the conference included a resolution on equal rights and responsibilities for men and women.

763.   U.S. Congress. Senate. Committee on Finance. *Tax Reform Proposals - VI, Hearing.* 99th Cong., 1st sess., 19 June 1985. 185p. Y4.F49:S.hrg.99-246/pt.6. Testimony within this hearing on tax reform proposals specifically addresses the treatment of women under the existing tax code. The tax burden of low and middle income women, particularly female heads of household, is examined, and various tax reform proposals are analyzed for their impact on women.

764.   U.S. Congress. Senate. Committee on the Judiciary. *Sex Discrimination in the United States Code Reform Act of 1985, Report on S. 86.* S. Rept. 99-194, 99th Cong., 1st sess., 1985. 98p. Serial 13625. Report on a bill to remove gender-based discrimination from the *U.S. Code* provides a history of efforts to eliminate sex discrimination in laws and an overview of categories of laws amended by S. 86. The report also briefly identifies laws not affected by S. 86, notably the miliary draft.

765.   U.S. Congress. Senate. Committee on the Judiciary. Subcommittee on the Constitution. *Summary of Hearings before the Senate Subcommittee on the Constitution, on the Impact of the Proposed Equal Rights Amendment.* by Leslie W. Gladstone, et al. 99th Cong., 1st sess., 1985. Committee print. 140p. Y4.J89/2:S.prt.99-93. Summary of hearings held in 1983-84 on the impact of the proposed Equal Rights Amendment is organized under the topics of education, the military, abortion, veterans' programs, social security, homosexual rights and family law. Proposed and implied exceptions in the ERA and the experience of state's with ERA's are also reviewed.

766.   U.S. National Park Service. *Special History Study: Women's Rights National Historical Park, Seneca Falls, New York.* by Sandra S. Weber. Washington, DC: GPO, 1985. 178p. I29.2:W84/2. Background material on the buildings in the Women's Rights National Historical Park links the buildings and their former occupants with the 1848 Seneca Falls Women's Rights Convention. Separate chapters describe Seneca Falls in 1848, the convention in the Wesleyan Chapel, and the roles of Elizabeth Cady Stanton, Amelia Bloomer, and Mary Ann McClintock in the convention.

767.   U.S. National Park Service. *Women's Rights National Historical Park.* Washington, DC: The Service, 1985. 89p. I29.2:W84. Description of the plan for the Women's Rights National Historic Park in the area around Seneca Falls, New York, site of the 1848 women's rights convention, includes maps of Seneca Falls and Waterloo, New York in 1856 and descriptions of the buildings to be preserved.

768.   U.S. Congress. House. Committee on Veterans' Affairs. *Elimination of Gender-Based Language Distinctions in Title 38, United States Code, Report to Accompany H.R. 5047.* H. Rept. 99-735, 99th Cong., 2d sess., 1986. 68p. Serial 13705. Reports a bill removing gender-specific language from sections of Title 38 of the *U.S. Code* relating to veterans benefit programs.

769.   U.S. Congress. House. Committee on Interior and Insular Affairs. *Increasing the Amount Authorized to be Appropriated for Acquisition at the Women's Rights National Historical*

Park, Report to Accompany H.R. 2952. H. Rept. 100-395, 100th Cong., 1st sess., 1987. 4p. Serial 13809. Additional funds will allow for the purchase and removal of a movie theater located adjacent to the Wesleyan Chapel, site of the 1848 Seneca Falls Convention.

770.   U.S. National Park Service. *Historic Structure Report: Historical Data Section, Wesleyan Chapel, Women's Rights National Historical Park, New York.* by Sharon A. Brown. Washington, DC: GPO, 1987. 302p. I29.88:W84. Lengthy document describes the history of the Wesleyan Chapel, site of the Seneca Falls Women's Rights Convention. Events held in the chapel, the physical changes, and evolving changes in use are covered in detail. A separate chapter describes the 1848 Women's Rights Convention with reference to records detailing the planning and proceedings of the Convention. Copious footnotes document the sources of information.

771.   U.S. Congress. House. Committee on Interior and Insular Affairs. *Increasing the Amount Authorized to be Appropriated with Respect to the Sewall-Belmont House National Historic Site, Report to Accompany H.R. 2203.* H. Rept. 100-611, 100th Cong., 2d sess., 1988. 5p. Serial 13893. Favorably reports a bill raising the appropriation limit for the Sewall-Belmont House National Historic Site and adding direction to the Secretary of the Interior to develop a statement for Management, a Statement of Interpretation, a Scope of Collections Statement and a Historic Structure Report for the property.   The Sewall-Belmont House was the home of Alice Paul and headquarters for the National Woman's Party.

772.   U.S. Congress. Senate. Committee on Energy and Natural Resources. *Increasing the Amount Authorized to be Appropriated for Acquisition at the Women's Rights National Historical Park, Report to Accompany H.R. 2952.* S. Rept.100-532, 100th Cong., 2d sess., 1988. 5p. Serial 13866 See 769 for abstract.

773.   U.S. Congress. Senate. Committee on Energy and Natural Resources. *Sewall-Belmont House National Historic Site, Report to Accompany S. 1682.* S. Rept.100-356, 100th Cong., 2d sess., 1988. 6p. Serial 13860. See 771 for abstract.

774.   U.S. Congress. Senate. Committee on Energy and Natural Resources. Subcommittee on Public Lands, National Parks and Forests. *Miscellaneous Parks and Public Lands Measures, Hearing on H.R. 2530, H.R. 2952, H.R. 3559, H.R. 4050, H.R. 4212, H.R. 4315, S. 1290, S. 2565, S. 2586, Part 2.* 100th Cong., 2d sess., 2 Aug. 1988. 110p. Y4.En2:S.hrg.100-313/pt.2. National Park Service statements express the service's views on miscellaneous park and public land bills, including a bill to allow the purchase of a final piece of land at the Women's Rights National Historic Park in Seneca Falls, New York.

775.   U.S. Congress. Senate. Committee on Energy and Natural Resources. Subcommittee on Public Lands, National Parks and Forests. *Miscellaneous Proposals Related to Historic Preservation, Hearing on S. 1052, S. 1513, S. 1682, S. 1690.* 100th Cong., 2d sess., 14 Apr. 1988. 148p. Y4.En3:S.hrg.100-704. Hearing on miscellaneous Parks Service bills presents testimony supporting increased appropriations for the maintenance of the Sewall-Belmont House National Historic Site. The house is former headquarters of the National Woman's Party. A brief history of the National Woman's Party and the women's rights movement is provided.

776.   U.S. Congress. Senate. Committee on Foreign Relations. Subcommittee on Terrorism, Narcotics and International Operations. *Issues Relating to the United Nations Convention on the Elimination of All Forms of Discrimination against Women, Hearing.* 100th Cong., 2d sess., 5 Dec. 1988. 140p. Y4.F76/2:S.hrg.100-1039. Women representing a wide spectrum of organizations testify in favor of ratification of the UN Convention on the Elimination of All Forms of Discrimination against Women.   Comments focus on

continuing gender bias in the U.S. while highlighting improvements in the status of women since the early 1970s. Economic discrimination against women and the changes in women's lives are described.

777.   U.S. Dept. of Justice. Office of Legal Policy. *Redefining Discrimination: "Disparate Impact" and the Institutionalization of Affirmative Action, Report to the Attorney General.* Washington, DC: GPO, 1988. 158p. J1.96:D63. Report examines the findings of discrimination under civil rights legislation focusing on the concept of disparate impact and its interpretation by the courts. Title VII of the Civil Rights Act of 1964 and its interpretation by the courts is the focus of the report, but other anti-discrimination laws, including Title IX of the Education Amendments of 1972, are also examined. In addition to court interpretation, the report reviews the legislative intent of acts supported by quotes from the congressional proceedings.

778.   U.S. National Archives and Records Administration. *Criminal Law, Voting Rights, United States v. Susan B. Anthony: "Prisoner Tried and Convicted," Indictment, January 24, 1873.* Washington, DC: The Administration, 1989. poster. AE1.110/3:V94.

779.   U.S. National Park Service. *McClintock House, First Wesleyan Methodist Church and Stanton House, Women's Rights National Historical Park, Seneca Falls, New York.* by Carol Petravage. Washington, DC: GPO, 1989. 62p. I29.88/2-2:M45. Historic furnishings report for the Women's Rights National Historical Park highlights the known information on the daily life of Elizabeth Cady Stanton in Seneca Falls and provides excerpts of correspondence containing clues to the furnishings of the McClintock and Stanton Houses.

780.   U.S. Congress. Senate. Committee on Foreign Relations. *Convention on the Elimination of All Forms of Discrimination against Women, Hearing.* 101st Cong., 2d sess., 2 Aug. 1990. 109p. Y4.F76/2:S.hrg.101-1119. Hearing on ratification of the U.N. Convention on the Elimination of All Forms of Discrimination against Women presents testimony on discrimination against women world-wide. Witnesses stress the need for the U.S. to take a leadership role in ratifying the convention. The extent to which U.S. law already adheres to the convention is discussed, and places where the convention provides broader protection against gender discrimination are noted.

781.   U.S. Congress. Senate. Committee on the Judiciary. *Club Membership of Judicial Nominees, Hearing.* 101st Cong., 2d sess., 7 June 1990. 238p. Y4.J89/2:S.hrg.101-163. Hearing considers the issue of judicial nominees who belong to clubs with discriminatory membership policies. Witnesses debate the role such clubs play in career advancement and the implications of membership for a nominee's sensitivity to discrimination cases. At the center of the debate is a Senate resolution stating that potential judicial nominees should not belong to such clubs.

SERIALS

782.   U.S. Citizens' Advisory Council on the Status of Women. *Women in [year].* Washington, DC: GPO, 1970-1975. annual. Y3.In8/21:2W84/year. Annual report reviews the legal status of women for the year covered and council recommendations on the major issues such as the ERA, maternity benefits, education, and credit. Provides an excellent overview of legislation and judicial actions affecting the status of women.

783.   U.S. Commission on Civil Rights. *Civil Rights Digest.* Washington, DC: The Commission, 1968-1979, vol. 1-11. quarterly. CR1.12:vol./no. Continued by *Perspectives* (785). Journal provides semi-scholarly articles on a wide range of civil rights issues, including women's issues, with a focus on current legislation.

784. U.S. Commission on Civil Rights. *Civil Rights Update.* Washington, DC: The Commission, June 1980 - Feb. 1986. monthly. CR1.15:date. Newsletter summarizes areas of current Civil Rights Commission investigations and highlights significant court decisions on civil rights.

785. U.S. Commission on Civil Rights. *New Perspectives.* Washington, DC: GPO, 1984 - . quarterly. Publication suspended Winter 1986 to Winter 1988. CR1.12:year/no. Continues *Perspectives* (786). Journal covers a wide array of civil rights issues, many of them relating to women, such as pension equity, sexual harassment, and educational equity.

786. U.S. Commission on Civil Rights. *Perspectives.* Washington, DC: GPO, 1980 - 1983. quarterly. CR1.12:year/no. Continues *Civil Rights Digest* (783), continued by *New Perspectives* (785).

787. U.S. Commission on Civil Rights. *The State of Civil Rights: A Report of the United States Commission on Civil Rights.* Washington, DC: GPO, 1976 - 1983. annual. CR1.2:C49/5/year. Summarizes the year's events, major court cases, legislation and government action in the area of civil rights.

788. U.S. Defense Fuel Supply Center. Federal Women's Program Committee. *Not for Women Only.* Washington, DC: GPO, 197? - 1978. irreg. D7.30:nos. Diverse collection of information on all aspects of women's rights provides specific information on women's issues at the Defense Fuel Supply Center.

789. U.S. Federal Reserve System. Board of Governors. *Annual Report to Congress on the Equal Credit Opportunity Act.* Washington, DC: The Board, 1976 - . 1st. - . annual. FR1.60:year. Brief review of enforcement of the Equal Credit Opportunity Act provides few details of compliance or violations, but rather gives a summary of overall compliance performance.

790. U.S. Women's Bureau. *Family and Property Law, [State].* Washington, DC: GPO, 1956 - 1967. rev. irreg. L13.17:(cutter)/year. Summarizes state laws relating to women and property rights, marriage and divorce, and parents and children.

   Arizona. 1956, revised 1957. L13.17:Ar4i.
   California. 1960, revised 1961. L13.17:C12.
   Colorado. 1957, revised 1965. L13.17:C71.
   Delaware. 1957. L13.17:D37.
   Florida. 1957. L13.17:F66.
   Idaho. 1957. L13.17:Id1.
   Indiana. 1957. L13.17:In2.
   Iowa. 1957, revised 1961, 1962, 1964, 1966. L13.17:Io9.
   Kansas. 1957. L13.17:K13.
   Kentucky. 1957. L13.17:K41.
   Maryland. 1957-1962. revised yearly. L13.17:M36.
   Massachusetts. 1956, revised 1965. L13.17:M38.
   Michigan. 1960, revised 1961 and 1962. L13.17:M58.
   Nebraska. 1956. L13.17:N27.
   New Jersey. 1967. L13.17:N42j.
   New Mexico. 1958, revised yearly 1960-1962. L13.17:N42m.
   New York. 1967. L13.17:N42y.
   North Carolina. 1957, revised 1959. L13.17:N81c.
   North Dakota. 1957, revised 1958. L13.17:N81d.
   Ohio. 1957, revised 1958, 1961-1962, 1966-1969, 1971. L13.17:Oh3.
   Oklahoma. 1957. L13.17:Ok4.

Oregon. 1956, revised yearly 1958-1961. L13.17:Or3.
South Carolina. 1957. L13.17:So8c.
Tennessee. 1957. L13.17:T25.
Texas. 1957. L13.17:T31.
Utah. 1957. L13.17:Ut1.
Vermont. 1957. L13.17:V59.
Washington. 1957. L13.17:W27.
Wisconsin. 1957. L13.17:W75.
Wyoming. 1957, revised yearly 1961-1963. L13.17:W99.

791. U.S. Women's Bureau. *The Legal Status of Women in the United States, Report for [State].* Bulletin no. 157-no. Washington, DC: GPO, 1938 - 1966. rev. irreg. L13.3:157-no. Reports provide concise summaries of state statutes relating to women in the areas of contracts and property, marriage and divorce, parents and children, and political rights. Revised editions and addenda (a) were issued on an irregular basis.

Alabama. 1938, revised 1948, 1953(a), 1959, 1964(a). L13.3:157-1.
Alaska. 1958. L13.3:157-51.
Arizona. 1938, revised 1948, 1953(a), 1958. L13.3:157-2.
Arkansas. 1938, revised 1948, 1953(a), 1959, 1964(a). L13.3:157-3.
California. 1938, revised 1948, 1953(a), 1957, 1963. L13.3:157-4.
Colorado. 1938, revised 1948, 1953(a), 1959, 1966. L13.3:157-5.
Connecticut. 1938, revised 1948, 1953(add)., 1957, 1962. L13.3:157-6.
Delaware. 1938, revised 1948, 1953(a), 1957, 1962. L13.3:157-7.
District of Columbia. 1938, revised 1948, 1953(a), 1959, 1964. L13.3:157-8
Florida. 1938, revised 1948, 1953(a), 1959, 1965. L13.3:157-9.
Georgia. 1938, revised 1948, 1953(a), 1959, 1963. L13.3:157-10.
Hawaii. 1959. L13.3:157-52. The 1948 report on territories (568) covers Hawaii.
Idaho. 1938, revised 1948, 1953(a), 1956, 1965. L13.3:157-11.
Illinois. 1938, revised 1948, 1953(a), 1956, 1965. L13.3:157-12.
Indiana. 1938, revised 1948, 1953(a), 1960. L13.3:157-13.
Iowa. 1938, revised 1948, 1953(a), 1960. L13.3:157-14.
Kansas. 1938, revised 1948, 1953(a), 1958. L13.3:157-15.
Kentucky. 1938, revised 1948, 1953(a), 1959, 1964. L13.3:157-16.
Louisiana. 1938, revised 1948, 1953(a), 1956. L13.3:157-17.
Maine. 1938, revised 1948, 1953(a), 1958, 1964(a). L13.3:157-18.
Maryland. 1938, revised 1948, 1953(a), 1959, 1966. L13.3:157-19.
Massachusetts. 1938, revised 1948, 1953(a), 1956, 1962, 1966. L13.3:157-20.
Michigan. 1938, revised 1948, 1953(a), 1956, 1963. L13.3:157-21.
Minnesota. 1938, revised 1948, 1953(a), 1960, 1964. L13.3:157-22.
Mississippi. 1938, revised 1948, 1953(a), 1960. L13.3:157-23.
Missouri. 1938, revised 1948, 1953(a), 1957, 1963(a). L13.3:157-24.
Montana. 1938, revised 1948, 1953(a), 1960. L13.3:157-25.
Nebraska. 1938, revised 1948, 1953(a), 1956, 1964. L13.3:157-26.
Nevada. 1938, revised 1949, 1953(a), 1958, 1964. L13.3:157-27.
New Hampshire. 1938, revised 1948, 1953(a), 1960. L13.3:157-28.
New Jersey. 1938, revised 1948, 1953(a), 1960. L13.3:157-29.
New Mexico. 1938, revised 1948, 1953(a), 1956, 1962. L13.3:157-30.
New York State. 1938, revised 1948, 1953(a), 1960. L13.3:157-31.
North Carolina. 1938, revised 1948, 1953(a), 1957, 1964. L13.3:157-32.
North Dakota. 1938, revised 1948, 1953(a), 1960. L13.3:157-33.
Ohio. 1938, revised 1948, 1958, 1963. L13.3:157-34.
Oklahoma. 1938, revised 1948, 1953(a), 1960. L13.3:157-35.
Oregon. 1938, revised 1948, 1953(a), 1957. L13.3:157-36.
Pennsylvania. 1938, revised 1948, 1953(a), 1957, 1965. L13.3:157-37.

Rhode Island. 1938, revised 1948, 1960. L13.3:157-38.
South Carolina. 1938, revised 1948, 1953(a), 1960. L13.3:157-39.
South Dakota. 1938, revised 1948, 1953(a), 1960. L13.3:157-40.
Tennessee. 1938, revised 1948, 1953(a), 1960. L13.3:157-41.
Texas. 1938, revised 1948, 1953(a), 1959, 1964. L13.3:157-42.
Utah. 1938, revised 1948, 1959, 1964(a). L13.3:157-43.
Vermont. 1938, revised 1948, 1953(a), 1959, 1964(a). L13.3:157-44.
Virginia. 1938, revised 1948, 1953(a), 1957. L13.3:157-45.
Washington. 1938, revised 1948, 1953(a), 1957, 1963. L13.3:157-46.
West Virginia. 1938, revised 1948, 1953(a), 1956, 1962. L13.3:157-47.
Wisconsin. 1938, revised 1948, 1953(a), 1957, 1964. L13.3:157-48.
Wyoming. 1938, revised 1948, 1953(a), 1960. L13.3:157-49.

792. U.S. Women's Bureau. *The Legal Status of Women in the United States, U.S. Summary.* by Sara Louise Buchanan. Bulletin no. 157. Washington, DC: GPO, 1938 - 1956. 89p. L13.3:157. Summary volume reviews the legal status of women in each state and identifies nation-wide trends. Revised editions were issued in 1948 and 1956, a supplement was issued in 1943, and a cumulative supplement covers 1938 to 1945.

793. U.S. Women's Bureau. *Women's Eligibility for Jury Duty.* Washington, DC: GPO, 1945-1950. irreg. L13.2:J97/year. Leaflet summarizes state laws on women's eligibility for jury duty.

5

Suffrage and Political Participation

Published documents on the campaign for woman suffrage in the United States begin with a series of petitions to Congress in 1870. Most of these petitions were merely printed as miscellaneous documents without response. The exception is the memorial of Victoria C. Woodhull, which was not only printed, but which was the subject of both majority and minority reports (795, 798-799).

The first published hearing on a constitutional amendment guaranteeing a woman's right to vote was printed in 1878 and featured the arguments of the National Woman Suffrage Association as presented by Elizabeth Cady Stanton and Matilda Joslyn Gage (806). For the next forty years hearings and reports debate the issue of woman suffrage. The battle begun by Stanton, Gage and Susan B. Anthony was continued by Carrie Chapman Catt, Dr. Anna Howard Shaw and Alice Paul. It is difficult to single out any particular hearing from this time period. Taken as a whole they reflect both the consistency and the changes in the arguments for and against woman suffrage. In general, proponents discussed the issue as a matter of justice and a right of citizenship while noting the role of women in the labor force and the need for working women to protect themselves through the ballot. Particularly in the early years, opposition arguments centered on the dire effects of suffrage on women's morality and on the threat to the home. Their refrain year after year was that women did not want the vote and that the suffrage issue should be left to the states. The hearings also reflect a tendency on both sides to appeal to the prejudice against blacks and immigrants.

As woman suffrage was adopted in the various states their experience was used by both sides, usually with opponents charging corruption and supporters sighting the good accomplished (854, 858, 866, 876). Some of the more unique woman suffrage documents include a 1910 hearing which presents a petition of 404,825 supporters categorized by occupation (854), and the detailed report, with photographs, of the District of Columbia Police Department's handling of crowd control at the March 3, 1913 woman suffrage parade (870). Starting in 1904 the hearings and reports also document the movement to secure by federal law the right of women to vote for Representatives (846) and for Senators (861).

At the same time as the campaign for a constitutional amendment on suffrage the issue of suffrage in territories and potential states was also considered. The issue of woman suffrage in Utah was closely tied to the issue of polygamy (815, 820). When Wyoming was considered for admission as a state arguments were advanced against its admission because its Constitution guaranteed woman suffrage (826). In the case of Hawaii, the Territorial Legislature requested that Congress amend the Organic Act to authorize woman suffrage (891, 896-971).

After 1919 the topic of women's political participation did not appear in government publications again until 1939 and 1940 when episodes of the "Gallant American Women" radio series featured the history of woman suffrage and the role of women in government (910-911). Starting in 1945 a regular flow of publications profiled women in Congress (914, 927, 933) and in state legislatures (916, 917, 920). At about the same time, interest in the political status of women around the world increased, and a number of Women's Bureau publications described the extent of woman suffrage and political participation outside the United States. Many of the documents on the status of women found in Chapter 1, General Works, also document women's political status.

794. U.S. Congress. Senate. *Memorial of C.E. McKay, Remonstrating against the Right of Suffrage Being Granted to Women.* S. Misc. Doc. 48, 41st Cong., 2d sess., 1870. 3p. Serial 1408. Argument against universal suffrage for women warns of an increase in the ignorant vote threatening the safety of the Republic.

795. U.S. Congress. Senate. *Memorial of Victoria C.Woodhull Praying the Passage of a Law Carrying into Execution the Right Vested by the Constitution in Citizens of the United States to Vote, without Regard to Sex.* S. Misc. Doc. 16, 41st Cong., 3d sess., 1870. 2p. Serial 1442. Memorial of Dec. 19, 1870 by Victoria C. Woodhull states the case for women's voting rights under the 14th and 15th Amendments and asks Congress to enact laws to ensure citizens the right to vote without regard to gender.

796. U.S. Congress. Senate. *Petition of H.C. Ingersoll Praying that the Right of Suffrage Be Granted to Women in the District of Columbia.* S. Misc. Doc. 47, 41st Cong., 2d sess., 1870. 2p. Serial 1408. Petition asks that women of the District of Columbia be given suffrage subject to qualifications regarding literacy, property ownership, and moral character.

797. U.S. Congress. House. *Woman Suffrage: Memorial of the St. Louis Women Suffrage Association.* H. Misc. Doc. 40, 42d Cong., 1st sess., 1871. 1p. Serial 1472. Memorial urges Congress to submit a woman suffrage amendment to the constitution.

798. U.S. Congress. House. Committee on the Judiciary. *[Memorial of] Victoria C. Woodhull.* H. Rept. 22, 41st Cong., 3d sess., 1871. 4p. Serial 1464. Rejects the pro-woman suffrage interpretation of the 14th Amendment as presented in the memorial of Victoria C. Woodhull (795).

799. U.S. Congress. House. Committee on the Judiciary. *[Memorial of] Victoria C. Woodhull, Views of the Minority.* H. Rept. 22, part 2, 41st Cong., 3d sess., 1871. 7p. Serial 1464. Minority views on the ability of Congress to secure women the right to vote cites the past history of women in positions of power, the right to vote under common law, and the argument for using the 14th Amendment as a basis for securing women's right to vote. The report relies heavily on legal opinions and other works defining the concept of citizen.

800. U.S. Congress. Senate. Committee on the Judiciary. *[Memorial of Elizabeth Cady Stanton, Isabell Bucher Hooker, Elizabeth S. Bladen, Olympia Brown, Susan B. Anthony, and Josephine J. Griffin, Citizens of the United States, Praying for the Enactment of a Law, during the Present Session of Congress, to Assist and Protect Them in the Exercise of Their Right and the Right of All Women, to Participate in the Elective Franchise, Which the Memorialists Claim They are Entitled to under the Constitution of the United States].* S. Rept. 21, 42d Cong., 2d sess., 1872. 5p. Serial 1483. Argument of the committee refutes the claim of the memorialists' that the right of woman suffrage is guaranteed by the Constitution under Article IV Section 4 and under the 14th Amendment.

801.   U.S. Congress. House. *Suffrage in Utah: Memorial of the New York Woman Suffrage Society, Protesting against the Sixth Section of the Bill regarding Utah*. H. Misc. Doc. 95, 42d Cong., 3d sess., 1873. 1p. Serial 1572. Brief memorial against a clause restricting suffrage in the Territory of Utah to male citizens cites the positive influence of the women's vote on the elimination of the practice of polygamy.

802.   U.S. Congress. House. Committee on the Judiciary. *Argument upon the Petition of 600 Citizens Asking for the Enfranchisement of the Women of the District of Columbia, Jan. 21, 1874 by Francis Miller, Esq.* 43d Cong., 1st sess., 21 Jan. 1874. Washington, DC: Gibson Brothers, Printers, 1874. 8p. Report on a petition requesting that Congress take action to ensure women the right to vote in the District of Columbia. The petition was in response to a decision of the Supreme Court of the District of Columbia which affirmed that the 14th Amendment gave women the right to vote, but also stated that Congress must provide the means by amending the act establishing the government of the District of Columbia by eliminating the word "male".

803.   U.S. Congress. House. *Memorial from the New York Woman Suffrage Society, in Reference to the Centennial*. H. Misc. Doc. 45, 44th Cong., 1st sess., 1876. 1p. Serial 1698. Protests the taxation of female citizens of the U.S. to pay for the Centennial Exhibition "which celebrates the freedom of only one-half that people."

804.   U.S. Congress. Senate. *Memorial of Women, Citizens of the United States, Asking for the Establishment of a Government in the District of Columbia Which Shall Secure to Women the Right to Vote*. S. Misc. Doc. 40, 44th Cong., 1st sess., 1876. 2p. Serial 1665. Formal statement of representatives of the National Women's Suffrage Association and the District of Columbia Women's Franchise Association requests that Congress establish a government for the District of Columbia which includes the franchise for women.

805.   U.S. Congress. Senate. *Resolution [to Allow Women to be Heard before the Senate on the Issue of Woman Suffrage]*. S. Misc. Doc. 12, 45th Cong., 2d sess., 1878. 1p. Serial 1785.

806.   U.S. Congress. Senate. Committee on Privileges and Elections. *Arguments in Behalf of a Sixteenth Amendment to the Constitution of the United States, Prohibiting the Several States from Disfranchising United States Citizens on Account of Sex, and Protest against Woman Suffrage*. 45th Cong., 2d sess., 11-12 Jan. 1878. 45p. Greenwood SPri 45-A. Delegates of the National Woman Suffrage Association presenting arguments for a constitutional amendment include Elizabeth Cady Stanton and Matilda Joslyn Gage. Testimony argues the need for woman suffrage and speaks to democratic principles and the rights of women as citizens. Some statements reflect the view of women voters as future agents of reform. The dissenting statement advances the argument that marriage is a sacred union and can only have one voice, i.e. the husband.

807.   U.S. Congress. Senate. *Memorial of Elizabeth Cady Stanton, Matilda Joslyn Gage, and Susan B. Anthony, Officers of the National Woman Suffrage Association, Asking for the Passage of Senate Resolution No. 12, Providing for an Amendment to the Constitution Protecting the Rights of Women Citizens, and Also Asking that the House Judiciary Committee be Relieved from Further Consideration of a Similar Resolution*. S. Misc. Doc. 45, 45th Cong., 3d sess., 1879. 2p. Serial 1833.

808.   U.S. Congress. Senate. Committee on the Judiciary. *Woman Suffrage- Arguments before the Committee on the Judiciary*. H.Doc. 20, 46th Cong., 2d sess., 1880. 22p. Serial 1929. Arguments of delegates to the Woman Suffrage Convention focus on women's need to protect themselves and their ability to earn a living, and on women's status as citizens and their subsequent right to the full protection of the laws and the ballot. The Supreme

Court's decision in the case of *Minor v. Happersett* (88 US 162) is reviewed and is compared to the Dred Scott decision. Susan B. Anthony makes a particularly eloquent speech on the principal of universal suffrage and the evils of disfranchisement.

809. U.S. Congress. Senate. *Resolution [That the Committee on "The Extension of Suffrage to Women, or the Removal of Their Disabilities," be Directed to Examine into the State of the Law Regulating the Right of Suffrage in the Territory of Utah.]* S. Misc. Doc. 34, 47th Cong., 1st sess., 1882. 1p. Serial 1993.

810. U.S. Congress. Senate. Committee on Woman Suffrage. *[On the Joint Resolution (S. 60) Proposing an Amendment to the Constitution of the United States to Secure the Right of Suffrage to All Citizens without Regard to Sex] Part 1.* S. Rept. 686, 47th Cong., 1st sess., 1882. 6p. Serial 2007. Report gives a concise history of the women's rights moment in the U.S. and provides appropriate quotes on the woman suffrage issue.

811. U.S. Congress. Senate. Committee on Woman Suffrage. *[On the Joint Resolution (S. 60) Proposing an Amendment to the Constitution of the United States to Secure the Right of Suffrage to All Citizens without Regard to Sex] Views of the Minority, Part 2.* S. Rept. 686, part 2, 47th Cong., 1st sess., 1882. 3p. Serial 2007. Minority report recommends rejection of the amendment on the grounds that a question such as woman suffrage, whose outcome would affect public welfare and the relations of public and private life, should be left to the States.

812. U.S. Congress. Senate. Select Committee on Woman Suffrage. *Arguments of the Women-Suffrage Delegates before the Committee on the Judiciary of the United States Senate, January 23, 1880.* S. Misc. Doc. 74, 47th Cong., 1st sess., 1882. 26p. Serial 1993. Delegates to the 12th Washington Convention of the National Woman Suffrage Association present arguments for woman suffrage. The various approaches include the vote as a tool to address social issues, taxation without representation, and the issue of civil rights. The primary witness is Susan B. Anthony who stresses women's need for political power and the expediency of the constitutional amendment approach.

813. U.S. Congress. House. Select Committee on Woman Suffrage. *Woman Suffrage, Report to Accompany H. Res. 225.* H. Rept. 1997, 47th Cong., 2d sess., 1883. 2p. Serial 2160. Favorable report on H. Res. 255 provides a concise summary of the arguments for woman suffrage.

814. U.S. Congress. House. Committee on the Judiciary. *Extending the Right of Suffrage to Women, Report to Accompany H. Res. 25.* H. Rept. 1330, 48th Cong., 1st sess., 1884. 8p. Serial 2257. Unfavorable report on a woman suffrage amendment denies women's right to vote as citizens and rejects comparison to the conditions of black men prior to the 13th, 14th and 15th Amendments. The report indicates that the states should first show overwhelming support of this issue. Minority views express support for the Amendment, or support the majority decision but disagree with the reasoning presented. The report indicates a great deal of dissention within the committee on this subject.

815. U.S. Congress. House. Committee on the Territories. *Reorganization of the Legislative Power of Utah Territory, Views of the Minority, to Accompany Bill H.R. 6765.* H. Rept. 1351, part 2, 48th Cong., 1st sess., 1884. 57p. Serial 2257. Discussion on the governing of Utah and the influence of the Mormon Church reviews the issue of polygamy and woman suffrage.

816. U.S. Congress. Senate. Committee on Woman Suffrage. *[On the Joint Resolution (S. Res. 19) Proposing an Amendment to the Constitution of the Untied States] Report to Accompany S.R. 19.* S. Rept. 399, part 1, 48th Cong., 1st sess., 1884. 31 p. Serial 2175.

Report on a proposed woman suffrage amendment prints the arguments presented to the Committee by Lillie Devereux Blake, Susan B. Anthony, and others on Mar. 7, 1884, and reprints Senate Misc. Doc. 74 (812) which includes arguments before the Committee on the Judiciary.

817. U.S. Congress. Senate. Committee on Woman Suffrage. *[On the Joint Resolution (S. Res. 19) Proposing an Amendment to the Constitution of the United States] Report to Accompany S.R. 19, Views of the Minority.* S. Rept. 399, part 2, 48th Cong., 1st. sess., 1884. 8p. Serial 2175. Argument based on divine intent in the roles of men and women rejects the proposed amendment as causing women to "leave their sacred labors at home."

818. U.S. Congress. House. *Woman Suffrage Convention, Resolution.* H. Misc. Doc. 23, 49th Cong., 2d sess., 1886. 1p. Serial 2488. Resolution grants use of the Hall of the House of Representatives for the use of the 19th National Woman's Suffrage Convention.

819. U.S. Congress. House. Committee on the Judiciary. *Woman Suffrage, Report to Accompany H. Res. 109.* H. Rept. 2289, 49th Cong., 1st sess., 1886. 3p. Serial 2442. Unfavorable report without comment on H. Res. 109 includes views of the minority on the importance of woman suffrage.

820. U.S. Congress. Senate. *Woman Suffrage in Utah, Petition of Mrs. Agnes F. Newman.* S. Misc. Doc. 122, 49th Cong., 1st sess., 1886. 9p. Serial 2346. Petition calls for the passage of Section 7 of the Edmunds bill, which specifically strips women of the elective franchise in Utah. The petition discusses voter fraud in Utah and the voting requirements and practices relating to female voters. The basic argument is that disenfranchising the women will loosen the Mormon hold on Utah government.

821. U.S. Congress. Senate. Select Committee on Woman Suffrage. *Report to Accompany S. Res. 5 [Proposing an Amendment to the Constitution of the United States Extending the Right of Suffrage to Women].* S. Rept. 70, part 1, 49th Cong., 1st sess., 1886. 38p. Serial 2355. Favorable report on a proposed woman suffrage amendment examines the weaknesses of arguments against woman suffrage and reviews the action toward woman suffrage in the states. Appendix reprints arguments in favor of woman suffrage before the Select Committee on Woman Suffrage, Mar. 7, 1884 (816), and before the Senate Committee on the Judiciary, Jan. 23, 1880 (808).

822. U.S. Congress. Senate. Select Committee on Woman Suffrage. *Views of the Minority to Accompany S. Res. 5 [Proposing an Amendment to the Constitution of the United States Extending the Right of Suffrage to Women].* S. Rept. 70, part 2, 49th Cong., 1st sess., 1886. 10p. Serial 2355. Minority report against woman suffrage consists primarily of excerpts from "Letters from a Chimney Corner," written by an unidentified Chicago woman. The excerpts discuss male and female roles and women's power in the home. Reprinted is S. Rept. 399, part 2, 48th Congress (816) and minority views on S. Res. 19, which also argue woman's higher purpose in life and the potential danger of suffrage.

823. U.S. Congress. Senate. Committee on Woman Suffrage. *Hearing before the Committee on Woman Suffrage, United States Senate, April 2, 1888.* S. Misc. Doc. 114, 50th Cong., 1st sess., 1888. 21p. Serial 2517. Delegates from the International Women's Council, including Elizabeth Cady Stanton, Frances E. Willard, and Julia Ward Howe, present statements in support of woman suffrage. The longest statement is by Stanton, who reviews the constitutional basis for woman suffrage and addresses the arguments raised against it.

824. U.S. Congress. Senate. Committee on Woman Suffrage. *Report to Accompany S. Res. 11 [Proposing an Amendment to the Constitution Prohibiting the Denial or Abridgement of the*

Right to Vote by the United States or by any States on Account of Sex]. S. Rept. 2543, 50th Cong., 2d sess., 1889. 67p. Serial 2618. Favorable report provides a good summary of the philosophical arguments for the enfranchisement of women. The appendix reprints the statements of delegates to the International Woman's Council presented before the Committee on Woman Suffrage, Apr. 2, 1888, and the hearing held Jan. 24, 1889 before the Committee on Woman Suffrage.

825. U.S. Congress. Senate. Committee on Woman Suffrage. *View of the Minority to Accompany S. Res. 11 [Proposing an Amendment to the Constitution Prohibiting the Denial or Abridgment of the Right to Vote by the United States or by any State on Account of Sex].* S. Rept. 2543, part 2, 50th Cong., 2d sess., 1889. 37p. Serial 2618. Minority report against woman suffrage reprints past House and Senate reports against the amendment and other letters and essays on women's place in society, her importance to the family, and her lack of desire for the vote. The Supreme Court opinion in *Minor v. Happersett* is also furnished.

826. U.S. Congress. House. *Admission of Wyoming into the Union, Views of the Minority.* H. Rept. 39, part 2, 51st Cong., 1st sess., 1890. 36p. Serial 2807. Arguments against the admission of Wyoming as a state focus on Article 6 of the state's constitution granting women equal suffrage and propose amending the state constitution to restrict suffrage to men. Four appendices present specific arguments against woman suffrage. The longest of these statements, by Goldwin Smith, addresses arguments for woman suffrage based on natural rights, the war issue and women's need to defend her rights. The statement reviews the history of republics and asserts that women are better protected through the actions of men. Appendix 4 presents an essay by Adeline D.T. Whitney which sets forth the place of woman prescribed by her role as wife and mother and postulates that the home can only suffer through the elective franchise for women.

827. U.S. Congress. House. Committee on the Judiciary. *Right of Suffrage to Women, Views of the Minority.* H. Rept. 2254, part 2, 51st Cong., 1st sess., 1890. 2p. Serial 2813. Brief statement opposed to a woman suffrage amendment reviews state action on woman suffrage in 1889 and early 1890.

828. U.S. Congress. House. Committee on the Judiciary. *Woman Suffrage, Report to Accompany H. Res. 60.* H. Rept. 2254, 51st Cong., 1st sess., 1890. 4p. Serial 2813. Report on H. Res. 60, to amend the Constitution to prohibit voting discrimination based on gender, discusses the status of women in the U.S. and the justice of woman suffrage.

829. U.S. Congress. Senate. Committee on Woman Suffrage. *Report to Accompany S. Res. 1 [Joint Resolution Proposing an Amendment to the Constitution of the United States, Extending the Right of Suffrage to Women].* S. Rept. 1576, 51st Cong.,1st sess., 1890. 3p. Serial 2711. Favorable report briefly justifies equal voting privilege for women.

830. U.S. Congress. House. Committee on the Judiciary. *Hearing of the Woman Suffrage Association.* 52d Cong., 1st sess., 18 Jan. 1892. 8p. Greenwood (52)HJ-1. Hearing on a constitutional amendment on woman suffrage features statements by Elizabeth Cady Stanton, Lucy Stone, Isabella Beecher Hooker, and Susan B. Anthony. Eloquent speeches demand woman suffrage for the common good and also speak to the cause of women's education. One of the more unique arguments is advanced by Stone who proposed that women, being acquainted with the economy of the home budget, would bring economy to the government.

831. U.S. Congress. Senate. Select Committee on Woman Suffrage. *Woman Suffrage.* 52d Cong., 1st sess, 20 Jan. 1892. 16p. Greenwood (52)SS-1. Short speeches from state

woman suffrage association leaders highlight the arguments for woman suffrage noting the good done in Wyoming and Kansas through woman suffrage.

832.　U.S. Congress. Senate. *Memorial of Caroline F. Corbin for American Women Remonstrates to the Extension of Suffrage to Women, Praying for a Hearing before Congress.* S. Misc. Doc. 28, 52d Cong., 2d sess., 1893. 11p. Serial 3064. Petition against woman suffrage presents arguments supporting women's place in society as dictated by nature, and warns of the harm to the home which would follow woman suffrage. An essay entitled "The Home Versus Women's Suffrage" brands woman suffrage as a socialistic attempt to destroy christian homes and bring about polygamy and free love.

833.　U.S. Congress. Senate. Select Committee on Woman Suffrage. *Report to Accompany S.R. 129 [in Relation to Petition of the National Woman's Suffrage Association of Massachusetts].* S. Rept. 1143, 52d Cong., 2d sess., 1893. 6p. Serial 3072. Report of a joint resolution on woman suffrage recommends its passage and very briefly reviews the supporting arguments focusing on the inherent justice of such an amendment and the success of woman suffrage in Wyoming. The minority report against the amendment turns on the issue of states rights and adopts S. Rept. 47-686 part 2 (811) as its own.

834.　U.S. Congress. Senate. Committee on the District of Columbia. *Report to Accompany S. 1717 [to Authorize the Appointment of Women as School Trustees in the District of Columbia.]* S. Rept. 281, 53d Cong., 2d sess., 1894. 1p. Serial 3179.

835.　U.S. Congress. Senate. Committee on Woman Suffrage. *Hearing before the Committee on Woman Suffrage.* S. Misc. Doc. 121, 53d Cong., 2d sess., 1894. 30p. Serial 3171. Representatives from across the nation present arguments for woman suffrage. Alice Stone Blackwell addresses the anti-suffrage argument that women do not want the vote, and the success of woman suffrage in Wyoming, Kansas, and New Jersey is reviewed. The Rev. Anna Shaw highlights the benefits of woman suffrage and Sara Winthrop Smith presents the constitutional argument.

836.　U.S. Congress. House. Committee on the Judiciary. *Hearing of the National American Woman Suffrage Association.* 54th Cong., 1st sess., 28 Jan. 1896. 21p. Y4.J89/1:W84/1. Statements of representatives of the National American Woman Suffrage Association, lead by Susan B. Anthony, address the justice of women voting, taxation without representation, and the raising of better citizens through enfranchised mothers. Testimony describes woman suffrage as being "in harmony with the evolution of the race," and refutes the argument that women do not want the vote.

837.　U.S. Congress. Senate. Committee on the District of Columbia. *Suffrage in the District of Columbia.* 54th Cong., 1st sess., 24 Mar. 1896. 18p. Greenwood (54)SD-1. Hearing testimony on a proposal to provide the District of Columbia with a representative government includes a plea to eliminate the word "male" from the bill and include women in the right to suffrage in the District of Columbia.

838.　U.S. Congress. Senate. Committee on Woman Suffrage. *Report on Hearing before the Committee on Woman Suffrage.* S. Doc. 157, 54th Cong., 1st sess., 1896. 23p. Serial 3353. Women from 19 states present their arguments in favor of woman suffrage describing the status of women and the logic and justice of woman suffrage.

839.　U.S. Congress. Senate. Committee on Woman Suffrage. *Views of the Minority to Accompany S. Res. 106 [to Amend the Constitution for Woman Suffrage].* S. Rept. 787. 54th Cong., 1st sess., 1896. 3p. Serial 3365. Views against a woman suffrage amendment concentrates on states rights and the difference between the case of former slaves and women as it relates to the power of Congress to impose suffrage requirements.

840. U.S. Congress. House. Committee on the Judiciary. *Hearing on House Joint Resolution 68.* 55th Cong., 2d sess., 15 Feb. 1898. 20p. Greenwood HJ55-A. Statements of proponents of a woman suffrage amendment examine the history of school suffrage for women, municipal suffrage in Kansas and woman suffrage in Wyoming, Colorado, Utah, Idaho, and other countries. Alice Stone Blackwell points out that reforms for women have always been brought about by the insistence of a few and not by majority demand.

841. U.S. Congress. Senate. Committee on Woman Suffrage. *Report of Hearing before the Committee on Woman Suffrage.* 55th Cong., 2d sess., 15 Feb. 1898. 24p. Y4.W84:W84/1. Technically not a hearing, this report is a collection of speeches including William Lloyd Garrison on "The Nature of a Republican Form of Government"; May Wright Sewall on "Fitness of Women to Become Citizens from the Standpoint of Education and Mental Development"; the Rev. Anna Garlin Spencer on "Fitness of Women to Become Citizens from the Standpoint of Moral Development"; Laura Clay on "Fitness of Women to Become Citizens from the Standpoint of Physical Development"; Harriet Stanton Blatch on "Women as a Economic Factor"; Florence Kelly on "The Working Woman's Need of the Ballot"; Marlana W. Chapman on "Women as Capitalists and Taxpayers"; Henry B. Blackwell on "Woman Suffrage and the Home"; and, finally, Elizabeth Cady Stanton on the "Significance and History of the Ballot." Stanton's piece deals primarily with the immigrant vote and educational qualifications for voters rather than a qualification based on sex.

842. U.S. Congress. House. Committee on the Judiciary. *Woman Suffrage, Hearing.* 56th Cong., 1st sess., 13 Feb. 1900. 35p. Greenwood HJ56-B. Arguments for and against a woman suffrage amendment to the constitution include an elegant argument by Lillie Devereux Blake based on the constitution, and a written statement by Elizabeth Cady Stanton calling for a constitutional amendment prohibiting the taxation or inclusion in counts to determine representation of any person who is denied the vote. The economic basis of woman suffrage and the growing intellectual status of American women are addressed. Those opposed to the amendment point to failed state constitutional amendment attempts as proof that only a small minority of women want the vote.

843. U.S. Congress. Senate. Committee on Woman Suffrage. *Hearing before the United States Senate Committee on Woman Suffrage.* 56th Cong., 1st sess., 13 Feb. 1900. 45p. Y4.W84:W84/2. Hearing primarily of supporters of woman suffrage includes a detailed history of congressional action on the woman suffrage question and related political and civil rights issues. Also includes a detailed report on municipal suffrage in Kansas, with statistics on the number of women registered and voting, and a report of the good done in Colorado by adoption of woman suffrage. Reviews the history of women's political and civil rights in great Britain and the movement toward limited woman suffrage in Europe and Australia, with a chart showing the extent of woman suffrage worldwide. Carrie Chapman Catt describes the state of the woman suffrage movement in 1900 in the U.S. and, along with Susan B. Anthony, describes the barriers to securing woman suffrage by popular vote. Brief statement in opposition argues the unfairness of the federal amendment approach, women's incapability to serve in high political office, on juries, or in the military, and the potential for disharmony in the home.

844. U.S. Congress. House. Committee on the Judiciary. *Woman Suffrage, Hearing.* 57th Cong., 1st sess., 18 Feb. 1902. 23p. Greenwood HJ57-F. Hearing on a woman suffrage amendment to the Constitution holds up the example of woman suffrage in Australia and New Zealand, and reports on woman suffrage in Russian municipal elections. Sweden, Norway, and England are also discussed and the situation in Wyoming and Idaho is described. Carrie Chapman Catt asks the committee to investigate woman suffrage in the U.S. to establish the facts regarding the operation of woman suffrage in the states and silence the objections of opponents.

845. U.S. Congress. Senate. Committee on Woman Suffrage. *Woman Suffrage, Hearing on the Joint Resolution (S.R. 53) Proposing an Amendment to the Constitution of the United States Extending the Right of Suffrage to Women.* 57th Cong., 1st sess., 18 Feb. 1902. 39p. Y4.W84:W84/3. Testimony in favor of a woman suffrage amendment discusses the question of literate women versus illiterate men voting, and the right of women to have a voice in laws which affect them as property owners, taxpayers, workers, and mothers. A rebuttal to an anti-woman suffrage publication of the Massachusetts Association Opposed to the Further Extension of Suffrage to Women is included. Speakers also present evidence based on the extension of suffrage to women in Norway, Australia, and Sweden. The Rev. Anna H. Shaw closes the hearing by refuting the argument that woman suffrage has been a failure where tried.

846. U.S. Congress. House. Committee on Election of President, Vice-President and Representative in Congress of the House of Representatives. *Right of Woman to Vote for Members of the House of Representative, Hearing on the Bill (H.R. 12042, by Mr. French) to Protect the Right of Women Citizens of the United States to Register and Vote for Members of the House of Representatives.* H. Doc. 378, 58th Cong., 3d sess., 15,16 Dec. 1904. 11p. Serial 4832. House hearing on a bill to secure women the right to vote for members of the House of Representatives includes a speech on the constitutional aspects of congressional suffrage for women. Comments by Representative French of Ohio illustrates the favorable outcome of woman suffrage in that state.

847. U.S. Congress. House. Committee on the Judiciary. *Woman's Suffrage.* 58th Cong., 2d sess., 16 Feb. 1904. 22p. Y4.J89/1:W84/2. Testimony of women from the state of Colorado focuses on the use of the vote by women in that state. Playing to prejudices of the day, the issue of the enfranchisement of immigrants, the illiterate, and blacks, while white native born women are denied the vote, is stressed.

848. U.S. Congress. Senate. Committee on Woman Suffrage. *Hearing on Bill (S. 2728) to Protect the Right of Women Citizens of the United States to Register and Vote for Members of the House of Representatives.* 58th Cong., 3d sess., 17 Dec. 1904. 11p. Y4.W84:W84/5. Eloquent speech of Clara Bewick Colby on the constitutional ability of Congress to give women the vote in the election of members of the House of Representatives quotes from legislative and judicial sources on citizenship and the right of suffrage. Other speakers describe evils which would not exist if women had the ballot, and present examples of cases where Congress has enfranchised or disenfranchised classes of people.

849. U.S. Congress. Senate. Committee on Woman Suffrage. *Hearing on the Joint Resolution (S.R. 4) Proposing an Amendment to the Constitution of the United States Extending the Right of Suffrage to Women and the Bill (S. 2728) to Protect the Right of Women Citizens of the United States to Register and Vote for Members of the House of Representatives.* 58th Cong., 2d sess., 16 Feb. 1904. 40p. Y4.W84:W84/4. Eloquent speeches of woman suffrage advocates lead by Susan B. Anthony present the case for woman suffrage as a just and necessary thing. The focus is on the need for women to have a voice in the making of laws which effect them as property holders, workers and homemakers. The need to address discrimination in job opportunities and wages, and the argument that women will raise more civic minded children if they themselves are involved in public affairs, are noted in support of suffrage. Also discussed is the role of the liquor interests in defeating woman suffrage in California.

850. U.S. Congress. House. Committee on the Judiciary. *Hearings on H.J. Res. 86, Proposing an Amendment to the Constitution of the United States, Extending the Right of Suffrage to Women.* 59th Cong., 1st sess., 15 Feb. 1906. 20p. Greenwood HJ59-J. The usual arguments for woman suffrage are advanced including the growing involvement of women

in public life through reform movements and the problems in the state-by-state approach. The history and philosophy of government play a large part in the argument for women's right to vote.

851. U.S. Congress. House. Committee on the Judiciary. *Hearing on Woman Suffrage, H.J. Res. 112.* 60th Cong., 1st sess., 3 Mar. 1908. 50p. Y4.J89/1:W84/3. Testimony supporting a woman suffrage amendment paints a picture of the U.S. lagging behind other countries in the question of political rights for women. The advances of women in all aspects of American life and their participation in education and labor is noted. One argument advanced is that nearly all women are good, therefor, the women's vote would be almost entirely on the side of morality. Also raised is the issue of the immigrant vote, and objections to woman suffrage are dealt with point-by-point.

852. U.S. Congress. Senate. Select Committee on Woman Suffrage. *Hearing on Joint Resolution (S.R.47) Proposing an Amendment to the Constitution of the United States Providing that the Right of Citizens of the United States to Vote Shall Not Be Denied or Abridged by the United States or by Any State on Account of Sex.* S. Doc. 409, 60th Cong., 1st sess., 3 Mar. 1908. 24p. Serial 5269. Hearing on a woman suffrage amendment includes the usual array of speakers lead by Anna Shaw, with statements by Barbara A. Lockwood, Ida Husted Harper, Carrie Chapman Catt, and others. A common theme is the extension of woman suffrage around the world and the difficulty of achieving woman suffrage in the U.S. when approached state by state.

853. U.S. Congress. Senate. *Memorial of Mr. Vere Goldwaite.* S. Doc. 630, 60th Cong., 2d sess., 1909. 19p. Serial 5407. Extended discussion examines the constitutional issues surrounding the memorialist's proposed bill securing women's right to vote for members of the House of Representative and for presidential electors.

854. U.S. Congress. House. Committee on the Judiciary. *Woman Suffrage, Hearing on H.J. Res. 151 and H.J. Res. 153.* 61st Cong., 2d sess., 19 April 1910. 48p. Y4.J89/1:W84/4. Arguments mostly for a woman suffrage amendment to the Constitution includes the presentation of a petition signed by 404,825 people with the number of signatures broken down by occupation. The need for woman suffrage is argued from the viewpoint of homemaker and worker, and Florence Kelly testifies as to the status of protective labor laws and the need for women to have a voice in protecting themselves. Opposition witnesses state that entry into the political arena would be injurious to women and that they lack the stamina for political participation. They also contend that the women voters of Colorado were easily duped into supporting corrupt politicians. Reprinted in opposition testimony is a treatise on the effect of the entrance of mothers into the political arena, which claims that it would lead to the loss of the "finer sensibilities" and "mother feelings" and finally the decline of the race.

855. U.S. Congress. Senate. *The Right of Suffrage: Memorial of the National American Woman Suffrage Association Demanding the Recognition by Congress of the Right to Vote for the Women of the United States.* S. Doc. 519, 61st Cong., 2d sess., 1910. 2p. Serial 5659. Memorial asks that Congress insure women's right to vote by amending the fifteenth article of the Constitution and provides a concise summary of the arguments for woman suffrage.

856. U.S. Congress. Senate. Committee on Woman Suffrage. *Should Woman Have Equal Suffrage?, Statement of Hon. John F. Shafroth, Governor of Colorado on Senate Joint Resolution 81.* 61st Cong., 2d sess, 19 Apr. 1910. 8p. Greenwood Swo 61-A. Statement supporting woman suffrage considers the questions will women use the vote for the public good?, will only disreputable women vote?, will women vote at all?, and will the vote lead men to lose respect for women?

857.   U.S. Congress. Senate. Committee on Woman Suffrage. *Woman Suffrage, Hearing on Senate Joint Resolution 81.* 61st Cong., 2d sess., 19 Apr. 1910. 39p. Y4.W84:W84/6. Arguments in favor of an amendment to the constitution granting woman suffrage are presented by Anna Howard Shaw, Carrie Chapman Catt, and others. The inequalities suffered by women and the right to the opportunity to correct them through the vote is a recurring theme. Speakers representing women lawyers, teachers, physicians, college women, and writers discuss the reasons for woman suffrage. The primary argument is that an immense public good will come of giving women the vote. Also included is an essay by Governor John F. Shafroth of Colorado, "Should Women Have Equal Suffrage." Shafroth's statement was also printed separately (856).

858.   U.S. Congress. House. Committee on Judiciary. *Woman Suffrage, Hearing.* 62d Cong., 2d sess., 13 Mar. 1912. 104p. Y4.J89/1:W84/5-2. Witnesses in support of a constitutional amendment for woman suffrage, lead by Jane Addams, present the argument that the vote is necessary for women to continue effectively in philanthropic work and to protect themselves as workers. Also described at length is the effect and operation of woman suffrage in Colorado with particular reference to the major objections raised against woman suffrage. Provides a time-line showing progress world-wide in equal suffrage. Opposing arguments stress that women do not want the vote, that woman suffrage would double the ignorant vote, that woman suffrage states lag behind others in protective labor laws, and that the suffragist are primarily socialists. Also included is a compilation of quotes against woman suffrage by "eminent persons".

859.   U.S. Congress. House. Committee on Judiciary. *Woman Suffrage, Hearing, Statement of Dr. Mary E. Walker.* 62d Cong., 2d sess., 14 Feb. 1912. 14p. Y4.J89/1:W84/5-1. Statement argues that the Constitution already guarantees women the right to vote and that state laws limiting voting to males are unconstitutional.

860.   U.S. Congress. Senate. *Equal Suffrage in Colorado, Speech Delivered in the House of Representatives, Wednesday, April 24, 1912, in Consideration of Bill (H.R. 38) to Confer Legislative Authority on the Territory of Alaska.* by Edward T. Taylor. S. Doc. 722, 62d Cong., 2d sess., 1912. 55p. Serial 6178. Argument for woman suffrage is long on rhetoric and only loosely based on the Colorado experience. The basic points made are the civic good arising from the female vote and the need to protect women workers. Includes a timeline showing progress in woman suffrage from 1838 to 1911 world wide.

861.   U.S. Congress. Senate. Committee on Woman Suffrage. *Woman Suffrage, Hearing.* 62d Cong., 2d sess., 16 Feb. 1912. 12p. Y4.W84:W84/7. Speech by Mrs. James Bennett before the Committee on Woman Suffrage supporting the right of women to vote in the popular election of Senators quotes heavily from the Bible and argues that if black men have the vote, so should white women.

862.   U.S. Congress. Senate. Joint Committee of the Committee on the Judiciary and the Committee on Woman Suffrage. *Woman Suffrage, Hearings.* S. Doc. 601, 62d Cong., 2d sess., 23 Apr. 1912. 32p. Serial 6176. Testimony on an amendment ensuring woman suffrage stresses women's need for the vote to protect and improve the home, to protect their interests as workers, and to protect them from a life of prostitution. Objection to the amendment is put forward in a five page barrage of questions implying that woman suffrage is a failure and would cause more harm than good. Letters from the National Association Opposed to Woman Suffrage stress the state's right to establish suffrage qualifications and raise the specter of the foreign and black "ignorant" vote.

863.   U.S. Congress. House. Committee on Election of President, Vice President, and Representative in Congress. *Woman Suffrage, Hearings on H.R. 26950.* 62d Cong., 3d sess., 31 Jan. 1913. 63p. Y4.El2/1:W84. Hearing on a bill to extend suffrage to women

in elections for members of the House of Representatives advances the argument that women help clean up politics and promote the moral good of the nation. The constitutionality of the law and the experience of woman suffrage states is examined. Anti-suffragists argue that women wield sufficient influence through existing channels, and that politics will divide women, hampering reform efforts. The voter fraud practiced by corrupt women in Denver elections is described. The idea is also advanced that only morally and intellectual fit persons of either sex should be allowed to vote.

864.   U.S. Congress. House. Committee on Rules. *Committee on Woman Suffrage, Hearing on Resolution Establishing a Committee on Woman Suffrage.* 63d Cong., 2d sess., 3-5 Dec. 1913. 214p. Y4.R86/1:W84o. Proponents state that women have come before the House Committee on the Judiciary to present the case for woman suffrage since 1869 and that, given the lack of action by that committee, a committee on woman suffrage should be established. Witnesses include Anna Shaw, Jane Addams, Ida Husted Harper and others. Although the primary point is that the issue deserves a committee which will take the time to hear arguments and report out a resolution, some discussion naturally follows on the progress of and desire for woman suffrage. Anti-suffragist speak against woman suffrage and a special committee on the grounds that most women are opposed to woman suffrage. Also printed is an attack on feminism and the argument that woman suffrage is a failure that degrades women. In rebuttal the proponents submitted figures on the extent of suffrage organizations, a compilation of quotes from "eminent persons" supporting woman suffrage, and a rebuttal to the assertion that suffrage would hurt the protective labor laws movement.

865.   U.S. Congress. Senate. *Interference with the Suffrage Procession: Letter from the President of Board of Commissioners of the District of Columbia, Transmitting Copies of the Official Orders and a Statement by the Superintendent of Police Relating to the Interference with the Suffrage Procession in Washington, D.C., on March 3, 1913.* S. Doc. 1, 63d Cong., special sess., 1913. 20p. Serial 6507. Reprint of official correspondence relating to the efforts of the District police department to prevent interference with the March 3, 1913 suffrage parade. Orders relating to the parade are printed along with a brief account of the action taken that day.

866.   U.S. Congress. Senate. *Woman Suffrage, Address Opposing an Amendment of the United States Extending the Right of Suffrage to Women.* by Annie Bock. S. Doc. 160, 63d Cong., 1st sess., 1913. 10p. Serial 6536. Statement details why woman suffrage is a failure in California and why, as a former suffrage supporter, Bock works against the further extension of woman suffrage. Bock also describes a link between woman suffrage, socialism, and anarchy.

867.   U.S. Congress. Senate. *Woman Suffrage Amendment: Proceeding in the United States Senate, July 31, 1913, upon the Presentation of Petitions Favoring the Adoption of S.J. Res. No. 1, "A Resolution proposing an amendment to the Constitution of the United States extending the right of suffrage to Women," Together with the Report of the Senate Committee on Woman Suffrage Recommending Its Passage.* S. Doc. 155, 63d Cong., 1st sess., 1913. 46p. Serial 6536. Reprints S. Rept. 64 (872) and portions of the *Congressional Record* on S.J. Res. 1. Many of the statements made by Senators discuss the function of woman suffrage in the states of Oregon, Utah, Colorado and California and summarize arguments refuting opposition claims.

868.   U.S. Congress. Senate. *Woman Suffrage: Reports and Hearings Relative to Joint Resolutions Proposing Amendments to the Constitution of the United States Providing that the Right of Citizens of the Citizens of the United States to Vote Shall Not Be Denied or Abridged by the United States or by Any State on Account of Sex.* S. Doc. 1035, 62d Cong., 3d sess., 1913. 100p. Serial 6365. Reprints S. Rept. 686, 47th Congress (810);

S. Rept. 399 (816) and H. Rept. 1330, 48th Congress (814); S. Rept. 1143 and views of the minority, 52d Congress (833); and the hearing before a Joint Committee of the Committee on the Judiciary and the Committee of Woman Suffrage of the Senate on "Woman Suffrage", S. Doc. 601, 62d Congress (862).

869.   U.S. Congress. Senate. Committee on the District of Columbia. *Report Pursuant to S. Res. 499, of March 4, 1913, Directing Said Committee to Investigate the Conduct of the District Police and Police Department of the District of Columbia in Connection with Woman's Suffrage Parade on March 3, 1913, with Hearings and List of Witnesses.* S. Rept. 53, 63d Cong., 1st. sess., 29 May 1913. 79p. Serial 6512. Committee report precedes the hearings and summarizes the information provided by police, spectators and parade participant witnesses. The opinion of the committee was that some police officers did little to control the crowd, but that the Police Department acted properly and the problem was with individual officers. The congressional resolution was also faulted for not designating that the streets be cleared earlier in advance of the parade.

870.   U.S. Congress. Senate. Committee on the District of Columbia. Subcommittee Conducting Investigation under S. Res. 499. *Suffrage Parade, Hearing under S. Res. 499, on March 4, 1913, Directing Said Committee to Investigate the Conduct of the District Police and Police Department of the District of Columbia in Connection with the Women's Suffrage Parade on March 3, 1913, Part 1.* 63rd Cong., 1st and Special sess., 6 Mar. - 17 Apr. 1913. 749p. Y4.D63/2:W84/1. Hearing investigates the woman suffrage parade of the 3rd of March to determine if the police made adequate preparations and took appropriate action to control the crowds. Testimony generally indicated that the police did little to control the crowds and in some cases encouraged the jeering. Numerous photographs of the parade are included in the hearing record. Testimony is taken from onlookers, parade participants, and police officers and officials as to the actions of the crowds and police that day.

871.   U.S. Congress. Senate. Committee on Woman Suffrage. *Woman Suffrage, Hearings on S. J. Res. 1.* 63rd Cong., 1st sess., 19 - 26 Apr. 1913. 97p. Y4.W84:W84/9. Hearing begins with the arguments of those opposed to a woman suffrage amendment lead by Mrs. Arthur M. Dodge. Basic arguments focus on women's higher purpose, state rights, the increase in the black and Asian vote, the mental strain of politics, women's lack of desire for the vote, the advances in the education of women and protection of women workers achieved without the vote, and the socialist and anti-home and family views of suffragists. Testimony in favor of the amendment discusses women's effect in suffrage states and addresses the charge of socialism and militancy. Proponents charge that women already influence all aspects of the life of the country and that they should have the vote so as to better educate their children to be citizens. The most common argument, however, is that women are citizens and should have the vote on purely democratic principles.

872.   U.S. Congress. Senate. Committee on Woman Suffrage. *Woman Suffrage, Report to Accompany S.J. Res. 1.* S. Rept. 64, 63d Cong., 1st sess., 1913. 8p. Serial 6510. Reports S.J. Res. 1, a woman suffrage amendment to the Constitution, citing the change in social conditions in the U.S. as the impetuous for such an amendment. Also included in the report is a chronology of gains in equal suffrage world wide from 1838 to 1913. Reprints S. Doc. 519, 61st Congress (855), a memorial of the National American Woman Suffrage Association.

873.   U.S. Congress. House. Committee on Election of President, Vice President, and Representative in Congress. *Woman Suffrage, Hearings on H.R. 9393.* 63d Cong., 3d sess., 17 Dec. 1914. 35p. Y4.El2/1:W84/2. Argument for a bill to provide women the right to vote in the election of Members of Congress notes the absence of anything in the Constitution to prevent the law and its potential as a safe test of woman suffrage. A

history of women's acknowledged right to vote in England and early America is presented as is the Supreme Courts' record on the question of citizenship and voting rights. Particular attention is paid to the case of *Minor v. Happersett* and to discussions of constitutional intent.

874. U.S. Congress. House. Committee on the Judiciary. *Woman Suffrage, Hearing.* 63d Cong., 2d sess., 3 Mar. 1914. 109p. Y4.J89/1:W84/7. Testimony in support of several woman suffrage resolutions, lead by the Federal Women's Equality Association and the National Woman Suffrage Association, addresses arguments of states rights, voter apathy among women in the suffrage states, family discord on account of differing political beliefs, and gender differences in voting. A history of congressional action on the woman suffrage question is part of the testimony. There is also talk in the hearing about holding the party in power responsible if the suffrage amendment is not favorably reported. Opposition testimony focuses on the argument that women do not want the vote but also raises the specter of an increased foreign vote and a rather bizarre argument that woman suffrage might lead to policies which would "plunge this country into war". Witnesses also warn that women are not knowledgeable of the world outside the home and that to become so they must neglect the home. Statement against feminism analyzes speeches and writing to show that feminism is anti-motherhood and would strip women of all privileges to economic support by men.

875. U.S. Congress. House. Committee on the Judiciary. *Woman Suffrage, Report to Accompany H.J. Res. 1.* H. Rept. 653, 63d Cong., 2d sess., 1914. 1p. Serial 6559. Report without recommendations on a woman suffrage amendment.

876. U.S. Congress. Senate. *Woman Suffrage, Address Written by a Committee of Women of Southern California for Presentation to the Committee of Woman Suffrage of the United States Senate in Favor of an Amendment to the Constitution of the United States Extending the Right of Suffrage to Women.* S. Doc. 488, 63d Cong., 2d sess., 1914. 22p. Serial 6594. Statement on the operation of woman suffrage in California provides information, by city, on voter registration and turnout by gender, place of voting, votes on social issues, and the role of women's organizations in educating women in public affairs. Also list laws of interest to women passed by the 1913 California State Legislature and provides excerpts from comments of leading citizens on the operation of woman suffrage in California.

877. U.S. Congress. Senate. Committee on the Judiciary. *Woman Suffrage: Views of the Minority of the Committee of the Judiciary, House of Representatives, 48th Congress, 1st Session, as Submitted by Hon. Thomas B. Reed.* S. Doc. 497, 63d Cong., 2d sess., 1914. 6p. Serial 6594. Excerpt from H. Rept. 48-1330 (814) supports woman suffrage.

878. U.S. Congress. Senate. Committee on Woman Suffrage. *Woman Suffrage, Report to Accompany S.J. Res. 128.* S. Rept. 468, 63d Cong., 2d sess., 1914. 3p. Serial 6552. Reports a resolution on a constitutional amendment requiring states, upon the petition of 8 percent of the legal voters, to hold an election on woman suffrage and declaring a simple majority of the vote as sufficient for passage. The purpose of the amendment was to bypass the provision of state constitutions which placed insurmountable barriers to the adoption of woman suffrage.

879. U.S. Congress. Senate. Committee on Woman Suffrage. *Woman Suffrage, Hearings on S. J. Res. 1 and S. J. Res. 2.* 64th Cong., 1st sess., 15-20 Dec. 1915. 75p. Y4.W84:W84/10. Hearing primarily of those in support of the amendment is lead by Anna Howard Shaw of the National Association for Woman Suffrage. The first witnesses focus on the conditions in Southern states, the appropriateness of the constitutional amendment approach, and the "negro vote" argument of opponents. The case of Ohio and Michigan, often touted by anti-suffragists as proof that the movement was losing

momentum, is examined. The history of the elective franchise is reviewed. Witnesses also argue that women need the vote to conduct the traditional business of being a woman and that with war approaching the energy of women would be needed elsewhere and therefore the question must be settled. Opponents argue states rights and attribute the passage of state woman suffrage to the influence of Mormonism, socialism, populism, and insurgency. They also argue that women will accomplish more by remaining nonpartisan and that women don't want the vote, citing the defeat of woman suffrage in a Massachusetts special election.

880.   U.S. Congress. House. Committee on Election of President, Vice President, and Representative in Congress. *Woman Suffrage, Hearings on H.R. 379.* 64th Cong., 1st sess., 27-28 Mar. 1916. 30p. Y4.El2/1:W84/3. Hearing on a bill to ensure women equal suffrage in the election of members of Congress presents arguments concerning congressional authority to pass such a law. Voter apathy among women in suffrage states is the primary argument of opponents, while the supporters argue that women have always been citizens and are entitled to vote. An analysis of revellent court cases is presented.

881.   U.S. Congress. House. Committee on Judiciary. *Woman Suffrage, Hearings.* 64th Cong., 1st sess., 16 Dec. 1915, 1 Feb. 1916. 141p. Y4.J89/1:W84/8. Arguments for a woman suffrage amendment are made by Anna Howard Shaw, Carrie Chapman Catt, Alice Stone Blackwell, and Alice Paul. Arguments highlight the woman suffrage movement and the difficulties in amending some state constitutions. Much of the talk is of liquor interests campaigning against woman suffrage. Alice Paul's testimony is marked by discussion of the Congressional Union's past efforts to unseat political candidates opposing woman suffrage. Opposition is based on states rights with a general consensus that women should not be involved in politics, can do more good without the vote, and have better protective laws in non-suffrage states. One man speaking for the opposition cites the deleterious effects on womanhood as already evidenced by women out marching and speaking on street corners.

882.   U.S. Congress. House. Committee on the Judiciary. *Woman Suffrage, Hearings.* 64th Cong., 1st sess., 1 June 1916. 143-166p. Y4.J89/1:W84/9. Statements of support by members of the House on the "Susan B. Anthony amendment" urge that woman suffrage be brought to a vote.

883.   U.S. Congress. House. Committee on the Judiciary. *Woman Suffrage, Report to Accompany H.J. Res. 1.* H. Rept. 1216, 64th Cong., 2d sess., 1916. 1p. Serial 7110. Reports the woman suffrage amendment without recommendation.

884.   U.S. Congress. Senate. *Woman Suffrage, Argument Submitted by the National Antisuffrage Association in Opposition to the Adoption of the So Called Susan B. Anthony Proposed Amendment to the Constitution of the United States Extending the Right to Suffrage to Women.* S. Doc. 408, 64th Cong., 1st sess., 1916. 27p. Serial 6952. Basic arguments raised in opposition to woman suffrage assert that only a minority want it, that women cannot enforce the law, that women's work is in a different sphere, that woman suffrage is socialistic, feministic, and anti-family, and that it is based on gender antagonism.

885.   U.S. Congress. Senate. Committee on Woman Suffrage. *Woman Suffrage, Report to Accompany S.J. Res. 1.* S. Rept. 35, 64th Cong., 1st sess., 1916. 5p. Serial 6897. Passage of S.J. Res. 1, the woman suffrage amendment, is recommended based on the doctrine of popular sovereignty and on the fitness of women to wield the ballot as evidenced by the role of women in WWI society. The argument that state woman suffrage did not result in great social advances is rejected as invalid criteria for the enfranchisement of any group.

886. U.S. Congress. House. Committee on Rules. *Amendment to Rules, Report to Accompany H. Res. 12.* H. Rept. 163, 65th Cong., 1st sess., 1917. 1p. Serial 7254. Recommends passage of a resolution creating the Committee on Woman Suffrage.

887. U.S. Congress. House. Committee on Rules. *Creating a Committee on Woman Suffrage in the House of Representatives, Hearing on H. Res. 12.* 65th Cong., 1st sess., 18 May 1917. 214p. Y4.R86/1:W84. Generally brief statements describe why a committee on woman suffrage should be established to conduct hearings on the issue of federal action toward woman suffrage.

888. U.S. Congress. House. Committee on the Judiciary. *Woman Suffrage, Hearings.* 65th Cong., 1st sess., 15 May 1917. 167-239pp. Y4.J89/1:W84/10. Statements for and against woman suffrage feature representatives of the National Woman's Party presenting the supporting arguments. In this hearing woman suffrage is presented as a necessary war measure. The argument that it is costly to grant suffrage state-by-state and to prolong the passage of a federal amendment is presented. One witness is questioned closely on the use of militant tactics to attain suffrage, and the electoral clout of women is also discussed. Also discusses the question of whether women will be more patriotic and more willing to work for the war effort if granted suffrage. An attempt is made to draw a connection between prohibition and woman suffrage. Opponents state that women do not want the vote and that the suffragists do not believe in democracy.

889. U.S. Congress. House. Committee on the Judiciary. *Woman Suffrage, Report to Accompany H.J. Res. 1.* H. Rept. 219, 65th Cong., 2d sess., 1917. 1p. Serial 7307. Report recommends an addition to the proposed woman suffrage amendment providing for a seven year time limit for ratification.

890. U.S. Congress. Senate. *Woman Suffrage, an Article on the Biological and Sociological Aspects of the Woman Question.* by Mrs. Annie Riley Hale. S. Doc. 692, 64th Cong., 2d sess., 1917. Serial 7125. Argument against the feminist conception of women's development and role in society links greater differentiation between the sexes to a higher degree of civilization. The primary argument defines women's role as the physical and moral improvement of the race and warns that feminism will lead to racial degradation. The article also speaks of the "outpost of feminism" lurking behind the drive for woman suffrage.

891. U.S. Congress. Senate. Committee on Pacific Islands and Puerto Rico. *Woman Suffrage in Hawaii, Report to Accompany S. 2380.* S. Rept. 108, 65th Cong., 1st sess., 1917. 3p. Serial 7249. Report favors a bill granting the legislature of the Territory of Hawaii the power to provide women with the vote. Women's role in wartime society is advanced in support of woman suffrage, noting the response of the women of England and Russia to the crisis.

892. U.S. Congress. Senate. Committee on Woman Suffrage. *Woman Suffrage, Hearing on S.J. Res. 2.* 65th Cong., 1st sess., 20 Apr. - 15 May 1917. 97p. Y4.W84:W84/12. Carrie Chapman Catt organized the first day of testimony on behalf of the National Woman's Suffrage Association supporting a constitutional amendment on woman suffrage. Chapter VI of Catt's *Woman Suffrage by Federal Constitutional Amendment* is reprinted providing a point-by-point analysis of the major objections advanced by opponents of woman suffrage. Representative Jeannette Rankin described the features of state constitutions which make passage of state amendments difficult. The major points addressed by witnesses are concerns over massive voting by "bad" women and the argument that women don't want the burden of the vote. The second day of testimony was presented by representatives of the National Woman's Party. Witnesses describe women's contributions to America in past times of war and the inevitability of federal woman

suffrage. The contributions and labor conditions of women workers are also advanced as reasons for woman suffrage. The third day of testimony covers opposing arguments and includes an attack on Catt's previously mentioned work as mean spirited and dishonest and rebuts the assertion of dishonesty in state suffrage elections.

893.   U.S. Congress. Senate. Committee on Woman Suffrage. *Woman Suffrage: Report to Accompany S.J. Res. 2.* S. Rept. 130, 65th Cong., 1st sess., 1917. 1p. Serial 7249.

894.   U.S. Congress. House. Committee on Rules. *Constitutionality of Vote Adopting Prohibition and Suffrage Amendments, Hearing on H. Res. 254.* 65th Cong., 2d sess., 4 Mar. 1918. 9p. Y4.R86/1:C76/2. Very brief hearing consists mostly of submitted documents questioning the validity of votes in the House on the prohibition and suffrage amendments. The point of contention was that only two thirds of the members present voted for the amendments, not two thirds of the House of Representatives.

895.   U.S. Congress. House. Committee on Woman Suffrage. *Extending the Right of Suffrage to Women, Hearings on H.J. Res. 200.* 65th Cong., 2d sess., 3-7 Jan. 1918. 330p. Y4.W84:W84/13. Representatives from the National American Woman Suffrage Association and the National Women's Party state the case for the woman suffrage amendment while the National Association Opposed to Woman Suffrage leads the opposition. Both sides discuss the effect of the women's vote, whether women want the vote, the issue of the "colored women's vote" and the "foreign vote", the proper method of achieving woman suffrage, and the "feminization" of the country.

896.   U.S. Congress. House. Committee on Woman Suffrage. *Woman Suffrage in Hawaii, Hearings on S. 2380 and H.R. 4665.* 65th Cong., 2d sess., 29 Apr. 1918. 12p. Y4.W84:H31. Hearing considers a bill to give the legislature of Hawaii the right to decide the question of woman suffrage in Hawaii. Testimony reveals that woman suffrage has already been accepted in Hawaii, and that the territory is only awaiting congressional action.

897.   U.S. Congress. House. Committee on Woman Suffrage. *Woman Suffrage in Hawaii, Report to Accompany S. 2380.* H. Rept. 536, 65th Cong., 2d sess., 1918. 4p. Serial 7307. Favorable report on a bill giving the legislature of Hawaii the authority to decide the woman suffrage question in Hawaii quotes heavily from the hearing and particularly notes that the Hawaiian legislature instigated the bill.

898.   U.S. Congress. House. Committee on Woman Suffrage. *Woman Suffrage, Minority Views to Accompany H.J. Res. 200.* H. Rept. 234, part 2, 65th Cong., 2d sess., 1918. 3p. Serial 7307. Argument against a woman suffrage amendment is based on the state's right to confer suffrage. Provides quotes from past and present political leaders on the extension of suffrage and the federal amendment approach.

899.   U.S. Congress. House. Committee on Woman Suffrage. *Woman Suffrage, Report to Accompany H.J. Res. 200.* H. Rept. 234, 65th Cong., 2d sess., 1918. 6p. Serial 7307. Favorable report on the woman suffrage amendment charts the progress of woman suffrage in the U.S. and abroad and prints excerpts of the communiques from governors of several states supporting the federal amendment.

900.   U.S. Congress. Senate. *Equal Suffrage, Address of the President of the United States Delivered in the Senate of the United States on September 30, 1918.* by Woodrow Wilson. S. Doc. 284, 65th Cong., 2d sess., 1918. 4p. Serial 7330. Supportive speech for the woman suffrage amendment stresses a speedy and favorable conclusion as necessary to the winning of the war. The basic gist of the speech is that the U.S., the great Democracy,

must set the example for the war torn world and that the moral sense of women will be needed to address the problems after the war.

901. U.S. Congress. House. Committee on Woman Suffrage. *Woman Suffrage, Report to Accompany H.J. Res. No. 1.* H. Rept. 1, 66th Cong., 2d sess., 1919. 1p. Serial 7592.

902. U.S. Congress. House. Committee on Woman Suffrage. *Woman Suffrage, Report to Accompany H.J. Res. 440.* H. Rept. 1167, 65th Cong., 3d sess., 1919. 1p. Serial 7455.

903. U.S. Congress. House. Committee on Woman Suffrage. *Woman Suffrage, Report to Accompany H.R. 14604.* H. Rept. 1160, 65th Cong., 3d sess., 1919. 1p. Serial 7455. Favorable report on a bill to protect women's right to vote for congressmen.

904. U.S. Congress. Senate. Committee on the District of Columbia. *Protestant Episcopal Church in the District of Columbia, Report to Accompany H.R. 5032.* S. Rept. 60, 66th Cong., 1st sess., 1919. 1p. Serial 7590. Due to the fact that the right to vote in parish meetings in the Protestant Episcopal Church in the District of Columbia was governed by an act of the Legislative Assembly of D.C., the bill reported was necessary to give women the right to vote in parish meetings.

905. U.S. Congress. House. Committee on the Territories. *Qualifying Women for Delegate from Hawaii to the House of Representatives, Report to Accompany H.R. 11590.* H. Rept. 1082, 67th Cong., 2d sess., 1922. 2p. Serial 7957. Reports a bill to amend a provision of the Organic Act of Hawaii limited eligibility for election to the territorial legislature to male citizens and hence limited eligibility for election as delegates to Congress to male citizens.

906. U.S. Congress. Senate. Committee on Territories and Insular Possessions. *Amending Organic Act of Territory of Hawaii, Report to Accompany H.R. 11590.* S. Rept. 807, 67th Cong., 2d sess., 1922. 2p. Serial 7951. See 905 for abstract.

907. U.S. Congress. House. Committee on Insular Affairs. *Confer the Right to Vote to Women of Puerto Rico, Report to Accompany H.R. 7010.* H. Rept. 1895, 70th Cong., 1st sess., 1928. 1p. Serial 8838. Reports a bill to amend the Organic Act of Puerto Rico so as to prohibit gender discrimination in the right to vote.

908. U.S. Congress. Senate. Committee on Territories and Insular Possessions. *Woman Suffrage in Puerto Rico, Hearing on S. 753.* 70th Cong., 1st sess., 25 Apr. 1928. 28p. Y4.T27/2:P83/4. Hearing presents arguments for and against a bill prohibiting discrimination based on gender in the right to vote in Puerto Rico. Opponents primarily use the self-government argument and witnesses accuse the National Women's Party of using blackmail to achieve passage of "feminist" legislation.

909. U.S. Congress. Senate. Committee on Territories and Insular Possessions. *Conferring the Right to Vote upon Puerto Rican Women, Report to Accompany H.R. 7010.* S. Rept. 1454, 70th Cong., 2d sess., 1929. 2p. Serial 8977. Report on a bill to amend the Organic Act of Puerto Rico in order to grant women the right to vote includes minority views opposing the bill as unnecessary interference with local self-government.

910. U.S. Office of Education. *Gallant American Women #6, Women are People, December 5, 1939.* by Jane Ashman. Washington, DC: The Office, 1939. 23p. FS5.15:6. The fight for woman suffrage and the women who led the battle are highlighted in the sixth "Gallant American Women" radio broadcast.

911.   U.S. Office of Education. *Gallant American Women #29, Women in Politics and Government, May 20, 1940.* Washington, DC: The Office, 1940. 27p. FS5.15:29. The fight for woman suffrage and the growing presence of women in government positions are revealed in the vignettes of this episode of the "Gallant American Women" radio series. Women's role in local government is also described, stressing the morality angle.

912.   U.S. Congress. House. Committee on the Judiciary. *Women's Enfranchisement Day, Report to Accompany H.J. Res. 255.* H. Rept. 1139, 79th Cong., 1st sess., 1945. 1p. Serial 10935.

913.   U.S. Dept. of State. Office of Intelligence Research. Interim Research and Intelligence Service. *Implications of Woman Suffrage in Japan.* OIR Report Series IV no. 3289. Washington, DC: The Office, 1945. 4p. S1.57:3289. Classified report analyzes postwar women's organizations in Japan, their potential for political activity, and the political influence of their leaders in relation to potential woman suffrage.

914.   U.S. Library of Congress. Legislative Reference Service. *Women in Congress of United States [with a List of Sources].* by George L. Kackley. Washington, DC: The Service, 1945. 15p. LC14.2W84. History of women in Congress provides basic information on date elected or appointed and provides a chronological list of women serving in Congress.

915.   U.S. Women's Bureau. *Replies to the ECOSOC Questionnaire on the Legal Status and Treatment of Women, Part I, Public Law, Sections A and B: Franchise and Public Office.* Washington, DC: The Bureau, 1947. 23p. L13.2:Ec7/pt.1/sec.A,B. Summarizes, in response to the UN Economic and Social Council questionnaire, state and federal laws guaranteeing equality of women with men, the right to vote, qualifications to vote, marriage and the right to vote, and eligibility to hold public office. Relevant court cases and provisions of state constitutions and codes are cited.

916.   U.S. Women's Bureau. *Women Serving in 1949 State Legislatures.* Washington, DC: The Bureau, 1949. 6p. L13.2:W84/25. Lists women serving in state legislatures by state, body, and party affiliation.

917.   U.S. Women's Bureau. *Women Serving in 1951 State Legislatures.* Washington, DC: The Bureau, 1951. 6p. L13.2:L52. See 916 for abstract.

918.   U.S. Women's Bureau. *Woman Suffrage among the Nations.* Washington, DC: The Bureau, 1952. 9p. L13.2:Su2/952. Brief description of the history and extent of the voting rights of women around the world. Earlier edition published in 1950.

919.   U.S. Women's Bureau. *Political Status of Women in the Other American Republics, February 1958: Notes for Reference.* Washington, DC: The Bureau, 1958. 18p. L13.2:P75/958. Concise summary of women's political participation in American Republics other than the U.S. covers topics such as the right to vote and to hold political office and past history of election and appointment of women to government positions. Countries included are Argentina, Bolivia, Brazil, Chile, Columbia, Costa Rica, Cuba, Dominican Republic, Ecuador, El Salvador, Guatemala, Haiti, Honduras, Mexico, Nicaragua, Panama, Paraguay, Peru, Uruguay, and Venezuela. Earlier edition published in 1957.

920.   U.S. Women's Bureau. *Women in State Governments as Secretaries of State and Members of State Legislatures, June 1961.* Washington, DC: The Bureau, 1961. 12p. L13.2:G74/2.

921.   U.S. Women's Bureau. *Political Rights of Women in Member Nations of the United Nations.* Washington, DC: The Bureau, 1962. 19p. L13.2:P75/3. Country summaries

provide a chronology of the extension of political rights to women in member nations of the United Nations.

922. U.S. Women's Bureau. *Political Rights of Women in Member Nations of the United Nations.* Women in the World Today International Report no. 2. Washington, DC: GPO, 1963. 19p. L13.23:2. Information from United Nations Report no. A/5456, *Constitution, Electoral Laws and Other Legal Instruments Relating to the Political Rights of Women,* presented in summary form, includes lists of countries by extent of women's voting rights. The history of women's voting rights in each country is summarized.

923. U.S. Women's Bureau. *Women in High-Level Elective and Appointive Positions in National Government.* Women in the World Today International Report no. 1. Washington, DC: GPO, 1963. 18p. L13.23:1. Charts provide information by country on the number of women in legislatures and lists titles of women in high-level positions.

924. U.S. Women's Bureau. *Progress of Women around the World, Recent Notes.* Washington, DC: The Bureau, 1965. 3p. L13.2:P94/4/965. Notes advances in the political rights of women in other countries.

925. U.S. Library of Congress. *Sources for Songs of the Woman's Suffrage Movement.* Washington, DC: The Library, 1969. 1p. LC1.12/2:Su3.

926. U.S. Post Office Department. *6-cent Woman Suffrage Commemorative Postage Stamp Will Be First Put on Sale on August 26, 1970 at Adams, Massachusetts.* Washington, DC: GPO, 1970. poster. P1.26/2:W84/4.

927. U.S. Congress. Joint Committee on Arrangements for the Commemoration of the Bicentennial. *Women in Congress 1917-1976.* Washington, DC: GPO, 1976. 112p. Y4.B47:W84. Highlights of the political careers of women serving in Congress from 1917 to 1976 includes portraits.

928. U.S. National Commission on the Observance of International Women's Year. *Women in Elective and Appointive Office: A Workshop Guide.* Washington, DC: GPO, 1977. 37p. Y3.W84:10/18. Guide to conducting a workshop on women in public office includes a fact sheet with national data and a resource lists of publications, films, and speakers.

929. U.S. Dept. of Housing and Urban Development. Office of Policy Development and Research. *Women in Public Service, toward Agenda Setting.* by Diane Rothbard Margolis, Center for the American Woman and Politics. Washington, DC: GPO, 1980. 108p. HH1.2:W84/9/v.2. Volume II reports on the Center for the American Woman in Politics' study of women's groups in politics and government. Various organizations of women public officials across the country are identified and their goals and agendas are examined. The establishment of these organizations, their structures, their relationship to parent organizations, and their reasons for forming their program activities are also discussed.

930. U.S. Dept. of Housing and Urban Development. Office of Policy Development and Research. *Women in Public Service, Volume III: Changing the Opportunity Structure for Women in the Public Sector.* by Center for the American Woman and Politics. Washington, DC: GPO, 1980. 90p. HH1.2:W84/9/v.3. Presents 33 program options, based on the first two volumes, designed to increase the number of women in government and to increase their effectiveness. Programs cover changing stereotypes, recruiting, skills development, networking and mentoring, and areas of further research.

931.   U.S. Library of Congress. Manuscript Division. *The Blackwell Family, Carrie Chapman Catt, and the National American Woman Suffrage Association: A Register of Their Papers in the Library of Congress.* rev. ed. Washington, DC: The Division, 1985. 121p. LC4.10:44. Register lists the papers, correspondence and other materials located in the Manuscript Division of the Library of Congress on the Blackwell family, Carrie Chapman Catt, and the National American Woman Suffrage Association. Blackwell family members represented in the collection are Alice Stone Blackwell, Elizabeth Blackwell, Henry Blackwell, and Lucy Stone.

SERIALS

932.   U.S. Government Printing Office. *Documents and Debates Relating to Initiative, Referendum, Lynching, Elections, Prohibition, Woman Suffrage, Political Parties, District of Columbia, List of Publications for Sale by Superintendent of Documents.* Price List 54. Washington, DC: GPO, 1924-1931. 10th - 17th editions. GP3.9:54.

933.   U.S. Women's Bureau. *Women in the ... Congress.* Washington, DC: The Bureau, 80th - 89th Congresses, 1947 - 1965. biennial. L13.2:W84/22/year (80th -84th), L13.20:year (85th - 89th). Biographical sketches of women serving in Congress.

6

Citizenship and Immigration

Congressional hearings and reports document the slow evolution of the independent citizenship of married women. Women's citizenship was first considered as a separate issue at a 1912 hearing on the situation of native-born American women who remained in the United States after marriage to an alien (936). At issue was the right of the women in suffrage states to vote in the period between the marriage and the husband's naturalization, since the woman's citizenship followed that of her husband under the Citizenship Act of March 2, 1907. In 1914 a bill was considered for the repatriation of women married to aliens and living abroad upon termination of the marriage (939).

The first extensive hearing on the citizenship of married women was held in 1917. At the hearing supporters cited the injustices under the existing law, but lawmakers expressed more concern over the possible conflict with the laws of other nations (944). In 1922 a compromise bill on the independent citizenship of married women, the Cable Act, was passed (950, 951) and the next twenty years saw constant amendment of the act to correct technical problems. Many of the problems were the result of the highly restrictive immigration quotas set by the Immigration Act of 1924. Since the Cable Act required the women to establish residence in the United States prior to repatriation, the immigration quotas created an insurmountable barrier to native-born women married to aliens prior to the Cable Act but who wished to resume citizenship (955, 962, 965).

The question of women married to ineligible aliens, i.e. Asians, but who continued to reside in the U.S. was also considered (957, 961, 967). Another area of discrimination against women married to aliens was in the exemption of alien husbands from immigration quotas. A hearing on establishing equality in this area reflects concern over the possibility of a "marriage mill" to circumvent immigration laws (967, 973). A number of technical problems regarding native-born Hawaiian women married to aliens prior to the Cable Act also resulted in a steady stream of bills between 1932 and 1940. Gender equity in the ability to transmit citizenship to children born abroad was considered in earnest beginning in 1930 (967, 969, 975-976, 978). A detailed history of the citizenship status of women in the U.S. to 1933 is included in the hearing *American Citizenship Rights of Women* (977). An overview of the effect of marriage on nationality world wide as of 1928 is provided in *Effect of Marriage Upon Nationality, Hearing* (959), a statement by Emma Wold of the National Woman's Party.

934. U.S. Congress. House. Committee on Immigration and Naturalization. *Naturalization of Wives of Insane Aliens, Report to Accompany S. 9443*. H. Rept. 2149, 61st Cong., 3d sess., 1911. 2p. Serial 5848. Favorable report on a bill to provide for the naturalization of the wife of an alien who became insane prior to naturalization. The bill allows the wife

to take out a homestead and be naturalized without any declaration of intent. The letter from District Court Judge Page Morris explaining the need for the bill is included.

935.   U.S. Congress. Senate. Committee on Immigration. *Amending Laws Relating to Bureau of Immigration and Naturalization, Report to Accompany S. 9443.* S. Rept. 1056, 61st Cong., 3d sess., 1911. 1p. Serial 5840. Reports, with amendment, a bill for the naturalization of the wife and minor children of an alien who becomes insane before being naturalized.

936.   U.S. Congress. House. Committee on Foreign Affairs. *Relating to Expatriation of Citizens, Hearing.* 62d Cong., 2d sess., 14 April 1912. 26p. Y4.F76/1:C49. Hearing considers the issue of suffrage in the case of a woman married to an alien while continuing to reside in the U.S., notably the case of American-born women in suffrage states who lost the right to vote for several years while their husbands waited to be naturalized. Amendment to the immigration and naturalization laws was sought to relieve the situation of these women. The question of a married woman's citizenship is also discussed in testimony.

937.   U.S. Dept. of the Interior. General Land Office. *Citizenship of Married Women [Circular to] to Registers and Receivers.* Circular no. 44. Washington, DC: The Office, 1912. 1p. I 21.4:44. Circular to registers calls their attention to the fact that under the act of March 2, 1907 the wife's citizenship follows that of her husband. Registers are reminded to ascertain the date of a woman's marriage and proof of husband's citizenship if married after passage of the act.

938.   U.S. Congress. House. *Certificate of Title to Homestead Entry by a Female American Citizen Who Has Intermarried with an Alien, Conference Report to Accompany H.R. 11745.* H. Rept. 1172, 63d Cong., 2d sess., 1914. 1p. Serial 6560.

939.   U.S. Congress. House. Committee on Foreign Affairs. *Expatriation of Citizens and Their Protection Abroad, Report to Accompany H.R. 1991.* H. Rept. 771, 63d Cong., 2d sess., 1914. 4p. Serial 6559. Reports a bill allowing American women who marry aliens and who leave the U.S. to resume their citizenship upon the termination of the marriage. Appended correspondence reviews the existing interpretation of the law.

940.   U.S. Congress. House. Committee on the Public Lands. *Marriage of Homestead Entrywoman with an Alien, Report to Accompany H.R. 11745.* H. Rept. 665, 63d Cong., 2d sess., 1914. 2p. Serial 6559. See 941 for abstract.

941.   U.S. Congress. Senate. Committee on Public Lands. *Marriage of Homestead Entrywoman with an Alien, Report to Accompany H.R. 11745.* S. Rept. 679, 63d Cong., 2d sess., 1914. 1p. Serial 6553. Reports a bill allowing a homestead entrywoman to retain title to the entry upon her marriage to an alien so long as her husband is eligible for citizenship.

942.   U.S. Congress. House. Committee on Immigration and Naturalization. *Restriction of Immigration, Hearing on H.R. 558, Statements of Miss Grace Abbott, Clarence N. Goodwin, James A. Gallivan, Stephen Oswsky, John Kulamer, John F. Smulski, Louis E. Levy.* 64th Cong., 1st sess., 20, 21 Jan. 1916. 33p. Y4.Im6/1:Im6/8-3. Testimony relating to the proposed literacy test as a means of restricting immigration features Grace Abbott, of Hull House and the Immigrants' Protective League of Chicago, speaking on the education of women and the resultant exclusionary effect of a literacy test on women.

943.   U.S. Dept. of State. *Registration of Widows and Divorced Women.* Washington, DC: The Department, 1916. 2p. S1.4/2:475. Memo to diplomatic and consular officers reminds them of the provisions of the Citizenship Act of March 2, 1907 and urges them to make

certain that 1) divorced wives and widows of American citizens residing abroad are aware that they must register with an American consulate within one year of termination of the marital relation, if they wish to retain their American citizenship, and 2) that American born widows and divorced wives of aliens know that they must register with an American consulate within one year after termination of marital relation in order to reserve their American citizenship.

944. U.S. Congress. House. Committee on Immigration and Naturalization. *Relative to Citizenship of American Women Married to Foreigners, Hearings.* 65th Cong., 2d sess., 13 Dec. 1917. 58p. Y4.Im6/1:C49. Hearing considers a bill introduced by Representative Jeanette Rankin to provide for a woman to retain her citizenship upon marriage to an alien unless she formally renounces her citizenship. Injustices, both general and specific cases, under the existing system are highlighted. The Committee's primary concern is the apparent conflict with the laws of others countries.

945. U.S. Congress. House. Committee on the Judiciary. *To Amend Section 4067, Revised Statutes, Report to Accompany H.R. 9504.* H. Rept. 285, 65th Cong., 2d sess., 1918. 2p. Serial 7307. Reports a bill to extend the "alien enemy law" to include women.

946. U.S. Congress. House. Committee on Immigration and Naturalization. *Proposed Changes in Naturalization Laws, Hearings, Statements of Mrs. Maud Wood Park, Hon. John Jacob Rogers.* 66th Cong., 2d sess., 28 Feb. 1920. 19p. Y4.Im6/1:N21/5. Testimony considers the question of independent citizenship for women, particularly in reference to the citizenship of women married to aliens. The question of allowing an alien wife to be naturalized independent of the husband is discussed. The citizenship of children under the various proposals is also explored. Under the proposed bills, the American woman who intermarries only retained her citizenship so long as she resided in the U.S.

947. U.S. Congress. House. Committee on Interstate and Foreign Commerce. *Alien Property Custodian Act, Hearing on H.R. 12651 and H.R. 12884.* 66th Cong., 2d sess., 23 Mar.-27 April 1920. 83p. Y4.In8/4:A/4. Hearing describes typical cases under the Trading with the Enemy Act where American-born women married to German citizens had their property confiscated as a result of the act. The bills proposed would amend the act to allow women to reclaim their property.

948. U.S. Congress. House. Committee on Interstate and Foreign Commerce. *Proposed Amendments to the Trading with the Enemy Act, Hearing, H.R. 15081, H.R. 15155, and H.R. 15634.* 66th Cong., 3rd sess., 11 Jan. 1921. 26p. Y4.In8/4:T67/5. Hearing considers amendments to the Trading with the Enemy Act relating to the return of property to women married to Germans. The proposed amendment effects the clause which requires that female American citizens must be born in the U.S. to take advantage of the act, by changing it to indicate only that she was a citizen of the U.S. prior to the war, married the German prior to the war, and that the property was not obtained from a German or Austrian source subsequent to January 1, 1917.

949. U.S. Congress. House. Committee on Immigration and Naturalization. *Immigration, Hearing.* 67th Cong., 2d sess., 13 Dec. 1921 - 13 Feb. 1922. 504p. Y4.Im6/1:Im6/11. Hearing explores immigration conditions in European countries and searches for a way to improve immigration law in the United States. Testimony describes a home for girls recently immigrated who do not have relatives to go to and who come here engaged to an American but who are not yet married. Lengthy testimony of Miss Genevieve Forbes, a newspaper reporter for the Chicago Tribune who travelled posing as an immigrant from Ireland, describes the treatment of women immigrants travelling third class at Ellis Island.

950.   U.S. Congress. House. Committee on Immigration and Naturalization. *Naturalization and Citizenship of Women, Hearings; Statements of Mrs. Maud Wood Park, Fred K. Nielson.* 67th Cong., 2d sess., 8 June 1922. 569-591pp. Y4.Im6/1:W84. Statements of Maud Wood Park and Fred K. Nelson discuss H.R. 11773, a bill introduced by Representative John L. Cable to address the separate citizenship status of women. The proposed bill was a compromise which did not grant women completely equal citizenship in most cases. Park describes the need for the legislation while Nielson comments on technical aspects.

951.   U.S. Congress. House. Committee on Immigration and Naturalization. *Naturalization of and Citizenship of Married Women, Report to Accompany H.R. 12022.* H. Rept. 1110, 67th Cong., 2d sess., 1922. 3p. Serial 7957. Favorably reports the Cable bill, a measure providing for the independent citizenship of married women both in naturalization and marriage to an alien. In the Serial Set edition, page 2 of this report was printed as page 2 of Report 1112, *American Merchant Marine*, whose page 2 was printed in the citizenship report.

952.   U.S. Dept. of State. *Period of Validity and Amendment of Passports of American Women Married to Aliens, Dec.12, 1922.* General Instruction Circular no. 859; Diplomatic Serial 164. Washington, DC: The Department, 1922. 1p. S1.4/2:859. Memo to diplomatic and consular officers details past passport restrictions for women going abroad for the purpose of marriage to an alien. Officers are authorized to amend the passports of women married abroad after the Cable Act to reflect the married name since such women were then issued a normal one year passport.

953.   U.S. Dept. of the Interior. General Land Office. *Citizenship of Married Women, [Instructions to] Registers and Receivers.* Circular no. 857. Washington,DC: GPO, 1922. 2p. I21.4:857. Circular reprints the Cable Act and reminds registers and receivers of Land Offices that applications of married women for entry on public lands must include facts of marital status and citizenship.

954.   U.S. Congress. House. Committee on Immigration and Naturalization. *Citizenship of Wives of Americans in the Foreign Service, Hearing on H.R. 6073.* 68th Cong., 1st sess., 12 Feb. 1924. 24p. Y4.Im6/1:C49/2. Addresses problems created by the Cable Act of 1922 which required an alien wife to reside in the U.S. for one year before becoming an American citizen. The women lost their original citizenship upon marriage, but did not immediately take the citizenship of their American husband. Eliminating this provision for foreign service personnel is the topic of the bill and hearing.

955.   U.S. Congress. House. Committee on Immigration and Naturalization. *Granting Nonquota Status to American-born Women Married to Aliens Prior to the Passage of the Cable Act, Report to Accompany H.R. 6238.* H. Rept. 659, 69th Cong., 1st sess., 1926. 2p. Serial 8532. Reports a bill reconciling provisions of the Cable Act of 1922 and the Immigration Act of 1924 which made it nearly impossible for some American-born women formerly married to aliens to resume their U.S. citizenship. The bill allowed these women to enter the U.S. as non-quota immigrants so that they could meet the one year residence requirement of the Cable Act.

956.   U.S. Congress. House. Committee on Immigration and Naturalization. *Immigration and Citizenship of American-born Women Married to Aliens, Hearings on H.R. 4057, H.R. 6238, H.R. 9825.* 69th Cong., 1st sess., 23 Mar. 1926. 45p. Y4.Im6/1:W84/2. Hearings consider bills to amend the Cable Act of 1922 to remedy the discrimination against women who lost their citizenship through marriage to an alien prior to passage of the Cable Act by allowing them to regain their citizenship through simple paperwork. International laws of citizenship and specific cases are the focus of the bulk of testimony

with considerable discussion of "what ifs". Congressman Adolph Sabath provides antagonistic questioning of Emma Wold, emphasizing the few cases of American women marrying titled Europeans.

957. U.S. Congress. Senate. Committee on Immigration. *Naturalization and Citizenship of Married Women, Hearing on S. 2969.* 69th Cong., 1st sess., 24 Mar. 1926. 22p. Y4.Im6/2:W84. Hearing considers amending the Cable Act to remove discrimination in the matter of citizenship against expatriates and women married to ineligible aliens. The primary issue is repatriation of women upon death or divorce of an alien husband and repealing section 3 of the Cable Act which required such women to go through the naturalization process as a quota immigrant. One point of discussion is the effect of current citizenship laws on the property rights of American women living abroad.

958. U.S. Congress. House. Committee on Immigration and Naturalization. *Amendments to Immigration Act of 1924, Nonquota and Preference Provisions-Certificates of Arrival-Nurses and Teachers in Porto Rico, Hearing on H.J. Res. 234, H.R. 8540, H.R. 159.* 70th Cong., 1st sess., 27 Mar.- 10 April 1928. 126p. Y4.Im6/1:Im6/17. Immigration hearing discusses a bill to admit, outside the quota, a limited number of women, primarily Catholic nurses and religious teachers from Spain, to Porto Rico. Also discussed are preference systems within the quotas to reunite families, primarily by allowing naturalized American men to bring their wives and children to the United States.

959. U.S. Congress. House. Committee on Immigration and Naturalization. *Effect of Marriage upon Nationality, Hearing.* 70th Cong., 1st sess., 19 May 1928. 58p. Y4.Im6/1:M34. Statement by Emma Wold, Legislative Secretary of the National Woman's Party, provides a comprehensive summary of the effect of marriage on the citizenship and naturalization of women around the world. Relevant statutes of the countries, translated where necessary, are reprinted.

960. U.S. Congress. House. Committee on Immigration and Naturalization. *Amending Cable Act to Permit the Wife of a Native-Born American Citizen and World War Veteran to Join Her Husband in the United States, Report to Accompany S. 3691.* H. Rept. 1697, 71st Cong., 2d sess., 1930. 5p. Serial 9193. Favorable report on amending the Cable Act to allow certain alien wives of American-born citizens to enter the U.S. as nonquota immigrants. A minority view rejects the bill on the grounds that it is a special measure designed to address the case of Anna Minna Venzke Ulrich, who was deemed ineligible for citizenship, and whose powerful friends sought to gain her admittance through this bill.

961. U.S. Congress. House. Committee on Immigration and Naturalization. *Amendment of the Women's Citizenship Act of 1922, Hearings on H.R. 10208.* 71st Cong., 2d sess., 6 Mar. 1930. 42p. Y4.Im6/1:W84/3-4. Hearing on amendments to remove discrimination against women who lose their American citizenship through marriage to an ineligible alien or through residence abroad enters into a technical discussion of the citizenship rights of women under the Cable Act.

962. U.S. Congress. House. Committee on Immigration and Naturalization. *Citizenship and Naturalization of Married Women, Report to Accompany H.R. 10960.* H. Rept. 1036, 71st Cong., 2d sess., 1930. 4p. Serial 9191. Reports a bill removing technical barriers to the citizenship and naturalization of married women under the Expatriation Act of 1907, the Cable Act of 1922, and the Immigration Act of 1924. The primary focus is the U.S. residency requirement for resuming citizenship upon the dissolution of marriage to an alien and the problems encountered by native-born American women living abroad who could not return to the U.S. due to the immigration quotas. Some specific examples of hardship under the existing laws are described.

963.   U.S. Congress. House. Committee on Immigration and Naturalization. *Proposed Amendments to the Immigration Act of 1924, Hearings on H.R. 5645, H.R. 5646, H.R. 5647, H.R. 5648, H.R. 6852, H.R. 7703.* 71st Cong., 2d sess., 27 Jan., 4 Feb. 1930. 283-371pp. Y4.Im6/1:Im6/19. Hearing considers bills relating to admission to the United States of alien husbands of American wives, and mothers and fathers of American citizens, without regard to quotas. Strong anti-immigration testimony also includes views supporting a wife's obligation to give up all, including her citizenship, if she marries an alien.

964.   U.S. Congress. Senate. Committee on Immigration. *Amending Cable Act to Permit the Wife of a Native-born American Citizen and World War Veteran to Join Her Husband in the United States, Report to Accompany S. 3691.* S. Rept. 442, 71st Cong., 2d sess., 1930. 3p. Serial 9185. The highly restrictive nature of this bill is noted in a favorable report on allowing certain alien wives to enter the U.S. without reference to quotas.

965.   U.S. Congress. Senate. Committee on Immigration. *Citizenship and Naturalization of Married Women, Report to Accompany H.R. 10960.* S. Rept. 614, 71st Cong., 2d sess., 1930. 10p. Serial 9186. Report includes major amendments to a bill eliminating technical difficulties encountered by American women married to aliens and living abroad who wished to resume their citizenship on the death of or divorce from their spouse. The difficulties arose from the combined effect of the Cable Act of 1922 and the Immigration Act of 1924. The House Report 1036 (962), which provides examples of the cases addressed by this bill, is appended.

966.   U.S. General Land Office. *Citizenship of Married Women, [Instructions to] Registers and Receivers.* Circular no. 857. Washington, DC:GPO, 1930. 2p. I21.4:857/2. Circular reprints the Cable Act and reminds registers and receivers of Land Offices that application by married women for entry of public lands must include facts of martial state and citizenship.

967.   U.S. Congress. House. Committee on Immigration and Naturalization. *Amendment to the Women's Citizenship Act of 1922, and for Other Purposes, Hearings on H.R. 14684, H.R. 14685, H.R. 16303.* 71st Cong., 3d sess., 17 Dec. 1930, 23 Jan. 1931. 33p. Y4.Im6/1:W84/4. The several bills under consideration relate to a female American citizen's right to retain or resume her citizenship after marriage to an alien ineligible for American citizenship. Also dealt with is the transfer of citizenship from parent to child by broadening the interpretation to include mothers as well as fathers. The case of alien husbands of U.S. citizens under immigration laws is considered with concern expressed over the possibility of a "marriage mill" to circumvent immigration quotas. Throughout the hearing an intense prejudice against Asian immigrants is evident. Several examples given by witnesses illustrates the effect of current law on the citizenship of American-born women married to aliens of Asian descent.

968.   U.S. Congress. House. Committee on Immigration and Naturalization. *Citizenship and Naturalization of Married Women, Report to Accompany H.R. 16975.* H. Rept. 2693, 71st Cong., 3d sess., 1931. 3p. Serial 9327. Reports a bill removing the "remaining" inequities in the area of citizenship and naturalization of married women. Specifically the bill addresses barriers to the resumption of citizenship for women married to an alien and residing in a foreign country.

969.   U.S. Congress. House. Committee on Immigration and Naturalization. *Relating to Naturalization and Citizenship Status of Certain Children of Mothers Who Are Citizens of the United States, and Relating to the Removal of Certain Distinctions in Matters of Nationality, Hearings on H.R. 5489.* 72 Cong., 1st sess., 7 Jan. 1931. 31p. Y4.Im6/1:C43/2. Hearing examines amendments to laws governing citizenship which

would allow women to transmit their citizenship equally with men to children born abroad, grant citizenship to illegitimate children of American men born abroad, and enact a blanket provision prohibiting distinctions based on sex in laws relative to nationality, citizenship and naturalization.

970. U.S. Dept. of State. *Act of 1922, Sept. 22 [Relative to Naturalization and Citizenship of Married Women] as Amended by Acts of July 3, 1930 and Mar. 3, 1931.* Washington, DC: GPO, 1931. 3p. S7.2:W84. Reprint of the Cable Act incorporates amendments made in 1930 and 1931.

971. U.S. General Land Office. *Naturalization and Citizenship of Married Women.* Circular no. 1248. Washington, DC: GPO, 1931. 5p. I21.4:1248. Circular to registers of Land Offices reprints the Cable Act as amended and outlines the information relating to marriage and citizenship which a married woman or widow must provide upon application or entry under the public land laws.

972. U.S. Congress. House. Committee on Immigration and Naturalization. *Naturalization of Certain Women Born in Hawaii, Report to Accompany H.R. 10829.* H. Rept. 1067, 72d Cong., 1st sess., 1932. 2p. Serial 9492. Barriers to reacquiring citizenship faced by native-born Hawaiian women born prior to the annexation of Hawaii and who lost their citizenship through marriage to an ineligible alien are addressed by the bill reported.

973. U.S. Congress. House. Committee on Immigration and Naturalization. *To Exempt from the Quota Husbands of American Citizen Wives and to Limit the Presumption that Certain Alien Relatives May Become Public Charges, Hearings on H.R. 5869, H.R. 7614, S. 2656.* 72d Cong., 1st sess., 18 Dec. 1931, 14 Jan. 1932. 102p. Y4.Im6/1:Q5/8. Hearings examine the problems of female American citizens whose alien husbands were refused entry to the United States based on the belief that the husband would become a public charge. Most of the wives involved held jobs and had substantial savings. One major concern of immigration authorities was whether the marriage was an attempt to circumvent the immigration laws of the U.S.

974. U.S. Congress. Senate. Committee on Immigration. *Hawaiian Naturalization, Report to Accompany H.R. 10829.* S. Rept. 825, 72d Cong., 1st sess., 1932. 2p. Serial 9488. See 972 for abstract.

975. U.S. Congress. House. Committee on Immigration and Naturalization. *Provide Equality in Matters of Citizenship between American Men and Women and to Clarify Status of Their Children, Report to Accompany H.R. 3673.* H. Rept. 131, 73d Cong., 1st sess., 1933. 4p. Serial 9774. The bill reported gives American women an equal ability to transmit citizenship to their children.

976. U.S. Congress. House. Committee on Immigration and Naturalization. *Relating to Naturalization and Citizenship Status of Children Whose Mothers are Citizens of the United States, and Relating to the Removal of Certain Inequities in Matters of Nationality, Hearings on H.R. 3673, H.R. 77.* 73rd Cong., 1st sess., 28 Mar. 1933. 60p. Y4.Im6/1:C43/3. Hearing considers proposed legislation to ensure that children of an alien man and an American women born abroad have the same American citizenship rights as the children of an American male and an alien female.

977. U.S. Congress. Senate. Subcommittee of the Committee on Immigration. *American Citizenship Rights of Women, Hearing on S. 992, S. 2760, S. 3968 and S. 4169.* 72d Cong., 2d sess., 2 Mar. 1933. 76p. Y4.Im6/2:W84/2. Hearing is, in fact, a report by former Congressman John L. Cable on the history of women's citizenship rights in America. The actions and court cases leading up to the Married Women's Independent

Citizenship Act of September 22, 1922, the Cable Act, are reviewed. Relevant congressional documents relating to women's citizenship are reprinted in the appendix and a table of related court cases is provided. Includes a chronology of the effect of marriage on a women's citizenship in the United States to 1922 and additional comments on perfecting the law.

978.   U.S. Congress. Senate. Committee on Immigration. *Provide Equality in Matter of Citizenship between American Men and American Women and to Clarify Status of Their Children, Report to Accompany H.R. 3673.* S. Rept. 865, 73d Cong., 2d sess., 1934. 3p. Serial 9770. Favorably reports a bill establishing an equal ability of both the father and the mother to transmit citizenship to children.

979.   U.S. Immigration and Naturalization Service. *Alien Woman Who Married a Citizen, or Whose Husband was Naturalized, Subsequent to 12 Noon (E.S.T.), May 24, 1934.* Form C-59-La. Washington, DC: The Service, 1934. 1p. L15.13:937/La. States the rules governing application for citizenship for married women.

980.   U.S. Congress. House. Committee on Immigration and Naturalization. *To Repatriate Native-born Women Who Lost Nationality by Marriage to an Alien, Report to Accompany H.R. 4354.* H. Rept. 279, 74th Cong., 1st sess., 1935. 3p. Serial 9886. Reports a bill to correct an omission from the Cable Act which created difficulties for women who married aliens prior to the act and who desired to regain their U.S. citizenship after the termination of marital relations.

981.   U.S. Congress. Senate. Committee on Immigration. *To Repatriate Native-born Women Who Married Aliens, Report to Accompany S. 2912.* S. Rept. 847, 74th Cong., 1st sess., 1935. 2p. Serial 9879. Reports, with minor amendments, a bill to provide an easy method of repatriation for women who lost their citizenship through marriage to an alien prior to passage of the Cable Act and whose marital relation had since been terminated.

982.   U.S. Dept. of State. *Act of Sept. 22, 1922, as Amended by Acts of July 3, 1930, Mar. 3, 1931 and May 24, 1934, Relative to Naturalization and Citizenship of Married Women.* Washington, DC: State, 1935. 3p. S1.2:N219/2. Reprints the Cable Act of 1922 incorporating 1930, 1931, and 1934 amendments.

983.   U.S. Congress. House. Committee on Immigration and Naturalization. *Repatriation of Certain Native-born American Women Citizens, Report to Accompany S. 2912.* H. Rept. 2106, 74th Cong., 2d sess., 1936. 4p. Serial 9992. Background on the Cable Act is provided in this report on a bill modifying the process of repatriation upon termination of the marriage for women married to aliens prior to passage of the Cable Act.

984.   U.S. Immigration and Naturalization Service. *Citizenship and Naturalization of Women.* General Order no. 235. Washington, DC: The Service, 1936. L15.9:235. Transmittal of Public Law no. 793, 74th Congress, relating to the resumption of citizenship of native-born women married to an alien prior to the Cable Act indicates changes to the naturalization regulations for the enforcement of the act.

985.   U.S. Immigration and Naturalization Service. *Alien Woman Who Married a Citizen, or Whose Husband was Naturalized, Subsequent to September 22, 1922, and Prior to 12 Noon (E.S.T.), May 24, 1933.* Washington, DC: GPO, 1937. 1p. L15.13:937/K. Details rules governing application for citizenship for an alien woman married to a citizen.

986.   U.S. Immigration and Naturalization Service. *Widow and Minor Children of Deceased Declarant.* Form C-59-A. Washington, DC: GPO, 1937. 1p. L15.13:937/A. Presents

rules on filing for citizenship for the wife and children of a man who died after declaration of intent but before becoming a citizen.

987. U.S. Immigration and Naturalization Service. *Wife and Minor Children of an Insane Declarant.* Form C-59-B. Washington, DC: GPO, 1937. 1p. L15.13:937/B. Prints rules governing application for citizenship for the wife and children of a male who became insane after filing a declaration of intent.

988. U.S. Immigration and Naturalization Service. *Women (Native Born Citizen) Who Prior to September 22, 1922, Lost American Citizenship by Marriage to an Alien, and Whose Martial Status with Alien Has or Shall Have Terminated.* Form C-59-N. Washington, DC: GPO, 1937. 1p. L15.13:937/N. Rules on citizenship of native-born American women who lost citizenship through marriage to an alien and who have since terminated that marriage are presented.

989. U.S. Immigration and Nationalization Service. *Women Who Prior to September 22, 1922, Lost American Citizenship: (1) by Marriage to an Alien; or (2) through Loss of United States Citizenship by Her Husband, or (3) by Residence Abroad after Marriage to an Alien.* Form C-59-M. Washington, DC: GPO, 1937. 2p. L15.13:937/M. Presents rules governing application for citizenship of women who were citizens but who lost their citizenship.

990. U.S. Congress. House. Committee on Immigration and Naturalization. *Amending Act Relating to Naturalization of Certain Women Born in Hawaii, Report to Accompany H.R. 7780.* H. Rept. 1800, 75th Cong., 3d sess., 14 Feb. 1938. 3p. Serial 10233. Reports a bill correcting technical problems with the Cable Act and its amendments relating to women born in Hawaii prior to annexation and who were not residing in the U.S. on July 2, 1932, the enactment date of the amendment to the Cable Act including these Hawaiian women.

991. U.S. Congress. Senate. Committee on Immigration. *Amending Act Relative to Naturalization of Certain Women Born in Hawaii, Report to Accompany H.R. 7780.* S. Rept. 2198, 75th Cong., 3d sess., 1938. 2p. Serial 10230. See 990 for abstract.

992. U.S. Congress. House. Committee on Immigration and Naturalization. *Amending Act Relating to Naturalization of Certain Women Born in Hawaii, Report to Accompany H.R. 159.* H. Rept. 122, 76th Cong., 1st sess., 1939. 3p. Serial 10296. Report on technical corrections to the Act of July 2, 1932 for the restoration of citizenship to certain women born in Hawaii prior to U.S. annexation who lost their citizenship through marriage to an alien.

993. U.S. Congress. House. Committee on Immigration and Naturalization. *Repatriating Native-Born Women Residents of the United States Who Have Heretofore Lost Their Citizenship by Marriage to an Alien, Report to Accompany H.R. 4185.* H. Rept. 869, 76th Cong., 1st sess., 1939. 3p. Serial 10299. Reports a bill to allow a native-born woman who lost her citizenship by marriage to an alien before the Cable Act, but who has continued to reside in the U.S., to regain her citizenship by taking an oath of allegiance even though she remains married to an alien.

994. U.S. Congress. House. Committee on Immigration and Naturalization. *Amending Subsection (D) of Section 4 of the Act Approved May 26, 1924 (43 Stat. L. 155; U.S.C., Title 8, Sec.204(d)), Report to Accompany H.R. 8753.* H. Rept. 1725, 76th Cong., 3d sess., 1940. 2p. Serial 10441. Reports a bill to give alien women equal privileges as extended to men for entry to the U.S. without regard to quotas if they are a minister, or professor of a college, academy, seminary or university.

995. U.S. Congress. Senate. Committee on Immigration. *Amending an Act Entitled "An Act relating to the naturalization of certain women born in Hawaii" Approved July 2,1932, Report to Accompany H.R. 159.* S. Rept. 1925, 76th Cong., 3d sess., 1940. 3p. Serial 10431. See 992 for abstracts.

996. U.S. Congress. Senate. Committee on Immigration. *Repatriating Native-Born Women Residents of the United States Who Have Heretofore Lost Their Citizenship by Marriage to an Alien, Report to Accompany H.R. 4185.* S. Rept. 1926, 76th Cong., 3d sess., 1940. 3p. Serial 10431. See 993 for abstract.

997. U.S. Congress. House. Committee on Immigration and Naturalization. *Amending the Nationality Act of 1940, Report to Accompany H.R. 5554.* H. Rept. 1240, 77th Cong., 1st sess., 1941. 3p. Serial 10557. Reports a measure which would extend to women and minor children the same protection of their citizenship as accorded to men under the Nationality Act of 1940. The bill protects the citizenship of a naturalized woman living abroad with her native-born American husband.

998. U.S. Congress. House. Committee on Immigration and Naturalization. *Amending the Nationality Act of 1940, Report to Accompany H.R. 4743.* H. Rept. 1632, 77th Cong., 2d sess., 1942. 4p. Serial 10661. Favorable report on a bill allowing the wives of persons who lost their U.S. citizenship due to military services with an allied country in WWI to become citizens by taking an oath. The men in question were allowed to regain their citizenship through an oath and this bill allows their wives to regain citizenship in the same manner if the marriage took place prior to passage of the Cable Act.

999. U.S. Congress. House. Committee on Immigration and Naturalization. *Repatriating Native-born Women Residents of the United States, Report to Accompany H.R. 7275.* H. Rept. 2499, 77th Cong., 2d sess., 1942. 2p. Serial 10664. The bill here reported corrects an omission in the Nationality Act of 1940 relative to the repatriation of native-born women who lost their American citizenship through marriage to an alien but who continued to reside in the United States.

1000. U.S. Congress. Senate. Committee on Immigration. *Amending the Nationality Act of 1940, Report to Accompany H.R. 5554.* S. Rept. 1675, 77th Cong., 2d sess., 1942. 2p. Serial 10659. Reports a bill to prevent the naturalized wife, husband, or minor child of an American citizen from losing his or her citizenship through residence abroad.

1001. U.S. Congress. House. Committee on Immigration and Naturalization. *Repatriating Native-born Women Residents of the United States, Report to Accompany H.R. 1289.* H. Rept. 183, 78th Cong., 1st sess., 1943. 2p. Serial 10761. Reports a bill to provide a simple method of repatriation for native-born American women who lost their citizenship through marriage to an alien prior to passage of the Cable Act and who have continued to reside in the Unites States.

1002. U.S. Congress. House. Committee on Immigration and Naturalization. *Facilitating the Admission to the United States of Husbands, Wives, and Children of United States Citizen Men and Women Who Have Served Honorably in the Armed Forces of the United States during the Present World War, Report to Accompany H.R. 714.* H. Rept. 1073, 79th Cong., 1st sess., 1945. 3p. Serial 10935. Favorable report on a bill which would, among other things, give husbands of service women the same nonquota status in entering the U.S. as was already granted to alien wives of servicemen.

1003. U.S. Congress. House. Committee on Immigration and Naturalization. *Repatriating Native-born Women Residents of the United States, Report to Accompany H.R. 384.* H. Rept. 189, 79th Cong., 1st sess., 1945. 3p. Serial 10931. Reports a measure to provide an easy method of repatriation for native-born women who lost their citizenship through marriage to an alien prior to the passage of the Cable Act and who continued to reside in the United States.

1004. U.S. Congress. House. Committee on Interstate and Foreign Commerce. *Amending Section 32(A)(2) of the Trading with the Enemy Act, Report to Accompany H.R. 5960.* H. Rept. 1842, 80th Cong., 2d sess., 1948. 4p. Serial 11211. Reports a bill allowing women citizens married to Germans, Japanese, Bulgarian, Hungarian and Rumanian citizens to reclaim property seized under the Trading with the Enemy Act so long as they did not actively support the enemy.

1005. U.S. Women's Bureau. *Replies to the ECOSOC Questionnaire on the Legal Status and Treatment of Women, Part I, Public Law, Section G: Nationality.* Washington, DC: The Bureau, 1948. 8p. L13.2:Ec7/pt.1/sec.G. Answers to a U.N. Economic and Social Council questionnaire details the effect of U.S. marriage and divorce laws on the nationality of a woman and her children.

1006. U.S. Women's Bureau. *Replies to the ECOSOC Questionnaire on the Legal Status and Treatment of Women, Part I, Public Law, Section G: Nationality (Supplemental Replies Requested).* Washington, DC: The Bureau, 1948. 8p. L13.2:Ec7/pt.1/sec.G/supp. Additional information on the laws of the U.S. governing the nationality of married persons and the laws of domicile supplements the original response to a U.N. Economic and Social Council questionnaire (1005).

7

Homemaking and Home Economics Education

Documents in this chapter represent only some of the published documents on homemaking, home economics education, and extension work in home demonstration. Documents were selected for inclusion primarily for the insight they provide into the lives of women at that period in time. In particular the home demonstration reports reveal the lifestyle and concerns of farm women in both the role of mother and homemaker and as a contributor to family income. In 1915 the USDA published two lengthy reports, *Domestic Needs of Farm Women* (1012) and *Economic Needs of Farm Women* (1013). These reports, based on letters sent to the USDA by farm women, reflect the home management concerns and economic situation of women in rural areas. In 1919 the USDA conducted a survey whose results were published in *The Farm Woman's Problem* (1020). This report provides background on the work of farm women and discusses the presence of "amenities" such as running water and telephones. The reports were used to focus home demonstration programs to meet women's needs. Regular status reports on home demonstration highlight the types of activities and provide basic statistics on agents and participants. Reports reviewing the history and progress of home demonstration were also issued periodically. (1034, 1089, 1094, 1098). The work of the agents is described in slide show scripts from 1930 and 1936 (1035, 1056).

The home economics education publications included primarily review secondary school programs and continuing education for adult women. One of the most interesting is *Home Economics for More Girls*, the proceedings of a 1927 conference of home economics supervisors (1033). The contributions of participants, as they discuss programs offered and curricular design, reveal much about existing assumptions on women's lives. The needs of adult women are addressed in a number of publications including *Homemaking Education Programs for Adults and Out-of-School Youth* (1059) and *Homemaking Education Programs for Adults* (1062) in the 1930's, a 1949 publication, *Frontiers in Homemaking Education Programs for Adults* (1083), and 1958's *Homemaking Education Programs for Adults* (1099).

A number of publications issued since 1930 focus on college level home economics with particular attention paid to enrollment and the placement of graduates (1039, 1092, 1096, 1101, 1109). A statistical report, *Home Economics in Degree-Granting Institutions* (1117), was issued between 1949 and 1962. World War II prompted a series of reports on adapting the college curriculum, including home economics, to meet wartime needs (1075, 1077). These reports encouraged program revision to focus on family adjustment to wartime conditions while continuing to provide professional career programs in home economics.

Also addressing the problems of homemakers in wartime were the reports of the Consumer Compliance Survey. These surveys collected information from housewives on knowledge and attitudes toward price control (1078-1079), rationing (1080-1081), and rent control (1082). The role of women as homemakers was extolled in two of the radio scripts for the "Gallant American Women" series (1067, 1071). Another area of homemaking explored was the expenditure patterns of working wives, usually compared to full-time homemakers (1103, 1106, 1108). A report series on the legal status of homemakers was published in 1977 and 1978. These and other reports on the status of homemakers are located in Chapter 4, Discrimination and Women's Rights.

1007. U.S. Dept. of Agriculture. Office of Experiment Stations. *Farmers' Institutes for Women.* by John Hamilton. Office of Extension Circular no. 85. Washington, DC: GPO, 1909. 16p. A10.4:85. Argues that rural women require better education in domestic science, and that the most natural means for accomplishing this is through the existing farmers institutes. The report provides a sample constitution for a county association of women and a copy of the constitution of the Illinois Association of Domestic Science. Summaries of women's institutes held in various states and territories in 1908 are included.

1008. U.S. Dept. of Agriculture. *List of Free and Available Publications of the Department of Agriculture of Interest to Farm Women.* Washington, DC: The Department, 1913. 11p. A1.2:W84.

1009. U.S. Bureau of Education. *Education for the Home, Part 2: The States and Education for the Home, Rural Schools, Elementary Schools, High Schools, Normal Schools, Technical Institutes, Various Agencies and Organizations.* by Benjamin R. Andrews. Bulletin 1914, no. 37. Washington, DC: GPO, 1914. 207p. I16.3:914/37.

1010. U.S. Bureau of Education. *Education for the Home, Part 3: Colleges and Universities.* by Benjamin R. Andrews. Bulletin 1914, no. 38. Washington, DC: GPO, 1914. 106p. I16.3:914/38.

1011. U.S. Bureau of Education. *Education for the Home, Part 4: List of References on Education for the Home; Cities and Towns Teaching Household Arts.* by Benjamin R. Andrews. Bulletin 1914, no. 39. Washington, DC: GPO, 1915. 61p. I16.3:914/39.

1012. U.S. Dept. of Agriculture. Office of the Secretary. *Domestic Needs of Farm Women.* USDA Report no. 104. Washington, DC: GPO, 1915. 100p. A1.8:104. The second report based on letters from women addressing the question of how the USDA can better meet the needs of farm housewives focuses on home management needs. Major themes of letter excerpts include kitchen planning, modern conveniences, electricity, sanitation, and beautifying the farm. Appendices list publications of various agencies which cover some of the issues raised by the report.

1013. U.S. Dept. of Agriculture. Office of the Secretary. *Economic Needs of Farm Women.* USDA Report no. 106. Washington, DC: GPO, 1915. 100p. A1.8:106. Fourth report based on the letters of farm women deals with the economic side of farm women's lives. Excerpts from the letters indicate that although money is spent on the latest in farm machinery, updating household appliances is a low priority. Another common theme is a desire for recognition of the financial contribution of the women's work on the farm and the women's need to have some money of their own. The financial plight of the farmer and the effect on farm women is also discussed at length. Appendices list publications of various agencies which may be of interest to farm women.

1014. U.S. Bureau of Education. *Principles and Policies in Home Economics Education.* by Henrietta W. Calvin. Home Economics Circular no. 4. Washington, DC: GPO, 1918. 12p. I16.25:4. Guidelines on goals for home economics education for both secondary and adult audiences are presented.

1015.   U.S. Food Administration. *Program for Woman Who Has Pledged Herself to Thrift for World Relief.* Washington, DC: The Administration, 1918. 2p. Y3.F73/2:W84.

1016.   U.S. Bureau of Education. *Home Economics.* by Henrietta W. Calvin and Carrie Alberts Lyford. Bulletin 1918, no. 50. Washington, DC: GPO, 1919. 38p. I16.3:918/50. Provides an overview of progress in home economics education from 1916 to 1918.

1017.   U.S. Federal Board of Vocational Education. *Education in Home Economics: Brief Survey of the Promotion of Home Economics Education.* Washington, DC: The Board, 1919. 6p. VE1.15:135. The importance of homemaking education for the girls and women of the United States is described noting child welfare and family economy as key factors. Types of home economics programs and the groups they are geared toward are outlined, and the areas of potential progress made by the Vocational Education Act are delineated. Finally, areas of the Vocational Education Act that need improvement are noted.

1018.   U.S. Treasury Dept.. *Ten Lessons in Thrift, Published for Use of Women's Clubs.* Washington, DC: GPO, 1919. 16p. T1.27/32:T41/2. Outline of lessons for women's clubs on family finances describes family accounting, the household budget, conservation of things and of living, and thrift in municipal affairs.

1019.   U.S. Dept. of Agriculture. *Status and Results of Home Demonstration Work, Northern and Western States, 1919.* by Florence E. Ward. Circular no. 141. Washington, DC: GPO, 1920. 25p. A1.14/2:141. Outcomes of extension work with women in 1919 is presented in tabular form. As a result of an influenza epidemic, home nursing became an area of extension work in addition to the usual work in clothing, food preparation, and home management.

1020.   U.S. Dept. of Agriculture. Office of the Secretary. *The Farm Woman's Problems.* Florence E. Ward. Circular no. 148. Washington, DC: GPO, 1920. 19p. A1.14/2:148. A 1919 survey of 10,000 farm homes in 33 northern and western states determined the number of hours farm women worked, the types of work they did, amenities such as running water, sewing machines and telephones available to them, and distances from schools and health care. The report discusses the results of the survey and ways that the home demonstration agents can and have helped alleviate some of the problems.

1021.   U.S. Treasury Dept. Federal Reserve District 5, War Loan Organization. *Budgets for Business Women.* Washington, DC: GPO, 1920. 8p. T1.27:32:B85/2. Advises women on setting a budget so that money can be put aside in savings.

1022.   U.S. Bureau of Education. *Present Status of Home Economics Education.* Home Economics Circular no. 10. Washington, DC: GPO, 1921. 8p. I16.25:10. Overview describes the status of home economics in the U.S. and in selected countries.

1023.   U.S. Dept. of Agriculture. *Status and Results of Home Demonstration Work, Northern and Western States, 1920.* by Florence E. Ward. Circular no. 141. Washington, DC: GPO, 1921. 30p. A1.14/2:178. Annual report provides information on various home demonstration projects including dollars saved through making and remodeling clothing and number of washing machines introduced. A large portion of the report is devoted to describing child nutrition programs.

1024.   U.S. Bureau of Education. *Home Economics Education.* by Henrietta W. Calvin. Bulletin 1923, no. 6. Washington, DC: GPO, 1923. 19p. I16.3:923/6. Reviews progress in Home Economics Education from 1920 to 1922.

1025. U.S. Bureau of the Census. *The Women Home-maker in the City: A Study of Statistics Relating to Married Women in the City of Rochester, N.Y. at the Census of 1920.* Washington, DC: GPO, 1923. 49p. C3.2:H75. Study of married women homemakers in the city of Rochester looks at household responsibility, children, women and mothers working for money, other persons living in the household who could help with housework or with care of children, members of family working for money, foreign born women by ability to speak English, domicile status of women who are or have been married, and ages of children. Some data is broken down by American-born versus foreign-born women.

1026. U.S. Congress. House. Committee on Agriculture. *Various Resolutions Relating to Agriculture, Hearings.* 67th Cong., 4th sess., 19-23 Feb. 1923. 37p. Y4.Ag8/1:Ag8/8. Hearing examines H.J. Res 432 relating to the employment of women in extension work. The resolution charges that women extension workers were discharged without hearing for the purpose of replacing them with "favorite henchmen of the administration." The question of whether any women were improperly dismissed due to Department of Agriculture pressure is answered in a letter from the state extension director indicating no such interference.

1027. U.S. Dept. of Agriculture. *Status and Results of Home Demonstration Work, Northern and Western States, 1921.* by Florence E. Ward. Circular no. 285. Washington, DC: GPO, 1923. 26p. A1.14/2:285. In addition to describing the various home demonstration activities, this report provides data on numbers of families adopting new practices as a result of extension work. Although the number of agents had not changed significantly, the number of women belonging to extension organizations increased by 35,800 from 1920. Emphasis in the report is placed on clothing and home management.

1028. U.S. Dept. of Agriculture. *Home Demonstration Work, 1922.* by Grace E. Frysinger. Circular no. 314. Washington, DC: GPO, 1924. 44p. A1.14/2:314. In addition to assessing the results of home demonstration work for 1922, this report gives considerable attention to the structure and methods of extension work.

1029. U.S. Federal Board of Vocational Education. *List of Responsibilities of Day School Home Economics Teacher on Job, as Set Up at Southern Regional Conference, Held at Hot Springs, Ark, June 16-24, 1925.* Miscellaneous series no. 642. Washington, DC: The Board, 1925. 11p. VE1.15:642. Charts give a breakdown of the instructional and management functions of home economics programs and indicates whether the responsibility for training the teacher for these tasks rests with the teacher-training institution or with the supervisors.

1030. U.S. Dept. of Agriculture. *Home Demonstration Work, 1923.* by Ola Powell Malcolm. Circular no. 399. Washington, DC: GPO, 1926. 48p. A1.14/2:399. Report of home demonstration activities for the year 1923 focuses on home improvement and beautification, gardening and canning, dairying, poultry raising, textiles and handicrafts, marketing of home products, health, and education activities such as rallies and camps for farm women.

1031. U.S. Bureau of Education. *Achievements in Home Economics Education.* by Emeline S. Whitcomb. Bulletin 1927, no. 35. Washington, DC: GPO, 1927. 26p. I16.3:927/35. Includes basic statistics on courses offered and enrollment in home economics at the high school level.

1032. U.S. Bureau of Education. *Trends in Home-Economics Education, 1926-28.* by Emeline S. Whitcomb. Bulletin 1929, no. 25. Washington, DC: GPO, 1927. 22p. I16.3:929/25.

1033. U.S. Office of Education. *Home Economics for More Girls, Proceedings of National Conference of Supervisors of Home Economics, Ashville, N.C., June 20, 1927.* Home Economics Letter no. 2. Washington, DC: The Office, 1927. 35p. I16.51:2. Conference attempted to reach a consensus on the need for home economics education at the elementary, junior and senior high school level and on the curriculum for such programs. Participants contributed information on the types of programs they were offering noting local conditions which influenced their choices. Many of the assumptions on women's lives are clearly stated as the basis for curriculum decisions.

1034. U.S. Dept. of Agriculture. *Home Demonstration Work under the Smith-Lever Act, 1914-1924.* by Florence E. Ward. Circular no. 43. Washington, DC: GPO, 1929. 36p. A1.4/2:43. Chronicles the first ten years of federally supported home economics extension work and provides some background from earlier, usually land-grant college sponsored, programs starting in the early 1870's. Basic statistics on participation in the various home demonstration programs are provided along with data on number of white and black women extension agents in various states and yearly funding for home demonstration work from all sources from 1919 to 1924.

1035. U.S. Extension Service. *Home Demonstration Agent Friend of Farm Women.* Washington, DC: The Service, 1930. 12p. A43.5/8:259. Script for a slide show outlines the work of home demonstration agents.

1036. U.S. Extension Service. *Home Demonstration Work, 1929, Central States.* by Grace E. Frysinger. Circular no. 129. Washington, DC: The Service, 1930. 17p. A43.5/6:129. Review of home demonstration program expenditures and expansion of local leadership programs for 1929 in the central states also describes the work done by the agents and the program focus in general terms. Summary information is also provided on teaching methods, special events, and publicity.

1037. U.S. Extension Service. *Trends in Extension Work in Home Economics.* by C.W. Warburton. Circular no. 133. Washington, DC: The Service, 1930. 11p. A43.5/6:133. Description of trends in home demonstration work details the organization for developing local leaders and attempts to ensure relevance in the home demonstration program. Methods utilized to reach and teach farm women are explained. Reviews the typical program focus areas.

1038. U.S. Federal Board for Vocational Education. *Agent's Report of Home Economics Education for 1929-30.* by Edith M. Thomas. Washington, DC: The Board, 193?. 7p. VE1.15:1193. Trends in the use of "home projects" and evening classes for adult women are applauded in this report on home demonstration work in the southern region for 1929-30. Also noted is a changing focus on solving the immediate problems of homemakers. Training of home economics teachers is discussed at some length.

1039. U.S. Office of Education. Educational Extension Division. *Home Economics Instruction in Higher Institutions, Including Universities, Colleges, Teachers Colleges, Normal Schools, and Junior Colleges, 1928-29.* Pamphlet no. 3. Washington, DC: GPO, 1930. 23p. I16.43:3. Statistical report details the number of courses offered, FTE teachers and students enrolled in home economics classes at institutions having a 4-year curriculum in home economics leading to a baccalaureate degree and at institutions offering courses but not granting degrees.

1040. U.S. Extension Service. *Opportunities for Older Girl in Extension Program.* by Gertrude L. Warren. Circular no. 166. Washington, DC: The Service, 1931. 10p. A43.5/6:166. Extension programs for older girls are viewed as an opportunity to develop the girl's awareness of community issues and family responsibilities. The role of 4-H in the psychological development of the girl and her adjustment are stressed along with opportunities for leaders to help the older farm girl make wise decisions regarding staying on the farm and handling her finances. The 4-H club leader is encouraged to work with parents to understand their daughter's needs.

1041. U.S. Extension Service. *The Problem of Reaching and Influencing Farm Women Not in Home Demonstration Clubs.* Circular no. 156. Washington, DC: The Service, 1931. 6p. A43.5/6:156. Results of a study of nonmembers of home demonstration clubs in Kentucky, New Jersey, and South Carolina reports on reasons given for not joining clubs and on the level of interest in participating in extension activities.

1042. U.S. Extensions Service. *Report of Home Demonstration Work, 1930.* by Madge J. Reese. Circular no. 170. Washington, DC: The Service, 1931. 60p. A43.5/6:170. Review of home demonstration work for 1930 highlights some of the major events and influences of the year including organization of home demonstration in the territories of Alaska and Hawaii. Describes the major program areas and some of the methods used in home demonstration, and includes highlights of work with black populations. Provides data on project enrollment by state and program area.

1043. U.S. Extension Service. Office of Cooperative Extension Work. *Home Demonstration Work, Central States, 1930.* Washington, DC: The Service, 1931? 26p. A43.5/2:H75/5. Report describes the organization, activities, and funding for home demonstration in 13 central states briefly mentioning individual activities at the state level.

1044. U.S. Extension Service. Office of Cooperative Extension Work. *Home Demonstration Work, Eastern States, 1930.* by Florence L. Hall. Washington, DC: The Office, 1931? 12p. A43.5/2:H75/6. The 1930 report on home demonstration in eastern states describes special campaigns on topics of clothing, gardening, kitchen improvement, and child development and care.

1045. U.S. Office of Education. *A Symposium on Home and Family Life in a Changing Civilization.* Bulletin 1931, no. 5. Washington, DC: GPO, 1931. 34p. I16.3:931/5. Proceedings of the Second Regional Conference on Homemaking held at Ames, Iowa, November 10 and 11, 1930, includes a section on the "Effect of the New Women's Movement".

1046. U.S. Extension Service. *Home Demonstration Work, 1931.* by Grace E. Frysinger. Circular no. 177. Washington, DC: The Service, 1932. 17p. A43.5/6:177. Reports on home demonstration work in 1931 briefly describes selected state and local programs within the context of economic stress and the farm family. The work of local home demonstration groups in relief activities is also highlighted.

1047. U.S. Extension Service. *Meeting the Needs of Older Rural Girls.* by Gertrude L. Warren. Circular no. 180. Washington, DC: The Service, 1933. 10p. A43.5/6:180. Describes activities of 4-H clubs for 16 to 20-year-old girls including home-management work and social activities, and reports the opinions of 4-H leaders on the special problems and needs of older rural girls.

1048. U.S. Extension Service. *Planning Program of Extension Work for Older Farm Girls.* Circular no. 194. Washington, DC: The Service, 1933. 37p. A43.5/6:194. Discusses the needs of farm women between the ages of 15 and 25 who have outgrown 4-H club work, but who are not yet ready for adult home demonstration groups. The report reviews the number and status of these young women, and notes the low participation of unmarried young women in home demonstration activities. Existing efforts to reach young women through extension are highlighted. As a basis for recommending programs for young women, their psychological characteristics, interests and desires are reviewed citing existing surveys of older girl's interests.

1049. U.S. Extension Service. *Report of Home Demonstration Work, 1933.* by Florence L. Hall. Circular no. 206. Washington, DC: The Service, 1934. 17p. A43.5/6:206. Report describes major projects in home demonstration work in 1933.

1050. U.S. Extension Service. *Home Demonstration Work Comes of Age.* Circular no. 222. Washington, DC: The Service, 1935. 10p. A43.5/6:222. The evolution of home demonstration work and official support in word and legislation from the federal government is presented.

1051. U.S. Extension Service. *Report of Home Demonstration Work, 1934.* by Madge J. Reese. Circular no. 228. Washington, DC: The Service, 1935. 16p. A43.5/6:228. Reviews progress in home demonstration work and major project results for 1934.

1052. U.S. Federal Housing Administration. *Ways for Women to Participate in the Better Housing Program.* Washington, DC: GPO, 1935. 4p. leaflet. Y3.F31/11:2W84/2. Suggestions for women desiring to participate in the Better Housing Program include pointing out to retailers the need to modernize their stores, making club members aware of the Better Housing Program, and modernizing club houses using Modernization Credit Loans.

1053. U.S. Federal Housing Administration. *Woman's Opportunity in the Better Housing Program.* Washington, DC: The Administration, 1935. 12p. leaflet. Y3.F31/11:2W84. Tells the story of two women who helped their families and their communities by securing home modernization and home building loans through the Better Housing Program.

1054. U.S. Bureau of Home Economics, U.S. Bureau of Agricultural Economics, and U.S. Cooperative Extension Service. *A Summary of Some of the Papers Presented at the Farm Family Living Outlook Conference, Washington, D.C., October 28 to November 2, 1935.* Miscellaneous Extension Publication no. 23. Washington, DC: The Bureau, 1936. 24p. A43.5/18:23. Briefly summarizes conference papers on topics such as farm homemakers activities to increase farm income, homemaking education, use of homemaker's leisure time, and regional field agent reports.

1055. U.S. Extension Service. *County Home Economics Extension Programs, Excerpts from Annual Reports of State and County Extension Agents, 1934.* Circular no. 233. Washington, DC: The Service, 1936. 20p. A43.5/6:233. Excerpts from the annual reports of state and county extension agents illustrate programs and methods in home economics extension.

1056. U.S. Extension Service. *Home Demonstration Work.* by Florence L. Hall. Film-Strip Series no. 411. Washington, DC: The Service, 1936. 3p. A43.5/8:411. Describes the slides in a program on the work performed by home demonstration agents.

1057. U.S. Extension Service. *Report of Home Demonstration Work, 1935.* Circular no. 249. Washington, DC: The Service, 1936. 25p. A43.5/6:249. Trends affecting home demonstration work, such as rural electrification and consumer education, and major project results for 1935 are described.

1058. U.S. Extension Service. Division of Cooperative Extension. *Home Demonstration Exhibits at the Third Triennial Conference of the Associated Country Women of the World.* Washington, DC: The Service, 1936. 17p. A43.5/18:32. Photographs and one page summaries of conference exhibits highlight aspects of home demonstrations work.

1059. U.S. Office of Education. Vocational Division. *Homemaking Education Programs for Adults and Out-of-School Youth.* Washington, DC: The Office, 1936. 165p. I16.54/5:1809. Describes the place of homemaking education in the adult education movement and the types of programs in adult homemaking education. Procedures for organizing these classes and sample course materials are provided.

1060. U.S. Extension Service. *Aims and Objectives of Home Demonstration Work.* by C.W. Warburton. Washington, DC: The Service, 1937. 4p. A43.5/6:265. The objectives and aims of home demonstration work are described in terms of the tight financial situation on most farms and the desire to improve family living conditions. Agents are urged to try to understand the problems of the very poor farm families and to provide practical assistance in addressing farm women's problems.

1061. U.S. Extension Service. *Expansion of Home-Economics Work under Baukhead-Jones Act.* by Madge J. Reese. Circular no. 256. Washington, DC: The Service, 1937. 8p. A43.5/6:256. Provides an overview of the growth of home economics extension, the development of trained staff, and the future personnel needs to meet the home demonstration demand. Objectives of home demonstration work and its contribution to a brighter farm outlook are reviewed.

1062. U.S. Office of Education. *Homemaking Education Program for Adults.* Vocational Education Bulletin no. 195. Washington, DC: GPO, 1938. 125p. I16.54/3:195. Discusses the place of homemaking education within the adult education movement and provides some guidance on planning an adult homemaking education program. Training and education of home economics teachers is reviewed and suggestions for methodology in teaching adult homemaking classes is covered. Finally, illustrations from existing adult homemaking programs are presented.

1063. U.S. Extensions Service. *Report of Home Demonstration Work, 1937.* by Florence L. Hall. Circular no. 294. Washington, DC: The Service, 1938. 23p. A43.5/6:294. Report of progress in home demonstration work in 1937 discusses new trends in rural electrification and consumer education and highlights successful programs in nutrition, clothing, home management, and other areas. Describes projects geared toward supplementing income and cooperation with other agencies such as the W.P.A.

1064. U.S. Office of Education. Vocational Education Division. *The Placement of Graduates the First Year after Graduation from Home Economics Education Programs in Institutions Reimbursed from Federal Vocational Funds for the Five-Year Period 1932-37: Home Economics Education.* Washington, DC: The Office, 1938. 11p. I16.54/5:2104. Data on placement by region of home economics education program graduates includes number of graduates and number teaching, in positions other than teaching, continuing study, married, and not placed for 1932-37 and 1936-37. Also compares placement of graduates for the entire U.S. in 1927-32, 1932-37, and 1936-37. Implications of these figures for program focus are discussed.

1065. U.S. Extension Service. *Home Demonstration Work Moves Forward.* by Ola Powell Malcolm. Circular no. 303. Washington, DC: The Service, 1939. 37p. A43.4:303. The 1936 annual report on home demonstration work focuses on the program's efforts in improving rural family finances. State reports are heavily quoted in relation to specific program areas. Information on home demonstration work with black women and girls and with women in Alaska and Puerto Rico is included.

1066. U.S. Housing Authority. Informational Service Division. *American Homemakers Help Design Low Rent Dwellings.* Washington, DC: The Authority, 1939. 3p. I40.2:L95/3.

Informational release on a laboratory to design the layout of low rent housing describes the role of housewives as project consultants.

1067. U.S. Office of Education. *Gallant American Women #4, Women the Providers, November 21, 1939.* by Jane Ashman. Washington, DC: The Office, 1939. 23p. FS5.15:4. The fourth in the "Gallant American Women" radio series celebrates the roll of women in preparing food for the family around a Thanksgiving theme.

1068. U.S. Agricultural Adjustment Administration. *Digest of Rural-Urban Women's Conversations, Held on Invitation of Secretary of Agriculture, Washington, D.C.* Washington, DC: GPO, 1940. 40p. A55.2:W84. Presents excepts from a dialogue between 25 rural women and 25 urban women on problems facing America. Questions for discussion include how to achieve abundance in America, educational opportunity, the role of the Dept. of Agriculture in solving the problem of abundance, and agricultural policy from the homemakers prospective.

1069. U.S. Extension Service. *Progress in Home Demonstration Work: Statistical Analysis of Trends.* by Gladys Gallup and Florence L. Hall. Circular no. 319. Washington, DC: The Service, 1940. 37p. A43.4:319. Through statistics this report presents a picture of home demonstration work with a specific emphasis on home demonstration work in 1938. Maps illustrate the proportion of agents' time spent on various activities by state.

1070. U.S. Extension Service. *Selected Statistical Data Regarding Home Demonstration Work, 1939.* by Grace E. Frysinger. Washington, DC: The Service, 1940. 8p. A43.2:H 75/2. Provides data on home demonstration clubs and agents by state, size of jurisdiction and specialty, and furnishes some data on agents by race.

1071. U.S. Office of Education. *Gallant American Women, #28, the American Home, May 13, 1940. 25p. FS5.15:28.* by Jane Ashman. Washington, DC: The Office, 1940. 25p. FS5.15:28. This episode of the "Gallant American Women" radio series is a tribute to women as homemakers depicting women as instigators of progress in the home, making it more comfortable and bringing others to accept new techniques and technological advances.

1072. U.S. Extension Service. *On the Home Front in Rural America: Home Demonstration Work, 1940.* by Florence L. Hall. Circular no. 370. Washington, DC: The Service, 1941. 14p. A43.4:370. Annual report on home demonstration work for 1940 focuses on nutrition and home improvement with brief descriptions of other activities.

1073. U.S. Office of Education. Vocational Division. *Home Economics in Public High Schools, 1938-39.* Vocational Division Bulletin no. 213. Washington, DC: GPO, 1941. 114p. FS5.123:213. Primary focus of this study was the extent to which home economics is taught in the nation's secondary schools and the enrollment of students in home economics courses by grade and sex.

1074. U.S. Extension Service. *Farm Women on the Home Front: Annual Report of Home Demonstration Work, July 1, 1941 - June 30, 1942.* by Florence L. Hall. Circular no. 390. Washington, DC: The Service, 1942. 14p. A43.4:390. Annual report looks at the traditional aspects of home demonstration work through the eyes of a nation at war. Emphasis is placed on nutrition, extending existing resources, and cooperating with the war effort.

1075. U.S. Office of Education. *Adjustments of College Curriculum to Wartime Conditions and Needs: Report 20, Home Economics.* Washington, DC: The Office, 1943. 4 parts. FS5.33:20/pt.1-4. See 1077 for abstract.

1076.   U.S. Bureau of Agricultural Economics. *How City Housewives Respond to War Food Programs.* Washington, D.C.: The Bureau, 1944. 12p. A36.2:H81/2. Interviews with city housewives provide information on their awareness of war food programs and their willingness to follow the program suggestions.

1077.   U.S. Office of Education. *Adjustments of College Curriculum to Wartime Conditions and Needs: Report 21, Home Economics.* Washington, DC: The Office, 1944. 4 parts. FS5.33:21/pt.no. Report speaks to the role home economics programs can play in helping families adjust to wartime conditions and the need for programs to provide occupational proficiency. The types of students to recruit and some curriculum adjustments to ensure revellent courses are discussed. Part 2, "How to Achieve Improvements in Home Economics Programs," discusses effective family life education, faculty development, and guidance needs. Adjustments in scheduling, requirements, and course contact in home economics as a result of the war are discussed in Part 3. Part 4 describes ways to provide personal and family life education in home economics programs to help students adjust to the war while continuing to provide quality programs for students with professional goals.

1078.   U.S. Office of Price Administration. *Women and Prices.* OPA Consumer Compliance Study Part 1. Washington, DC: The Office, 1944. 23p. Pr32.4202:C76/pt.1. Based on a December 1943 survey of 5000 housewives who do their own shopping, this report summarizes knowledge and attitudes toward price control. Women were asked to define ceiling prices and describe how the prices were set. Other questions asked concerned knowledge of ceiling prices when shopping, knowledge of price controlled items, attitudes toward price evasion, attitude toward reporting violations, acceptance of price control, and attitudes toward continuing price controls after the war. Attitudes toward price controls are further analyzed by group characteristics, such as stores shopped at, educational level, race, and place of residence.

1079.   U.S. Office of Price Administration. *Women and Prices.* Second Consumer Compliance Survey Part 1. Washington, DC: The Office, 1944. 23p. Pr32.4202:C76/2/pt.1. Results of a second survey of housewives knowledge and attitudes relating to price control conducted in mid-1944 provides comparisons to information collected in the first survey (1078).

1080.   U.S. Office of Price Administration. *Women and Rationing.* OPA Consumer Compliance Study Part 2. Washington, DC: The Office, 1944. 25p. Pr32.4202:C76/part.2. See 1081 for abstract.

1081.   U.S. Office of Price Administration. *Women and Rationing: Attitudes, Beliefs, Experience, Knowledge...Compliance Behavior.* Second Consumer Compliance Survey Part 2. Washington, DC: The Office, 1944. 18p. Pr32.4202:C76/2/pt.2. Findings of a June 1944 survey of 4,865 housewives is compared to results of a similar December 1943 survey on women's knowledge and attitudes toward rationing. Questions asked concern adequacy of rations and feelings of depravation, ability to get rationed items, taking items off the ration list, knowledge of rationing, and experience in seeking extra allowances from ration boards. Also surveyed attitudes toward compliance enforcement, experience with rationing violations, and attitudes on the fairness of OPA price controls.

1082.   U.S. Office of Price Administration. *Women and Rent Control.* OPA Consumer Compliance Study, Part 5. Washington, DC: The Office, 1944. 3p. Pr32.4202:C76/pt.5. Report of information gained from personal interviews with 5,000 women in December 1943 covers knowledge and approval of rent control.

1083.   U.S. Office of Education. Vocational Division. *Frontiers in Homemaking Education Programs for Adults.* by Elizabeth Riner. Vocational Division Bulletin no. 239.

Washington, DC: GPO, 1949. 63p. FS5.123:239. Some of the topics covered in this guide to setting up home economics programs for adult women include class content, presenting information to catch the women's interest, and scheduling classes to fit the housewife's schedule. Also covers the details of starting and evaluating programs.

1084.   U.S. Extension Service. *A Report on Home Demonstration Work, November 1949.* by Mena Hogan. Circular no. 463. Washington, DC: The Service, 1950. 25p. A43.4:463. Report on home demonstration work in 1949 highlights both traditional work with rural families and the increasing demand for home demonstration agents in urban areas. Problems of recruiting and retaining home demonstration agents are addressed.

1085.   U.S. Extension Service. *Women in a Free World.* by M.L. Wilson. Washington, DC: The Service, 1950. 7p. A43.21:W84. Talk given at the annual meeting of the National Home Demonstration Council, Biloxi, Mississippi, October 19, 1950, gives a general overview of home demonstration work with a particular emphasis on activities promoting world understanding. The anti-communist rhetoric is minimal.

1086.   U.S. Human Nutrition and Home Economics Bureau. *Workload of Farm Homemakers, Address by Gertrude S. Weiss, Head, Family Economics Division, Bureau of Human Nutrition and Home Economics, Agricultural Research Administration, Department of Agriculture, at 29th Annual Agricultural Outlook Conference, Washington, D.C., Oct. 30, 1951.* Washington, DC: The Bureau, 1951. 3p. A77.702:H75/3. General speech describes the farm and nonfarm work of rural homemakers and the effect of labor-saving devices on their work load.

1087.   U.S. Office of Education. Vocational Division. *Home Economics in Colleges and Universities of the United States.* by Beuleh I. Coon. Vocational Division Bulletin no. 244. Washington, DC: GPO, 1951. 58p. FS5.123:244. Reviews home economics courses and research at the college level.

1088.   U.S. Extension Service. *A Look at Home Demonstration Work.* by Madge J. Reese. Circular no. 483. Washington, DC: The Service, 1952. 24p. A43.4:483. Home demonstration work in 1951 with both farm and urban families is presented. The Service's traditional role of teaching home management and improving communities is described. Encouraging the establishment of rural library services and promoting the understanding of different cultures were programs undertaken by many local groups.

1089.   U.S. Extension Service. *Progress in Home Demonstration Work: A Statistical Analysis of Trends, 1910-1950.* by Amelia S. Gordy and Gladys G. Gallup. Circular no. 479. Washington, DC: GPO, 1952. 37p. A43.4:479. Detailed analysis of home demonstration work chronicles the rise in the number of home demonstration agents and in women serving as voluntary local leaders. Yearly data on number of agents and number of clubs show the growth of home demonstration work, and maps illustrate data for states in 1950. Through statistics the report draws a picture of the type of work performed by a home demonstration agent.

1090.   U.S. Office of Education. *Homemakers in the Defense Program: Implications for Education in Home Economics.* Washington, D.C.: The Office, 1952. 17p. FS5.11:3403. Presents the philosophy supporting homemakers entry into wartime employment and provides guidance on selling the idea to local communities. Discusses the integration of these ideas into home economics programs.

1091.   U.S. Foreign Agriculture Service. Foreign Training Division. *Report on the Institute in Home Economics Extension for Latin American Women, January 29 to May 31, 1953.* Washington, DC: The Service, 1954. 20p. A67.2:H75. Describes a program which brought women from 14 Latin American countries to the U.S. to observe home economic extension programs in the U.S. The problems in the participant's home countries to which knowledge gained at the institute could be applied is summarized. The report gives a general impression of the activities of the women while in the United States.

1092. U.S. Office of Education. Division of Vocational Education. Home Economics Education Branch. *Home Economics in Schools and Colleges of the U.S.A.* Washington, DC: The Office, 1954. 7p. FS5.11:3306/2. Summarizes information on enrollment and curriculum in home economics in schools and colleges. Earlier edition published in 1953.

1093. U.S. Office of Education. *Education for Homemaking in the Secondary Schools of the United States.* by Bernice Mallory and Mary Laxson Buffum. Office of Education Special Series no. 4. Washington, DC: GPO, 1955. 32p. FS5.41:4. The purpose of education for home and family living in the school curriculum and the various factors which influence the development of home economic programs are the focus of this publication. In addition to the discussion of the topics covered in home economics classes, the role of Future Homemakers of America clubs is also highlighted.

1094. U.S. Federal Extension Service. *Changing Styles of Home Demonstration Work, 1910- 1917, Today, Tomorrow.* Washington, DC: The Service, 1956. 30p. A43.2:H75/11. Changes in the farm home between 1910 and 1955 and in the work of home demonstration agents in response to the changes are described in this overview of home demonstration work. Ages and education of farm women and their interests are reviewed as is the progress of amenities in the farm home. Charts illustrating the information presented supplement the text.

1095. U.S. Housing and Home Finance Agency. *Women's Congress on Housing.* Washington, DC: GPO, 1956. 82p. HH1.2:W84. Homemakers voice their opinions on improving modern homes through design of space, use of appliances, and enhancement of appearance.

1096. U.S. Office of Education. Division of Vocational Education. *Factors Influencing Enrollment in Home Economics, a Summary of Those Factors Which Seem to Have Influenced Increased Enrollment at 28 Colleges and Universities in 1955-56.* Washington, DC: The Office, 1957. 15p. FS5.11:3520. Responses of state home economic supervisors in areas where home economics had shown a significant increase in enrollment express ideas on what factors contributed to the increase.

1097. U.S. Office of Education. Division of Vocational Education. Home Economics Branch. *Overview of Nature and Scope of Homemaking in Schools and Colleges.* Washington, DC: The Office, 1957. 8p. FS5.11:3306/4. See 1092 for abstract.

1098. U.S. Federal Extension Service. *Progress in Home Demonstration Work, 1910-56.* by Amelia S. Gordy. Circular no. 516. Washington, DC: The Service, 1958. 39p. A43.4:516. Report on the growth in the field of home economics extension from 1910 to 1956 looks at staffing patterns and characteristics of agents and at the changes in methods agents use to reach individuals. Provides data on the number of homes reached by subject matter of program and briefly describes the growth of home demonstration work in urban areas and outside the U.S.

1099. U.S. Office of Education. Vocational Division. *Homemaking Education Programs for Adults.* Vocational Division Bulletin no. 268. Washington, DC: GPO, 1958. 62p. FS5.123:268. Although the title uses non-sexist language, the publication is primarily geared toward setting up home economics programs for housewives. Some of the areas covered are program setup, course offerings, and building community interest.

1100. U.S. Federal Extension Service. *These Are the Women Who Are Members of Home Demonstration Organizations in the United States.* Circular no. 528. Washington, DC: The Service, 1959? 16p. A43.4:528. Membership in home demonstration organizations is examined by age, education, place of residence, family income, employment, and home economics training.

1101. U.S. Office of Education. *Enrollment in Home Economics Education and Placement of Graduates: A 10-Year Summary, 1947 to 1956-57.* Washington, DC: GPO, 1959. 13p. FS5.11:3571. Study of enrollment in home economics programs between 1947 and 1957 also examines placement of graduates and the effect of marriage on their employment. Provides statistics on enrollment of juniors and seniors in home economics by academic year, 1947/48 to 1956/57, change in enrollment by region and academic year, and number and placement of home economics education graduates in the year following graduation by academic year and region.

1102. U.S. Agricultural Research Service. *Energy Expenditures of Women Performing Selected Activities.* by Martha Richardson and Earl C. McCracken. Home Economics Research Report no. 11. Washington, DC: GPO, 1960. 24p. A1.87:11. The amount of energy required by women to perform basic activities was measured in the hope that the data could be used to develop energy saving methods of performing common household chores.

1103. U.S. Agricultural Research Service. Household Economics Research Division. *Food Consumption and Dietary Levels as Related to Employment of Homemaker, United States - by Region.* Household Food Consumption Survey 1955 Report no. 15. Washington, DC: GPO, 1960. 130p. A1.86:15. Comparison of food consumption patterns in families with an employed wife and with a nonemployed wife showed little difference in the nutritional value of food served. More money was spent on food per person in households with an employed wife and more of the food dollar was spent on meat, poultry and fish, bakery products, and beverages. Families with a working wife were also more likely to eat out. Data is presented by urban and rural area and by region.

1104. U.S. Office of Education. *Studies of Home Economics in High School and in Adult Education Programs, 1955-58.* Washington, DC: GPO, 1960. 185p. FS5.283:83005. Review of current research on home economics in high school and extension programs includes studies of course content and student interest. Student and homemaker needs in relation to home economics programs are described.

1105. U.S. Office of Education. *Management Problems of Homemakers Employed Outside the Home, Resources for Teaching.* by Mildred Weigley Wood. Vocational Division Bulletin no. 289. Washington, DC: GPO, 1961. 153p. FS5.283:83009. Curriculum guide for teaching high school and adult women home management skills focuses on coping with home responsibility while employed outside the home.

1106. U.S. Agricultural Research Service. *Job-Related Expenditures and Management Practices of Gainfully Employed Wives in 4 Georgia Cities.* Home Economics Research Report no. 15. Washington, DC: GPO, 1962. 40p. A1.87:105. Report of a study of the income and job-related expenses of gainfully employed wives in four Georgia cities compares the home management practices of employed and non-employed wives. Factors such as eating out, use of frozen and canned foods, home baking, home food preservation, home sewing, and consumer debt are analyzed by income and family size.

1107. U.S. Office of Education. *Home Economics in the Public Secondary Schools.* Washington, DC: GPO, 1962. 156p. FS5.283:83010. Report presents data on the extent of home economics programs, enrollment, and curriculum characteristics in high schools with most of the data presented for vocational and nonvocational programs by region. Also provides information on home economics programs aimed at boys.

1108.   U.S. Agricultural Research Service. *Job-Related Expenditures and Management Practices of Gainfully Employed Wives in Ohio.* by Emma G. Holms. Home Economics Research Report no. 27. Washington, DC: GPO, 1964. 39p. A1.87:27. A study of employed and non-employed wives in Ohio looked at earnings and job related expenses for rural and non-rural women. Most of the employed women pooled their earnings with their husbands to pay household expenses. Employed wives were likely to pay for child care and laundry service, but other housework showed little difference. Ownership of the home and of home appliances was related more to age and income than employment status of the wife.

1109.   U.S. Office of Education. *Enrollment in Home Economics Education and Employment Status of Graduates the First Year Following Graduation, 1962-63.* Washington, DC: GPO, 1964. 13p. FS5.283:83012. Report of data presents a brief analysis of home economics education enrollment and employment of graduates. Includes enrollment by level and state, and employment status of persons prepared to teach vocational programs.

1110.   U.S. Post Office Dept. *5-Cent Homemakers Commemorative Postage Stamp, Available at Your Local Post Office Oct. 27, 1964.* Washington, DC: GPO, 1964. poster. P1.26/2:H75/3.

1111.   U.S. Consumer Product Safety Commission. *Remarks of the Honorable Barbara Hackman Franklin at the Conference "The Woman as a Consumer," Louisiana State University, Baton Rouge, Louisiana, November 20, 1974.* Washington, DC: The Commission, 1974. 11p. Y3.C76/3/10F85. Address ties the women's movement to the consumer safety movement and reviews what women as consumers are doing for product safety.

1112.   U.S. Social Security Administration. Office of Research and Statistics. *Economic Value of Housewife.* by Wendyce H. Brody. Research and Statistics Note 1975, no. 9. Washington, DC: The Office, 1975. 5p. HE3.28/2:975/9. Describes various approaches to determining the economic value of work performed by housewives and provides a determination of such value based on research performed by Walker and Gauger. Values are reported by race and age, and for nonemployed white women ages 35-39 by age and number of children. Average value of a housewife in 1972 was determined to be $4,705.

1113.   U.S. Congress. House. Committee on Education and Labor. Subcommittee on Elementary, Secondary, and Vocational Education. *Hearings on Reauthorization of the Vocational Education Act of 1963, Part 6: Consumer and Homemaking Education, Hearings on H.R. 66.* 97th Cong., 1st sess., 12,13 Nov. 1981. 264p. Y4.Ed8/1:V85/9/pt.6. Hearings on reauthorization of consumer and homemaking education portions of the Vocational Education Act of 1963 stress the importance of education in parenting and consumer skills. The changing demographics of homemaking education is detailed noting increasing enrollment by boys, students from disadvantaged backgrounds, and the differently-abled. The way consumer and homemaking education programs are meeting the needs of local areas are illustrated in a brief state-by-state review. Several case studies illustrate the benefits for women of consumer and home economics education. The question of incorporating consumer and home economics into the total vocational program funding pool is addressed noting possible adverse effects when programs to place graduates in paid employment are stressed. Some witnesses, noting research showing that women who take home economics courses earn less, question the advisability of targeting disadvantaged women for home economics training instead of more profitable classes.

SERIALS

1114.   U.S. Federal Housing Administration. *Women's Page Clip Sheet, Particularly Suited for Women's Pages and Sections.* Washington, DC: The Administration, 1935. vol. 1 nos. 1-5. weekly. Y3.F31/11:15/1-no. Copy pages provide newspaper articles on home repair and improvement and interior design. Continued by *Women's Page Feature* (1115).

1115.   U.S. Federal Housing Administration. *Women's Page Feature; with Women's Page Housing Shorts.* Washington, DC: The Administration, 1935-36. nos. 1 - 66. weekly. Y3.F31/11:25/no. Continues *Women's Page Clip Sheet* (1114).

1116.   U.S. Office of Education. *Enrollments in Home Economics Courses in Land Grant Institutions.* Washington, DC: The Office, 1952/53 - 1954/55. irreg. FS5.11:3463/no. Enrollment in home economics courses at land grant institutions is reported by sex and home economics program major.

1117.   U.S. Office of Education. Division of Vocational Education. *Home Economics in Degree-Granting Institutions.* Washington, DC: GPO, 1949-1962. biennial. FS5.11:2557 (1949-1958), FS5.283:83008 (1959-1962). Statistical profile of home economics enrollment and program structure at degree-granting institutions provides data by sex on undergraduate and graduate majors in home economics and course enrollment by non-home economics majors; undergraduate enrollment in home economics by sex and by region and state; women enrolled in home economics, 1949-1959; undergraduate men enrolled in home economics, 1949-1959; institutions reporting graduate majors, number of graduate majors, and degrees conferred, 1949-1959; number of home economics students, faculty, courses offered, degrees granted, and credits required for undergraduate degree in home economics by institution, 1959; and areas of home economic majors and fields for which graduates in home economics are prepared by institution, 1959.

8

Education of Women

Some of the earliest documents related specifically to women are the petitions of state legislatures requesting land grants to establish female colleges. Between 1830 and 1898 the legislatures of Alabama, Connecticut, Indiana, Michigan, and Mississippi passed such resolutions. For the District of Columbia these pre-1900 requests for assistance centered on preventing juvenile delinquency through funding of the Orphan Asylum and Female Free School of Alexandria. Of particular interest is the first annual report, issued in 1833, which discusses the evils of irregular school attendance (1120). Later, in 1959, the education of girls in the District of Columbia was again briefly considered in the report on amending the charter of the Sisters of the Visitation in order to facilitate the establishment of a preparatory school and junior college for women (1155).

Two bibliographies provide reference to sources on the education of women from the late 1800s through the 1920s (1143) and 1930s (1148). Several substantial reports from the Bureau of Education describe the philosophy of the day on the education of women. In 1883 the bureau published data on coeducation in public schools accompanied by a review of the pros and cons of coeducation (1133). The effect of class and race on the education of southern women in explored in *Southern Women in the Recent Educational Movement in the South* (1094). A 1918 bulletin, *The Curriculum of the Woman's College,* examines college socialization and career choice (1142). A three part report on adjusting college curriculum to meet wartime needs ties physical education to the World War Two war effort (1152). The status of women's education in 1963 is detailed in the report of the Committee on Education of the President's Commission on the Status of Women, which emphasized continuing education for adult women and guidance counseling for girls (1156). Education for adult women was also stressed in Women's Bureau documents of the 1960s and 1970s. A 1975 report of the National Center of Education Statistics reviews the literature on barriers to postsecondary education for women (1170).

Two major series characterize the documents since 1976. The first, from the National Advisory Council on Women's Educational Programs, is a series of nine documents examining the establishment and operation of women's studies programs. Some of the areas examined include teaching effectiveness (1189), the impact on campus (1190), the relationship to vocational choice (1192), faculty development (1193), and the incorporation of women's studies in graduates' lives (1195). The second series is made up of reports from a series of National Institute of Education sponsored conferences held in the late 1970s on the educational and occupational needs of special populations of women. The conference reports review the educational attainment of Native American, Asian-Pacific-American, Hispanic, White Ethnic, and African American women, and look at the role of culture and identify needed areas of research for each group (1180, 1197-1200). The majority of documents on the education of women since 1970 deal with discrimination in educational opportunity and with federal efforts to ensure educational equity. These documents are described in Chapter 9, Educational Equity. Home economics education is described in

Chapter 7, and documents on vocational education and career guidance are covered in Volume Two.

1118. U.S. Congress. House. *Application of Alabama for Land for Female Academics in That State, a Joint Memorial.* 21st Cong., 1st sess., 1830. 1p. American State Papers: VIII. Public Lands. Vol. 6, no. 794. Memorial of the legislature of Alabama requests a grant of land in each county of Alabama to support the establishment of academies to ensure the proper and necessary education of females.

1119. U.S. Congress. House. *District of Columbia; Petition of the Manager of the Female Orphan Asylum of Georgetown D.C.* H. Doc. 31, 22d Cong., 2d sess., 1833. 1p. Serial 233. Petition requests funding for the Female Orphan Asylum of Georgetown.

1120. U.S. Congress. House. Committee for the District of Columbia. *First Annual Report of the Orphan Asylum and Female Free School of Alexandria.* H. Doc. 65, 22d Cong., 2d sess., 1833. 6p. Serial 234. More rhetoric than solid information characterizes this report on the first year of the Orphan Asylum and Female Free School of Alexandria. The primary focus is on cost and numbers of orphans and destitute girls served although the report does discuss the "remediless evil" of irregular attendance by the girls.

1121. U.S. Congress. Senate. *Application of Alabama for a Grant of Land to the Male and Female Academies in Tuscumbia, Joint Memorial.* 23rd Cong., 1st sess., 1834. 1p. American State Papers: VIII. Public Lands. Vol. 6, no. 1176. Memorial of the legislature of Alabama requests land grants for the Male and Female Academies of Tuscumbia, Alabama and the Elizabeth Academy in Franklin County.

1122. U.S. Congress. House. Committee for the District of Columbia. *Orphan Asylum and Female Free School of Alexandria, Report to Accompany Bill H.R. No. 64.* H. Rept. 35, 28th Cong., 1st sess., 1844. 1p. Serial 445. Report responds to a petition of Mrs. E. Smith and sixteen other women for a charter of incorporation for the Orphan Asylum and Female Free School of Alexandria and for a grant of land in the city of Washington.

1123. U.S. Congress. House. Committee for the District of Columbia. *Orphan Asylum and Free School, to Accompany Bill H.R. No. 250.* H. Rept. 312, 29th Cong., 1st sess., 1846. 1p. Serial 489. Reports a bill to incorporate the Orphan Asylum and Alexandria Female Free School.

1124. U.S. Congress. Senate. *Resolution of the Legislature of Indiana in Favor of a Grant of Land for the Indiana Normal University for the Education of Females.* S. Misc. Doc. 100, 32d Cong., 1st sess., 1852. 1p. Serial 629.

1125. U.S. Congress. House. *Joint Resolution of the Legislature of Michigan Asking for a Donation of Public Lands to Endow Female Colleges.* H. Misc. Doc. 22, 38th Cong., 1st sess., 1864. 1p. Serial 1199.

1126. U.S. Congress. House. *Joint Resolution of the State of Michigan Asking for Donations of Public Lands to Endow Female Colleges.* H. Misc. Doc. 19, 38th Cong., 1st sess., 1864. 1p. Serial 1199.

1127. U.S. Congress. Senate. *Resolution of the Legislature of Michigan in Favor of an Appropriation of Lands to Endow Female Colleges in the Several States.* S. Misc. Doc. 12, 38th Cong., 1st sess., 1864. 1p. Serial 1177.

1128. U.S. Congress. Senate. *Resolutions of the Legislature of Connecticut, in Favor of a Donation of Lands to Endow Female Colleges in the Several States.* S. Misc. Doc. 121, 39th Cong., 1st sess., 1866. 1p. Serial 1239.

1129. U.S. Congress. House. *Resolution of the Legislature of Michigan, Asking for an Appropriation of Lands by Congress to Endow Female Colleges in Several States.* H. Misc. Doc. 5, 40th Cong., 1st sess., 1867. 1p. Serial 1312.

1130. U.S. Congress. Senate. *Resolution of the Legislature of Michigan, in Favor of a Donation of Lands to Endow Female Colleges in the Several States.* S. Misc. Doc. 49, 39th Cong., 2d sess., 1867. 1p. Serial 1278.

1131. U.S. Congress. House. *Memorial of the Legislature of Mississippi, Relation to the Reneau Female University of Mississippi.* H. Misc. Doc. 217, 42d Cong., 2d sess., 1872. 2p. Serial 1527.

1132. U.S. Bureau of Education. *Coeducation of the Sexes in Public Schools.* Circular of Information 1883, no. 2. Washington, DC: GPO, 1883. 30p. I16.5:883/2. Data on cities providing coeducation in public schools in 1882 reviews some of the reasons for and against coeducation.

1133. U.S. Bureau of Education. *Southern Women in the Recent Educational Movement in the South.* Circular of Information 1892, no. 1. by Rev. A.D. Mays. Washington, DC: GPO, 1892. 300p. I16.5:892/1. Detailed monograph explores the education of Southern women and is, in many ways, a discourse on southern culture and economics pre- and post-Civil War. Discusses the factors of class and race in the education of Southern women.

1134. U.S. Congress. House. Committee on the District of Columbia. *Public School Trustees, District of Columbia, Report to Accompany S. 1717.* H. Rept. 1782, 53rd Cong., 3rd sess., 1895. 1p. Serial 3346. Reports a bill authorizing the appointment of women as public school trustees in the District of Columbia. An amendment increased the board size by two and limiting the number of women on the board to two.

1135. U.S. Congress. Senate. Committee on Public Lands. *[Mississippi Industrial Institute and College for the Education of White Girls of the State of Mississippi in the Arts and Science.]* S. Rept. 855, 53rd Cong., 3rd sess., 1895. 1p. Serial 3289.

1136. U.S. Congress. House. Committee on the Public Lands. *Grant of Certain Lands to the State of Alabama.* H. Rept. 1376, 54th Cong., 1st sess., 1896. 1p. Serial 3461. Favorably reports S. 2461, a bill granting lands to Alabama for the use of the Industrial School for Girls of Alabama and the Tuskegee Normal and Industrial Institution.

1137. U.S. Congress. House. Committee on the Public Lands. *Industrial School for Girls of Alabama.* H. Rept. 393, 54th Cong., 1st sess., 1896. 1p. Serial 3458. Report recommends a land grant for the Industrial School for Girls of Alabama, a school for the industrial and classical education of poor white girls in the state.

1138. U.S. Congress. House. Committee on the Public Lands. *Grant of Certain Lands to the State of Alabama.* H. Rept. 293, 55th Cong., 2d sess., 1898. 2p. Serial 3718. Favorable report on S. 2768, a land grant for the Industrial School for Girls of Alabama and the Tuskegee Normal and Industrial Institute.

1139.   U.S. Congress. Senate. Committee on Public Lands. *Grant of Certain Lands to the State of Alabama.* S. Rept. 433, 55th Cong., 2d sess., 1898. 2p. Serial 3620. See 1138 for abstract.

1140.   U.S. Office of Indian Affairs. *Some Things that Girls Should Know How to Do and Hence Should Learn How to Do When in School.* Washington, DC: GPO, 1911. 23p. I20.8:G44. Outline of lessons to be taught to girls in Indian schools includes cooking, housekeeping, care of the sick, and care of animals.

1141.   U.S. Dept. of Agriculture. Office of the Secretary. *Educational Needs of Farm Women.* USDA Report no. 105. Washington, DC: GPO, 1915. 88p. A1.8:105. Third report based on letters from women suggesting ways the USDA could better meet the needs of farm housewives focuses on educating children and on the existing agricultural extension service. The need for farm children to be educated closer to home appears frequently and there is a common complaint that schools don't teach children to live on the farm but encourage them to leave for the city. The major point made regarding adult education of farm women is that the education must come to them because they are limited in their ability to travel.

1142.   U.S. Bureau of Education. *The Curriculum of the Woman's College.* by Louise Robinson. Bureau of Education Bulletin 1918, no. 6. Washington, DC: GPO, 1918. 140p. I16.3:918/6. Description of the curriculum of women's colleges, particularly Vassar, Wellesley, Radcliff, Barnard, and Mount Holyoke, examines the relation between majors and vocations, and discusses the socialization of women's colleges.

1143.   U.S. Bureau of Education. *List of References on Education of Women in the United States.* Washington, DC: GPO, 1923. 7p. I16.10/5:19. Bibliography of books, journal articles, and conference proceedings which address the question of educating women cites works published between the 1890's and 1922.

1144.   U.S. Bureau of Education. *Athletics for Women.* by J.F. Rogers. Physical Education Series no. 4. Washington, DC: GPO, 1924. 4p. I16.40:4. Concern for the health of women entering into athletics led to the formation of the Women's Division of the National Athletic Federation. The resolutions of their executive committee are reported.

1145.   U.S. Bureau of Education. *Parent-Teacher Associations and Foreign-born Women.* Home Economics Circular no. 5. Washington, DC: GPO, 1924. 4p. I16.13:5. Describes how PTAs can help integrate foreign-born women into American society by teaching them homemaking skills.

1146.   U.S. Bureau of Indian Affairs. *Organization Plan for Girls' Advisor, Superintendent, Principal, Girls' Advisor; Responsibilities and Duties.* Washington, DC: The Bureau, 193? 3p. I20.8:G44/3. Lists the duties and responsibilities of the girls' advisor as a counselor to the girls, and in an administrative capacity in conducting the school, working with matron, laundresses and seamstresses, and supervising the dormitories.

1147.   U. S. Bureau of the Indian Affairs. *The Indian Girl: Her Social Heritage, Her Needs, and Her Opportunities.* by Josette Frank, Child Study Association of America. Prepared for the Commission of Indian Affairs. Lawrence, KS: Haskell Institute, 1932. 18p. I20.2:G44. Discussion of the sociological and psychological factors which may influence the behavior of girls sent to Government Indian schools emphasizes conflicts between Indian culture and the school society.

1148.   U.S. Office of Education. *Good References on Education of Women.* by Martha R. McCabe. Office of Education Bibliography no. 4. Washington, DC: GPO, 1936. 16p.

116.46:4/2. Annotated list of books and reports on the education and vocational training of women mostly includes references from the 1930's but some date back to the early 1900's. Earlier edition published in 1931.

1149.   U.S. Congress. House. *Letter from the Acting Director of the Bureau of the Budget: Correspondence from the President of the United States Transmitting a Letter of the Acting Director of the Bureau of the Budget and to Ask the Congress to Give Consideration to the Suggestions Contained Therein.* H. Doc. 683, 75th Cong., 3rd sess., 1938. 5p. Serial 10265. Letter examines the problems related to the Receiving Home for Children and the National Training School for Girls in the District of Columbia and transmits a proposal for disposition of the girls remanded by the courts to the Training School which Congress did not fund past July 1, 1938. The proposals focus on expanding the facilities at the Industrial Home School for Colored Children at Blue Plains and placing more children in foster homes.

1150.   U.S. Office of Education. *Gallant American Women #10, Women of Learning, January 2, 1940.* Washington, DC: The Office, 1940. 24p. FS5.15:10. Changing attitudes toward the education of women are highlighted by the radio script vignettes featuring characters such as Abigail Adams, Mercy Warren, and Hannah Adams.

1151.   U.S. Office of Education. *Gallant American Women #11, Women as Teachers, January 9, 1940.* Washington, DC: The Office, 1940. 23p. FS5.15:11. The role of women as teachers and as supporters of education for women is the theme of this radio script.

1152.   U.S. Federal Security Administration. Office of Education. *Adjustments of College Curriculum to Wartime Conditions and Needs: Report 16; Physical Education for Women, General Aspects.* Washington, DC: The Office, 1943. 3 parts. FS5.33:16/pt.1-3. Report on the adaptation of physical education requirements to wartime needs suggests vigorous activities, "promotion of an attitudes of joy in bodily movement," emergency skills learning, and student-faculty planning of activities to develop practices in democratic techniques. Part I discusses staff and facilities and the need for emotionally stable, happy teachers. Coping with limited financial resources is also stressed. Part II describes how the group activities in physical education classes can be used to strengthen understanding of democratic principles and encourage individual initiative. Attempts to tie physical education activities to war work focus on leadership and group dynamic skills. Also discusses the more traditional role of physical education in developing agility, muscular strength, courage, endurance, flexibility, and the ability to relax. Part III discusses organization of the total recreational program stressing appropriate activity levels, democratic principles, guidance and morale, and evaluation of fitness.

1153.   U.S. Women's Bureau. *Replies to the ECOSOC Questionnaire on the Legal Status and Treatment of Women, Part I, Public Law, Section D: Educational and Professional Opportunities.* Washington, DC: The Bureau, 1947. 33p. L13.2:Ec7/pt.1/sec.D. Answers to the UN Economic and Social Council questionnaire on state and federal laws regarding education for girls covers compulsory education, availability of public school for girls, access to college education, and equality of college and professional opportunities. Provides citations to state codes governing school laws and professional occupation licensing laws, and presents statistics by sex and state on school enrollment, high school graduates, enrollment in federally aided vocational classes, enrollment in teacher training courses, higher education enrollments, and professional school enrollments.

1154.   U.S. Congress. Senate. *Communication from the President of the United States Transmitting a Proposed Supplemental Appropriation for the District of Columbia, Fiscal Year 1953, Amounting to $86,000.* S. Doc. 119, 82d Cong., 2d sess., 1952. 2p. Serial 11593. Transmits a supplemental budget appropriation to cover the cost of plans and specifications for an Industrial Home School for Colored Girls to replace the National School for Girls.

1155.   U.S. Congress. Senate. Committee on the District of Columbia. *Supplementing and Modifying the Act of May 24, 1928 (6 Stat 383, Ch. CXII), insofar as It Relates to the Corporation Powers of the Sisters of the Visitation, of Georgetown in the District of Columbia, Report to Accompany H.R. 4282.* S. Rept. 288, 86th Cong., 1st sess., 1959. 2p. Serial 12150. Committee favorably reports amending the charter of the Sisters of the Visitation to clarify their organization and the operation of Georgetown Visitation Preparatory School and Georgetown Visitation Junior College, schools established to provide education for girls.

1156.   U.S. President's Commission on the Status of Women. *Report of Committee on Education to President's Commission on the Status of Women.* Washington, DC: GPO, 1963. 71p. Pr35.8:W84/Ed8. Working from a philosophy that women's education and career should not displace traditional responsibilities of women in the home and community, the report emphasizes continuing education for adult women. Financial aid and guidance counseling as they affect girls and women are explored. Finally, the report makes recommendations on education for home, health, and family.

1157.   U.S. Women's Bureau. *The Impact of Education, Address by Esther Petersen, Assistant Secretary of Labor and Director of the Women's Bureau, at the Symposium on Man and Civilization: The Potential of Woman, University of California School of Medicine, San Francisco, Calf., Jan. 26, 1963.* Washington, DC: The Bureau, 1963. 16p. L13.12:P44/6. Women's career patterns as they relate to education form the basis of this speech which stresses the tendency for high school and college educated women to work before marriage, drop out of the labor market for a few years for childrearing, then return to the labor market. A broad-based education which would allow these women to train for specific jobs later on and the need for continuing education program are noted. Government programs to make education more accessible to women after high school and later in life are also promoted. Adapting the college system to adult women's needs is discussed.

1158.   U.S. Women's Bureau. *Why Continuing Education Programs for Women?* Washington, DC: The Bureau, 1963. 8p. L13.2:Ed8/2. The return of mature women to college and to the labor force market is described in this publication which notes some of the adjustments higher education should make to accommodate their needs. Reports the results of a study of women 15 years after college which examined their employment and education expectations and the types of educational services they required. Briefly describes continuing education programs already in place for mature women. Appendix includes a list of educational services and continuing education programs for mature women and a selected reading list of related materials.

1159.   U.S. Women's Bureau. *Needs and Opportunities in Our Society for Educated Women, [addressed by Esther Peterson, at Itasca State Park, Minnesota, Sept. 7, 1962.]* Washington, DC: The Bureau, 1964. 12p. L13.2:W84/41. The educational needs of women, particularly housewives who married young, are discussed in this speech by Esther Peterson. The need for educated women in the home, in the labor force, and as volunteers is stressed with supporting statistics. The need for new approaches to guidance counseling for women and women's lack of geographic mobility are noted.

1160.   U.S. Women's Bureau. *Fact Sheet on the Educational Attainment of Nonwhite Women and Men.* Washington, DC: The Bureau, 1965. 2p. L13.2:Ed8/4. Later editions published as *Fact Sheet on the Educational Attainment of Nonwhite Women* (1212).

1161. U.S. Dept. of Labor. *Who's Afraid of the Educated Woman? Address by Secretary of Labor W. Willard Wirtz before Bryn Mawr Club of Washington, Washington, D.C., Mar. 12, 1966.* by W. Willard Wirtz. Washington, DC: The Dept., 1966. 7p. L1.13:W74/67. Humorous speech quotes historians and philosophers on the subject of the educated woman.

1162. U.S. Women's Bureau. *Continuing Education Programs for Women.* Women's Bureau Pamphlet no. 10. Washington, DC: GPO, 1966. 31p. L13.19:10. Describes the needs of mature women for continuing education programs and summarizes programs offered around the country. Later editions published in 1968 and 1971 (1165).

1163. U.S. National Institutes of Health. *Special Report on Women and Graduate Study.* Resources for Medical Research Report no. 13. Washington, DC: GPO, 1968. 94p. FS2.22/33:13. Describes the result of a study of the obstacles to graduate study by women and the major factors which would allow more women to complete their graduate training. Women's career decisions and changes in expectations over a three year period are analyzed. Financial and family concerns were the major obstacles to graduate study identified.

1164. U.S. Office of Education. Office of Economic Opportunity. *Model Programs, Childhood Education: Mother's Training Program, Urbana, Illinois.* Washington, DC: GPO, 1970. 19p. HE5.220:20147. Describes a program to train disadvantaged mothers to teach their own children, resulting in new attitudes for the mothers and educational gains for the children.

1165. U.S. Women's Bureau. *Continuing Education Programs and Services for Women.* Women's Bureau Pamphlet no. 10, revised. Washington, DC: GPO, 1971. 167p. L36.112:10. General discussion explores why women are returning to finish college degree programs and the types of programs necessary to meed their needs. The majority of the publication is a list of programs geared toward or suitable for women continuing their education, arranged by state and institution. Earlier editions published in 1966 (1162) and 1968.

1166. U.S. Women's Bureau. *Plans for Widening Women's Educational Opportunities.* Washington, DC: The Bureau, 1972. 13p. L36.102:Ed3. Paper outlines how educational institutions can and should alter their programs to accommodate the educational needs of mature women and to encourage girls and women to explore nontraditional career paths. Programs which are trying to meet these needs are described.

1167. U.S. National Advisory Council on Extension and Continuing Education. *Question of Opportunity: Women and Continuing Education.* by Kathryn L. Mulligan. Washington, DC: The Council, 1973. 33p. Y3.Ex8:2W84. Review and analysis of the literature on continuing education programs for adult women highlights the factors which affect women's ability to take advantage of educational opportunities, and notes the lack of commitment on the part of university administrators to programs designed for adult women. The financial assistance available to women and the problem of part-time status are described. Finally, federal programs and legislation which impact women's education are reviewed with an overview of past funding and program emphasis for women's programs.

1168. U.S. Women's Bureau. *Continuing Education for Women: Current Developments.* Washington, DC: GPO, 1974. 13p. L36.102:Ed8/2. Describes innovative programs for mature women students and how these programs have begun to change approaches to counseling high school and college women. Special programs set up for low income women, single women, women offenders and union women, and the role of consortiums and extension programs are described. Research and evaluation of these programs is reviewed along with efforts to disseminate information on programs and the problems of funding continuing education.

1169. U.S. Women's Bureau. *Get Credit for What You Know*. Leaflet no. 56. Washington, DC: GPO, 1974. 8p. leaflet. L36.110:56. Describes programs for getting the GED and college credit by examination. Colleges study opportunities available in a flexible course structure such as the "open university", are noted.

1170. U.S. National Center for Educational Statistics. *Barriers to Women's Participation in Post Secondary Education: A Review of Research and Commentary as of 1973-74*. Washington, DC: GPO, 1975. 74p. HE19.311:W84. Women of equal ability were less likely than their male counterparts to enter degree programs and were more likely to leave school before completing their degree. This review of the literature examines the factors which contribute to this trend such as admissions and financial aid practices, curriculum design, faculty attitudes, social constrains and psychological factors.

1171. U.S. Dept. of Health, Education, and Welfare. Education Division. *Focus on Women: A Guide to Programs and Research in the Education Division*. Washington, DC: The Department, 1976? 37p. HE19.8:W84. Presents information on women-related programs and research funded by the Office of the Assistant Secretary for Education, Office of Education, and National Institute of Education.

1172. U.S. National Center for Educational Statistics. *Women's Participation in First-Professional Degree Programs in Medicine, Dentistry, Veterinary Medicine, and Law, 1969-70 through 1974-75*. by Mary Diederich Ott. Washington, DC: GPO, 1976. 29p. HE19.302:W84/2/969-75. Furnishes data documenting the increase in enrollment of women in first-professional degree programs in medicine, dentistry, veterinary medicine and law with statistics on acceptance, enrollment, and degrees awards 1969/70 to 1974/74.

1173. U.S. National Center for Educational Statistics. *Women's Representation among Recipients of Doctor's and First Professional Degrees, 1970-71 through 1974-75*. by Mary Diederich Ott. Washington, DC: GPO, 1976. 13p. HE19.302:W84/970-75. Data on number of doctor's and first professional degrees awarded by sex and specialty and percentage of degrees conferred on women for each specialty by year, 1970/71 to 1975/75, is furnished.

1174. U.S. National Advisory Council on Women's Educational Programs. *Educational Needs of Rural Women and Girls*. Washington, DC: GPO, 1977. 71p. Y3.Ed8/6:2Ed8. Report on consultations held by the National Advisory Council on the educational needs of rural women and girls discusses the recommendations of the council and related issues such as health education, health care and political participation. Includes a review of federal and national education programs that impact rural women and a short annotated bibliography.

1175. U.S. National Advisory Council on Women's Educational Programs. *Seven Years Later: Women's Studies Programs in 1976*. by Florence Howe. Washington, DC: The Council, 1977. 104p. Y3.Ed8/6:2St9/976. Study of the status of women's studies programs reviews enrollment, faculty, governance structures, and funding in fifteen mature women's studies programs. Also looks at the impact of women's studies on individuals and institutions and makes recommendations for federal government support of women's studies.

1176. U.S. National Institute of Education. *Grants for Research on Education and Work, Spring 1977*. Washington, DC: The Institute, 1977. 50p. HE19.202:G76/2/977. Application information for Women and Mathematics career awareness grants.

1177. U.S. National Institute of Education. Education and Work Group. *Women and Mathematics: Research Perspectives for Change*. by Lynn H. Fox, et al. NIE Papers in

Education and Work no. 8. Washington, DC: GPO, 1977. 207p. HE19.212:8. Research review on women and mathematics looks at the effect of sex role socialization on mathematics participation and achievement and at the influence of selected cognitive, affective, and educational variables on sex-related differences in mathematics learning and studying. Also examines the role of biological factors on sex-related differences in mathematics achievement.

1178. U.S. Dept. of Health, Education, and Welfare. Fund for the Improvement of Postsecondary Education. *Reports from the Fund: Projects/Women.* Washington, DC: GPO, 1978. 11p. HE19.9:R29. Describes projects funded by the Fund for the Improvement of Postsecondary Education which were geared toward improving the postsecondary educational experience of women.

1179. U.S. National Advisory Council on Women's Educational Programs. *Problems in Assessing the Impact of Education Division Programs on Girls and Women.* by JoAnn M. Steiger. Washington, DC: The Council, 1978. 23p. Y3.Ed8/6:2P94. Examination of the difficulty in assessing the impact of education programs on girls and women stresses the lack of data and the lack of information on what data is collected by sex and by race/ethnicity. Also notes the lack of analysis of existing data to determine differential impact by sex and race/ethnicity.

1180. U.S. National Institute of Education. Women's Research Program. Educational Equity Group. *Conference on the Educational and Occupational Needs of Black Women, December 16-17, 1975.* Washington, DC: The Institute, 1978. 2 vol. HE19.202:Ed8/6/v.1-2. Through background papers and subsequent discussion conference participants identified needed research on the educational and occupational needs of black women and recommended NIE action to stimulate research in this area. Volume one contains an overview and the recommendations while volume two reprints the nine background papers.

1181. U.S. Office of Education. *Finding Funds for Programs Related to Women's Education and Other Opportunities for Women.* by Ruth B. Ekstrom and Aileen Wehren. Washington, DC: GPO, 1978. 85p. HE19.102:W84/2. Provides information on writing a funding request and profiles funding opportunities through foundations and federal agencies.

1182. U.S. Dept. of Education. Office of Education, Business and Labor Affairs. *Guide for the Preparation of Proposals for the Pre-Freshman and Cooperative Education for Minorities and Women in Engineering (PREFACE) Program- 1980.* Washington, DC: The Office, 1979. 8p. E1.33:0012/2. Details of the PREFACE program accompany guidelines for colleges and universities submitting proposals.

1183. U.S. National Advisory Council on Women's Educational Programs. *Working Women Speak: Education, Training, Counseling Needs.* Washington, DC: The Council, 1979. 43p. Y3.Ed8/6:2W89. Review of the status of working women and reports from National Council on Working Women dialogues focus on the educational and training needs of women workers.

1184. U.S. National Center for Educational Statistics. *Degree Awards to Women: An Update.* Washington, DC: GPO, 1979. 33p. HE19.302:W84/4. Reports data on bachelor's, master's, doctoral, and first professional degrees awarded to women in 1977 including percentage of women among degree recipients and distribution of degrees by sex, discipline division and field of study.

1185. U.S. National Institute of Mental Health. *Questions Women Most Often Ask about National Institute of Mental Health Research Grants.* Washington, DC: GPO, 1979. 7p. leaflet. HE20.8102:W84/979. Earlier edition issued in 1978.

1186. U.S. Congress. Senate. Committee on Labor and Human Resources. *Education Amendments of 1980, Report to Accompany S. 1839.* S. Rept. 96-733, 96th Cong., 2d sess., 1980. 430p. Serial 13324. One of the programs authorized by the Education Amendments of 1980 was a demonstration program which encouraged educational programs for working women at the worksite.

1187. U.S. Dept. of Education. *Selected List of Postsecondary Education Opportunities for Minorities and Women.* by Linda Byrd-Johnson and Carol J. Smith. Washington, DC: GPO, 1980. 106p. ED1.2:P94/980. Scholarship and fellowship opportunities are described by field and selected programs specifically for women are listed. The basics of federally sponsored financial aid are explained. Earlier editions published in 1978 and 1979.

1188. U.S. National Advisory Council on Women's Educational Programs. *Sexual Harassment: A Report on the Sexual Harassment of Students.* by Frank J. Till. Washington, DC: The Council, 1980. 87p. ED1.2:Se9. Excerpts of reports from individual students tell of their experience with sexual harassment on campus and how they responded it. The report also describes how the institutions responded to the report. The report is primarily a collection of personal experiences, not a comprehensive study. Part II of the report provides technical information regarding the legality of sexual harassment.

1189. U.S. National Institute of Education. *The Effectiveness of Women's Studies Teaching.* by Nancy M. Porter and Margaret T. Eileenchild. Washington, DC: GPO, 1980. 76p. HE19.220:T22. Report reviews the research to date on the effectiveness of teaching in women's studies and identifies areas of needed research.

1190. U.S. National Institute of Education. *The Impact of Women's Studies on the Campus and the Disciplines.* by Florence Howe and Paul Lauter. Washington, DC: GPO, 1980. 132p. HE19.220:C15. Review of the literature on the effect of women's studies programs on campuses and in professional organizations found a growing tendency for women's studies to be accepted as a legitimate field of study, but pointed out a lack of longitudinal research documenting the impact of women's studies programs.

1191. U.S. National Institute of Education. *Re-Entry Women Involved in Women's Studies.* by Blanche Glassman Hersh. Washington, DC: GPO, 1980. 57p. HE19.220:R25. Overview of the relationship between re-entry women and women's studies reviews the history and research literature, and identifies some of the problems associated with research in these areas.

1192. U.S. National Institute of Education. *The Relationship between Women's Studies, Career Development, and Vocational Choice.* by Christine E. Bose and Janet Priest-Jones. Washington, DC: GPO, 1980. 59p. HE19.220:C18. Report reviews the literature on the relationship between women's studies courses and career aspirations, and suggests areas for further research.

1193. U.S. National Institute of Education. *Women's Studies as a Catalyst for Faculty Development.* by Elizabeth Ness Nelson and Kathryn H. Brooks. Washington, DC: GPO, 1980. 43p. HE19.220:C28. Review of the available literature on the role of women's studies in faculty development and results of a survey of women's studies programs found some indications of an impact on faculty development, but noted a lack of research to document the level of impact. Report includes several proposals to improve information and research on the faculty development activities of women's studies programs.

1194. U.S. National Institute of Education. *Women's Studies Evaluation Handbook.* by Mary Ann Millsap, et al. Washington, DC: GPO, 1980. 63p. HE19.208:W84. Practical guide to the evaluation of women's studies programs provides descriptions of various methods of evaluation with specific reference to women's studies goals and objectives. Appendix B abstracts several research studies on women's studies programs.

1195. U.S. National Institute of Education. *Women's Studies Graduates.* Washington, DC: GPO, 1980. 174p. ED1.312:W84. Study looks at how women with degrees in women's studies use those degrees in their careers and how they incorporate their feminist views into their lives.

1196. U.S. National Institute of Education. *Women's Studies in the Community College.* Washington, DC: GPO, 1980. 43p. HE19.220:C73. Review of the literature found almost no documentation on women's studies courses at the community college level. The report recommends that NIE conduct further research in this area.

1197. U.S. National Institute of Education. Program of Teaching and Learning. *Conference on the Educational and Occupational Needs of American Indian Women.* Washington, DC: GPO, 1980. 312p. ED1.311:In2. American Indian women representing tribes from all regions of the U.S. met to discuss research on the needs of American Indian women. Papers presented explore the employment and educational needs of women within the context of tribal society. Recommendations for research emphasis of federal agencies are based on the papers. Includes some background statistics on the occupations and education of American Indian women.

1198. U.S. National Institute of Education. Program of Teaching and Learning. *Conference on the Educational and Occupational Needs of Asian-Pacific-American Women.* Washington, DC: GPO, 1980. 390p. ED1.311:As4. Conference papers examine the early socialization of Asian-Pacific women and its effect on their educational goals and attainment. The special problems of Asian-Pacific women married to U.S. military personnel is the topic of one of the papers. Recommendations for a federal research agenda include collection of data on Asian-Pacific women and the encouragement of research sensitive to the issues identified.

1199. U.S. National Institute of Education. Program on Teaching and Learning. *Conference on the Education and Occupational Needs of Hispanic Women.* Washington, DC: GPO, 1980. 301p. ED1.311:H62. Representative Hispanic women activists and higher education faculty and administrators presented background papers at this conference on the educational and occupational needs of Hispanic women. The participants identified areas where policies and research are needed and made recommendations, many of which focus on federal, state and local programs for the Hispanic community. Includes background statistics on Hispanic women and educational attainment and earnings.

1200. U.S. National Institute of Education. Program on Teaching and Learning. *Conference on the Education and Occupational Needs of White Ethnic Women.* Washington, DC: GPO, 1980. 240p. ED1.311:Et3. The education and social needs of white ethnic women are examined in the presented papers and discussion at the conference. The need to encourage career opportunities for white ethnic girls and to foster leadership skills, while recognizing the desire to preserve the heritage of ethnic groups, is stressed.

1201. U.S. Veterans Administration. Office of Reports and Statistics. *Women Veterans - Use of Educational Benefits under the GI Bill.* Washington, D.C.: GPO, 1981. 26p. VA1.57:81-1. Analysis of use of the GI Bill by female post-Korean veterans found that women entered the service at a higher educational level than males, but were less likely to continue their education on the GI Bill.

1202. U.S. National Institutes of Health. Division of Research Grants. *NIH Programs of Special Interest to Minorities and Women.* Bethesda, MD: The Institutes, 1984. folder and cards. HE20.3002:M66/4. Each card describes an NIH grant or fellowship program of interest to women.

1203. U.S. National Science Foundation. *A Directory of Federal R & D Agencies' Science and Engineering Programs for Women, Minorities, and Physically Handicapped Persons.* Washington, DC: The Foundation, 1985. 27p. NS1.50:M66. Directory describes department and agency research programs which target women, minorities and the physically handicapped. Most programs target faculty members and research scientists, but some are aimed at high school and college students.

1204. U.S. Congress. House. Committee on Government Operations. Human Resources and Intergovernmental Relations Subcommittee. *Civil Rights Enforcement by the Department of Education.* 100th Cong., 1st sess., 23 Apr. 1987. 398p. Y4.G74/7:Ed8/7. Hearing examines Department of Education Office of Civil Rights enforcement activities and in particular looks at charges of backdating documents and encouraging individuals to drop complaints.

1205. U.S. Congress. House. Committee on Science, Space, and Technology. Subcommittee on Science, Research and Technology. *Women, Minorities, and the Disabled in Science and Technology, Hearing.* 100th Cong., 2d sess., 28 June 1988. 183p. Y4.Sci2:100/134. While stressing the need to recruit women and minorities to science and engineering, hearing witnesses point out the fiscal and psychological barriers to their entrance into these fields. Factors that predict success for women and minorities as scientists and engineers, particularly the role of women's and predominantly black colleges, are noted. Special precollege programs to prepare students, mainly minority students, for college work are highlighted.

1206. U.S. Congress. House, Committee on Science, Space and Technology. Subcommittee on Science, Research and Technology. *Science and Technology Education at Community Colleges, Hearing.* 101st Cong., 1st sess., 11 Apr. 1989. 216p. Y4.Sci2:101/34. Hearing on the state of science and technology education at community colleges focuses on the quality of that education and on improving the flow of those students into baccalaureate and eventually Ph.D. programs. Most witnesses note the need to encourage women and minorities to enter scientific and technical fields, but only one witness specifically discusses the number of adult women matriculating at community colleges and suggests ways to encourage those women to pursue technology-related fields.

1207. U.S. Congress. Senate. Committee on Governmental Affairs. *Crisis in Science and Math Education, Hearing.* 101st Cong., 1st sess., 9 Nov. 1989. 134p. Y4.G74/9:S.hrg.101-561. Witnesses at a hearing on meeting the nation's need for scientists and engineers focus on the need to improve science and mathematics education at the secondary school level. One point repeatedly made in testimony is the need to change societal attitudes and teacher preconceptions which discourage female and minority students from taking and excelling in math and science classes.

1208. U.S. Congress. Senate. Committee on Labor and Human Resources. *Crisis in American Math, Science and Engineering Education, Hearing.* 101st Cong., 1st sess., 14 Nov. 1989. 77p. Y4.L11/4:S.hrg.101-459. Improving math and science education at the primary and secondary school level is the main focus of a hearing on the decline of math and science in postsecondary education. The factors that discourage women and minorities from pursuing post-secondary education in these fields are examined.

1209. U.S. Task Force on Women, Minorities, and the Handicapped in Science and Technology. *Changing America: The New Face of Science and Engineering, Final Report.* Washington, DC: The Task Force, 1989. 46p. Y3.W84/3:2Am3/2. Final report of the Task Force summarizes the representation of women, minorities, and the handicapped in science and engineering education and makes recommendations on the role of business, educational systems, and federal research in improving the situation.

1210. U.S. Congress. Senate. Committee on Labor and Human Resources. *Excellence in Mathematics, Science, and Engineers Education Act of 1990, Report to Accompany S. 2114.* S. Rept. 101-412, 101st Cong., 2d sess., 1 Aug. 1900. 35p. Report recommends a bill aimed at improving science and engineering education and increasing female and minority participation in science and technology fields.

SERIALS

1211. U.S. Office of Education. Home Economics Division. *Reading Course for Girls.* Washington, DC: The Office, 1915-1924. irreg. I16.12:5/rev. no.

1212. U.S. Women's Bureau. *Fact Sheet on the Educational Attainment of Nonwhite Women.* Washington, DC: The Bureau, 1966 -1968. annual. L13.2:Ed8/6/year. Published earlier as *Fact Sheet on the Educational Attainment of Nonwhite Women and Men* (1160).

1213. U.S. Women's Bureau. *Fact Sheet on the Educational Attainment of Women.* Washington, DC: The Bureau, 1965 - 1969. irreg. L13.2:Ed8/5/year. Summary data highlights trends in the educational attainment of women from 1900.

1214. U.S. Women's Bureau. *Trends in the Educational Attainment of Women.* Washington, DC: GPO, 1965 - 1969. irreg. L13.2:Ed8/3/year. Analysis and supporting statistics on trends in the educational attainment of women since 1900 looks at the number of degrees earned and at women as a percentage of all degrees by type of degree. Also examines the relationship between educational attainment of women and their employment patterns.

9

Educational Equity

The decade of the 1970s saw a focus in federal legislation on equal educational opportunity for women. In 1970 Congress held extensive hearings on discrimination against women in education and its effect on income and employment (1215). Title IX of the Education Amendments of 1972 and the Women's Educational Equity Act were two major pieces of legislation passed in the early 1970s. The hearings on WEEA explore in some depth the problem of gender discrimination at all levels and the need for research and demonstration programs (1220-1221). The programs conducted under WEEA are described in its annual report (1315) and in hearings on the undermining of WEEA by the Reagan Administration (1293) and on WEEA reauthorization (1302, 1306).

The majority of the documents deal with the implementation and application of Title IX. A major series of workshop manuals explore Title IX implementation issues for administrators, teachers, and the community at the elementary-secondary and postsecondary levels (1256-1270). One of the biggest issues surrounding Title IX was its application to intercollegiate athletics. As early as 1974 and again in 1975 attempts were made to protect intercollegiate athletics revenues from Title IX requirements (1225, 1229). The implementation of Title IX in athletics is reviewed in HEW regulations and guidelines (1230, 1231) and in manuals designed to clarify compliance for school officials (1247, 1260, 1263, 1270). A good overview of the equity issues in women's athletics can be found in the U.S. Commission on Civil Right's report, *More Hurdles to Clear: Women and Girls in Competitive Athletics* (1276).

With the Supreme Court's decision in *Grove City College v. Bell* (465 U.S. 555), Title IX again became the center of controversy. Congress responded with legislation aimed at ensuring Title IX's application to institutions, not just programs, receiving federal assistance. The hearing held in 1982, *Guaranteed Student Loan and Civil Rights Enforcement* (1283), was the first in a series of hearings where Title IX enforcement, abortion, and religious institutions are discussed at length in relation to indirect federal aid (1290, 1292, 1294-1297, 1301). Harsh criticism is leveled at the Department of Education's Office of Civil Rights' Title IX enforcement effort in both a 1988 committee print and in a 1989 hearing (1309, 1313). Equity in education is also discussed in some of the general works on discrimination against women cited in Chapter 4. Consult the index to locate these references. For documents on discrimination in vocational education and career counseling, consult Volume Two.

1215. U.S. Congress. House. Committee on Education and Labor. Special Subcommittee on Education. *Discrimination against Women, Hearings on Section 805 of H.R. 16098.* 96th Cong., 2d sess., 17 June - 31 July 1970. 1261p. Y4.Ed8/1:W84/3/pt.1-2. Hearing testimony presents facts on discrimination against women in education with a focus on post-secondary education. Relationships between educational attainment and poverty, and women's changing role in the work force, are explored. Reprints several articles and pamphlets on women's work and education and presents numerous articles on salaries of college and university teachers by sex, doctorates awarded to women by field, and the employment of women and men at United Press International.

1216. U.S. Congress. House. Committee on Education and Labor. *Higher Education Act of 1971, Report Together with Supplemental, Additional, and Individual Views to Accompany H.R. 7248.* H. Rept. 92-554, 92d Cong., 1st sess., 1971. 257p. Serial 12932-4. Among the provisions of the bill reported are sections prohibiting sex discrimination in programs receiving federal funding and removing exemptions for persons employed in educational institutions from the equal employment provisions of the Civil Rights Act. Also eliminated is the exemption from the equal pay provisions of the Fair Labor Standards Act of people employed in executive, administrative, or professional positions. Discussion of the sex equity provision is minimal, although one additional view stresses support of this section of the act.

1217. U.S. Citizens' Advisory Council on the Status of Women. *Need for Studies of Sex Discrimination in Public Schools.* Washington, DC: GPO, 1972. 11p. Y3.In8/21:2Se9. Outline of areas of probable sex discrimination in elementary and secondary schools is designed as a guide for local groups desiring to take action to eliminate discrimination. A list of publications and related court decisions is provided.

1218. U.S. Congress. House. *Education Amendments of 1972, Conference Report to Accompany S. 659.* H. Rept. 92-1085, 92d Cong., 2d sess., 1972. 220p. Serial 12974-3. Conference report on the Education Amendments of 1972 delineates the House and Senate amendments to a bill prohibiting discrimination on the basis of gender in educational programs and the conference committee's decision on each amendment.

1219. U.S. Congress. Senate. *Education Amendments of 1972, Conference Report to Accompany S. 659.* S. Rept. 92-798, 92d Cong., 2d sess., 1972. 229p. Serial 12971-3. See 1218 for abstract.

1220. U.S. Congress. House. Committee on Education and Labor. Subcommittee on Equal Opportunities. *The Women's Educational Equity Act, Hearings on H.R. 208, Part 1.* 93rd Cong., 1st sess., 25 July - 13 Sept. 1973. 622p. Y4.Ed8/1:W84/5/pt.1. Hearings on the Women's Educational Equity Act presents testimony on the extent of gender discrimination in elementary, secondary, and postsecondary education. Witnesses describe gender bias in textbooks and vocational counseling. Data from studies on sex and race of textbook characters is reported.

1221. U.S. Congress. Senate. Committee on Labor and Public Welfare. Subcommittee on Education. *Women's Educational Equity Act of 1973, Hearings on S. 2518.* 93rd Cong., 1st sess., 17 Oct., 9 Nov. 1973. 426p. Y4.L11/2:W84. Hearing on the Women's Educational Equity Act documents continued discrimination against women at all educational levels and stresses the need for government support for research and programs to eliminate inequities.

1222. U.S. Dept. of Health, Education and Welfare. Office for Civil Rights. *Higher Education Guidelines Executive Order 11246.* Washington, DC: GPO, 1973. 86p. HE1.6/3:H53. Addressing itself primarily to college and university administrators, this publication reviews the executive orders and resulting regulations prohibiting discrimination by federal contractors. Specifically addressed are common discriminatory personnel practices in higher education and the development of affirmative action programs. Appendices reprint relevant documents including Titles VI and VII of the Civil Rights Act of 1964, Title IX of the Education Amendments of 1972, and *Federal Register* guidelines.

1223. U.S. Congress. House. *Education Amendments of 1974, Conference Report to Accompany H.R. 69.* H. Rept. 93-1211, 93rd Cong., 2d sess., 1974. 209p. Serial 13061-6. Identical to S. Rept. 93-1026 (1225).

1224. U.S. Congress. House. *White House Conference on Library and Information Services, Conference Report to Accompany S.J. Res. 40.* H. Rept. 93-1619, 93rd Cong., 2d sess., 1974. 13p. Serial 13061-11. Identical to S. Rept. 93-1409 (1226).

1225. U.S. Congress. Senate. *Education Amendments of 1974, Conference Report to Accompany H.R. 69.* S. Rept. 93-1026, 93rd Cong., 2d sess., 1974. 209p. Serial 13057-5. Conference report resolves House and Senate differences on the Education Amendments of 1974 including a Senate amendment to Title IX of the Education Amendments of 1972 which would exempt revenue producing intercollegiate athletic activities. Also accepted in the report are Senate amendments authorizing the "Women's Educational Equity Act of 1973" and establishing an Advisory Council on Women's Educational Programs.

1226. U.S. Congress. Senate. *White House Conference on Library and Information Services, Conference Report to Accompany S.J. Res. 40.* S. Rept. 93-1409, 93rd Cong., 2d sess., 1974. 13p. Serial 13057-12. Among the numerous amendments attached to S.J.Res. 40 is a Senate amendment to amend Title IX of the Education Amendments of 1972 to exempt the membership practices of certain social fraternities and sororities and voluntary youth organizations including YMCA, YWCA, Girl Scouts, Boy Scouts, and Campfire Girls.

1227. U.S. Congress. House. Committee on Education and Labor. Subcommittee on Equal Opportunities. *Hearing on House Concurrent Resolution 330 (Title IX Regulation).* 94th Cong., 1st sess., 14 July 1975. 71p. Y4.Ed8/1:R31. Discussion of HEW's regulations for implementation of Title IX rejects sections of the regulations which Subcommittee members say exceed the intent of Congress. The regulations rejected involve internal grievance procedures, self-assessment, and proof of religious exemption. Statements submitted for the record comment on Title IX in general and the adequacy of the proposed regulations in particular. The issue of athletics is raised repeatedly.

1228. U.S. Congress. House. Committee on Education and Labor. Subcommittee on Postsecondary Education. *Sex Discrimination Regulations, Hearings.* 94th Cong., 1st sess., 17 - 26 June 1975. 664p. Y4.Ed8/1:Se9/2. Extensive hearing explores regulations implementing Title IX of the Education Amendments of 1972.

1229. U.S. Congress. Senate. Committee on Labor and Public Welfare. Subcommittee on Education. *Prohibition of Sex Discrimination, 1975, Hearings on S. 2106.* 94th Cong., 1st. sess., 16, 18 Sept. 1975. 441p. Y4.L11/2:Se9/975. Hearing explores the issue of Title IX requirements for distribution of revenue from contributions to athletic programs to achieve gender equality in sports programs. The proposed bill would exempt funds needed to sustain a revenue producing sport from Title IX requirements. Much of the testimony against the amendment of Title IX provides background on existing differentials in spending on men's and women's athletics at the college and university level.

1230. U.S. Dept. of Health, Education, and Welfare. Office for Civil Rights. *Elimination of Sex Discrimination in Athletic Programs.* Washington, DC: GPO, 1975. 11p. HE1.2:Se9. Memorandum provides guidelines for school administrators on compliance with Title IX in the first year after the regulations become effective.

1231. U.S. Dept. of Health, Education, and Welfare. Office for Civil Rights. *Final Title IX Regulation Implementing Education Amendments of 1972 Prohibiting Sex Discrimination in Education.* Washington, DC: GPO, 1975. 43p. HE1.6:Ed8. Final Title IX regulations provide interpretation and examples of the application of regulations implementing Title IX of the Education Amendments of 1972 prohibiting sex discrimination in federally assisted education programs. The effect of Title IX on physical education, athletics, admissions, financial aid and school organizations is discussed.

1232. U.S. Office of Education. Bureau of Postsecondary Education. Division of International Education. *Minimum Targets to be Achieved during Decade, United States Report on American Education, Progress Achieved in the Education and Training of Women for U.N. Second Development Decade Review.* Washington, DC: The Bureau, 1975. 22p. HE5.75/a:T17. Overview of educational equity in the United States highlights legislation passed in the 60's and 70's impacting equal educational opportunity for women. Statistics, presented mainly as graphics, illustrate the distribution of enrollment and educational attainment of men and women in the United States. Provides statistics on bachelor's, master's, and doctor's degrees conferred in 1970/71 by sex and detailed major field of study. Finally, the report discusses public policy toward education and vocational counseling of women.

1233. U.S. Congress. House. Committee on Education and Labor. Subcommittee on Select Education. *Oversight Hearing on the National Institute of Education, Hearing.* 94th Cong., 2d sess., 4 Feb. 1976. 52p. Y4.Ed8/1:N21i/4/976. Oversight hearing assesses the record of the National Institute of Education in addressing the educational needs and concerns of minorities and women. Witnesses make a case for ensuring through whatever means possible that the NIE conducts research relevant to the needs of women and minorities and that all areas of research take these groups into consideration. Alternative education programs aimed at minorities and, to a lesser extent, girls are noted.

1234. U.S. Congress. Senate. Committee on Labor and Public Welfare. *Education Amendments of 1976, Report Together with Supplemental Views to Accompany S. 2657.* S. Rept. 94-1186, 94th Cong., 2d sess., 1976. 464p. Serial 13130-9. Among the programs affected by S. 2657 are the Women's Educational Equity Act and state vocational education programs directed at overcoming sex discrimination and sex stereotyping in occupations. The report also focuses on the need to make career education responsive to the changing roles of women.

1235. U.S. Office of Education. *Complying with Title IX: The First Twelve Months.* by Shirley McCune and Martha Matthews, Resource Center on Sex Roles in Education. Washington, DC: GPO, 1976. 28p. HE19.102:T53/5. Overview of requirements for compliance in the first year of Title IX includes notification of policy, designation of Title IX coordinator, grievance procedures, institutional self-evaluation, and assurance of compliance. Sample policies and checklists for compliance are provided.

1236. U.S. Office of Education. *Identifying Discrimination: A Review of Federal Antidiscrimination Laws and Selected Case Examples.* by Shirley McCune and Martha Matthews, Resource Center on Sex Roles in Education. Washington, DC: GPO, 1976. 16p. HE19.102:D63. The antidiscrimination aspects of Titles VI and VII of the Civil Rights Act of 1964, The Equal Pay Act of 1963, Title IX of the 1972 Education Amendments, Executive Order 11246 and Titles VII and VIII of the PHSA are illustrated through examples of prohibited practices in local education agencies and postsecondary education.

1237.   U.S. Office of Education. Women's Program Staff. *Equal Education Opportunity.* by Resource Center on Sex Roles in Education. Washington, DC: GPO, 1976. leaflet. HE1.43:Eq2/2.

1238.   U.S. Office of Education. Women's Program Staff. *A Handbook for Workshops on Sex Equality in Education.* by Mary Ellen Verheyden-Hilliard. Washington, DC: GPO, 1976. 80p. HE19.108:Se9. Resource materials for leaders of gender equity in education workshops includes tips on structuring the workshop and factual material to supplement issue discussions. Appendices reprint important laws, regulations and guidelines.

1239.   U.S. Congress. House. Committee on Education and Labor. Subcommittee on Elementary, Secondary, and Vocational Education. *Part 7: Special Projects Act and Miscellaneous Programs, Hearings on H.R. 15.* 95th Cong., 1st sess., 13-20 July 1977. 827p. Y4.Ed8/1:Ed2/2/pt.7. Included in this hearing is discussion of the Women's Educational Equity Act and the role WEEA should play in implementing Title IX. Witnesses review the history of WEEA's implementation and note past WEEA funded projects while stressing the need for better funding. A lengthy discussion of sex discrimination in education is included, and ways to strengthen WEEA are examined.

1240.   U.S. National Advisory Council on Women's Educational Programs. *Efforts Toward Sex Fairness in the Use of Education Division Funds.* by JoAnn M. Steiger and Eleanor Szanton. Washington, DC: GPO, 1977. 84p. Y3.Ed8/6:2Se9. Analysis of efforts to assure sex fairness in federally funded programs in education examines formula grant programs, discretionary programs, and student financial aid programs. Incudes statistics on female student aid recipients by program and type of institution, and age distribution by occupational program and female enrollment in 1972 and 1975.

1241.   U.S. National Advisory Council on Women's Educational Programs. *Sex Bias: Education Legislation and Regulations.* by Grace L. Mastalli. Washington, DC: The Council, 1977. 39p. Y3.Ed8/6:2Se9/2. Examines sex equity issues in federal education legislation and recommends corrective action. Programs examined include Women's Educational Equity Act, the Career Education Incentive Act, Title IV of the Higher Education Act of 1965, Title IV of the Civil Rights Act of 1964, Title VIII of the Higher Education Act of 1965, Title III of the Education Amendments of 1976, and the Elementary and Secondary Education Act.

1242.   U.S. National Commission on the Observance of International Women's Year. *Education: A Workshop Guide.* Washington, DC: GPO, 1977. 81p. Y3.W84:10/4. Guide to conducting a workshop on women and education includes a workshop outline, fact sheets on Title IX in relation to sports and vocational education, and a list of A/V materials and resource people.

1243.   U.S. National Institute of Education. *Improving Equity in Postsecondary Education: New Directions for Leadership.* by Judith M. Gappa. Washington, DC: GPO, 1977. 50p. HE19.202:Eq5. The Equity Workshop held at Keystone, Colorado, July 17-20, 1977 dealt with the state of sex and race equity in higher education, both for students and faculty. Sessions discussed the continued underrepresentation of women and minorities in spite of affirmative action and identified focus areas for future efforts.

1244.   U.S. Office of Education. *Complying with Title IX: Implementing Institutional Self-Evaluation.* by Shirley McCune and Martha Matthews, Resource Center on Sex Roles in Education. Washington, DC: GPO, 1977. 141p. HE19.102:T53/4. Guide to self-evaluation for Title IX compliance gives specific examples of administrative practices and procedures to evaluate the gender-fairness of programs. Areas addressed include access to courses, counseling, student marital or parental status, athletics, financial assistance, and employment.

1245. U.S. Office of Education. *Freedom of Reach for Young Children: Nonsexist Early Childhood Education.* by Tish Henslee and Peg Jones, Resource Center on Sex Roles in Education. Washington, DC: GPO, 1977. 58p. HE19.108:N73. Complete overview of nonsexist early childhood education defines goals of nonsexist education and offers suggestions for nonsexist teaching-learning activities. Also provides information on dealing with parents and with the community, and includes a bibliography of other resources.

1246. U.S. Office of Education. *A Student Guide to Title IX.* by Myra Sadker, Resource Center on Sex Roles in Education. Washington, DC: GPO, 1977. 45p. HE19.108:St9/2. Primer on sex discrimination in education written for the high school student provides examples of discriminatory behavior and examines the obvious and the more subtle effects of discriminatory behavior. Explains in simple language what is allowed and what is prohibited under Title IX in the areas of course selection, physical education, financial aid, vocational education, pregnant students, and college recruitment.

1247. U.S. Office of Education. *Title IX and Physical Education: a Compliance Overview.* by Resource Center on Sex Roles in Education. Washington, DC: GPO, 1977. 29p. HE19.102:T53/7. Summary of the basic requirements of Title IX as they effect the physical education curriculum and the employment of physical education staff is written to help schools insure compliance.

1248. U.S. Office of Education. *Title IX Grievance Procedures: An Introductory Manual.* by Shirley McCune and Martha Matthews, Resource Center on Sex Roles in Education. Washington, DC: GPO, 1977. 111p. HE19.108:T53. Manual on developing and evaluating grievance procedures for sex discrimination under Title IX of the Education Amendment of 1972 includes sample forms and records.

1249. U.S. Office of Education. *Title IX of the Education Amendments of 1972: A Summary of the Implementing Regulation.* by Resource Center on Sex Roles in Education. Washington, DC: GPO, 1977. 16p. HE19.102:T53/3. Summary of the implementing regulations of Title IX issued in June 1975 describes the regulations in the areas of general provisions, coverage, administration, treatment of students in educational programs and activities, and employment.

1250. U.S. Office of Education. *Title IX: Selected Resources.* by Resource Center on Sex Roles in Education. Washington, DC: GPO, 1977. 9p. HE19.102:T53. Annotated bibliography of resources on Title IX of the 1972 Education Amendments includes journal articles and publications of national organizations and state agencies.

1251. U.S. Office of Education. *Why Title IX?* by Shirley McCune and Martha Matthews, Resource Center on Sex Roles in Education. Washington, DC: GPO, 1977. 8p. HE19.102:T53/2. Reviews the research supporting the assertion that women have been discriminated against in education.

1252. U.S. Congress. House. Committee on Education and Labor. *Education Amendments of 1978, Report Together with Additional and Supplemental Views to Accompany H.R. 15.* H. Rept. 95-1137, 95th Cong., 2d sess., 1978. 455p. Serial 13204-4. One of the changes proposed in this lengthy report on extending the major federal elementary and secondary school aid programs is an upgrading of women's educational equity programs. Activities previously conducted under WEEA, particularly activities in support of Title IX, are highlighted and the reasons for making WEEA a separate program from the Special Projects Act are set forth.

1253. U.S. Congress. Senate. Committee on Human Resources. Subcommittee on Health and Scientific Research. *National Science Foundation Authorization Act of Fiscal Years 1979 and 1980 and the Women in Science and Technology Equal Opportunity Act, Hearing on S. 2549, S. 2550.* 95th Cong., 2d sess., 10 Apr. 1978. 262p. Y4.H88:N21s/2. Hearing discusses authorization for the NSF and the Women in Science and Technology Equal Opportunity Act. Witnesses and materials submitted for the record describe the representation of women and minorities in science and technology fields. The ways in which educational systems filter women and minorities out of scientific and technical fields of study are described. The role that the NSF can play in encouraging women in science and technology fields is examined.

1254. U.S. National Advisory Council on Women's Educational Programs. *The Unenforced Law: Title IX Activity by Federal Agencies Other than HEW.* by Nancy J. Bolles. Washington, DC: GPO, 1978. 55p. Y3.Ed8/6:2L41. A survey of agencies identified programs subject to Title IX of the Education Amendments of 1972 and ascertained the level of enforcement actions taken by those agencies. Intra-governmental coordination of enforcement is examined within the context of the survey results.

1255. U.S. National Institute of Education. *Educational Equity Research Grants Program.* Washington, DC: The Institute, 1978. 42p. HE19.202:Ed8/5. Information on focus programs and application procedures for Educational Equity Research Grants.

1256. U.S. Office of Education. *Implementing Title IX and Attaining Sex Equity: A Workshop Package for Elementary-Secondary Educators, Participant's Notebook.* by Shirley McCune and Martha Matthews, Resource Center on Sex Roles in Education. Washington, DC: GPO, 1978. 155p. HE19.141/2:P25. Notebook for participants in a workshop on implementing Title IX includes background materials, work sheets and an annotated bibliography of resources.

1257. U.S. Office of Education. *Implementing Title IX and Attaining Sex Equity: A Workshop Package for Elementary-Secondary Educators, the Administrator's Role.* by Shirley McCune and Martha Matthews, Resource Center on Sex Roles in Education. Washington, DC: GPO, 1978. 158p. HE19.141/2:Ad6. Guide for persons conducting a workshop for school administrators responsible for Title IX compliance includes sessions on assessing problems, compliance procedures, the role of the Title IX coordinator, implementing grievance procedures, self-evaluations, and monitoring implementation.

1258. U.S. Office of Education. *Implementing Title IX and Attaining Sex Equity: A Workshop Package for Elementary-Secondary Educators, the Community's Role.* by Shirley McCune and Martha Matthews, Resource Center on Sex Roles in Education. Washington, DC: GPO, 1978. 141p. HE19.141/2:C73. Guide for facilitators of community sessions on Title IX implementation covers topics such as the community's role in shaping school policy, the knowledge base needed for attaining sex equity, monitoring and enforcement strategies, and organizational skills necessary to effect change.

1259. U.S. Office of Education. *Implementing Title IX and Attaining Sex Equity: A Workshop Package for Elementary-Secondary Educators, the Context of Title IX.* by Shirley McCune and Martha Matthews, Resource Center on Sex Roles in Education. Washington, DC: GPO, 1978. 74p. HE19.141/2:C76. Facilitator's guide for conducting a workshop on the basic provisions of Title IX covers the legal context of Title IX and sex role socialization.

1260. U.S. Office of Education. *Implementing Title IX and Attaining Sex Equity: A Workshop Package for Elementary-Secondary Educators, the Physical Activity Specialist's Role.* by Barb Landers, Resource Center on Sex Roles in Education. Washington, DC: GPO, 1978. 249p. HE19.141/2:P56. Materials for conducting a workshop on attaining gender equity in athletics outlines sessions on the need for achieving gender equity in athletics, the legal requirements, and planning for sex equity programs and personnel. Includes charts to use in the sessions.

1261.   U.S. Office of Education. *Implementing Title IX and Attaining Sex Equity: A Workshop Package for Elementary-Secondary Educators, the Teacher's Role.* by Shirley McCune, et al., Resource Center on Sex Roles in Education. Washington, DC: GPO, 1978. 180p. HE19.141/2:T22. Guidelines and materials for conducting a workshop on eliminating sex bias in classroom management and instructional materials is geared toward elementary and secondary teachers.

1262.   U.S. Office of Education. *Implementing Title IX and Attaining Sex Equity: A Workshop Package for Elementary-Secondary Educators, the Title IX Regulation and Grievance Process.* by Martha Matthews, Resource Center on Sex Roles in Education. Washington, DC: GPO, 1978. 123p. HE19.141/2:R26. Outline and participant's materials for conducting a workshop on examining and implementing Title IX grievance procedures.

1263.   U.S. Office of Education. *Implementing Title IX and Attaining Sex Equity: A Workshop Package for Postsecondary Educators, Implications of Title IX for Postsecondary Physical Education and Athletic Personnel.* by Celeste Ulrich and Pearl Berlin, Resource Center on Sex Roles in Education. Washington, DC: GPO, 1978. 59p. HE19.141:P56. Supplementary reading materials for athletic personnel are intended to provide a deeper understanding of the need for Title IX and of the process of eliminating sex bias from postsecondary athletics.

1264.   U.S. Office of Education. *Implementing Title IX and Attaining Sex Equity: A Workshop Package for Postsecondary Educators, Participant's Notebook.* by Martha Matthews and Shirley McCune, Resource Center on Sex Roles in Education. Washington, DC: GPO, 1978. 191p. HE19.141:P25. Participant materials for a workshop on Title IX and postsecondary education includes reading materials and work sheets on implementing Title IX through identifying bias, initiating grievance procedures, and encouraging action. Notebook includes a bibliography of print and non-print resource materials.

1265.   U.S. Office of Education. *Implementing Title IX and Attaining Sex Equity: A Workshop Package for Postsecondary Educators, Planning for Change.* by Shirley McCune and Martha Matthews, Resource Center on Sex Roles in Education. Washington, DC: GPO, 1978. 67p. HE19.141:P69. Packet provides information and resource materials for conducting a workshop on taking action to achieve sex equity in postsecondary education as required by Title IX.

1266.   U.S. Office of Education. *Implementing Title IX and Attaining Sex Equity: A Workshop Package for Postsecondary Educators, the Administrator's Role.* by Shirley McCune and Martha Matthews, Resource Center on Sex Roles in Education. Washington, DC: GPO, 1978. 167p. HE19.141:Ad6. Outline and materials for a workshop on Title IX compliance for administrators, Title IX coordinators, and trustees in postsecondary education covers compliance procedures, grievance procedures, self-evaluation, and compliance monitoring.

1267.   U.S. Office of Education. *Implementing Title IX and Attaining Sex Equity: A Workshop Package for Postsecondary Educators, the Context of Title IX.* by Shirley McCune and Martha Matthews, Resource Center on Sex Roles in Education. Washington, DC: GPO, 1978. 86p. HE19.141:C76. Workshop materials focus on understanding the legal context of Title IX and on the need for the law to encourage sex equity in postsecondary education.

1268.   U.S. Office of Education. *Implementing Title IX and Attaining Sex Equity: A Workshop Package for Postsecondary Educators, the Teacher Educator's Role.* by Shirley McCune and Martha Matthews, Resource Center on Sex Roles in Education. Washington, DC: GPO, 1978. 156p. HE19.141:T22. Materials for a workshop on sex equity in teacher education promote awareness of sex bias in the K-12 curriculum and the need to eliminate bias in teacher education and in the teaching profession.

1269. U.S. Office of Education. *Implementing Title IX and Attaining Sex Equity: A Workshop Package for Postsecondary Educators, the Title IX Regulation and Grievance Process.* by Shirley McCune and Martha Matthews, Resource Center on Sex Roles in Education. Washington, DC: GPO, 1978. 122p. HE19.141:R26. Workshop guide provides resource materials and session outlines focusing on Title IX regulations and the process of implementing grievance procedures in postsecondary institutions.

1270. U.S. Office of Education. *Implementing Title IX in Physical Education and Athletics, Application Booklet for Physical Activity Specialists.* by Barb Landers, Resource Center on Sex Roles in Education. Washington, DC: GPO, 1978? 121p. HE19.102:T53/8. Guide to the application of Title IX to physical education and athletics at the primary and secondary school level includes case scenarios to illustrate legal and illegal actions under Title IX and helps clarify what would constitute sex discrimination in funding and participation in athletics. Guidelines provide concrete information on implementing Title IX.

1271. U.S. National Council on Women's Educational Programs. *Women's Educational Equity Act: Projects.* Washington, DC: GPO, 1979. 36p. Y3.Ed8/6:2W84. The first of four WEEA sponsored projects described is designed to show high school girls the options open to them. Career development for women offenders is the focus of the second program. The third project is a model girls' and women's sports commission to promote women in athletics. The final project is directed at making high school students aware of the effects of sex stereotyping so that they can take leadership roles in implementing Title IX.

1272. U.S. National Institute of Education. *Women's Educational Equity Research Grants Announcement.* Washington, DC: GPO, 1979. 47p. HE19.202:W84. Information on applying for Women's Educational Equity Research Grants includes a list of past projects funded.

1273. U.S. Commission on Civil Rights. *Characters in Textbooks: A Review of the Literature.* Clearinghouse Publication no. 62. Washington, DC: GPO, 1980. 19p. CR1.10:62. Review of the literature on the portrayal of minorities, older persons, and women in textbooks found that stereotypes were prevalent in most textbooks used in the 1970's.

1274. U.S. Commission on Civil Rights. *Enforcing Title IX.* Washington, DC: GPO, 1980. 78p. CR1.2:En2/7. Analysis of the enforcement of Title IX of the Education Amendments of 1972 provides an extensive review of the literature. Past enforcement efforts of the Office for Civil Rights are sharply criticized noting that adequate steps had not been taken to improve their civil rights enforcement effort.

1275. U.S. Commission on Civil Rights. *Fair Textbooks: A Resource Guide.* Clearinghouse Publication no. 61. Washington, DC: GPO, 1980. 430p. CR1.10:61. Resource guide lists materials on textbook evaluation, curriculum guidelines, administrative guidelines, state statutes, conferences, resource lists and nonprint materials as they relate to eliminating negative portrayals of women, minorities and the handicapped in textbooks.

1276. U.S. Commission on Civil Rights. *More Hurdles to Clear: Women and Girls in Competitive Athletics.* Clearinghouse Publication no. 63. Washington, DC: GPO, 1980. 87p. CR1.10:63. Progress in guaranteeing avenues for women to participate in sports and the Title IX enforcement efforts of HEW are the focus of this report. Includes statistics on the number and percentage of boys and of girls participating in sports, the number and percentage of men and of women participating in intramural sports at NCAA colleges, and intercollegiate athletics at colleges by program availability and participation by sex.

1277. U.S. Congress. House. Committee on Education and Labor. Subcommittee on Select Education. *To Extend the Authorization of Appropriations for the National Institute of Education, Hearings.* 96th Cong., 2d sess., 5,6 Feb. 1980. 164p. Y4.Ed8/1:N21i/7. Examination of the activities and performance of the National Institute of Education focuses on its mission to promote educational equity. Programs for bilingual education and for teacher understanding of black vernacular English are described. Discussion of work in the area of sex equity is minimal.

1278. U.S. Dept. of Education. *Sex Equity Ideabook for the District of Columbia Public Schools.* by American University Educational Equity Institute. Washington, DC: GPO, 1980. 182p. ED1.8:Se9/ideabook. Collection of activities and resource materials to encourage sex equity at the primary and secondary levels introduces students to the concept of sex bias.

1279. U.S. Dept. of Education. *Sex Equity Resource Directory for the District of Columbia Public Schools.* by American University Educational Equity Institute. Washington, DC: GPO, 1980. 166p. ED1.8:Se9. Bibliography of print and non-print materials which can be incorporated into curricula to eliminate sex bias also lists individuals and organizations as possible resources.

1280. U.S. Commission on Civil Rights. Montana Advisory Committee. *Access to the Legal Profession in Montana.* Washington, DC: GPO, 1981. 30p. CR1.2:M76/2. Since most attorneys practicing in Montana are graduates of the University of Montana School of Law the Advisory Committee focused their study of access to the legal profession on the school's admissions and financial aid policies. The committee recommended that the University increase its efforts in recruiting of minorities and women, advertise the possibility of part-time study, and improve financial aid.

1281. U.S. National Advisory Council on Women's Educational Programs. *Title IX: The Half Full, Half Empty Glass.* Washington, DC: GPO, 1981. 68p. Y3.Ed8/6:2T53. Overview of the effects of Title IX looks at the impact of the law on enrollments, student services and activities, admissions, and degrees in higher education institutions, employment of women in education, and athletics. Insight into the problems of sex discrimination and the success in breaking down barriers are revealed through personal accounts. Summary statistics on women's athletics, women faculty by academic rank, degrees earned by women, and enrollment of women in professional schools are furnished.

1282. U.S. National Institute of Education. *Sex Equity in Education: NIE-Sponsored Projects & Publications, 1981.* Washington, DC: GPO, 1981. 313p. ED1.302:Se9. Abstracts of current sex equity projects funded by NIE and of publications available primarily from ERIC cover topics of women in mathematics and science, elementary and secondary school practices, careers and employment, women educators, women with special needs, and women and minorities in higher and continuing education.

1283. U.S. Congress. House. Committee on Education and Labor. Subcommittee on Postsecondary Education. *Guaranteed Student Loan and Civil Rights Enforcement, Hearings.* 97th Cong., 2d sess., 12-19 May 1982. 271p. Y4.Ed8/1:St9/18. Hearing witnesses discuss the issues surrounding the applicability of federal non-discrimination laws, notably Title IX, to private educational institutions whose students receive Guaranteed Student Loans. Testimony supports strong enforcement of civil rights laws at educational institutions and focuses on the Administration's action in response to the U.S.

district court's decision in *Grove City College v. Bell.* The requirements for institutions under Title IX are reviewed along with testimony on the improvement in women's status in educational institutions under Title IX.

1284.   U.S. Congress. House. Committee on the Judiciary. Subcommittee on Civil and Constitutional Rights. *Civil Rights Enforcement in the Department of Education, Hearing.* 97th Cong., 2d sess., 30 Sept. 1982. 100p. Y4.J89/1:97/98. Witnesses examine the failure of the Department of Education to adequately enforce Title VI, Title IX, and section 504. Evidence of inaction by the Departments' Office of Civil Rights is presented and suggestions for improvement are put forward. The enforcement of Title IX and intercollegiate athletics is specifically addressed.

1285.   U.S. Commission on Civil Rights. *Statement of the U.S. Commission on Civil Rights on Civil Rights Enforcement in Education.* Washington, DC: The Commission, 1983. 10p. CR1.2:Ed8/11. The ability of the federal government to enforce the protection granted under Title VI of the Civil Rights Act of 1964 and Title IX of the Education Amendments of 1972 are examined in relation to court decisions in *Bob Jones University v. U.S.* and *Grove City College v. Bell.*

1286.   U.S. Congress. House. Committee on Education and Labor. Subcommittee on Elementary, Secondary, and Vocational Education and U.S. Congress. House. Committee on Post Office and Civil Service. Subcommittee on Investigations. *Hearings on the Department of Education's Proposed Reorganization and Reduction-in-Force, Joint Hearing.* 98th Cong., 1st sess., 2 Aug., 27 Sept. 1983. 214p. Y4.Ed8/1:Ed8/65. Witnesses discuss the importance of the migrant education program and the Women's Educational Equity Act program, both targeted in the reorganization and reduction-in-force proposals for the Department of Education. Reagan administration efforts to eliminate the WEEA program are cited as the cause for the proposed reduction of WEEA staff.

1287.   U.S. Congress. House. Committee on Education and Labor. Subcommittee on Postsecondary Education and U.S. Congress. House. Committee on the Judiciary. Subcommittee on Civil and Constitutional Rights. *Hearings on Higher Education Civil Rights Enforcement, Joint Hearings.* 98th Cong., 1st. sess., 17 - 25 May 1983. 438p. Y4.Ed8/1:C49/5. The primary focus of this hearing is on the activities of the Department of Education and the Department of Justice in enforcing Title VI of the Civil Rights Act of 1964. Some testimony concerns charges that the departments were actively engaged in undermining the enforcement of Title IX of the Education Amendments of 1972.

1288.   U.S. General Accounting Office. *Procedures for Making Grant Awards under Three Department of Education Discretionary Grant Programs: Report.* Washington, DC: The Office, 1983. 78p. GA1.13:HRD-83-68. Investigation examines the grant awards process for the Women's Educational Equity Act Program, the National Institute of Education's Unsolicited Proposal Program and the Talent Search Program. The report reviews the legislation and regulations governing each program, the selection and training of reviewers, procedures for reviewing and selecting grant applications, and the procedures for determining funding. The investigation also collected information on the gender and race/ethnicity of reviewers.

1289.   U.S. Congress. House. *Education Amendments of 1984, Conference Report to Accompany S. 2496.* H. Rept. 98-1128, 98th Cong., 2d sess., 1984. 55p. Serial 13601. Differences between the House and Senate versions of the Education Amendments of 1984 which affect women primarily involve administrative provisions and funding levels of the Women's Education Equity Act.

1290. U.S. Congress. House. Committee on Education and Labor. *Civil Rights Act of 1984, Report Together with Supplemental and Additional Views to Accompany H.R. 5490.* H. Rept. 98-829, part 2, 98th Cong., 2d sess., 1984. 53p. Serial 13593. Reports a bill whose primary purpose is to overturn the *Grove City College v. Bell* decision which limited the coverage of Title IX of the Education Amendments of 1972. The desirability of clarifying the intent of Congress in applying the provision of Title IX, Section 504 of the Rehabilitation Act of 1973, the Age Discrimination Act of 1975, and Title VI of the Civil Rights Act of 1964 to an entire institution when a part of that institution received federal funds is discussed. The significance of the *Grove City* decision and testimony on its effects are reviewed in detail with an emphasis on the Title IX issue.

1291. U.S. Congress. House. Committee on Education and Labor. *Educational Amendments of 1984, Report Together with Minority and Supplemental Views to Accompany H.R. 11.* H. Rept. 98-748, 98th Cong., 2d sess., 1984. 123p. Serial 13590. Favorable report on an omnibus education bill includes reauthorization of the Women's Educational Equity Act grant programs. Progress made under WEEA in addressing sex equity issues is summarily reviewed, and a general description of the need to continue the program is provided.

1292. U.S. Congress. House. Committee on Education and Labor and U.S. Congress. House. Committee on the Judiciary. Subcommittee on Civil and Constitutional Rights. *Civil Rights Act of 1984, Joint Hearings on H.R. 5490.* 98th Cong., 2d sess., 9 - 22 May 1984. 308p. Y4.Ed8/1:C49/6. Hearing on a bill to clarify the application of Title IX of the Education Amendments of 1972, Section 504 of the Rehabilitation Act of 1973, the Age Discrimination Act of 1975, and Title VI of the Civil Rights Act of 1964 discusses reaction to the *Grove City* decision. Testimony highlighting the continuing need for strong federal anti-discrimination laws focuses on education.

1293. U.S. Congress. House. Committee on Education and Labor. Subcommittee on Elementary, Secondary, and Vocational Education. *Hearing on Women's Educational Equity Act, Hearing on H.R. 11.* 98th Cong., 2d sess., 5 Apr. 1984. 206p. Y4.Ed8/1:W84/6. Testimony reviews the accomplishments of the Women's Educational Equity Act in promoting women's education and documents the undermining of WEEA by the Reagan administration. Reprints an excellent review of WEEA, *Catching Up: A Review of the Women's Educational Equity Act Program* by the Citizens Council on Women's Education. Ways to protect the program from future tampering by hostile administrations are discussed.

1294. U.S. Congress. House. Committee on the Judiciary. *Civil Rights Act of 1984, Report to Accompany H.R. 5490.* H. Rept. 98-829, part 1, 98th Cong., 2d sess., 1984. 47p. Serial 13593. Report recommends a bill to clarify the application of Title IX of the Education Amendments of 1972, Section 504 of the Rehabilitation Act of 1973, the Age Discrimination Act of 1975, and Title VI of the Civil Rights Act of 1964 in the wake of *Grove City College* decision. The report reviews the legislative intent of the four civil rights measures and the effect of *Grove City* on Title IX enforcement. Testimony on the effect of the decision is summarized and the need for clarifying legislation is presented.

1295. U.S. Congress. Senate. Committee on Labor and Human Resources. Subcommittee on Education, Arts and Humanities and Subcommittee on the Handicapped. *Civil Rights Act of 1984, Joint Hearing on S. 2568.* 98th Cong., 2d sess., 24 May, 26 June 1984. 394p. Y4.L11/4:S.hrg.98-1137/pt.1-2. Hearing held in response to the *Grove City College v. Bell* decision, which interprets Title IX as applying to educational programs rather to institutions, explores the implications of the decision. The proposed legislation would clarify Title IX and section 504 of the Rehabilitation Act of 1973 to guarantee institution-wide application. Testimony is primarily in support of the measure and illustrates progress still to be made in educational equity. Those testifying against the measure cite the potential for intrusion into state affairs and unintended effects of discouraging institutions from accepting federal financial aid students, many of whom are minorities. Part two of the hearings includes more testimony against the bill from the Moral Majority, private schools, hospital associations, and other interested parties.

1296. U.S. Congress. Senate. Committee on the Judiciary. Subcommittee on the Constitution. *Civil Rights Act of 1984, Hearing on S. 2568.* 98th Cong., 2d sess., 30 May, 5 June 1984. 575p. Y4.J89/2:S.hrg.98-934. Hearing considers the proposed Civil Rights Act of 1984 which would clarify the application of Title IX of the Education Amendments of 1972, Section 504 of the Rehabilitation Act of 1973, the Age Discrimination Act of 1975, and Title VI of the Civil Rights Act of 1964 in the wake of the *Grove City* decision. The implications of *Grove City* for all federal programs containing anti-discrimination clauses is examined. Some opposition to the bill is based on federal interference and the Court's interpretation of enrollment of students receiving federal financial aid as federal funding for the purpose of applying Title IX. In particular this question of indirect aid and private colleges is discussed.

1297. U.S. Congress. House. Committee on Education and Labor and U.S. Congress. House. Committee on the Judiciary. Subcommittee on Civil and Constitutional Rights. *Civil Rights Restoration Act of 1985, Joint Hearing.* 99th Cong., 1st sess., 4 Mar. - 2 Apr. 1985. 1329p. Y4.Ed8/1:99-87. Witnesses at extensive hearings held in five states and the District of Columbia describe the importance of civil rights legislation in ensuring equal educational and employment opportunities. The effect of the *Grove City* decision is discussed at length in testimony supporting legislation to clearly define wider institutional application of Title IX and other civil rights legislation. The evidence of continued discrimination against women in education is stressed. The concerns of some religious denominations over the abortion issue and the proposed Civil Rights Restoration Act of 1985 are expressed. Other opposition statements claim the act is an attempt to further expand federal power into the private sector. In addition to representatives of women's organizations, witnesses appearing in support of the bill include advocates for the disabled and for racial and ethnic minorities.

1298. U.S. Congress. House. Committee on Education and Labor. Subcommittee on Postsecondary Education. *Reauthorization of the Higher Education Act, Nontraditional Students, Volume 3, Hearings.* 99th Cong., 1st sess., 9,10 July 1985. 197p. Y4.Ed8/1:99-45. The major focus of this hearing on reauthorization of funding under the Higher Education Act of 1965 is the nontraditional student. Considerable discussion supports a bill, H.R. 2111, which would authorize a grant program for child care services. Witnesses link the availability of affordable child care to women's ability to attend college. The need for more equitable federal student financial aid programs for part-time students is also stressed and rules governing AFDC recipient eligibility and student assistance programs are reviewed.

1299. U.S. Congress. House. Committee on Government Operations. Subcommittee on Intergovernmental Relations and Human Relations. *Investigation of Civil Rights Enforcement by the Department of Education.* 99th Cong., 1st sess., 18 July, 11 Sept. 1985. 427p. Y4.G74/7:Ed8/5. Investigation examines the performance of the Department of Education's Office of Civil Rights in enforcing Title VI of the Civil Rights Act of 1964, Title IX of the Education Amendments of 1972, and section 504 of the Rehabilitation Act of 1973. Questions regarding inadequacies in general compliance reviews and in investigations of individual complaints are addressed by OCR representatives and the *Adams v. Bennett* case is discussed.

1300. U.S. Congress. House. Committee on Government Operations. Subcommittee on Intergovernmental Relations and Human Resources. *Limits on the Dissemination of Information by the Department of Education, Hearing.* 99th Cong., 1st sess., 13 Nov. 1985. 166p. Y4.G74/7:Ed8/6. Investigation of the role of the Department of Education's Publications and Audio Visual Advisory Council examined charges that PAVAC was censoring the dissemination of education research materials, particularly products of the Women's Educational Equity Act Program.

1301. U.S. Congress. Senate. Committee on Labor and Human Resources. *Proposed Grove City Legislation, Religious Liberty, and Private Education, Hearings.* 99th Cong., 1st sess., 17 July, 20 Sept. 1985. 243p. Y4.L11/4:S.hrg.99-467. Hearing on legislation to counter the *Grove City College v. Bell* decision restricting Title IX requirements on sex discrimination to the educational program receiving funds expresses concern over the definition of "federally assisted" programs in relation to religious institutions. The issue of student services and abortion is predominant.

1302. U.S. Congress. House. Committee on Education and Labor. *School Improvement Act of 1987, Report Together with Additional Views to Accompany H.R. 5.* H. Rept. 100-95, 100th Cong., 1st sess., 1987. 317p. Serial 13801. Favorable report on a bill authorizing numerous education programs provides background on the current state of education. Among the education programs revised and extended is the Women's Educational Equity Act. The importance of WEEA as the only federal funding source for women's educational equity programs at all levels is stressed and changes to WEEA in this bill include a higher appropriation and placement of the program under the Office of Educational Research and Improvement.

1303. U.S. Congress. House. Committee on the Judiciary. Subcommittee on Civil and Constitutional Rights. *Sex and Race Differences in Standardized Tests, Oversight Hearings.* 100th Cong., 1st sess., 23 Apr. 1987. 305p. Y4.J89/1:100/93. Witnesses present testimony relating to the lower SAT and ACT scores of women and minorities. Much of the debate centers on whether women's standardized test scores, particularly in mathematics, really predict college success, as the College Board contends. The domino-effect of low standardized test scores and women's economic life is explored. Articles highlighting gender and racial bias in test questions, with examples, are reprinted.

1304. U.S. Congress. Senate. Committee on Labor and Human Resources. *Civil Rights Restoration Act of 1987, Hearings on S. 557.* 100th Cong., 1st. sess., 19 Mar., 1 Apr. 1987. 679p. Y4.L11/4:S.hrg.100-374. Testimony against a bill to override the *Grove City* decision focuses on health insurance and health services in relation to abortion.

1305. U.S. Congress. Senate. Committee on Labor and Human Resources. *The Civil Rights Restoration Act of 1987, Report Together with Minority Views, to Accompany S. 557.* S. Rept. 100-64, 100th Cong., 1st sess., 1987. 38p. Serial 13733. Report on a bill intended to reverse the Supreme Court decision in *Grove City College V. Bell* summarizes the implications of the *Grove City* decision. Minority views cite concern over the abortion issue and religious institutions under the bill presented.

1306. U.S. Congress. Senate. Committee on Labor and Human Resources. *The Robert T. Stafford Elementary and Secondary Education Improvement Act of 1987, Report to Accompany S.373.* S. Rept. 100-222, 100th Cong., 1st sess., 1987. 249p. Serial 13775. The Women's Educational Equity Act is among the programs provided for in this bill revising and extending education programs. The purpose of WEEA and the continued need for the program in the wake of the *Grove City* decision are stressed. Changes made in WEEA include decreased appropriation, elimination of the National Advisory Council on Women's Educational Programs, and movement of the program placing it under the administration of the Office of Educational Research and Improvement.

1307. U.S. Dept. of Education. Office of Elementary and Secondary Education. *Application for Grants under Women's Educational Equity Act Program.* Washington, DC: The Office, 1987. 31p. ED1.2:W84. Details grant application procedures and regulations for the Women's Educational Equity Act Program, a program to promote educational equity for women and girls through the development of educational materials and model programs.

1308. U.S. Congress. House. *Elementary and Secondary Education, Conference Report to Accompany H.R. 5.* H. Rept. 100-567, 100th Cong., 2d sess., 1988. 424p. Serial 13892. Differences between the House and Senate versions of a massive elementary and secondary education improvement act are noted and settled in this conference report. One of the programs reauthorized was the Women's Educational Equity Act program.

1309. U.S. Congress. House. Committee on Education and Labor. Majority Staff. *Report on the Investigation of the Civil Rights Enforcement Activities of the Office of Civil Rights, U.S. Department of Education.* 100th Cong., 2d sess., 1988. Committee print. 284p. Y4.Ed8/1:100-FF. Detailed report on civil rights enforcement by the Department of Education's Office of Civil Rights focuses on OCR's management and case handling practices, and addresses charges that OCR encouraged complainants to drop charges. Charts and tables illustrate OCR's case handling in the 1980s.

1310. U.S. Dept. of Education. Office of Civil Rights. *Sexual Harassment: It's Not Academic.* Washington, DC: The Office, 1988. 13p. ED1.2:Se9/3. Pamphlet discusses sexual harassment aspects of Title IX and provides guidance on development of a sexual harassment grievance procedure.

1311. U.S. Dept. of Education. Office for Civil Rights. *Title IX and Sex Discrimination.* Washington, DC: GPO, 1988. 8p. ED1.2:Se9/2. Brief description notes who is covered by Title IX, how it is enforced and how to file a complaint.

1312. U.S. Dept. of Education. Office for Civil Rights. *El Titulo IX y la Discriminacion por Razon de Sexo.* Washington, DC: GPO, 1988. 8p. ED1.2:Se9/2/spanish. Spanish edition of *Title IX and Sex Discrimination* (1311).

1313. U.S. Congress. House. Committee on Education and Labor. *Hearing on the Federal Enforcement of Equal Education Opportunity Laws, Hearing.* 101st Cong., 1st sess., 28 Nov. 1989. 371p. Y4.Ed8/1:101-73. Testimony strongly critical of the Department of Education's Office of Civil Rights describes the failure of government agencies under the Bush Administration to enforce equal educational opportunity statutes. Representatives of the OCR defend the agency's track record and stress their inability to act on certain cases between the *Grove City* decision in February 1984 and passage of the Civil Rights Restoration Act in 1988. Most of the testimony focuses on continuing racial discrimination, but sex discrimination and discrimination against the handicapped are also reviewed in relation to OCR actions.

SERIALS

1314. U.S. Dept. of Education. *Higher Education Opportunities for Minorities and Women: Annotated Selections.* Washington, DC: GPO, 1982 - . annual. ED1.42:year. List of undergraduate and graduate programs which provide grants, scholarships and fellowships with an emphasis on minority and female students includes a section on federal financial aid programs.

1315. U.S. Dept. of Education. *Women's Educational Equity Act Program, Annual Report.* Washington, DC: GPO, 1976 - . annual. HE19.136:year (1976-1979); ED1.44:year (1980 -). Annual report on grants and contracts issued under the Women's Educational Equity Act Program analyzes the distribution of grant money and abstracts individual projects funded. Reports for 1976 through 1979 were issued by the Office of Education; the report for 1982 was called *Educational Equity: A Continuing Quest.*

1316. U.S. Dept. of Education. Women's Educational Equity Communication Network. *Resources in Women's Educational Equity.* Washington, DC: GPO, 1977-1980. irreg. ED1.17/2:vol./no.; HE19.128:W84/2/vol./no. Abstracts of dissertations, journal articles, ERIC documents, and films on women's educational equity drawn from databases such as ABI/Inform, ERIC, NICEM, MEDLARS, NTIS and others.

1317. U.S. National Advisory Council on Women's Educational Programs. *Annual Report.* Washington, DC: GPO, 1975 - 1981. 1st. - 7th. annual. Y3.Ed8/6:1/year. Report on the activities of the Advisory Council and their recommendations to the executive branch on promoting educational equity for women includes discussion of Title IX of the Education Amendments of 1972 and the Women's Educational Equity Act. Some years have distinctive titles.

1318. U.S. Office of Education. Women's Educational Equity Communication Network. *Resources in Women's Educational Equity: Special Issue.* San Francisco, CA: The Network, Dec.1979-Apr. 1980. irreg. HE19.128:W84/4/spec. no. Bibliography lists materials for instruction, description and evaluation of educational curricula, programs and treatments, and research on women's educational equity.

10

Health

Government documents on women's health have dealt mainly with substance abuse and cancer of the female reproductive system. A few examine women's health in general. House and Senate hearings held in 1919 discuss physical fitness for women while considering assistance to the United States Training Corps for Women, a group dedicated to military style drill for women and to training in sanitation (1320, 1321). Other documents include a 1945 review of illness and injury rates by gender (1330) and a 1978 annotated bibliography on *Women and the Health System* (1367). The issue of women in medical research is considered in *Women and Their Health* (1361), a collection of papers from a 1975 conference. Serious discussion of the exclusion of women subjects from most health research came in numerous 1990 congressional hearings, including a general hearing on women's health issues (1544), and specific hearings on a requirement to include women subjects in research funded by the National Institutes of Health (1559, 1565). National health insurance as a women's issue is explored in a report of the Secretary's Advisory Committee on the Rights and Responsibilities of Women (1402).

The mental health of women is first considered in an 1875 House Executive Document requesting funds to build a separate building for female patients at the Government Hospital for the Insane (1319). Concepts of women's mental illness are described in a 1965 study of the functioning of a halfway house for female psychiatric patients (1338). Older women and mental health issues were considered in a 1983 Administration on Aging working paper which discussed policy options (1419).

Substance abuse is a common theme in publications on women's health. The first document specifically addressing the issue of women and drug addiction was a 1939 Public Health Service report discussing the psychological reasons for women's opium addiction and the need for treatment alternatives (1328). The problem of alcohol abuse among women was reviewed in 1976 Senate hearings (1354), and in the same year the House reported out of committee a bill requiring states to address the needs of alcoholic women (1353). Another hearing, held in 1979 explored the medical treatment of women with mental and emotional problems and the link to abuse of prescription drugs (1372).

Starting in 1979 a wealth of substantial documents on women and substance abuse were issued. The National Center for Alcohol Education developed a training program on providing services to alcoholic women and published a resource book, trainer manual, and session outline cards (1376-1378). The same year the National Drug Abuse Center for Training and Resource Development published *Women in Treatment II* (1379-1380). The participant and trainer manuals provide information on research on substance abuse among women and are designed for the training of service providers. Also in 1979 the NIDA published *Psychosocial Characteristics of Drug-Abusing Women* (1384) and *Addicted Women: Family Dynamics, Self Perceptions, and*

Support Systems (1386). Statistical publications from 1980 includes NIAAA's *Alcoholism and Alcohol Abuse among Women: Research Issues* (1394) and the NIDA's *Women in Drug Abuse Treatment, 1979* (1395), a statistical analysis of women in treatment. Another NIDA publication of note is *Treatment Services for Drug Dependent Women*, a two volume review of all aspects of treating drug dependent women (1416). Treatment services are also described in *Advances in Alcoholism Treatment Services for Women* (1422). Short summaries of research on women and non-medical drug use are provided in *Women and Drugs* (1424), and *Women and Alcohol Use* (1518) reviews research published between 1980 and 1988. The problems of drug abuse among pregnant women and mothers are highlighted in a wealth of hearings held in 1989 and 1990. Although the motivating factor behind the hearings was the effect of drug abuse on child welfare, the treatment and service needs of women were often discussed.

The state of research and treatment options for breast cancer are reviewed in numerous reports and congressional hearings. Treatment options are the focus of a 1976 Senate hearing (1355) and in 1978 the National Cancer Institute published a detailed report, *Consensus Development Meeting on Breast Cancer Screening* (1368). The National Cancer Institute's *Breast Cancer Digest* provides caregivers with information on medical care and support programs for breast cancer patients (1374) and its *ICRDB Cancergram* series provides abstracts of recent literature (1581). Materials on breast cancer published between 1970 and 1978 are listed in an NCI produced bibliography (1373), and citations on the treatment of early-stage breast cancer are listed in a 1990 National Library of Medicine bibliography (1578). Survey results on the knowledge and attitudes of women and their spouses are presented in *Breast Cancer: A Measure of Progress in Public Understanding* (1390). Other documents describe government-sponsored research on breast cancer (1403), the cost-effectiveness of radical mastectomy (1411), and the need for federal support for mammography (1447, 1474, 1492, 1502, 1550).

Cervical cancer screening was another common topic of documents. Hearings on the Clinical Laboratory Improvement Act detail the incidence and consequences of false negative Pap smear results (1496, 1497, 1562). The cost-effectiveness of Pap smear coverage under Medicare is examined in a 1990 Office of Technology assessment report (1579). Other health issues explored in documents include the effect of Diethylstilbestrol on daughters exposed *in utero*, cervical and uterine cancer, osteoporosis, smoking, toxic shock syndrome, eating disorders, the dangers of silicone breast implants, and research on RU 486. The beginnings of acknowledgement of the growing incidence of women with AIDS is seen in 1989 when the Public Health Service published *Women and AIDS: Initiatives of the Public Health Service* (1541), and in 1990 when the issue was raised in congressional hearings on the health care crisis (1549). Other chapters providing information on women's health are Chapter 11, Fertility and Maternity, and Chapter 13, Birth Control and Abortion. Documents on the occupational health of women are found in Volume Two.

1319. U.S. Congress. House. *Government Hospital for the Insane: Letter from the Secretary of the Interior, Relative to the Erection of a New Building to be Devoted Solely to the Detention and Treatment of Female Patients at the Insane Asylum.* H. Ex. Doc. 136, 43d Cong., 2d sess., 1875. 9p. Serial 1648. Correspondence relevant to the plan to erect a separate building for female patients at the Government Hospital for the Insane cites overcrowding at the existing facility as the primary motivation for the proposal although the desirability of separate facilities for male and female patients is discussed.

1320. U.S. Congress. House. Committee on Military Affairs. *War Department Equipment and Facilities for United States Training Corps for Women, Miss Susanna Cocroft, Hearings on H.R. 4096.* 66th Cong., 1st sess., 1 Oct. 1919. 23p. Y4.M59/1:W84. Testimony of Susanna Cocroft, commandant of the United States Training Corps for Women, describes the origin, structure, and purpose of the corps which operates camps for the development of physical fitness among women. Cocroft petitioned Congress to allow the use Army of facilities and advisors to further their program.

1321.   U.S. Congress. Senate. Committee on Military Affairs. *National Training Camps for Women, Hearing on H.R. 4096.*   96th Cong., 1st. sess., 30 Oct. 1919.   18p. Y4.M59/2:W84. Hearing discusses allowing the United States Training Corps for Women to use Army facilities. The corps began as a physical exercise program to improve the health of women employed as government clerks and expanded to a general program of physical training camps for women. Additional statements include excerpts of letters from women on the corps experience.

1322.   U.S. Public Health Service. *For Girls [Facts about Venereal Diseases].* by American Social Hygiene Association. Washington, DC: The Service, 1919. 16p. T27.20:16/2.

1323.   U.S. Public Health Service. *Healthy Womanhood is Hope of Every Girl, Every Woman Who Looks Forward to Motherhood Wants Healthy Well-Formed Children.* N.p., 1919. 1p. T27.20:13/2. Flyer on venereal disease.

1324.   U.S. Public Health Service. *On Guard [Sex Information for Girls and Young Women].* Washington, DC: The Service, 1919. 14p. T27.20:8. Pamphlet discusses the meaning of sex, urges healthy lifestyles during menstruation, and describes clothing and posture's effect on reproductive health. Girls are also advised not to "thoughtlessly stimulate the sex emotions of their men friends" and are warned of the dangers of frequent "spooning." The misuse of sex and venereal disease are also covered.

1325.   U.S. Congress. House. Committee on Indian Affairs. *Girls Dormitory at Lapwai Indian Sanatorium, Report to Accompany H.R. 192.* H. Rept. 133, 68th Cong., 1st sess., 1924. 1p. Serial 8226.

1326.   U.S. Congress. Senate. Committee on Indian Affairs. *To Provide for a Girls' Dormitory at the Fort Lapwai Sanatorium, Lapwai, Idaho, Report to Accompany H.R. 192.* S. Rept. 271, 68th Cong., 1st sess., 1924. 2p. Serial 8220.

1327.   U.S. Public Health Service. *Healthy Happy Womanhood, Pamphlet for Girls and Young Women.* Washington, DC: GPO, 1934. 16p. T27.20:60/3. Pamphlet for young women gives advice on physical fitness, hygiene, the female reproductive system, the "sex urge", and venereal disease. Earlier editions published in 1920 and 1929.

1328.   U.S. Public Health Service. *Drug Addiction among Women.* by Lawrence Kolb. Washington, DC: The Service, 1939. 13p. T27.2:D84/2. Discusses the characteristics of drug abuse among women as compared to men before and after criminalization. Reviews the problems of the opium addict and psychological reasons for women's addiction, and stresses the need to provide treatment alternatives for female addicts so that prison is not their only alternative. A brief bibliography is included.

1329.   U.S. Children's Bureau. *Peggy Dreams of Nursing, May 5,1942.* Children in Wartime no. 6. Washington, DC: The Bureau, 1942. 9p. L5.44:6. Tells the story of a maladjusted mother who depends too much on her daughter for companionship. Peggy, the daughter, plays nurse alone in her room to escape the constant company of her mother.

1330.   U.S. Federal Security Agency. Committee on Physical Fitness. *Some Facts about Fitness of Girls and Women.* by Dorothy LaSalle. Washington, DC: The Agency, 1945. 5p. FS12.2:G44. Charts and tables profile illness and injury rates of men and women, the adequacy of diets of women college students, and high school enrollment of girls in physical education and health education.

1331.   U.S. National Cancer Institute. *Breast Self Examination.* Washington, DC: GPO, 1951. 1p. folded. FS2.22:B74

1332. U.S. National Institutes of Health. *A Chance to Live: a Cancer Test For Women.* Washington, DC: GPO, 1957. 1p. folded. FS2.22:C16/16. Flyer describes a uterine cancer cell test.

1333. U.S. Army, Navy and Air Force. *Hygiene Educational Guide for Women Officers and Women Officer Candidates of Armed Forces.* Army Pamphlet 21-44; Navy Publication NAVMED P-5060; Air Force Manual AFM 160-44. Washington, DC: GPO, 1958. 40p. D101.22:21-44/2. Hygiene guide for women officers describes the physiology of the female reproductive system and the psychology of human sexual development. The manual goes on to discuss management of sexual problems including illicit sex, sexually transmitted diseases, pregnancy, and homosexuality.

1334. U.S. National Cancer Institute and The American Cancer Society. *Cancer of Female Reproductive Organs.* Health Information Series no. 77. Washington, DC: GPO, 1959. 25p. FS2.50:77. Informational pamphlet on uterine, cervical, ovarian and other types of cancers of the female reproductive system. Other editions were published in 1949 (FS2.57:3) and 1954.

1335. U.S. Public Health Service. *Morbidity from Cancer in the United States.* by Harold F. Dorn and Sidney J. Cutler. Public Health Monograph no. 56. Washington, DC: GPO, 1959. 207p. FS2.62:56. Study of morbidity from cancer in 10 metropolitan areas looks at variations according to age, sex, race, geographic region, marital status, primary site and histological site.

1336. U.S. Agricultural Research Service. Human Nutrition Research Division. *Metabolic Response of Young Women to Standardized Diet.* by Ruth M. Leverton, et al. Home Economics Research Report no. 16. Washington, DC: GPO, 1962. 45p. A1.87:16. Report describes results of a study of the metabolic response of college women to a standardized diet and to altered levels of magnesium and pantothenic acid.

1337. U.S. Public Health Service. *Socioeconomic Distribution of Cervical Cancer in Relation to Early Marriage and Pregnancy.* by Frank E. Lundin, et al. Public Health Monograph no. 73. Washington, DC: GPO, 1964. 41p. FS2.62:73. Study of the relation between cervical cancer, age at first marriage and first pregnancy, and socioeconomic status is based on data from a survey of women in Memphis, Tennessee.

1338. U.S. Social and Rehabilitation Service. *Halfway House, Sociocultural and Clinical Study of Rutland Corner House, Transitional Aftercare Residence for Female Psychiatric Patients.* by David Landy and Milton Greenblatt. Washington, DC: The Service, 1965. 136p. FS13.202:H13. Reprinted in 1968 under SuDoc HE17.2:H13. Study of the functioning of a halfway house for female psychiatric patients examines how such a house "works" in the rehabilitation process. Through a description of the operation of the house the report provides insight into the concepts of women and mental illness in the 1950s and 1960s and into the course of treatment for female patients. Describes numerous cases and the treatment process with an emphasis on the role the "house culture." Data is provided on resident characteristics including educational level, pre- and post-hospital occupational status, type of treatment, and probable cause of mental illness. An interesting sidelight of the report is the history of the house, which was established in 1877 as a home for working women and which functioned as a sheltered workshop for "unfortunate women" through the early 1950s.

1339. U.S. Public Health Service. *Age at Menopause.* Washington, DC: GPO, 1966. 20p. HE20.6209:11/19. Report describes age at menopause, with consideration of operative and natural menopause, based on data from the U.S. Health Examination Survey of Adults, 1960-62.

1340. U.S. Public Health Service. *A Message to Women about Cancer Screening.* Washington, DC: GPO, 1969. leaflet. FS2.50/3:5.

1341. U.S. Congress. House. Committee on Government Operations. Subcommittee on Intergovernmental Operations. *Regulation of Diethylstilbestrol (DES); Its Use as a Drug for Humans and in Animal Feeds, Part 1, Hearings.* 92d Cong., 1st sess., 11 Nov. 1971. 111p. Y4.G74/7:D56/pt.1. Informational hearing on DES explores the reports of carcinogenicity in humans and animals. Of particular concern are studies linking cancer of the vagina in young women to mother's use of DES during pregnancy. Witnesses also attempt to assess the cancer risk to humans of DES residue in animals fed the drug.

1342. U.S. National Clearinghouse for Smoking and Health. *Women and Smoking, the Latest, in Brief.* Washington, DC: GPO, 1971. 6p. leaflet. HE20.2602:W84.

1343. U.S. Public Health Service. *Age at Menarche, United States.* Washington, DC: GPO, 1973. 29p. HE20.6209:11/133. A report on age at menarche of American women analyzes variations in age at menarche associated with race, region, family income, place of residence, educational level, height, weight, and skinfold thickness, as estimated from the Health Examination Survey conducted during the period 1960 to 1970.

1344. U.S. Centers for Disease Control. *Surprising News about Women and Smoking.* Washington, DC: GPO, 1974. 2p. leaflet. HE20.7002:Sm7/5.

1345. U.S. Centers for Disease Control. *Twenty-Five Years Ago They Would Have Given Us Some Dumb Reasons for Not Smoking.* Washington, DC: The Center, 1974. poster. HE20.7014:Sm7.

1346. U.S. National Cancer Institute. *Make Breast Examination a Health Habit.* Bethesda, MD: The Institute, 1974. 12p. HE20.3152:B74.

1347. U.S. National Clearinghouse for Alcohol Information. *Sociocultural Aspects of Alcohol Use and Alcoholism, Part G: Cultural Groups, Women Alcohol Abusers.* Subject Area Bibliography 1-B-5. Washington, DC: GPO, 1974. 15p. HE20.8311/2:1-B-5. Annotated bibliography covers English and foreign language articles on all aspects of women as users of alcohol.

1348. U.S. National Clearinghouse for Smoking and Health. *You're Young, You're Female, and You Smoke.* Washington, DC: GPO, 1974. 1p. HE20.7002:Sm7/4.

1349. U.S. National Institute of Mental Health. *Women and Mental Health: A Selected Annotated Reference, 1970-1973.* Washington, DC: GPO, 1974. 254p. HE20.8113:W84/970-73. Extensive annotated bibliography of journal articles and audio-visual materials written or produced between 1970 and 1973 on factors which affect women's mental health covers topics of abortion, alcoholism, divorce, motherhood, rape, and singleness.

1350. U.S. Congress. House. Committee on Interstate and Foreign Commerce. Subcommittee on Health and the Environment. *Diethylstilbestrol (DES), Hearing on Title I of S. 963.* 94th Cong., 1st sess., 16 Dec. 1975. 78p. Y4.In8/4:94-69. Representatives of women's health organizations, experts in obstetrics and gynecology, and FDA officials testify as to the carcinogenic potential of DES. The therapeutic use of DES by women and its possible effects on offspring are examined. Relevant sections of the *Federal Register* on the approval of DES as a postcoital oral contraceptive are reprinted. The primary points of contention are the danger posed to humans when DES is used in cattle, and the use of the drug as a "morning after" pill.

1351. U.S. Congress. Senate. Committee on Labor and Public Welfare. Subcommittee on Health and U.S. Congress. Senate. Committee on the Judiciary. Subcommittee on Administrative Practice and Procedure. *Regulation of Diethylstilbestrol (DES), 1975, Joint Hearing on S. 963.* 94th Cong., 1st sess., 27 Feb. 1975. 304p. Y4.L11/2:D56/975. Hearing on a bill to ban the administration of DES to animals intended for food and to place a one-year ban on interstate commerce in DES intended for use as a postcoital contraceptive reviews the evidence of a link between DES used by mothers and vaginal cancer in daughters. The routine use of DES as a "morning after" contraceptive is criticized.

1352. U.S. National Institute on Alcohol Abuse and Alcoholism. *Alcohol Abuse and Women: a Guide to Getting Help.* by Marian Sandmaier. Washington, DC: GPO, 1975. 25p. HE20.8308:W84 Provides an overview of why women develop drinking problems, how to identify the problem drinker, and the treatment process.

1353. U.S. Congress. House. Committee on Interstate and Foreign Commerce. *Extension of the Comprehensive Alcohol Abuse and Alcoholism Prevention, Treatment and Rehabilitation Act of 1970, Report to Accompany H.R. 12677.* H. Rept. 94-1092, 94th Cong., 2d sess., 1976. 25p. Serial 13134-6. Proposed extension of programs under the Comprehensive Alcohol Abuse and Alcoholism Prevention, Treatment and Rehabilitation Act of 1970 includes a requirement that each state survey and identify the need for prevention and treatment programs for women and that the state program specifically target their needs. Some discussion of the need for programs on female alcoholism is presented.

1354. U.S. Congress. Senate. Committee on Labor and Public Welfare. Subcommittee on Alcoholism and Narcotics. *Alcohol Abuse among Women: Special Problems and Unmet Needs, 1976, Hearing.* 94th Cong., 2d sess., 29 Sept. 1976. 421p. Y4.L11/2:Al1/12/976. Report reviews current research on and experience with the needs of alcoholic women. Reprints reports on alcohol abuse among subpopulations of women including black women and lesbian women, and the suitability of the recovery setting for women alcoholics. Includes a selective annotated bibliography.

1355. U.S. Congress. Senate. Committee on Labor and Public Welfare. Subcommittee on Health. *Breast Cancer, 1976, Hearing.* 94th Cong., 2d sess., 4 May 1976. 96p. Y4.L11/2:B74/976. Expert witnesses discuss the treatment options for breast cancer with disagreement over radical mastectomy versus less extensive surgical approaches. The use of chemotherapy and the participation of the patient in selecting treatment options are also discussed. The hearing record provides a review of current research on treatment outcomes.

1356. U.S. Congress. Senate. Committee on Labor and Public Welfare. Subcommittee on Health and U.S. Congress. Senate. Committee on the Judiciary. Subcommittee on Administrative Practice and Procedure. *Oral Contraceptives and Estrogens for Postmenopausal Use, 1976, Joint Hearing.* 94th Cong., 2d sess., 21 Jan. 1976. 292p. Y4.L11/2:C76/4. Panel discussion of the numerous health risks related to estrogen use is accompanied by reprints of articles on the effects of its long term use.

1357. U.S. National Cancer Institute. *Information for Physicians, DES Exposure In Utero, Vaginal and Cervical Cancers and Other Abnormalities Associated with Exposure In Utero to Diethylstilbestrol and Related Synthetic Hormones.* Washington, DC: GPO, 1976. 11p. HE20.3152:D26.

1358. U.S. National Institute on Alcohol Abuse and Alcoholism. *De Mujer a Mujer: Hablemos Sobre el Alcoholismo - from Women to Women: A Conversation on Alcoholism.* Rockville, MD: The Institute, 1976. leaflet. HE20.8302:W84.

1359. U.S. National Institutes of Health. *What Every Woman Should Know about High Blood Pressure.* Washington, DC: The Institutes, 1976? [5]p. leaflet. HE20.3202:B62/11.

1360. U.S. Health Resources Administration. *HRA Council for Women and Health.* Rockville, MD: The Administration, 1977. leaflet. HE20.6002:W89/2.

1361. U.S. Health Resources Administration. *Women and Their Health: Research Implications for a New Era.* Rockville, MD: The Administration, 1977. 104p. HE20.6512/3:W84. Papers presented at the conference, Women and Health: Research Implications for a New Era, held August 1-2, 1975, San Francisco, California, include the following: "Problems of Research in Women's Health," "Methodological Issues: Choice of Variables, Ethics, Design," "New Ways of Viewing Key Questions for Investigation," "Substantive Research Issues: Tensions and Divergences in Utilization, Access, and Recourse to Health Care for Women and Contracting Methodologies," and "Questions for the Future."

1362. U.S. National Cancer Institute. *Cigarette Smoking among Teen-agers and Young Women.* Rockville, MD: The Institute, 1977? 31p. HE20.3152:C48. Results of a study of smoking habits of teenage and young women provide insight into the extent of smoking among these groups, the social status of young female smokers, the attitudes and knowledge of smoking's consequences among smokers, and the exposure to anti-smoking messages. Teenage girls are compared to teenage boys and to young women. A brief analysis of findings is presented.

1363. U.S. National Commission on the Observance of International Women's Year. *Health: a Workshop Guide.* Washington, DC: GPO, 1977. 81p. Y3.W84:10/8. Fact sheets and resource guide for conducting a workshop on women and health covers the topics of gynecology, alcohol and drug abuse, mental health, and occupational health.

1364. U.S. National Institute on Alcohol Abuse and Alcoholism. *Alcohol Programs for Women: Issues, Strategies and Resources.* by Marian Sandmaier. Washington, DC: GPO, 1977. 26p. HE20.8302:W84/2/review. Manual provides background information on treatment programs for alcoholic women. The extent of alcohol abuse among women, the existing treatment programs, and prevention/education programs for women are reviewed. Also provides a guide to informational resources and sources of funding.

1365. U.S. National Institute on Alcohol Abuse and Alcoholism. *Decisions and Drinking, Reflections in a Glass, a Course for Women.* Rockville, MD: The Institute, 1977. kit. HE20.8302:D35/2 Educational kit on women and alcoholism includes a facilitator's handbook, masters for handouts, outline cards, and take-home summaries for each session.

1366. U.S. Congress. House. Committee on Government Operations. Intergovernmental Relations and Human Resources Subcommittee. *Quality of Scientific Evidence in FDA Regulatory Decisions (The Adoption of an Antismoking Warning in Oral Contraceptive Pill Labeling), Hearing.* 95th Cong., 2d sess., 4 Oct. 1978. 293p. Y4.G74/7:Sci2/2. Hearing reviews studies linking smoking and heart attacks in users of oral contraceptives, although tobacco industry representatives claim the studies are inconclusive. At issue is the FDA's decision to require an antismoking warning on oral contraceptive labels. The research reports on which the decision to require labeling was based are reprinted in the hearing record.

1367. U.S. Health Resources Administration. *Women and the Health System: Selected Annotated References.* Health Planning Bibliography Series no. 4. Washington, DC: GPO, 1978. 57p. HE20.6112/2:4. Bibliography provides lengthy annotations of articles on a variety health-related subjects including health care, insurance, working women with sick children, and sex discrimination in health care professions.

1368. U.S. National Cancer Institute. *Consensus Development Meeting on Breast Cancer Screening.* Bethesda, MD: The Institute, 1978. 407p. HE20.3152:B74/5. Report of a meeting on breast cancer screening discusses the issues connected with mammography and thermography for breast cancer detection. Includes a review of the Breast Cancer Detection Demonstration Project and statements from concerned professionals and citizens. Statistics on breast cancer mortality and the risks of mammography are provided.

1369. U.S. National Library of Medicine. *Adverse Effects of Prenatal Exposure to Diethylstilbestrol (DES).* Bethesda, MD: The Library, 1978. 15p. HE20.3614/2:78-29. Citations from the MEDLINE data base cover adverse effects of prenatal exposure to DES in humans and experiments with DES in animals.

1370. U.S. Alcohol, Drug Abuse, and Mental Health Administration. *A Woman's Choice: Deciding about Drugs.* Washington, DC: GPO, 1979. 28p. HE20.8202:W84. Describes the stress factors in women's lives and various drugs that they may be tempted to abuse, including prescription drugs. A reading list and directory of state substance abuse agencies is provided.

1371. U.S. Congress. House. Committee on Interstate and Foreign Commerce. *Extension of Alcoholism and Drug Abuse Prevention and Treatment Authorities, Report to Accompany H.R. 3916.* H. Rept. 96-193, 96th Cong., 1st sess., 1979. 24p. Serial 13293. Reports a bill extending, with changes, programs authorized under the Comprehensive Alcohol Abuse and Alcoholism Prevention, Treatment and Rehabilitation Act of 1970 and the Drug Abuse Office and Treatment Act of 1972. Emphasizing programs for women and the elderly, the report highlights the growing problems of substance abuse among females.

1372. U.S. Congress. House. Select Committee on Narcotics Abuse and Control. *Women's Dependency on Prescription Drugs, Hearing.* 96th Cong., 1st sess., 13 Sept. 1979. 104p. Y4.N16:96-1-8. Hearing on the problems of women who are dependent on prescription drugs explores the roots of the problem focusing on the way women are treated for mental and emotional problems.

1373. U.S. National Cancer Institute. *Breast Cancer, Annotated Bibliography of Public, Patient, and Professional Information and Educational Materials.* Washington, DC: GPO, 1979. 71p. HE20.3165:B74/2. Annotated bibliography lists 201 books, leaflets, and audio-visual materials published on breast cancer between 1970 and 1978. Includes a subject index.

1374. U.S. National Cancer Institute. *The Breast Cancer Digest: A Guide to Medical Care, Emotional Support, Educational Programs, and Resources.* Bethesda, MD: The Institute, 1979. 165p. HE20.3158:B74/2. Provides background information on the incidence of breast cancer and the treatment options, its financial impact, and guidelines for coping with diagnosis and treatment. Describes informational and support resources available and model support programs. Includes a bibliography and index.

1375. U.S. National Cancer Institute. *Breast Self-Examination.* Bethesda, MD: The Institute, 1979. revised. 17p. HE20.3152:B74/979. Minor revision of *Make Breast Examination a Health Habit* (1346).

1376. U.S. National Center for Alcohol Education. *Services for Alcoholic Women: Foundations for Change, Resource Book.* Washington, DC: GPO, 1979. 326p. HE20.8302:W84/3. Resource book to support a training program on services to alcoholic women includes detailed information on designing treatment programs and provides selected reading materials on treatment approaches. Topics addressed in the articles include sex differences in helplessness, sex-role stereotypes and clinical judgements of mental health, feminism in therapy, Mexican-American women alcoholics, and alcoholism and the lesbian community. Also provides sample procedures for treatment programs, staff development resources, and a bibliography on staff development and client education resources.

1377. U.S. National Center for Alcohol Education. *Services for Alcoholic Women: Foundations for Change, Session Outline Cards.* Washington, DC: GPO, 1979. 112p. HE20.8302: W84/3/session. Series of cards outline training sessions designed for administrators of women's alcohol treatment programs.

1378. U.S. National Center for Alcohol Education. *Services for Alcoholic Women: Foundations for Change, Trainer Manual.* Washington, DC: GPO, 1979. 121p. HE20.8302:W84/3/ trainer. Trainer manual outlines a workshop for administrators of women's alcohol treatment programs. Sessions focus on evaluating and prioritizing programs and setting program goals.

1379. U.S. National Drug Abuse Center for Training and Resource Development. *Women in Treatment II: Participant Manual.* by Beth J. Gillispie and Irene Rubenstein Bush. Washington, DC: GPO, 1979. 452p. HE20.8208:W84/participant. Manual describes a course for persons providing services to women with substance abuse problems. Divided into ten modules, the course covers research on substance abuse patterns in women, women's life cycle, life stress counseling, family, suicide, victimization, sexuality, critical program components, and principles of counseling women.

1380. U.S. National Drug Abuse Center for Training and Resource Development. *Women in Treatment II: Trainer Manual.* by Beth J. Gillispie and Irene Rubenstein Bush. Washington, DC: GPO, 1979. 241p. HE20.8208:W84/trainer. See 1379 for abstract.

1381. U.S. National Institute of Mental Health. *Changing Directions in the Treatment of Women: A Mental Health Bibliography.* by Elyse Zukerman. Washington, DC: GPO, 1979. 494p. HE20.8113:W34/2. Annotated bibliography of literature related to the provision of mental health services to women focuses primarily on the period 1960 to 1977, although some materials on early theories of the psychology and biology of women are included. Criticism of traditional treatment approaches and research and new treatment approaches in response to the criticism are included.

1382. U.S. National Institute of Mental Health. *The Older Woman: Continuities and Discontinuities.* Washington, DC: GPO, 1979. 56p. HE20.3002:W84. Report of a workshop designed to stimulate research on the physical and mental health of women over seventy examines the sex and intimacy needs of older women, delivery of health service, and labor force participation.

1383. U.S. National Institute on Drug Abuse. *Characteristics of Drug-Abusing Women.* Washington, DC: GPO, 1979. 82p. HE20.8216/2-2:W84. Basically the same publication as *Psychosocial Characteristics of Drug-Abusing Women* (1384).

1384. U.S. National Institute on Drug Abuse. *Psychosocial Characteristics of Drug-Abusing Women.* by Marvin R. Burt, et al. Rockville, MD: The Institute, 1979. 82p. HE20.8216/2-2:W84/2. Report compares the characteristics of female and male abusers of illicit and psychotherapeutic drugs. Some characteristics examined include age, race/ethnicity, marital status, educational status and drug used. The findings of psychological studies of female drug abusers are reviewed.

1385. U.S. National Institute on Drug Abuse. *Specialized Therapeutic Community Program for Female Addicts.* Washington, DC: GPO, 1979. 21p. HE20.8216/3:T34/3. Report describes the findings of the Mabon Parents' Demonstration Program. The program offered a comprehensive treatment program to drug-addicted women and their dependent children through a therapeutic community approach.

1386. U.S. National Institute on Drug Abuse. Services Research Branch. *Addicted Women: Family Dynamics, Self Perceptions, and Support Systems.* Washington, DC: GPO, 1979. 136p. HE20.8216/2-2:W84/3. Analysis of data on heroin-addicted urban women examines self-perception and attitudes, social support structure, and family history comparing addicted women to male addicts and non-addicted women. Discusses the implications of the research for treatment approaches.

1387. U.S. Congress. Senate. Committee on Labor and Human Resources. Subcommittee on Health and Scientific Research. *Toxic Shock Syndrome, 1980, Hearing.* 96th Cong., 1st sess., 6 June 1980. 12p. Y4.L11/4:T66/980. In a brief hearing victims of TSS and the director of the Center for Disease Control discuss the symptoms of the newly recognized disease, toxic shock syndrome. At the time of the hearing the relationship with tampon use had not been established.

1388. U.S. Food and Drug Administration. *Toxic Shock Syndrome and Tampons.* Washington, DC:GPO, 1980. leaflet. HE20.4002:T66/3/983. Also 1980 and 1982 editions.

1389. U.S. National Cancer Institute. *The Best Patient is an Informed Patient.* Bethesda, MD: The Institute, 198? 6p. HE20.3152:B74/18. Patient education materials on breast cancer available from the National Canter Institute are listed.

1390. U.S. National Cancer Institute. *Breast Cancer: A Measure of Progress in Public Understanding, Technical Report.* Washington, DC: GPO, 1980. 291p. HE20.3152:B74/8. Survey of knowledge and attitudes of women and their spouses/partners concerning breast cancer looks at awareness among the general population and at differences in knowledge, attitude and practices related to breast cancer by characteristics of education, income, age, and racial/ethnic group.

1391. U.S. National Cancer Institute. *Breast Reconstruction: Creating a New Breast Contour after Mastectomy.* Bethesda, MD: The Institute, 1980. 28p. HE20.3152:B74/9. Basic information for patients describes breast reconstruction.

1392. U.S. National Cancer Institute. *Prenatal Diethylstilbestrol (DES) Exposure: Recommendations of the Diethylstilbestrol-Adenosis (DESAD) Project for the Identification and Management of Exposed Individuals.* Bethesda, MD: The Institute, 1980. 31p. HE20.3152:P91/2. Information for physicians describes examination procedures for women exposed to DES *in utero.*

1393. U.S. National Cancer Institute. *Questions and Answers about DES Exposure during Pregnancy and before Birth.* Bethesda, MD: The Institute, 1980. 16p. HE20.3152:D56/4.

1394. U.S. National Institute on Alcohol Abuse and Alcoholism. *Alcoholism and Alcohol Abuse among Women: Research Issues.* Research Monograph Series no. 1. Washington, DC: GPO, 1980. 256p. HE20.8315:1. Proceedings of a workshop on alcoholism and alcohol abuse among women held at Jekyll Island, Georgia, April 2-5,1978 discusses the current state of knowledge on women and alcohol. Workshop objectives were to identify key issues and to develop priorities for NIAAA research efforts.

1395. U.S. National Institute on Drug Abuse. *Women in Drug Abuse Treatment 1979.* National Institute on Drug Abuse Series C, no. 1. Washington, DC: GPO, 1980. 204p. HE20.8212/9:1. Data and analysis of statistics on women in drug abuse treatment in 1979 provides data on drug group used and age, education, employment status, marital status, race/ethnicity, health insurance coverage, and arrest history.

1396. U.S. National Institutes of Health. *Breast Cancer: A Measure of Progress in Public Understanding - Management Summary.* Washington, DC: GPO, 1980. 30p. HE20.3152:B74/8/sum. Results of a survey of adult women and their spouses/partners describes attitudes about and knowledge of breast cancer by age and socioeconomic status.

1397. U.S. National Institutes of Health. *DES Task Force Summary Report.* Bethesda, MD: The Institute, 1980. 68p. HE20.3152:D56/5/sum. Discusses the health effects of DES including breast cancer in DES mothers, reproductive tract abnormalities in DES sons, and cancer and tissue changes in DES daughters.

1398. U.S. Office of Women in Development. *Planning for Women and Health.* by Patricia Blair. Washington, DC: GPO, 1980. 52p. S18.55:H34. Report on the health problems of third world women discusses personal health, reproductive health, and occupational health. Argues for a development program approach which includes all women, not just pregnant and lactating women.

1399. U.S. Office on Smoking and Health. *The Health Consequences of Smoking for Women.* Washington, DC: GPO, 1980. 359p. HE20.2:Sm7/5. Review of the literature on women and cigarette smoking looks at patterns of smoking, morbidity and mortality related to smoking, pregnancy and smoking, and psychological and behavioral aspects of smoking by women. Statistics on characteristics of smokers, smoking related morbidity and mortality, and attempts to stop smoking by sex are provided.

1400. U.S. Public Health Service. *Office Visits by Women, National Ambulatory Medical Care Survey, United States, 1977.* Washington, DC: GPO, 1980. 66p. HE20.6209:13.45. Data on physician's office visits by women 15 years of age and over reports on age, sex, race, condition, and management of problems. Also provides data on family planning visits by patient characteristics and services rendered.

1401. U.S. Commission on Civil Rights. *Civil Rights Issues in Health Care Delivery: A Consultation Sponsored by the United States Commission on Civil Rights, Washington, D.C., April 15-16,1980.* Washington, DC: GPO, 1981. 960p. CR1.2:H34/3. Consultation participants concluded that minorities, women and older persons have less access to health care due to health care costs, the relocation of hospitals away from the inner city, and the low number of women and minorities in the medical profession. Several courses of action are proposed including denying Medicaid/Medicare payments to discriminatory hospitals and physicians.

1402. U.S. Dept. of Health and Human Services. Secretary's Advisory Committee on the Rights and Responsibilities of Women. *Women and National Health Insurance: Where Do We Go from Here?* Washington, DC: GPO, 1981. 22p. HE1.2:W84/6. Primer on the issue of national health insurance specifically addresses insurance as a women's issue and discusses structuring national health insurance to meet the needs of women.

1403. U.S. National Cancer Institute. Division of Cancer Biology and Diagnosis. *Breast Cancer Task Force Program and Related Projects.* Washington, DC: GPO, 1981. 420p. HE20.3152:B74/10. Summaries describe research projects on breast cancer supported by grants and contracts from the Breast Cancer Program Coordinating Branch of the National Cancer Institute and other funding sources. Includes a brief discussion of international cooperation in breast cancer research.

1404. U.S. National Institute on Alcohol Abuse and Alcoholism. *Here's To Your Health: Alcohol Facts for Women.* Rockville, MD: The Institute, 1981. [6]p. HE20.8302:H34/3.

1405. U.S. National Institute on Alcohol Abuse and Alcoholism. *Spectrum: Alcohol Problem Prevention for Women by Women.* Washington, DC: GPO, 1981. 91p. HE20.8302:Sp3/corr. Guide to planning alcohol abuse prevention programs reviews the topic of women and alcohol from historical and contemporary perspectives. Issues in planning programs are detailed and examples of existing alcohol problem prevention programs for women are provided. A resource section lists organizations, publications, and media programs related to alcohol abuse prevention.

1406. U.S. National Institute on Drug Abuse. *Women and Drug Abuse Treatment: Needs and Services.* Washington, DC: GPO, 1981. 25p. HE20.8216/2-2:W84/4. First part of this report reviews current theory on the needs of female drug abusers including medical, counseling, employment, and child care services. The findings of a study of services provided by women-oriented drug treatment programs are presented in part two. Data on age, race, and type of drug used, detailed data on type of service provided, and a bibliography are furnished.

1407. U.S. National Institute on Mental Health. *Anorexia Nervosa.* Literature Survey Series no. 1. Washington, DC:GPO, 1981. 196p. HE20.8134:1. Annotated bibliography lists books, journal articles, and dissertations from 1978 to 1980 on anorexia nervosa.

1408. U.S. National Institutes of Health. *The Search for Health: Cervical Cancer Screening, the Pap Smear.* Bethesda, MD: The Institutes,1981. 1p. HE20.3038:C33. Also issued in Spanish.

1409. U.S. National Library of Medicine. *Adverse Effects of Cosmetics.* Washington, DC: GPO, 1981. 17p. HE20.3614/2:81-11. Bibliography cites articles from the MEDLINE database describing the health hazards of cosmetics and the results of animal studies testing for adverse affects.

1410. U.S. Office of Technology Assessment. *The Implications of Cost-Effectiveness Analysis of Medical Technology. Background Paper #2: Case Studies of Medical Technologies. Case Study #15: Elective Hysterectomy: Cost, Risks, and Benefits.* Washington, DC: GPO, 1981. 33p. Y3.T22/2:2C82/no.2/case15. Review of research and statistics on the health risks and benefits of elective hysterectomies includes a cost-benefit analysis.

1411. U.S. Office of Technology Assessment. *The Implications of Cost-Effectiveness Analysis of Medical Technology. Background Paper #2: Case Studies of Medical Technologies. Case Study #17: Surgery for Breast Cancer.* Washington, DC: GPO, 1981. 29p. Y3.T22/2:2C82/no.2/case17. Report reviews data on health benefits and risks of surgery for breast cancer and analyzes the cost effectiveness of radical mastectomy.

1412. U.S. Public Health Service. *Use of Health Services by Women 65 Years of Age and Over, United States.* Washington, DC: GPO, 1981. 72p. HE20.6209:13/59. Report on utilization of non-federal hospitals, nursing homes and physicians by women 65 years of age and over describes patient characteristics, condition, management, and outcomes.

1413. U.S. Centers for Decease Control. *Questions and Answers on Toxic-Shock Syndrome.* Washington, DC: GPO, 1982. 2p. HE20.7002:T66.

1414. U.S. National Institute on Alcohol Abuse and Alcoholism. *For Women Who Drink...* Washington, DC: GPO, 1982. 13p. leaflet. HE20.8302:W84/4.

1415. U.S. National Institute on Alcohol Abuse and Alcoholism. *Women's Occupational Alcoholism Demonstration Project: Final Report.* Washington, DC: GPO, 1982. 67p. HE20.8302:W84/6/final. Final report reviews NIAAA funded projects focusing on improving Employee Assistance Program response to alcoholic women. Phase one of the project defined the extent of alcohol problems among female workers. Creating a special component in existing EAP programs for female employees was the focus of phase two, and phase three measured the effect of adding the special component.

1416. U.S. National Institute on Drug Abuse. *Treatment Services for Drug Dependent Women.* Washington, DC: GPO, 1981-1982. 2 vol. HE20.8217/2:D84/2/v.1-2. Comprehensive work on all aspects of treating drug dependent women includes discussion of support services, such as child care and employment development, as well as treatment methods.

1417. U.S. President's Council on Physical Fitness and Sports. Nutrition Advisory Committee of the National Women's Leadership Conference on Fitness. *Nutrition, Exercise, and Physical Fitness in Women: A Position Paper.* Washington, DC: GPO, 1982. 11p. HE20.102:W84. Summary information examines diet and nutrition as they relate to the health and physical fitness of women and the special needs of pregnant and lactating women.

1418. U.S. Public Health Service. *Use of Health Services for Disorders of the Female Reproductive System: United States, 1977-78.* Washington, DC: GPO, 1982. 40p. HE20.6209:13/63. Data on office visits and hospital stays of women for reproductive disorders are examined in terms of patient, physician and clinic characteristics.

1419. U.S. Administration on Aging. *Mental Health Concerns of Older Women.* by Donald E. Gelfand. National Policy Center On Women and Aging Working Paper no. 5. College Park, MD: The Center, 1983. 58p. HE23.3002:W84/2/wk. paper 5. Discussion of data on the prevalence of mental disorders among older women outlines policy options to address their mental health needs. Provides data on mental health admissions by diagnosis, sex and age; admissions for mental disorders by sex, age, and race; and admissions by sex, diagnosis and marital status.

1420. U.S. National Center for Health Statistics. *The Health of Women: A Bibliography.* Hyattsville, MD: The Center, 1983. 24p. HE20.6216:W84. Provides annotations of recent publications of the National Center for Health Statistics relating to the health status of women and their impact on the health services system.

1421. U.S. National Institute of Child Health and Human Development. *Facts about Anorexia Nervosa.* Bethesda, MD: The Institute, 1983? leaflet. HE20.3352:An3.

1422. U.S. National Institute on Alcohol Abuse and Alcoholism. *Advances in Alcoholism Treatment Services for Women.* Washington, DC: GPO, 1983. 93p. HE20.8302:Al1/19. Reports information gained from 45 treatment and occupation programs for alcoholic women in the areas of outreach, treatment, aftercare, and community support. Characteristics of women alcoholics and issues relating to their treatment are summarized. The appendix provides descriptions of NIAAA-funded women and alcoholism program projects.

1423. U.S. National Institute on Alcohol Abuse and Alcoholism. *Alcoholic Women: They Do Recover.* by Margaret Wilmore and Joan Volpe. Washington, DC: GPO, 1983. 46p. HE20.8302:W84/5/983. Manual is based on information from program director's of eight alcohol treatment programs funded by NIAAA and directed at meeting the treatment needs of alcoholic women. Outreach, treatment, community involvement, and implementation are discussed, and an appendix with descriptions of NIAAA-funded programs is provided. Earlier edition published in 1982.

1424. U.S. National Institute on Drug Abuse. *Women and Drugs.* Edited by Thomas J. Glynn, et al. Research Issues Series no. 31. Washington, DC: GPO, 1983. 360p. HE20.8214:31. Compilation of two to three page summaries of research covering all aspects of women and non-medical drug use includes a subject index and bibliography.

1425. U.S. National Institutes of Health. *An Atlas of Findings in the Human Female after Intrauterine Exposure to Diethylstilbestrol.* Washington, DC: GPO, 1983. 78p. HE20.3152:D56/6. Describes the known effects to women of prenatal exposure to diethylstilbestrol (DES) and methods of identifying DES related changes.

1426. U.S. National Institutes of Health. *The Menopause Time of Life.* Bethesda, MD: The Institute,1983. 20p. HE20.3002:M52/2. Presents basic facts on women's health during menopause, treatment for symptoms, and tips for staying healthy through menopause.

1427. U.S. National Institutes of Health. *The Search for Health: Anorexia Nervosa.* Bethesda, MD: The Institute, 1983. 1p. HE20.3038:An7. Also published in Spanish.

1428. U.S. National Library of Medicine. *Anorexia Nervosa and Bulimia.* Washington, DC: GPO, 1983. 20p. HE20.3614/2:83-15. Citations in English from the MEDLINE and CATLINE databases describe the diagnosis, treatment, and other aspects of anorexia nervosa and bulimia.

1429. U.S. National Library of Medicine. *Toxic Shock Syndrome.* Washington, DC: GPO, 1983. 17p. HE20.3614/2:82-24. Bibliography lists selected articles and monographs on toxic shock syndrome published between January 1979 and December 1982 drawn from the MEDLINE, CATLINE, and AVLINE databases.

1430. U.S. Public Health Service. *Sex Differences in Health and Use of Medical Care: United States, 1979.* Washington, DC: GPO, 1983. 24p. HE20.6209:3/24. Reports and analyzes statistics on sex differences in the incidence of illness and in the utilization of office-based physicians and short-stay hospitals.

1431. U.S. Administration on Aging. *The Effects of Retirement on the Health Status of Older Unmarried Women.* by Robyn Stone, Aging Health Policy Center, University of California. Washington, DC: The Administration, 1984. 91p. HE23.3002:R31/4. Research report examines findings on the relationship of retirement and economic well-being to the health status of unmarried older women. A review of the literature on the health of older women is provided and reasons for focusing on unmarried women for this research is noted. Work history was one of the factors considered.

1432. U.S. Congress. House. Committee on Energy and Commerce. Subcommittee on Health and the Environment. *Health and the Environment Miscellaneous, Part 5, Hearing.* 98th Cong., 2d sess., 15 Mar. - 24 Apr. 1984. 1031p. Y4.En2/3:98-151. Hearing on miscellaneous health measures includes discussion of the proposed set-aside for research on women and alcohol and on the federal role in health manpower programs. Information on the problems of alcoholic women and summaries of ADAMHA research projects focusing on alcoholism among women are included.

1433. U.S. Congress. House. Select Committee on Aging. Subcommittee on Health and Long-Term Care. *Progress in Controlling Breast Cancer, Hearing.* 98th Cong., 2d sess., 28 June 1984. 293p. Y4.Ag4/2:C16/3. Expert witnesses and women who have survived breast cancer testify on the current status of treatment for breast cancer and on the need to increase accessibility of breast cancer screening for early detection and treatment. The issue of health insurance and Medicare coverage for mammography is discussed with particular reference to the detection of breast cancer in older women. The hearing provides a good overview of state-of-the-art early detection projects.

1434. U.S. Congress. Senate. Committee on Labor and Human Resources. *Alcohol Abuse, Alcoholism and Drug Abuse Amendments of 1984, Report to Accompany S. 2615.* S. Rept. 98-477, 98th Cong., 2d sess., 1984. 41p. Serial 13558. Report on a bill authorizing NIAAA and NIDA programs describes the provisions providing funding for research on women and substance abuse. The tendency for past research to focus on males and the need for research focused on women is noted.

1435. U.S. Congress. Senate. Committee on Labor and Human Resources. *The Alcohol and Drug Abuse and Mental Health Services Block Grant Amendments of 1984, Report Together with Additional Views to Accompany S. 2303.* S. Rept. 98-381, 98th Cong., 2d sess., 1984. 45p. Serial 13557. One of the block grants authorized is a special emphasis demonstration program aimed at the prevention and treatment of alcoholism, alcohol abuse and drug abuse among women. Hearing testimony stressing the need for substance abuse programs aimed at women is summarized.

1436. U.S. National Cancer Institute. *The Breast Cancer Digest: A Guide to Medical Care, Emotional Support, Educational Programs, and Resources.* 2d ed. Bethesda, MD: The Institute, 1984. 212p. HE20.3158:B74/2/984. See 1374 for abstract.

1437. U.S. National Cancer Institute. *Participation in Clinical Trials of the Treatment of Early-Stage Breast Cancer at the National Cancer Institute.* Bethesda, MD: The Institute, 1984. 14p. leaflet. HE20.3152:B74/11/974.

1438. U.S. National Cancer Institute. *Radiation Therapy: A Treatment for Early Stage Breast Cancer.* Washington, DC: GPO, 1984. 20p. leaflet. HE20.3152:R11/2.

1439. U.S. National Cancer Institute. Office of Cancer Communication. *Breast Cancer Screenage.* Washington, DC: GPO, 1984. 7p. HE20.3182/2:B74. Briefly describes NCI research and projects on breast cancer screening.

1440. U.S. National Cancer Institute. Office of Cancer Communication. *A Followup Study of Mothers Exposed to Diethylstilbestrol in Pregnancy.* by Alice C. Hamm. Washington, DC: GPO, 1984. 6p. HE20.3182/3:D56. Study describes the incidence of breast cancer in DES mothers.

1441. U.S. National Center for Health Services Research. *Women and Divorce: Health Insurance Coverage, Utilization and Health Care Expenditures.* Washington, DC: GPO, 1984. 16p. HE20.6513/2:W84/corr. Paper presented at the Annual Meeting of the American Public Health Association, November 15, 1983 analyzes statistics on health care coverage and health status of divorced women as compared to married women. Includes statistics on insurance coverage, reliance on Medicaid, and out-of-pocket health care expenditures by marital and employment status for the year 1977.

1442. U.S. National Institute of Child Health and Human Development. *NICHD Research Highlights and Topics of Interest.* Bethesda, MD: The Institute, 1984. 2p. HE20.3364:P56. Report of research and activities at NICHD includes a summary of research on exercise during pregnancy and on treatment of women with hyperprolacinemia.

1443. U.S. National Institutes of Health. *Older Women Need Estrogen and Calcium to Prevent Osteoporosis, NIH Panel Concludes.* Washington, DC: The Institute, 1984. 1p.

HE20.3038:Os7. Brief report details the known risk of osteoporosis in postmenopausal women, provides a simple explanation of the progress of the disease, and reviews prevention behaviors.

1444. U.S. National Library of Medicine. *Pelvic Inflammatory Disease.* by Jacque-Lynne Schulman. Washington, DC: GPO, 1984. 18p. HE20.3614/2:84-22. Brief overview accompanies citations to journal articles in English on Pelvic Inflammatory Disease (PID).

1445. U.S. National Library of Medicine. *Premenstrual Syndrome.* by Jacque-Lynne Schulman. Washington, DC: GPO, 1984. 10p. HE20.3614/2:84-11. Journal articles and some monographs from the MEDLINE database on the symptoms and treatment of Premenstrual Tension Syndrome are listed.

1446. U.S Public Health Service. *The U.S. Public Health Service, Region V, Department of Health and Human Services Conference on Women's Health Issues, January 25, 1984.* Chicago, IL: The Service, 1984. various pagings. HE20.2:W84. Report describes a conference organized around panel discussions on "The Female Child Adolescent," "Women and Adulthood," "Women and Aging," and "Women and Social Change." Topics covered at sessions include teenage pregnancy, women's diet and diseases, sex bias in medical research, handicapped women, prescription drug abuse, alcoholism, and nursing home care.

1447. U.S. Congress. House. Select Committee on Aging. Subcommittee on Health and Long-term Care and U.S. Congress. House. Select Committee on Aging. Task Force on Social Security and Women. *Breast Cancer Detection: The Need for a Federal Response, Joint Hearing.* 99th Cong., 1st sess., 23 Oct. 1985. 169p. Y4.Ag4/2:C16/5. Hearing witnesses recount personal experiences with breast cancer and describe the screening process for early detection. The importance of early detection and the role the federal government should play in making early detection possible are examined.

1448. U.S. Congress. Senate. Committee on Labor and Human Resources. Subcommittee on Aging. *Osteoporosis, Hearing.* 99th Cong., 1st sess., 20 June 1985. 261p. Y4.L11/4:S.hrg.99-231. Hearing witnesses review the prevalence and treatment of osteoporosis and describe educational activities aimed at preventing the condition. A list of osteoporosis-related research funded by the National Institute of Arthritis, Diabetes, and Digestive and Kidney Diseases in fiscal year 1984 is provided. Women who suffer from osteoporosis testify on their experience.

1449. U.S. Congress. Senate. Special Committee on Aging. *Prospects for Better Health for Older Women, Hearing.* 99th Cong., 1st sess., 15 Apr. 1985. 71p. Y4.Ag4:S.hrg.99-128. Hearing testimony highlights the health problems common to older women, preventive measures, and funding of current programs aimed at older women. Some of the topics covered include osteoporosis, arthritis, hypertension, and drug interactions.

1450. U.S. Food and Drug Administration. *Toxic Shock Syndrome and Tampons.* Washington, DC: GPO, 1985. leaflet. HE20.4002:T66/3/985.

1451. U.S. Food and Drug Administration. *Toxic Shock Syndrome is So Rare You Might Forget It Can Happen...* Rockville, MD: The Administration, 1985. 2p. HE20.4002:T66/4.

1452. U.S. National Cancer Institute. *Lo Que Usted Necesita Saber Sobre la Displasia, el Cancer Incipiente y el Cancer Invasivo de la Cerviz.* Washington, DC: GPO, 1985. 4p. HE20.3152:D99/984/spanish.

1453. U.S. National Cancer Institute. *What You Need to Know about Dysplasia, Very Early Cancer and Invasive Cancer of the Cervix.* Bethesda, MD: The Institute, 1985. 14p. HE20.3152:D99/985. Editions also published in 1980 and 1984.

1454. U.S. National Cancer Institute. Office of Cancer Communications. *Oral Contraceptives and Cancer Risk.* Washington, DC: GPO, 1985. 7p. HE20.3182:Or1. Summarizes research findings on contraceptive users and breast cancer, ovarian and endometrial cancer, and cervical cancer.

1455. U.S. National Cancer Institute. Office of Cancer Communications. *Recently Reported Health Effects of Exposure before Birth and during Pregnancy to Synthetic Estrogen Diethylstilbestrol (DES).* Washington, DC: GPO, 1985. 10p. HE20.3182/3:D56/2. Review summarizes recent research on the risk of cancer to reproductive organs in young men and women exposed *in utero* to DES and in mothers exposed to DES during pregnancy.

1456. U.S. National Institute on Alcohol Abuse and Alcoholism. *Women and Alcohol Problems: Tools for Prevention.* Washington, DC: GPO, 1985. 27p. HE20.8308:W84/2. Describes prevention measures for women with alcohol problems on three different levels. Level one, primary prevention, focuses on stopping alcohol problems before they start. Level two targets women at risk of becoming alcoholic and level three involves getting women with alcohol abuse problems into treatment.

1457. U.S. National Institutes of Health. *En Busca de Buena Salud: Las Mujeres Mayores Necesitan Estrogeno y Calcio Para Impedir la Osteoporosis, Segur Concluye un Panel de NIH.* Bethesda, MD: The Institutes, 1985? 1p. HE20.3038:Os7/spanish.

1458. U.S. National Institutes of Health. *The Search for Health: Teenage Girls and Smoking.* Bethesda, MD: The Institutes, 1985? 1p. HE20.3038:T22.

1459. U.S. National Institutes of Health. *The Search for Health: Women and Osteoporosis.* Bethesda, MD: The Institutes, 1985? 1p. HE20.3038:Os7/2.

1460. U.S. National Library of Medicine. *Adjuvant Chemotherapy for Breast Cancer.* by Charlotte Kenton. Washington, DC: GPO, 1985. 39p. HE20.3614/2:85-14. Bibliography drawn from citations in the MEDLINE database from January 1980 - August 1985 details the controversy over the use of adjuvant chemotherapy for breast cancer.

1461. U.S. Public Health Service. Task Force on Women's Health Issues. *Women's Health: Report of the Public Health Service Task Force on Women's Health Issues.* Washington, DC: The Service, 1985. 2 vol. HE20.2:W84/2/v.1-2. Volume one of the report, reprinted from *Public Health Reports*, v. 100 no. 1, presents the recommendations of the Task Force and provides concise summaries of the subcommittee reports followed by a brief bibliography. The full reports of the Task Force are presented in volume two. These reports provide an excellent overview of the literature on social factors affecting women's health, women's physical health and well-being, health concerns of older women, and substance abuse and mental health of women.   Factors of poverty, labor force participation, status as an ethnic or cultural minority, and physical or mental disability are noted in relation to women's health. Briefly discusses the problem of gender-related bias in health research methodology.

1462. U.S. Congress. House. Select Committee on Aging. Subcommittee on Retirement Income and Employment. Task Force of Social Security and Women. *Older Women's Health.* 99th Cong., 2d sess., 5 Feb. 1986. 67p. Y4.Ag4/2:W84/10. Hearing on the health concerns of older women highlights the issue of poverty and health status, and reviews federal health programs' ability to meet older women's needs. Presents testimony on the major health problems of older women including Alzheimer's and osteoporosis. Background statistics provided include sex-specific mortality rates by cause and health statistics by sex.

1463. U.S. Congress. Senate. Committee on Labor and Human Resources. *Alcohol, Drug Abuse, and Mental Health Amendments of 1986, Report to Accompany S. 2595.* S. Rept. 99-333, 99th Cong., 2d sess., 8 July 1986. 49p. Serial 13676. Reports a bill reauthorizing NIAAA and NIDA for 5 years with a new provision requiring the Secretary of HHS to produce public service announcements on the health risks to women of cigarette smoking.

1464. U.S. Food and Drug Administration. *Women's Health Message from the Food and Drug Administration (FDA) about Mammography.* Washington, DC: GPO, 1986. 15p. HE20.4002:M31. Guidance for women on mammography includes basic information and questions to ask when selecting a mammography center. A bibliography of publications on breast cancer from the National Cancer Institute and reprints of articles relating to breast cancer from *FDA Consumer* magazine are furnished.

1465. U.S. Human Nutrition Information Service. Nutrition Monitoring Division. *Low-Income Women 19-50 Years and Their Children 1-5 Years, 1 Day, 1985.* Hyattsville, MD: The Division, 1986. 186p. A111.9/3:85-2. See 1477 for abstract.

1466. U.S. Human Nutrition Information Service. Nutrition Monitoring Division. *Women 19-50 Years and Their Children 1-5 Years, 1 Day, 1985.* Washington, DC: GPO, 1986. 102p. A111.9/3:85-1. See 1478 for abstract.

1467. U.S. National Cancer Institute. *Breast Cancer: Understanding Treatment Options.* Washington, DC: GPO, 1986. 17p. HE20.3152:B74/14/986. Also issued in 1984.

1468. U.S. National Cancer Institute. *Cancer of the Uterus: Research Report.* Washington, DC: GPO, 1986. 13p. HE20.3166:Ut2/986. Brief review describes the incidence, causes and prevention, detection and treatment of cervical cancer and endometrial cancer. Earlier edition published in 1983.

1469. U.S. National Cancer Institute. *What You Need to Know about Cancer of the Ovary.* Bethesda, MD: The Institute, 1986. 16p. HE20.3152:Ov1/986. Also issued in 1979.

1470. U.S. National Institute on Drug Abuse. Division of Clinical Research. *Women and Drugs: A New Era for Research.* Edited by Barbara A. Ray and Monique C. Braude. Research Monograph Series no. 65. Washington, DC: GPO, 1986. 105p. HE20.8216:65. Excellent overview of research on women and drugs highlights the need to consider gender differences when designing research on drug abuse and misuse. Among the topics covered are the effects of gender on health, the role of sex hormones in behavior, the extent of drug abuse among women, gender differences in drug use patterns, and the role of societal, economic and physiological factors on substance abuse patterns among women and men.

1471. U.S. President's Council on Physical Fitness and Sports. *Proceedings, the National Women's Leadership Conference on Fitness, Proceedings, April 6-7, 1984, Washington, D.C.* Washington, DC: The Council, 1986? 72p. HE20.102:W84/2. Papers presented at a conference on women and physical fitness focus on the importance of exercise for girls and women and touches on specific issues such as older women, eating disorders, working women, school age women, psychological aspects of fitness, and nutrition.

1472. U.S. Public Health Service. Coordinating Committee on Women's Health Issues. *National Conference on Women's Health, June 17-18, 1986, Bethesda, Maryland.* Washington,

DC: GPO, 1986. various paging. HE20.4002:W84; HE20.4002:W84/speck.; HE20.4002:W84/eval. Conference packet includes the program for the National Conference on Women's Health, biographical information on conference speakers, and an evaluation questionnaire.

1473. U.S. Alcoholism, Drug Abuse and Mental Health Administration. *Useful Information on... Anorexia Nervosa and Bulimia.* Rockville, MD: The Administration, 1987. 14p. HE20.8102:An7.

1474. U.S. Congress. House. Committee on Ways and Means. Subcommittee on Health. *Medicare Coverage for Mammography Examinations, Hearing.* 100th Cong., 1st sess., 3 Nov. 1987. 107p. Y4.W36:100-47. The importance of mammography for early detection and treatment of breast cancer is stressed in testimony urging Medicare coverage of mammography for asymptomatic women. The cost of mammography and the need to ensure quality services are explored.

1475. U.S. Congress. House. Select Committee on Children, Youth, and Families. *Eating Disorders: The Impact on Children and Families, Hearing.* 100th Cong., 1st sess., 31 July 1987. 157p. Y4.C43/2:Ea8. Witnesses describe the characteristics and treatment of anorexia nervosa and bulimia, particularly within the family context. Ways families contribute to the psychological state of anorexic adolescents and the involvement of the family in therapy are discussed.

1476. U.S. Food and Drug Administration. *A Special Topic Conference: Osteoporosis.* Bethesda, MD: The Administration, 1987. 5 parts. HE20.4002:W84/987/pt. 1-5. Information on an FDA National Conference on Women's Health special topic conference on osteoporosis includes booklets on conference goals and agenda, conference CEU and evaluation form, general conference information, conference program and patient education sampler.

1477. U.S. Human Nutrition Information Service. Nutrition Monitoring Division. *Low-Income Women 19-50 Years and Their Children 1-5 Years, 1 Day: 1986.* Hyattsville, MD: The Service, 1987. 166p. A111.9/3:86-2. Data from the Continuing Survey of Food Intakes by Individuals compares spring 1986 data on the diets of low-income women and their children to data collected in the 1985 survey (1465).

1478. U.S. Human Nutrition Information Service. Nutrition Monitoring Division. *Women 19-50 Years and Their Children 1-5 Years, 1 Day: 1986.* Hyattsville, MD: The Service, 1987. 98p. A111.9/3:86-1. A one day sample of the dietary habits of women 19-50 years of age and their young children, taken in the spring of 1986, is compared to earlier data (1466).

1479. U.S. National Cancer Institute. *Adjuvant Therapy: Facts for Women with Breast Cancer.* Washington, DC: GPO, 1987. 10p. HE20.3152:B74/17/987. Also issued in 1984.

1480. U.S. National Cancer Institute. *Breast Biopsy: What You Should Know.* Washington, DC: GPO, 1987. 12p. HE20.3152:B74/15/987. Also issued in 1984.

1481. U.S. National Cancer Institute. *Breast Cancer: We're Making Progress Every Day.* Bethesda, MD: The Institute, 1987. 12p. HE20.3152:B74/13/987. Editions also published in 1981 and 1983.

1482. U.S. National Cancer Institute. *Breast Reconstruction: A Matter of Choice.* Bethesda, MD: The Institute, 1987. 21p. HE20.3152:B74/9/987. Informational pamphlet describes breast reconstruction. Also published in 1984 and 1986.

1483. U.S. National Cancer Institute. *Did You Know...There is a Special Study at the National Cancer Institute for Women with Early Breast Cancer?* Washington, DC: GPO, 1987. 17p. HE20.3152:B74/19. Description for potential participants provides details of a randomized study comparing mastectomy and lumpectomy plus radiation therapy in the treatment of early breast cancer.

1484. U.S. National Cancer Institute. *Mastectomy: A Treatment for Breast Cancer.* Washington, DC: GPO, 1987. 24p. HE20.3152:M39/987. Informational pamphlet on the medical and psychological aspects of mastectomy. Also issued in 1984.

1485. U.S. National Cancer Institute. *La Prueba Pap: Un Metoda Para el Diagostico del Cancer de la Cerviz.* Washington, DC: GPO, 1987. 11p. HE20.3152:P19/2/987/spanish. Also issued in 1985.

1486. U.S.National Cancer Institute. *Report of the DES Task Force.* Bethesda, MD: The Institute, 1987. 31p. HE20.3152:D56/5/985. Update of the 1978 report on the adverse effects of DES analyzes the literature on the incidence of breast cancer in women who took DES during pregnancy and on the cancer risks for DES daughters.

1487. U.S. National Cancer Institute. *Study Links Alcohol Consumption to Breast Cancer.* Bethesda, MD: The Office, 1987. 1p. HE20.3182/3:A/1. Reports the results of a study indicating that consuming moderate amounts of alcohol may increase the risk of developing breast cancer.

1488. U.S. National Heart, Lung, and Blood Institute. *Coronary Heart Disease in Women: Reviewing the Evidence, Identifying the Needs: A Summary of the Proceedings, January 26-28, 1986, Bethesda, Maryland.* by Elaine D. Eaker, et al. Bethesda, MD: The Institute, 1987. 48p. HE20.3202:C81/5. Workshop proceedings explore gender differences in coronary heart disease (CHD). Research on CHD in women examines risk factors, behaviors, estrogen, and diabetes. The recognition of CHD in women by the medical community and current research issues are also discussed.

1489. U.S. National Institutes of Health. *The Healthy Heart Handbook for Women.* by Marian Sandmaier. Washington, DC: GPO, 1987. 32p. HE20.3208:H34/3. Booklet describes the risk factors associated with coronary heart disease and particularly notes the physical characteristics and habits linked to heart disease in women. Modifying behavior to reduce the risk is stressed and women are cautioned to consider the heart disease risks associated with oral contraceptive use.

1490. U.S. National Institutes of Health. *Menopause Poses No Problems for a Majority of Women Says NIA Study.* Washington, DC: The Institutes, 1987. 1p. HE20.3038:M52/2. Summary report of a longitudinal study of natural menopause dispels many negative ideas about women's experience of menopause. Differences in the impact of menopause on women who experience natural menopause and women who have undergone surgical menopause is noted.

1491. U.S. National Institutes of Health. *Not Far Enough: Women vs. Smoking, a Workshop for Women's Groups and Women's Health Leaders.* Washington, DC: GPO, 1987. 27p. HE20.3152:W84. Workshop papers report on morbidity and mortality linked to women's smoking, and on the tobacco industry's targeting of women through advertising and by funding women's organizations.

1492. U.S. Office of Technology Assessment. *Breast Cancer Screening for Medicare Beneficiaries: Effectiveness, Costs to Medicare and Medicaid Resources Required.* Washington, DC: GPO, 1987. 147p. CIS 87-J952-71. Overview of issues surrounding the provision of mammography for Medicare clients examines the cost and effectiveness of mammography for early detection of breast cancer. The paper notes that, while the cost of routine screening for Medicare recipients is not offset in saving in treatment costs, the impact on mortality from breast cancer could be significant. Data from studies on the long term effectiveness of mammography is included.

1493. U.S. Public Health Service. *Hysterectomies in the United States, 1965-84.* Washington, DC: GPO, 1987. 32p. HE20.6209:13/92. Trends in hysterectomies from 1965 through 1984 are examined by age, region, race, diagnosis, surgical approach, and by whether a bilateral oophorectomy was performed.

1494. U.S. Surgeon General. *Alcohol Abuse and Women Today.* by C. Everett Koop. Bethesda, MD: The Service, 1987. 1p. HE20.2:Al1. Brief piece on women and alcohol abuse notes the role of women's careers in encouraging alcohol abuse and briefly suggests avenues to help women abusers.

1495. U.S. Veterans Administration. Biometrics Division. Statistical Policy and Research Services. Office of Information Management and Statistics. *Female Veterans' Usage of VA Hospitalization, Fiscal Year 1986.* by Elizabeth M. Ahuja. Biometrics Monograph no. 21. Washington, DC: The Administration, 1987. 26p. VA1.67:21. Detailed statistics on usage of VA hospitals by female veterans in 1986 covers discharges by sex; discharges by age and sex; and VA medical center utilization by age and sex, marital status, geographic distribution, length of stay, service-connected disability status, and principle diagnosis.

1496. U.S. Congress. House. Committee on Energy and Commerce. Subcommittee on Health and the Environment. *Clinical Laboratory Improvement Act, Hearing on H.R. 4325, H.R. 4927 and H.R. 4928.* 100th Cong., 2d sess., 6 July 1988. 364p. Y4.En2/3:100-167. Hearing considers bills to regulate all clinical laboratories. Testimony focuses on the quality of testing and on the controversy over inaccurate Pap smear results. Negligence and kickbacks in Pap smear work and ways to ensure valid laboratory results are discussed. The structure of Medicaid and Medicare payment rules and their tendency to encourage physician's offices to do their own, less accurate, lab work is also discussed.

1497. U.S. Congress. House. Committee on Energy and Commerce. Subcommittee on Oversight and Investigations. *Clinical Laboratories, Hearings.* 100th Cong., 2d sess., 10 Mar., 27 July 1988. 552p. Y4.En2/3:100-146. Investigation of the practices of clinical laboratories reveals problems of high false result reports, overcharging for Medicaid patients, and kickbacks to doctors. The severe consequences of undetected cervical cancer due to false negative Pap smear results are examined.

1498. U.S. Congress. House. Committee on Government Operations. Subcommittee on Human Resources and Intergovernmental Relations. *Therapeutic Drugs and AIDS: Development, Testing, and Availability, Hearings.* 100th Cong., 2d sess., 28-29 Apr. 1988. 448p. Y4.G74/7:D84/24. Hearing testimony explores the AIDS drug development and testing process with heavy criticism of the limited scope of drug trials. The exclusion of children and women from the clinical trials is noted as is a tendency to exclude minorities and drug users. Much of the discussion centers on the NIAID AIDS clinical trials protocol and the need to expand trials and stop the use of placebos.

1499. U.S. Congress. House. Committee on Small Business. Subcommittee on Regulation and Business Opportunities. *Potential Health Hazards of Cosmetic Products, Hearings.* 100th Cong., 2d sess., 14 July, 15 Sept. 1988. 608p. Y4.Sm1:100-67. Hearing witnesses debate the safety of cosmetic products both for cosmeticians and consumers. Failure to label products as health hazards for cosmetologists and the failure to adequately test ingredients for long term health hazards are discussed. Also noted is the rush to market "anti-aging" products such as Retin-A before they have been thoroughly tested. Most of the testimony centers on the amount of control the FDA should have over cosmetic products.

1500. U.S. Congress. House. Committee on the District of Columbia. *Authorizing the Conveyance to the Columbia Hospital for Women of Certain Parcels of Land in the District of Columbia, and for Other Purposes, Report Together with Minority Views to Accompany H.R. 4700.* H. Rept. 100-1085, part 1, 100th Cong., 2d sess., 1988. 16p. Favorable report with minority views supports the sale of land to the Columbia Hospital for Women. The majority report cites the history of the Columbia Hospital and the need for the planned National Women's Health Resources Center. The minority report rejects the bill on the grounds that the Columbia Hospital had ignored use restrictions on federal land conveyed to it previously.

1501. U.S. Congress. House. Committee on the District of Columbia. Subcommittee on Fiscal Affairs and Health. *Conveyance of Land to the Columbia Hospital for Women, Hearing and Markup on H.R. 2909 and Clean Bill H.R. 4700 and H.R. 4236.* 100th Cong., 1st and 2d sess., 4 Aug. 1987 - 28 Sept. 1988. 164p. Y4.D63/1:100-7. Hearing considers bills conveying land to the Columbia Hospital for Women for the site of the National Women's Health Resource Center. The history of the hospital and the unique role the center will play in addressing women's health concerns are stressed by supporters.

1502. U.S. Congress. Senate. Committee on Finance. Subcommittee on Health. *Preventive Health Care for the Elderly, Hearing.* 100th Cong., 2d sess., 6 Jan. 1988, Miami, FL. 169p. Y4.F49:S.hrg.100-451. Within this hearing on preventive health care and the elderly is discussion of the incidence of breast cancer among women over 65 and the effectiveness of mammography. The cost of mammography and the need to ensure its affordability for elderly women on fixed incomes is stressed. Successful prevention programs targeting the elderly, particularly ethnic minorities, are described.

1503. U.S. Congress. Senate. Committee on Labor and Human Resources. *Cancer Detection in Women and Other Health Concerns, Hearing.* 100th Cong., 2d sess., 8 June 1988, Salt Lake City, UT. 137p. Y4.L11/4:S.hrg.100-804. Hearing on health concerns of women presents information in the incidence of breast cancer and cervical cancer. The need for early detection, long term health care, programs on depression and substance abuse among women, and access to treatment programs is stressed.

1504. U.S. Congress. Senate. Committee on Labor and Human Resources. *Cancer Detection in Women, Hearing.* 100th Cong., 2d sess., 28 Jan. 1988. 250p. Y4.L11/4:S.hrg.100-529. Hearing testimony reviews procedures for cancer detection in women focusing on early detection of breast cancer using mammography and on the reliability of laboratory screening of Pap smears for cervical cancer.

1505. U.S. Dept. of the Army. *Safer Sex Sense: A Survival Manual for Women.* Washington, DC: The Dept., 1988? leaflet. D101.6/5:Se9/2. Informational pamphlet for women describes ways the HIV virus is transmitted and "safe sex" practices to avoid contracting AIDS.

1506. U.S. Human Nutrition Information Service. Nutrition Monitoring Division. *Low-Income Women 19-50 Years and Their Children 1-5 Years, 4 Days: 1985.* Hyattsville, MD: The Service, 1988. 220p. A111.9/3:95-5. Data from a survey of the diets of low income women age 19 to 50 and their young children reports food intake by food groups and age, household income, region, and Food Stamp program status. Data on percentage of food energy from protein, fat, fatty acids, and carbohydrates, and on general eating habits is given.

1507.   U.S. National Cancer Institute. *Breast Exams, What You Should Know.* Washington, DC: GPO, 1988. 10p. HE20.3152:B74/7/988. Editions issued in 1980, 1983, 1984, and 1985.

1508.   U.S. National Cancer Institute. *Breast Lumps: Questions & Answers.* Washington, DC: GPO, 1988. 23p. HE20.3152:B74/12/988. Earlier editions called *Questions and Answers about Beast Lumps* were issued in 1981 and 1983.

1509.   U.S. National Caner Institute. *NCI Takes Action after Discontinuing Women's Health Trial.* Bethesda, MD: The Institute, 1988. 3p. HE20.3182/8:W84. NCI statement describes the purpose of the Women's Health Trial, a study of the link between diet and breast cancer, and the reasons behind the decision to discontinue the study.

1510.   U.S. National Cancer Institute. *Reversal of Alhylating Agent and Platinum Resistance in Ovarian Cancer.* by Robert F. Ozols, et al. Bethesda, MD: The Institute, 1988. 3p. HE20.3182/3:Am3/8. Press release describes research showing the potential for buthionine sulfoximine and aphidicolin to reverse drug resistance in the treatment of advanced ovarian cancer.

1511.   U.S. National Cancer Institute. *Study Shows Mammography Beneficial for Women Both Over and Under Age 50.* Bethesda, MD: The Institute, 1988. 4p. HE20.3182:M31 or HE20.3182/3:M31. Summary report describes results of an NCI study showing significant reduction in breast cancer deaths for women in the 40 to 49 age group as well as in women aged 50 and older through regular screening with mammography.

1512.   U.S. National Cancer Institute. *What You Need To Know about Cancer of the Uterus.* Bethesda, MD: The Institute, 1988. 25p. HE20.3152:Ut2/2/988. Informational booklet describes the symptoms and treatment of cancer of the uterus. Also published in 1980.

1513.   U.S. National Cancer Institute. *What You Should Know: Breast Lumps.* Bethesda, MD: The Institute, 1988. 7p. HE20.3152:B74/20. Booklet describes methods of early detection of breast cancer.

1514.   U.S. National Cancer Institute. Office of Cancer Communications. *National Cancer Institute Breast Cancer Research: An Overview.* Bethesda, MD: The Institute, 1988. 4p. HE20.3182:B74. Fact sheet summarizes NCI research programs on breast cancer.

1515.   U.S. National Cancer Institute. Office of Cancer Communications. *Primary Treatment Is Not Enough for Early Stage Breast Cancer.* Washington, DC: GPO, 1988. 7p. HE20.3182:Ea7. Reviews research on successful treatment of early stage breast cancer with adjuvant therapy following primary treatment.

1516.   U.S. National Heart, Lung, and Blood Institute. *Facts about -- Women: Heart Disease and Stroke.* Bethesda, MD: The Institute, 1988. 2p. HE20.3202:W84. Fact sheet on heart disease focuses on risk factors such as blood cholesterol level, high blood pressure and cigarette smoking, and on their significance for women.

1517.   U.S. National Institute on Aging. *Health Resources for Older Women.* Gaithersburg, MD?: The Institute, 1988. 76p. HE20.3852:H34/988. Common health concerns of older women are described and related organizations and additional readings are listed after each section. Information resources for other areas of concern such as housing, financial planning, and widowhood are also listed.

1518. U.S. National Institute on Alcohol Abuse and Alcoholism. *Women and Alcohol Use: A Review of the Research Literature.* Rockville, MD: The Institute, 1988. 64p. HE20.8302:W84/7. Report reviews the research published between 1980 and early 1988 on women and alcohol consumption. Studies cover research methods, epidemiology, social surveys, biological features, and psychological correlates of women's alcohol use, and treatment issues.

1519. U.S. National Institutes of Health. *Why Do Women Live Longer Than Men?* Bethesda, MD: The Institute, 1988? 1p. HE20.3038:W84. Brief report summarizes biological and psychosocial differences between men and women that contribute to the gender gap in life expectancy. Atherosclerotic heart disease and a higher incidence of high-risk behaviors are noted as major contributors to men's lower life expectancies.

1520. U.S. Army. Social Work Service. *AIDS is a Women's Health Issue.* Washington, DC: The Service, 1989? 4p. D101.2:Ac7/4. Basic facts on the incidence of AIDS in women accompanies brief information on HIV transmission and behaviors that increase or decrease the risk of contracting the virus.

1521. U.S. Congress. House. Committee on Energy and Commerce. Subcommittee on Health and the Environment. *Antidrug Abuse Appropriations Authorization, Hearing.* 101st Cong., 1st sess., 30 Oct. 1989. 62p. Y4.En2/3:101-105. Hearing on funding for anti-drug abuse programs focuses on the treatment needs of pregnant women. The main thrust of testimony is on the need to get pregnant women in drug abuse treatment programs early and on the lack of sufficient program "slots" for all women needing such care.

1522. U.S. Congress. House. Committee on Small Business. Subcommittee on Regulation, Business Opportunities, and Energy. *Unqualified Doctors Performing Cosmetic Surgery: Policies and Enforcement Activities of the Federal Trade Commission - Part II, Hearing.* 101st Cong., 1st sess., 13 May 1989. 599p. Y4.Sm1:101-11. Witnesses describe the financial and physical harm suffered by the victims of unqualified doctors performing cosmetic surgery. The false advertising and dangers of various cosmetic procedures are described. Individual cases of death and disfigurement are described and the tendency for victims to be women is noted.

1523. U.S. Congress. House. Committee on the District of Columbia. *Columbia Hospital for Women - Conveyance of Land, Markups on H.R. 1523 and Clean Bill H.R. 2031.* 101st Cong., 1st sess., 23 Mar., 27 Apr. 1989. 47p. Y4.D63/1:101-2. Brief committee session considers a bill to allow the sale of federal government land in the District to the Columbia Hospital for Women. Plans for the site, which would house the National Women's Health Resource Center, are included in the hearing record.

1524. U.S. Congress. House. Select Committee on Aging. Subcommittee on Human Services. *International Perspectives on Osteoporosis.* 101st Cong., 1st sess., 1989. Committee print. 137p. Y4.Ag4/2:Os7. Proceedings of a forum on osteoporosis reviews the current body of knowledge on the epidemiology of osteoporosis. International cooperation in research and emerging racial and geographical differences in osteoporosis risks are summarized. Finally, actions to prevent osteoporosis and educational efforts in the U.S. are reviewed with examples and a bibliography of patient education materials.

1525. U.S. Congress. House. Select Committee on Children, Youth and Families. *Born Hooked: Confronting the Impact of Perinatal Substance Abuse, Hearing.* 101st Cong., 1st sess., 27 Apr. 1989. 269p. Y4.C43/2:P41. The growing problem of drug use among pregnant women is explored both in terms of the effect on infant health and the impact on the welfare system. The failure of the drug treatment system to address the needs of women coupled with barriers to prenatal care are cited as major problems. Drug treatment programs which address the multiple service needs of pregnant and postpartum women are discussed. The punitive treatment of these women by the legal system is also noted.

1526. U.S. Congress. Senate. Committee on Governmental Affairs. *Missing Links: Coordinating Federal Drug Policy for Women, Infants, and Children, Hearing.* 101st Cong., 1st sess., 31 July 1989. 154p. Y4.G74/9:S.hrg.101-515. Testimony explores the effect of drug abuse on the lives of women and their offspring and discusses ways to improve treatment options to pregnant women. The need to identify female drug abusers early in pregnancy and to coordinate all of the services these women need in addition to basic drug abuse treatment are examined. The lack of open slots in treatment programs and ways federal maternity and child health programs could provide support for local efforts are discussed.

1527. U.S. Congress. Senate. Committee on Labor and Human Resources. Subcommittee on Children, Family, Drugs and Alcoholism. *Drug Addicted Babies: What Can Be Done?. Hearing.* 101st Cong., 1st sess., 9 Oct. 1989. Indianapolis, IN. 89p. Y4.L11/4:S.hrg.101-396. Protection of infants and of the rights of mothers are discussed in testimony on the state response to drug abuse among pregnant women. The extent of substance abuse among pregnant women and mothers of young children is discussed with witnesses stressing the need for early pregnancy intervention. The practice of prosecuting the pregnant woman when drug use is identified is examined in debate over the advisability of using coercion to force the mother into treatment.

1528. U.S. Congress. Senate. Committee on the Judiciary and U.S. Congress. Senate. Committee on Governmental Affairs. *A View from the Front Lines: Wisconsin's Response to the President's Antidrug Policy, Joint Hearing.* 101st Cong., 1st sess., 11 Sept. 1989. Milwaukee, WI. 87p. Y4.J89/2:S.hrg.101-1044. Hearing exploring the operation of President Bush's antidrug policy focuses on education, treatment, and drug user identification. Working with families is discussed and the possibilities for creating more supportive treatment programs directed at women users are looked at in detail.

1529. U.S. Food and Drug Administration. *FDA Special Topic Conference on Osteoporosis, National Conference on Women's Health Series, Directory of Registrants.* Washington, DC: GPO, 1989. 46p. HE20.4037/3:W84/987.

1530. U.S. General Accounting Office. *Breast Cancer: Patients' Survival.* Washington, DC: The Office, 1989. 53p. GA1.13:PEMD-89-9. Concise report reviews the impact of adjuvant chemotherapy on the survival rate of women after breast cancer surgery. While the report shows little change in survival rate since the use of adjuvant chemotherapy was introduced, the writers stress the need for further study. Possible reasons the survival rate has not shown the expected increase are noted.

1531. U.S. General Accounting Office. *Federal Real Property: Conflicting Appraisals of Land Near Columbia Hospital for Women.* Washington, DC: The Office, 1989. 7p. GA1.13:GGD-90-15. Brief report explains the reasons for the high GAO appraisal of federal land under consideration for sale to the Columbia Hospital for Women.

1532. U.S. National Cancer Institute. *Cancer of the Ovary, Research Report.* by Karen McCrory Pocinki. Bethesda, MD: The Institute, 1989. 18p. HE20.3166:Ov1. Overview of the diagnosis and treatment of ovarian cancer and the possible risk factors provides a clear, concise explanation of the current state of knowledge.

1533. U.S. National Cancer Institute. *Long-Term Postmenopausal Hormone Therapy Increase Breast Cancer Risk.* Bethesda, MD: The Institute, 1989. 4p. HE20.3182:P84. Research summary reviews study results showing a higher incidence of breast cancer among Swedish women using replacement hormones for menopausal symptoms over a long period of time.

1534. U.S. National Cancer Institute. *La Prueba Pap: Un Metodo Para Diagnostica Cancer del Cuello del Utero.* Bethesda, MD: The Institute, 1989. 12p. HE20.3152:P19/2/989/ spanish. Spanish language booklet provides patient information on pap smear procedures.

1535. U.S. National Cancer Institute. *What You Need to Know about Breast Cancer.* Bethesda, MD: The Institute, 1989. 32p. HE20.3152:B74/6/989. Informational pamphlet presents basic facts on breast cancer. Earlier editions published in 1978, 1984, 1985, and 1988.

1536. U.S. National Institutes of Health. *Long-Term Postmenopausal Hormone Increases Breast Cancer Risk.* Bethesda, MD: The Institutes, 1989. 1p. HE20.3038:P84. Brief report reviews research showing increased risk of breast cancer in women using replacement hormones for menopausal symptoms. Comments from Dr. Robert Hoover of the National Cancer Institute provide some perspectives on the findings as they relate to short-term hormone replacement and long term use of estrogen to decrease the risk of osteoporosis.

1537. U.S. National Institutes of Health. *Osteoporosis.* Bethesda, MD: The Institutes, 1989. 10p. HE20.3031:Os7. Informational booklet describes the symptoms, treatment and prevention of osteoporosis.

1538. U.S. National Institutes of Health. Clinical Communications Center. *Preparing for a Pelvic Exam.* by Lorene M. Kimzey and Nelly Rivera. Bethesda, MD: The Institute, 1989. 5p. HE20.3002:P36. Patient information booklet provides information on what to expect when given a pelvic exam.

1539. U.S. National Institutes of Health. Clinical Communications Center. *Preparing for an Endometrial Biopsy.* Bethesda, MD: The Institutes, 1989. 5p. HE20.3002:En2. Booklet provides patient information to understand the procedures in an endometrial biopsy.

1540. U.S. Office of Family Planning. *Improving the Quality of Clinician Pap Smear Technique and Management, Client Pap Smear Education, and the Evaluation of Pap Smear Laboratory Testing: A Resource Guide for Title X Family Planning Projects.* Washington, DC: GPO, 1989. 100p. HE20.8:P19. Review of Pap smear procedures for clinicians discusses techniques, quality control, patient management and education, and reporting requirements. A 189-item bibliography on screening for cervical cancer in provided.

1541. U.S. Public Health Service. Coordinating Committee on Women's Health Issues. *Women and AIDS: Initiatives of the Public Health Service.* Washington, DC: GPO, 1989. various paging. HE20.2:W84/3. Report lists AIDS-related activities of PHS agencies and offices which relate to women. Highlights of grants, contracts, and publications are provided.

1542. U.S. Congress. House. Committee on Energy and Commerce. *Breast and Cervical Cancer Mortality Prevention Act of 1990, Report to Accompany H.R. 4790.* H. Rept. 101-543, 101st Cong., 2d sess., 1990. 21p. Reports a bill creating a grant program under the PHSA targeting preventive screening and referral services for breast and cervical cancer. Background materials review the barriers to regular screening for these cancers and examine the role of mammography and Pap smears in reducing mortality from breast and cervical cancers.

1543. U.S. Congress. House. Committee on Energy and Commerce. Subcommittee on Health and the Environment. *Drug Treatment Issues, Hearings.* 101st Cong., 2d sess., 30 Apr., 4 May 1990. 276p. Y4.En2/3:101-177. Hearings on the national drug abuse strategy and on drug treatment focuses on programs for pregnant women. A representative of the ACLU describes the treatment of pregnant women identified as drug users in the justice system, particularly prosecution for endangering the child and the potential for abortion to avoid prosecution. Cases illustrative of the courts' treatment of addicted pregnant women are summarized. The work at Chrysalis House, Inc., a chemical dependency treatment facility for women, is described. The response of ADAMHA to drug treatment needs, particularly programs for pregnant women, is explored.

1544. U.S. Congress. House. Committee on Energy and Commerce. Subcommittee in Health and the Environment. *Women's Health, Hearings.* 101st Cong., 2d sess., 23,25 Apr. 1990. 262p. Y4.En2/3:101-141. The first day of hearings considers legislation to fund breast and cervical cancer detection and treatment programs. The bill under review would fund demonstration projects for screening through state Medicaid programs. Testimony focuses on the potential for regular mammography and Pap smears to reduce mortality from breast and cervical cancer and on ways to encourage regular screening among women. The second day of hearings considers bills to fund contraceptive and infertility research. One area of debate centers on abortifacient drugs, such as RU-486, and whether the bill would fund research in this area. The need for more research on remedies for infertility and safe and effective contraceptives is described. Also discussed is the effect on drug research in general of a proposed clause prohibiting NIH research on drugs with an abortifacient effect.

1545. U.S. Congress. House. Committee on Government Operations. Government Activities and Transportation Subcommittee. *Columbia Hospital: Conveyance of GSA Land, Hearings on H.R. 2031.* 101st Cong., 2d sess., 23 May, 2 Oct. 1990. 447p. Y4.G74/7:C72/2. The transfer of land to the Columbia Hospital for Women is considered in hearing testimony. Witnesses discuss women's health issues and the role the proposed National Women's Health Research Center would play in promoting education and research in women's health.

1546. U.S. Congress. House. Committee on Government Operations. Human Resources and Intergovernmental Relations Subcommittee. *Is the FDA Protecting Patients from the Dangers of Silicone Breast Implants? Hearing.* 101st Cong., 2d sess., 18 Dec. 1990. 426p. Y4.G74/7:Si3/2. Personal stories and research results begin to outline the health risks of silicone breast implants. Witnesses describe chronic illness and other major health impacts caused by leakage from the implants while others note the role of implants in the psychological recovery from mastectomy. Criticism of the FDA's review of silicone breast implant safety and the inability of the FDA to get patient education materials finished and distributed is the focus of testimony.

1547. U.S. Congress. House. Committee on Small Business. Subcommittee on Regulation, Business Opportunities, and Energy. *RU 486: The Import Ban and Its Effect on Medical Research, Hearing.* 101st Cong., 2d sess., 19 Nov. 1990. 285p. Y4.Sm1:101-85. Medical researchers describe the potential of RU 486 for the treatment of a number of disorders and diseases including many, such as Cushings syndrome, which primarily affect women. The FDA is criticized for its ban on the importation of RU 486 based on its use as an abortifacient.

1548. U.S. Congress. House. Committee on the Budget. Task Force on Human Resources. *Health Care Crisis: Problems of Cost and Access for Children of Color, Hearing.* 101st Cong., 2d sess., 19 Nov. 1990. 82p. Y4.B85/3:101-5-14. Hearing witnesses discuss health care access in California and the deficiencies in the MediCal system. Much of the testimony centers on the health care needs of low income women, particularly with reference to prenatal care and AIDS. Difficulties faced by women in qualifying for MediCal and in finding prenatal care providers who will accept MediCal patients are examined. The lack of research and awareness regarding HIV and women is discussed.

1549. U.S. Congress. House. Committee on the Budget. Task Force on Human Resources. *Health Care Crisis, Problems of Cost and Access, Hearing.* 101st Cong., 1st sess., 31 Oct., 5 Nov. 1990. 168p. Y4.B85/3:101-5-13. Examination of the health care system and access to health care for low income persons provides diverse views on the issue of access to prenatal care and the impact on women and children of the existing system. Discussion also deals with health care and people with AIDS or HIV+ persons including specific testimony on treatment of women with AIDS, the failure of the system to diagnose AIDS in women, and the needs of HIV+ women with children.

1550. U.S. Congress. House. Committee on Ways and Means. Subcommittee on Health. *Medicare Benefit Improvements Act of 1990, Hearing on H.R. 3880.* 101st Cong., 2d sess., 27 Feb. 1990. 94p. Y4.W36:101-76. One of the major benefit additions to Medicare considered in this hearing is mammography screening. The incidence of breast cancer and the role of early detection in preventing mortality is stressed by supporters of mammography's inclusion in Medicare benefits. The cost of the benefit and how to finance it are also discussed along with hospice care and home health services.

1551. U.S. Congress. House. Committee on Ways and Means. Subcommittee on Human Resources. *The Enemy Within: Crack-Cocaine and American's Families.* 101st Cong., 2d sess., 12 June 1990. Committee print. 93p. Y4.W36:WMCP101-30. Report on the impact of cocaine on the child welfare system examines statistics and research on the use of cocaine among women of childbearing age. The effect of crack cocaine use on parental behavior and the treatment options which address the welfare of mother and child are reviewed.

1552. U.S. Congress. House. Select Committee on Aging. Subcommittee on Health and Long-Term Care. *Breast Cancer: Race for the Cure, Hearing.* 101st Cong., 2d sess., 16 May 1990. 125p. Y4.Ag4/2:C16/7. The incidence of breast cancer in the U.S. and the state of research on prevention and treatment is examined in hearing testimony. The focus of the hearing is a bill to increase funding for breast cancer research by $25 million. Witnesses express support for Medicaid, Medicare and private health plan coverage of mammography.

1553. U.S. Congress. House. Select Committee on Aging. Subcommittee on Housing and Consumer Interests. *Women Health Care Consumers: Short Changed on Medical Research and Treatment, Hearing.* 101st Cong., 2d sess., 24 July 1990. 174p. Y4.Ag4/2:W84/13. Hearing on women and medical treatment focuses primarily on the tendency of medical researchers to develop treatment theories based on research which excludes women. Much of the discussion centers on research funding by the NIH, charges of preference to male researchers, and the need to require funded projects to include women subjects in most cases. The exclusion of women subjects from heart disease research is repeatedly noted.

1554. U.S. Congress. House. Select Committee on Children, Youth, and Families. *Beyond the Stereotypes: Women, Addiction, and Perinatal Substance Abuse, Hearing.* 101st Cong., 2d sess., 19 Apr. 1990. 197p. Y4.C43/2:St4. Hearing testimony explores the extent of substance abuse among women of childbearing age and the consequences for infant mortality and welfare costs. Funding and intervention opportunities are the topic of testimony on targeting treatment programs to pregnant women. Although much of the discussion centers on drug abuse, the problem of alcohol abuse among women is also noted. Successful intervention programs for women are described.

1555. U.S. Congress. House. Select Committee on Children, Youth, and Families. *Getting Straight: Overcoming Treatment Barriers for Addicted Women and Their Children, Hearing.* 101st Cong., 2d sess., 23 Apr. 1990. Detroit, MI. 174p. Y4.C43/2:T71. The need for residential treatment programs for addicted women and their children is emphasized in a hearing focusing on Detroit and the programs of the Eleonore Hutzel Recovery Center. Witnesses stress the need for improved flexibility in government programs such as Medicaid to help support these and similar programs. Aspects of good substance abuse programs for women and infants are noted, and coordination among service providers is discussed.

1556.   U.S. Congress. House. Select Committee on Children, Youth, and Families. *Law and Policy Affecting Addicted Women and Their Children, Hearing.* 101st Cong., 2d sess., 17 May 1990. 327p. Y4.C43/2:L41. Hearing witnesses discuss treatment approaches to chemical dependency among women, particularly pregnant women, and the need for a national focus on providing services to these groups. Legal aspects of drug addiction and pregnancy are reviewed and government support for outreach programs are stressed. The failure of states to implement treatment programs targeting pregnant women and mothers, in spite of a federal mandate for some funding, is noted.

1557.   U.S. Congress. Senate. Committee on Finance. *Infant Victims of Drug Abuse, Hearing.* 101st Cong., 2d sess., 28 June 1990. 263p. Y4.F49:S.hrg.101-1216. The problem of "crack babies" and the factors affecting treatment-seeking behavior among pregnant women is the focus of this hearing on infant and child victims of drug abuse. Treatment options which do not automatically separate the mother from her children are explored. The need to target more drug treatment programs to women is also emphasized.

1558.   U.S. Congress. Senate. Committee on Labor and Human Resources. *Breast and Cervical Cancer Mortality Prevention Act of 1990, Report Together with Additional Views to Accompany S. 2283.* S. Rept. 101-380, 101st Cong., 2d sess., 1990. 32p. Report reviews evidence supporting the value of mammography and Pap smears in improving the survival rate for women with breast cancer or cervical cancer. To encourage early detection, the bill reported authorizes a state grant program to make quality cancer screening available to women.

1559.   U.S. Congress. Senate. Committee on Labor and Human Resources. *National Institutes of Health Reauthorization Act of 1990, Report to Accompany S. 2857.* S. Rept. 101-459, 101st Cong., 2d sess., 1990. 63p. Report on reauthorizing certain institutes of the NIH includes background on Title II, which requires the inclusion of women and minorities in clinical research, on the establishment of an Office of Women's Health Research, and on the creation of a data bank on women's health and gender differences research.

1560.   U.S. Congress. Senate. Committee on Labor and Human Resources. *Substance Abuse in Pregnancy: Economic and Social Costs, Hearing.* 101st Cong., 2d sess., 11 Apr. 1990. Seattle, WA. 110p. Y4.L11/4:S.hrg.101-860. Testimony and reports presented at a Seattle hearing highlight the effect of substance abuse among pregnant women on social service agencies. Treatment approaches for chemically dependent pregnant women and mothers described focus on a holistic view which addresses the social service as well as the drug abuse treatment needs of the woman.

1561.   U.S. Congress. Senate. Committee on Labor and Human Resources. *Tobacco Product Education and Health Protection Act of 1990, Hearing on S. 1883.* 101st Cong., 2d sess., 20 Feb. 1990. 240p. Y4.L11/4:S.hrg.101-707/pt.1. Hearing on ways to counteract the impact of tobacco advertising on young people includes analysis of tobacco advertising targeting young women.

1562.   U.S. Congress. Senate. Committee on Labor and Human Resources and U.S. Congress. Senate. Committee on Governmental Affairs. Subcommittee on Oversight of Government Management. *Oversight of Implementation of the Clinical Laboratory Improvement Act of 1988, Joint Hearing.* 101st Cong., 1st sess., 9 Mar. 1990. 80p. Y4.L11/4:S.hrg.101-

862. Study results showing significant errors in laboratory reports for Pap smears accompanies testimony examining HHS's failure to establish regulations under the Clinical Laboratory Improvement Amendments of 1988. The continued need to ensure accurate cervical cancer screening is stressed.

1563. U.S. Congress. Senate. Committee on Labor and Human Resources. Subcommittee on Children, Family, Drugs and Alcoholism. *Falling through the Crack: The Impact of Drug-Exposed Children on the Welfare System, Hearing.* 101st Cong., 2d sess., 8 Mar. 1990. 216p. Y4.L11/4:S.hrg.101-846. The extent of the problem of babies born to drug addicted mothers is explored in a hearing on the child welfare system's attempts to deal with the problem. The factors that keep pregnant drug users from receiving prenatal care are explored, and theories on providing supportive treatment services to addicted mothers are described.

1564. U.S. Congress. Senate. Committee on the Judiciary. *One-Year Drug Strategy Review, Hearing on the First Anniversary of the President's National Drug Control Strategy.* 101st Cong., 2d sess., 5-6 Sept. 1990. 165p. Y4.J89/2:S.hrg.101-1206. Hearing on the effectiveness of President Bush's drug control program focuses primarily on drug traffic control and the success of efforts to control the narcotics business. Some testimony is included on treatment programs and on the need to reach pregnant women who are using drugs.

1565. U.S. General Accounting Office. Human Research Division. *National Institutes of Health: Problems in Implementing Policy on Women in Study Populations.* by Mark V. Nadel. Washington, DC: The Office, 1990. 13p. GA1.5/2:T-HRD-90-38. Testimony of Nadel before the House Committee on Energy and Commerce details the failure of NIH to implement its policy on the inclusion of women in study populations. The delay in the issuance of implementation guidelines and inconsistencies in application are noted.

1566. U.S. National Cancer Institute. *Breast Cancer: Do the Right Thing, Get a Mammogram.* Bethesda, MD: The Institutes, 1990. 2p. HE20.3152:B74/22.

1567. U.S. National Cancer Institute. *Questions and Answers about Breast Calcification.* Bethesda, MD: The Institutes, 1990. 2p. HE20.3152:B74/23.

1568. U.S. National Cancer Institute. *Radiation Therapy: A Treatment for Early Stage Breast Cancer.* Bethesda, MD: The Institute, 1990. 21p. HE20.3152:R11/2/990. Patient booklet describes the procedures involved in radiation therapy for early stage breast cancer and provides information on aftercare.

1569. U.S. National Cancer Institute. *Smart Advice for Women 40 and Over: Have a Mammogram.* Bethesda, MD?: The Institute, 1990. leaflet. HE20.3152:M31/2.

1570. U.S. National Cancer Institute. *Surviving Breast and Prostate Cancer.* Bethesda, MD: The Institute, 1990? 1p. HE20.3152:B74/21. Pictorial presentation illustrates survival rates for breast cancer and prostate cancer by race and survival rates for all types of cancer by race and sex.

1571. U.S. National Cancer Institute. *What You Need to Know about Cancer of the Cervix.* Bethesda, MD: The Institute, 1990. 28p. HE20.3152:C33/990. Booklet describes the nature of cervical cancer and the treatment options.

1572. U.S. National Center for Health Statistics. *Breast Cancer Risk Factors and Screening: United States, 1987.* by Deborah A. Dawson and Gary B. Thompson. Hyattsville, MD: The Center, 1990. 60p. HE20.6209:10/172. Data from the 1987 National Health

Interview Survey is used to estimate risk factors and preventive behaviors for breast cancer in the United States. The results focus on women over forty and are broken down by race and age. Preventive practices are examined by socioeconomic characteristics. An extensive list of references is included.

1573. U.S. National Institute on Alcohol Abuse and Alcoholism. *Alcohol and Women.* Alcohol Alert No. 10. Rockville, MD: The Institute, 1990. 4p. HE20.8322:10. Review of the research literature on alcoholism and alcohol abuse among women is accompanied by a commentary by NIAAA Director Enoch Gordis. The commentary notes concern over the limited extent of women's participation in treatment programs and the absence of women as subjects in alcohol studies.

1574. U.S. National Institutes of Health. *Cigarette Smoking - Risk Factor for Cardiovascular Disease for Women.* Bethesda, MD: The Institutes, 1990. 1p. HE20.3038:C48. Fact sheet summarizes the health risk to women from smoking with a focus on the increased risk of cardiovascular disease.

1575. U.S. National Institutes of Health. *The Healthy Heart - for Women.* Bethesda, MD: The Institute, 1990. 1p. HE20.3038:H35/3. Fact sheet describes the risks of cardiovascular disease and the factors associated with increased risk for women.

1576. U.S. National Institutes of Health. *High Blood Cholesterol - A Risk Factor for Cardiovascular Disease for Women.* Bethesda, MD: The Institutes, 1990. 1p. HE20.3038:C45/4. Fact sheet details the risk of coronary heart disease for women with high blood cholesterol.

1577. U.S. National Institutes of Health. *High Blood Pressure - A Risk Factor for Cardiovascular Disease for Women.* Bethesda, MD: The Institutes, 1990. 1p. HE20.3038:H53/2. Fact sheet reviews information on the risk of cardiovascular disease in women with high blood pressure.

1578. U.S. National Library of Medicine. *Treatment of Early-Stage Breast Cancer, January 1985 through May 1990, 668 Citations.* by Naomi Miller and F. Andrew Dorr. Washington, DC: GPO, 1990. 26p. HE20.3615/2:90-6. Bibliography lists books, book chapters, and journal articles on management of early-stage breast cancer.

1579. U.S. Office of Technology Assessment. *The Costs and Effectiveness of Cervical Cancer Screening in Elderly Women.* by Charlette Muller, et al. Preventive Health Services under Medicare Background Paper 4. Washington, DC: GPO, 1990. 88p. Y3.T22/2:2C33. Review of existing research on cervical cancer in elderly women accompanies an analysis of the cost-effectiveness of cervical cancer screening. The review section covers the incidence of cervical neoplasia and its diagnosis and treatment in elderly women as well as reviewing the accuracy and effectiveness of Pap smears. Finally, the implications of cost-effectiveness findings for Medicare coverage are examined.

SERIALS

1580. U.S. Alcohol, Drug Abuse, and Mental Health Administration. *Memorandum on Women's Alcohol, Drug Abuse, and Mental Health Issues.* Rockville, MD: The Administration, 1987? - . quarterly. HE20.8019:date. Newsletter highlights ADAMHA research and workshops relating to women. A special issue on "Women and AIDS" was issued in September 1987.

1581. U.S. National Cancer Institute. *ICRDB Cancergram: Breast Cancer, Diagnosis, Treatment, Pre-Clinical Biology.* Washington, DC: GPO, 1977- . irreg. Title varies. HE20.3173/2:CT09/date. Informational abstracts describe recent articles on breast cancer.

11

Fertility and Maternity

Government interest in maternity has primarily focused on maternal mortality and pregnancy outcome. This chapter describes selected documents on prenatal care, childbirth, and fertility. Numerous other documents describing prenatal care from a child health perspective, although relevant to women's lives, were excluded. Also excluded are general vital statistics reports on natality. Documents on fertility which were included focus on deferential fertility and socioeconomic characteristics. Some of the more unique reports include an Immigrant Commission study, *Fecundity of Immigrant Women* (1588), reports on characteristics and trends in wanted and unwanted childbearing between 1968 and 1972 (1739) and 1973 and 1988 (1787), and *Future Fertility of Women by Present Age and Parity: Analysis of American Historical Data, 1917-80* (1766).

Most documents on government sponsored maternity programs are listed in Chapter 12, however congressional support for the Columbia Hospital for Women and Lying-In Asylum is documented here. The earliest government documents on maternal health are the detailed annual reports of the hospital which were published by the Government Printing Office between 1866 and 1917 (1790). Trends in maternal mortality in the U.S. and in other countries were a major government concern in the early 1900's. The Children's Bureau routinely published data on maternal mortality rates and brought out a major research report in 1917, *Maternal Mortality from All Conditions Connected with Childbirth in the United States and Certain Other Countries* (1596). Other substantial reports on maternal mortality were published in 1926 (1612), 1934 (1623), and 1953 (1582), with numerous shorter statistical reports and chartbooks published in between. Early work on maternity care focused on access in rural areas. Results of surveys by the Children's Bureau published in 1919 and 1923 describe maternity and infant care in rural areas of Kansas (1597), Wisconsin (1600), Montana (1601), Mississippi (1604), and Georgia (1608). The use of midwives as a way to improve maternity care is discussed in a 1929 report on the situation in Denmark (1618), a 1941 manual for teaching midwives (1652), and a 1984 report on out-of-hospital deliveries (1714).

Obstetrical practices are also a topic of government documents, particularly since the mid-1970's. In 1978 the Senate held hearings on obstetrical practices in the United States at which the health implications of cesarean sections, fetal monitors, and other procedures were discussed (1734). The actions of HEW to ensure safe obstetrical practices are examined in a 1979 report of the General Accounting Office (1741). The most complete review of cesarean childbirth is found in the 1982 report of the Consensus Development Conference on Cesarean Childbirth (1754). Possible factors contributing to an increased usage of cesarean sections are examined in the 1984 report *Who Receives Caesareans: Patient and Hospital Characteristics* (1762).

The employment of pregnant women is briefly dealt with in a 1942 leaflet on standards of maternity care for women in industry. More detailed reports on pregnancy and employment include a 1976 report *Occupational Health Problems of Pregnant Women* (1727), and a 1978 NIOSH publication, *Guidelines on Pregnancy and Work* (1736). Other documents on pregnancy and occupational health are found in Volume Two. Although some documents on substance abuse and pregnancy are listed below, most are included with other documents on substance abuse in Chapter 10, Health.

1582. U.S. Congress. Senate. *Letter of the Secretary of the Interior, Communicating a Report from the Surgeon General of the Expenditures of the Columbia Hospital for Women and Lying-In Asylum.* S. Ex. Doc. 2, 41st Cong., 2d sess., 1869. 2p. Serial 1405. Report of expenditures from Dec. 5, 1868 to June 30, 1869 for the Columbia Hospital for Women and Lying- In Asylum.

1583. U.S. Congress. House. *Columbia Hospital for Women, Letter from the Acting Secretary of the Interior, Relative to an Appropriation of $30,000 for Purchasing a Site for the Columbia Hospital for Women.* H. Ex. Doc. 249, 42d Cong., 2d sess., 1872. 2p. Serial 1515.

1584. U.S. Congress. House. *Columbia Hospital for Women, Letter from the Acting Secretary of the Interior, Relative to an Appropriation for the Completion of the Columbia Hospital for Women, in the District of Columbia.* H. Ex. Doc. 154, 42d Cong., 3d sess., 1873. 2p. Serial 1567.

1585. U.S. Congress. House. *Columbia Hospital, Letter from the Secretary of the Interior, Relative to an Appropriation Required for Completing the Purchase of the Grounds Surrounding the Columbia Hospital.* H. Ex. Doc. 128, 43d Cong., 2d sess., 1875. 1p. Serial 1648.

1586. U.S. Congress. House. *Letter from the Secretary of the Treasury, Transmitting a Copy of a Communication from the Commissioner of the District of Columbia Submitting a Supplemental Estimate of Appropriation for Columbia Hospital.* H. Doc. 549, 57th Cong., 1st sess., 1902. 3p. Serial 4361. Details requests for funding for a new elevator and for an additional operating room at the Columbia Hospital.

1587. U.S. Immigrant Commission. *Abstract of Report on Fecundity of Immigrant Women.* by Joseph A. Hill. Washington, DC: The Commission, 1911. 52p. Y3.Im6:W84/2. Full report issued as S. Doc. 282, 61st Congress (1588).

1588. U.S. Immigrant Commission. *Occupations of the First and Second Generations of Immigrants in the United States; Fecundity of Immigrant Women.* Reports of the Immigrant Commission vol. 28. S. Doc. 282, 61st Cong., 2d sess., 1911. 826p. Serial 5664. The first report in this volume provides a detailed examination with supporting statistics on employment of first and second generation Americans by occupation and country of origin or parentage. Data is broken down by sex, occupation, generation, and country of origin for the U.S. and states. The second report analyzes data from the 1900 Census for Rhode Island, Ohio, and Minnesota on birth rates for immigrant and native white women in the U.S. and analyzes the data by parentage and nativity, average number of years married and average number of children born.

1589. U.S. Congress. Senate. *Infant Mortality and Its Relation to Employment of Mothers.* Report on Condition of Woman and Child Wage-Earners in the United States vol. XIII. S. Doc. 645, 61st Cong., 2d sess., 1912. 174p. Serial 5697. Detailed examination of still birth and infant mortality looks for links between mother's employment and mortality rates.

Provides detailed data on causes of infant death in Massachusetts industrial cities but fails to show any link between employment of mother while pregnant and infant mortality rates. The return of the mother to work after childbirth is also examined as is the type of care the children receive and the character of the food the child receives. The study found that high infant morality rates among children whose mothers returned to work was linked to improper feeding habits.

1590. U.S.Congress. House. *Columbia Hospital for Women and Lying-In Asylum, Letter from the Acting Secretary of the Treasury, Transmitting Copy of a Communication from the Secretary of the Interior Submitting an Estimate of Appropriation in the Sum of $200,000 for the Completion of the Building for the Columbia Hospital for Women and Lying-In Asylum, Washington, D.C.* H. Doc. 749, 63d Cong., 2d sess., 1914. 3p. Serial 6758.

1591. U.S. Congress. House. *Columbia Hospital for Women, Letter from the Acting Secretary of the Treasury, Transmitting Copy of Communication of the Secretary of the Interior, Submitting an Estimate of Appropriation in the Sum of $75,725, for Special Equipment and Furnishing to Complete the Building for the Columbia Hospital for Women and Lying-In Asylum.* H. Doc. 1474, 63d Cong., 3d sess., 1915. 3p. Serial 6892.

1592. U.S. Congress. Senate. *Columbia Hospital for Women and Lying-In Asylum, Letter from the Secretary of the Interior, Transmitting a Letter of the Superintendent of the Capitol Building and Grounds, Relative to the Completion of the Building for the Columbia Hospital for Women and Lying-In Asylum, and Recommending that Provision be Made for the Proper Custody of the Structure.* S. Doc. 24, 64th Cong., 1st sess., 1915. 6p. Serial 6954.

1593. U.S. Congress. House. *Columbia Hospital for Women and Lying-In Asylum, Letter from the Secretary of the Treasury, Transmitting a Copy of a Communication from the Secretary of the Interior, Submitting an Estimate of Appropriation in the Sum of $16,344 for Expansion Connected with Recently Completed Columbia Hospital for Women and Lying-In Asylum, Washington, D.C.* H. Doc. 786, 64th Cong., 1st sess., 1916. 3p. Serial 7102.

1594. U.S. Congress. House. *Columbia Hospital for Women and Lying-In Asylum, Letter from the Secretary of the Treasury, Transmitting Copies of Communications from the Secretary of the Interior Submitting a Supplemental Estimate of Appropriations for the Columbia Hospital for Women and Lying-In Asylum for the Fiscal Year, 1917.* H. Doc. 1310, 64th Cong., 1st sess., 1916. 3p. Serial 7102.

1595. U.S. Congress. House. *Report of the Completion of Columbia Hospital for Women and Lying-In Asylum, with Recommendations, Letter from the Secretary of the Interior, Transmitting Copy of Letter from Superintendent of United States Capitol Building and Grounds, Reporting Completion of the Columbia Hospital for Women and Lying-In Asylum and Making Recommendations Regarding the Custodial Care Thereof.* H. Doc. 500, 64th Cong., 1st sess., 6 Jan. 1916. 6p. Serial 7101. Exact duplicate of S. Doc. 24 (1592).

1596. U.S. Children's Bureau. *Maternal Mortality from All Conditions Connected with Childbirth in the United States and Certain Other Countries.* Publication no. 19. Washington, DC: GPO, 1917. 66p. L5.20:19. Discussion of trends in maternal mortality in the United States and in selected foreign countries furnishes statistics on maternal deaths and death rates by cause and race for states and selected cities, and maternal death rates for 16 countries for selected years.

1597. U.S. Children's Bureau. *Maternity and Infant Care in a Rural County in Kansas.* Publication no. 26. Washington, DC: GPO, 1917. 50p. L5.20:26. A survey of maternity care in a Kansas county looks at place of confinement, maternity care received, cost of childbearing, and mothers work activities before and after childbirth.

1598. U.S. Children's Bureau. *Saving Mothers.* Washington, DC: GPO, 1917. 3p. L5.2:M85. Describes the factors contributing to continued high maternal death rates in the U.S. and the need for community action to ensure proper maternity care.

1599. U.S. Children's Bureau. *Care of the Mother: Welfare of Child is Wrapped Up in That of Mother.* Dodger no. 2. Washington, DC: GPO, 1918. 2p. leaflet. L5.17:2. Reprinted twice with slight revision in 1919 and revised again in 1939.

1600. U.S. Children's Bureau. *Maternity and Infant Care in Two Rural Counties in Wisconsin.* by Florence Brown Sherborn and Elizabeth Moore. Publication no. 46. Washington, DC: GPO, 1919. 92p. L5.11:4 or L5.20:46. Survey of maternity care and child welfare in a northern and a southern county of Wisconsin examines maternity care, mother's work before and after childbearing, and infant welfare. Also looks at the activities of Wisconsin state and local agencies on behalf of mothers and children.

1601. U.S. Children's Bureau. *Maternity Care and the Welfare of Young Children in a Homestead County in Montana.* by Viola I. Paradise. Publication no. 34. Washington, DC: GPO, 1919. 98p. L5.20:34. Survey of maternity care and child welfare in a typical homesteading county in Montana provides insight into mother and child welfare in pioneer areas. Specific areas surveyed include maternity care, cost of childbirth, mother's work before and after childbearing, housing and sanitation, infant care, and state and county activities for mothers and children in rural areas.

1602. U.S. Public Health Service. *Motherhood.* Keep Well Series no. 8. Washington, DC: GPO, 1919. 8p. leaflet. T27.22:8. Information on reducing maternal mortality through prenatal health was written for a general audience.

1603. U.S. Children's Bureau. *Maternal Mortality Rates per 100 Births, Latest Available Figures Up to 1917.* Chart Series no. 5. Washington, DC: The Bureau, 1921. 1p. L5.19:5.

1604. U.S. Children's Bureau. *Maternity and Child Care in Selected Rural Areas of Mississippi.* by Helen M. Dart. Publication no. 88. Washington, DC: GPO, 1921. 60p. L5.20:88. Information on maternity care and child welfare was gathered through home interviews in selected rural counties of Mississippi. Factors examined include prenatal and maternity care, attendant at confinement, costs, maternal mortality, mother's work before and after childbearing, and the care of young children.

1605. U.S. Children's Bureau. *Save the Youngest: Seven Charts on Maternal and Infant Mortality, with Explanatory Comment.* Publication no. 61, rev. Washington, DC: GPO, 1921. 15p. L5.20:61. Brief look at maternal and infant mortality for the U.S. draws comparisons to other countries.

1606. U.S. Congress. House. *Appropriation for Columbia Hospital for Women, Communication from the President of the United States, Transmitting, with a Letter from the Director of the Bureau of the Budget, an Estimate of Appropriation for the District of Columbia for the Fiscal Year Ending June 30, 1924, for the Columbia Hospital for Women and Lying-In Asylum, $20,000.* H. Doc. 509, 67th Cong., 4th sess., 1922. 2p. Serial 8215.

1607. U.S. Children's Bureau. *Maternal Mortality Thermometer, Deaths from Puerperal Causes per 1,000 Live Births, from Latest Figures Available.* Washington, DC: The Bureau, 1923. 1p. L5.19/2:M41.

1608.   U.S. Children's Bureau. *Maternity and Infant Care in a Mountain County in Georgia.*
Publication no. 120. Washington, DC: GPO, 1923. 58p. L5.20:120. Describes maternity
and child care, infant mortality, and mother's work in a mountain county in Georgia. Also
discusses use of patent medicines and home remedies by pregnant women and babies, and
state activities relating to maternity and infancy.

1609.   U.S. Children's Bureau. *The Hygiene of Maternity and Childhood: Outlines for Study.*
Publication no. 90. Washington, DC: GPO, 1924. 372p. L5.20:90. Primary focus of
publication is on health in early childhood, however, some discussion of hygiene in relation
to confinement and lying-in is included.

1610.   U.S. Children's Bureau. *Minimum Standards for Prenatal Care.* Folder no. 1, rev.
Washington, DC: GPO, 1924. 7p. leaflet. L5.22:1/2. Later editions published under the
title *The Expectant Mother* (1662).

1611.   U.S. Children's Bureau. *Standards of Prenatal Care: An Outline for the Use of
Physicians.* Publication no. 153. Washington, DC: GPO, 1925. 42p. L5.20:153.

1612.   U.S. Children's Bureau. *Maternal Mortality: The Risk of Death in Childbirth and from
All Diseases Caused by Pregnancy and Confinement.* by Robert Morse Woodbury.
Publication no. 158. Washington, DC: GPO, 1926. 163p. L5.20:158. Provides statistical
data on deaths arising from childbirth by cause and characteristics of mother with some
comparative statistics for selected foreign countries. Discusses the factors in puerperal
mortality and preventive measures including protective legislation and maternity care.

1613.   U.S. Congress. House. Committee on the District of Columbia. *To Authorize the Refund
of $25,000 to the Columbia Hospital for Women and Lying-In Asylum, Report to
Accompany H.R. 9450.* H. Rept. 864, 69th Cong., 1st sess., 1926. 2p. Serial 8533. See
1615 for abstract.

1614.   U.S. Congress. House. Committee on the District of Columbia. *Refund of $25,000 to the
Columbia Hospital for Women and Lying-In Asylum, Report to Accompany S. 2729.* H.
Rept. 1129, 69th Cong., 1st sess., 1926. 2p. Serial 8534. See 1615 for abstract.

1615.   U.S. Congress. Senate. Committee on the District of Columbia. *Authorizing the Refund
of $25,00 to the Columbia Hospital for Women and Lying-In Asylum, Report to Accompany
S. 2729.* S. Rept. 601, 69th Cong., 1st sess., 1926. 4p. Serial 8525. Favorable report
on refunding $25,000 to the Columbia Hospital for Women and Lying-In Asylum provides
a concise summary of the purpose of the hospital and of joint federal and District of
Columbia support of the hospital. The refund refers to a surplus acquired by the hospital
through donations and charges to non-charity patients and intended for the construction of
nurses quarters, but which the 1923 appropriations bill had required to be turned over to
the U.S. Treasury.

1616.   U.S. Congress. House. *Buildings, Columbia Hospital for Women, Communication from
the President of the United States, Transmitting Supplemental Estimate of Appropriations
for the District of Columbia for the Fiscal Year Ending June 30, 1927, for the Construction
and Equipment of the Nurses' Home for the Columbia Hospital for Women and Lying-In
Asylum, $35,000.* H. Doc. 743, 69th Cong., 2d sess., 1927. 2p. Serial 8735.

1617.   U.S. Children's Bureau. *What Is Happening to Mothers and Babies in the District of
Columbia?* by Dorothy Reed Mendenhall. Washington, DC: GPO, 1928. 27p.
L5.2:M85/3. Study of infant and maternal mortality by race in the District of Columbia
area emphasizes the need for wider availability of prenatal care in areas of high mortality.
Maternal and infant mortality and stillbirths were notably higher for blacks.

1618. U.S. Children's Bureau. *Midwifery in Denmark.* by Dorothy Reed Mendenhall. Washington, DC: GPO, 1929. 14p. L5.2:D41. Paper delivered at the Fifth Annual Conference of State Directors in charge of the local administration of the Maternity and Infancy Act of 1928 describes the lower maternal mortality rate in Scandinavian countries as compared to the U.S. and reviews the history of the practice of midwifery in Denmark. The training and duties of midwives are described and information on salaries, pensions and midwives associations is furnished.

1619. U.S. Bureau of the Census. *Ratio of Children to Women, 1920, Study in Differential Rate of Natural Increase in United States.* Census Monograph no. 11. Washington, DC: GPO, 1931. 242p. C3.30:11. Study of differential fertility examines factors such as race, nativity, employment, type of residence, and marital status related to population growth as reflected in the ratio of children to women. Provides data by state and by metropolitan area with some comparative data for England and Wales on marriage and family size.

1620. U.S. District of Columbia. Gallinger Municipal Hospital. *Rules and Regulations for Guidance of Obstetrical Department of Gallinger Municipal Hospital, Washington, D.C.* Washington, DC: The Hospital, 1931. 11p. DC54.6/2:Ob7. Detailed rules and regulations for the care and treatment of gynecology and obstetrics patients at Gallinger Municipal Hospital in the District of Columbia clearly defines authority to perform procedures and the routine procedures to be carried out for most patients.

1621. U.S. District of Columbia. Health Dept. *Suggestions for Expectant Mothers.* N.p., 1931. 2p. DC14.2:P91.

1622. U.S. Children's Bureau. *Maternal Deaths: A Brief Report of a Study Made in 15 States.* Publication no. 221. Washington, DC: GPO, 1933. 60p. L5.20:221. Summary of Children's Bureau Publication 223 (1623) looks at causes and conditions associated with maternal death.

1623. U.S. Children's Bureau. *Maternal Mortality in Fifteen States.* Publication no. 223. Washington, DC: GPO, 1934. 234p. L5.20:223. Study of maternal mortality in fifteen states looks at cause of death and characteristics of the women including race, place of residence, age, and legitimacy of child. Other factors examined were maternal care, operations, cesarean sections, abortions, puerperal septicemia, embolism, toxemia, puerperal hemorrhage, and ectopic gestation.

1624. U.S. Post Office Dept. *Commemorative Postage Stamp in Honor of Mothers; [Issued by] 3d Assistant Postmaster General.* Washington, DC: The Office, 1934. 1p. P4.2:M85/3.

1625. U.S. Post Office Dept. *Mothers' Day, May 13 [1934, Announcement Regarding Special Commemorative Postage Stamp, Issued by] 3d Assistant Postmaster General.* Washington, DC: The Office, 1934. 1p. P4.3:M85/4.

1626. U.S. Children's Bureau. *Comparability of Maternal Mortality Rates in the United States and Certain Foreign Countries.* by Elizabeth C. Tandy. Publication no. 229. Washington, DC: GPO, 1935. 24p. L5.20:229. Briefly examines maternal mortality rates in the United States and in selected foreign countries. Discusses the comparability of the rates based on methods of classifying cause of death and furnishes a bibliography of statistical reports for the seventeen countries discussed.

1627. U.S. Children's Bureau. *Maternal Mortality in Counties of the United States, 1930-34.* Fort Humphreys, DC: Engineer Reproduction Plant, Army, 1936. map. L5.14:M41.

1628. U.S. Children's Bureau. *Causes of Maternal Mortality, United States, 1935.* Washington, DC: The Bureau, 1937. poster. L5.14:M41/2/935. Also issued in a smaller format under SuDoc number L5.14:M41/3/935.

1629. U.S. Children's Bureau. *Infant and Maternal Mortality among Negroes.* by Elizabeth Tandy. Publication no. 243. Washington, DC: GPO, 1937. 34p. L5.20:243. Statistical report reviews the status of maternal mortality among black women and the trend in maternal mortality throughout the period of record.

1630. U.S. Children's Bureau. *Live Births in Urban and Rural Districts of Each State by Person in Attendance, United States, 1935.* Table BS-3. Washington, DC: The Bureau, 1937. 3p. L5.37:BS-3.

1631. U.S. Children's Bureau. *Maternal Mortality in the United States, 1935.* Washington, DC: The Bureau, 1937. map. L5.14:M41/4/935.

1632. U.S. Children's Bureau. *Number of Live Births in Each State, 1935, Source, Reports of the Bureau of the Census.* Washington, DC: The Bureau, 1937. map. L5.14:B53. Smaller version issued under SuDoc Number L5.14:B53/2.

1633. U.S. Children's Bureau. *Trend of Birth Rates in the United States and Certain Foreign Countries.* Table BS-2. Washington, DC: GPO, 1937. 1p. L5.37:BS-2. Table shows birth rates for U.S. and selected countries between 1915 and 1935.

1634. U.S. Children's Bureau. *Trend of Maternal Mortality by Color, U.S. Expanding Birth-Registration Area and States with 1,500 or More Negro Live Births per Year, 1915-35.* Table MM-3. Washington, DC: The Bureau, 1937. 2p. L5.37:MM-3.

1635. U.S. Children's Bureau. *Trend of Maternal Mortality in the United States and Certain Foreign Countries, 1915-35.* Table MM-6. Washington, DC: The Bureau, 1937. 1p. L5.37:MM-6.

1636. U.S. Children's Bureau. *Trend of Maternal Mortality in Urban and Rural Districts, U.S. Expanded Birth Registration Area by States, 1915-35.* Table MM-2. Washington, DC: The Bureau, 1937. 4p. L5.37:MM-2.

1637. U.S. Children's Bureau. *Maternal Mortality, by Cause, 1915-36, United States Expanded Birth Registration Area.* Washington, DC: The Bureau, 1938. 1p. chart. L5.19/2:M41/2.

1638. U.S. Children's Bureau. *Maternal Mortality in the United States, 1936.* Washington, DC: The Bureau, 1938. map. L5.14:M41/4/936.

1639. U.S. Children's Bureau. *Number of Live Births in Each State, 1936, Source, Reports of the Bureau of the Census.* Washington, DC: The Bureau, 1938. map. L5.14:B53/2/936.

1640. U.S. Children's Bureau. *Proceedings of the Conference on Better Care for Mothers and Babies, Held in Washington, D.C., January 17-18, 1938.* Publication no. 246. Washington, DC: GPO, 1938. 171p. L5.20:246. Conference proceedings focus on the provision of prenatal and infant care and on public education methods for maternal and infant health.

1641. U.S. Children's Bureau. *Better Care for Mother and Child.* Washington, DC: GPO, 1939. 20p. L5.2:M85/5. Graphic presentation of data on infant and maternal mortality.

1642. U.S. Office of Education. *Gallant American Women #26, Children First, Apr. 30, 1940.* by Jane Ashman. Washington, DC: The Office, 1940. 24p. FS5.15:26. Women as protectors of children is the theme of this episode of the "Gallant American Women" radio series. Includes a reference list of sources consulted.

1643. U.S. Bureau of the Census. *Average Number of Children per Woman in Butler County, Ohio, 1930: Study in Differential Fertility.* Washington, DC: The Bureau, 1941. 81p. C3.2:C437. The average number of children per woman in Butler County Ohio is analyzed to determine its relation to factors of age, age at marriage, duration of marriage, residence, birth-residence of parents, monthly rental costs, and employment of women.

1644. U.S. Children's Bureau. *Better Care for Mother and Child.* Washington, DC: GPO, 1941. poster. L5.14:M85/2.

1645. U.S. Children's Bureau. *Better Care for Mother and Child.* Publication no. 278. Washington, DC: GPO, 1941. 19p. L5.20:278. Chartbook illustrates maternal and infant mortality rates and causes in the U.S. and data on attendant at birth.

1646. U.S. Children's Bureau. *Causes of Maternal Death Point the Way to Cures.* Washington, DC: The Bureau, 1941. poster. L5.14:M41/5.

1647. U.S. Children's Bureau. *Causes of Maternal Death, United States, 1939.* Chart MM-39-A. Washington, DC: The Bureau, 1941. [2]p. L5.14:M41/7.

1648. U.S. Children's Bureau. *Do Many More Mothers Die in Some States of This Country than in Others?* Washington, DC: The Bureau, 1941. poster. L5.14:M85/7.

1649. U.S. Children's Bureau. *Do Many More Mothers Die in This Country than in Countries of Our Ancestors?* Washington, DC: The Bureau, 1941. poster. L5.14:M85/5.

1650. U.S. Children's Bureau. *How to Make Motherhood Safer, Adequate Care before, during, and after Childbirth is the Right of Every Mother.* Washington, DC: GPO, 1941. poster. L5.14:M85/3.

1651. U.S. Children's Bureau. *In Single Year 148,000 Deaths, Doctors Say at Least 1 Out of 2 Maternal Deaths Can Be Prevented.* Washington, DC: The Bureau, 1941. poster. L5.14:D34.

1652. U.S. Children's Bureau. *Manual for Teaching Midwives.* Publication no. 260. Washington, DC: GPO, 1941. 139p. L5.20:260. Manual of basic midwife tasks designed for the training of non-professional midwives describes antiseptic techniques, the basic tools, and the actions of the midwife at each stage of delivery. Provides insight into the childbirth experience for poor women since they are the presumed beneficiaries of this training.

1653. U.S. Children's Bureau. *Maternal Deaths in Relation to Time of Delivery, United States, 1939.* Chart MM-39-3. Washington, DC: The Bureau, 1941. 2p. L5.14:M41/6.

1654. U.S. Children's Bureau. *What Are We Doing to Make Motherhood Safer?* Washington, DC: GPO, 1941. poster. L5.14:M85/4.

1655. U.S. Children's Bureau. *Where Are Babies Born?* Washington, DC: GPO, 1941. poster. L5.14:B11/2.

1656. U.S. Children's Bureau. *Who Are the Mothers That Die?* Washington, DC: The Bureau, 1941. poster. L5.14:M85/6.

1657. U.S. Children's Bureau. *Who Attended Mothers At Delivery?* Washington, DC: The Bureau, 1941. poster. L5.14:M85/8.

1658. U.S. Children's Bureau. *Why Do These Mothers Die?* Washington, DC: The Bureau, 1941. poster. L5.14:M85/9.

1659. U.S. Children's Bureau and U.S. Women's Bureau. *Standards for Maternity Care and Employment of Mothers in Industry.* Washington, DC: The Bureau, 1942. 4p. L5.2:M41/10. Advice on employment policies and recommendations on care of pregnant women workers was written for employers.

1660. U.S. Bureau of the Census. *Population, Differential Fertility 1940 and 1910: Fertility for States and Large Cities.* Washington, DC: GPO, 1943. 281p. C3.940-2:P81/22. Statistics for U.S. regions, states, metropolitan areas and cities on number of children by race, age, and martial status of mother also provides statistics on fertility and age at marriage, and fertility and duration of marriage.

1661. U.S. Children's Bureau. *Birth, Infant Mortality, Maternal Mortality: Graphic Presentation.* Publication no. 288. Washington, DC: GPO, 1943. 71p. L5.20:288. Tables and charts provide information from 1940 on number and characteristics of births, infant mortality, and maternal mortality by cause. Some data is furnished by age and race.

1662. U.S. Children's Bureau. *The Expectant Mother.* Folder no. 1, rev. Washington, DC: GPO, 1943. 10p. L5.22:1/4. For earlier title see 1610. Other editions under this title published in 1936.

1663. U.S. Children Bureau. *Maternity Care in United States, Planning for Future, Speech Delivered at Annual Meeting of American Gynecological Society, Hershey, Pa., June 19, 1944.* by Edwin F. Daily. Washington, DC: The Bureau, 1944. 11p. L5.47:M41. Key topics of this speech on the future of maternity care in the U.S. are the training of more obstetricians, the building of more hospitals, and the government support to ensure maternity care regardless of family income. Future problems of paying for maternity care in low-income families are examined in relation to maternity care costs. The administration of a nation-wide maternity care plan is outlined.

1664. U.S. Coordinator of Inter-American Affairs Office. Division of Health and Sanitation. *Bibliography for Maternal and Child Health Program.* by Janet W. Mackie. N.p., 1944. 13p. Pr32.4602:M41. Annotated bibliography lists source materials for instruction of mothers in prenatal care, infant care, nutrition, and malaria and source materials on public health programs and the training of midwives.

1665. U.S. Bureau of the Census. *Population, Differential Fertility 1940 and 1910: Women by Number of Children Ever Born.* Washington, DC: GPO, 1945. 410p. C3.940-2:P81/29. Presents data on children born to women and to women ever married by age of women, race, urban/rural areas and regions by characteristics including martial status, age at marriage, duration of marriage, parentage, region or country of birth, years in U.S., education, literacy and rental value of home.

1666. U.S. Bureau of the Census. *Population, Differential Fertility, 1940 and 1910: Women by Number of Children under 5 Years Old.* Washington, DC: The Bureau, 1945. 263p. C3.940-2:P81/28. Statistics on number of children under 5 years of native white and black women are classified by social and economic characteristics of the woman and her family for 1910 and 1940. Characteristics examined include age, race/nativity, marital status, age at marriage, parentage, education, migration status, employment status, occupation of husband, tenure of home, rental value of home, and region of birth. Social characteristics are reported for U.S. and for urban and rural areas.

1667. U.S. Children's Bureau. *Health and Welfare Services for Mothers and Children in the Union of Soviet Socialist Republics.* by Anna Kalet Smith. Washington, DC: The Bureau, 1945. 40p. L5.2:H34/7. Information collected from published Soviet sources describes the system for delivery of health and welfare services for mothers and children in the USSR. Describes the authority of various agencies for maternal and child health and the operation of maternity clinics and homes, establishment of paternity and collection of support, day nurseries, and child health programs. Protective labor legislation and social insurance legislation related to mothers and children is reviewed.

1668. U.S. Children's Bureau. *Charts on Births, Infant and Childhood Mortality, Maternal Mortality 1946.* Washington, DC: The Bureau, 1946. various paging. FS3.202:B53/946. Tables and charts provide state data on birth, infant mortality and maternal mortality rates.

1669. U.S. Children's Bureau. *Fight for Better Maternal and Child Health.* Washington, DC: The Bureau, 1946. 3p. L1.2:C43/2.

1670. U.S. Children's Bureau. *Standards and Recommendations for Hospital Care of Maternity Patients.* Publication no. 314. Washington, DC: GPO, 1946? 22p. L5.20:314. Standards and recommendations for hospital care of maternity patients describe medical and nursing staff, facilities, and maternity unit procedures.

1671. U.S. Bureau of the Census. *Population, Differential Fertility, 1940 and 1910: Fertility by Duration of Marriage.* Washington, DC: GPO, 1947. 338p. C3.940-2:P81/34. Reports statistics on duration of marriage by race and age of woman and number of children ever born, for U.S. and urban and rural areas. Provides data on total children ever born by employment status and occupation of husband and by education of woman and duration of marriage.

1672. U.S. Children's Bureau. *Maternal and Infant Mortality in 1944, an Inquiry into Differential Mortality.* Statistical Series no. 1. Washington, DC: GPO, 1947. 17p. FS3.214:1. Analysis of statistics of maternal and infant mortality for 1944 found lower death rates than in 1943 and a growing trend towards hospital births. Other areas studied were differences by race and geographic region in infant and maternal mortality and in birth attendant.

1673. U.S. Children's Bureau. *Charts on Infant, Childhood and Maternal Mortality, 1946.* Washington, DC: GPO, 1949. 76p. FS3.202:B53/946. See 1676 for abstract.

1674. U.S. Children's Bureau. *Further Progress in Reducing Maternal and Infant Mortality: The Record of 1945 and 1946.* Statistical Series no. 4. Washington, DC: GPO, 1949. 27p. FS3.214:4. Examines trends in maternal and infant mortality in the U.S. by race, state, person in attendance, rural and urban area, age of mother, and cause of death including self-induced abortion.

1675. U.S. Bureau of the Census. *Estimated Net Reproduction Rates for the White Population, by Counties: Apr. 1935, to Apr. 1940.* Current Population Reports Series P-20, no. 29. Washington, DC: The Bureau, 1950. 18p. C3.186:P-20/29.

1676. U.S. Children's Bureau. *1947 Chartbook: Infant and Childhood Mortality, Maternal Mortality, Natality: Trend Data for the United States, Profile Data for Each State.*

Washington, DC: The Bureau, 195? 93p. FS3.202:B53/947. Mortality rates for infants, children, and women in childbirth is presented in table and chart format for states.

1677.   U.S. Children's Bureau. *Changes in Infant, Childhood, and Maternal Mortality Over the Decade 1939-1948: A Graphic Analysis.* Statistical Series no. 6. Washington, DC: The Bureau, 1950. 31p. FS3.214:6. Presents, via charts and tables, state statistics on maternal mortality and births by person in attendance and race for 1948 with some comparison to 1939 data.

1678.   U.S. Children's Bureau. *Charts on Infant, Childhood and Maternal Mortality, 1949.* Statistical Series no. 9. Washington, DC: GPO, 1951. 33p. FS3.214:9. Infant, childhood and maternal mortality rates are provided by state and race and by cause for 1949 with data on trends in births by attendant and race, 1935-1949, and maternal mortality by race, 1915-1949.

1679.   U.S. Children's Bureau. *Infant and Maternal Mortality in Metropolitan and Outlying Counties, 1944-1948.* by Eleanor P. Hunt and Bronson Price. Statistical Series no. 12. Washington, DC: The Bureau, 1952. 62p. FS3.214:12. Charts present infant and maternal mortality statistics by state and type of county, i.e. lesser metropolitan, semi-rural, etc.

1680.   U.S. Congress. House. Committee on the District of Columbia. *Authorizing the Conveyance to the Columbia Hospital for Women and Lying-In Asylum of Certain Parcels of Land in the District of Columbia, Report to Accompany H.R. 7253.* H. Rept. 1942, 82d Cong., 2d sess., 1952. 2p. Serial 11577.

1681.   U.S. Congress. Senate. Committee on the District of Columbia. *Authorizing the Conveyance to the Columbia Hospital for Women and Lying-In Asylum of Certain Parcels of Land in the District of Columbia, Report to Accompany H.R. 7253.* S. Rept. 1786, 82d Cong., 2d sess., 1952. 3p. Serial 11568.

1682.   U.S. Children's Bureau. *Main Causes of Infant, Childhood and Maternal Mortality 1939-1949 in Terms of the Sixth Revision of the International Lists.* Statistical Series no. 15. Washington, DC: The Bureau, 1953. 14p. FS3.214:15. Report attempts to compare infant, childhood and maternal mortality rates by cause for the period 1939 to 1949, taking into account the revision of the International Lists of Diseases and Cause of Death.

1683.   U.S. Bureau of the Census. *Fertility by Social and Economic Status, for Puerto Rico, 1950.* 1950 Census of Population, Series PC-14, no. 21. Washington,DC: GPO, 1954. 28p. C3.950-4:PC-14/21. Basic statistics on characteristics of Puerto Rican women for the 1950 Census includes urban-rural residence, marital status, ability to speak English, literacy, educational attainment, birth or residence in San Juan, farm residence, and labor force status. Tables provide statistics on number of children ever born by characteristics of the women and age cohorts.

1684.   U.S. Bureau of the Census. *Fertility by Duration of Marriage, 1950.* 1950 Census of Population Series PC-14, no. 22. Washington, DC: GPO, 1956. 15p. C3.950-4:PC-14/22. Summary statistics from the 1950 Census details the number of children born by duration of marriage, age, and educational attainment, and by duration of marriage, age of woman and occupation of husband.

1685.   U.S. Bureau of the Census. *Estimated Net Reproduction Rates for the White Population, by Counties, Apr. 1945 to 1950 and 1935 to 1940.* Current Population Reports Series P-20, no. 4. Washington, DC: GPO, 1957. 28p. C3.186:P-23/4.

1686. U.S. Children's Bureau. *Perinatal, Infant and Maternal Mortality, 1954.* by Eleanor P. Hunt and Ruth R. Moore. Statistical Series no. 42. Washington, DC: GPO, 1957. 32p. F3.214:42. Reports birth rates by race (1909-54) and person in attendance (1935-54), and maternal mortality by race (1915-54) and cause of death (1944 & 1954). Statistics on perinatal, infant and childhood mortality are also furnished.

1687. U.S. Dept. of Health, Education and Welfare. *Perinatal,Infant, Childhood, and Maternal Mortality, 1955.* by Eleanor P. Hunt and Ruth R. Moore. Statistical Series no. 50. Washington, DC: The Bureau, 1958. 43p. FS3.214:50. See 1686 for abstract.

1688. U.S. Federal Extension Service. *Satisfactions and Concerns of Mothers.* by Jewell G. Fessenden and Edward V. Pope. Circular no. 527. Washington, DC: The Service, 1959? 13p. A43.4:527. The satisfactions of motherhood are examined in this 1957 study of white home demonstration members. Age of mother, income, age of children at home, and education level of mother are compared to expressed satisfaction with motherhood. Study also looks at mother's concerns with children's behavior.

1689. U.S. Bureau of the Census. *Marriage, Fertility, and Childspacing, Aug. 1959.* Current Population Reports Series P-20, no. 108. Washington, DC: GPO, 1961. 55p. C3.186:P-20/108. Reports statistics on number of children ever born by age, race, marital status, and labor force status of mother; percent of women ever married by age, by year of birth and race; number of children ever born by birth order and by age, race and year of birth of women; age of women at completion of childbearing by race, marital status, number of children ever born, and year of birth of women; age at first marriage by year of first marriage, marital status, and race; distribution of births by interval since first marriage by year of first marriage; and birth intervals by number of children ever born, race, and year of first marriage.

1690. U.S. Children's Bureau. *Current Problems of Maternity Care [Lecture] by Arthur J. Lesser, Director, Division of Health Services, Delivered May 10, 1963, at School of Public Health, University of California, Berkeley.* by Arthur J. Lesser. Washington,DC: The Bureau, 1963. 13p. FS14.110/2:L56. Paper reveals the decreasing access of poor urban women to proper maternity care and the related health problems of their babies. The factors which contribute to inadequate prenatal care are described.

1691. U.S. Children's Bureau. *Maternal and Newborn Care in Fallout Shelters, Project 2406.* Washington, DC: Children's Bureau, 1963. 55p. FS14.102:F19/2. Guidelines for preparation for maternity care in fallout shelters discusses treatment of spontaneous abortion, delivery, and after care of infant and mother. The guidelines are based on one month in a shelter and a list of references is included.

1692. U.S. Bureau of the Census. *Women by Number of Children Ever Born, Fertility of Women by Social, Economic, and Housing Characteristics.* 1960 Census of Population, Subject Report PC(2)pt.3A. Washington, DC: GPO, 1964. 323p. C3.223/10:960/v.2/pt.3A. Data for 1960 on women by number of children ever born examines age, race, nativity, region, type of residence, marital status, age at first marriage, educational attainment, employment status, occupation of husband, occupation of woman, family income, and other factors.

1693. U.S. Children's Bureau. *Aspects of Maternal and Child Health in Developing Regions. Second Jessie M. Bierman Annual Lecture in Maternal and Child Health.* by Derrick B. Jelliffe. Washington, DC: The Bureau, 1964. 22p. FS14.110/2:J39. Lecture describes the problem of infant and maternal mortality in tropical developing countries and the early death of women from Maternal Depletion Syndrome, the continuous cycle of pregnancy, overwork and inadequate diet. Factors to consider in planning maternal and child health service in these countries are set forth. Adapting approaches to service delivery to meet local conditions is stressed, and training, research, and gaining public support are reviewed.

1694.   U.S. Public Health Service. *Maternity Care Utilization and Financing.* Health Economics Series no. 4. Washington, DC: GPO, 1964. 201p. FS2.99:4. Variety of data from surveys on maternity care and insurance benefits provides statistics on perinatal hospital care, convalescent time, complications, and federal and private maternity and dependent care insurance coverage.

1695.   U.S. Children's Bureau. *Recent Demographic Trends and Their Effects on Maternal and Child Health Needs and Services.* Washington, DC: GPO, 1966. 20p. FS14.110:H91. Changes in urban/rural distribution of the childbearing and new born population are analyzed as they relate to maternal and infant mortality. Mortality rates for nonwhite mothers and infants are compared to the white population.

1696.   U.S. National Center for Health Statistics. *Infant, Fetal, and Maternal Mortality, United States, 1963.* by Mary A. McCarthy. Washington, DC: GPO, 1966. 64p. FS2.85/2:20/no.3.

1697.   U.S. Public Health Service. *Seasonal Variation of Births, United States, 1933-63.* Washington, DC: GPO, 1966. 59p. HE20.6209:21/9. Examination of seasonal patterns of births in the United States for 1933-63, considers factors of race, geographic region, live-birth order, age of mother, and legitimacy status. The report identifies changes in patterns over time and draws international comparisons. Includes a discussion of factors associated with seasonality of births and possible causes.

1698.   U.S. Public Health Service. *Fertility and Educational Attainment, Puerto Rico, 1962.* Washington, DC: GPO, 1967. 20p. HE20.6209:21/12. Analysis relates fertility and characteristics of births to the educational attainment of the parents of children born in Puerto Rico in 1962.

1699.   U.S. Bureau of the Census. *Childspacing: Spacing of Successive Births to Women by Age, Duration of Marriage and Other Characteristics.* 1960 Census of Population, Subject Report PC(2)pt.3B. Washington, DC: GPO, 1968. 185p. C3.223/10:960/v.2/pt.3B. Reports data on childspacing by age, type of residence, duration of marriage, educational attainment, race, age of first marriage, and other factors.

1700.   U.S. Bureau of the Census. *Women by Children under 5 Years Old, Current Fertility by Social and Economic Characteristics of Women and Their Families.* 1960 Census of Population, Subject Report PC(2)pt.3C. Washington, DC: GPO, 1968. 140p. C3.223/10:960/v.2/pt.3C. Statistics on fertility by characteristics of the mother include marital status, race, age, residence, duration of marriage, educational attainment, employment status, occupational groups, family income and other factors.

1701.   U.S. Office of Aviation Medicine. *Impact Injury to Pregnant Female and Fetus in Lap Belt Restraint.* Aviation Medical Report AM68-24. Washington, DC: The Office, 1968. 16p. TD4.210:68-24. Reviews the medical evidence and experimental findings to date concerning the use of automobile and airplane lap belts by pregnant women.

1702.   U.S. Bureau of the Census. *Marriage, Fertility, and Childspacing, June 1965.* Current Population Reports P-20, no. 186. Washington, DC: GPO, 1969. 76p. C3.186:P-20/186. Statistical report details the number of children ever born by age and marital status of mother, employment status and occupation of husband, and age difference between husband and wife. Provides data on age at first marriage by educational attainment, 1940-1964;

labor force status by age at first marriage; and intervals between births by characteristics of mother and families.

1703. U.S. Bureau of the Census. *Women by Number of Own Children under 5 Years Old, 1968 and 1967.* Current Population Reports P-20, no. 184. Washington, DC: GPO, 1969. 35p. C3.186:P-20/184. Brief analysis of data on women by number of own children under 5 years old looks at trends from 1940 considering factors of race, residence, educational attainment, labor force status, family income, and occupation of husband.

1704. U.S. Bureau of the Census. *Changes in the Average Number of Children Ever Born to Women: 1960 to November 1969.* Current Population Reports Series P-20, no. 196. Washington, DC: GPO, 1970. 2p. C3.186:P-20/196.

1705. U.S. Bureau of the Census. *Fertility of the Population, January 1969.* Current Population Reports Series P-20, no. 203. Washington, DC: GPO, 1970. 15p. C3.186:P-20/203. Statistical report details number of children ever born by age, marital status and race of mother in 1969, with some comparative data for earlier years. Also reports on children ever born by region and type of residence, educational attainment, labor force status, and poverty-nonpoverty area.

1706. U.S. Bureau of the Census. *Women by Number of Own Children under 5 Years Old, March 1969.* Current Population Reports Series P-20, no. 205. Washington, DC: GPO, 1970. 24p. C3.186:P-20/205. Reports statistics on age and marital status of women with children under 5 years old by race, 1910 to 1969. Also furnished data on race and age of women with children under 5 by region and type of residence, relationship to household head, educational attainment, and labor force status. Statistics on characteristics of husbands when present including husbands income, family income, labor force status, and occupation are provided.

1707. U.S. Bureau of the Census. *Fertility Indicators.* Current Population Reports Series P-23, no. 36. Washington, DC: GPO, 1971. 56p. C3.186:P-23/36. Furnishes data on birth rates, cohort fertility, age, marital status, fertility by social and economic characteristics, child spacing, illegitimacy, birth expectations, contraception, and attitudes toward abortion.

1708. U.S. Bureau of the Census. *Fertility Variations by Ethnic Origin: November 1969.* Current Population Reports Series P-20, no. 226. Washington, DC: GPO, 1971. 28p. C3.186:P-20/226. Presents statistics on fertility by age, race/nativity, ethnic origin, marital status, years of school completed, relation to household head, labor force status and family income.

1709. U.S. Bureau of the Census. *Previous and Prospective Fertility, 1967.* Current Population Reports Series P-20, no. 211. Washington, DC: GPO, 1971. 35p. C3.186:P-20/211. Statistical report provides data by race on previous and prospective fertility of American women by residence, education, poverty status, age at first marriage, and children ever born.

1710. U.S. National Institutes of Child Health and Human Development. *Birth Rate and Population Growth in United States.* Washington, DC: GPO, 1971. 12p. leaflet. HE20.3352:B53. Basic information on birthrate trends in the U.S. since the 1920s accompanies speculation on future trends in the birth rate and population growth.

1711. U.S. Bureau of the Census. *Birth Expectations Data, June 1971.* Current Population Reports Series P-20, no. 232. Washington, DC: GPO, 1972. 6p. C3.186:P-20/232. Report provides data on birth expectations, expected number of additional births and total births for wives 18 to 39; children ever born by age, race, and marital status in 1965,

1969, and 1971; and women ever married by number of children ever born by age and race, 1971.

1712.   U.S. Bureau of the Census. *Fertility and Family Composition for the United States: 1970.* 1970 Census of Population, Supplementary Report PC(S1)-21. Washington, DC: GPO, 1972. 4p. C3.223/12:970/21.

1713.   U.S. Health Services and Mental Health Administration. *Should Pregnant Women Use Safety Belts? Yes!* Washington, DC: GPO, 1972. leaflet. HE20.2852:P91.

1714.   U.S. National Institute of Neurological Diseases and Strokes. *Women and Their Pregnancies, Collaborative Perinatal Study of National Institute of Neurological Disease and Stroke.* by Kenneth R. Niswander, et al. Washington, DC: GPO, 1972. 540p.+ 2 fiche. HE20.3502:P91. Data on characteristics of women and their pregnancies is related to pregnancy outcome. Factors examined include demographic characteristics of mothers, maternal conditions during pregnancy, labor and delivery, and complications of pregnancy and labor.

1715.   U.S. Bureau of the Census. *Age at First Marriage and Children Ever Born, for the United States: 1970.* 1970 Census of Population, Supplementary Report PC(S1)-34. Washington, DC: GPO, 1973. 10p. C3.223/12:970/34. Statistics on persons ever married and mean age at first marriage of persons 30 to 49 years old are reported by race and sex, marital status, race of spouse, educational attainment, occupational group, and income in 1969. Also reports data on children ever born and marital status of women by age and race, 1970; and number of children ever born per 1,000 women 35 to 44 years old by type of residence, state of birth, ethnic group, marital status, age at first marriage, educational attainment, labor force status, occupational group of husband, and income of husband in 1969.

1716.   U.S. Bureau of the Census. *Fertility of Women by Education and Family Income for the United States: 1970.* 1970 Census of Population, Supplementary Report PC(S1)-51. Washington, DC: GPO, 1973. 13p. C3.223/12:970/51. Statistical report details years of school completed for women 15 years old and over by number of children ever born, age, and race, 1970, and family income in 1969 for wives 15 to 44 years old by number of children ever born and age of woman.

1717.   U.S. Bureau of the Census. *Women by Number of Children Ever Born.* 1970 Census of Population, Subject Reports PC(2)pt.3A. Washington, DC: GPO, 1973. 404p. C3.223/10:970/v.2/pt.3A. Fertility of American women is reported by marital status, age, race, place of residence, duration of marriage, educational attainment, age at first marriage, employment status and occupational group, income of husband, family income, and other factors.

1718.   U.S. Bureau of Community Health Services. *Research to Improve Health Services for Mothers and Children.* MCH Research Series no. 2-5. Washington, DC: GPO, 1974. 4 vol. HE20.5114:nos. Brief summaries of research conducted under Title V of the Social Security Act covers topics such as pregnant adolescents, prenatal care and nutrition, abortion, and family planning services.

1719.   U.S. Bureau of the Census. *Fertility Expectations of American Women, June 1973.* by Wilson H. Grabil and Maurice J. Moore. Current Population Reports Series P-20, no. 265. Washington, DC: GPO, 1974. 62p. C56.218:P-20/265.

1720.   U.S. Bureau of the Census. *Fertility Histories and Birth Expectations of American Women, June 1971.* Current Population Reports Series P-20, no. 263. Washington, DC: GPO,

1974. 147p. C56.218:P-20/263. Report on fertility provides data on births cumulated to successive ages, cumulated to successive intervals since first marriage, intervals between births, and birth expectations for white and black women by year of birth, metropolitan-nonmetropolitan residence, years of school completed, occupation of husband, and family income; children ever born by characteristics of mother and family; and fertility of remarriage.

1721. U.S. National Institute on Drug Abuse. *Drugs and Pregnancy: The Effects of Nonmedical Use of Drugs on Pregnancy, Childbirth, and Neonates.* Edited by Patricia Ferguson, Thomas Lennox and Dan J. Lettieri. Research Issues Series no. 5. Washington, DC: GPO, 1974. 154p. HE20.8214:5. Summarizes research on the effects of LSD, heroin, and methadone on pregnancy, childbirth and newborns.

1722. U.S. Bureau of Community Health Services. *Infant, Maternal, and Childhood Mortality in the United States, 1968-1973.* by Joseph Garfinkel, et al. Washington, DC: GPO, 1975. 34p. HE20.5102:In3/4/968-73. Data and analysis of statistics on infant, maternal and childhood mortality in the United States, between 1968 and 1973, provides state and regional data on maternal mortality by race and cause.

1723. U.S. Bureau of Community Health Services. *Studies in Maternal Health: Research to Improve Health Services for Mother and Children.* Washington, DC: GPO, 1975. 37p. HE20.5114/2:M41. Summaries highlight research on services for pregnant teenagers, school-age mothers, and therapeutic abortions.

1724. U.S. Bureau of the Census. *Childspacing and Current Fertility.* 1970 Census of Population, Subject Reports PC(2)pt.3B. Washington, DC: GPO, 1975. 485p. C3.223/10:970/v.2/pt.3B. Statistics for 1970 describe childspacing and fertility by characteristics of race, occupation, labor force status, family income, times married, duration of marriage and other factors.

1725. U.S. Bureau of the Census. *Illustrative Projections of First Births for the United States, 1975 to 2000.* Current Population Reports Series P-25, no. 613. Washington, DC: GPO, 1975. 8p. C3.186:P-25/613. Report gives estimated and projected total births and first births, 1940 to 2000; estimated and projected total fertility rates and fertility rates by age, 1925 to 2000; and mean and median age of childbearing, 1925 to 2000.

1726. U.S. Bureau of the Census. *Fertility History and Prospects of American Women, June 1975.* Current Population Reports Series P-20, no. 288. Washington, DC: GPO, 1976. 15p. C56.218:P-20/288. Statistical report on births to date by age and race; additional births expected by age, race, Spanish origin, years of school completed, residence, age at first marriage, and educational attainment; children ever born to women 15 to 49 by age, race, and marital status; and birth intervals since first marriage began.

1727. U.S. Department of Health, Education, and Welfare. Office of the Secretary. *Occupational Health Problems of Pregnant Women.* by Vilma R. Hunt. Washington, DC: GPO, 1976. 161p. HE1.2:P91. Report on the history and current status of women and work, particularly during pregnancy, reviews federal agency reporting and regulating activities and shortfalls in occupational safety of pregnant women. Provides statistics on employed women by occupation, number of children born to married women and childlessness, age of employed women by occupation, and women employed by trimester. An annotated bibliography is included.

1728. U.S. Bureau of Community Health Services. *Studies in Maternal Health II: Research to Improve Health Services for Mothers and Children.* Washington, DC: GPO, 1977. 28p. HE20.5114/2:M41/977. Summarizes research projects on indigent primigravid pregnancy, prenatal services in Puerto Rico, postpartum adjustment, and maternal health and family solidarity in Appalachia.

1729.   U.S. Public Health Service. *Birth and Fertility Rates for States and Metropolitan Areas, United States.* Washington, DC: GPO, 1977. 48p. HE20.6209:21/27. Presents data on birth and fertility rates for geographic divisions, states, and selected SMSA's and cities during the years 1969-71. Differences in rates by place of residence and birth characteristics, including age of mother, live birth order, race, and legitimacy, are detailed. Rates are also furnished for specific racial or national origin groups and for native and foreign-born women.

1730.   U.S. Public Health Service. *Trends in Fertility in the United States.* Washington, DC: GPO, 1977. 41p. HE20.6209:21/28. An analytic study of recent and long-term fertility trends in terms of period and cohort measures emphasizes changes occurring during the period 1970-73. Variations in fertility of major population groups by race and place of residence are described.

1731.   U.S. Bureau of the Census. *Perspectives on American Fertility.* Current Population Reports Series P-23, no. 70. Washington, DC: GPO, 1978. 67p. C3.186:P-23/70. Reports statistics on historical trends in fertility, family formation and dissolution, birth expectations, geographical and educational variations and fertility, pregnancy and childbearing outside of marriage, contraceptive use and abortion.

1732.   U.S. Bureau of the Census. *Trends in Childspacing, June 1975.* Current Population Reports Series P-20, no. 315. Washington, DC: GPO, 1978. 123p. C3.186:P-20/315. Data on childspacing is presented including births cumulated to successive ages, births cumulated to successive intervals from first marriage, and intervals between births by race, residence, husbands occupation, family income, and years of school completed.

1733.   U.S. Congress. House. Committee on Interstate and Foreign Commerce. Subcommittee on Health and the Environment. *In-Vitro Fertilization - Oversight Hearing.* 95th Cong., 2d sess., 4 Aug. 1978. 117p. Y4.In8/4:95-134. The process of in-vitro fertilization and the ethical issues it raises are discussed in testimony which tries to balance the benefits to infertile couples with future legal and ethical considerations. One of the issues identified is the potential for surrogate mothers.

1734.   U.S. Congress. Senate. Committee on Human Resources. Subcommittee on Health and Scientific Research. *Obstetrical Practices in the United States, 1978, Hearings.* 95th Cong., 2d sess., 17 Apr. 1978. 226p. Y4.H88:Ob7/978. Hearing on obstetrical practices and their impact on the health of mother and newborn examines the use of fetal monitors, cesarean sections, induced labor, and drugs in pregnancy and labor.

1735.   U.S. National Institute for Occupational Safety and Health. *Comprehensive Bibliography on Pregnancy and Work.* Washington, DC: GPO, 1978. 137p. HE20.7114:P91. Bibliography lists English and foreign language books and journal articles on women, pregnancy and occupational health.

1736.   U.S. National Institute for Occupational Safety and Health. *Guidelines on Pregnancy and Work.* Washington, DC: GPO, 1978. 73p. HE20.7111:P91. Guide for doctors to use when advising patients on work during pregnancy discusses particular problems encountered during pregnancy and their effect on the ability to work. Includes a list of resources and contact persons.

1737.   U.S. National Institute on Drug Abuse. Services Research Branch. *Drug Dependency in Pregnancy: Clinical Management of Mother and Child.* Washington, DC: GPO, 1978.

117p. HE20.8216/2-2:P91. Review of the literature on the complications for mother and child of drug dependency during pregnancy and on successful treatment methods covers management during pregnancy, delivery, postpartum, and continuing care. Revised edition published in 1979.

1738. U.S. Public Health Service. *Characteristics of Births, United States, 1973-1975.* Washington, DC: GPO, 1978. 49p. HE20.6209:21/30. Statistical profile of characteristics of live births includes educational attainment of parents, birth weight, period of gestation, prenatal care, sex ratios, month of birth, attendant at birth and place of delivery, plurality, illegitimacy, interval since last live birth and last pregnancy, and outcome of last pregnancy. Emphasis is on births occurring in 1973, however, data for 1974 and 1975 are included in the summary and the discussion of trends.

1739. U.S. Public Health Service. *Wanted and Unwanted Childbearing in the United States, 1968, 1969, and 1972 National Natality Survey.* Washington, DC: GPO, 1978. 56p. HE20.6209:21/32. Reports results of a study of legitimate live births by whether they were wanted at the time they occurred, wanted later, or not wanted at all, as reported by the mother. Discusses trends and variations in relation to race, live-birth order, age of mother, expectations of future births, age at marriage, duration of marriage, education, income and religious preference.

1740. U.S. Bureau of Community Health Services. *Selected Natality Characteristics for Single Live Births, United States, 1974.* Washington, DC: GPO, 1979. 62p. HE20.5102:N19/974. Data and analysis of statistics on single live births in the U.S. discusses factors such as maternal age, onset of prenatal care, total birth order, mother's education, wedlock status, interpregnancy interval, race, and size of place of residence. Some data is shown by state or urbanized area.

1741. U.S. General Accounting Office. *Evaluating Benefits and Risks of Obstetric Practices - More Coordinated Federal and Private Efforts Needed.* Washington, DC: The Office, 1979. 68p. GA1.13:HRD-79-85. Study of the actions taken by HEW to ensure safe obstetric practices in the U.S. describes actions taken to date and areas which could be improved.

1742. U.S. National Center for Child Abuse and Neglect. *Selected Reading on Mother-Infant Bonding.* Washington, DC: GPO, 1979. 115p. HE23.1210:M85. Reprints twelve research articles on mother-infant bonding, particularly as it relates to child abuse and neglect.

1743. U.S. Peace Corps. Information Collection and Exchange. *Preparation for Childbirth: A Health Workers Manual.* Washington, DC: The Corps, 1979. reprinted 1985. 88p. PE1.10:R-55. Written for the use of Peace Corps health workers in Columbia, the manual describes ways to prepare uninformed women for a comfortable and satisfying childbirth experience.

1744. U.S. Public Health Service. *Trends in Breastfeeding among American Mothers.* Washington, DC: GPO, 1979. 39p. HE20.6209:23/3. Report of statistics on breastfeeding of first- and second-born babies looks at year of mother's birth and year of babies birth classified by race/ethnicity, geographic region, and socioeconomic characteristics.

1745. U.S. Bureau of the Census. *A Compilation of Age-Specific Fertility Rates for Developing Countries.* International Research Document no. 7. Washington, DC: GPO, 1980. 154p. C3.205/6:7.

1746. U.S. Centers for Disease Control. Bureau of Epidemiology. Family Planning Evaluation Division. *Texas Fertility: Childbearing Patterns and Trends.* Atlanta, GA: The Center, 1980. 77p. HE20.7011/29:950-77. Fertility trends and patterns for Texas are analyzed by age, ethnic group, and legitimacy statewide and for health services areas in 1977 with selected comparative data from 1950.

1747. U.S. Congress. House. Select Committee on Narcotics Abuse and Control. *The Use of Drugs during Pregnancy.* 96th Cong., 2d sess., 6 Feb. 1980. 99p. Y4.N16:96-2-2. Hearing on the physical and psychological effects of drug abuse during pregnancy examines the scope of the problems and current treatment services.

1748. U.S. National Institutes of Health. *Pregnancy and Diabetes: Select Annotations.* Washington, DC: GPO, 1980. 38p. HE20.3316:P91. Annotated bibliography of recent books, journal articles, and audio-visual materials on pregnancy and diabetes is divided by resources for the general public and patients and those for health professionals.

1749. U.S. National Institutes of Health. Task Force on Cesarean Childbirth. *Consensus Development Conference on Cesarean Childbirth: Draft Report.* Washington, DC: GPO, 1980. 551p. HE20.3030:980/draft. Draft report of the Task Force examines the reasons for cesarean childbirth and specifically discusses epidemiologic information, medical, obstetrical and neonatal problems, behavioral studies on mothers and infants, and ethical and economic concerns.

1750. U.S. Wright-Patterson Air Force Base. *Prenatal Exercise Program.* Washington, DC: GPO, 1980. 16p. D301.2:P92.

1751. U.S. Army. *Instructional Booklet for Maternity Patients: Ireland Army Hospital, U.S. Army Armor Center, Fort Knox, Kentucky.* Washington, DC: GPO, 1981. 41p. D101.2:M41. Advises pregnant women on diet, exercise, and the common discomforts of pregnancy.

1752. U.S. Public Health Service. *Socioeconomic Differentials and Trends in the Timing of Births.* Washington, DC: GPO, 1981. 49p. HE20.6209:23/6. Report on birth probabilities within first marriages analyzes trends and differentials by race, Hispanic origin, education, farm origin, religion, and timing of first birth.

1753. U.S. Public Health Service. Office of the Assistant Secretary for Health. *The Surgeon General's Workshop on Maternal and Infant Health.* Washington, DC: GPO, 1981. 55p. HE20.2:M41/2. Workshop papers present views on services for maternal and infant health, progress made, and problems identified in health services provision.

1754. U.S. National Institutes of Health. *Cesarean Childbirth: Report of a Consensus Development Conference.* Washington, DC: GPO, 1982. 537p. HE20.3002:C33/2. Final report of the Task Force on Cesarean Childbirth provides an historical overview of cesarean childbirth and presents existing epidemiological information. Reviews the medical problems for mother and child in cesarean birth and reports on behavior studies of mothers and infants. The ethical, legal, and economic concerns related to cesarean birth are also reviewed. Provides data on cesarean birth and associated complications by age of mothers.

1755. U.S. Public Health Service. *Working Women and Childbearing, United States.* Washington, DC: GPO, 1982. 53p. HE20.6209:23/9. Statistics for currently married women 15 to 44 years of age details age at first marriage, number of children ever born, interval between births, and expected completed family size by labor force participation, income, occupation, age, race and education.

1756. U.S. Bureau of the Census. *Fertility Decline in Developing Countries.* International Research Document no. 9. Washington, DC: GPO, 1983. 20p. C3.205/6:9. Reports and analyzes data on crude birth rates and fertility rates of countries in Asia, Africa and Latin America, 1950 to 1980. Years covered varies by country due to availability of data.

1757. U.S. Bureau of the Census. *International Fertility Indicators.* Current Population Reports Series P-23, no. 123. Washington, DC: GPO, 1983. 59p. C3.186:P-23/123. Statistics for selected countries accompany a description of the relation between religious and socioeconomic factors and fertility, age patterns of fertility, contraceptive practices by age and education level of women, and induced abortions.

1758. U.S. National Institute of Child Health and Human Development. *Facts about Cesarean Childbirth.* Bethesda, MD: The Institute, 1983? 13p. leaflet. HE20.3352:C33.

1759. U.S. National Institutes of Health. *The Search for Health: NICHD Panel Makes Recommendations to Decrease Cesarean Childbirth Rates.* Bethesda, MD: The Institutes, 1983. 1p. HE20.3038:C33/2. Also published in Spanish.

1760. U.S. Bureau of the Census. *Childspacing among Birth Cohorts of American Women, 1905 to 1959.* Current Population Reports Series P-20, no. 385. Washington, DC: GPO, 1984. 117p. C3.186:P-20/385. Reports data by race and Spanish origin on births cumulated to successive ages for birth cohorts of women and years of school completed, age and marital status, age at completion of childbearing, interval between first marriage and first birth, interval between first marriage and successive births, and intervals between births.

1761. U.S. Health Resources and Services Administration. Division of Maternal and Child Health. *Maternal and Child Health and Crippled Children Services: Inventory of Data Sources.* Washington, DC: GPO, 1984. 154p. HE20.9102:M41. Describes 27 national data bases with information relevant to maternal and child health.

1762. U.S. National Center for Health Services Research. *Who Receives Caesareans: Patient and Hospital Characteristics.* Hospital Cost and Utilization Project Research Note no. 4. Rockville, MD: The Center, 1984. 18p. HE20.6514:4. Study looks at possible contributing factors to the growing percentage of cesarean births. Statistics on the number of cesarean births by age, race, payment source, and number or nature of diagnosis in hospital with and without neonatal intensive care unit are furnished.

1763. U.S. Public Health Service. *Birth and Fertility Rates for States, United States, 1980.* Washington, DC: GPO, 1984. 31p. HE20.6209:21/42. Presents birth and fertility rates for 1980 for geographic divisions and states. Rates are shown by place of residence according to socioeconomic characteristics of mother and characteristics of birth and for Hispanic and non-Hispanic populations.

1764. U.S. Public Health Service. *Midwife and Out-of-Hospital Deliveries, United States.* Washington, DC: GPO, 1984. 43p. HE20.6209:21/40. Analyzes the demographic characteristics and pregnancy history of mothers and birth weight of babies delivered in a nonhospital setting or by a midwife in a hospital setting.

1765. U.S. Public Health Service. *Patterns of Ambulatory Care in Obstetrics and Gynecology: The National Ambulatory Medical Care Survey, United States, January 1980-December 1981.* Washington, DC: GPO, 1984. 62p. HE20.6209:13/76. Report on medical care provided during office visits to obstetricians and gynecologists examines patterns of medical care, patients' reason for visit and diagnosis, and utilization of patient management techniques.

1766. U.S. Bureau of the Census. *Future Fertility of Women by Present Age and Parity: Analysis of American Historical Data, 1917-80.* Current Population Reports Series P-23, no. 142. Washington, DC: GPO, 1985. 63p. C3.186:P-23/142. Fertility statistics for white and nonwhite women gives parity by cohort for selected birth cohorts between 1868 and 1966 and for selected calendar years between 1917 and 1980.

1767. U.S. Bureau of Health Care Delivery and Assistance. Division of Maternal and Child Health. *The Maternal & Child Health Research Grants Program: Inventory of Projects.* Washington, DC: The Division, 1986. 71p. HE20.9102:M41/2. Describes current maternal and child health research projects and lists projects completed to date.

1768. U.S. National Center for Health Statistics. *Maternal Weight Gain and the Outcome of Pregnancy, United States, 1980.* Washington, DC: GPO, 1986. 25p. HE20.6209:21/44. Report and analysis of statistics on maternal weight gain and pregnancy outcomes provides data on weight gain during pregnancy by race, prepregnancy weight, smoking habit, socioeconomic status, age of mother, live-birth order, and marital status. The incidence of low birth weight babies is then examined by characteristics of mother's maternal weight gain.

1769. U.S. National Institutes of Health. *Research Shows that Pregnant Women Can Safety Continue to Exercise.* Bethesda, MD: The Institutes, 1986. 1p. HE20.3038:P91/2. Report highlights research indicating that continued exercise during pregnancy is not harmful to the mother or the fetus and is unlikely to stimulate premature labor.

1770. U.S. Navy. *Childbirth Education.* by R. Spinks. Bremerton, WA: Naval Hospital, 1986. 42p. D201.2:C43. Manual for expectant mothers provides information on diet and exercise, sex, prenatal care, childbirth, and common postpartum problems.

1771. U.S. Congress. House. Select Committee on Children, Youth, and Families. *Alternative Reproductive Technologies: Implications for Children and Families, Hearing.* 100th Cong., 1st sess., 21 May 1987. 235p. Y4.C43/2:T22/4. The legal and ethical issues of alternative reproduction technologies, particularly in vitro fertilization, are explored. Technology of embryo transfer and gamete intrafallopian transfer are reviewed. One of the issues of IVF is the embryo's status as "human life" and whether there is an obligation to implant all such embryos. Possibilities for detecting genetic abnormalities in the embryo prior to implantation and embryo research are also discussed.

1772. U.S. Public Health Service. *Fecundity, Infertility, and Reproductive Health in the United States, 1982.* Washington, DC: GPO, 1987. 51p. HE20.6209:23/14. Statistics for women 15-44 years of age on fecundity status, infertility, spontaneous pregnancy loss, pelvic inflammatory disease, cesarean section, and smoking and drinking during pregnancy is reported by race, age, marital status, and socioeconomic characteristics.

1773. U.S. Congress. House. Committee on Energy and Commerce. *Comprehensive Alcohol Abuse, Drug Abuse, and Mental Health Amendments Act of 1988, Report to Accompany H.R. 4907.* H. Rept. 100-927, 100th Cong., 2d sess., 1988. 147p. Serial 13902. Favorable report on extension of Alcohol, Drug Abuse and Mental Health Administration programs includes background on the effects of drug abuse on pregnant women and their babies. The bill directs NIDA and the Office of Substance Abuse Prevention to allocate funds for research and services targeting substance abuse among pregnant women.

1774. U.S. Congress. House. Committee on Government Operations. Subcommittee on Human Resources and Intergovernmental Relations. *Medical and Social Choices for Infertile Couples and the Federal Role in Prevention and Treatment, Hearing.* 100th Cong., 2d sess., 14 July 1988. 297p. Y4.G74/7:M46/4. Major themes explored by witnesses are the lack of insurance, VA coverage of infertility treatment, and the ethical issues of human reproductive technology experiments. The failure of the Secretary of HHS to appoint an Ethics Advisory Board is the center of discussion of NIH's failure to support research on reproductive technologies such as in vitro fertilization and embryo transfer.

1775. U.S. Congress. Senate. Committee on Commerce, Science, and Transportation. Subcommittee on the Consumer. *Alcohol Warning Labels, Hearing on S. 2047.* 100th Cong., 2d sess., 10 Aug. 1988. 174p. Y4.C73/7:S.hrg.100-925. Members of Congress and witnesses debate the need for health warning labels on alcoholic beverage containers focusing primarily on warning pregnant women so as to prevent fetal alcohol syndrome.

1776. U.S. National Library of Medicine. *Pregnancy in the Older Woman.* by Jacqueline Van De Kamp. NLM Current Bibliographies in Medicine no. 88-1. Washington, DC: GPO, 1988. 15p. HE20.3615/2:88-1. Provides citations to 327 journal articles, dissertations and monographs from the NLM database on topics related to pregnancy in later life.

1777. U.S. Public Health Service. *Health Aspects of Pregnancy and Childbirth, United States, 1982.* Washington, DC: GPO, 1988. 74p. HE20.6209:23/16. Statistical report describes characteristics of prenatal care including timing of first prenatal visit, source of prenatal care, smoking and alcohol use during pregnancy, low birth weight, and method of payment for delivery.

1778. U.S. Air Force. *Luke AFB Prenatal Handbook.* Luke AFB, AZ?: Luke Air Force Base, 1989. 135p. D301.6/5:P91. Detailed handbook on pregnancy and childbirth reviews prenatal care, diet and exercise, postpartum care, and infant care. Administrative information for active duty women who become pregnant is also included.

1779. U.S. Congress. House. Committee on Government Operations. *Infertility in America: Why is the Federal Government Ignoring a Major Health Problem? Eighth Report by the Committee on Government Operations Together with Dissenting and Additional Views.* H. Rept. 101-389, 101st Cong., 1st sess., 1989. 35p. Report summarizes hearing testimony on barriers to infertility treatment and research in federal programs. Most of the report deals with the failure of HHS to appoint an Ethics Advisory Board to oversee IVF research and the failure of the Veteran's Administration to provide infertility services to veterans.

1780. U.S. Congress. House. Committee on Small Business. Subcommittee on Regulation, Business Opportunities, and Energy. *Consumer Protection Issues Involving In Vitro Fertilization Clinics, Hearing.* 101st Cong., 1st sess., 9 Mar. 1989. 1300p. Y4.Sm1:101-34. Witnesses discuss the lack of regulation of in vitro fertilization and gamete intrafallopian transfer and the success rates in the booming infertility treatment industry. Extensive data from a survey of IVF/GIFT clinics is provided.

1781. U.S. Congress. House. Committee on Small Business. Subcommittee on Regulation, Business Opportunities, and Energy. *Medical Liability and the Delivery of Obstetrical Care, Hearing.* 101st Cong., 1st sess., 12 Oct. 1989. 106p. Y4.Sm1:101-34. The availability of obstetrical care is examined in hearing testimony exploring the lack of competent obstetrical care for low and middle-income women. The impact of malpractice insurance costs on the practice of obstetrics is identified as a major factor in availability.

1782. U.S. National Agriculture Library. *Maternal and Infant Nutrition Education Materials, January 1981 - October 1988: 152 Citations.* by Holly Berry Irving. Quick Bibliography Series 89-44. Beltsville, MD: USDA 1989. 23p. A17.18/4:89-44. Annotated bibliography of educational materials on maternal and infant nutrition was compiled from the AGRICOLA database. Both print and non-print materials are included.

1783. U.S. National Center for Health Statistics. *Trends and Variations in First Births to Older Women, 1970-86.* Hyattsville, MD: The Center, 1989. 27p. HE20.6209:21/47. Analysis of data from live birth certificates describes trends in first-time childbearing by women over thirty for the years 1970 to 1986. Trends in delayed childbearing by educated women and nonmarital childbearing are discussed. Access to prenatal care and health characteristics of mother and infant are noted. Most statistics are presented for all women with details for white and black women.

1784. U.S. National Institute of Child Health and Human Development. *Understanding Gestational Diabetes: A Practical Guide to a Healthy Pregnancy.* N.p.: The Institute, 1989. 46p. HE20.3358:G33. Information booklet for expectant mothers with gestational diabetes describes the causes of the condition, and the implications for pregnancy and delivery. Diet, exercise, and routine steps to control the condition are described.

1785. U.S. National Center for Health Statistics. *Birth and Fertility Rates by Education, 1980 and 1985.* Hyattsville, MD: The Center, 1990. 40p. HE20.6209:21/49. Report on birth and fertility rates in the U.S. focuses on the changes between 1980 and 1985 in births to well-educated older women. Data is reported for all races, whites and blacks, and for married and unmarried mothers. Detailed statistics are presented for the 15 largest states and basic statistics are provided for the 47 reporting states.

1786. U.S. National Center for Health Statistics. *Fecundity and Infertility in the United States, 1965-88.* by William D. Mosher and William F. Pratt. NCHS Advance Data no. 192. Hyattsville, MD: The Center, 1990. 9p. HE20.6209:3/192. Provides data on fecundity in the U.S. by age and parity in 1976, 1982, and 1988 with breakdowns by surgically sterile, impaired fecundity, and fecund. Data on infertility among married couples and use of infertility services is also reported.

1787. U.S. National Center for Health Statistics. *Wanted and Unwanted Childbearing in the United States, 1973-88: Data from the National Survey of Family Growth.* Advance Data from the Vital and Health Statistics no. 189. Hyattsville, MD: The Center, 1990. 8p. HE20.6209:3/189. Survey results show a growing trend in unwanted childbearing and briefly examines unwanted birth by characteristics of the mother. Births to never-married women by wantedness status is reported for 1982 and 1988.

1788. U.S. National Library of Medicine. *Cocaine, Pregnancy, and the Newborn, January 1988 through March 1990, 486 Citations.* by Cynthia B. Love. Current Bibliographies in Medicine no. 90-7. Washington, DC: GPO, 1990. 24p. HE20.3615/2:90-7. Bibliography provides unannotated citations from the National Library of Medicine's MEDLINE, AVLINE, BIOETHICSLINE, CANCERLIT, CATLINE, HEALTH, POLINE and TOXLINE databases. The citations cover the period from 1988 to March 1990 and represent all aspects of the impact of cocaine use on pregnant women, new mothers, the fetus, neonates, and infants. In addition to medical aspects, the economic, legal and ethical considerations in maternal use of cocaine are covered. Publications on AIDS as it relates to cocaine and pregnancy are also included.

1789. U.S. Public Health Service. Region V. *Guidelines for Nutrition Care during Pregnancy.* by Irene Alton. Chicago, IL: The Service, 1990. 123p. HE20.8:N95. Handbook for management of pregnant women describes conditions related to nutrition. Each section provides a condition management outline covering goals, nutrition and exercise guidelines, client education and monitoring. A bibliography of sources used to compile the handbook is furnished.

SERIALS

1790. District of Columbia. *Annual Report, Columbia Hospital for Women and Lying-In Asylum.* [title varies]. Washington, DC: The Hospital, 1866-1917. 1st - 51st. annual. DC29.1:year. Annual report summarizes of the operation of the hospital and describes of special cases involving diseases of the female reproductive organs. Description based on 1887 edition.

1791. U.S. Bureau of the Census. *Birth Statistics for the Registration Area of U.S.* Washington, DC: GPO, 1915-1921. annual. C3.26:year.

1792. U.S. Bureau of the Census. *Birth, Still-Birth, and Infant Mortality Statistics for the Birth Registration Area of the United States.* Washington, DC: GPO, 1922-1932. annual. C3.26:year.

1793. U.S. Bureau of the Census. *Birth, Stillbirths and Infant Mortality Statistics for Continental U.S., Territory of Hawaii, Virgin Islands.* Washington, DC: GPO, 1933-1936. annual. C3.26:year. Report provides statistics on births by sex of child, race, age of mother, nativity of mother, and number of child for the U.S., states, counties, and rural and urban areas. Also furnishes data on stillbirths and infant mortality.

1794. U.S. Bureau of the Census. *Differential Fertility.* [title varies] Current Population Reports Series P-20, nos. 8, 18, 27, 46, 65, 84, 147. Washington, DC: GPO, 1946-1964. irregular. C3.186:P-20/nos. Data on women with children under 5 by age and marital status, place of residence, labor force status and occupation of father, and presence or absence of parent is reported.

1795. U.S. Bureau of the Census. *Fertility of American Women.* Washington, DC: GPO, 1975 - . annual. C3.186:P-20/nos.; C3.186/10:year. Detailed report of data on current and predicted fertility of American women specifically examines trends in labor force status of mothers of newborns, premarital childbearing, age patterns in childbearing, and birth expectations. Most of the data is reported by race and marital status with some data on educational attainment, occupation, place of residence, and family income for current fertility.

1796. U.S. Bureau of the Census. International Demographic Statistics Center. *World Fertility Pattern for the Period...* Washington, DC: GPO, 1950-55 - 1980. irregular. C3.205/3:WCF-year and C3.62/2:F41/year.

1797. U.S. Children's Bureau. *Prenatal Care.* Publication no. 4. Washington, DC: GPO, 1913 - 1944. irregularly revised. FS3.209:4/rev. no.; L5.20:4/rev. no. Signs of pregnancy, diet and personal hygiene, complications and how to avoid them, preparations for confinement, and outfits for the baby are a few of the topics covered in this handbook for expectant mothers.

1798. U.S. Congress. House. "Annual Report of Directors of the Columbia Hospital for Women and Lying-In Asylum." In *Annual Report of the Secretary of the Interior.* H. Ex. Doc. 1, 40th - 46th Cong., 1867-1879. Brief report on the Columbia Hospital for Women and Lying-In Asylum was included in the House Executive Document 1, the *Annual Report of the Secretary of the Interior* for the years 1867 to 1879. A more detailed report in the operation of the hospital was published separately.

1799. U.S. Maternal and Child Health Service. *Publications of the Maternal and Child Health Service.* Washington, DC: GPO, 1970-1972. annual. HE20.2759:P96/year.

1800.   U.S. National Institute of Child Health and Human Development. *Research Reports from the NICHD.* Bethesda, MD: The Institute, 1988 - . irreg. HE20.3364/2:year/no. Brief summaries describe the results of research sponsored by the NICHD. Maternal health and pregnancy outcomes are the focus of most reports. Infertility and contraceptive effects are also covered.

1801.   U.S. Public Health Service. *Natality Statistics Analysis, United States.* Washington, DC: GPO, 1962-1967. annual. HE20.6209:21/nos. An analytical study of recent fertility trends in terms of period and cohort measures discusses variations in fertility of major population groups by race and place of residence, including Puerto Rico and the Virgin Islands. Also discusses characteristics of live births including birth weight, period of gestation, attendant at birth, month of birth, plurality, sex and legitimacy.

12

Federal Maternal
Health Programs

Aid to the states for the purpose of promoting maternal and child health was a topic of intense controversy when it was first explored in congressional hearings. Advocates came to the hearings and presented facts on maternal and infant mortality and reported on successful state programs. The opponents rejected the entire concept of federal assistance and expressed fears of interference in state affairs, compulsory medicine, and government intrusion onto the family. In the 1921 hearing supporters were accused of advocating birth control and free love (1808). When the Sheppard-Towner Act was considered for extension in 1926, and again in 1929 and 1932, the same issues were raised, although in 1929 the program was labeled "communist-inspired" (1820) and 1932's hearing included strong opposition from Catholic women's societies (1827). The House report for the 1929 extension provides a good review of the history of federal aid to the states and of the individuals and organizations supporting the program (1821). During World War Two the problem of providing adequate maternity care to the wives of servicemen was addressed by the Emergency Maternity and Infant Care program. Most of the EMIC documents relate to the appropriation of additional funds to meet the unanticipated demand for the program (1842).

The problems with a 1945 bill, the "Maternal and Child Welfare Act of 1945," are noted in the report of the Children's Bureau Advisory Committee report (1848). The effect of a means test is one of the issues discussed in the report, and the same issue was the point of debate at a 1946 hearing on federal maternal and child welfare assistance (1851688). Financial need and access to prenatal care again became an issue for federal action in the mid-1970's when the problems of uninsured mothers were considered (1863). In the early 1980's the need for prenatal care funding was again raised, this time in relation to Medicaid and the coverage of women in households with an unemployed wage-earner or first-time pregnant women who would qualify for AFDC after the birth of the child (1868). The problems in obtaining prenatal care faced by uninsured women were again discussed in the 1987 hearing *Infants at Risk* (1718), and at hearings in 1987 (1718), 1989 (1887-1888), and 1990 (1893, 1895-1896, 1898). Programs supported by the Maternal and Child Health Service are reviewed in an annual publication beginning in 1970 (1904) and in other periodic reports (1881, 1884). Day care, abortion, and adolescent pregnancy are some of the areas routinely addressed. The large number of publications focusing on the child health aspects of maternal and child health programs were excluded from this bibliography.

1802. U.S. Congress. House. Committee on Labor. *Hygiene of Maternity and Infancy, Hearing on H.R. 12634.* 65th Cong., 3d sess., 15, 28 Jan. 1919. 60p. Y4.L11:M41. Hearing considers a bill providing monies to the states for the promotion of hygiene of maternity and infancy. The Children's Bureau, which would implement the act, provides figures and graphs illustrating rates and causes of maternal and infant mortality in the U.S. with comparative statistics for other countries. Witnesses describe the success of a Wisconsin program to teach maternal and child hygiene. Objections are made to the creation of state boards for maternal and child hygiene when many states already have a state board of health.

1803.   U.S. Congress. House. Committee on Labor. *Maternity Aid and Infant Hygiene, Report to Accompany H.R. 12634.* H. Rept. 1062, 65th Cong., 3d sess., 1919. 6p. Serial 7455. Report goes over the basic components of the proposed federal maternity and infant hygiene program stressing the placement of the program with the Children's Bureau and the role of the state boards. The problems of maternal and infant mortality in rural areas are reviewed.

1804.   U.S. Congress. House. Committee on Interstate and Foreign Commerce. *Public Protection of Maternity and Infancy, Hearings on H.R. 10925.* 66th Cong., 3d sess., 20 - 29 Dec. 1920. 194p. Y4.In8/4:M41. Hearing on the Sheppard-Towner bill establishing a cooperative federal-state effort to promote maternal and infant health through matching grants to the states focuses on infant death rates and on ways education can lower the rates. The activities of the Children's Bureau are described and social work related to maternal and infant mortality in New York and other areas is examined. There is some discussion of whether the Public Health Service or the Children's Bureau should administer the act. Opponents of Sheppard-Towner call it unnecessary and an infringement on medical freedom and suggest that it will open the door to compulsory medicine.

1805.   U.S. Congress. Senate. Committee on Public Health and National Quarantine. *Protection of Maternity and Infancy, Report to Accompany S. 3259.* S. Rept. 650, 66th Cong., 2d sess., 1920. 4p. Serial 7649. Review of the rates of maternal and infant mortality and of state efforts to reduce them form the basis of this favorable report on a cooperative federal-state maternal and child health program.

1806.   U.S. Congress. House. Committee on Interstate and Foreign Commerce. *Protection of Maternity and Infancy, Report to Accompany S. 1039.* H. Rept. 467, 67th Cong., 1st sess., 1921. 7p. Serial 7921. Report includes amendments to a bill to provide for cooperation between the federal government and the states in the promotion of maternal and infant health.

1807.   U.S. Congress. House. Committee on Interstate and Foreign Commerce. *Protection of Maternity and Infancy, Report to Accompany S. 3259.* H. Rept. 1255, 66th Cong., 3d sess., 1921. 6p. Serial 7776. Favorable report on the Sheppard-Towner maternity and infancy bill details the amendments by the Senate and the further proposed amendments by the House Committee. A history of the major supporters of the bill is given with some basic background on maternal and infant mortality with an emphasis on rural areas.

1808.   U.S. Congress. House. Committee on Interstate and Foreign Commerce. *Public Protection of Maternity and Infancy, Hearings on H.R. 2366.* 67th Cong., 1st sess., 12 - 23 July 1921. 278p. Y4.In8/4:M41/2. Hearing on the Sheppard-Towner bill for cooperation between federal and state government in the protection of maternity and infancy covers the basic topics of maternal and infant mortality rates in the United States and abroad, the organization and effectiveness of maternal and child hygiene work in New York and in other countries, and organizational options for a cooperative effort. The hearing is characterized by very convoluted exchanges on the right of the government to "meddle" with the health of mothers and children. Objections presented center on federal interference in the practice of medicine. One of the more interesting objections to the bill comes from a doctor who complains that nurses are unwilling to work more than 8 hours a day and that this bill will make nurse recruiting harder by providing high paying jobs with 8-hour days. The hearing degenerates at one point into an argument over whether the Children's Bureau endorses the Russian system of maternity benefits.

1809. U.S. Congress. Senate. Committee on Education and Labor. *Protection of Maternity and Infancy, Report to Accompany S. 1039*. S. Rept. 61, 67th Cong., 1st sess., 1921. 7p. Serial 7918. Reports a version of the Sheppard-Towner bill establishing a cooperative federal-state maternal and child health program with an added section to prevent agents from entering a home over the objections of the parents. Reports from the previous Congress are reprinted.

1810. U.S. Congress. Senate. Committee on Education and Labor. *Protection of Maternity, Hearing on S. 1039*. 67th Cong., 1st sess., 25, 28 Apr. 1921. 152p. Y4.Ed8/3:M41. Testimony on the Sheppard-Towner bill includes charges that it is backed by advocates of birth control and "free love" along with the more common objections to the bill as the first step toward socialism and compulsory medicine. Concerns are also expressed over possible "snooping" in homes and interference with families under the bill. Advocates of the bill discuss the need for such a measure and examine the proposed administration of the act.

1811. U.S. Congress. House. Committee on Interstate and Foreign Commerce. *Extension of Welfare and Maternity and Infancy Act to Puerto Rico, Report to Accompany H.R. 6142*. H. Rept. 346, 68th Cong., 1st sess., 1924. 2p. Serial 8227. Reports a bill extending Sheppard-Towner Act to cover maternal and infant health assistance to Puerto Rico.

1812. U.S. Congress. House. Committee on Interstate and Foreign Commerce. *Public Protection of Maternity and Infancy - Porto Rico, Hearing on H.R. 6142*. 68th Cong., 1st sess., 19 Feb. 1924. 20p. Y4.In8/4:P83. Hearing on extending Sheppard-Towner provisions to include Puerto Rico talks in general about health conditions there with the primary focuses on child health.

1813. U.S. Children's Bureau. *Text of Act of November 23, 1921, for the Promotion of the Welfare and Hygiene of Maternity and Infancy and Maximum Amounts Available to the States*. Publication no. 95. Washington, DC: GPO, 1925. 7p. L5.20:95. Reprints the text of the act creating the Board of Maternity and Infant Hygiene. Revised edition issued in 1926 under SuDoc number L5.20:95/4.

1814. U.S. Children's Bureau. *Proceedings of the Third Annual Conference of State Directors in Charge of the Local Administration of the Maternity and Infancy Act (Act of Congress of November 23, 1921) Held in Washington, D.C., January 11-13, 1926*. Publication no. 157. Washington, DC: GPO, 1926. 207p. L5.20:157. Presentations discuss prenatal care programs, midwife classes, child health service delivery, public education programs, mother's classes, and cooperation between state maternal and child health agencies and private sector organizations.

1815. U.S. Congress. House. Committee on Interstate and Foreign Commerce. *Extension of Public Protection of Maternity and Infancy Act, Hearing on H.R. 7555*. 69th Cong., 1st sess., 14 Jan. 1926. 59p. Y4.In8/4:M41/3. Testimony of Maud Wood Park, Grace Abbott and others on the extension of Sheppard-Towner cites work done since its enactment to improve maternal and child health. The unfavorable comparison of U.S. maternal and infant mortality rate to rates worldwide is made. Opposition witnesses reject Sheppard-Towner as paternalistic and as an unnecessary intrusion of the federal government into state and family affairs.

1816. U.S. Congress. House. Committee on Interstate and Foreign Commerce. *To Amend the Maternity Act, Report to Accompany H.R. 7555*. H. Rept. 575, 69th Cong., 1st sess., 1926. 14p. Serial 8532. The role of federal aid to the states is examined in this report on the extension of portions of the 1921 Sheppard-Towner Act. The progress made in the battle against maternal and infant mortality is reviewed and data on infant mortality and maternal mortality by state is presented for 1915 to 1924. The minority report considers the entire maternal welfare program unconstitutional and a needless appropriation of federal funds.

1817.   U.S. Congress. Senate. *Maternity and Infancy Act: Letters and Extracts from Letters Commending the Maternity and Infancy Act.* S. Doc. 120, 69th Cong., 1st sess., 1926. 32p. Serial 8558. Brief letters and excerpts of letters from mothers, physicians, and other observers describe the help and instruction received through the State Boards of Health and supporting the continuation of Sheppard-Towner.

1818.   U.S. Congress. Senate. Committee on Education and Labor. *Amend the Maternity Act, Report to Accompany H.R. 7555.* S. Rept. 745, 69th Cong., 1st sess., 1926. 3p. Serial 8526. Favorable report on a bill to extend the federal contribution to state maternal and infant welfare activities for an additional year declines to extend the program for 2 years since the program was not viewed as a permanent federal government function.

1819.   U.S. Children's Bureau. *Proceedings of the Fourth Annual Conference of State Directors in Charge of the Local Administration of the Maternity and Infancy Act (Act of Congress of November 23, 1921) Held in Washington, D.C., January 11-13, 1927.* Publication no. 181. Washington, DC: GPO, 1927. 167p. L5.20:181. Report on current studies in maternal and child welfare covers training obstetrical nurses, breast-feeding demonstrations, mother's classes, administration of programs, and general nurse training.

1820.   U.S. Congress. House. Committee on Interstate and Foreign Commerce. *Child Welfare Extension Service, Hearing on H.R. 14070.* 70th Cong., 2d sess., 24,25 Feb. 1929. 290p. Y4.In8/4:C43/5. Hearing discusses a replacement for Sheppard-Towner to provide money to states for maternal and infant health programs. The maternal and child welfare movement is opposed in most cases as socialized medicine and an interference in state governance, although one lengthy statement goes so far as to say it is communist-inspired and will lead to the break up of the family and legalized abortion. On the proponents side the work of the Children's Bureau under Sheppard-Towner is reviewed. Disagreement exists as to whether such legislation has any effect on maternal and infant mortality rates.

1821.   U.S. Congress. House. Committee on Interstate and Foreign Commerce. *Extension of Maternity and Infancy Act, Report to Accompany H.R. 17183.* H. Rept. 2751, 70th Cong., 2d sess., 1929. 22p. Serial 8980. Favorable report on extending the provisions of the Sheppard-Towner Act for five years reviews the history of the act and the progress made in maternal and infant welfare programs under its authority. The history of federal aid to the states is also reviewed and a list of some of the individuals and organization supporting the measure is given. Supplemental tables provide statistics on funding to states and territories, trends in infant mortality, and trends in maternal mortality by state, 1915-1927. A minority view objects to the continuation of the program on the basis that such work should be controlled and funded by the states.

1822.   U.S. Congress. Senate. Committee on Commerce. *To Amend the Maternity Act, Report to Accompany S. 255.* S. Rept. 369, 71st Cong., 2d sess., 1930. 16p. Serial 9185. Favorable report on a bill similar to the Sheppard-Towner Act includes a letter from the Dept. of Labor supporting the bill and reprints H. Rept. 575 (1816) and S. Rept. 745 (1818), 69th Congress.

1823.   U.S. Congress. House. Committee on Interstate and Foreign Commerce. *Maternity and Infancy, Minority Views to Accompany S. 255.* H. Rept. 2485, part 2, 71st Cong., 3d sess., 1931. 6p. Serial 9326. Views opposed to a bill to renew and expand the provisions of Sheppard-Towner are based on the argument that the federal funding approach is of questionable constitutionality, that the power of the federal government will be expanded under such encouragement to cover issues of eugenics and birth control, and that it is unfair for the few states which contribute the majority of taxes to support the domestic programs of other states.

1824. U.S. Congress. House. Committee on Interstate and Foreign Commerce. *Maternity and Infancy, Report to Accompany S. 255.* H. Rept. 2485, 71st Cong., 3d sess., 1931. 8p. Serial 9326. Reports with significant amendments a bill for a rural health and maternal and infant health federal-state cooperative program. The need for federal leadership in the area of public health is specifically addressed.

1825. U.S. Congress. House. Committee on Interstate and Foreign Commerce. *Maternity and Infancy, Report to Accompany H.R. 7525.* H. Rept. 101, 72d Cong., 1st sess., 1932. 7p. Serial 9491. The responsibility of the federal government for health and welfare of the nation and the need to coordinate the work of the Children's Bureau and the Public Health Service are noted in support of a federal-state cooperative rural health and maternal and child health bill.

1826. U.S. Congress. Senate. Committee on Commerce. *Amend the Maternity Act, Report to Accompany S. 572.* S. Rept. 428, 72d Cong., 1st sess., 1932. 10p. Serial 9487. Reports a bill establishing a combined public health and maternal and infant health program with federal funding dependent upon application of an equal amount of state funds. The issue of the need for instruction and health care for maternity and infancy is reviewed and special needs due to the Depression are noted.

1827. U.S. Congress. Senate. Committee on Commerce. *Federal Cooperation with States in Promotion of General Health of Rural Population of the United States and Welfare and Hygiene of Mothers and Children, Hearings on S. 572.* 72d Cong., 1st sess., 4,5 Feb. 1932. 418p. Y4.C73/2:R88. Testimony primarily in opposition to a bill to provide federal matching funds for maternal and child welfare programs points to the failure of the Sheppard-Towner Act to reduce maternal mortality, but primarily centers on issues of Federalism and cost. Some discussion on why maternal mortality is still relatively high focuses on the high incidence of interference by doctors during labor. Objections from Catholic women's societies center on intrusion of the government into family affairs. Includes considerable information on state maternal and infant welfare programs under Sheppard-Towner and provides data on infant and maternal mortality trends in the United States.

1828. U.S. Congress. Senate. Committee on Commerce. *Maternity and Infancy Hygiene, Minority Report to Accompany S. 572.* S. Rept. 428, part 2, 72d Cong., 1st sess., 1932. 7p. Serial 9487. Opposition to federal aid for maternal and infant hygiene programs is based on the argument that the Sheppard-Towner Act did little to affect mortality rates and that it undermines local support for public health programs. Opponents also consider such legislation an intrusion into local affairs and a precursor to greater federal control.

1829. U.S. Children's Bureau. *Grants to States for Maternal and Child Welfare under Social Security Act Approved August 14, 1935, Title 5, Parts 1,2,3, Maternal and Child-Health Services, Services for Crippled Children, Child Welfare Services.* Maternal and Child Welfare Bulletin no. 1. Washington, DC: GPO, 1935. 20p. L5.34:1. Summarizes regulations and general apportionment of funds. Corrected edition issued in 1936.

1830. U.S. Children's Bureau. *Report of Director of Maternal and Child Health Division of Children's Bureau as of April 1, 1937.* Washington, DC: The Bureau, 1937. 5p. L5.2:M41/2. Overview of state maternal and child health activities under Title V of the Social Security Act reviews administrative services, medical care, public health nursing, and physician education. Briefly notes some of the demonstration programs.

1831. U.S. Children's Bureau. *Federal and State Cooperation in Maternal and Child Welfare Services under the Social Security Act.* Maternal and Child Welfare Bulletin no. 2. Washington, DC: GPO, 1938. 111p. L5.34:2. Also issued as Children's Bureau Publication no. 254, L5.20:254. Describes federal allocations and state programs, January 1936 - June 1937, for maternal and child health services, services for crippled children, and child-welfare services. Provides data on expenditures by program and state.

1832. U.S. Children's Bureau. *Federal and State Cooperation in Maternal and Child Welfare under Social Security Act Approved August 14, 1935, Title 5, Parts 1,2,3, Maternal and Child-Health Services, Services for Crippled Children, Child Welfare Services: Summary for 5 Months Ended June 30, 1936, Preliminary Summary of Fiscal Year 1937.* Publication no. 254, revised. Washington, DC: GPO, 1940. 111p. L5.20:254/1-2. Also issued as Maternal and Child Welfare Bulletin no. 2 revised.

1833. U.S. Children's Bureau. *Grants to States for Maternal and Child Welfare under Social Security Act of 1935 and the Social Security Act Amendments of 1939.* Publication no. 253. Washington, DC: GPO, 1940. 24p. L5.20:253/4. Also issued as Maternal and Child Welfare Bulletin no. 1, revised. Describes the provisions of Title V grants for maternal and child health services, services for crippled children, and child welfare services. Data on the amount of federal grants per state under each program for the fiscal year ending June 30, 1941 is given.

1834. U.S. Children's Bureau. *Maternal and Child-Health Services under the Social Security Act Title V, Part 1: Development of Programs, 1936-1939.* Publication no. 259. Washington, DC: GPO, 1941. 109p. L5.20:259. Describes the development of state and local programs to improve health services for expectant mothers and young children and to train professional workers in these areas. Includes data on federal funding for these programs by state, maternal mortality rates for the years of the program, and number of counties with services by state.

1835. U.S. Children's Bureau. *Maternity Care at Public Expense in Six Counties in New York State, July 1, 1935 -June 30, 1936.* Publication no. 267. Washington, DC: GPO, 1941. 84p. L5.20:267. Study examines publicly funded maternity care in six counties representing farming, mountainous, and suburban areas in New York State. Areas of study include outcome of pregnancy, duration and extent of care, state and local expenditures, place of delivery and attendant.

1836. U.S. Children's Bureau. *Administrative Policies, Emergency Maternity and Infant Care Program.* EMIC Information Circular no. 1. Washington, DC: GPO, 1943. 22p. L5.46:1. Details application policies, authorization for care, and authorized services under EMIC as well as qualifications for physicians and nurses and minimum requirements for hospital facilities.

1837. U.S. Children's Bureau. *Maternity and Infant Care for Wives and Infants of Enlisted Men in the Armed Forces.* Folder no. 29. Washington, DC: The Bureau, 1943. 6p. leaflet. L5.22:29. Revised editions published in April and August 1944 and October 1945.

1838. U.S. Children's Bureau. *Maternity and Infant Care for Wives and Infants of Men in the Armed Forces.* Washington, DC: The Bureau, 1943. 5p. leaflet. L5.2:M41/3.

1839. U.S. Children's Bureau. *Progress Reports, Maternal and Child Health Services, Social Security Act, Title V, Part 1, Fiscal Years Ended June 30, 1941 and June 30, 1942.* Washington, DC: The Bureau, 1943. 22p. L5.2:M41/7/941-42. Data for states on staff and services under the Maternal and Child Health Service program is presented including education of staff members, services for which payment was made, prenatal clinics, amount of medical and hospital care paid for, and organized home-delivery nursing service.

1840. U.S. Children's Bureau. *Types of Health Activities Benefiting Negro Mothers and Children under Federal-Aid Programs for Maternal and Child-Health Services and Services for Crippled Children.* Washington, DC: The Bureau, 1943. 10p. L5.2:N31/2. Description of maternal and child health programs dealing primarily with black women and their children focuses mostly on rural areas. The responsibility of black public health nurses for prenatal care and supervision of midwives is common to most of the programs described. The progress in ensuring the attendance of a physician at birth is also emphasized. Both rural and urban programs are described.

1841. U.S. Congress. House. Committee on Appropriations. *Emergency Maternity and Infant Care for Wives of Enlisted Men in the Armed Forces- Additional Appropriation, Fiscal Year 1944.* H. Rept. 708, 78th Cong., 1st sess., 1943. 4p. Serial 10763. See 1842 for abstract.

1842. U.S. Congress. Senate. Committee on Appropriations. *Emergency Maternity and Infant Care for Wives of Enlisted Men in the Armed Forces- Additional Appropriations, Fiscal Year 1944, Report to Accompany H.J. Res. 159.* S. Rept. 413, 78th Cong., 1st sess., 1943. 3p. Serial 10756. Report recommends early enactment of a bill appropriating additional funds for the EMIC program due to unanticipated demand for the program. Table shows the number of cases authorized under EMIC by state.

1843. U.S. Children's Bureau. *For Your Wife and Your Baby, Help from Uncle Sam to Keep Them Safe.* Washington, DC: GPO, 1944. 4p. leaflet. L5.2:W63.

1844. U.S. Congress. House. *Communication from the President of the United States Transmitting a Draft of Proposed Provisions Pertaining to an Appropriation for the Fiscal Year 1945, in the Form of Amendments to the Budget for the Department of Labor for Said Fiscal Year.* H. Doc. 524, 78th Cong., 2d sess., 1944. 2p. Serial 10878. Extends EMIC program to wives of aviation cadets, makes 1945 funds available in 1944, and changes the ability of states to use funds to meet administrative costs.

1845. U.S. Congress. House. Committee on Appropriations. *Emergency Maternity and Infant Care for Wives of Enlisted Men in Armed Forces- Additional Appropriations, Fiscal Year 1944, Report to Accompany H.R. 271.* H. Rept. 1419, 78th Cong., 2d sess., 1944. 2p. Serial 10846.

1846. U.S. Congress. Senate. Committee on Appropriations. *Making an Additional Appropriation for the Fiscal Year 1944 for Emergency Maternity and Infant Care for Wives of Enlisted Men in the Armed Forces, Report to Accompany H.J. Res. 271.* S. Rept. 864, 78th Cong., 2d sess., 1944. 2p. Serial 10841. Report on appropriations for EMIC includes a table showing cases and costs by state.

1847. U.S. Children's Bureau. *Recommendations for Expansion of Maternal and Child Health and Crippled Children's Programs, Adopted by Steering Committee on Health Services, Advisory to Children's Bureau, Washington, January 28, 1945.* Washington, DC: The Bureau, 1945. 8p. L5.2:M41/9. Reports the recommendation of the Steering Committee on Health Services for expanding maternal and child health programs to ensure adequate maternity and infant care in all parts of the country.

1848. U.S. Children's Bureau. *Report of Annual Meeting of Children's Bureau Advisory Committee on Maternal and Child Health Services and on Services for Crippled Children, November 8 and 9, 1945.* by Allan C. Butler. Washington, DC: The Bureau, 1945. 11p.

L5.2:C86/11. Reprinted in 1946 under SuDoc number FS3.202:M41/945. Report of the Children's Bureau advisory committee on Senate Bill 1318, the "Maternal and Child Welfare Act of 1945," expresses concern over federal agency jurisdiction, the need for a means test, the scope of services, coordination with other medical care programs, and expansion of nurse-midwife training.

1849.   U.S. Children's Bureau. *Maternal and Child Welfare, Legislation, Report to Children's Bureau Advisory Committee on Maternal and Child Health Services and Services for Crippled Children.* Washington, DC: The Bureau, 1946. 6p. FS3.202:M41/3/945. Report focuses on the failure of the Senate Committee on Education and Labor to report out the Maternal and Child Welfare Act, the testimony presented at the hearing, and the House Committee on Labor amendments to the bill.

1850.   U.S. Congress. House. Committee on Labor. *Maternal and Child Welfare Act of 1946, Report to Accompany H.R. 3922.* H. Rept. 2662, 79th Cong., 2d sess., 1946. 13p. Serial 11026. Section-by-section description of a federal aid program for the improvement of maternal and child health and child welfare focuses primarily on child health.

1851.   U.S. Congress. Senate. Committee on Education and Labor. *Maternal and Child Welfare.* 79th Cong., 2d sess., 21, 22 June 1946. 391p. Y4.Ed8/3:M41/2. Discussion emphasizes the need for federal assistance to ensure adequate health care for pregnant women and young children with the primary focus placed on child welfare. Much of the opposition to the bill centers on the provision which provides services regardless of financial need. Work of the Children's Bureau and other projects related to maternal and infant health are highlighted. Provides supporting statistics on number and percentage of births by race and person in attendance, 1935 and 1943; maternal deaths by cause, 1933 and 1943; maternal mortality by age, 1933 and 1943; and maternal mortality by state, 1942 and 1943.

1852.   U.S. Children's Bureau. *The Emergency Maternity and Infant Care Program.* Folder no. 29. Washington, DC: GPO, 1947. leaflet. FS3.210:29. Other editions published in 1944.

1853.   U.S. Congress. House. Committee on Ways and Means. *Comments by Interested Individuals and Organizations on H.R. 3386, the Maternal and Child Health and Mental Retardation Planning Amendments of 1963.* 88th Cong., 1st sess., 1963. Committee print. 135p. Y4.W36:M41/3. Collection of comments submitted by individuals and organizations supporting continued federal funding for maternal and child welfare programs focus on prenatal care and infant health although there is some mention of maternal mortality.

1854.   U.S. Congress. House. Committee on Ways and Means. *Maternal and Child Health and Mental Retardation Planning Amendments of 1963, Report to Accompany H.R. 7544.* H. Rept. 637, 88th Cong., 1st sess., 1963. 21p. Serial 12543. Favorable report on amending the Social Security Act to fund programs of maternal and child health focuses on reducing the incidence of mental retardation. Minority views include a tirade against the welfare system as encouraging illegitimacy.

1855.   U.S. Congress. Senate. Committee on Finance. *Maternal and Child Health and Mental Retardation, Report to Accompany H.R. 7544.* S. Rept. 551, 88th Cong., 1st sess., 1963. 14p. Serial 12535. Report on amending the Social Security Act to provide funding to states for the expansion of maternal health programs discusses how such programs might reduce mental retardation among lower income groups.

1856.   U.S. Maternal and Child Health Service. *Health Services for Mothers and Children under Title 5 Social Security Act.* Washington, DC: GPO, 1970. 13p. HE20.2752:H34. Overview of the types of programs and services authorized under Maternal and Child

Health Service programs provides a review of research and demonstration projects supported and details the level of appropriations authorized for each type of project.

1857. U.S. Congress. House. Committee on Ways and Means. *One-Year Extension of Special Project Grant Authority under Maternal and Child Health Service Program, Report to Accompany H.R. 9410.* H. Rept. 1143, 92d Cong., 2d sess., 1972. 7p. Serial 12974-3.

1858. U.S. Health Services and Mental Health Administration. *Programs of the Maternal and Child Health Service.* Washington, DC: GPO, 1972. 11p. leaflet. HE20.2752:P94/3. Later edition published in 1973.

1859. U.S. Bureau of Community Health Services. *Maternal and Child Health Services Programs and Project Guidelines.* Washington, DC: GPO, 1976. 34p. HE20.5102:M41/4. Guidelines for state agencies in administrating maternal and child health programs under Title V of the Social Security Act, Section 505.

1860. U.S. Bureau of Community Health Services. *The Maternity and Infant Care Projects, Reducing Risks for Mothers and Babies.* Washington, DC: GPO, 1976. 19p. HE20.5102:M41/2. Describes general maternal and infant care programs and cites some specific examples of model programs.

1861. U.S. Bureau of Community Health Services. *Program Guidance Material, Health Services for Mothers and Children.* Rockville, MD: The Bureau, 1976. looseleaf. HE20.5108:H34/2. Handbook provides information on the legislative base, regulations, and program component guidelines for agencies providing Title V services to mothers and children.

1862. U.S. Congress. House. Committee on Interstate and Foreign Commerce. Subcommittee on Health and the Environment. *Maternal and Child Health Care Act - 1976, Supplemental Hearing on H.R. 12937, H.R. 14309, and H.R. 14822 and H.R. 14497.* 94th Cong., 2d sess., 13 Sept. 1976. 270p. Y4.In8/4:94-117. Hearing considers bills to provide a national system of maternal and child health care.

1863. U.S. Congress. House. Committee on Interstate and Foreign Commerce. Subcommittee on Health and the Environment. *Maternal and Child Health Care Act - 1977, Hearing on H.R. 1702.* 95th Cong., 2d sess., 4,5 Jan. 1978. 379p. Y4.In8/4:95-86. Primary focus of the bill discussed is prenatal and child health care for uninsured mothers. An interesting side bar to the discussion is testimony on the role of nurse practitioners in the delivery of health care.

1864. U.S. Department of Agriculture. Food and Nutrition Service. *Evaluation of the WIC Migrant Demonstration Project: A Final Report.* by Development Associates, Inc. Washington, DC: GPO, 1979. 179p. A98.2:W84. The WIC Migrant Demonstration Project was designed to help ensure that pregnant women and children of migrant families received the benefits of the WIC program. This study of the success of the project gathered extensive information on the women and children involved.

1865. U.S. Congress. Senate. Committee on Labor and Human Resources. *Oversight on Efforts to Reduce Infant Mortality and to Improve Pregnancy Outcome, Hearing.* 96th Cong., 2d sess., 30 June 1980. 700p. Y4.L11/4:In3/3. Oversight hearing on federal maternal and child health services primarily centers on the adequacy of programs to improve pregnancy outcomes and infant mortality. The safety of obstetrical practices and the utilization of nurse midwives is also discussed. Several witnesses raise the issue of adolescent pregnancy and anti-abortion groups also state their views.

1866.   U.S. National Institute of Child Health and Human Development. *Research Programs of the Center for Research for Mothers and Children at the National Institute of Child Health and Human Development.* Washington, DC: GPO, 1982. 11p. HE20.3352:R31/5. Describes the research agendas of the branches and sections of the Center for Research for Mothers and Children. Later edition published in 1987.

1867.   U.S. Congress. House. *Making Appropriations to Provide Emergency Expenditures to Meet Neglected Urgent Needs, to Protect and Add to the National Wealth, Resulting in Not Make Work but Productive Jobs for Women and Men and to Help Provide for the Indigent and Homeless for the Fiscal Year 1983, and for Other Purposes, Conference Report to Accompany H.R. 1718.* H. Rept. 98-44, 98th Cong., 1st sess., 1983. 39p. Serial 13534. Conference bill provides that up to 20% of community and migrant health center funds go for hospital care of pregnant women and newborns with no other means of paying for such care. The conference agreement renewed an amendment earmarking Social Services Block Grant funds for child day care.

1868.   U.S. Congress. House. Committee on Energy and Commerce. *Medicare and Medicaid Budget Reconciliation Amendments of 1983, Report Together with Supplemental and Minority Views to Accompany H.R. 4136.* H. Rept. 98-442, part 1, 98th Cong., 1st sess., 1983. 133p. and errata. Serial 13544. Among the provisions of this Medicare-Medicaid program bill is an extension of Medicaid coverage with 100% federal matching funds for pregnant women in households where the wage earner is unemployed and to first-time pregnant women who would not be covered under existing AFDC programs until after the birth of the child.

1869.   U.S. Congress. House. Committee on Energy and Commerce. Subcommittee on Health and the Environment. *Health Budget Proposals, Hearings on Medicaid Maternal and Child Health Initiatives, Medicare Cost Savings - H.R. 1106, H.R. 3590.* 98th Cong., 1st sess., 15,18 July 1983. 387p. Y4.En2/3:98-54. The first day of hearing testimony examines budget proposals for Medicaid Maternal and Child Health Programs, stressing the importance of prenatal care and the need of federal funding to assure such care for first-time pregnant women. Witnesses note the problems peculiar to pregnant adolescents.

1870.   U.S. Congress. Joint Economic Committee. Subcommittee on Economic Goals and Intergovernmental Policy. *Impact of Federal Spending Cuts on Maternal and Child Health Care, Hearing.* 98th Cong., 1st sess., 17 Nov. 1983. 148p. Y4.Ec7:F31/10. Current data on access to prenatal care by race is stressed repeatedly in this hearing highlighting the effect of federal budget cuts on maternal and child health programs. The primary focus of testimony is on the effect of prenatal care on pregnancy outcome and on the long term cost implications of treating unhealthy babies whose mothers received late or no prenatal care.

1871.   U.S. Congress. Senate. Committee on Finance. *Health Care for Unemployed Workers, Report Together with Additional Views to Accompany S. 951.* S. Rept. 98-193, 98th Cong., 1st sess., 1983. 68p. Serial 13509. Section 203 of this bill to provide medical coverage for unemployed workers and their families also would require states to provide Medicaid coverage to pregnant women who would be eligible for AFDC after the birth of the child with coverage beginning at medical determination of pregnancy.

1872.   U.S. Congress. Senate. Committee on Finance. Subcommittee on Health. *Maternal and Child Health Block Grant, Hearing.* 98th Cong., 2d sess., 20 June 1984. 210p. Y4.F49:S.hrg.98-1020. The gap in coverage for pregnant women and their children who live below the poverty line is one of the topics in this hearing on the Maternal and Child Health Block Grant program. Primary focus of the hearing is on administration of the programs.

1873. U.S. Department of Agriculture. Food and Nutrition Service. *Efforts to Promote Breastfeeding in the Supplemental Food Programs.* Washington, DC: GPO, 1984. 4p. A98.9:236/2. Both the WIC and the Food Stamp program have specific provisions to encourage breastfeeding. These requirements and other USDA activities to encourage breastfeeding are described and a bibliography of additional reading is provided. Earlier edition published in 1982.

1874. U.S. General Accounting Office. *Maternal and Child Health Block Grant: Program Changes Emerging under State Administration.* Washington, DC: GPO, 1984. 116p. GA1.13:HRD-84-35. Changes in the structure of Maternal and Child Health Block Grants, resulting in shifting emphasis of priorities and allocation of funds, is described. Services included in MCH block grants are maternal health and adolescent pregnancy programs. Includes statistics on changes in state expenditures for programs.

1875. U.S. Congress. House. *Consolidated Omnibus Budget: The Conciliation Act of 1985, Conference Report to Accompany H.R. 3128.* H. Rept. 99-453, 99th Cong., 1st sess., 1985. 718p. Serial 13662. Conference report on an omnibus budget bill highlights House and Senate versions of a bill covering multiple aspects of the federal budget. Provisions of the conference committee bill include mandatory coverage of pregnant women by Medicaid when they meets the AFDC requirements regardless of the employment status of the husband. Also covered is a one year extension of a program to train AFDC recipients as homemaker/home health aides. A House proposed teen pregnancy program and an anti-abortion provision for SBA loans were eliminated in the conference version. A House amendment providing for a study of Agent Orange effects in female veterans was dropped due to its inclusion in another bill.

1876. U.S. Congress. House. Committee on Energy and Commerce. *Indian Health Care Amendments of 1985, Report Together with Minority Views, to Accompany H.R. 14326.* H. Rept. 99-94, part 2, 99th Cong., 1st sess., 1985. 92p. Serial 13646. Included in the bill reported here is a program to reduce maternal and infant mortality rates among Native American populations. The views of the Administrator of the Health Resources and Health Services Administration are included in the report, and the program proposed by this bill is criticized in relation to the stated acceptable maternal mortality and infant mortality rate in the first 28 days.

1877. U.S. Congress. House. Committee on Energy and Commerce. *Medicare and Medicaid Budget Reconciliation Amendments of 1985, Report Together with Minority Views to Accompany H.R. 3101.* H. Rept. 99-265, part 1, 99th Cong., 1st sess., 1985. 134p. Serial 13654. Maternity coverage of Medicaid for low-income two parent families is one of the areas covered by the provisions of this bill. Under the bill, states would be required to extend Medicaid coverage for prenatal care to pregnant women in families that meet the AFDC income and resources standards without regard to family composition.

1878. U.S. Congress. House. Committee on Interior and Insular Affairs. *The Authorizing and Amending the Indian Health Care Improvement Act, and for Other Purposes, Report to Accompany H.R. 1426.* H. Rept. 99-94, part 1, 99th Cong., 1st sess., 1985. 100p. Serial 13646. Favorable report on a measure authorizing Indian health care programs describes the health status of the Native American population in relation to the general population. The bill requires the development and implementation of a plan to reduce infant and maternal mortality rates among Native Americans.

1879. U.S. Congress. Senate. Select Committee on Indian Affairs. *Indian Health Care Amendments of 1985, Report to Accompany S. 277.* S. Rept. 99-62, 99th Cong., 1st sess., 1985. 89p. Serial 13619. Reports a bill authorizing a number of health care programs aimed at reducing the disparity between the health status of Native Americans and that of the general population. Title VII of the proposed act directs the Secretary of Health and Human Services to initiate programs to reduce infant and maternal mortality and fetal alcohol syndrome among the Native American population.

1880.   U.S. General Accounting Office. *Need to Foster Optimal Use of Resources in the Special Supplemental Food Program for Women, Infants, and Children (WIC): Report to the Secretary of Agriculture.* Washington, DC: The Office, 1985. 99p. GA1.13:RCED-85-105. Report stresses the need for better management of the WIC program noting the specific need to better target high risk groups such as pregnant adolescents.

1881.   U.S. Health Resources and Services Administration. *Health Mothers, Healthy Babies: A Compendium of Program Ideas for Serving Low-Income Women.* Washington, DC: GPO, 1986. 168p. HE20.9102:L95. Description of program characteristics, staffing, outreach, educational programs, educational materials, and successes is drawn from a survey of programs directed toward maternal and child health in low-income groups. Specific topics covered include pregnancy, prenatal services, postnatal programs, breastfeeding, nutrition, substance abuse, rural populations, Native Americans, and adolescent pregnancy.

1882.   U.S. Congress. House. Committee on Government Operations. Subcommittee on Human Resources and Intergovernmental Relations. *Infants at Risk: Is the Federal Government Assuring Prenatal Care for Poor Women? Hearing.* 100th Cong., 1st sess., 30 Sept. 1987. 225p. Y4.G74/7:In3/21. Discussion of government policy affecting access to prenatal care among low income women reviews the importance of prenatal care to positive pregnancy outcomes. Barriers to prenatal care faced by poor and uninsured women are explored. Hospital and clinic policies on uninsured women and the risk this poses to mother and child in a high-risk pregnancy are discussed, particularly in relation to the difficulty the borderline poor have in establishing Medicaid eligibility. The role of cost in the failure to obtain prenatal care among the poor is debated.

1883.   U.S. Congress. Senate. Committee on Finance. *Medicaid, Medicare, and Maternal and Child Health Block Grant Budget Issues, Hearing.* 100th Cong., 1st sess., 10 July 1987. 154p. Y4.F49:S.hrg.100-398/pt.2. Hearing primarily discusses the Maternal and Child Health Block Grant program focusing on the inability of many women to afford prenatal care and the resulting cost of health care for seriously or chronically ill children. The Medicaid rules which impoverish the spouse of the nursing home resident are also examined.

1884.   U.S. Health Resources and Services Administration. Division of Maternal and Child Health. *The Maternal and Child Health Research Grants Program: Inventory of Projects.* Washington, DC: GPO, 1987. 76p. HE20.9102:M41/2. Describes projects in progress and lists completed projects as of September 1986 funded by Maternal and Child Health Research Grants Program. Most of the projects focus on child health, but some deal with low-income maternity care and adolescent pregnancy programs.

1885.   U.S. Congress. House. Select Committee on Hunger. *Strategies for Expanding the Special Supplemental Food Program for Women, Infants, and Children [WIC] Participation: A Survey of WIC Directors, Report.* 100th Cong., 2d sess., 1988. Committee print. 37p. Y4.H89:St8. Results of a survey of state WIC directors describes the financial, physical, and behavioral barriers to expanding WIC participation. Ways to improve outreach for prenatal care and nutrition services are detailed. The report appendix includes a chronology of the WIC program and data on WIC participation trends.

1886.   U.S. Congress. Senate. Committee on Finance. *Children's Primary Care and Chronic Health Care Issues, Hearings.* 100th Cong. 2d sess., 24,26 May 1988. 404p. Y4.F49:S.hrg.100-1024. First of two hearings focuses on the role of prenatal care in reducing infant mortality and considers federal and state options to ensure early access to prenatal care for low income women. The second hearing presents testimony on health care for chronically ill children and discusses approaches to improving outcomes and easing family burdens.

1887.   U.S. Congress. House. Committee on Energy and Commerce. Subcommittee on Health and the Environment. *Medicare and Medicaid Initiatives, Hearings.* 101st Cong., 1st sess., 8 Feb., 8 June 1989. 645p. Y4.En2/3:101-46. First day of hearings on Medicare and Medicaid initiatives focuses on infant mortality. Access to obstetrical care is the main topic as witnesses discuss barriers to improving access to health care. Rural health care, reimbursement of certified nurse midwives, and practitioner liability are areas examined.

1888.   U.S. Congress. House. Select Committee on Children, Youth, and Families. *Caring for New Mothers: Pressing Problems, New Solutions, Hearing.* 101st Cong., 1st sess., 24 Oct. 1989. 277p. Y4.C43/2:M85. Hearing witnesses stress the importance of prenatal care for positive pregnancy outcomes and the barriers to such care in the United States. Women's attitudes and knowledge regarding prenatal care and pregnancy risks are reviewed, and the role of federal and state programs, notably WIC and Medicaid, are discussed.

1889.   U.S. Congress. Senate. Committee on Finance. *Health Care Coverage for Children, Hearing.* 101st Cong., 1st sess., 20 June 1989. 242p. Y4.F49:S.hrg.101-568. Hearing considers extending Medicaid coverage to pregnant women and children in families with incomes up to 130% of the federal poverty level. Most statements focus on preventing infant mortality through better prenatal care and witnesses stress the lack of insurance coverage of maternity care for low-income families.

1890.   U.S. Dept. of Defense. *CHAMPUS Maternity Care.* Washington, DC: The Dept., 1989. leaflet. D2.18:8/989. Describes the maternity care provisions of CHAMPUS, the military health insurance program.

1891.   U.S. General Accounting Office. *Medicaid: State Expanded Coverage for Pregnant Women, Infants and Children.* Washington, DC: The Office, 1989. 23p. GA1.13:HRD-89-90. Report provides an overview with graphs showing the expansion of Medicaid coverage to pregnant women under OBRA 1986 and OBRA 1987. Detailed information is provided by state on eligibility for prenatal care under Medicaid and on infant mortality rates.

1892.   U.S. Health Care Financing Administration. Bureau of Quality Control. *Maternal and Infant Health: Medicaid Strategies to Save Lives and Money, a State's Opportunity.* Washington, DC: GPO, 1989. 6p. HE22.2:M46/23. Outline of steps to improve Medicaid programs for prenatal care at the state level notes the outreach and eligibility process, recruitment and retention of providers, and improvements to service delivery.

1893.   U.S. Congress. House. Committee on the Budget. Task Force on Human Resources. *Health Care Crisis: Problems of Cost and Access, Hearings.* 101st Cong., 2d sess., 23-24 Aug. 1990. 156p. Y4.B85/3:101-5-10. Access to health care in California is the focus of hearings held in Fresno and Modesto. Recurring themes of testimony include cultural differences in approaches to medical treatment and their effect on health care for South East Asian-Americans and also the lack of prenatal care and its effect on pregnancy outcomes. Much of the discussion in on the Medi-Cal system and on ways to improve Medicaid to meet the needs of low incomes women and children.

1894.   U.S. Congress. House. Committee on the Budget. Task Force on Human Resources. *Women, Infants, and Children (WIC): The Current Crisis, Hearing.* 101st Cong., 2d sess.,

27 June 1990. 133p. Y4.B85/3:101-5-9. Hearing explores the problems faced by the States in funding the WIC program. The effect of the inadequate funding levels on the ability to serve all needy women and their children is emphasized. Short-term and long-term proposals to address the distribution of WIC funds to the states are discussed.

1895. U.S. Congress. House. Committee on Ways and Means. Subcommittee on Health. *Health Insurance for Children and Pregnant Women, Hearing.* 101st Cong., 2d sess., 20 Mar. 1990. 102p. Y4.W36:101-78. Hearing witnesses discuss the long term costs of the failure to receive prenatal care and support proposals to ensure that all pregnant women and infants have access to health care.

1896. U.S. Congress. House. Select Committee on Children, Youth, and Families. *Ensuring Healthy Babies in Upstate New York: Pressing Problems, Promising Strategies, Hearing.* 101st Cong., 2d sess., 16 July 1990. Syracuse, NY. 199p. Y4.C43/2:B11. Hearing explores barriers to prenatal care for women in upstate New York focusing on Medicaid coverage, provider availability, and the role of poverty and drug abuse in failure to seek care. Community-based programs to provide prenatal care and the need to coordinate Medicaid and WIC are discussed. The role of domestic violence in failure to seek prenatal care is also examined.

1897. U.S. Congress. House. Select Committee on Hunger and Senate. Committee on Agriculture. *National WIC Evaluation: Reporting and Followup Issues, Joint Hearing.* 101st Cong., 2d sess., 24 Jan. 1990. 190p. Y4.H89:101-13. The GAO report of the same title is at the center of this hearing devoted to speeches supporting WIC and criticizing the USDA rewrite of portions of the National WIC Evaluation report. Further evaluation of the effect of the WIC program on maternal and child nutrition and health is discussed.

1898. U.S. Congress. Senate. Committee on Governmental Affairs. Subcommittee on General Services, Federalism, and the District of Columbia. *Prenatal Care in the 1990's: Assuring a Healthy Start, Hearing.* 101st Cong., 2d sess., 26 Mar. 1990. Philadelphia, PA. 33p. Y4.G74/9:S.hrg.101-682. Brief hearing describes early prenatal care intervention programs, particularly the use of advocates to speed determination of Medicaid eligibility. Ways federal programs can work with local agencies to get at-risk women into prenatal care early are explored with reference to changing Medicaid eligibility rules.

SERIALS

1899. U.S. Bureau of Community Health Services. *Maternal and Child Health Programs: Legislative Base.* Rockville, MD: The Bureau, 1975-1980. irreg. HE20.5102:M41/year. Reprint of federal laws relating to maternal and child health programs includes Titles V, XI, and XIX of the Social Security Act, Title II of the Social Security Amendments of 1972, Title VI of the Civil Rights Act, and related regulations.

1900. U.S. Children's Bureau. *Maternal and Child Health Services.* Statistical Series nos. 38, 49, 53, 58, 62, 68, and 77. Washington, DC: GPO, 1955-1963. annual. FS3.214:no. Although the focus of the report is on health services to children, some statistics of maternal health services, including use of midwives for delivery and number of practicing midwives by state, are included.

1901. U.S. Children's Bureau. *Preliminary Monthly Statistical Report on EMIC Program.* Washington, DC: The Bureau, May 16 - Dec. 16, 1944. nos. 1-8. monthly. L5.50:944/no. Provides data by state on number of cases authorized, completed, closed without payment, and incomplete for the month and to date under the Emergency Maternity and Infant Care program.

1902. U.S. Children's Bureau. *The Promotion of the Welfare and Hygiene of Maternity and Infancy: The Administration of the Act of Congress of November 23, 1921.* Children's Bureau Publication no. 137, 146, 156, 178, 186, 194, and 203. Washington, DC: GPO, 1923-1931. annual. L5.20:nos. Annual report for the fiscal year on state and federal administration of maternal and child health care under the Sheppard-Towner Act details state programs and progress in education, prenatal care, and use of midwives.

1903. U.S. Health Services and Mental Health Administration. Maternal and Child Health Service. *Maternal and Child Health Service Programs, Administering Agencies and Legislative Base.* Washington, DC: GPO, 1971-1973. annual. HE20.2752:P94/2/year. List of state agencies and project sites for maternal and child health programs also reprints enabling legislation.

1904. U.S. Health Services and Mental Health Administration. Maternal and Child Health Service. *The Maternal and Child Health Service Reports on Promoting the Health of Mothers and Children.* Washington, DC: GPO, 1970 - . annual. HE20.2751:year (1970-1973), HE20.5401:year (1974-). Describes programs offered under Maternal and Child Health Service programs including day care, family planning, and family life education. Relevant trends in areas such as day care, maternal mortality, and the changing status of legal abortion are also examined.

1905. U.S. Health Services and Mental Health Administration. Maternal and Child Health Service. *Maternal and Child Health Services of State and Local Health Departments, Fiscal Year...* MCHS Statistical Series. Washington, DC: GPO, FY1970 - 1976. annual. HE20.2760:2:no. Statistical report on the number of women and children served by federally-aided health care at the local level provides data on users of maternity medical clinics, maternity nursing services, classes for expectant parents, family planning services, practicing midwives, and child services by state.

1906. U.S. National Institute of Child Health and Human Development. Center for Research for Mothers and Children. *Progress Report.* Bethesda, MD: The Institute, 1982 - . irreg. HE20.3351/2:year. Report on program activities and research highlights of the Center focuses on fetal development, pregnancy and birth, nutrients and hormones in growth and development, prevention of mental retardation, and human learning behavior.

1907. U.S. National Institute of Child Health and Human Development. Maternal and Child Health Research Committee. *Annual Report, Maternal and Child Health Research Committee, National Institutes of Health.* Bethesda, MD: The Institute, 1973/74 - . annual. HE20.3001/2:M41/year.

13

Birth Control
and Abortion

The issue of birth control first recieved significant discussion in government documents in 1924 when Congress considered lifting the ban on the importation and mail distribution of contraceptive information (1908). The Depression sparked another attempt between 1931 and 1934 to amend the Tariff Act and the Criminal Code to allow limited distribution of information on birth control methods and contraceptive devices. Margaret Sanger was the chief witness at these hearings where advocates stressed the need for poor families to limit childbearing (1909, 1911-1915). It wasn't until 1970 that proposals to amend the Tariff Act and the Criminal Code relative to contraceptive devices were again reported out of committee (1941-1942).

Adoption of family planning as a government initiative doesn't appear until the early 1960's. In 1962 the National Institute of Health published the results of a world-wide survey of birth and population control research (1916) and in 1966 Congress held its first hearing on funding family planning services (1918). Hearings and reports on funding family planning services appear regularly since that time. The many facets of population planning and the religious issues involved are reviewed in the 1971 hearing, *Declaration of U.S. Policy on Population Stabilization by Voluntary Means...* (1952). The need for subsidized family planning in each state and county is analyzed in a 1968 report by Planned Parenthood for the Office of Economic Opportunity (1937). A good overview of both foreign and domestic family planning issues is provided by the 1979 document, *Final Report of the Select Committee on Population* (2036).

Two major issues emerged over the years in federal family planning programs. The provision of services to adolescents and the notification of parents before providing services was one issue. Although numerous documents from Congress and various agencies had earlier discussed the problem of adolescent pregnancy, it wasn't until 1981 that parental consent became a major issue (2066-2067). This question of the adolescent's right to privacy versus parental rights figures in most family planning service hearings from that date. Government approaches to the problem of adolescent pregnancy are covered more fully in Chapter 14, Illegitimacy and Adolescent Pregnancy.

The big issue of the 1970s and the 1980s both in relation to family planning funding and on its own, was abortion. Scattered references to abortion are found in early birth control hearings (1911, 1914). Documents supporting legalized abortion prior to *Roe v. Wade* (410 U.S. 113) include the 1970 hearings on family planning programs (1944) and a brief Women's Bureau review of state abortion laws (1950). Basic data on abortions under liberalized state laws is provided in a 1971 publication of the Maternal and Child Health Service (1957). An amendment to a 1973 family planning bill allowed persons or institutions to refuse to perform abortions for religious or moral reasons (1967). The issue of federal funding of abortions is raised in 1975 hearings on health services programs (1992), and a 1977 GAO report reviews abortion guidelines in HEW family planning programs (2001). The 1970's debate on federally funded programs and abortion is not entirely represented in the documents here since abortion restrictions were often attached to appropriations bills and other measures whose hearings are not included in this bibliography. Their existence is reflected in the Senate report on a bill which continues such a prohibition in the use of Labor, HEW, Defense, Foreign Operations and District of Columbia appropriations (2037). Throughout the eighties the issue of abortion counseling and federal funding was raised at almost every family planning services hearing. The federal abortion funding restrictions are debated at length in the 1985 hearing on a bill to ensure that the Civil Rights Act of 1984 could not be used to protect abortion rights (2104).

The first hearings on amending the Constitution to prohibit abortion were held in 1974. This extensive three part hearing provides a wealth of material supporting both sides of the abortion debate (1977-1979). Another useful document is the 1975 Commission on Civil Rights report, *Constitutional Aspects of the Right to Limit Childbearing*, which provides a detailed examination of the constitutional issues of abortion (1990). Extensive hearings on the abortion issue were held in 1975 (1944), 1976 (2004), and in 1981 (2068, 2070-2071). In 1983 Congress considered the proposed Human Life Federalism Amendment, which stated that the Constitution did not guarantee the right to an abortion (2092, 2093). The federal response to the violence aimed at clinics providing abortion services is explored in hearings held in 1985 and 1986 (2108). The medical and psychological impact of abortion on the woman were considered in a 1989 hearing and report (2126-2127). In 1990 hearings were held on the proposed Freedom of Choice Act, a measure designed to protect abortion rights (2133). Data on abortion in the U.S. can be found in many of the hearings and in the Centers for Disease Control's annual report, *Abortion Surveillance* (2140).

Family planning in developing countries is also addressed in documents, primarily in the hearings on Agency for International Development programs. A review of the population assistance programs can be found in the annual publication *Population Program Assistance, Aid to Developing Nations by United States, Other Nations, and International and Private Agencies* (2138) and in *Assistance for Family Planning Programs in Developing Countries, Jan. 1967* (1944). Extensive discussion of U.S. policy on population assistance is provided in the 1978 House Select Committee on Population hearings *Population and Development* (2019-2021) and in a 1984 hearing, *U.S. Policy of Population Assistance* (2099). In its 1990 report, *Foreign Assistance: AID's Population Program*, the General Accounting Office questioned AID's commitment to encouraging family planning programs (2135).

Another area of government scrutiny is contraceptive development and safety. A number of substantial reports address the safety of oral contraceptives (1921, 1934, 1945), intrauterine devices (1966, 1971, 1993), Depo-Provera (1972, 2001, 2016), diethylstilbestrol (1972, 2001), and the Today Contraceptive Sponge (2089). Also examined is the use of new technologies such as Norplant (2008, 2104). The safety of Depo-Provera is debated in hearings on aid to developing countries (2021-2022, 2054) and in relation to the Indian Health Service (2112). Additional documents on family planning services are located in Chapter 14, Illegitimacy and Adolescent Pregnacny, and in Chapter 16, Public Assistance and Poverty.

1908. U.S. Congress. House. Committee on the Judiciary. *Cumins-Vaile Bill, Joint Hearings on H.R. 6542 and S. 2290.* 68th Cong., 1st. sess., 8 Apr., 9 May 1924. 79p. Y4.J89/1:C86/3. Hearing on a bill to remove language from the Criminal Code and the Tariff Act which classify contraceptive information and devices as obscene, and therefore prohibit their distribution through the mail, discusses family size, quality of children, and birth rates among the "inferior" classes. The opposition argues that the information should come directly from a physician and proposes a resolution "To Promote the Dignity, Purity and Stability of the Family." The degradation of the family through birth control is also a common theme. Proponents speak mainly to the ability to raise good children through birth control. Letters from women personally describing the need for birth control information are inserted in the record.

1909. U.S. Congress. Senate. Committee on the Judiciary. Subcommittee on S. 4582. *Birth Control, Hearing on S. 4582.* 71st Cong., 3rd sess., 13-14 Feb. 1931. 84p. Y4.J89/2:B53. Hearing considers a bill to modify the Tariff Act and the Criminal Code to allow birth control information and supplies to be shipped to physicians, hospitals, clinics and patients. Proponents, including Margaret Sanger, discuss the social and medical need for birth control information. Opposition calls the birth control movement communist inspired and predicts more immoral behavior if birth control is available. Includes a chart summarizing state laws relating to contraception.

1910. U.S. Congress. House. Committee on Ways and Means. *Amend the Tariff Act of 1930 and the Criminal Code, Adverse Report to Accompany H.R. 11082.* H. Rept. 1435, 72d Cong., 1st sess., 1932. 2p. Serial 9493. Bill to amend the Tariff Act and the Criminal Code relative to the distribution of contraceptive devices and information is adversely reported on the grounds that the committee only has jurisdiction over the tariff provisions and that with the existing economic unrest it is unwise to discuss birth control.

1911. U.S. Congress. House. Committee on Ways and Means. *Birth Control, Hearing on H.R. 11082.* 92d Cong., 1st sess., 19-20 May 1932. 149p. Y4.W36:B53. Proponents of a bill to amend the Tariff Act and the Criminal Code to allow doctors and hospitals freer access to birth control research and supplies discuss the need for better access to birth control with a special emphasis on families of the unemployed. Primary witness for the bill is Margaret Sanger. Testimony includes some case histories from birth control clinics and the problem of criminal abortions is briefly discussed. Arguments pro and con center on moral issues and Malthusian theory. A summary of state legislation on birth control is provided.

1912. U.S. Congress. Senate. Committee of the Judiciary. *Birth Control, Hearing on S. 4436.* 72d Cong., 1st sess., 24,30 June 1932. 35p. Y4.J89/2:B53/3. Originally confidential hearing on amending the Tariff Act and the Criminal Code as regards availability of birth control information and devices is primarily a dialogue with Margaret Sanger on types of contraceptive devices and practices worldwide. The methods used by practitioners to distribute information and supplies in the U.S., in spite of federal laws, are described. The second day of the hearing presents briefly the moral argument against wider distribution of birth control information. An additional statement by Sanger appended to the hearing briefly outlines the goals of the major organizations in the birth control movement.

1913. U.S. Congress. Senate. Committee on the Judiciary. Subcommittee on S. 4436. *Birth Control, Hearings on S. 4436.* 72d Cong., 1st sess., 12 - 20 May 1932. 151p. Y4.J89/2:B53/2. Hearing examines a bill to allow the importation of birth control devices and literature and to modify the Criminal Code to allow the circulation through the mail of contractive devices and information to hospitals and clinics, physicians and pharmacists. Arguments in support by Margaret Sanger and others are based on social welfare, eugenics and population control. Opposition is based primarily on moral grounds although some arguments claim physical and nervous damage to women who use contraceptive devices. Includes a summary of state laws regulating contraceptives.

1914. U.S. Congress. House. Committee on the Judiciary. *Birth Control, Hearing on H.R. 5978.* 73rd Cong., 2d sess., 18-19 Jan. 1934. 245p. Y4.J89/1:B53. Hearing considers modification of the United States Penal Code by lifting the prohibition on sending or receiving through the U.S. mail information or supplies pertaining to contraception when sent to physicians, hospitals, and pharmacists. Margaret Sanger is one of the primary witnesses. The problems of poor women and contraception and health are stressed. Death rates from abortion are also presented in arguments for wider distribution of birth control information. Early court rulings on mailing information on abortion and birth control are reviewed. Also includes data on the use and efficiency of contraception. The Reverend

Charley E. Coughlin and other opposition witnesses reject the bill as sanctioning immorality and express concerns over a declining population.

1915. U.S. Congress. Senate. Committee on the Judiciary. Subcommittee on S. 1842. *Birth Control Hearings on S. 1842.* 73rd Cong., 2d sess., 1 - 27 Mar. 1934. 175p. Y4.J89/2:B53/4. Hearing considers a bill to amend the Criminal Code to allow shipment of birth control information and supplies to physicians. Drawing parallels to the prohibition of liquor, proponents argue that birth control information should come from doctors rather than bootlegged from drug stores. Opposition predicts moral decay and the ruin of the Nation if birth control is sanctioned. Much discussion centers on the problem of families on relief and the ability to limit childbearing among the poor.

1916. U.S. National Institute of Health. *Survey of Research on Reproduction Related to Birth Control as of Jan. 1, 1963.* Washington, DC: The Institute, 1963. 250p. FS2.22:R29/963. Survey of research world-wide related to birth and population control lists sponsor, funds granted, and principle investigators, and provides a brief description of the research. Earlier edition issued in 1962.

1917. U.S. Children's Bureau. *Family Planning.* Washington, DC: GPO, 1966. leaflet. FS14.102:F21.

1918. U.S. Congress. Senate. Committee on Labor and Public Welfare. Subcommittee on Employment, Manpower and Poverty. *Family Planning Program, Hearing on S. 2993.* 89th Cong., 2d sess., 10 May 1966. 135p. Y4.L11/2:F21. Testimony on a bill to provide federal funds to private organizations involved in providing family planning services to low income women reviews the existing federal role in family planning and discusses the proper role of government in this area. The need for and approach to family planning services are detailed on both a national and international level. The policy of the Catholic Church on birth control is the topic of several statements.

1919. U.S. Dept. of Health, Education and Welfare. *Report on Family Planning: Activities of the U.S. Department of Health, Education, and Welfare in Family Planning, Fertility, Sterility, and Population Dynamics.* Washington, DC: GPO, 1966. 35p. FS1.2:F21/2. Report on family planning related activities in the Welfare Administration, Public Health Service, Office of Education, and the Food and Drug Administration includes a summary of projects in progress.

1920. U.S. Dept. of Health, Education, and Welfare. Office of the Assistant Secretary for Program Coordination. *Maternal and Child Health Care Programs.* Program Analysis 1966, no. 6. Washington, DC: GPO, 1966. 77p. FS1.29:966/6. Most of the programs described in this document focus on child health issues, however, family planning programs are also reviewed.

1921. U.S. Food and Drug Administration. Advisory Committee on Obstetrics and Gynecology. *FDA Report on the Oral Contraceptives.* Washington, DC: GPO, 1966. 104p. FS13.102:C76/2. Review of research on oral contraceptives examines the areas of utilization, thromboembolic disease, carcinogenic potential, metabolic effects and efficacy. Also includes a review by pharmaceutical companies involved in the manufacture of oral contraceptives.

1922. U.S. Agency for International Development. Office of Technical Cooperation and Research. *Assistance for Family Planning Programs in Developing Countries, Jan. 1967.* Washington, DC: The Office, 1967. 80p. S18.2:F21. Country-by-country summary of family planning activities and assistance in 53 LDC's furnishes basic background statistics such as birth rate and infant mortality rates. For later editions see *Population Program Assistance...* (2138).

1923. U.S. Office of Economic Opportunity. Community Action Program. *Community Action for Health: Family Planning.* rev.ed. Washington, DC: GPO, 1967. 27p. PrEx10.9/3:F21/967. Primer for agencies on participation in the Office's family planning program gives the conditions for use of OEO grant funds and guidelines on program operation. Earlier edition published in 1966.

1924. U.S. Agency for International Development. *AID Policy of Family Planning and Population Growth.* by William S. Gaud. Washington, DC: The Agency, 1968. 13p. S18.2:F21/2. Overview profiles AID policy and programs on family planning assistance in LDC's.

1925. U.S. Agency of International Development. Office of the War on Hunger. *Population Challenge, U.S. Aid and Family Planning in Less-Developed Countries.* Washington, DC: The Office, 1968. 20p. S18.2:P81. Overview of AID family planning assistance and activities in India, Pakistan, Turkey, Taiwan, the Philippines, Korea, and Latin America focuses on cooperation between developing countries and the United States.

1926. U.S. Children's Bureau. *Project Grants to Provide Family Planning Services, P.L. 90-248.* Washington, DC: GPO, 1968. leaflet. FS17.202:F21/3.

1927. U.S. Children's Bureau. *Selected References for Social Workers on Family Planning, Annotated List.* Washington, DC: GPO, 1968. 23p. FS17.212:F21. Citations cover delivery and philosophy of family planning with a section on studies of attitudes toward family planning and another on descriptions of family planning service programs.

1928. U.S. Dept. of Health, Education, and Welfare. *Family Planning: Nationwide Opportunities for Action.* Washington, DC: GPO, 1968. 40p. FS1.2:F21/2/968. Reviews the various ways federal agencies support family planning services for the poor, and looks at education efforts including sex education in secondary schools.

1929. U.S. Dept. of Health, Education, and Welfare. Deputy Assistant Secretary for Population and Family Planning. *The School of Social Work's Responsibilities in Family Planning Education.* by Katherine Brownell Oettinger. Washington, DC: GPO, 1968. 16p. FS1.2:F21/3. Address before the Family Planning Session of the Annual Program of the Council of Social Work Education, January 26, 1968, in Minneapolis, presents information on social work, federal policy, and family planning education. The problems of teenage pregnancy, health, and economic well-being are discussed in the family planning context.

1930. U.S. Food and Drug Administration. Advisory Committee on Obstetrics and Gynecology. *Report on Intrauterine Contraceptive Devices.* Washington, DC: GPO, 1968. 101p. FS13.102:C76/3. Comprehensive review of the use and possible risks of IUD's looks at the history, carcinogenic potential, death and critical illness, and proposed legislation related to the use of IUDs. Includes a 350-item bibliography.

1931. U.S. Indian Health Service. *Computerized Projected Analysis of Indian Health Service Family Planning Program.* by Gerald L. Portney. Washington, DC: The Administration, 1968. 16p. FS2.2:In25/19. Report of data on birth control users and non-users and subsequent births among American Indian and Alaska Native beneficiaries considers the implications for future workload of the Indian Health Service program.

1932. U.S. Office of Economic Opportunity. *Conference Report on Family Planning.* Washington, DC: GPO, 1968. 15p. PrEx10.2:F21/2. General information on the OEO family planning program gives practical advice from a series of regional conferences sponsored by the OEO.

1933. U.S. President's Committee on Population and Family Planning. *Population and Family Planning, Transition from Concern to Action.* Washington, DC: GPO, 1968. 43p. Pr36.8:P81/P81. Recommendations of the President's Committee on Population and Family Planning include increased funding for family planning programs directed at low income women and a stronger population and family planning research effort.

1934. U.S. Food and Drug Administration. Advisory Committee on Obstetrics and Gynecology. *Second Report on the Oral Contraceptives.* Washington, DC: GPO, 1969. 88p. FS13.102:C76/2/969. Report reviews progress made on recommendations from the 1966 report (1921) and presents the results of the Task Force's examination of oral contraceptive utilization and effectiveness, and of carcinogenesis, biological effects, and thromboembolic disorders associated with their use.

1935. U.S. National Clearinghouse for Mental Health Information. *International Family Planning, 1966 - 1968.* by David L. Kasdon. Washington, DC: GPO, 1969. 62p. FS2.22/13:F21/2. Annotated journal article references on international aspects of family planning covers topics of economic, demographic, and cultural aspects of family planning, government policies, IUD's and oral contraceptives, and abortion.

1936. U.S. Office of Economic Opportunity. *Family Planning.* Washington, DC: GPO, 1969. 4p. leaflet. PrEx10.23:6130-3.

1937. U.S. Office of Economic Opportunity. *Need for Subsidized Family Planning Services, United States, Each State and County, 1968 Report.* by Center for Family Planning Program Development, Planned Parenthood - World Population. Washington, DC: GPO, 1969. 255p. PrEx10.23:6130-6. Presents information by county on the need for family planning services based on demographic factors such as presence of a large migrant population, number of medically indigent women, and infant mortality rates. Data on availability of family planning programs and potential resources for programs is also furnished.

1938. U.S. Congress. House. *Family Planning Services and Population Research Act of 1970, Conference Report to Accompany S. 2108.* H. Rept. 91-1667, 91st Cong., 2d sess., 1970. 9p. Serial 12884-8. Conference committee report presents a further amendment of the Family Planning Services and Population Research Act of 1970, an act to improve access to family planning services and to expand population research activities.

1939. U.S. Congress. House. Committee on Interstate and Foreign Commerce. *Family Planning Services and Population Research Act of 1970, Report to Accompany H.R. 19318.* H. Rept. 91-4172, 91st Cong., 2d sess., 1970. 27p. Serial 12884-6. Report recommends a totally revised H.R. 1938, a bill to improve and expand the availability of family planning services and information and to coordinate domestic family planning activities. The need for family planning services and research is reviewed and past government programs and presidential policy are summarized.

1940. U.S. Congress. House. Committee on Interstate and Foreign Commerce. Subcommittee on Public Health and Welfare. *Family Planning Services, Hearing on H.R. 15159, H.R. 9107, H.R. 9108, H.R. 9109, and H.R. 11123 and S. 2108.* 91st Cong., 2d sess., 3 - 7 Aug. 1970. 469p. Y4.In8/4:91-70. Hearing testimony discusses the need for increased access to family planning services and presents data on contraceptive use. The issue of poverty and family planning is raised as are issues relating to marital status, abortion, and the Catholic Church's stand on birth control.

1941.   U.S. Congress. House. Committee on Ways and Means. *Articles Intended for Preventing Conception, Report to Accompany H.R. 4605.* H. Rept. 91-1105, 91st Cong., 2d sess., 1970. 8p. Serial 12884-3. Reports a bill to remove restrictions on the importing and mailing of contraceptive information and devices while retaining restrictions on mailing such items to the general public unless solicited. Excerpts from departmental reports reflect the changing attitude toward contraceptive availability.

1942.   U.S. Congress. Senate. Committee on Finance. *Articles Intended for Preventing Conception, Report to Accompany H.R. 4605.* S. Rept. 1472, 91st Cong., 2d sess., 1970. 7p. Serial 12881-7. Reports a bill amending the Tariff Act of 1930 and the U.S. Code by removing language prohibiting the importing, transporting and mailing of contraceptive devices.

1943.   U.S. Congress. Senate. Committee on Labor and Public Welfare. *Expanding, Improving, and Better Coordinating the Family Planning Services and Population Research Activities of the Federal Government, Report to Accompany S. 2108.* S. Rept. 1004, 91st Cong., 2d sess., 1970. 21p. Serial 12881-3. Favorable report with amendments on a bill to guarantee access to family planning services and to increase government support of family planning research describes the need for expanded family planning services. Includes a brief history of federal family planning programs with quotes from past presidents on the issue of family planning.

1944.   U.S. Congress. Senate. Committee on Labor and Public Welfare. Subcommittee on Health. *Family Planning and Population Research, 1970, Hearings on S. 2108, S. 3219.* 91st Cong., 1st and 2d sess., 8 Dec. 1969 - 19 Feb. 1970. 541p. Y4.L11/2:F21/2. Primary focus of testimony is on the inadequacy of HEWs leadership role in family planning research and service provision. Views express support for legalized abortion and also opposition to S. 2108 as coercive birth control. The state of family planning services in the U.S., particularly for the poor, is reviewed and the case for a link between large families and poverty is made. Witnesses suggest actions to improve administration of family planning programs under HEW agencies. Current and future contraceptive methods are reviewed and a list of ongoing federally funded population research projects is included.

1945.   U.S. Congress. Senate. Select Committee on Small Business. Subcommittee on Monopoly. *Competitive Problems in the Drug Industry, Part 16: Oral Contraceptives, Hearings.* 91st Cong., 2d sess., 14 Jan.-4 Mar. 1970. 5821-7324pp. Y4.Sm1/2:D84/pt.16/v.1-3. Expert witnesses explore all aspects of the safety of oral contraceptives and discuss the availability of risk information to women. Volume one focuses on the physical effects of oral contraceptives. Volume two examines the risks of contraceptives and the government, pharmaceutical company, and physician's role in educating the public. Appendix material in volume three includes the two FDA reports on oral contraceptives, numerous articles from women's magazines and medical and scientific journals on the risks of contraceptive use and unwanted pregnancies, and summary results of oral contraceptive studies.

1946.   U.S. Dept. of Health, Education, and Welfare. Office of the Assistant Secretary for Planning and Evaluation. *Family Planning Service Programs: An Operational Analysis.* Program Analysis 1970, no. 1. Washington, DC: GPO, 1970. 109p. HE1.29:970/1. Analysis of the effectiveness of methods of organizing family planning clinics looks at the areas of patient registration, services offered, and characteristics of facilities and personnel.

1947.   U.S. Indian Health Service. Desert Willow Training Center. *Family Planning for Better Health and Happiness.* Washington, DC: GPO, 1970. 16p. HE20.2652:F21. Picture book provides information on family planning methods.

1948. U.S. Office of Economic Opportunity. Community Action Program. *If You're Not Ready for Another Baby.* by Carolina Population Center. Washington, DC: GPO, 1970. 20p. PrEx10.23:6130-4.

1949. U.S. Office of Economic Opportunity. Community Action Program. *Planning Your Pregnancy.* Washington, DC: GPO, 1970. 15p. leaflet. PrEx10.23:6130-5.

1950. U.S. Women's Bureau. *Abortion Laws.* Washington, DC: The Bureau, 1970. 6p. L13.2:Ab7. Review of the status of state abortion laws and of constitutional challenges to existing laws reveals a strong bias toward the liberalization of such laws.

1951. U.S. Congress. Senate. Committee on Government Operations. Subcommittee on Executive Reorganization and Government Research. "Population Change in the United States and the Development of Family Planning Services." In *Government Research on the Problems of Children and Youth: Background Papers Prepared for the 1970-71 White House Conference on Children and Youth.* 92d Cong., 1st sess., 1971. Committee print. 484p. Y4.G74/6:C43. Part of a collection of papers for the White House Conference on Children and Youth, this paper reviews trends in family size and child spacing, and briefly discusses the implications for poverty. Contraceptive use, illegal abortion and illegitimacy are also touched on. Implications of fertility trends for government population programs are discussed, and current and projected funding is reviewed.

1952. U.S. Congress. Senate. Committee on Labor and Public Welfare. Special Subcommittee on Human Resources. *Declaration of U.S. Policy on Population Stabilization by Voluntary Means, 1971, Hearings on S.J. Res. 108.* 92d Cong., 1st sess., 5 Aug. - 3 Nov. 1971. 834p. Y4.L11/2:P81. Testimony discusses world fertility trends and zero population growth and their implications for government programs and policies relating to family planning. Questions of religious issues and the abortion on demand controversy are addressed. Family planning program goals are reviewed and factors influencing lower infant and maternal mortality rates and illegitimate births are debated. Statement by Ellen Peck describes the media's, particularly women's magazines', romanticized view of maternity.

1953. U.S. Congress. Senate. Committee on Labor and Public Welfare. Special Subcommittee on Human Resources. *Report of the Secretary of Health, Education, and Welfare Submitting Five-Year Plan for Family Planning Services and Population Research Programs.* 92d Cong., 1st sess., 12 Oct. 1971. 560p. Y4.L11/2:F21/3. Presents HEW's five-year plan for population research programs, family planning service delivery, and the family planning statistical program. Appendices review fiscal year 1970 federally supported population research, FDA and AID research programs, family planning needs and cost estimates, and delivery methods for family planning services. Includes statistics on family planning patients by type of provider and estimated unmet need, family planning dropout rates, and projected 1971 and 1975 family planning services by type of provider.

1954. U.S. Government Printing Office. *Social Services, Aging, Family Planning, Handicapped, Medicaid, Nursing Homes, Pensions and Retirement, Poverty, Social Security and Social Welfare.* Washington, DC: GPO, 1971. 35p. GP3.9:78. Lists publications available from the Superintendent of Documents.

1955. U.S. Health Services and Mental Health Administration. *Family Planning Services Project Grants of the National Center for Family Planning Services Policies and Guidelines for Applicants.* Washington, DC: The Administration, 1971. 12p. HE20.2008:F21/971.

1956. U.S. Health Services and Mental Health Administration. *The Social Worker and Family Planning, Based on the Proceedings of the 1969 Annual Institute for Public Health Social*

Workers. Washington, DC: GPO, 1971. 127p. HE20.2752:So1. Conference papers discuss the role of the social worker in family planning and touches on issues such as abortion counseling, medical and cultural aspects of family planning, and training social workers.

1957. U.S. Maternal and Child Health Service. *The Effect of Changes in the State Abortion Laws.* Washington, DC: GPO, 1971. 28p. HE20.2752:Ab7. Analysis of statistics on legal and illegal abortions looks at the effect of the trend toward liberalization of abortion laws. Summarizes state penal codes regarding abortion and presents statistics by state on number of abortions, state or out-of-state residence, and abortions by race, age, and marital status. Also provides data on gestation and morbidity by abortion method.

1958. U.S. Maternal and Child Health Service. *Selected References for Social Workers on Family Planning: An Annotated List.* Washington, DC: GPO, 1971. 38p. HE20.2759:So1. Annotated bibliography lists current books, journal articles, conference proceedings, and federal, state, and international documents on family planning services.

1959. U.S. Office of Economic Opportunity. *Provisional Inventory of Family Planning Clinics in the United States, 1970.* by Center for Family Planning Program Development. Planned Parenthood - World Population. Washington, DC: GPO, 1971. 187p. PrEx10.23:6130-9.

1960. U.S. Congress. House. *Communicable Disease Control Amendments Act of 1972, Conference Report to Accompany S. 3442.* H. Rept. 92-1376, 92d Cong., 2d sess., 1972. 14p. Serial 12974-5. Conference report resolves, among other issues, the Senate amendment increasing the authorized appropriation for project grants and contracts for family planning services under Title X of the Public Health Service Act.

1961. U.S. Congress. House. *Social Security Amendments of 1972, Conference Report to Accompany H.R. 1.* H. Rept. 92-1605, 92d Cong., 2d sess., 1972. 67p. Serial 12974-7. Settles conflicting House and Senate amendments to a bill to change programs under OASDI, AFDC and other Social Security Act programs including family planning services to AFDC recipients.

1962. U.S. Congress. Senate. Committee on Labor and Public Welfare. Special Subcommittee on Human Resources. *Family Planning Services Authorization, Fiscal Year 1973, Hearing.* 92d Cong., 2d sess., 17 Apr. 1972. 134p. Y4.L11/2:F21/4. Testimony on funding for Title X of the Public Health Service Act focuses on provision of family planning services and research, and on the costs of providing these services.

1963. U.S. Congress. Senate. Committee on Labor and Public Welfare. Special Subcommittee on Human Resources. *Progress Report on the Five-Year Plan for Family Planning Services and Population Research Programs.* 92d Cong., 2d sess., 1972. Committee print. 157p. Y4.L11/2:F21/3/972. Report on HEW family planning and population research and education programs details amount of grants and name of service provider or research project. Also provides some basic statistics on family planning services and characteristics of recipients.

1964. U.S. Dept. of Housing and Urban Development. *Family Planning.* Washington, DC: GPO, 1972. 4 vol. HH1.2:F21. Four part guide details planning and administration of family planning programs as part of a local health care system. Part one provides background information on family planning, part two focuses on planning, organization of local resources, and grant applications, part three discusses personnel and facilities, and part four covers program evaluation and outreach.

1965. U.S. Congress. House. Committee on Foreign Affairs. *U.S. Aid to Population/Family Planning in Asia.* 93rd Cong., 1st sess., 1973. Committee print. 50p. Y4.F76/1:As4/10. Evaluation of population control programs in Korea, the Philippines, Indonesia, Thailand, and Malaysia provides information, by country, on population pressures, policies and programs, and AID and other sources of foreign assistance. The progress and problems of the programs and the problems of U.S. assistance are reviewed. The report urges coordination of AID population, health and nutrition programs.

1966. U.S. Congress. House. Committee on Government Operations. Intergovernmental Relations Subcommittee. *Regulation of Medical Devices (Intrauterine Contraceptive Devices), Hearing.* 93rd Cong., 1st sess., 30 May- 13 June 1973. 576p. Y4.G74/7:M46. Hearing on FDA regulation of medical devices focuses on IUDs examining their use and the accounts of IUD-related morbidity and mortality. Actions which should be taken by the FDA to regulate IUDs are reviewed.

1967. U.S. Congress. House. Committee on Interstate and Foreign Commerce. *Health Programs Extension Act of 1973, Report to Accompany H.R. 7806.* H. Rept. 93-227, 93d Cong., 1st sess., 1973. 35p. Serial 13020-2. Reports legislation to temporarily extend the authority for twelve health-related programs including family planning programs under Title X of the PHSA. An amendment to the bill would allow institutions receiving federal funds to refuse to allow sterilization procedures or abortions if it is contrary to the religious or moral beliefs of the personnel or institution.

1968. U.S. Congress. House. Committee on Interstate and Foreign Commerce. Subcommittee on Public Health and Environment. *Oversight of HEW Health Programs, Hearing.* 93rd Cong., 1st sess., 1 Mar. 1973. 126p. Y4.In8/4:93-7. Oversight hearing on HEW health programs examines, among other programs, family planning services and nurse recruitment activities.

1969. U.S. Congress. Senate. Committee on Land and Public Welfare. Special Subcommittee on Human Resources. *Family Planning Services and Population Research Amendments of 1973, Hearings on S. 1708 and S. 1632.* 93rd Cong., 1st sess., May 1973. 761p. Y4.L11/2:F21/2/973. Witnesses on federal family planning services and population research programs include representatives from HEW on program focus and results, Planned Parenthood and other family planning service providers on family planning needs, and religious groups on the government role in family planning. Among the issues debated are abortion and parental rights.

1970. U.S. Congress. Senate. Committee on Labor and Public Welfare. Subcommittee on Health. *Health Care in China, 1973, Hearing.* 93d Cong., 1st sess., 4 May 1973. 265p. Y4.L11/2:C44/973. Informative hearing on health care in China focuses on family planning policy and programs, acupuncture, and cooperative day care. A number of articles discussing population policy, social services and health services in China are included in the hearing record.

1971. U.S. Congress. Senate. Committee on Labor and Public Welfare. Subcommittee on Health. *Medical Device Amendments, 1973, Hearings on S. 2368, S. 1446, S. 1337.* 93d Cong., 1st sess., 14,17 Sept. 1973. 1184p. Y4.L11/2:M46/17/973. Hearing on legislation to amend the federal Food, Drug and Cosmetic Act discusses the need to ensure the safety of medical devices. The medical problems associated with intrauterine devices (IUDs) and the lack of FDA oversight on their availability and advertising are discussed in depth.

1972. U.S. Congress. Senate. Committee on Labor and Public Welfare. Subcommittee on Health. *Quality of Health Care - Human Experimentation, 1973, Part 1, Hearings.* 93d Cong., 1st sess., 21,22 Feb. 1973. 336p. Y4.L11/2:H34/32/973/pt.1. Hearing testimony discusses the protection of human subjects in drug research and particularly focuses on the misuse of Depo-Provera and diethylstilbestrol(DES) as contraceptives. Evidence of widespread, unapproved use of these drugs is examined and the FDA's role in curbing their use is discussed.

1973.   U.S. Congress. Senate. Committee on the Judiciary. Subcommittee on Criminal Law and Procedures. *Reform of the Federal Criminal Laws, Hearing on S. 1 and S. 1400, Part IX.* 93d Cong., 1st sess., 25 July - 27 Sept. 1973. 6479-6803pp. Y4.J89/2:C86/12/pt.9. Hearing on the federal criminal code examines primarily the death penalty and the insanity defense. One point of debate is the definition of "human being" and "person" as it would affect the criminal status of induced abortion. An anti-abortion witness provides statements and reprints of articles supporting the criminalization of abortion. Articles describe the failure of liberal abortion policies in Japan and present the medical, social and ethical issues of abortion and fetal experimentation.

1974.   U.S. General Accounting Office. *Assistance to Family Planning Programs in Southeast Asia, Agency for International Development: Report to Congress.* Washington, DC: The Office, 1973. 53p. GA1.13:F21. Review of the use of funds under Title X of the Foreign Assistance Act for family planning programs in Laos, the Philippines, Thailand, and Indonesia points out conflicts between family planning and area social and political beliefs. The use of the funds by AID for maternal and child welfare programs prompts a recommendation for coordination of family planning, health, and nutrition programs under Title X.

1975.   U.S. Congress. House. *Health Revenue Sharing and Health Services Act of 1974, Conference Report to Accompany H.R. 14214.* H. Rept. 93-1524, 93rd Cong., 2d sess., 1974. 102p. Serial 13061-11. Among the programs authorized in the bill discussed are family planning programs and rape prevention and control programs. Major differences existed in the House and Senate versions relating to family planning program administration, and the rape prevention and control program was added by the Senate.

1976.   U.S. Congress. House. Committee on Interstate and Foreign Commerce. Subcommittee on Public Health and Environment. *Health Services and Health Revenue Sharing, Part 2, Hearings on H.R. 11511, H.R. 11518, H.R. 11845, H.R. 12892.* 93d Cong., 2d sess., 14 - 22 Feb. 1974. 663-1307pp. Y4.In8/14:93-87. Family planning funding is among the topics discussed by hearing witnesses who mostly support the extension and expansion of family planning services under the Family Planning Services and Population Act of 1970. Witnesses discuss the need for contraceptive research, the interaction of family planning and poverty, and the benefits under the program to date. Graphics included in the hearing record illustrate the progress in family planning under federal programs between 1967 and 1973 and the characteristics of the population served. The need to involve women in contraceptive development and to ensure the safety of contraceptive drugs is noted.

1977.   U.S. Congress. Senate. Committee on the Judiciary. Subcommittee on Constitutional Amendments. *Abortion, Part 1, Hearings on S.J.Res. 119 and S.J.Res. 130.* 93rd Cong., 2d sess., 6 March - 10 April 1974. 729p. Y4.J89/2:Ab7/pt.1. Testimony and extensive supporting statements primarily reflect the views of a multitude of religious denominations on the abortion issue and on the need for an amendment to the Constitution to protect the fetus. Testimony for the amendment focuses on moral issues while testimony against cites political and practical implementation issues.

1978.   U.S. Congress. Senate. Committee on the Judiciary. Subcommittee on Constitutional Amendments. *Abortion, Part 2, Hearings on S.J. Res. 119 and S.J. Res. 130.* 93d Cong., 2d sess., 24 July 1974. 999p. Y4.J89/2:Ab7/pt.2. Second part of hearings present testimony, mostly opposed, on a proposed constitutional amendment guaranteeing the fetus a "right to life." The medical and psychological consequences of abortion and denial of abortion are examined, and the preservation of legalized abortion in the case of genetic defects is defended. A wealth of articles, papers, and other material submitted for the record detail the effects of liberal abortion laws on fertility, women's physical and mental health, and use of contraception. Trends in the number of women crossing state lines for abortions is also documented as are characteristics of reported abortions. The issue of abortion in rape cases is also examined.

1979. U.S. Congress. Senate. Committee on the Judiciary. Subcommittee on Constitutional Amendments. *Abortion, Part 3, Hearings on S.J. Res. 119 and S.J. Res. 130.* 93d Cong., 2d sess., 21 Aug. - 8 Oct. 1974. 475p. Y4.J89/2:Ab7/pt.3. Continued hearings on a proposed constitutional amendment prohibiting abortion includes testimony for both sides of the issue although primarily anti-abortion in tenor. Among the witnesses are representatives of Feminists for Life and Catholics for a Free Choice as well as law school professors who discuss the constitutionality of the *Roe v. Wade* decision and the proposed amendment. A considerable number of anti-abortion articles and reports are reprinted in the hearing record.

1980. U.S. Congressional Research Service. *China's Experience in Population Control, the Elusive Model.* Washington, DC: GPO, 1974. 45p. Y4.F76/1:C44/13. Background report on the politics and policies of population control in China discusses the obstacles overcome in establishing a policy of limiting family size. The report addresses the relationship between the changing role of women and the success of family planning policies and outlines the role of the health system and the means of fertility control.

1981. U.S. National Center for Family Planning Services. *Family Planning, Contraception, and Voluntary Sterilization: An Analysis of Laws and Policies in the United States, Each State and Jurisdiction (as of September 1971.)* Washington, DC: GPO, 1974. 337p. HE20.5102:F21. Summarizes federal laws and policies on family planning, contraception, and voluntary sterilization, and profiles the programs involved. Also discusses trends and variations in state laws governing family planning services, particularly as they relate to eligibility requirements and minors. State health and welfare policies related to birth control are reviewed, and statistics on state family planning expenditures are provided.

1982. U.S. National Library of Medicine. *Adverse Effects of Oral Contraceptives, Jan. 1970 - June 1974, 943 Citations.* by Geraldine D. Nowak. Washington, DC: GPO, 1974. 66p. HE20.3614/2:74-20. Literature search provides citations from the MEDLARS database on adverse effects of oral contraceptives.

1983. U.S. Bureau of Community Health Service. *The Extra Advantages of Family Planning.* Washington, DC: GPO, 1975. 9p. leaflet. HE20.5102:F21/4.

1984. U.S. Bureau of Community Health Services. *Family Planning and Health.* Washington, DC: GPO, 1975. 10p. leaflet. HE20.5102:F21/3.

1985. U.S. Bureau of Community Health Services. *Family Planning for Completed Families.* Washington, DC: GPO, 1975. 8p. leaflet. HE20.5102:F21/6.

1986. U.S. Bureau of Community Health Services. *International MCH Projects, Research to Improve Services for Mothers and Children.* Washington, DC: GPO, 1975. 36p. HE20.5102:In8. Summary of research projects on maternal and child health under the Special Foreign Currency Program includes a study of the effect of an intensive contraception program on abortion rates in Yugoslavia.

1987.   U.S. Bureau of Community Health Services. *Planning Your Future Includes Family Planning.* Washington, DC: GPO, 1975. 9p. leaflet. HE20.5102:F21/5.

1988.   U.S. Bureau of Community Health Services. *Practical Suggestions for Family Planning Education.* Washington, DC: GPO, 1975. 93p. HE 20.5102:F21/2. Guide to structuring family planning education programs covers approaching clients, use of A/V materials, and basic program content. Includes a bibliography.

1989.   U.S. Bureau of the Census. International Statistical Programs Center and U.S. Agency for International Development. *Family Planning Statistics: 1965 to 1973, Africa, Asia, Latin America.* Washington, DC: GPO, 1975. 74p. C56.226:FP-73. Data on new acceptors of family planning services in 50 countries in Africa, Asia, and Latin America for 1965-73 includes statistics on client revisits and contraceptives distributed by type of contraceptive.

1990.   U.S. Commission on Civil Rights. *Constitutional Aspects of the Right to Limit Childbearing.* Washington, DC: The Commission, 1975. 223p. CR1.2:C43. Review of the abortion issue from a legal and constitutional perspective examines in detail proposed constitutional amendments to limit abortion. Appendices include texts of proposed constitutional amendments to restrict abortions and the text of the Supreme Court decisions in *Roe v. Wade* and *Doe v. Bolton.*

1991.   U.S. Congress. House. Committee on Interstate and Foreign Commerce. *Health Revenue Sharing and Health Services Act of 1975, Report Together with Separate, Additional and Minority Views to Accompany H.R. 4925.* H. Rept. 94-192, 94th Cong., 1st sess., 1975. 252p. Serial 13099-3. Among the programs authorized in the bill reported are Title X family planning programs and rape prevention and control programs. Background information is provided on the history of and need for each program and on the intent of the legislation.

1992.   U.S. Congress. House. Committee on Interstate and Foreign Commerce. Subcommittee on Health and the Environment. *Health Services Programs, Hearing.* 94th Cong., 1st sess., 19 Feb. 1975. 278p. Y4.In8/4:94-4. Among the health services programs discussed by hearing witnesses is federal family planning revenue sharing. The bills under consideration would also authorize the establishment of a National Center for the Prevention and Control of Rape. Brief testimony supports funding for family planning services and touches on the issue of federal funding of abortion. Policy on natural family planning methods is discussed. Testimony also briefly discusses maternal and child health programs and supports the need for research and demonstration programs to address the problem of rape.

1993.   U.S. Congress. Senate. Committee on Labor and Public Welfare. Subcommittee on Health and U.S. Congress. Senate. Committee on the Judiciary. Subcommittee on Administrative Practice and Procedure. *Food and Drug Administration Practice and Procedure, 1975, Joint Hearings.* 94th Cong., 1st sess., 28,29 Jan. 1975. 449p. Y4.L11/2:F73/4/975. First day of hearings on FDA practices examines the issues surrounding the marketing of the Dalkon Shield IUD. Advisory committee reports and journal articles detailing the health risks of the Dalkon Shield are included in the hearing record. Testimony presents a number of views on the adequacy of the FDA's response to reported problems with the IUD.

1994.   U.S. Congress. Senate. Committee on the Judiciary. Subcommittee on Constitutional Amendments. *Abortion, Part IV, Hearings on S.J. Res. 6, S.J. Res. 10 and 11, and S.J. Res. 91.* 94th Cong., 1st sess., 10 Mar. - 8 July 1975. 1001p. Y4.J89/2:Ab7/pt.4. Hearings on proposed constitutional amendments relating to abortion presents arguments from both sides of the legalized abortion issue. Abortion court cases are examined and in particular the issue or women's rights versus rights of the father and the fetus are explored. Supporters of abortion alternatives and pregnancy support services also express their views. Statements and resolutions on legalized abortion from religious, medical, and other groups are included in the hearing record. Medical, ethical, and legal arguments are presented. The action, effectiveness, and safety of contraceptive methods are discussed.

1995. U.S. General Accounting Office. *Improving Federally Assisted Family Planning Programs, Department of Health, Education and Welfare.* Washington, DC: The Office, 1975. 73p. GA1.13:MWD-75-25. Review of federally assisted family planning programs in Illinois, Pennsylvania, and Texas found that delivery of services to welfare recipients needs to be improved as does the economy and efficiency of programs. A report of a survey of welfare recipients of childbearing age describes the number using family planning services, the number wishing to use such services, and how recipients learned of federally supported services.

1996. U.S. Public Health Service. *An Inventory of Family Planning Service Sites: Institutional Characteristics, United States, 1974.* Washington, DC: GPO, 1975. 47p. HE20.6209:14/15. Data from the National Inventory of Family Planning Services describes service sites' geographic and physical location, the agency or project responsible for its operation, funding source, primary purpose, length of time in operation, medical services performed, and contraceptive methods provided.

1997. U.S. Bureau of Community Health Services. *Family Planning Methods of Contraception.* Washington, DC: GPO, 1976. leaflet. HE20.5102:C76/976. Earlier edition published in 1973.

1998. U.S. Bureau of Community Health Services. *A Guidebook for Family Planning Education.* Washington, DC: GPO, 1976. 93p. HE20.5108:F21/2. Objectives and approaches to incorporating family planning education into provision of family planning services.

1999. U.S. Bureau of Community Health Services. *A Self-Instructional Booklet to Aid in the Understanding of Female Physical Examination for Contraception.* Rockville, MD: The Bureau, 1976. 19p. HE20.5102:C76/2.

2000. U.S. Bureau of Community Health Services. *A Self-Instruction Booklet to Aid in Understanding Female Sterilization.* Rockville, MD: The Bureau, 1976. 13p. HE20.5102:St4.

2001. U.S. Congress. House. Committee on Government Operations. *Use of Advisory Committee by the Food and Drug Administration, Eleventh Report.* H. Rept. 94-787, 94th Cong., 2d sess., 1976. 91p. Serial 13136-2. Critical report on the FDA's use of advisory committees specifically addresses the work of committees on DES for use as a "morning after" birth control drug and on the contraceptive Depo-Provera.

2002. U.S. Congress. House. Committee on Intergovernmental Relations. *U.S. Development Aid Programs in West Africa.* by John H. Sullivan and John C. Chester. 94th Cong., 2d sess., 22 Mar. 1976. Committee print. 56p. Y.4.In8/16:Af8. Part one of this staff survey mission report examines family planning programs in Nigeria, Ghana, Sierra Leone, Ivory Coast, Upper Volta, and Senegal. Political reluctance among country leaders to commit to family planning projects is noted, and the need to integrate family planning and health services is stressed. United States aid to family planning programs in each country is detailed. The report also criticizes the operations of the International Planned Parenthood Federation.

2003. U.S. Congress. House. Committee on Post Office and Civil Service. Subcommittee on Census and Population. *Population, Hearings.* 94th Cong., 1st and 2d sess., 23 Oct. 1975 - 20 July 1976. 266p. Y4.P84/10:94-65. Within this hearing focusing on population research is support for governmental subsidized family planning programs and discussion of the problems of teenage pregnancy. Changing societal attitudes toward the role of women and family size, and access to family planning services are reviewed. Some discussion of abortion rates and policy is presented. The problems of poverty in Appalachia and birth rates are examined. Problems of illegal immigrants and trends in migration are also reviewed.

2004. U.S. Congress. House. Committee on the Judiciary. Subcommittee on Civil and Constitutional Rights. *Proposed Constitutional Amendments on Abortion, Hearings.* 94th Cong., 2d sess., 4 Feb. - 26 March 1976. 1089p. Y4.J89/1:94-46/pt.1-2. Hearing on proposed constitutional amendments on abortion examines the constitutional, moral, philosophical, and medical issues, and provides the *Doe v. Bolton* and *Roe v. Wade* decisions and the texts to over sixty resolutions on abortion. The various theological approaches to the beginning of life are a major point of discussion as are the various legal approaches to abortion control.

2005. U.S. Dept. of Health, Education and Welfare. Office of the Assistant Secretary for Planning and Evaluation/Health. *Improving Family Planning Services for Teenagers.* by Urban and Rural Systems Associates. Washington, DC: The Office, 1976. 129p. HE1.2:F21/4. Study examined factors which affect accessibility of family planning clinics to teens, actions to attract teens to clinics, and the success of efforts so far. Also discusses barriers to effectively reaching teens such as community attitude and legislation.

2006. U.S. Dept. of Health, Education, and Welfare. Office of the Assistant Secretary for Planning and Evaluation/Health. *Improving Family Planning Services for Teenagers: Executive Summary.* by Urban and Rural Systems Associates. Washington, DC: The Office, 1976. 31p. HE1.2:F21/4/sum. Study of the provision of family planning services for teenagers found that in most cases public supported services were not effective in reaching this population group, and that most clinics lacked a strong commitment to providing contraceptive care to teenagers.

2007. U.S. Bureau of Community Health Services. *Program Guidelines for Project Grants for Family Planning Services under Section 1001, Public Health Service Act.* Rockville, MD: The Bureau, 1977. 58p. HE20.5108:F21/977. Earlier edition published in 1976.

2008. U.S. Center for Population Research. Contraceptive Development Branch. *Proceedings, Drug Delivery Systems.* Washington, DC: GPO, 1977. 414p. HE20.3352:D84. Workshop on research into new systems for delivery of contraceptive drugs describes local delivery of drugs to the uterus or cervix by means of removable devices, and systematic delivery from biodegradable implants or injectable microcapsules.

2009. U.S. Commission on Civil Rights. Wyoming Advisory Committee. *Abortion Services in Wyoming.* Washington, DC: GPO, 1977. 66p. CR1.2:Ab7. Investigation into the availability of abortion services in Wyoming found that the lack of abortion services at Wyoming public hospitals resulted in 50% of women having abortions going out-of-state compared to 10% nationally. Several of the hospitals had unconstitutional prohibitions or regulations regarding abortions in their by laws.

2010. U.S. Congress. House. Committee on International Relations. *Foreign Assistance Legislation for Fiscal Year 1978, Part 1, Hearings.* 95th Cong., 1st sess., 16 Mar. - 18 Apr. 1977. 419p. Y4.In8/16:F76/8/978/pt.1. Hearing on foreign assistance legislation presents lengthy discussion of population planning programs. Supporters of population assistance programs point to a growing acceptance of family planning and to the need to include women in AID family planning programs. Opponents reject the contraceptive programs as anti-family and oppose funding of International Planned Parenthood Federation over the abortion issue. Much of the testimony for and against population planning assistance focuses on the role of the IPPF.

2011. U.S. General Accounting Office. *Problems in Administration of Family Planning Programs in Region VIII, Department of Health, Education, and Welfare.* Washington, DC: The Office, 1977. 34p. GA1.13:HRD-77-42. Report on administrative problems in the HEW Region VIII Family Planning Program discusses miscommunication regarding abortion guidelines.

2012. U.S. Public Health Service. *Utilization of Family Planning Services by Currently Married Women 15 - 44 Years of Age, United States, 1973.* Washington, DC: GPO, 1977. 36p. HE20.6209:23/1. Race, age, and socioeconomic variables are analyzed for married women using family planning services.

2013. U.S. Bureau of Community Health Services. *Evaluation Handbook for Family Planning Programs.* by Jack Reynolds, et al. Washington, DC: GPO, 1978. 337p. HE20.5108:F21/3. Detailed guide to conducting an evaluation of services includes examples of program design and performance evaluation of family planning projects.

2014. U.S. Bureau of Community Health Services. Office for Family Planning. *Family Planning, Contraception, Voluntary Sterilization and Abortion: An Analysis of Laws and Policies in the United States, Each State and Jurisdiction (as of October 1, 1976 with 1978 Addenda).* by Alan Guttmacher Institute. Washington, DC: GPO, 1978. 380p. HE20.5102:F21/976. Analysis of federal and state laws and policies relating to family planning, contraception, voluntary sterilization and abortion pays particular attention to services to minors and to eligibility requirements. Includes profiles of state laws and agency policies on birth control and abortion services, and presents statistics on family planning expenditures by state.

2015. U.S. Congress. House. Committee on Interstate and Foreign Commerce. *Health Services Amendments of 1978, Report Together with Separate Views to Accompany H.R. 12370.* H. Rept. 95-1191, 95th Cong., 2d sess., 1978. 80p. Serial 13201-7. Reports a bill authorizing health service programs including Title X family planning programs activities. Background information on the federal programs providing family planning services is provided.

2016. U.S. Congress. House. Select Committee on Population. *Depo-Provera Debate, Hearings.* 95th Cong., 2d sess., 8-10 Aug. 1978. 794p. Y4.P81:95/12. Hearing testimony explores the debate over the FDA's decision against the use of Depo-Provera (medroxyprogesterone acetate) as a contraceptive. The international implications of the FDA decision and the history of the FDA's action on Depo-Provera focuses in particular on its advantages for developing countries with high fertility rates. Appendix materials provide details of research on Depo-Provera's possible health risks.

2017. U.S. Congress. House. Select Committee on Population. *Fertility and Contraception in America: Contraceptive Technology and Development, Hearings, Volume III.* 95th Cong., 2nd sess., 7-9 Mar. 1978. 599p. Y4.P81:95/4. Representatives from the FDA, research institutes, pharmaceutical companies, and professors in the field of obstetrics/gynecology discuss the effectiveness of current contraception methods, the need for better methods, and the process of developing them. The current status of funding for contraceptive research is reviewed and areas where more funds are needed are highlighted. FDA approval of Depo-Provera is discussed. Provides statistics on pregnancy rates by contraception methods, and diaphragm use by age, ethnicity, marital status and number of previous pregnancies.

2018.   U.S. Congress. House. Select Committee on Population. *Fertility and Contraception in America: Domestic Fertility Trends and Family Planning Services, Hearings, Volume I.* 95th Cong., 2nd sess., 21 Feb. - 16 June 1978. 535p. Y4.P81:95/2. Topics covered in this hearing on family planning services include abortion, the effectiveness of natural family planning methods, counseling services for pregnant women, family planning and AID, the best way to meet family planning needs in the U.S., and the need for research and services for infertility. The teenage pregnancy issue is a common theme.

2019.   U.S. Congress. House. Select Committee on Population. *Population and Development: Overview of Trends, Consequences, Perspectives, and Issues, Hearings, Volume 1.* 95th Cong., 2d sess., 18-20 Apr. 1978. 770p. Y4.P81:95/6. Hearing debates policies on population control and development of countries to sustain their people. Among the topics discussed are the desire of LDCs for population control assistance and the role contraceptives should play. Some witnesses charge that women in LDCs are used as guinea pigs for contraceptive testing. The issue of abortion is raised in some testimony. Human rights and coercive population control programs are also touched on. Natural methods for child spacing, particularly breast feeding, are promoted. The need to include women in development efforts is also explored.

2020.   U.S. Congress. House. Select Committee on Population. *Population and Development: Research in Population and Development, Needs and Capacities, Vol. 3, Hearings.* 95th Cong., 2d sess., 2-4 May 1978. 575p. Y4.P81:95/8. Testimony on the current state of fertility and contraceptive research in developing countries stresses the risks and benefits of contraceptive use versus childbearing for women in poor, underdeveloped areas. Needed areas of research, including the effect of oral contraception on malnourished women, are discussed. Of particular interest is a report on cultural attitudes in LDC's on contraception, abortion, sterilization, and family size. The Agency for International Development's policies and funding levels are also examined.

2021.   U.S. Congress. House. Select Committee on Population. *Population and Development: Status and Trends of Family Planning/Population Programs in Developing Countries, Vol. 2, Hearings.* 95th Cong., 2d sess., 25-27 Apr. 1978. 672p. Y4.P81:95/7. Hearing exploring the role of the Agency for International Development in family planning programs focuses specifically on family planning needs and programs in Latin America, Columbia, Brazil, Kenya, Egypt, Bangladesh and Asia. The need for contraceptives, particularly Depo-Provera, and the role of cultural attitudes are discussed. The need to utilize women in implementing family planning and maternal and child health programs is also briefly considered. The involvement of non-U.S. funded groups in supporting family planning services is described for the various countries represented. A list of AID population and family planning projects funded between 1965 and 1975 provides a description of the project, the dollars funded, and the completion date.

2022.   U.S. Congress. House. Select Committee on Population. *Population and Development Assistance, Report.* 95th Cong., 2d sess., 1978. 124p. Y4.P81:95/D. Report of the findings from hearings before the Select Committee on Population reviews the role of population planning in development programs and the policy of AID on population planning. The acceptance of family planning in developing countries and the role of the IPPF is discussed. Contraceptive research and development is reviewed with particular attention to the risks and benefits of Depo-Provera. Organizational problems within AID are summarized and recommendations for AID policy are presented.

2023. U.S. Congress. Senate. Committee on Human Resources. *Voluntary Family Planning Services, Population Research, and Sudden Infant Death Syndrome Amendments of 1978, Report to Accompany S. 2522.* S. Rept. 95-822, 95th Cong., 2d sess., 1978. 97p. Serial 13197-3. Reports a bill to increase appropriations for family planning services, education and research and to emphasize service to sexually active adolescents. Also included is a directive to stress natural family planning methods and a clause prohibiting project employees from being compelled to act regarding abortion or sterilization when it is against their personal conscience. Gives a basic overview of family planning programs under Title X of the PHSA and of organizational changes made by S. 2522.

2024. U.S. Congress. Senate. Committee on Human Resources. Subcommittee on Child and Human Development. *Family Planning Services and Population Research Act Extension of 1978, Hearing on S. 2522.* 95th Cong., 2nd sess., 24 Feb. 1978. 889p. Y4.H88:F21. Hearing on extending the Family Planning Services and Population Research Act of 1970 for an additional five years discusses coordination of federally funded family planning programs and the special problems of providing services for teenagers. Also examines the FDA and contraceptive approval process and current trends in contraceptive research and development. Witnesses attack the Planned Parenthood organization.

2025. U.S. Congress. Senate. Select Committee on Small Business. Subcommittee on Monopoly and Anticompetitive Activities. *Competitive Problems in the Drug Industry: The Risks and Benefits of Oral Contraceptives.* by Congressional Research Service. 95th Cong., 2d sess., 1978. 124p. CIS78-S722-11. Using testimony from the 1970 hearing before the subcommittee this report describes health issues related to contraceptive use. Recent research relating contraceptive drug use to health problems is examined and the FDA's regulatory actions are reviewed. The FDA's oral contraceptive labeling requirements from the *Federal Register* (31 June 1978) are reprinted.

2026. U.S. Dept. of Health, Education, and Welfare. *A Report on Family Planning Services and Population Research.* Washington, DC: GPO, 1978. 160p. HE1.2:F21/5. Descriptive report looks at the state of family planning and at progress made since 1971. The focus is on use patterns of existing programs with little commentary on deficiencies in the current system.

2027. U.S. Food and Drug Administration. *Contraception: Comparing the Options.* Washington, DC: GPO, 1978. chart. HE20.4002:C76.

2028. U.S. National Center for Health Statistics. *Directory, Family Planning Service Sites, United States.* Washington, DC: GPO, 1978. 177p. HE20.6202:F21/2.

2029. U.S. National Library Of Medicine. *Adverse Effects of Oral Contraceptives.* by Julia F. Sollenberger. Washington, DC: GPO, 1978. 49p. HE20.3614/2:78-9. English language citations from the MEDLINE database for the period July 1974 through December 1977 review the adverse effects of oral contraceptives.

2030. U.S. Public Health Service. *Information for Women: Your Sterilization Operation.* Washington, DC: GPO, 1978. 9p. HE20.8:St4/2. Basic information on birth control options and on sterilization procedures.

2031. U.S. Bureau of Community Health Services. *Catalog of Family Planning Materials.* Washington, DC: GPO, 1979. 144p. HE20.5102:F21/8. Bibliography lists booklets and audiovisual materials on family planning.

2032.   U.S. Bureau of Community Health Services. *The Choice is Yours.* Washington, DC: GPO, 1979. 22p. HE20.5102:C45. Information on birth control methods is presented in a quiz format.

2033.   U.S. Bureau of Community Health Services. *Natural Family Planning.* Washington, DC: GPO, 1979. leaflet. HE20.5102:F21/9.

2034.   U.S. Bureau of Community Health Services. Office of Family Planning. *A Decision-Making Approach to Sex Education: A Curriculum Guide and Implementation Manual for a Model Program with Adolescent and Parents.* Washington, DC: GPO, 1979. 296p. HE20.5108:Se9.

2035.   U.S. Congress. House. Committee on Interstate and Foreign Commerce. *Technical Corrections to Health Laws, Report to Accompany S.J. Res. 14.* H. Rept. 96-187, 96th Cong., 1st sess., 1979. 33p. Serial 13293. Technical corrections to 95th Congress legislation affecting the PHSA includes a corrected appropriation of $120.8 million for Title X family planning and population research activities. The appropriation was erroneously printed as $3.6 million.

2036.   U.S. Congress. House. Select Committee on Population. *Final Report of the Select Committee on Population.* H. Rept. 95-1842, 95th Cong., 2d sess., 1979. 75p. Serial 13203-3. Report provides an overview of U.S. population facts and trends including fertility, contraceptive use, adolescent pregnancy, legal and illegal immigration, and domestic consequences of U.S. population changes. The report also examines population planning in LDCs and the role of AID. Each section is followed by recommendations on program administration and funding, program strategies, and research needs. The problems in the area of adolescent contraception and sex education are particularly emphasized.

2037.   U.S. Congress. Senate. Committee on Appropriation. *Continuing Appropriations, 1980, Report to Accompany H.J. Res. 402.* S. Rept. 96-334, 96th Cong., 1st sess., 1979. 10p. Serial 13245. One aspect of the bill reported here is a continuation of a prohibition of the use of federal funds appropriated for Labor-HEW, Defense, Foreign Operations and the District of Columbia for abortion.

2038.   U.S. Food and Drug Administration. The Medical Device and Drug Advisory Committee on Obstetrics and Gynecology. *Second Report on Intrauterine Contraceptive Devices.* Washington, DC: GPO, 1979. 102p. HE20.4002:In8. Update of the 1968 report on IUDs (1930) reviews recent research on their history, biologic action, utilization and effectiveness, adverse reactions, chemical management, and regulation. Includes a bibliography of 297 references.

2039.   U.S. Public Health Service. *Contraceptive Utilizations, United States.* Washington, DC: GPO, 1979. 48p. HE20.6209:23/2. Report of data on contraceptive usage by married women, never married women with offspring, and widowed, divorced, and separated women examines contraceptive methods used by race, age, and socioeconomic variables.

2040.   U.S. Public Health Service. *Patterns of Aggregate and Individual Changes in Contraceptive Practice, United States, 1965-1975.* Washington, DC: GPO, 1979. 23p. HE20.6209:3/7. Analyzes data on contraceptive methods used by couples in their first marriage from 1965 to 1975 and on changes in the choice of contraceptive method of women interviewed in 1970 and 1975.

2041.   U.S. Agency for International Development. Bureau for Asia. *Third Evaluation of the Thailand National Family Planning Program.* A.I.D. Program Evaluation Report no. 3.

Washington, DC: The Agency, 1980. 111p. S18.52/4:3. Description and evaluation of the National Family Planning Program in Thailand, which began in 1971, discusses programs, funds, results, and recommendations for the future.

2042. U.S. Army. *Contraception.* DA Pamphlet 40-10. Washington, DC: The Department, 1980. 20p. D101.22:40-10. Cutesy pamphlet reviews contraceptive methods.

2043. U.S. Bureau of Community Health Services. *Can You Picture Birth Control for Teens?* Washington, DC: GPO, 1980. leaflet. HE20.5102:B53.

2044. U.S. Bureau of Community Health Services. *Choices: You and Sex.* Rockville, MD: The Bureau, 1980. 16p. HE20.5102:C45/2.

2045. U.S. Bureau of Community Health Services. *Family Planning in Primary Care Settings: Guidelines for Non-Title-X BCHS Projects Providing Family Planning Services.* Rockville, MD: The Bureau, 1980. 28p. HE20.5108:F21/4. Basic information on approaches to providing education, counseling, and medical services for family planning specifically addresses dealing with adolescents.

2046. U.S. Bureau of Community Health Services. *Family Planning Services: A Guide for Client Education.* by Los Angeles Regional Family Planning Council, Inc. Washington, DC: GPO, 1980. 225p. HE20.5108:F21/6. Detailed guidelines for family planning client education during visits to clinics covers topics of contraception, cancer, and sexually transmitted diseases.

2047. U.S. Bureau of Community Health Services. *Have You Solved the Body Puzzle?* Washington, DC: GPO, 1980. leaflet. HE20.5102:B53/2.

2048. U.S. Bureau of Community Health Services. *Here's the Word on Birth Control for Teens.* Washington, DC: GPO, 1980. leaflet. HE20.5102:B53/4.

2049. U.S. Bureau of Community Health Services. *Many Teens Are Saying "No."* Washington, DC: GPO, 1980. leaflet. HE20.5102:N66/2.

2050. U.S. Bureau of Community Health Services. *Methods of Contraception Including Reproductive Anatomy and Physiology.* by Planned Parenthood Federation of America. Rockville, MD: The Bureau, 1980? 60p. HE20.5102:C76/4. Flip boards outline methods of contraception with illustrations.

2051. U.S. Bureau of Community Health Services. *Project Teen Concern: An Implementation Manual for an Educational Program to Prevent Premature Parenthood and Venereal Disease.* Washington, DC: GPO, 1980. 152p. HE20.5108:T22. Description of a model sex education program aimed at preventing teenage pregnancy and venereal disease includes details on class sessions and guidance on building community support.

2052. U.S. Bureau of Community Health Services. *You'd Be Amazed How Many Teens Say "No."* Washington, DC: GPO, 1980. leaflet. HE20.5102:N66.

2053. U.S. Centers for Disease Control. Family Planning Evaluation Division. *Surgical Sterilization Surveillance: Hysterectomy in Women Aged 15-44.* Atlanta: The Center, 1980. 15p. HE20.7011/30-2:970-75. Summary statistics for 1970 to 1975 on women obtaining hysterectomies are presented by geographic region, age, race, marital status, timing in relation to pregnancy, surgical approach, length of hospital stay, and characteristics of hospital.

2054. U.S. Congress. House. Committee on Foreign Affairs. Subcommittee on International Economic Policy and Trade. *Export of Hazardous Products, Hearings on H.R. 6587.* 96th Cong., 2d sess., 5 June - 9 Sept. 1980. 421p. Y4.F76/1:H33. Hearing on legislation to amend the Export Administration Act of 1979 to control export of substances banned in the U.S. includes considerable discussion of the available risk/benefit information on Depo-Provera. The advantages of the injectable contraceptive for use in developing countries are put forward by supporters, while opponents point to possible risks to users and to breast-fed infants.

2055. U.S. Congress. Senate. Committee on Foreign Relations. *World Population Trends, Hearings on U.S. Population Policy and Programs.* 96th Cong., 2d sess., 29 Apr., 5 June 1980. 348p. Y4.F76/2:W89/3. Family planning methods and government policy are discussed from a worldwide perspective. The U.S. policy on family planning assistance and the use of natural family planning methods are explored. The state of family planning in the U.S. and in LDCs is reviewed, and AID policy on approaches to family planning are examined.

2056. U.S. Health Services Administration. *A Self-Instruction Booklet to Aid in the Understanding of Contraception.* Washington, DC: GPO, 1980. 30p. HE20.5102:C76/3/980. Earlier edition published in 1976.

2057. U.S. National Library of Medicine. *Adverse Effects of Intrauterine Devices.* NLM Literature Search no. 80-13. Washington DC: GPO, 1980. 20p. HE20.3614/2:80-13. English citations from the MEDLINE database report the adverse effects to women and to the fetus of intrauterine devices.

2058. U.S. Public Health Service. *Contraceptive Efficiency among Married Women Aged 15-44 Years, United States.* Washington, DC: GPO, 1980. 62p. HE20.6209:23/5. Report of a study of contraceptive effectiveness analyzes, by socioeconomic and demographic groups, the percentage of women who failed to prevent an unplanned pregnancy.

2059. U.S. Bureau of Community Health Services. *Designing Your Family Planning Evaluation Program.* Washington, DC: GPO, 1981. 90p. HE20.5102:F21/11. Step-by-step guide to designing family planning education discusses setting objectives, identifying resources, designing program evaluation, and staff development.

2060. U.S. Bureau of Community Health Services. *Family Planning Services for Disabled People: A Manual for Service Providers.* by Ebon Research Systems. Washington, DC: GPO, 1981. 185p. HE20.5108:F21/7. Guide to providing family planning services for disabled people includes access considerations, interpersonal interaction, and contraceptive considerations for specific disabilities.

2061. U.S. Center for Health Promotion and Education. Family Planning Education Division. *The Family Planning Evaluation Division Publications, 1967-1980.* Atlanta: The Center, 1981? 35p. HE20.7019:F21. Bibliography lists journal articles reporting results of Family Planning Education Division studies.

2062. U.S. Center for Population Research. *The Walnut Creek Contraceptive Drug Study.* Washington, DC: GPO, 1974-1981. 3 vol. HE20.3362/6:C76/v.1-3. Study of the adverse effects of oral contraceptive use provides a statistical profile of the health of oral contraceptive users at the beginning of the study in volume one, and presents data on the effect of steroid contraceptive drugs on the health status of users in volume two. Volume three compares morbidity and mortality among women users and non-users of oral contraceptives.

2063. U.S. Centers for Disease Control. *Current Awareness in Family Life and Sex Education.* Washington, DC: GPO, 1981. 54p. HE20.7026:F21/2. Annotated bibliography lists English and foreign language books, journal articles, conference proceedings, and reports on family life and sex education received by the Center for Health Promotion and Education.

2064. U.S. Centers for Disease Control. *Family Planning Evaluation Divisions Publications.* Washington, DC: The Center, 1981. 53p. HE20.7026:F21. Lists books, journal articles, and technical reports by the staff of the Family Planning Evaluation Division of the Center for Health Promotion and Education.

2065. U.S. Congress. House. Committee on Energy and Commerce. *Health and the Environment Miscellaneous, Part 1, Hearings.* 97th Cong., 1st sess., 4 Feb. - 3 Apr. 1981. 573p. Y4.En2/3:97-16. Hearing on miscellaneous health issues and programs includes testimony on office worker health, particularly employer policies on health hazards and fertile women, and on adolescent pregnancy programs. Most testimony is in support of family planning programs and several witnesses voice opposition to anti-abortion legislation. Anti-abortion witnesses oppose a federal role in family planning and sex education. The nurse shortage is also explored noting the problem of low salaries.

2066. U.S. Congress. Senate. Committee on Labor and Human Resources. *Oversight of Family Planning Programs, 1981, Hearing.* 97th Cong., 1st. sess., 31 March 1981. 381p. Y4.L11/4:F21/2/981. Oversight hearing on Title X family planning programs touches on all of the major issues including natural methods, abortion, and services to teenagers. The continued problem of teenage pregnancy in the U.S. is examined and issues of federal funding for family planning are highlighted by witnesses. Patient confidentiality versus parental rights is a major point of debate. Planned Parenthood is the target of several attacks in the testimony.

2067. U.S. Congress. Senate. Committee on Labor and Human Resources. Subcommittee on Aging, Family and Human Services. *Oversight on Family Planning Programs under Title X of the Public Health Services Act, 1981, Hearing.* 97th Cong., 1st sess., 23 June, 28 Sept. 1981. 326p. Y4.L11/4:F21/3. Oversight hearings on Title X family planning programs focus on issues of teenage pregnancy and the parent's role. The effectiveness of birth control availability as a way of reducing teen pregnancy, the adequacy of outreach programs for poor women, and the role of the federal government in providing family planning services are topics addressed. Results of the GAO review of Title X program effectiveness are highlighted.

2068. U.S. Congress. Senate. Committee on the Judiciary. Subcommittee on Separation of Powers. *The Human Life Bill, Hearings on S. 158.* 97th Cong., 1st. sess., 23 Apr.- 18 June 1981. 1124p. Y4.J89/2:J-97-16/v.1-2. Extensive hearing presents testimony from experts, concerned organizations and individuals from both sides of the legalized abortion debate. Physical, psychological, and moral arguments are presented from each perspective, and the question of when human life begins is a major point of debate. The legal impact of S. 158, which would grant the fetus status as a person for civil rights enforcement, is discussed in relation to birth control, rape, and the Constitution. The legal history of abortion is examined with each side of the controversy presenting a different interpretation of the motives behind past abortion laws.

2069. U.S. Congress. Senate. Committee on the Judiciary. Subcommittee on Separation of Powers. *The Human Life Bill - S. 158, Report Together with Additional and Minority Views.* 97th Cong., 1st sess., 1981. 53p. Y4.J89/2:H88/7. Report presents the Committee's reasoning and intent in favorably reporting S. 158, the Human Life Bill, which legally defines human life as existing at conception and extends the protection of the

14th Amendment to the fetus. The constitutionality of the bill is the primary issue of the additional and minority views. Scientific evidence of when life begins and the Supreme Courts decision in *Roe v. Wade* are major points in the report.

2070.   U.S. Congress. Senate. Committee on the Judiciary. Subcommittee on the Constitution. *Constitutional Amendments Relating to Abortion, Hearings on S.J. Res. 17, S.J. Res. 18, S.J. Res. 19, and S.J. Res. 110, Volume 1.* 97th Cong., 1st sess., 5 Oct. - 16 Dec. 1981. 1244p. Y4.J89/2:J-97-62/v.1. Extensive hearing on the abortion issue includes a detailed examination of the legal and constitutional questions of *Roe v. Wade* and of the proposed constitutional amendment. The health and moral issues are discussed from both the pro-choice and anti-abortion views. Also discusses the impact the anti-abortion amendment would have on contraceptive availability. Detailed statistics on abortion in the U.S. are provided including abortion rates and ratios by state, characteristics of women receiving abortions, legal abortions by weeks of gestation and procedure, abortions by number of previous abortions, legal abortions by patient characteristics and state, legal abortions obtained by teenagers, death-to-case rate of legal abortions, and abortions performed out-of-state. Also provides information on grounds for legal abortion by country and number of abortions by age and marital status of mother for selected countries.

2071.   U.S. Congress. Senate. Committee on the Judiciary. Subcommittee on the Constitution. *Constitutional Amendments Relating to Abortion, Hearings on S.J. Res. 17, S.J. Res. 18, S.J. Res. 19, and S.J. Res. 110, Volume 2 - Appendix.* 97th Cong., 1st. sess., 5 Oct. - 16 Dec. 1981. 781p. Y4.J89/2:J-97-62/v.2. Supporting material for the hearing on constitutional amendments to limit abortion provides a wide range of reprinted material including excepts from philosophy books, legal interpretations, articles on abortion before and after *Roe v. Wade* on the health consequences of abortion, and public opinion polls on the abortion issue. Also provides detailed statistics on abortion in the U.S. and worldwide, and reprints the decisions in *Roe v. Wade* and *Doe v. Bolton.* Statistics presented include age of women receiving abortions by year and country; legal abortion in England by country of residence; distribution of legal abortions by marital status, country and year; distribution of legal abortions by number of prior abortions, age, and marital status for selected countries; and death-to-case ratios by country and year.

2072.   U.S. General Accounting Office. *Family Planning Clinics Can Provide Services at Less Cost but Clearer Federal Policies Are Needed.* Washington, DC: GPO, 1981. 72p. GA1.13:HRD-81-68. Examination of ways to reduce Title X family planning service costs focus on elimination of unnecessary medical procedures and enforcement of fee collections. Also discusses conflicts between fee based Title X services and free Title XX services.

2073.   U.S. Public Health Service. *Family Planning Visits by Teenagers: United States, 1978.* Washington, DC: GPO, 1981. 24p. HE20.6209:13/58. Examination of family planning clinic visits by women under 20 provides details by race and geographic region and by patient sociodemographic characteristics, visit status, prior and current contraceptive method, and medical services provided.

2074.   U.S. Public Health Service. *Teenagers Who Use Organized Family Planning Services: United States, 1978.* Washington, DC: GPO, 1981. 18p. HE20.6209:13/57. Data on family planning clinic usage by women under age 20 examines social and demographic characteristics as related to pregnancy history, pre- and post-visit contraceptive use, and medical services received. Information is compared to pregnancy history and contraceptive use for women age 20 and over.

2075.   U.S. Public Health Service. *Use of Services for Family Planning and Infertility: United States.* Washington, DC: GPO, 1981. 41p. HE20.6209:23/8. Statistics on use of contraceptive and infertility services by currently married women reports the percent of women who ever used family planning services, who currently use family planning services, and who used infertility services, by race or Hispanic origin, age, and socioeconomic variables.

2076. U.S. Congress. House. Committee on Energy and Commerce. Subcommittee on Health and the Environment. *Health and the Environment Miscellaneous, Part 7, Hearings.* 97th Cong., 2d sess., 4 Feb. - 8 March 1982. 368p. Y4.En2/3:97-128. Hearing on miscellaneous health programs includes discussion of a proposed requirement that the parents of adolescents seeking family planning services be informed when contraceptives are prescribed at Title X funded clinics. Most witnesses justify parental notification citing parental rights and health risks. Opponents base their arguments on the negative impact on teenage access to birth control information.

2077. U.S. Congress. House. Committee on Foreign Affairs. Subcommittee on Inter-American Affairs. *Population and Development in Latin America and the Caribbean, Hearing.* 97th Cong., 2d sess., 8 Sept. 1982. 130p. Y4.F76/1:P81/2. Past attitudes and current policies on family planning in Latin America and the Caribbean are reviewed as witnesses discuss the benefits of family planning from an economic development perspective. Financing of family planning programs and continued opposition in some countries are reviewed.

2078. U.S. Congress. Senate. Committee on Labor and Human Resources. Subcommittee on Aging, Family, and Human Resources. *Health Aspects of Adolescent Sex, 1982.* 97th Cong., 2d sess., 19 Apr. 1982. 92p. Y4.L11/4:H34/17. Hearing on adolescent sexual activity reviews issues of young women and contraceptive methods, and the incidence and consequences of venereal disease in adolescents.

2079. U.S. Congress. Senate. Committee on the Judiciary. *Human Life Federalism Amendment, Report Together with Additional and Minority Views, to Accompany S. J.Res. 110.* S. Rept. 97-465, 97th Cong., 2d sess., 1982. 69p. Serial 13450. Reports a proposed constitutional amendment declaring that the Constitution contains no right to an abortion and giving Congress the power to legislate with respect to abortion. The report cites the need to restrict abortion on demand and to place the debate over abortion with the legislative branch of government and remove it from the courts. The effect of *Roe v. Wade* on abortion law in the U.S. and subsequent court cases defining the scope of restrictive abortion laws are reviewed. The report also discusses abortion methods and the social impact of the *Roe* decision. Discrepancies in public opinion polls on abortion are also explored.

2080. U.S. General Accounting Office. *Restrictions on Abortion and Lobbying Activities in Family Planning Programs Need Clarification.* Washington, DC: The Office, 1982. 36p. GA1.13:HRD-82-106. The areas in need of clarification relating to abortion and the activities of family planning programs receiving Title X funds are outlined.

2081. U.S. Office of Technology Assessment. *World Population and Fertility Planning Technologies in the Next 20 Years.* Washington, DC: GPO, 1982. 243p. Y3.T22/2:2P81. Comprehensive overview of the current status and projected technologies affecting fertility change reviews the projections and implication for population growth, and summarizes current research and development in contraception. Factors influencing the acceptance, distribution, and use of fertility planning technologies in LDCs and the role of U.S. population assistance program are discussed.

2082. U.S. Office of Technology Assessment. *World Population and Fertility Planning Technologies, the Next 20 Years: Summary.* Washington, DC: GPO, 1982. 27p. Y3.T22/2:2P81/summ. See 2081 for abstract.

2083.   U.S. Public Health Service. *Basic Data on Visits to Family Planning Service Sites: United States, 1980.* Washington, DC: GPO, 1982. 32p. HE20.6209:13/68. Estimate of the use of family planning services in 1980 is broken down by social and demographic characteristics.

2084.   U.S. Public Health Service. *Basic Data on Women Who Use Family Planning Clinics, United States, 1980.* Washington, DC: GPO, 1982. 46p. HE20.6209:13/67.

2085.   U.S. Public Health Service. *Trends in Contraceptive Practice: United States, 1965-76.* Washington, DC: GPO, 1982. 47p. HE20.6209:23/10. Examines contraceptive use by currently married women in 1965, 1973 and 1976 by race, age, education, and religion.

2086.   U.S. Bureau of Community Health Services. *Family Planning Methods of Contraception: Family Planning Healthier Babies When You Want Them.* Washington, DC: GPO, 1983. [8]p. leaflet. HE20.5102:C76/980.

2087.   U.S. Center for Health Promotion and Education. Division of Reproductive Health. *Family Planning Methods and Practice: Africa.* Atlanta, GA: Centers for Disease Control, 1983. 329p. HE20.7002:F21/2/africa. Handbook on family planning approaches places the information within the context of the social and health status of African women. Information on contraceptive methods is very detailed, and the risks and benefits of each method are clearly delineated. Unique considerations in providing family planning services in Africa are also examined.

2088.   U.S. Congress. House. Committee on Energy and Commerce. Subcommittee on Health and the Environment. *Health and the Environment Miscellaneous, Part 1, Hearings.* 98th Cong., 1st sess., 9 May - 1 Aug. 1983. 399p. Y4.En2/3:98-52. The majority of this hearing focuses on the issue of therapeutic abortions, unintended pregnancy and federal abortion policy. The psychological and social effects of unintended pregnancy are explored. Both sides of the issue discuss the evidence of a link between unwanted pregnancy and child abuse. Much of the debate focuses on morbidity and mortality rates associated with abortions.

2089.   U.S. Congress. House. Committee on Government Operations. Intergovernmental Relations and Human Resources Subcommittee. *FDA's Approval of the Today Contraceptive Sponge, Hearing.* 98th Cong., 1st sess., 13 July 1983. 520p. Y4.G74/7:F73/8. The statistical methods used by the FDA in analyzing the carcinogenic risks of the Today Contraceptive Sponge are criticized by witnesses. Studies on the carcinogenicity of the chemical components of the sponge are reviewed and the manufacturer, Vorhauer Laboratories Inc., defends the safety of the contraceptive device. Correspondence and reports related to the FDA approval of the sponge are reprinted.

2090.   U.S. Congress. House. Committee on Post Office and Civil Service. Subcommittee on Civil Service. *Study of Effort to Exclude Planned Parenthood from Participation in Combined Federal Campaign.* by Andrea Nelson. 98th Cong., 1st sess., 1983. 379p. Y4.P84/10:P21/5. Report on the efforts of the director of the Office of Personnel Management to exclude Planned Parenthood from the Combined Federal Campaign provides a concise summary of the conflict and reprints related OPM hearings and documents.

2091.   U.S. Congress. House. Select Committee on Children, Youth, and Families. *Teen Parents and Their Children: Issues and Programs, Hearing.* 98th Cong., 1st. sess., 20 July 1983. 200p. Y4.C43/2:T22. The primary topic of this hearing on teenage pregnancy is the effect of sex education and contraceptive availability on the sexual activity of teenagers. Moral issues and parental notification for dispensing birth control are also recurring topics.

2092. U.S. Congress. Senate. Committee on the Judiciary. *Human Life Federalism Amendment, Report on S.J. Res. 3.* S. Rept. 98-149, 98th Cong., 1st sess., 1983, 72p. Serial 13508. Reviews the impact of *Roe V. Wade* on abortion law in the U.S. and discusses the intent of S.J. Res. 3, which proposes an amendment stating that the Constitution does not guarantee the right to an abortion. The report focuses on removing the abortion debate from the courts and placing it in the states legislatures and Congress. Public opinion on the abortion issue is reviewed. Opposition views to the bill are appended.

2093. U.S. Congress. Senate. Committee on the Judiciary. Subcommittee on the Constitution. *Legal Ramifications of the Human Life Amendment, Hearings on S.J. Res. 3.* 98th Cong., 1st. sess., 28 Feb., 7 Mar. 1983. 262p. Y4.J89/2:S.hrg.98-381. Testimony and accompanying material focus on *Roe v. Wade* from a legal standpoint and on the morbidity and mortality from illegal abortions prior to *Roe.*

2094. U.S. National Institutes of Health. *En Busca de Buena Salud: La Pildora y el Cancer - Noticias Alentadoras.* Bethesda, MD: The Institutes, 1983. 1p. HE20.3038:P64/spanish.

2095. U.S. National Institutes of Health. *The Search for Health: The Pill & Cancer, Reassuring News.* Bethesda, MD: The Institutes, 1983. 1p. HE20.3038:P64.

2096. United States-Mexico Border Health Association. *The U.S.-Mexico Border: Contraceptive Use and Maternal Health Care in Perspective.* El Paso, TX: The Assoc., 1983. 110p. HE20.7002:C76/3. Results of U.S. and Mexican surveys of fertility, contraceptive use, and maternal health along the U.S.-Mexico border are presented separately. The reports examine data in the areas of fertility, unplanned fertility, contraceptive use, source of contraceptive, need for family planning services, and attitudes toward family planning services. Information is also presented on prenatal care, abortion, smoking and alcohol consumption. The U.S. study reports data separately for Hispanics and Anglos and for married and unmarried women.

2097. U.S. Congress. House. Committee on Energy and Commerce. *Titles X and XX and Preventive Health Services Block Grants, Report Together with Dissenting Views to Accompany H.R. 5600.* H. Rept. 98-804, 98th Cong., 2d sess., 1984. 18p. Serial 13592. Report supports extension of family planning programs under Titles X of the PHSA, the Adolescent Family Life program under Title XX, and the Preventive Health and Health Services Block grant program, a program which provides services for rape victims and rape prevention. Although the bill makes no significant changes in any of the programs, the intent of each program is carefully described to alleviate confusion over the interpretation of program provisions. Dissenting views express concern over undermining parental authority.

2098. U.S. Congress. House. Committee on Energy and Commerce. Subcommittee on Health and the Environment. *Health and the Environment Miscellaneous, Part 3, Hearings.* 98th Cong., 1st and 2d sess., 12 Dec. 1983 - 27 Apr. 1984. 1114p. Y4.En2/3:98-121. Topics examined in this series of hearings include federal abortion policy, implementation of Title X family planning programs, and the adolescent family life demonstration project.

2099. U.S. Congress. House. Committee on Post Office and Civil Service. Subcommittee on Census and Population. *U.S. Policy on Population Assistance, Hearing.* 98th Cong., 2d sess., 25 July 1984. 199p. Y4.P84/10:98-53. Testimony at a hearing on U.S. population policy focuses on the implications of withholding aid from organizations which provide abortion services. Also discussed is the administration's desire to downsize voluntary population planning and focus on free market economics to address population problems in developing countries. The effect of repeated pregnancies on women's health and the cultural attitudes which encourage continuous childbearing in developing countries are reviewed.

2100.   U.S. Congress. Senate. Committee on Labor and Human Resources. Subcommittee on Family and Human Resources. *Oversight on Family Planning Programs under Title X of the Public Health Service Act, 1984, Hearings.* 98th Cong., 2d sess., 5 Apr., 1 May 1984. 362p. Y4.L11/4:S.hrg.98-1077. Types of service provided, access to family planning services for poor women and teenagers, and funding to clinics providing abortion services or counseling are among the topics covered in this hearing on reauthorization of Title X of the PHSA.

2101.   U.S. National Institute of Child Health and Human Development. *Facts about Oral Contraceptives.* Washington, DC: GPO, 1984. 19p. leaflet. HE20.3352:Or1.

2102.   U.S. Congress. House. Committee on Energy and Commerce. *Extension of Title X, Report Together with Dissenting Views to Accompany H.R. 2369.* H. Rept. 99-159, 99th Cong., 1st sess., 1985. 17p. Serial 13648. Favorable report on a bill to revise and extend family planning programs under Title X of the PHSA briefly discusses the adequacy of the ban on the use of funds for abortion. The bill authorizes programs of federal aid to state and local family planning service providers, research on contraceptive development, and information and education programs aimed at adolescents and adults. The dissenting views support a parental notification requirement for adolescent family planning services.

2103.   U.S. Congress. House. Committee on Foreign Affairs. *International Security and Development Corporation Act of 1985, Report on H.R. 1555 Together with Dissenting, Supplemental and Additional Views.* H. Rept. 99-39, 99th Cong., 1st sess., 1985. 165p. Serial 13644. Among the foreign assistance programs authorized by the bill reported here are family planning programs. Clarified language is provided on funding for organizations which support abortion-related activities along with family planning programs, with specific mention of the International Planned Parenthood Federation.

2104.   U.S. Congress. House. Committee on Science and Technology. Subcommittee on Natural Resources, Agricultural Research, and Environment. *Contraceptive Technology, Hearing.* 99th Cong., 1st sess., 23 Apr. 1985. 214p. Y4.Sci2:99/83. Hearing on contraceptive development discusses new contraceptives, particularly the Norplant five-year contraceptive, and the effectiveness of natural family planning in developing countries. Several articles on natural family planning in LDCs are included in the record. The effectiveness of available contraceptives are examined, and the extent of misinformation on the risk of oral contraceptives is discussed.

2105.   U.S. Congress. Senate. Committee on the Judiciary. Subcommittee on the Constitution. *Abortion Funding Restriction Act, Hearing on S. 522.* 99th Cong., 1st sess., 2 Apr., 22 July 1985. 163p. Y4.J89/2:S.hrg.99-437. Hearing explores a bill to insure that the Civil Rights Act of 1984 could not be used to protect abortion rights, and to prohibit the use of federal funds to perform abortions except to save the life of the mother. Testimony discusses the legal ramifications of the bill, the Supreme Court and the abortion issue, and the constitutionality of the bill. Also examined is the extent of the definition of "use of federal funds" within programs and institutions.

2106.   U.S. Congress. Senate. Committee on the Judiciary. Subcommittee on the Constitution. *Fetal Pain, Hearing.* 99th Cong., 1st sess., 21 May 1985. 118p. Y4.J89/2:S.hrg.99-429. Witnesses from the scientific community debate the evidence on the ability of the human fetus to experience pain, focusing on the claims made about the abortion film *Silent Scream*. Federal abortion policy is discussed in relation to evidence of fetal pain.

2107. U.S. National Institute of Child Health and Human Development. *Special Initiative on Contraceptive Development, Fiscal Years 1986-1989*. Washington, DC: GPO, 1985. 45p. HE20.3352:C76/986-89. Describes research programs proposed as part of a special initiative on developing safe and convenient methods of contraception.

2108. U.S. Congress. House. Committee on the Judiciary. Subcommittee on Civil and Constitutional Rights. *Abortion Clinic Violence, Oversight Hearings*. 99th Cong., 1st and 2d sess., 6 Mar. 1985 - 17 Dec. 1986. 677p. Y4.J89/1:99/115. Hearing explores the problem of anti-abortion activists who sometime violently disrupt the operation of abortion clinics. Witnesses describe the actions taken against the clinics and the local law enforcement response, and discuss whether the violence and intimidation violates the civil rights of clinic patients. Both pro-choice and anti-choice advocates engage in often hostile interchanges with each other and with subcommittee members. Anti-choice advocates downplay the acts of violence as the work of extremists and clearly define the tactics they use and their justification. Whether the federal government has an obligation to investigate and attempt to control the violence is discussed.

2109. U.S. Congress. Senate. Committee on Labor and Human Resources. *Family Planning Amendments of 1986, Report Together with Additional Views to Accompany S. 881*. S. Rept. 99-297, 99th Cong., 2d sess., 1986. 25p. Serial 13674. Extension of voluntary family planning projects under Title X of the PHSA includes a demonstration project on the effect of written parental consent for birth control on the rate of unintended adolescent pregnancies. The report provides a brief history of family planning legislation and appropriations since 1970. Additional views object to parental notification.

2110. U.S. Food and Drug Administration. *Comparing Contraceptives*. Washington, DC: GPO, 1986. 8p. HE20.4010/a:C76/3. Revision of an article originally printed in *FDA Consumer* describes the effectiveness and health risks of various contraceptive methods.

2111. U.S. Public Health Service. *Contraceptive Use, United States, 1982*. Washington, DC: GPO, 1986. 52p. HE20.6209:23/12. Analysis by race, age, marital status and socioeconomic variables of history of contraceptive use examines contraceptive use at first intercourse, first method used, all methods ever used, and current contraceptive use.

2112. U.S. Congress. House. Committee on Interior and Insular Affairs. Subcommittee on General Oversight and Investigations. *Use of the Drug, Depo Provera, by the Indian Health Services, Oversight Hearing*. 100th Cong., 1st sess., 6 Aug. 1987. 232p. Y4.In8/14:100-33. Hearing investigates the Indian Health Service's use of Depo-Provera as an injectable contraceptive for mentally retarded women. The IHS defends its use of the drug while other witnesses charge that the IHS uses the drug because of its convenience without regard the concern over the health risks connected to its use. Information on the possible risks of Depo-Provera to women and their offspring is reviewed.

2113. U.S. Congress. Senate. Committee on Labor and Human Resources. *Family Planning Amendments of 1987, Hearing on S. 1366*. 100th Cong., 1st sess., 30 July 1987. 218p. Y4.L11/4:S. hrg.100-378. Hearing considers reauthorization of PHSA Title X funding for family planning services. Testimony centers around the issues of parental consent, abortion counseling, and the effectiveness of family planning services on teenage pregnancy rates.

2114. U.S. Congress. Senate. Committee on Labor and Human Resources. *Family Planning Amendments of 1987, Report Together with Minority and Dissenting Views to Accompany*

S. 1366. S. Rept. 100-286, 100th Cong., 2d sess., 1987. 32p. Serial 13859. Report on a bill revising and extending family planning programs under Title X of the PHSA describes programs and program requirements with some background on past research and services funded. The report also mentions the issue of parental notification for adolescent services and the committee's support of patient confidentiality in this area. Also supported in the report is the training of nurse practitioners as providers of family planning services.

2115.   U.S. National Center for Health Statistics. *Instruction Manual Part 10: Classification and Coding Instructions for Induced Termination of Pregnancy Records, 1988.* Washington, DC: GPO, 1987. 52p. HE20.6208/8:988.

2116.   U.S. Congress. House. *Proposed Legislation - President's Pro-Life Act of 1988, Message from the President of the United States Transmitting a Draft of Proposed Legislation to Prohibit the Use of Federal Funds for Abortions Except Where the Life of the Mother Be Endangered.* H. Doc. 100-204, 100th Cong., 2d sess., 1988. 3p. Serial 13877. Transmits a bill to prohibit the use of federal funds for abortion, stating the principle that the fetus is a living human being, that a right to an abortion is not secured by the Constitution, and that the Supreme Court erred in its decision in *Roe v. Wade*.

2117.   U.S. Congress. House. Committee on Energy and Commerce. Subcommittee on Health and the Environment. *Maternal, Child Health, and Family Planning Services, Hearings.* 100th Cong., 2d sess., 25 Feb., 22 Apr. 1988. 317p. Y4.En2/3:100-149. Brief hearing on improving access to health care for low income pregnant women and children is followed by a more extensive hearing on reauthorization of Title X family planning services. Administration witnesses support transfer of the administration of Title X to the states and reviews existing Title X programs. The abortion issue is discussed by several witnesses focusing on the extent of compliance with the abortion prohibition and on the negative consequences of the prohibition of abortion counseling on women's health. The questions surrounding services to teenagers are also debated.

2118.   U.S. General Accounting Office. *Development Assistance: Issues Concerning AID's Social Marketing for Change Program.* Washington, DC: GPO, 1988. 11p. GA1.13:NSIAD-89-29. Review of the Social Marketing for Change (SOMARC) Program, a contraceptive marketing program developed by AID for third-world countries, looks at charges that evaluators sanitized their report, and that the cost of the program is higher than reported. Discussion of the effectiveness of SOMARC, which subsidizes contraceptive costs for local retailers and develops sales promotion materials, is included with a focus on deficiencies in the program evaluation.

2119.   U.S. Congress. House. *Veto of H.R. 2939, Message from the President of the United States Transmitting His Veto of H.R. 2939, a Bill Making Appropriations for Foreign Operations, Export Financing, and Related Programs for the Fiscal Year Ending September 30, 1990, and for Other Purposes.* H. Doc. 101-113, 101st Cong., 1st sess., 1989. 77p. One of the reasons given by Bush for his veto of a foreign appropriations bill is a provision contributing funds to the United Nations Fund for Population Activities. The objection to the Fund is based on its support of a particular unnamed country whose population program includes coercive abortion. The President rejects as too weak a provision in the bill to ensure that funds are not used in countries which support a program of coercive abortion.

2120.   U.S. Congress. House. *Veto of H.R. 2990, Message from the President of the United States Transmitting His Veto of H.R. 2990, the "Departments of Labor, Health and Human Services, and Education, and Related Agencies Appropriations Act, 1990."* H. Doc. 101-102, 101st Cong., 1st sess., 1989. 37p. Presidential veto rejects the more permissive anti-abortion provisions of the Labor, Health and Human Services, and Education Department appropriations bill.

2121. U.S. Congress. House. *Veto of H.R. 3026, Message from the President of the United States Transmitting His Veto of H.R. 3026, the "District of Columbia Appropriations Act, 1990."* H. Doc. 101-105, 101st Cong., 1st sess., 1989. 20p. In a brief veto message, Bush returns the District appropriations bill citing its failure to adequately restrict the use of funding for abortion.

2122. U.S. Congress. House. *Veto of H.R. 3610, Message from the President of the United States Transmitting His Veto of H.R. 3610, a Bill Making Appropriations for the Government of the District of Columbia and Other Activities Chargeable in Whole or in Part Against the Revenue of Said District for the Fiscal Year Ending September 30, 1990, and for Other Purposes.* H. Doc. 101-114, 101st Cong., 1st sess., 1989. 20p. Bush's veto rejects the District appropriations bill for failing to restrict the use of congressionally appropriated local funds for abortion on demand.

2123. U.S. Congress. House. Committee on Appropriations. *Departments of Labor, Health and Human Services, and Education, and Related Agencies Appropriations Bill, 1990, Report to Accompany H.R. 3566.* H. Rept. 101-354, 101st Cong., 1st sess., 1989. 69p. Revised appropriations bill includes a strict limitation on the use of federal funds for abortion. The report details the veto of the first bill by President Bush because of its more liberal abortion provisions.

2124. U.S. Congress. House. Committee on Energy and Commerce. Subcommittee on Health and the Environment. *Federal Family Planning Program Reauthorization, Hearing on H.R. 930.* 101st Cong., 1st sess., 15 June 1989. 283p. Y4.En2/3:101-50. Hearing on extending the family planning program authorization under Title X of the PHSA reviews the progress in health care for women under the act and the controversy surrounding its implementation. The hearing primarily considers proposals to make Title X family planning programs state-administered block grants. The issues of abortion and services to adolescents are primary points of debate.

2125. U.S. Congress. House. Committee on Foreign Affairs. Subcommittee on International Operations. *The Effect of the Mexico City Policy on International Family Planning, Hearing.* 101st Cong., 1st sess., 21 Sept. 1989. 197p. Y4.F76/1:M57/12. Hearing explores U.S. policy prohibiting provision of family planning funding to international providers who perform abortions or provide abortion counseling. Testimony considers the effect on the health and well-being of women in developing countries of the Mexico City policy. The viewpoint of anti-abortion organizations is also expressed. The state of abortion and family planning in developing countries is reviewed by witnesses.

2126. U.S. Congress. House. Committee on Government Operations. *The Federal Role in Determining the Medical and Psychological Impact of Abortion on Women, Tenth Report by the Committee on Government Operations, Together with Dissenting and Additional Views.* H. Rept. 101-392, 101st Cong., 1st sess., 1989. 30p. Report on the federal government's role in researching abortion summarizes hearing testimony on the medical and psychological risks of abortion. The report emphasizes the testimony of Surgeon General C. Everett Koop and the report written for the Surgeon General but never published. Dissenting views charge the committee report with discrediting anti-abortion witnesses and slanting the report toward pro-choice views.

2127. U.S. Congress. House. Committee on Government Operations. Human Resources and Intergovernmental Relations Subcommittee. *Medical and Psychological Impact of Abortion, Hearing.* 101st Cong., 1st sess., 16 Mar. 1989. 346p. Y4.G74/7:M46/5.

Mostly balanced testimony from Surgeon General C. Everett Koop, experts in obstetrics and gynecology, and representatives of the American Psychological Association and the National Right to Life Committee review the research evidence of negative physical and psychological effects of abortion. Most testimony indicated few lasting harmful effects of first trimester abortion or stressed the need for better, methodologically sound, studies over a period of years.

2128.   U.S. Congress. Senate. Committee on Labor and Human Resources. *Family Planning Amendments of 1989, Hearing on S. 110.* 101st Cong., 1st sess., 9 May 1989. 203p. Y4.L11/4:S.hrg.101-419. Hearing on reauthorization of Title X family planning services includes discussion of abortion and the abortion counseling ban, services to adolescents, and the negative aspects of RU 486. The effectiveness of focusing adolescent pregnancy prevention programs on abstinence is debated.

2129.   U.S. Congress. Senate. Committee on Labor and Human Resources. *Family Planning Amendments of 1989, Report Together with Additional Views to Accompany S. 110.* S. Rept. 101-95. 101st Cong., 1st sess., 1989. 32p. Favorable report on revision and extension of Title X PHSA family planning programs highlights provisions relating to adoption referral services, clinical training of personnel, contraceptive research and development, adolescent family planning education, collection of statistical data, and research on the effect of parental consent requirements on adolescent use of family planning services. The bill also reauthorized the Title XX Adolescent Family Life program. Additional views of committee members focus on the abortion issue and on funding of school-based family planning clinics.

2130.   U.S. National Library of Medicine. *Wrongful Life: Births as the Result of Negligence: January 1970 through September 1988, 627 Citations.* Current Bibliographies in Medicine no. 88-18. Washington, DC: GPO, 1989. 23p. HE20.3615/2:88-18. Citations from National Library of Medicine databases cover the ethical and legal issues of birth as the result of negligence, and examine related issues of genetic counseling, abortion, contraception and pregnancy. The primary focus is on the legal aspects of the issue.

2131.   U.S. Congress. House. Committee on Energy and Commerce. *Family Planning Reauthorization Act of 1990, Report Together with Dissenting Views, to Accompany H.R. 5693.* H. Rept. 101-870, 101st Cong., 2d sess., 1990. 6p. Brief report on reauthorization of Title X PHSA family planning programs notes the committee's rejection of a parental notification amendment.

2132.   U.S. Congress. House. Committee on Energy and Commerce. Subcommittee on Health and the Environment. *Fetal Tissue Transplantation Research, Hearing.* 101st Cong., 2d sess., 2 Apr. 1990. 220p. Y4.En2/3:101-135. The bioethical issues surrounding fetal tissue transplantation research are explored in testimony focusing on the federal moratorium on FTTR and the abortion issue. Whether federally-funded FTTR would increase induced abortion is a central issue of testimony on the moratorium.

2133.   U.S. Congress. Senate. Committee on Labor and Human Resources. *Freedom of Choice Act of 1989, Hearing on S. 1912.* 101st Cong., 2d sess., 27 Mar, 23 May 1990. 282p. Y4.L11/4:S.hrg.101-876. A markedly divided committee examines the issue of legal abortion with views ranging from a total ban to abortion on demand up to viability. Medical evidence on fetal development is presented. Morbidity from illegal abortion is examined and opponents of legal abortion discuss the psychological impact of abortion on patients and their families.

2134.   U.S. Congress. Senate. Committee on the Judiciary. *Nomination of David H. Souter to be Associate Justice of the Supreme Court of the United States, Hearing.* 101st Cong., 2d sess., 13-19 Sept. 1990. 1198p. Y4.J89/2:S.hrg.101-1263. Confirmation hearing for Justice David Souter is marked by intense debate over the abortion issue and Souter's anti-abortion views. Souter's views on *Roe v. Wade* are explored and his position on anti-discrimination laws is discussed in-depth.

2135. U.S. Government Accounting Office. *Foreign Assistance: AID's Population Program.* Washington, DC: The Office, 1990. 68p. GA1.13:NSIAD-90-112. Review of AID policy on population assistance details changes in policy from active promotion of family planning in the 1970's to a more passive stance in the 1980's. The question of the extent to which AID actively encourages governments to adopt campaigns promoting smaller families is at issue. The report recommends that AID develop better management and evaluation procedures.

2136. U.S. General Accounting Office. *Foreign Assistance: Circumstances Surrounding a Family Planning Project.* Washington, DC: The Office, 1990. 13p. GA1.13:NSIAD-90-89. Reviews conflict regarding funding to the Family of the Americas Foundation, the organization selected to development natural family planning method educational materials for AID.

2137. U.S. National Center for Health Statistics. *Use of Family Planning Services in the United States: 1982 and 1988.* by William D. Mosher. Advanced Data from Vital and Health Statistics no. 1984. Hyattsville, MD: The Center, 1990. 8p. HE20.6209/3:184. Data reported on the use of family planning services includes age, race, poverty status, and service provider. The race and poverty status of users of family planning services are a particular focus, and trends in the use of subsidized services are examined.

SERIALS

2138. U.S. Agency for International Development. Office of Population. *Population Program Assistance, Aid to Developing Nations by United States, Other Nations, and International and Private Agencies.* Washington, DC: The Office, 1969 - 1973. annual. S18.2:P81/2/year. Summary of policies and trends in family planning assistance to developing countries focuses on programs of the U.S. government. Country profiles summarize related demographic information, population and family planning activities, and external sources of assistance.

2139. U.S. Bureau of Community Health Services. *Family Planning Digest.* Washington, DC: GPO, 1972 -. v.1-. bimonthly. HE20.2909:vol./no. (1972-1973); HE20.5111:vol./no. (1973-) Newsletter prepared by the Center for Family Planning Program Development of Planned Parenthood provides summaries of research on contraceptive use, family planning practices and contraceptive methods as well as notes on government sponsored programs.

2140. U.S. Centers for Disease Control. *Abortion Surveillance.* Washington, DC:GPO, 1972-. annual. HE20.7011/20:year. Annual summary of legal abortions in the United States presents data on abortions by age, race, period of gestation, number of previous abortions, state of residence, abortions outside state of residence, and type of procedure.

2141. U.S. Centers for Disease Control. *Annual Summary of Family Planning Services.* Atlanta: The Centers, 1972 - . annual. HE20.7002:F21. Summarizes of use of family planning services and presents statistics on age and number of living children, method of contraception, marital status, welfare status, race, male family planning patients, and the need for public family planning service by never married women, by age and race.

2142. U.S. Centers for Disease Control. Family Planning Evaluation Division. *Surgical Sterilization Surveillance: Tubal Sterilization and Hysterectomy in Women Aged 15-44.* Atlanta: The Center, 1979/80 - . biennial. HE20.7011/30:year. Continues *Surgical Sterilization Surveillance: Hysterectomy in Women Aged 15-44* (2053).

2143. U.S. Government Printing Office. *Family Planning.* Subject Bibliography 292. Washington, DC: GPO, 1980 - . irreg. GP3.22/2:292. Brief list identifies selected documents on family planning available from the Superintendent of Documents.

2144. U.S. Health Resources Administration. *Annual Report of the National Reporting System for Family Planning Services.* Washington, DC: GPO, 1974 - 1975. annual. HE20.6219:year. Detailed cross-tabulation of the sociodemographic characteristics of family planning patients and the services they received is presented for each state, selected territories, and the United States.

2145. U.S. National Center for Health Statistics. *Public Use Data Tape Documentation: Fetal Deaths Detail Record.* Hyattsville, MD: The Center, 1982? - . annual. HE20.6226/11:987.

2146. U.S. National Center for Health Statistics. Division of Health Resources Utilization Statistics. Family Planning Statistics Branch. *Provisional Data from the National Reporting System for Family Planning Services.* Hyattsville, MD: The Center, Oct.1975/Dec.1975 - . irreg. HE20.6202:F21/year. Detailed statistics, by state, profile the use of family planning clinics and characteristics of users. Some of the data collected includes race, ethnic origin, education, public assistance status, service provided, number of live births, number of living children, number of pregnancies, and birth control method used. In addition to the 50 states, data was also collected for the District of Columbia, Puerto Rico, Guam, and the U.S. Virgin Islands.

2147. U.S. National Clearinghouse for Family Planning Information. *Family Planning Grantees, Delegates, and Clinics.* Washington, DC: GPO, 1983 - . irreg. HE20.5119/3:year; HE20.33:year. Directory lists family planning grantees, delegate agencies which contract for services in a particular area, and the family planning clinics supported.

2148. U.S. National Institute of Child Health and Human Development. *Progress Report: Center for Population Research.* Washington, DC: GPO, 1985 - . annual. HE20.3351/3:year. Annual report on the research efforts of the Center for Population Research describes accomplishments relating to reproductive health, contraceptive development and evaluation, and demographic and behavioral aspects of family planning.

2149. U.S. National Institute of Child Health and Human Development. Contraceptive Development Contract Review Committee. *Annual Report, Contraceptive Development Contract Review Committee, National Institutes of Health.* Bethesda, MD: The Institute, 1974 - . annual. HE20.3001/2:C76/year.

14

Illegitimacy and Adolescent Pregnancy

The documents in this chapter discuss illegitimacy and teenage pregnancy from the perspective of social services. As the agency primarily concerned with child welfare, the Children's Bureau was the major producer of documents on the topic of birth out-of-wedlock. The early documents concern primarily the use of maternity homes and the advisability of adoption. One of the most interesting of these documents is the 1928 report, *Children of Illegitimate Birth Whose Mothers Have Kept Their Custody* (2155), which provides case histories of young women who decided to keep their children. The psychological aspects of unwed parenthood are explored from a Freudian perspective in a Children's Bureau reprint from the 1943 *American Journal of Orthopsychiatry* (2162). World War Two sparked a flurry of documents on services to unmarried mothers with a definite emphasis on a move away from a punishment mentality.

The 1960's war on poverty brought about a renewed interest in illegitimacy, this time with a pronounced focus on adolescents. Various Children's Bureau publications describe services to pregnant teenagers and discuss the advantages of a multi-service approach. Since the mid-1970s Congress has held hearings on a string of target programs for teenage mothers. First the School-Age Mother and Child Health Act (2182) was passed, followed by the Adolescent Health, Services, and Pregnancy Prevention and Care Act of 1978 (2191), the Adolescent Family Life Program, which was reauthorized repeatedly since 1981, and finally, the Adolescent Pregnancy Prevention, Care, and Research Grants Act of 1988 (2217).

Several information gathering hearings since the mid-1970s examined trends in adolescent pregnancy and the contributing factors to the problem. Among the most notable of these are *Adolescent Pregnancy* (2188) and *Fertility and Contraception in America: Adolescent and Pre-Adolescent Pregnancy* (2190), both held in 1978, the 1984 hearing *Adolescents in Crisis: Parental Involvement* (2202), and *Pregnancy among Black Teenagers* (2212) from 1986. Other reports of interest include *Teenage Pregnancy: What Is Being Done? A State-by-State Look* (2210, 2213) and the Public Health Service statistical report, *Trends in Teenage Childbearing, United States, 1970-81* (2205). The late 1980s focus on self-sufficiency is reflected in a 1990 Congressional Budget Office report, *Sources of Support for Adolescent Mothers* (2222). The legal issues of illegitimacy and child support are covered in Chapter 15; some additional documents discussing illegitimacy and the Aid to Families with Dependent Children program are found in Chapter 16, Public Assistance and Poverty.

2150. U.S. Children's Bureau. *Illegitimacy as a Child Welfare Problem, Part 2: A Study of Original Records in the City of Boston and the State of Massachusetts.* by Emma O. Lundberg and Katharine F. Lenroot. Publication no. 75. Washington, DC: GPO, 1921. 408p. L5.20:75. Results of a study of illegitimacy in Boston provide statistics on children born out-of-wedlock and relates the figures to infant mortality, parentage, characteristics of mother and father, care of the child, and provision of care by social agencies and by the parents. The legal issues of illegitimacy in Massachusetts and illegitimate children who become wards of the state are also reviewed.

2151. U.S. Children's Bureau. *Illegitimacy as a Child Welfare Problem, Part 3: Methods of Care in Selected Urban and Rural Communities.* Publication no. 128. Washington, DC: GPO, 1924. 260p. L5.20:128. Report describes assistance to unmarried mothers, characteristics of the parents of children born out-of-wedlock, care of unmarried mothers during confinement, and care of illegitimate child in Philadelphia, Milwaukee, and New York State. The results of Minnesota's illegitimacy legislation are also described.

2152. U.S. Children's Bureau. *The Welfare of Infants of Illegitimate Birth in Baltimore.* by Rene Rosenburg and A. Madorah Donahue. Publication no. 144. Washington, DC: GPO, 1925. 24p. L5.20:144. Study reports the effects on child survival of a Maryland law prohibiting the separation of a child younger than six months from its mother except under special circumstances. The effects of the law on social work agencies that provide care for unwed mothers are also examined.

2153. U.S. Children's Bureau. *Children of Illegitimate Birth and Measures for Their Protection.* by Emma O. Lundberg. Publication no. 166. Washington, DC: GPO, 1926. 20p. L5.20:166. General discussion reviews the prevalence and problems of birth out-of-wedlock and promotes preventive social measures and constructive legislation to alleviate the problem.

2154. U.S. Children's Bureau. *A Study of Maternity Homes in Minnesota and Pennsylvania.* Publication no. 167. Washington, DC: GPO, 1926. 92p. L5.20:167. Information on the facilities and administration of maternity homes in Minnesota and Pennsylvania covers topics of admission and postnatal care, recreation, and training for future employment.

2155. U.S. Children's Bureau. *Children of Illegitimate Birth Whose Mothers Have Kept Their Custody.* by A. Madorah Donahue. Publication no. 190. Washington, DC: GPO, 1928. 105p. L5.20:190. Study of case histories of mothers who kept their illegitimate children in their custody looks at the effect of the decision on the mother and the welfare of the child. Reviews the policies of the organization cooperating in the study in regard to keeping children and mothers together, plans for the care of the child, status of mother and children in the community, and sources of support of the children. Case histories of children whose mothers married are compared with cases where the mother did not marry.

2156. U.S. Children's Bureau. *Protective Case Work for Young People and Maternity Homes.* by Glenn Steele. Washington, DC: GPO, 1932. 16p. L5.20/a:P946. Report provides statistics on young people in supervised programs such as Big Brother and Big Sister programs and in maternity homes for unwed mothers. Maternity home data includes number of mothers and babies cared for, rate per population 15-44 years of age, average number of days care per women, average size of staff, and number of live birth, stillbirths, and infant and maternal deaths. All data is given for selected metropolitan areas.

2157. U.S. Children's Bureau. *List of References on Illegitimacy.* by Evangeline Kendall. Washington, DC: The Bureau, 1935. 8p. L5.40:Il6/935. Briefly annotated bibliography lists articles, books, and government reports on illegitimacy, mostly from the public welfare perspective.

2158. U.S. Children's Bureau. *List of References on Illegitimacy.* Washington, DC: The Bureau, 1939. 12p. L5.40:Il6/939. Annotated list of books and articles on the problems of children born out-of-wedlock covers the literature from 1926 to 1939.

2159. U.S. Children's Bureau. *Problems and Procedures in Adoption.* by Mary Ruth Colby. Publication no. 262. Washington, DC: GPO, 1941. 130p. L5.20:262. Study explores the existing legal procedures for adoption and the relationship between illegitimacy and adoption. Reports data on marital status of parents and status of birth for children for whom adoption petitions were filed, the relationship of petitioner to child, and characteristics of the adoptive parent.

2160. U.S. Children's Bureau. *The Use of the Social-Service Exchange in Situations Involving Birth Out-of-Wedlock.* Washington, DC: The Bureau, 1941. 8p. No SuDoc number. Discusses the special confidentiality problems involved in the practice of exchanging information between social service agencies when an unwed mother is involved.

2161. U.S. Children's Bureau. *Meeting Challenge of Today's Needs in Working with Unmarried Mother through Use of Institution.* Washington, DC: The Bureau, 1943. 9p. L5.47:In7/2. Paper given at the war regional meeting of the National Conference of Social Work, St. Louis, Mo., April 14, 1943, emphasizes the need to treat each unmarried mother as an individual. Both the physical and psychological needs of unmarried mothers are examined and arguments for and against placing the child for adoption are reviewed. The problems and strengths of maternity homes are discussed with an emphasis on the need for such homes to be less rigid and to shed the tendency to adopt a punishment mentality toward the mother.

2162. U.S. Children's Bureau. *Psychological Implications of Unmarried Parenthood.* by Florence Clothier. Washington, DC: The Bureau, 1943. 19p. L5.2:P21. Reprint from *The American Journal of Orthopsychiatry* (July 1943) discusses the importance of the role of motherhood in the emotional life of mature woman and the implications of unwed parenthood, particularly for women. Very Freudian interpretation of the psychological development of men and women and the role of parenthood in psychological maturity discusses female acceptance of inferiority and adolescent fantasies of rape and prostitution as they relate to unmarried pregnancy.

2163. U.S. Children's Bureau. *Shall I Keep My Baby? Nurse Has Golden Opportunities in Situations Involving Unmarried Mothers.* by Maud Morlock. Washington, DC: The Bureau, 1943. 4p. L5.2:B11/2. Reprint from *Trained Nurse and Hospital Review* (July 1942) discusses the emotional problems faced by the unwed mother as she decides whether to keep her baby or give it up for adoption. Nurses are encouraged to see that the woman gets sound advice from a social worker.

2164. U.S. Children's Bureau. *Unmarried Mothers in Wartime.* by Maud Morlock. Washington, DC: The Bureau, 1943. 13p. L5.47:Un5/5. Paper presented at the regional meeting of the National Conference of Social Work in New York, March 1943 and at the regional meeting in St. Louis, April 1943 (2161), in revised form.

2165. U.S. Children's Bureau. *Birth Out of Wedlock.* Washington, DC: The Bureau, 1945. 13p. L52.:B53/4. Children's Bureau policy on various matters related to birth out-of-wedlock are presented in this report. Birth certificate information, community services for unmarried mothers, adoption laws, and the right to support for illegitimate children of servicemen are the main topics. A report is also given of illegitimate birth rates during the war years with an estimate of legitimate children conceived prior to marriage. Finally, the report gives examples of successful social programs in local areas designed to assist unmarried mothers.

2166. U.S. Children's Bureau. *Factors Affecting Decision of Unmarried Mother to Give Up or Keep Her Child, Environmental Factors.* by Abigail Bosworth. Washington, DC: The Bureau, 1945. 8p. L5.47:Un5/3. Paper given at the National Conference of Social

Work, Cleveland, Ohio, May 26, 1944, examines point by point the role of factors such as community, financial security, culture, and social strata on an unwed mother's decision to give up her baby.

2167. U.S. Children's Bureau. *List of References on Illegitimacy.* Washington, DC: The Bureau, 1945. 11p. L5.40:Il6/945. Lists books, journal articles, and government publications on illegitimacy.

2168. U.S. Children's Bureau. *Services for Unmarried Mothers and Their Children.* Washington, DC: GPO, 1945. 18p. L5.2:Un5/2. Discusses the various problems and related services for unwed mothers including financial assistance, health care, and establishment of paternity. Outlines the services which should be provided and suggests which services should be provided at the state level and which at the community level. Federally funded programs for maternal and infant health and aid to dependent children are reviewed. In particular the publication notes problems of illegitimacy directly related to wartime, such as wives of servicemen becoming pregnant while the husband is overseas.

2169. U.S. Children's Bureau. *Services to Unmarried Mothers as Kate Waller Barrett Might Have Wanted Them Today.* by Maud Morlock. Washington, DC: The Bureau, 1945. 7p. L5.47:Un5. Paper read at the Conference of Florence Crittenton Homes, Toledo, Ohio, May 22, 1944, summarizes the contributions of Kate Waller Barrett to the provision of services to unwed mothers and points to the need to continue her work in securing humane treatment of unwed mothers.

2170. U.S. Children's Bureau. *Maternity Homes for Unmarried Mothers: A Community Service.* by Maud Morlock and Hilary Campbell. Publication no. 309. Washington, DC: GPO, 1946. 94p. L5.20:309. Discussion of maternity homes provides an historical overview of attitudes and treatment of unmarried mothers and highlights the trend toward a more supportive approach. Services provided in maternity homes and the role of social case workers are described.

2171. U.S. Children's Bureau. *Adolescent Unmarried Mother.* by Maud Morlock. Washington, DC: The Bureau, 1947. [2]p. FS3.202:Un5. Reprint from *Practical Home Economics* (May 1946) discusses the social, psychological, and medical problems of the unwed pregnant teenager and gives advice on how teachers can help the girl cope with her situation. The implications of keeping the baby or giving it up for adoption are reviewed.

2172. U.S. Social Security Administration. Bureau of Public Assistance. *Illegitimacy and Its Impact on the Aid to Dependent Children Program.* Washington, DC: The Bureau, 1960. 82p. FS3.2:Il6. Discussion of the problem of illegitimacy and its relation to the ADC program looks at trends in illegitimacy by race and area, causes of illegitimacy, and factors underlaying increases in the ADC caseload. Provides data on illegitimate births by race, ADC families with an unwed mother, status of father in ADC families, and employment status of mothers of illegitimate children. Includes a bibliography.

2173. U.S. Children's Bureau. *A Guide for the Development of Services in Public Welfare, Unmarried Parents.* Bureau of Public Assistance Report no. 45; Children's Bureau Publication no. 390-1961. Washington, DC: GPO, 1961. 63p. FS3.13:45 or FS14.111:390. What is being done and what should be done to aid unmarried parents, particularly unwed mothers, is the topic of this study. Includes discussion of prenatal care and living arrangements for unwed mothers as well as public assistance after the birth of the child. Provides an excellent bibliography on unwed parents.

2174. U.S. Children's Bureau. *Health Services for Unmarried Mothers.* by Elizabeth Herzog and Rose Bernstein. Publication no. 425-1964. Washington, DC: GPO, 1964. 61p.

FS14.111:425. The reasons unwed mothers do not seek prenatal care and the way services could be restructured to address the problem are the topics of this report. Among the specific issues addressed are the desire of unwed mothers to conceal their pregnancy, ignorance of the need for prenatal care, and varying eligibility requirements for subsidized prenatal care.

2175. U.S. Children's Bureau. *About the Poor, Some Facts and Some Fictions.* Publication 451. Washington, DC: GPO, 1968. 85p. FS17.210:451. Two of four papers presented here describe the incidence of unwed motherhood among the poor and its significance for social services. The breakdown of the black family, assumptions about the poor, and the culture of poverty are also covered.

2176. U.S. Children's Bureau. *Effective Patterns of Services to Unmarried Parents.* Washington, DC: The Bureau, 1968. 8p. FS17.217:G13. Speech on services to unwed pregnant teenagers focuses on community and administrative actions to meet their needs. Briefly looks at successful programs and outlines steps which should be taken on a local level.

2177. U.S. Children's Bureau. *Multiservice Programs for Pregnant School Girls.* Washington, DC: The Bureau, 1968. 47p. FS17.202:G44. Describes 35 programs providing education, health, and welfare services to pregnant teenagers who are excluded from school.

2178. U.S. Children's Bureau. *National Trends in Service to Unmarried Parents.* by Ursula M. Gallagher. Washington, DC: The Bureau, 1968. 10p. FS17.217:G13/2. Focus of this speech is on the case of the unwed mother, in particular teenage girls, and the types of social services they need. Existing programs in health services, education and social services are described, and possible areas of improvement in services to pregnant teenagers are put forward.

2179. U.S. Public Health Service. *Trends in Illegitimacy, United States, 1940-1965.* Washington, DC: GPO, 1968. 90p. HE20.6209:21/15. Describes recent trends and differentials in illegitimacy, particularly for the period 1955-65. Estimates of illegitimacy rates by race and age of mother are presented and changes in the incidence of illegitimacy over time and variations in illegitimacy by race, age of mother, live-birth order, and place of residence are discussed.

2180. U.S. Children's Bureau. *School Continues for Pregnant Teenagers.* by Marion Howard. Washington, DC: GPO, 1969. 3p. FS5.220:20115. General discussion outlines programs to help pregnant teenagers stay in school.

2181. U.S. Health Services and Mental Health Administration. *The Maternal and Child Health Service Reports on Research to Improve Health Services for Mothers and Children.* Washington, DC: GPO, 1973. 29p. HE20.2752:R31/973. Report on SSA Title V funded research and projects in maternal and child health includes several brief reports dealing with adolescent pregnancy.

2182. U.S. Public Health Service. *Teenagers: Marriages, Divorces, Parenthood, and Mortality.* Washington, DC: GPO, 1973. 42p. HE20.6209:21/23. Analysis of teenage marriage, divorce, parenthood, and mortality during the 1960's furnishes information on illegitimacy rates and ratios.

2183. U.S. Congress. Senate. Committee on Labor and Public Welfare. Subcommittee on Health. *School-Age Mother and Child Health Act, 1975, Hearing on S. 2538.* 95th Cong., 1st sess., 4 Nov. 1975. 878p. Y4.L11/2:Sch6/21/975. Discussion of the teenage pregnancy rate and of federal programs to address the problem covers a wide range of issues from the funding and philosophy of family planning services to medical, educational, and economic assistance to teenage mothers. Includes several studies of programs for care of unwed pregnant teenagers and a lengthy statement on approaches to teenage pregnancy by an anti-abortion organization. Much of the data from existing studies focuses on health care seeking behavior of pregnant teenagers. Reprints a bibliography, "Parenting Guide - Selected Resources and Materials 1965 - 1975," by the National Alliance Concerned with School-Age Parents.

2184.   U.S. Bureau of the Census. *Premarital Fertility.* Current Population Reports Series P-23, no. 63. Washington, DC: GPO, 1976. 52p.   C3.186:P-23/63. Statistical report on children born before first marriage and characteristics of mothers who conceive before marriage describes age, race, education, occupation of husband, occupation of wife, and years of first marriage.

2185.   U.S. Bureau of Community Health Services. *Studies in Adolescent Health, Research to Improve Health Services for Mothers and Children.* Washington, DC: GPO, 1977. 30p. HE20.5114/2:Ad7. Briefly summarizes federally funded projects on adolescent health including several programs aimed at school-age parents.

2186.   U.S. Health Services Administration. *Teenage Pregnancy, Everybody's Problem.* Washington, DC: GPO, 1977. 9p. HE20.5102:P91/3. Pamphlet provides a concise overview of the problem of adolescent pregnancy and prevention, abortion, and prenatal care.

2187.   U.S. National Commission on the Observance of International Women's Year. *Teenage Pregnancy.* Washington, DC: GPO, 1977. 50p. Y3.W84:10/16. Materials for a workshop on teenage pregnancy includes program ideas, fact sheets, regional/state data on teenage birthrates and abortions, and resource lists of publications, films and organizations.

2188.   U.S. Congress. House. Committee on Education and Labor. Subcommittee on Select Education. *Adolescent Pregnancy, Hearing on H.R. 12146.* 95th Cong., 2d sess., 24 July 1978. 320p. Y4.Ed8/1:Ad7. Hearing witnesses discuss the short term and long term consequences of teenage pregnancy from both health and economic angles. The cycle started by teenage pregnancy is examined and possibilities for breaking the cycle through education and family planning services are debated. Supplementary material provides statistics on births to 14- to 19-year-olds between 1920 and 1976 by age; out of wedlock births by age, 1960-1976; and sexual activity levels of teenagers.

2189.   U.S. Congress. House. Committee on Interstate and Foreign Commerce. Subcommittee on Health and the Environment. *Adolescent Health, Services, and Pregnancy Prevention Care Act of 1978, Hearing.* 95th Cong., 2nd sess., 28 June 1978. 251p. Y4.In8/4:95-113. Hearing presents the case for a bill to support community based teenage pregnancy prevention programs and to provide health care and social services to pregnant adolescents. Issues raised include parental consent, contraception and abortion.

2190.   U.S. Congress. House. Select Committee on Population. *Fertility and Contraception in America: Adolescent and Pre-Adolescent Pregnancy, Hearing, Volume II.* 95th Cong., 2nd sess., 28 Feb. - 2 Mar. 1978. 689p. Y4.P81:95/3. Testimony describes the extent of the teenage pregnancy problem and examines the contraceptive practices and abortion rates among teenage women. The educational and economic implications of teenage pregnancy are discussed and trends in placing illegitimate infants up for adoption are analyzed. The issue of the parental role in sex education and availability of contraceptives is explored. The federal role in funding sex education and family planning services for teenagers and related research is also reviewed. Statistics include birth rates for U.S. teenagers, 1910-1975, and out-of-wedlock births to teenagers 1960 and 1975 by race.

Reprints "Contraception Services for Adolescents: United States, Each State and County, 1975" by the Alan Guttmacher Institute and the "Interfaith Statement on Sex Education" by the U.S. Catholic Conference, National Council of Churches, and Synagogue Council of America.

2191. U.S. Congress. Senate. Committee on Human Resources. *Adolescent Health, Services, and Pregnancy Prevention and Care Act of 1978, Hearings on S. 2910.* 95th Cong., 2nd sess., 14 June 1978. 778p. Y4.H88:Ad7/2. Hearing on the needs of pregnant teenagers discusses the best way to prevent pregnancy and to provide support services to pregnant teenagers. While all testifying agree on the need to deal with the teenage pregnancy issue, disagreements are evident on prevention approaches, sex education, and the role of parents. One aspect of care repeatedly stressed is the need to help pregnant teenagers finish high school, and examples of model school programs are examined. Statistics illustrate the relationship between welfare dependency and age at birth of first child, and provide data on pregnancy outcome, out-of-wedlock births, and infant mortality rates for teenagers. Reprints "Adolescent Pregnancy and Childbearing - Growing Concerns for Americans," from *Population Bulletin* (v. 31, no. 2), which provides an excellent summary of trends and implications of teenage pregnancy.

2192. U.S. Congress. Senate. Committee on Human Resources. *Adolescent Health, Services, and Pregnancy Prevention and Care Act of 1978, Report to Accompany S. 2910.* S. Rept. 95-1206, 95th Cong., 2d sess., 1978. 39p. Serial 13197-12. Report with minority views describes the problems of adolescent pregnancy and details a proposed federal grant program to support local health and support services programs. A primary goal is to break the cycle of teenage pregnancy and lifelong welfare dependency. The socioeconomic consequences of teenage motherhood are described and the issue of providing unbiased counseling on all alternatives for a pregnant teenager are discussed. Minority views highlight the number of existing family planning and maternal health programs and express concern over the unbiased counselling issue.

2193. U.S. National Library of Medicine. *Adolescent Pregnancy, January 1975 through April 1978, 254 Citations.* Bethesda, MD: The National Library of Medicine, 1978. 16p. HE20.3614/2:78-8.

2194. U.S. Congress. Senate. Committee on Labor and Human Resources. Subcommittee on Child and Human Development. *Oversight on Adoption Reform Act (Public Law 95-266), Hearing.* 96th Cong., 2d sess., 17 Apr. 1980. 475p. Y4.L11/4:Ad7. Much of the discussion in this hearing on the Adoption Reform Act focuses on the desire of adopted children to locate their natural parents and on the psychological needs of the natural mother to know the fate of her child. The pros and cons of protecting the natural mother are debated in relation to a model adoption act for the states.

2195. U.S. Dept. of Health and Human Services. Office of the Assistant Secretary for Planning and Evaluation. Project Share. *Adolescent Pregnancy.* Washington, DC: GPO, 1980. 38p. HE1.18/4:Ad7. Annotated bibliography lists current books, reports and journal articles on services to pregnant adolescents and teenage fathers.

2196. U.S. National Institutes of Health. *Adolescent Pregnancy and Childbearing: Findings from Research.* by Catherine S. Chilman. Washington, DC: GPO, 1980. 339p. HE20.3002:Ad7/2. Research papers from the Conference on Determinants of Adolescent Pregnancy and Childbearing and from the Conference on Consequences of Adolescent Pregnancy and Childbearing look at the psychological, economic, and social consequences of teenage pregnancy and at teenager's contraceptive practices.

2197. U.S. Public Health Service. *Trends and Differentials in Births to Unmarried Women: United States, 1970-76.* Washington, DC: GPO, 1980. 74p. HE20.6209:21/36. An analysis of trends and differentials in childbearing by unmarried women discusses variations in relation to age of mother, live-birth order, race, educational attainment, and place of residence. Also examines the relationship of childbearing by unwed women to health factors such as low birth weight and prenatal care.

2198. U.S. Congress. Senate. *Adolescent Family Life, Report Together with Additional Views to Accompany S. 1090.* S. Rept. 97-161, 97th Cong., 1st sess., 1981. 32p. Serial 13401. Report recommends repeal of existing Adolescent Health Services and Pregnancy Prevention and Care programs and replacement with a new Title XX PHSA program. The proposed program is based on research and demonstration grants with the money divided between adolescent pregnancy prevention programs and services to pregnant adolescents. The bill mandates the involvement of parents when providing service to unemancipated minors and prohibits the use of program funds for abortion. Concerns over rising teenage pregnancy, abortion and illegitimate birth rates are expressed as is the need for a family and community centered approach.

2199. U.S. Congress. House. *Extending the Adolescent Family Life Demonstration Program, Conference Report to Accompany S. 2616.* H. Rept. 98-1154, 98th Cong., 2d sess., 1984. 3p. Serial 13602. Conference report fails to resolve the difficult issues which marked the difference between the House and Senate versions of a bill to extend the Adolescent Family Life program under Title XX of the PHSA. The agreement reached extends the Adolescent Family Life Program and the federal family planning programs under Title X for one year noting the intention to examine the issues through hearings in the 99th Congress.

2200. U.S. Congress. House. Select Committee on Children, Youth, and Families. *Federal Programs Affecting Children, Committee Print with Supplemental Views of Chairman George Miller, Supplemental Views of Congressman Thomas J. Bliley, Jr.* 98th Cong., 1st sess., Jan. 1984. 232p. Y4.C43/2:C43/7. Concise description of federal programs affecting children covers family planning, teenage pregnancy, and child support enforcement programs, as well as child care tax credits and public assistance programs, many of which are in aid of single mothers.

2201. U.S. Congress. Senate. Committee on Labor and Human Resources. *The Adolescent Family Life Act, Report to Accompany S. 2616.* S. Rept. 98-496, 98th Cong., 2d sess., 1984. 21p. Serial 13559. Report on extension of the Adolescent Family Life Demonstration Program provides background on the program designed to address the problems of adolescent pregnancy. The program emphasized adoption and agencies were only allowed to provide family planning services to teens who were already pregnant or were parents. Referrals to abortion services were only allowed if both the adolescent and her parent request the information. The rate of teenage sexual activity and pregnancy and the social and economic consequences of adolescent pregnancy are reviewed as background for the bill.

2202. U.S. Congress. Senate. Committee on Labor and Human Resources. Subcommittee on Family and Human Services. *Adolescents in Crisis: Parental Involvement, Hearing.* 98th Cong., 2d sess., 24 Feb. 1984. 253p. Y4.L11/4:S.hrg.98-903. Hearing to examine the need for parental involvement when teenagers use government subsidized services discusses drug abuse, mental illness, family planning, and sex education. The issue of mandatory parental notification for teenagers served under Title X family planning is examined from both the social and legal standpoints. A history of congressional intent and court review of parental consent requirements and Title X is provided.

2203. U.S. Congress. Senate. Committee on Labor and Human Resources. Subcommittee on Family and Human Services. *Reauthorization of the Adolescent Family Life Demonstration Project Act of 1981, Hearings.* 98th Cong., 2d sess., 24,26 Apr. 1984. 231p. Y4.L11/4:S.hrg.98-1209. Hearing testimony details the incidence and problems of adolescent pregnancy and the services offered under the Adolescent Family Life project authorized under Title XX of the PHSA. The emphasis in the programs on postponement of sexual activity and the family centered approach are highlighted. The adoption alternative for pregnant teens is studied at some length.

2204. U.S. National Library of Medicine. *Adolescent Parenthood.* by Charlotte Kenton. NLM Literature Search 84-15. Washington, DC: GPO, 1984. 11p. HE20.3614/2:84-15. Bibliography lists articles and some monographs on the health and psychological aspects of adolescent motherhood and studies on the adolescent father drawn from the MEDLINE database.

2205. U.S. Public Health Service. *Trends in Teenage Childbearing, United States, 1970-81.* Washington, DC: GPO, 1984. 22p. HE20.6209:21/41. An analytical review of recent trends and differentials in childbearing by teenagers furnishes breakdowns by age, race, marital status, and educational attainment.

2206. U.S. Congress. House. Committee on Energy and Commerce. Subcommittee on Health and Environment. *Pregnancy-Related Health Services, Hearings on Prevention of Low Birthweight, Adolescent Pregnancy and Reauthorization of Adolescent Family Life Act - H.R.927, Family Planning Act Reauthorization.* 99th Cong., 1st sess., 25 Feb. - 27 Mar. 1985. 499p. Y4.En2/3:99-13. The primary focus of hearing testimony is Title X family planning services and Title XX adolescent family life programs. The hearing on reauthorization of the Adolescent Family Life Act emphasizes health care and adoption counseling for pregnant teenage girls. Discussion of the Family Planning Act reauthorization covers the need for family planning services and the Planned Parenthood-abortion issue. Parental notification as a requirement for adolescent family planning services is a recurring theme. Several articles on comparative studies of adolescent pregnancy in the U.S. and in other developed countries are reprinted.

2207. U.S. Congress. House. Committee on Post Office and Civil Service. Subcommittee on Census and Population and U.S. Congress. House. Committee on Energy and Commerce. Subcommittee on Health and the Environment. *Demographics of Adolescent Pregnancy in the U.S., Joint Hearing.* 99th Cong., 1st sess., 30 April 1985. 127p. Y4.P84/10:99-5. Hearing testimony details trends in teenage pregnancy and childbearing in the U.S. and discusses the implications for family planning policy. Sex education, patterns of contraceptive use, and long-term social consequences of adolescent childbearing are explored. The Census Bureau provides a statistical profile of teenage childbearing in the U.S. by year, race, and marital status.

2208. U.S. Congress. House. Committee on Ways and Means. *Deficit Reduction Amendments of 1985, Report Together with Dissenting and Additional Dissenting Views to Accompany H.R. 3128.* H. Rept. 99-241, part 1, 99th Cong., 1st sess., 1985. 196p. Serial 13651. Among the programs authorized in this bill covering Medicare, AFDC, trade, and revenue is a teenage pregnancy block grant program aimed at children of AFDC families and at teenage AFDC parents.

2209. U.S. Congress. House. Committee on Ways and Means. Subcommittee on Public Assistance and Unemployment Compensation. *Teenage Pregnancy Issues, Hearing.* 99th Cong., 1st sess., 7 May 1985. 252p. Y4.W36:99-33. Testimony explores the problem of teenage pregnancy and its link to welfare dependency. Existing state and federal programs are described and the role of family planning and sex education in prevention programs are discussed. The incidence of adolescent pregnancy among black women is particularly stressed. Education and training programs for adolescent mothers are also discussed in terms of self-sufficiency. Several teenage mothers answer questions about raising a child as a teenager, welfare, their relationship with the father, and the effect of the pregnancy on their friends' sexual habits.

2210.   U.S. Congress. House. Select Committee on Children, Youth, and Families. *Teen Pregnancy: What is Being Done? A State-by-State Look.* 99th Cong., 1st sess., 1985. Committee print. 397p. Y4.C43/2:T22/3. Background information on teenage pregnancy provides information by state on births to teenagers by age of mother, abortions by age of woman, miscarriages by age of woman, and infant mortality by age of mother. Also reports on female adolescent school dropout rates, pregnant and parenting adolescents receiving AFDC, and adolescent unemployment rates. Describes programs for pregnant teenagers and state comments on federal aid programs.

2211.   U.S. National Center for Health Statistics. *An Evaluation of California's Inferred Birth Statistics for Unmarried Women.* Washington, DC: The Center, 1985. 28p. HE20.6209:2/97. Report examines the reliability of statistics on births to unmarried women in California by evaluating the accuracy of its inferential method of data production. The need to determine the rate of births to unmarried women in states such as California, which do not record marital status on the birth certificate, for social research is stressed.

2212.   U.S. Congress. House. Committee on Ways and Means. Subcommittee on Public Assistance and Unemployment Compensation. *Pregnancy among Black Teenagers, Hearing.* 99th Cong., 2d sess., 18 Feb. 1986. 416p. Y4.W36:99-60. The transcript of a CBS Reports episode "The Vanishing Family - Crisis in Black America" starts out this hearing on the problem of illegitimate births to black teenagers. The transcript reveals the culture of black teenagers in relation to illegitimacy. The need to address poverty and employment options as factors in teenage pregnancy are discussed as are programs to encourage teenagers to stay in school. The role of a broad spectrum of federal programs in addressing these problems is discussed.

2213.   U.S. Congress. House. Select Committee on Children, Youth, and Families. *Teenage Pregnancy: What is Being Done? A State-By-State Look, Report Together with Additional and Minority Views.* H. Rept. 99-1022, 99th Cong., 2d sess., 1986. 397p. Serial 13714. A survey of state experiences with the problem of teenage pregnancy forms the basis of this report which explores the extent of the problem and reviews state efforts to deal with the issue. Data reported and analyzed include teenage sexual activity and pregnancy rates, prenatal care, education and income prospects of pregnant teens, long term social consequences, and adoption. The problems faced by states in addressing teenage pregnancy and the relationship between federal programs and state efforts are discussed. The report includes state statistics showing the number of births to teenage mothers, abortions by age of mother, number of females dropping out of school due to pregnancy and child care responsibilities, and pregnant and parenting adolescents receiving AFDC. State-wide initiatives and recent policy changes are noted for each state. Lengthy minority views discuss the need for family involvement and the strengths and weakness of school-based programs.

2214.   U.S. Congress. Senate. Committee on Labor and Human Resources. *Adolescent Family Life Act of 1986, Report to Accompany S. 1566.* S. Rept. 99-298, 99th Cong., 2d sess., 1986. 7p. Serial 13674. An overview of the extent of the teenage pregnancy problem in the U.S. and of federal programs to address the problem is provided in this report reauthorizing the Adolescent Family Life Act. The bill makes little change in the act which focuses on postponement of adolescent premarital sexual activity and provides services to pregnant and parenting teens. The program stresses alternatives to abortion and promotes adoption as an alternative.

2215. U.S. General Accounting Office. *Teenage Pregnancy: 500,00 Births a Year but Few Tested Programs: Briefing Report to the Honorable John H. Chafee, United States Senate.* Washington, DC: The Office, 1986. 56p. GA1.13:PEMD-86-16-BR. The trends in teenage pregnancy and the effectiveness of demonstration programs to combat the problem are examined. Possibilities for future legislation in response to reports from the demonstration projects are presented, and an analysis of effective teen pregnancy programs is provided.

2216. U.S. Women's Bureau. *Employment-Focused Programs for Adolescent Mothers.* Washington, DC: GPO, 1986. 47p. L36.102:Ad5. Three basic models for developing the employability of adolescent mothers came out of a consultation with educators, health professionals, representatives of community-based programs, and federal agency representatives. The models presented here are the community based model, the school based model and the work study model.

2217. U.S. Congress. Senate. Committee on Labor and Human Resources. *Adolescent Pregnancy Prevention, Care, and Research Grants Act of 1988, Report to Accompany S. 1950 Together with Minority Views.* S. Rept. 100-591, 100th Cong., 2d sess., 1988. 73p. Serial 13867. Minority views object to S. 1950 on the basis that it turns the Adolescent Family Life Program way from its sexual abstinence-family involvement focus and stresses provision of information on family planning services and methods. Also objected to are requirements that clients be informed of the availability of abortion counseling and the elimination of restrictions on such counseling and on abortion referral. A history of federal programs focused on teen pregnancy and the economic and social consequences of adolescent motherhood are presented.

2218. U.S. Congress. House. Select Committee on Children, Youth and Families. *Caring for Young Black Children at Risk in Louisiana, Hearing.* 101st Cong., 1st sess., 14 July 1989. New Orleans, LA. 225p. Y4.C43/2:B27/2. Hearing on child care issues for black children in Louisiana focuses on developmental aspects of day care, but also discusses adolescent pregnancy and possible program approaches.

2219. U.S. Congress. Senate. Committee on Labor and Human Resources. *Adolescent Pregnancy Prevention, Care, and Research Grants Act of 1989, Report Together with Minority Views to Accompany S. 120.* S. Rept. 101-103 (star print), 101st Cong., 1st sess., 1989. 69p. Recommendations on reauthorization of the Adolescent Family Life Demonstration Projects provide background on trends in adolescent pregnancy in the United States. The results of adolescent pregnancy programs are briefly reviewed. A point of contention between majority and minority views is the issue of abortion counseling, which was banned under earlier law but was authorized under S. 120.

2220. U.S. Congress. Senate. Committee on Labor and Human Resources. *Current Patterns and Programs for Teenage Pregnancy Prevention: A Summary for Policy Makers.* by the Institute for Research and Evaluation. 101st Cong., 1st sess., 1989. Committee print. 31p. Y4.L11/4:S.prt.101-52. Review of teenage pregnancy prevention programs examines their primary strategies and considers research on predictors of sexual activity and pregnancy. Guidelines for policy approaches to teenage pregnancy are put forward.

2221. U.S. Congress. House. Committee on Energy and Commerce. *Adolescent Family Life Amendments of 1990, Report to Accompany H.R. 5692.* H. Rept.101-867, 101st Cong., 2d sess., 1990. 4p. Brief report recommends reauthorization of the Adolescent Family Life Program.

2222. U.S. Congressional Budget Office. *Sources of Support for Adolescent Mothers.* Washington, DC: The Office, 1990. 94p. Y10.2:Su7. Report on the extent of adolescent motherhood and the sources of financial support for teenage mothers reviews factors affecting income sources. Data on the extent and source of private support by marital status and living arrangement is examined focusing on parental support, support from husbands and absent fathers, and self-support. The use of public assistance, mainly AFDC, as a means of support is also reviewed by race, age and marital status. Government policy approaches to encourage self-sufficiency and reduce the problems of adolescent parenthood are presented. Supporting statistics from the Census Bureau and from the National Longitudinal Survey of Youth are incorporated in the report.

SERIALS

2223. U.S. National Center for Social Statistics. *Adoptions in (year).* Washington, DC: GPO, 1970- . annual. HE17.646:year. Reports adoption statistics by state for children born in wedlock or out-of-wedlock by relative or nonrelative petitioner, by race/ethnicity, and by type of placement.

2224. U.S. Office for Maternal and Child Health. *Food for the Teenager during Pregnancy.* Washington, DC: GPO, 1976-1978. annual rev. HE20.5102:P91/2/year.

15

Divorce and Child Support

The earliest document identified which dealt with a women's issue was the 1804 House of Representatives report on the petitions of several women of the District of Columbia who were seeking divorce from their husbands (2225). The question of divorce was also addressed between 1892 and 1924 in a series of attempts to grant Congress power to establish uniform marriage and divorce laws. The encouragement of the desertion of wife and children under disparate state laws was a common theme of reports and hearings at that time (2228, 2252, 2259, 2260). The issue of non-support of wife and children in the District of Columbia is described in a series of House and Senate reports beginning in 1906 and continuing through 1926. The reports include discussion of a 1910 amendment to the law expanding coverage to illegitimate children (2247) and of a 1926 bill placing nonsupport cases in the Juvenile Court and eliminating the sentence of hard labor (2261).

Starting in 1918 a steady flow of documents reviewed state and international laws on illegitimate children and detailed provisions for paternity establishment and the right to support (2254, 2255, 2258, 2262, 2264). The question of child support and the Aid to Families with Dependent Children is first raised in the 1960 report, *Support from Absent Fathers of Children Receiving ADC, 1955* (2271), locating absent parents was the focus of a 1964 meeting sponsored by the Bureau of Family Services (2274). The welfare reform process that began in the early 1970s returned repeatedly to the issue of child support. Child support enforcement as a component of AFDC is discussed in-depth in a number of hearings and reports including a 1973 hearing *Child Support and the Work Bonus* (2283), the 1976 report *Child Support Amendments* (2294), the 1983 *Child Support Enforcement Legislation, Hearing* (2321), *Child Support Enforcement Reform Proposals* (2332) in 1984, and 1987's two part hearing, *Welfare Reform or Replacement?* (2362-2363).

The interstate enforcement of support orders was the focus of hearings held in 1973 (2282), of Office of Child Support Enforcement reports issued in the mid-1980s (2137, 2145), and of General Accounting Office studies in 1989 and 1990 (2374, 2379). The GAO also examined state implementation of the Child Support Enforcement Amendments of 1984 and published a detailed report on child support enforcement provisions in state laws (2355). The establishment in 1976 of the Office of Child Support Enforcement resulted in a wealth of publications over the next decade on enforcement techniques and program administration, similar publications from 1981 on were issued by the National Institute for Child Support Enforcement.

The primary child support issues in the 1980s were the use of wage garnishment and income tax refund intercepts to collect support payments (2319-2320, 2323-2324), and the government role in collecting child support in non-AFDC cases. The main issues surrounding the Social Security Act Title IV-D program for non-AFDC child support collections centered on eligibility for services (2293) and the limits on collection fees which could be withheld by the state (2313, 2321). The effectiveness of the entire Child Support Enforcement Program for both AFDC and non-AFDC cases was reviewed in 1983 and 1984 congressional hearings and reports (2325, 2331, 2332), and in the Social Security Administration report, *Evaluation of the Child Support Enforcement Program, Final Report* (2328). Additional documents discussing child support and the AFDC program can be found in Chapter 15, Public Assistance and Poverty.

2225.   U.S. Congress. House. *Application for Divorces in the District of Columbia.* 8th Cong., 1st sess., 17 Feb. 1804. 1p. American State Papers: X. Miscellaneous no. 172. Serial 37. Having received several petitions of women wishing divorce from their husbands, the committee recommends that the district court of the District of Columbia be invested with the power to grant divorces.

2226.   U.S. Congress. Senate. Committee on Military Affairs. *Report upon Senate Resolution of May 22, 1888 [Amendment of Law to Prevent the Enlistment in Peace Time of Men with Wives without Notice to or Consent of Their Wives].* S. Rept. 2532, 50th Cong., 2d sess., 1889. 1p. Serial 2618. Report deemed such legislation unnecessary since regulations already stated "no man having a wife or minor child shall be enlisted without special authorizing from the Adjutant-General's office."

2227.   U.S. Dept. of Labor. *A Report on Marriage and Divorce in the United States, 1867 to 1886: Including an Appendix Relating to Marriage and Divorce in Certain Countries in Europe.* Washington, DC: GPO, 1891. rev. ed. 1074p. LA1.5:1. Detailed examination with statistics on laws of marriage and divorce in the United States describes the laws and the sectarian influences on marriage and divorce. Statistics provided include duration of marriage before divorce, place of divorce compared to place of marriage, divorces by cause for states and territories, duration of marriage by cause of divorce for states and territories, and divorces with reference to children for states and territories. Also summarizes marriage and divorce laws of selected foreign countries and furnishes statistics on number of marriages and divorces in some cases with cause of divorce and statistics on religion of each party when a difference exists.

2228.   U.S. Congress. House. Committee on the Judiciary. *Marriage and Divorce, Adverse Report to Accompany H. Res. 46.* H. Rept. 1290, 52d Cong., 1st sess., 1892. 8p. Serial 3045. Report against an amendment to the Constitution giving Congress the authority to set laws governing marriage and divorce states that domestic relations are a subject for state rather that federal law. The minority report discusses the inheritance and alimony problems arising from the disparity in state laws and the problems of desertion caused by lax divorce laws in some states and very limited laws in others. A letter reprinted from the *New York Law Journal* describes the confusion caused by existing marriage and divorce laws.

2229.   U.S. Congress. House. Committee on the Judiciary. *Marriage and Divorce, Report to Accompany H. Res. 23.* H. Rept. 1291, 52d Cong., 1st sess., 1892. 1p. Serial 3045. Adverse report refers to the House Report 1290 (2228).

2230.   U.S. Congress. Senate. Committee on Pensions. *Report to Accompany S. 1175 [to Require Payment of Pension Money to Wives in Cases where Male Pensioners Desert or Abandon Their Families, or Are Habitual Drunkards, or for Any Reason Fail and Neglect to Support Their Families].* S. Rept. 646, 53rd Cong., 2d sess., 1894. 1p. Serial 3192. Reports a bill to pay the pension to a wife in cases where the male pensioner fails to support his family, and amends the bill by requiring that the wife be of good character.

2231.   U.S. Congress. Senate. Committee on Pensions. *Report to Accompany S. 242 [Payment of Pension Money to Wives in Cases Where Male Pensioners Desert or Abandon Their*

Families]. S. Rept. 2, 54th Cong., 1st sess., 1895. 2p. Serial 3362. See 2230 for abstract.

2232. U.S. Congress. House. Committee on the Judiciary. *Territorial Divorces, Report to Accompany H.R. 5217.* H. Rept. 428, 54th Cong., 1st sess., 1896. 1p. Serial 3458. Reports a bill requiring one years continuous residence in a territory before being granted a divorce.

2233. U.S. Congress. Senate. Committee on Territories. *Report to Accompany H.R. 5217 [Making One Year's Residence in a Territory a Prerequisite to Obtaining a Divorce There].* S. Rept. 611, 54th Cong., 1st sess., 1896. 1p. Serial 3364. See 2232 for abstract.

2234. U.S. Congress. House. Committee in Invalid Pensions. *Pensions to Deserted Wife or Minor Children of a Soldier, Report to Accompany H.R. 1055 [Pensions for Deserted Wife or Child].* H. Rept. 781, 55th Cong., 2d sess., 1898. 1p. Serial 3719. Favorable report affirms the duty of a husband to support his wife and recommends passage of a bill to pay half of the pension to the wife or minor child deserted by a veteran drawing a pension.

2235. U.S. Congress. Senate. Committee on Pensions. *Amending Section 4766, Revised Statutes, Report to Accompany H.R. 1055 [Pensions for Deserted Wife or Child].* S. Rept. 1408, 55th Cong., 2d sess., 1898. 3p. Serial 3627. See 2234 for abstract.

2236. U.S. Congress. Senate. *Divorce Law for the District of Columbia, to Accompany Amendment to H.R. 9835, Relating to Improvement of District Divorce Law.* S. Doc. 174, 56th Cong., 2d sess, 1901. 4p. Serial 4042. Correspondence supports a move to pass a more restrictive divorce law for the District of Columbia which would allow divorce only on grounds of adultery with legal separation for drunkenness, cruelty, or desertion.

2237. U.S. Congress. Senate. *Paper Relating to Proposed Repeal of "New District Divorce Law."* S. Doc. 305, 57th Cong., 1st sess., 1902. 5p. Serial 4241. Response to a petition of the Bar Association of the District of Columbia to repeal the new divorce law and allow absolute divorce for the causes of desertion, drunkenness, cruelty and adultery reprints S. Doc.174, 56th Congress (2236), and the revised divorce code.

2238. U.S. Congress. House. Committee on the District of Columbia. *Neglect to Support or Abandonment of Wife or Minor Children, Report to Accompany H.R. 14515.* H. Rept. 1551, 59th Cong., 1st sess., 1906. 1p. Serial 4906. District of Columbia measure would make it a misdemeanor to abandon or fail to support a wife or minor children leaving them in "destitute or necessitous circumstances."

2239. U.S. Congress. Senate. Committee on the District of Columbia. *Abandonment of or Neglect to Provide for Wife, Etc., Report to Accompany S. 4303.* S. Rept. 1001, 59th Cong., 1st sess., 1906. 1p. Serial 4904. See 2238 for abstract.

2240. U.S. Congress. Senate. Committee on the District of Columbia. *Abandonment of Wife, etc., District of Columbia, Report to Accompany H.R. 14515.* S. Rept. 1498, 59th Cong., 1st sess., 1906. 1p. Serial 4904. See 2238 for abstract.

2241. U.S. Congress. Senate. Committee on the District of Columbia. *Adverse Report to Accompany S. 2319 [Modification of Marriage Settlement in Decree Granting Divorce].* S. Rept. 475, 59th Cong., 1st sess., 1906. 2p. Serial 4904. Adverse report on a bill allowing courts to modify or set aside divorce settlements made upon or for the benefit of the wife is accompanied by the opinion of the Corporation Council for the Commissioners of the District of Columbia.

2242. U.S. Congress. Senate. Committee on the Judiciary. *Uniform Marriage and Divorce Laws, Adverse Report to Accompany S.R. 9*. S. Rept. 4035, 59th Cong., 1st sess., 1906. 1p. Serial 4905.

2243. U.S. Bureau of the Census. *Marriage and Divorce, 1887-1906*. Bulletin no. 96. Washington, DC: GPO, 1908. 71p. C3.3:96. Statistical report furnishes data on trends in the number of marriages and divorces, 1887-1906; divorces by cause and party to which granted; duration of marriages ending in divorce; divorces by place of marriage and place of divorce; divorces by party to which granted, presence of children, and cause; and divorces contested, alimony asked, and alimony granted. Statistics are given by state.

2244. U.S. Bureau of the Census. *Marriage and Divorce, 1867-1906, Part 1: Summary, Laws, Foreign Statistics*. Washington, DC: GPO, 1909. 533p. C3.5:M34/pt.1. Summary of marriage and divorce laws of the states is accompanied by detailed statistics on marriage and divorce in states and territories, 1887 to 1906. Divorce statistics include cause and party to which granted, and duration of marriage. Also presents statutory regulations governing marriage and divorce in Austria, Hungary, Belgium, Bulgaria, Canada, Australia and New Zealand, Denmark, France, German Empire, England and Wales, Scotland, Ireland, Japan, Netherlands, Norway, Romania, Russian Empire, Servia, Sweden, and Switzerland.

2245. U.S. Bureau of the Census. *Marriage and Divorce, 1867-1906, Part 2: General Tables*. Washington, DC: GPO, 1909. 840p. C3.5:M34/pt.2. Tables for each state provide detailed statistics on divorce from 1887 to 1906 including divorces by cause and libellant; divorces by classified cause, libellant, whether or not contested, and service of notice; divorces by classified cause, libellant and duration of marriage; divorces by duration of marriage and libellant; number of years from separation to divorce; and cases involving children by cause and libellant. Summary statistics for the U.S. are provided showing divorce by classified cause, libellant, and duration of marriage.

2246. U.S. Congress. Senate. Committee on the District of Columbia. *Abandonment of Wife or Minor Children, Adverse Report to Accompany S. 2040*. S. Rept. 188, 61st Cong., 2d sess., 1910. 1p. Serial 5582. Committee favorably reports S. 3890 (2247) in lieu of S. 2040.

2247. U.S. Congress. Senate. Committee on the District of Columbia. *Abandonment of Wife or Minor Children, Report to Accompany S. 3890*. S. Rept. 185, 61st Cong., 2d sess., 1910. 2p. Serial 5582. The measure reported amends the act making abandonment and non-support of wife and or children a misdemeanor in D.C. to include illegitimate children.

2248. U.S. Congress. House. Committee on Public Lands. *Issuance of Homestead Patent, Report to Accompany H.R. 16296*. H. Rept. 743, 63d Cong., 2d sess., 1914. 4p. Serial 6559. Reports a bill allowing the title to a homestead claim to go to a deserted wife with an amendment providing that notice must be served upon the husband. Correspondence related to the bill describes the hardships of current practice for deserted wives of homesteaders.

2249. U.S. Congress. Senate. Committee on Public Lands. *Issuance of Homestead Patent for the Benefit of Deserted Wives, Report to Accompany H.R. 16296*. S. Rept. 752, 63d Cong., 2d sess., 1914. 2p. Serial 6553. See 2249 for abstract.

2250. U.S. Congress. House. Committee on the Judiciary. *Uniform Laws as to Marriage and Divorce, Hearing on H.J. Res. 48*. 64th Cong., 1st sess., 12 Apr. 1916. 59p. Y4.J89/1:M34. Hearing discusses the divorce laws in the U.S. with particular attention to the variation between state laws and the problems caused by states with liberal laws.

Reasonable causes for divorce are discussed assuming the woman as the aggrieved party. Questions of legitimacy of second marriages and children thereof are raised as arguments for a uniform federal law. Includes a chart showing residency requirements and causes for divorce by state.

2251. U.S. Children's Bureau. *Norwegian Laws concerning Illegitimate Children.* by Leifur Magnusson. Publication no. 31. Washington, DC: GPO, 1918. 37p. L5.20:31. Translation of Norwegian law concerning illegitimate children describes amendments to the inheritance laws, to laws on the property relations of husband and wife, and to laws on the dissolution of marriage. Laws on the care of children and the supervision of foster children are also included.

2252. U.S. Congress. House. Committee on the Judiciary. *Uniform Laws as to Marriage and Divorce, Hearings on H.J. Res. 187.* 65th Cong., 2d sess., 2 Oct. 1918. 112p. Y4.J89/1:M34/2. Hearing on a proposed amendment to the Constitution granting Congress the power to establish uniform laws of marriage and divorce discusses the rising divorce rates and the legal ambiguity of crossing state lines to divorce under more favorable laws. The legal status of divorce in statute and case law is examined. Support of children of divorce is cited repeatedly as a justification for federal action.

2253. U.S. Bureau of War Risk Insurance. *Digest of Law Relating to Common Law Marriage in States, Territories and Dependencies of United States.* Treasury Dept. Doc. 2834. Washington, DC: Treasury, 1919. 54p. T49.2:M34.

2254. U.S. Children's Bureau. *Illegitimacy Laws of the United States and Certain Foreign Countries.* by Ernst Freund. Publication no. 42. Washington, DC: GPO, 1919. 260p. L5.20:42. Reviews the legal concepts underlaying illegitimacy laws and discusses illegitimacy laws of the U.S. and other countries. The text of illegitimacy laws for each state are provided.

2255. U.S. Children's Bureau. *Illegitimacy as a Child Welfare Problem, Part 1, Brief Treatment of Prevalence and Significance of Birth Out of Wedlock, Child's Status, and State's Responsibility for Care and Protection.* by Emma O. Lundberg and Katharine F. Lenroot. Publication no. 66. Washington, DC: GPO, 1920. 105p. L5.20:66. Report looks at the prevalence of illegitimacy in foreign countries and the United States, reviews state laws relating to illegitimacy and support of the child, and highlights laws regarding illegitimacy in foreign countries. Includes a detailed bibliography of source material on illegitimacy in the U.S. and foreign countries.

2256. U.S. Congress. House. Committee on the Judiciary. *Uniform Marriage and Divorce Laws, Hearings on H.J. Res. 75 and H.J. Res. 108.* 66th Cong., 2d sess., 13 Jan. 1920. 25p. Y4.J89/1:M34/3. Hearing considers a proposed amendment to the constitution giving Congress the power to make laws defining and limiting the causes for divorce or authorizing uniform laws on marriage and divorce. Testimony discusses the relationship between divorce rates and "ill-devised" marriage laws and notes the alarming 1 in 12 divorce rate. The problem of the woman who makes an "unfortunate" marriage is advanced as an example of the need for divorce.

2257. U.S. Children's Bureau. *Standards of Legal Protection for Children Born Out-of-Wedlock: A Report of Regional Conferences.* Publication no. 77. Washington, DC: GPO, 1921. 158p. L5.20:77. Conference proceedings explore existing and ideal illegitimacy laws. Topics covered include paternity establishment, state supervision, and the responsibility of the father and of the mother.

2258.   U.S. Children's Bureau. *Illegitimacy Laws of the United States Passed During the Years 1919 to 1922, Inclusive.* Washington, DC: GPO, 1922. 35p. L5.13/a:Il6. State-by-state summary reviews laws governing the legal recognition and right to support for children born out-of-wedlock.

2259.   U.S. Congress. House. Committee on the Judiciary. *Constitutional Amendment Granting Congress Power to Establish Uniform Laws Relating to Marriage and Divorce, Hearing on H.J. Res. 83.* 67th Cong., 2d sess., 26 Jan. 1922. 11p. Y4.J89/1:M34/4. Statement of George P. Codd, Representative from Michigan and a former judge, on a proposed amendment to the Constitution giving Congress the authority to set uniform marriage and divorce laws, expounds on the evils of divorce and the problem of ex-husbands leaving a state to avoid payment of alimony and child support.

2260.   U.S. Congress. Senate. Committee on the Judiciary. Subcommittee on Senate Joint Resolution 5. *Marriage and Divorce (Amendment to the Constitution), Hearing on S.J. Res. 5.* 68th Cong., 1st sess., 11 Jan. 1924. 28p. Y4.J89/2:M34. Hearing examines a proposed Constitutional amendment giving Congress power to establish uniform laws on marriage and divorce, legitimacy of children, and care of children after divorce. The amendment was proposed by the General Federation of Women's Clubs. Testimony discusses the rising divorce rate and the need for uniformity of divorce laws to prevent persons from crossing state lines to evade the divorce laws of their state.

2261.   U.S. Congress. Senate. Committee on the District of Columbia. *Abandonment and Nonsupport of Wife or Children in the District of Columbia, Report to Accompany H.R. 4812.* S. Rept. 985, 69th Cong., 1st sess., 1926. 3p. Serial 8526. Reports a bill placing jurisdiction over non-support cases with the Juvenile Court of the District of Columbia and eliminating the sentence of "hard labor" in failure to pay child support cases. The bill was in response to *U.S. v. Moreland* in which the Supreme Court ruled that the Juvenile Court could not impose the "hard labor" sentence.

2262.   U.S. Children's Bureau. *Analysis and Tabular Summary of State Laws Relating to Illegitimacy in the United States, in Effect January 1, 1928 and the Text of Selected Laws.* by Marietta Stevenson. Chart no. 16. Washington, DC: GPO, 1929. 49p. L5.19:16. Chart summary of state laws relating to illegitimacy details rights and obligations of mother and father, action to establish paternity, legitimation, right of maintenance from the father and mother, and rights of inheritance. Selected laws are reprinted.

2263.   U.S. Children's Bureau. *Analysis and Tabular Summary of State Laws Relating to Jurisdiction in Children's Cases and Cases of Domestic Relations in the United States.* by Freda Ring Lyman. Chart no. 17. Washington, DC: GPO, 1930. 33p. L5.19:17. Analysis of court jurisdiction in children's cases and cases of domestic relations is followed by a chart summarizing jurisdictions and statutory authority, by state, in cases of juvenile delinquency, offenses against children, desertion and nonsupport, establishment of paternity, annulment of marriage, divorce, separate maintenance, adoption, and commitment of mentally retarded children.

2264.   U.S. Children's Bureau. *Paternity Laws: Analysis and Tabular Summary of State Laws Relating to Paternity and Support of Children Born Out-of-Wedlock in Effect January 1, 1938.* Chart no. 16. Washington, DC: GPO, 1938. 83p. L5.19:16/2. Summary of paternity laws in the United States is followed by charts providing basic information, by state, on father's responsibility for support, persons who may make complaint, court jurisdiction and procedure, judgement and enforcement of judgement, and person to whom support payments are made. Appendix reprints selected state laws.

2265.   U.S. Children's Bureau. *List of References on Marriage*. Washington, DC: The Bureau, 1940. 5p. L5.40:M34. Bibliography of books and magazine articles on marriage and divorce in the U.S. furnishes brief annotations.

2266.   U.S. Children's Bureau. *List of References on Marriage and Family Counseling*. Washington, DC: The Bureau, 1940. 3p. L5.40:M34/2. Annotated list cites journal articles published between 1931 and 1939 on marriage and family counseling.

2267.   U.S. Library of Congress. Division of Bibliography. *Marriage and Divorce, with Special Reference to Legal Aspects: a Selected Bibliography*. by Helen F. Conover. Washington, DC: Library of Congress, 1940. 55p. LC2.2:M34/940. Bibliography of both popular and scholarly books, articles, and government documents on marriage and divorce provides 574 references including materials published outside the U.S.

2268.   U.S. Air Force. *Military Personnel: Paternity Claims, June 16, 1952*. Special Regulation 35-70/2. Washington, DC: Air Force, [1952]. 2p. D301.6:35-70/2. Also issued in 1950.

2269.   U.S. Army. *Personnel: Paternity Claims*. Special Regulation no. 600-940-1. Washington, DC: GPO, 1953. 3p. D101.10:600-940-4.

2270.   U.S. Congress. Senate. Committee on District of Columbia. Subcommittee on the Judiciary. *Family Court for the District of Columbia*. 83d Cong., 2d sess., 24-26 Feb. 1954. 144p. Y4.D63/2:F21. Hearing on revising the handling of divorce cases in the District of Columbia provides insight into the judicial process in these cases, the problem of alimony and maintenance payments and enforcement of orders, and theory on the role of social workers in the mid-1950's. Testimony is primarily from lawyers opposing the bill on the basis that divorce is too complex for the proposed family court.

2271.   U.S. Army. *Personnel: Paternity Claims, October 29, 1956*. Special Regulation 608-99. Washington, DC: GPO, 1956. 4p. D101.10:608-99.

2272.   U.S. Bureau of Public Assistance. *Support from Absent Fathers of Children Receiving ADC, 1955*. by Saul Kaplan. Public Assistance Report no. 41. Washington, DC: GPO, 1960. 112p. FS3.13:41 Study of families with an absent father receiving ADC looks at the extent to which the father contributes to support, legal efforts to obtain support, and the ability of non-supporting fathers to pay.

2273.   U.S. National Center for Health Statistics. *Marriage and Divorce, Selected Bibliography of Statistically Oriented Studies*. Washington, DC: The Center, 1963. 8p. FS2.121:M34.

2274.   U.S. Bureau of Family Services. *Report of a Meeting on Coordination in Location of Absent Parents of Children Receiving Aid to Families with Dependent Children*. Washington, DC: The Administration, 1964. 12p. FS14.202:P21 Describes problems and procedures in locating absent parents to secure support for children in ADC families. Coordination between law enforcement and public welfare agencies is stressed.

2275.   U.S. Congress. Senate. Committee on Finance. *Payment of Pension to Wife and Children Where Veteran Has Disappeared, Report to Accompany H.R. 9961*. S. Rept. 1219, 89th Cong., 2d sess., 1966. 6p. Serial 12710-2. Recommends a bill amending the *U.S. Code* to permit payment of veterans' pension to the wife and children of a veteran whose whereabouts is unknown. Correspondence from the Veterans' Administration details the provisions of the bill and stresses the need for such legislation as a matter of equality of treatment.

2276.   U.S. Women's Bureau. *Divorce Laws as of July 1, 1965.* Washington, DC: The Bureau, 1966. 2p. L13.2:D64/965. Summary in chart form details state divorce laws showing grounds for divorce and the period before parties can remarry. Earlier edition published in 1964.

2277.   U.S. National Center for Health Statistics. *Marriage and Divorce, Bibliography of Statistical Studies.* rev. ed. Washington, DC: The Center, 1969. 9p. FS2.121:M34/969.

2278.   U.S. Bureau of the Census. *Social and Economic Variations in Marriage, Divorce, and Remarriage: 1967.* Current Population Reports Series P-20, no. 223. Washington, DC: GPO, 1971. 92p. C3.186:P-20/223. Statistical report presents data for males and females on marriage, divorce and remarriage and the probability of marriage, divorce, widowhood, and remarriage by year of first marriage, years of school completed, and age and number of children under 18 years.

2279.   U.S. Congress. Senate. Committee on Finance. *Welfare -Or Is It? Address of Hon. Russell B. Long, Chairman, Committee on Finance, and Supporting Material.* 92d Cong., 1st sess., 1971. Committee Print. 23p. Y4.F49:W45. Address to Congress by Russell B. Long on AFDC and issues of child support, the marriage disincentive, and child care provides supporting data on AFDC children and status of father.

2280.   U.S. Citizens' Advisory Council on the Status of Women. *The Equal Rights Amendment and Alimony and Child Support Laws.* Washington, DC: The Council, 1972. 11p. Y3.In8/21:2Eq2/2. Review of the legal status of a husband's obligation to support wife and children before and after divorce discussed the effect of the proposed Equal Rights Amendment. Existing research on collection of alimony and child support is reviewed.

2281.   U.S. Congress. Senate. Committee on Finance. *Welfare Reform: Child Support and Paternity Determination, Explanation of Committee Decisions.* 92d Cong., 2d sess., 19 May 1972. 14p. Y4.F49:W45/3 Report details committee decisions related to H.R. 1, the administration's welfare reform proposal, in the areas of child support, determination of paternity, location of deserting parents, and the garnishment of the wages of federal employees for support obligations.

2282.   U.S. Congress. House. Committee on the Judiciary. *Enforcement of Support Orders in State and Federal Courts, Hearing on H.R. 5405 and Related Bills.* 93d Cong., 1st sess., 25 Oct. 1973. 99p. Y4.J89/1:93-47. Brief testimony on bills to improve enforcement of child support orders across state lines argues against moving interstate enforcement to the federal courts and the criminalization of crossing state lines to avoid support orders. Emphasis is placed on encouraging states to better improve enforcement procedures. Some support is given to the bill as a method of decreasing federal AFDC payments. The legal subtleties of interstate enforcement of child support are discussed.

2283.   U.S. Congress. Senate. Committee on Finance. *Child Support and the Work Bonus, Hearing on S. 1842, S. 2081.* 93d Cong., 1st sess., 25 Sept. 1973. 282p. Y4.F49:C43/5. Two AFDC related measures, one to locate and establish paternity of absent fathers and to enforce child support and one to provide payments to low-income heads of families equal to 10 percent of their wages are discussed. The primary focus of witnesses is on child support. Statistics on contributions from absent fathers in AFDC families, income of AFDC families by source, reasons for discontinuing AFDC payments and AFDC families by status of father are included.

2284.   U.S. Congress. Senate. Committee on Finance. *Social Security Amendments of 1973, Report to Accompany H.R. 3153.* S. Rept. 93-553, 93d Cong., 1st sess., 1973. 279p. Serial 13017-7. Senate amendments to a bill making technical corrections in the Social

Security Act make substantial changes in child support programs. Additional views focus on the AFDC program and work incentives. Supporting statistics include data on child support collections on behalf of AFDC recipients by state for fiscal year 1973.

2285. U.S. Public Health Service. *100 Years of Marriage and Divorce Statistics, United States, 1867-1967.* Washington, DC: GPO, 1973. 61p. HE20.6209:21/24. Analysis of marriage and divorce statistics for the period 1867-1967 describes data collection procedures throughout the period, trends in national and area totals and rates, and characteristics of marriage and divorce.

2286. U.S. Assistance Payments Administration. *How They Do It: Child Support Payments Control, Massachusetts and Washington.* Washington, DC: The Administration, 1974. 100p. HE17.408/2:C43 Describes procedures for AFDC child support payment control programs in Massachusetts and Washington. Sample forms and supporting statistics on child support collections and enforcement costs are included.

2287. U.S. Citizens' Advisory Council on the Status of Women and U.S. Interdepartmental Committee on the Status of Women. *Recognition of the Economic Contribution of Homemakers and Protection of Children in Divorce Law and Practice.* Washington, DC: The Council, 1974. 14p. Y3.In8/21:2H75. Report explores the implications of the move toward no-fault divorce for alimony and child support. Specifically, the value of homemaking in divorce settlements under various proposed changes in the Uniform Marriage and Divorce Act is discussed and questions to be considered in drafting new approaches to divorce laws are suggested. Appendix summarizes the sections of the Uniform Marriage and Divorce Act which provide economic protection for dependent spouses and children, and also summarizes amendments proposed by the American Bar Association Family Law Section.

2288. U.S. Congress. Senate. Committee on Finance. *Social Services Amendments of 1974, Report to Accompany H.R. 17045.* S. Rept. 93-1356, 93d Cong., 2d sess., 1974. 57p. Serial 13057-12. Report with separate views on the Social Services Amendments of 1974 discusses child support programs and federal responsibility at some length. Family planning programs and the Work Incentive Program are mentioned. Includes data on child support collections on behalf of AFDC recipients in fiscal year 1973.

2289. U.S. Congress. Senate. Committee on Finance and House. and U.S. Congress. Senate. Committee on Ways and Means. *Social Services and Child Support: Summary of the Provisions of H.R. 17045.* 93d Cong., 2d sess., 1974. Committee print. 8p. Y4.F49:So1/38 Summarizes H.R. 17045, a bill moving general social services programs to a new Title XX of the SSA and providing for a more active federal role in monitoring state child support activities.

2290. U.S. Congress. House. Committee on Ways and Means. *Child Support Program Improvements, Report to Accompany H.R. 8598.* H. Rept. 94-368, 94th Cong., 1st sess., 1975. 27p. Serial 13099-6. Reports a bill amending Title IV of the SSA to improve the child support enforcement program. Changes in the child support laws would allow states more time to comply before losing AFDC funds and would lessen federal intrusion into state and local government responsibility for family law and child support. The individual right to privacy was also at issue.

2291. U.S. Congress. Senate. Committee on Finance. *Child Support Data and Materials.* 94th Cong., 1st sess., 1975. 183p. Y4.F49:C43/8/pt.2 Compilation of statistics related to child support enforcement and the success of enforcement in AFDC families details AFDC families by status of father, AFDC families by presence of child support order, extent to which court ordered child support is met, amount of child support payments, voluntary support order by amount, and AFDC families by number of child recipients.

2292.   U.S. Congress. Senate. Committee on Finance. *Provisions of State Laws and Other Data Relating to Wage Garnishment, Attachment and Assignment, and Establishment of Paternity.* 94th Cong., 1st sess., 1975. Committee print. 288p. Y4.F49:W12. Summary of the provisions of state laws and court decisions relating to the ability to garnish or assign wages and to the establishment of paternity was compiled as background for federal legislation on child support and establishment of paternity. Attached chart summarizes the provisions of state divorce laws and tables provide statistics on number of illegitimate children receiving AFDC.

2293.   U.S. Congress. House. Committee on Ways and Means. Subcommittee on Public Assistance. *Extension of Interim Assistance and Food Stamps for SSI Beneficiaries and Continuation of Federal-State Matching Funds for Nonwelfare Recipient Children, Executive Hearing.* 94th Cong., 2d sess., 10 June 1976. 7p. Y4.W36:F73. Very brief hearing discusses temporary extension of programs authorizing Food Stamps for SSI beneficiaries and federal matching funds for absent parent locator and child support collection services for non-AFDC families. Administration witnesses recommend authorization of federal funding of child support services for AFDC recipients or potential recipients only.

2294.   U.S. Congress. Senate. Committee on Finance. *Child Support Amendments, Report to Accompany H.R. 9889.* S. Rept. 94-1350, 94th Cong., 2d sess., 1976. 23p. Serial 13130-11. Total revision of H.R. 9889, a bill dealing with estate tax charitable contribution deductions, substitutes a measure amending title IV-D of the Social Security Act relating to child support. The amendments provide for the issuance of regulations relating to garnishment of wages, incentive payments for governmental units making child support collections, research and demonstration projects, and other administrative provisions. The report discusses AFDC and the need for child support enforcement to reduce the welfare roles.

2295.   U.S. General Accounting Office. *New Child Support Legislation -- Its Potential Impact and How to Improve It.* Washington, DC: GPO, 1976. 55p. GA1.13:MWD-76-63. Report examines the potential for improving child support collections for AFDC recipients based on program reviews in seven states. Past problems, limitations on program improvements, and recent child support legislation are analyzed. Additional legislative changes to improve program operation are recommended.

2296.   U.S. Office of Child Support Enforcement. *First Annual Report to the Congress on the Child Support Enforcement Program.* Washington, DC: GPO, 1976. 149p. HE1.53:976 Report on HEW implementation of the Child Support Enforcement Program presents its legislative background and describes the Parent Locator Service and state program activities. Provides 1976 data on state collections, expenditures, cases and actions.

2297.   U.S. Bureau of the Census. *Marriage, Divorce, Widowhood, and Remarriage by Family Characteristics: June 1975.* Current Population Reports Series P-20, no. 312. Washington, DC: GPO, 1977. 39p. C3.186:P-20/312. Presents data on marital history of husband and wife by level of education, age at divorce, age of youngest child at divorce, age at widowhood and number of children, age at widowhood and duration of widowhood, and living arrangements of children.

2298.   U.S. Congress. Senate. Committee on Finance. *For the Relief of Smith College, Northampton, Mass., Report to Accompany H.R. 1404.* S. Rept. 95-298, 95th Cong., 1st sess., 1977. 11p. Serial 13168-6. Among the riders attached to a bill providing for the duty free entry of carillon bells for Smith College are provisions funding child support collection and paternity establishment services for non-AFDC recipients and extending the deadline for submission of a HEW report on Title XX day care standards.

2299. U.S. Office of Child Support Enforcement. *Child Support Enforcement: Supplemental Report to the Congress for the Period Ending September 30, 1976.* Washington, DC: GPO, 1977. 160p. HE1.53:976/supp. Summary of the child support enforcement provisions in federal laws accompanies profiles of state child support programs.

2300. U.S. Office of Child Support Enforcement. *Guide for Determining the Ability of an Absent Parent to Pay Child Support.* by Mignon Sauber and Edith Taittonen. Washington, DC: GPO, 1977. 58p. HE1.6/3:C43 Presents a formula for determining the ability of an absent parent to pay child support intended for use by states enforcing federal AFDC child support enforcement rules.

2301. U.S. Office of Child Support Enforcement. *Office of Child Support Enforcement Auditor's Manual.* Washington, DC: GPO, 1977. 118p. HE3.508:Au2. Auditor's manual gives program objectives and procedures for the Child Support Enforcement Program.

2302. U.S. Office of Child Support Enforcement. *Paternity Determination: Techniques and Procedures to Establish the Paternity of Children Born Out of Wedlock.* Washington, DC: GPO, 1977. 38p. HE1.2:P27. Report describes methods of determining paternity and the judicial process of establishing paternity to enforce child support.

2303. U.S. Army. *Personal Affairs, Support of Dependents, Paternity Claims, and Related Adoption Proceedings.* Army Regulation 608-99. Washington, DC: GPO, 1978. 11p. D101.9:608-99.

2304. U.S. Office of Child Support Enforcement. *Child Support Enforcement: A Program Administered by Your Local Child Support Enforcement Agency.* Washington, DC: The Office, 1978. [4]p. leaflet. HE3.502:C43.

2305. U.S. Administration for Children, Youth and Families. *The Project to Determine the Legal and Social Benefits, Rights and Remedies Accruing to Illegitimate Children upon the Establishment of Paternity.* by Center for Health Services Research, University of Southern California. Washington, DC: The Administration, 1979. 58p. + 17 leaves. HE23.1002:Il6. Primary focus of the study reported is mothers' knowledge of the rights of her illegitimate child on the establishment of paternity and of the process and persons from whom she obtains such information. Summarizes the rights granted to illegitimate children under the paternity laws of each states.

2306. U.S. Bureau of the Census. *Divorce, Child Custody, and Child Support.* Current Population Reports Series P-23, no. 84. Washington, DC: GPO, 1979. 30p. C3.186:P-23/84. Statistical report on divorce rates from 1940 to 1978 provides data on children under 18 involved in parents' divorce, 1956-1976; two-parent and one-parent families by race, 1960-1978; characteristics of female-headed families; money income, poverty status, and child support payments received by divorced, separated, remarried and never married women, 1975; and characteristics of divorced and separated women by receipt of alimony payments.

2307. U.S. Congress. House. Committee of the Judiciary. Subcommittee on Civil and Constitutional Rights. *Dischargeability of Child Support, Hearing.* 96th Cong., 1st sess., 13 June 1979. 19p. Y4.J89/1:96/35. Brief hearing examines the issues of bankruptcy, child support obligations and federal AFDC policy.

2308.   U.S. Congress. Senate. Committee on Finance. *Staff Data and Materials on Child Support.* 96th Cong., 1st sess., 1979. Committee print. 76p. Y4.F49:C43/11. Report provides background data on establishment of paternity, location of parents, court ordered child support, child support collections for AFDC families, children receiving AFDC by status of father, 1948-1978, and related topics.

2309.   U.S. Family Support Administration. *Strengthening the American Family.* Washington, DC: The Administration, 198? leaflet. HE25.2:Am3. Overview of Family Support Administration programs briefly describes AFDC, the Child Support Enforcement Program, and the Teenage Pregnancy Prevention Initiative.

2310.   U.S. Office of Child Support Enforcement. *Child Support, a State-by-State Review.* Washington, DC: GPO, 198? leaflet. HE24.2:K54.

2311.   U.S. Office of Child Support Enforcement. *Child Support: An Agenda for Action.* Washington, DC: GPO, 198? 3p. HE24.2:K54/3. Reviews why child support enforcement is needed and how the Child Support Enforcement Program helps.

2312.   U.S. Office of Child Support Enforcement. *The Child Support Enforcement Program...a Close Up.* Washington, DC: GPO, 198? leaflet. HE24.2:K54/2.

2313.   U.S. Congress. House. Committee on Ways and Means. *Miscellaneous Revenue Act of 1981, Report on H.R. 4961 Together with Dissenting Views.* H. Rept. 97-404, 97th Cong., 1st sess., 1981. 75p. Serial 13437. One of the effects of H.R. 4961 is a change in the way states are allowed to charge fees for non-AFDC child support collection services. The problems with the existing method of allowing states to collect a fee equal to ten percent of the support payment is briefly described.

2314.   U.S. National Institute for Child Support Enforcement. *The Administrative Adjudication of Child Support Obligations.* by Fred Silvester and Dennis C. Cooper. Rockville, MD: The Institute, 1981. 88p. HE24.10:2. Reviews the background and development of child support obligations and discusses the adjudication of child support cases. A sample method for designing and implementing administrative legislation is provided.

2315.   U.S. National Institute for Child Support Enforcement. *Benefits of Establishing Paternity.* by Laurene T. McKillop. Washington, DC: GPO, 1981. 46p. HE24.10:1. Summary of the need and process for establishing paternity provides background information on the legal process and on the benefits, both economic and psychological, of paternity establishment.

2316.   U.S. National Institute for Child Support Enforcement. *Effective Enforcement Techniques for Child Support Obligations Handbook.* Washington, DC: GPO, 1982. 215p. HE24.8:En2. Handbook on child support enforcement provides information on case preparation, preliminary and judicial enforcement techniques, judicial defenses, the role of the IRS, alternative court systems, arrearage collection, prioritization of cases, and privacy. Summarizes current statutes and regulations and provides sample forms.

2317.   U.S. Office of Child Support Enforcement. *Child Support Enforcement Program Staffing and Organization Analysis: Final Report.* Rockville, MD: The Office, 1982. 199p. HE24.2:St1. Study of the organization and staffing of six large, urban child support enforcement programs focuses on effective allocation of staff and setting case priorities. A model for staffing state programs was developed based on information collected.

2318.   U.S. Office of Child Support Enforcement. *In the Best Interest of the Child: A Guide to State Child Support and Paternity Laws.* by Carolyn Royce Kastner and Lawrence R.

Young. Washington, DC: GPO, 1982. 155p. HE24.8:Su7. Discussion of the necessary components of effective state legislation for child support enforcement serves as a guide both to existing state legislation and for drafting legislation in the areas covered. Major topics discussed are enabling legislation, the judicial process, administrative procedures, paternity determination, and enforcement of support orders.

2319. U.S. Congress. House. Committee on Education and Labor. Subcommittee on Select Education. *Oversight Hearing on Child Support Enforcement, Hearing.* 98th Cong., 1st sess., 12 Sept. 1983. 100p. Y4.Ed8/1:C43/25. Hearings held in New York examine a bill requiring states to enforce court ordered child support through mandatory wage withholding. Social welfare officials, a judge, and divorced mothers discuss the economic implications for families when the father does not pay court-ordered child support.

2320. U.S. Congress. House. Committee on Ways and Means. *Child Support Enforcement Amendments of 1983, Report to Accompany H.R. 4325.* H. Rept. 98-527, 98th Cong., 1st sess., 1983. 77p. Serial 13545. Reports a bill to improve Title IV-D child support enforcement through income withholding, state-level administrative requirements, incentive payments to states, and the appointment in each state of a commission on child support. The shortcomings of present legislation and the intent of the amendments are detailed.

2321. U.S. Congress. House. Committee on Ways and Means. Subcommittee on Public Assistance and Unemployment Compensation. *Child Support Enforcement Legislation, Hearing.* 98th Cong., 1st sess., 14 July 1983. 360p. Y4.W36:98-41. Included in this hearing on improving child support enforcement is a Congressional Research Service report with statistics on family characteristics and support orders and information on proven child support collection techniques. Both AFDC and non-AFDC options currently available are reviewed and their inadequacies are noted. Costs of collection programs and low-cost ways to help non-AFDC mothers collect support are examined.

2322. U.S. Congress. Senate. Committee on Finance. *Staff Data and Materials on Child Support.* 98th Cong., 1st sess., 1983. Committee print. 79p. Y4.F49:S.prt.98-91. Statistical overview of child support provides yearly data on AFDC program operations, state program characteristics, state child support collections for AFDC and non-AFDC cases, number of AFDC child support enforcement cases, paternity establishments, and tax refund offsets. The report also gives an overview of paternity establishment and compares bills proposing changes in the child support enforcement program.

2323. U.S. Congress. Senate. Committee on Finance. Subcommittee on Oversight of the Internal Revenue Service. *Description of the Child Support Enforcement Program and of S. 150.* 98th Cong., 1st sess., 1983. Committee print. 10p. Y4.T19/4:D45/19. The current provisions of the federal tax refund offset program for the collection of delinquent child support payments are reviewed and court decisions involving the refund-offset provisions are noted.

2324. U.S. Congress. Senate. Committee on Finance. Subcommittee on Oversight of the Internal Revenue Service. *Tax Refund Offset Program for Delinquent Student Loans and Child Support Payments, Hearing on S. 150.* 98th Cong., 1st sess., 16 Sept. 1983. 136p. Y4.F49:S.hrg.498. The use of tax refund withholding to collect delinquent student loan and child support payments is discussed. The problems of the tax refund offset approach are examined and existing tax refund withholding programs for child support are reviewed. Possibilities for using the approach for non-AFDC cases and the legality of such actions are examined.

2325. U.S. Congress. Senate. Committee on Finance. Subcommittee on Social Security and Income Maintenance Programs. *Proposed Restructuring of the Child Support Enforcement*

Program, Hearing. 98th Cong., 1st sess., 15 Sept. 1983. 72p. Y4.F49:S.hrg.98-608. The principal witness in this hearing on child support enforcement is Margaret M. Heckler, Secretary, Department of Health and Human Services. The problems faced by women in collecting court-ordered child support and the areas of needed improvement in state and federal child support enforcement programs are described. Effective methods of collecting child support are discussed. An appended statement from the American Child Custody Alliance opposes the bill as a punitive measure towards the father.

2326. U.S. Congress. Senate. Committee on Labor and Human Resources. Subcommittee on Family and Human Services. *Broken Families, Hearings.* 98th Cong., 1st sess., 22,24 Mar. 1983. 306p. Y4.L11/4:S.hrg.98-195. Hearing examines the societal factors involved in the high divorce rate and the effects of divorce on children and on women and men. The primary focus is on the effects of child custody arrangements on the psycho-social development of the child and on the prospects for strengthening families.

2327. U.S. Congress. Senate. Committee on Labor and Human Resources. Subcommittee on Family and Human Services. *Broken Families, Hearings, Part 2.* 98th Cong., 1st sess., 22 Sept., 4 Oct. 1983. 379p. Y4.L11/4:S.hrg.98-195/pt.2. Continued hearing on the causes and consequences of divorce in America explores ways government policy can contribute to family stability. Child care and family planning services are two areas specifically mentioned.

2328. U.S. Social Security Administration. Office of Research and Statistics. *Evaluation of the Child Support Enforcement Program, Final Report.* Washington, DC: The Administration, 1983. 356p. HE3.2:C43/9/final. Study looks at the effectiveness of the Title IV-D Child Support Enforcement Program which encourages state governments to more actively pursue child support payments for both AFDC and non-AFDC families. The focus is on the financial impact of state and federal efforts, rather than the social effects. Statistics on program expenditures and collections for AFDC and non-AFDC cases, delinquencies on court ordered support payments, locating absent parents, and average amount of support orders are provided.

2329. U.S. Congress. House. *Child Support Enforcement Amendments of 1984, Conference Report to Accompany H.R. 4325.* H. Rept. 98-925, 98th Cong., 2d sess., 1984. 60p. Serial 13597. Reports a bill to improve IV-D child support enforcement programs for both AFDC and non-AFDC cases through mandatory income withholding, incentive payments to states, and administrative improvements. Major differences between the House and Senate bills and the conference committee compromise are highlighted.

2330. U.S. Congress. House. Committee on Armed Services. *Modification of Procedures for Payment of Military Retired Pay to Spouses and Former Spouses of Members of the Uniformed Services in Compliance with Court Orders, Report to Accompany H.R. 5027.* H. Rept. 98-700, 98th Cong., 2d sess., 1984. 11p. Serial 13590. Reports on technical corrections to the Uniformed Services Former Spouses Protection Act clarifying the authority to pay child support and alimony directly from military retired pay. The judicial and legislative background of court ordered support and military retirement pay is provided with an overview of existing garnishment problems.

2331. U.S. Congress. Senate. Committee on Finance. *Child Support Enforcement Amendments, Report to Accompany H.R. 4325.* S. Rept. 98-387, 98th Cong., 2d sess., 1984. 50p. Serial 13557. Reports a bill encouraging states to better administer Title IV-D child support enforcement programs and improving incentives to states to make child support enforcement services available to both AFDC and non-AFDC families. A new incentive formula, requirements for the enactment of laws establishing procedures, and automatic transfer of AFDC families to the non-AFDC program upon termination of AFDC are some of the bill's provisions. Background on the history and operation of federal-state child support enforcement programs is including along with data illustrating past program achievements.

2332. U.S. Congress. Senate. Committee on Finance. *Child Support Enforcement Program Reform Proposals, Hearings.* 98th Cong., 2d sess., 24, 26 Jan. 1984. 543p. Y4.F49:S.hrg.98-673. The state experience with child support enforcement and the status of child support collections in the U.S. are explored through hearings on proposals to improve the federal leadership role. Methods of collecting child support payments for AFDC and non-AFDC families are examined. The question of fathers' visitation rights are also discussed amid charges of prejudice against fathers by the divorce system.

2333. U.S. Office of Child Support Enforcement. *Child Support: An Annotated Legal Bibliography.* by Robert Horowitz and Diane Dodson. Washington, DC: GPO, 1984. 150p. HE24.13:L52. Annotated bibliography lists books, journal articles and government documents on establishing and enforcing child support. Chapters highlight articles on interstate and international child support, tax aspects of child support, and the effect of bankruptcy on support payments.

2334. U.S. Office of Child Support Enforcement. *Cost Benefit Analysis of Selected Child Support Enforcement and Collection Techniques.* Washington, DC: GPO, 1984. 145p. HE24.2:C82/final. Study examines the success and cost effectiveness of three methods of enforcing and collecting child support: 1) mandatory wage withholding, 2) administrative process and 3) state debt off-set. Statistics are furnished for comparative purposes on collections and administrative costs of child support programs in three study sites and nationally.

2335. U.S. Office of Child Support Enforcement. *Handbook on Child Support Enforcement.* Rockville,MD: The Office, 1984? 67p. HE24.8:K54. Simply worded handbook for single parents on child support enforcement covers topics of getting help, enforcement costs, locating absent parents, establishment of paternity, legal enforcement options, and interstate enforcement. Includes a glossary of child support terms.

2336. U.S. Office of Child Support Enforcement. *El Manteniminento de Menores...Una Nueva Ayuda Esta Disponible.* Rockville, MD: The Office, 1984? 8p. leaflet. HE24.2:M66.

2337. U.S. Office of Child Support Enforcement. *Model Interstate Income Withholding Act with Comments.* Rockville, MD: The Office, 1984. 38p. HE24.2:M72. Background information on the income withholding requirements of the 1984 Child Support Amendments includes clarifying comments on the provisions of the Act. A draft of a model interstate income withholding act is provided for state legislatures to help them meet the requirements.

2338. U.S. Office of Child Support Enforcement. *Review of Selected State Practices in Establishing and Updating Child Support Awards.* by National Institute for Socioeconomic Research. Rockville, MD: The Office, 1984. 92p. HE24.2:St2/2. Review examines formulas used by states in setting child support obligations and the methods used to update awards in response to changes in the situation of the obligator, the custodial parent, and the children. Close scrutiny was given to practices in Delaware, which had used a formula since 1979, and Colorado, which did not use a formula. Detailed information is also provided on practices in Wisconsin and Washington.

2339. U.S. Office of Child Support Enforcement and National Conference of State Legislatures. Child Support Enforcement Project. *Selected Exemplary State Child Support Laws: Income Withholding, State Income Tax Intercept, Expedited Judicial Administrative Procedures.*

by Carolyn R. Kastner and Deborah Dale. Rockville, MD: The Office, 1984. 43p. HE24.2:St2/4. Information for drafters of state child support laws provides examples of laws in Illinois, Georgia, Wisconsin, Michigan, Missouri, and Virginia.

2340. U.S. Office of Child Support Enforcement and National Conference of State Legislatures. Child Support Enforcement Project. *State Statutes and the Child Support Enforcement Amendments of 1984: A 54 Jurisdictional Analysis.* Rockville, MD: The Office, 1984. 138p. HE24.2:St2/3. Provides a state-by-state analysis of child support laws incorporating the provisions of the Child Support Enforcement Amendments of 1984. Areas of laws needing review and modification and new provisions which the state legislature should consider are noted. The District of Columbia, Guam, the U.S. Virgin Islands, and Puerto Rico are also included.

2341. U.S. Office of Child Support Enforcement. Child Support Technology Transfer Project. *A Guide to Drafting, Passing, and Implementing Beneficial Child Support Legislation.* Rockville, MD: The National Child Support Enforcement Reference Center, 1984. 54p. HE24.8:D78. Guide to establishing state legislation for effective child support orders and enforcement outlines the content of state child support laws. Advice on organizing the draft legislation, the legislative process, and preparing a legislative implementation plan is provided. Includes a case study of the process in Missouri.

2342. U.S. Congress. Senate. Committee on the Judiciary. Subcommittee on Juvenile Justice. *Parental Kidnapping and Child Support, Hearing.* 99th Cong., 1st sess., 19 July 1985. 52p. Y4.J89/2:S.hrg.99-469. The bulk of this hearing explores the problem of parental kidnapping across international boundaries. Briefer testimony is given on the issue of child support looking at issues of inadequate support orders and insufficient enforcement practices. The increasing cost of child support over time and the hassles of getting court ordered child support increased are noted in support of federal legislation requiring automatic cost of living adjustments to child support awards.

2343. U.S. General Accounting Office. *Child Support: State's Implementation of the 1984 Child Support Enforcement Amendments: Briefing Report to the Chairman, Subcommittee on Public Assistance and Unemployment Compensation, Committee on Ways and Means, House of Representatives.* Washington, DC: The Office, 1985. 21p. GA1.13:HRD-86-40BR. Briefing report provides a concise review of the results of a telephone survey on state implementation of the Child Support Enforcement Amendments. Exemptions and program implementation delays are reviewed.

2344. U.S. National Institute for Child Support Enforcement. *A Guide for Designing and Implementing an Administrative Process for Child Support Enforcement.* Washington, DC: GPO, 1985. 106p. HE24.8:Ad6. Explains the basics of an administrative process for child support enforcement including how the process works, drafting a statute, and implementation considerations. Chart illustrates the provisions of administrative process policies in sixteen states.

2345. U.S. National Institute for Child Support Enforcement. *Interviewing Skills for Child Support Workers - Handbook.* Washington, DC: GPO, 1985. 174p. HE24.8:In8. Handbook on interviewing skills discusses communication theory and cultural differences within the context of the child support interview.

2346. U.S. Office of Child Support Enforcement. *Costs and Benefits of Paternity Establishment: Executive Summary.* Rockville, MD: The Office, 1985. 19p. HE24.2: P27/2/exec. sum. Study of paternity cases examines the cost of establishing paternity and the amount of collections from resulting support obligation determinations. Also briefly looks at non-monetary benefits of paternity establishment.

2347. U.S. Office of Child Support Enforcement. *Development of Guidelines for Establishment and Updating Child Support Orders: Interim Report.* Washington, DC: GPO,1985. 164p. HE24.8:Su7/2. Information for states on establishing formulas for determining amount of child support awards illustrates the development and use of formulas in three states. Five formula systems with illustrative outcomes for different cases are also provided.

2348. U.S. Office of Child Support Enforcement. *Effective Child Support Enforcement Techniques: State Tax Intercept.* Washington, DC: GPO, 1985. 92p. HE24.8:St2. Guide for states gives advice on implementation of programs to recover overdue child support payments through intercepting income tax refunds.

2349. U.S. Office of Child Support Enforcement. *Interstate Child Support Collections Study: A Study to Determine Methods, Cost Factors, Policy Options, and Incentives Essential to Improving Interstate Child Support Collections, Final Report.* Washington, DC: GPO, 1985. 159p. HE24.2:In8. Study analyzes the shortcomings of current practice for enforcing child support orders across state lines and recommends action at the federal, state, and local level to more effectively collect child support payments. The Child Support Enforcement Amendments of 1984 and the Uniform Reciprocal Enforcement of Support Act are examined.

2350. U.S. Office of Child Support Enforcement. *Mandatory Income Withholding Implementation Monograph.* Rockville, MD: The Office, 1985. 56p. HE24.2:In2. Guide to implementing mandatory withholding for child support payments discusses the basic legal requirements, covers administrative considerations, and notes common problems.

2351. U.S. Office of Child Support Enforcement. *National Conference of State Legislatures Children and Youth Program Information Clearinghouse Reference List.* by Heather F. Maggard and Joan M. Smith. Washington, DC: GPO, 1985. 55p. HE24.13:St2. Briefly annotated bibliography of law review and journal articles, research reports, model laws, state statutes, and excerpts from books on children and youth issues covers child support enforcement, family and juvenile law, AFDC, teen pregnancy, and runway youth.

2352. U.S. Office of Child Support Enforcement. *Remedies under the Child Support Enforcement Amendments of 1984.* Rockville, MD: The Office, 1985. 143p. HE24.2:R28. Reviews the options available under the Child Support Enforcement Amendments of 1984 for the collection of delinquent child support payments. These options include income withholding, federal income tax refund offset, liens and bonds and other securities. Also examines methods of locating absent parents.

2353. U.S. Public Health Service. *Teenage Marriage and Divorce, United States, 1970-81.* Washington, DC: GPO, 1985. 23p. HE20.6209:21/43. An analysis of the trends in teenage marriage and divorce in the United States for the period 1970-81 is presented. Information provided includes geographic variations, marriage laws, age differences between spouses, previous marital status, race, educational attainment, duration of marriage, and children involved in divorce.

2354. U.S. Congress. House. Select Committee on Children, Youth and Families. *Divorce: The Impact on Children and Families.* 99th Cong., 2d sess., 19 June 1986. 184p. Y4.C43/2:D64. Hearing on the impact of divorce examines the economic implications of current divorce laws for women and children, child support issues, and the psychological consequences for children.

2355. U.S. General Accounting Office. *Child Support: States' Progress in Implementing the 1984 Amendments: Report to the Chairman, Subcommittee on Public Assistance and Unemployment Compensation, Committee on Ways and Means, House of Representatives.*

Washington, DC: The Office, 1986. 64p. GA1.13:HRD-87-11. Results of a GAO survey of state implementation of the 1984 Child Support Enforcement Amendments reports on legislative changes at the state level, expected implementation dates, and delays in implementation. Implementation is examined by 14 different provisions of the amendments including paternity establishment and mandatory wage withholding. Information on state officials' attitudes toward the potential effectiveness of the amendments is also reported.

2356.   U.S. Office of Child Support Enforcement. *Bankruptcy and Support Enforcement: How to Make Sure It Stays Owed to the Kids.* by John Replogle. Washington, DC: GPO, 1986. 42p. HE24.8:B22. Guide suggests ways to maintain collection of child support payments when the absent parent files Chapter 13 bankruptcy.

2357.   U.S. Office of Child Support Enforcement. *Compilation of Child Support and Related Regulations.* Washington, DC: GPO, 1986. 187p. HE24.15:86-01. Reprint of applicable sections of Title 45 of the *Code of Federal Regulations* on child support enforcement covers AFDC and Health and Human Services Department regulations.

2358.   U.S. Office of Child Support Enforcement. *Interstate Child Support Enforcement Laws Digest: URESA Laws.* Washington, DC: GPO, 1986. 3 vol. HE24.8:In8/2/v.1-3. Volumes 1 and 2 reprint state statutes and case law pertaining to interstate child support enforcement under the Uniform Reciprocal Enforcement of Support Acts (URESA). Volume three focuses on interstate laws relating to child support enforcement.

2359.   U.S. Office of Child Support Enforcement. *State Child Support Legislation and the 1984 Federal Amendments: A 54 Jurisdictional Analysis.* by Deborah Dale and Charles Brackney. Washington, DC: GPO, 1986. 164p. HE24.2:St2/5. The Child Support Enforcement Amendments of 1984 mandate state action for child support enforcement. The report analyzes the statutes of the states, the District of Columbia, Guam, Puerto Rico and the Virgin Islands with summaries of features of current laws which meet the mandates of PL98-378 and modifications and additions necessitated by the new law.

2360.   U.S. Office of Child Support Enforcement. *Summaries of Reports by State Commissioners on Child Support Enforcement.* Washington, DC: GPO, 1986. 185p. HE24.2:St2/6. Summary of reports by state commissioners on child support enforcement discusses administrative functions, interstate enforcement, child custody and visitation, and paternity establishment.

2361.   U.S. Office of Child Support Enforcement. *Wage Withholding for Child Support: An Employer's Guide.* Washington, DC: GPO, 1986. 24p. HE24.8:W12. Answers questions employers may have regarding court ordered wage withholding for child support.

2362.   U.S. Congress. Senate. Committee on Finance. Subcommittee on Social Security and Family Policy. *Welfare: Reform or Replacement? (Child Support Enforcement), Hearings.* 100th Cong., 1st sess., 23 Jan., 2 Feb. 1987. 448p. Y4.F49:S.hrg.100-335. Hearing addressing the problem of female-headed households below the poverty level examines proposals to replace AFDC. The concept that the parents should bear the financial burden of supporting the child forms the basis for discussion of approaches to child support enforcement. The witnesses discuss poverty and welfare reform focusing on issues of taxes, work requirements, and short-term dependency, as well as illegitimacy and child support. The role of federal, state, and local government in ensuring maintenance income for families is explored.

2363.   U.S. Congress. Senate. Committee on Finance. Subcommittee on Social Security and Family Policy. *Welfare: Reform or Replacement? (Child Support Enforcement - II), Hearings.* 100th Cong., 1st sess., 20 Feb. 1987. 421p. Y4.F49:S.hrg.100-395. The problems of child support enforcement are examined as witnesses describe the inadequacy of support awards and the difficulty faced by many mothers in collecting delinquent payments. The cost of going to court to collect payments is illustrated and the government role in enforcement is discussed. Witnesses review the performance of states in paternity determination and AFDC child support collections. A significant part of the hearing focuses on the rising cost of raising a child and the inadequacy of the average child support order.

2364. U.S. Office of Child Support Enforcement. *Development of Guidelines for Child Support Orders: Advisory Panel Recommendations and Final Report.* by the Advisory Panel on Child Support Guidelines and Robert G. Williams under a grant to the National Center for State Courts. Washington, DC: The Office, 1987. 287p. HE4.8:Su7/2/final. Report on the development of guidelines for establishing child support orders describes the benefits of using guidelines, the extent of inadequate orders, and possible legal barriers to guideline implementation. Details on constructing and enacting guidelines in the states are provided with examples of existing guidelines in several states. Economic background on the cost of childrearing is included.

2365. U.S. Office of Child Support Enforcement. Child Support Technology Transfer Project. *Public Affairs Handbook for Child Support Enforcement.* by Athena M. Kaye, et al. Washington, DC: GPO, 1987. 193p. HE24.8:P96. Guide for conducting public awareness campaigns on child support enforcement gives examples of and strategies for public service announcements, press releases and news paper articles, speeches, press interviews, and community relations.

2366. U.S. Office of Child Support Enforcement. Child Support Technology Transfer Project. *Service of Process Monograph.* by Barbara Roberts. Washington, DC: GPO, 1987. 37p. HE24.2:Se6. Information on the role of the service process step in the child support enforcement process is followed by a discussion of best practices.

2367. U.S. Office of Child Support Enforcement. Child Support Technology Transfer Project. and National Council of Juvenile and Family Court Judges. *A Guide for Judges in Child Support Enforcement.* by Michael R. Henry and Victoria S. Schwartz. 2d ed. Washington, DC: GPO, 1987. 251p. HE24.8:J87/987. Extensive treatise on the legal aspects of child support provides an overview of the child support problem and the feminization of poverty, and of the federal, state, and local role in child support enforcement. Establishing support obligations, paternity establishment, and the methods of enforcing child support obligations are specifically addressed. Other editions published in 1983 and 1986.

2368. U.S. Congress. House. Committee on Ways and Means. Subcommittee on Public Assistance and Unemployment Compensation. *Child Support Enforcement Program, Hearing.* 100th Cong., 2d sess., 23 Feb. - 2 Mar. 1988. 636p. Y4.W36:100-56. Advocates for a stronger Child Support Enforcement Program detail the continued problems encountered by women in collecting child support. State implementation of the Child Support Enforcement Amendments of 1984 is reviewed and witnesses suggest administrative and legislative approaches to improving enforcement. Gaps between official implementation of the 1984 amendments and the state of child support services are identified.

2369. U.S. General Accounting Office. *Problems GAO Identified in Work on Child Support Enforcement Program: Statement of Joseph F. Delfico, Senior Associate Director, Human Resources Division before the Subcommittee on Public Assistance and Unemployment Compensation, Committee on Ways and Means, House of Representatives.* by Joseph F. Delfico. Washington, DC: The Office, 1988. 9p. GA1.5/2:T-HRD-88-8. Testimony before a congressional subcommittee describes the results of the GAO study of child support enforcement. Remarks focus on the problems of interstate enforcement, notably the need for more automation, more uniform laws, and better staffing. The need to collect better data on child support enforcement is also stressed.

2370. U.S. National Institute for Child Support Enforcement. *Improving IV-A/IV-D Interface - Handbook.* Chevy Chase, MD: The Institute, 1988. 46p. HE24.8:In8/3. Handbook and trainer guide for workers in AFDC(IV-A) and Child Support Enforcement(IV-D) programs encourages the two programs to work effectively with each other in enforcing parental responsibility for child support.

2371. U.S. National Institute for Child Support Enforcement. *Improving IV-A/IV-D Interface, Training Guide.* Chevy Chase, MD: The Institute, 1988. various paging. HE24.8:In8/3/train. Trainer guide provides a canned presentation for AFDC (IV-A) and Child Support Enforcement (IV-D) program managers and workers. The training materials focus on the structure of IV-A and IV-D programs and present the case for coordination of programs. Individual modules describe the role of IV-A and IV-D personnel in improving child support collections.

2372. U.S. Congress. House. Committee on Ways and Means. Subcommittee on Human Resources. *The Child Support Enforcement Program: Policy and Practice.* by the Congressional Research Service. 101st Cong., 1st sess., 1989. Committee print. 175p. Y4.W36:WMCP101-19. Detailed report on the problem of fathers who fail to make child support payments reviews the operation and potential of the Child Support Enforcement Program. The report discusses the state/local role and the federal role in establishing child support orders and collecting support payments, and reviews the funding and performance of the Child Support Enforcement Program. Continuing issues in child support enforcement are also briefly considered. Included in the appendix are reprints of major child support legislation and selected state statistics.

2373. U.S. Family Support Administration. *An Explanation of Child Support Enforcement for Credit Grantors.* Washington, DC: GPO, 1989. 15p. HE25.8:C43. Review of the Child Support Enforcement Programs for credit grantors urges them to consider child support obligations when assessing credit risk. Companies are also encouraged to lobby for state regulations requiring the reporting of delinquent support payments to credit bureaus and the inclusion of support orders as a "trade line" on credit bureau reports.

2374. U.S. General Accounting Office. *Interstate Child Support: Case Data Limitations, Enforcement Problems, Views on Improvements Needed.* Washington, DC: the Office, 1989. 85p. GA1.13:HRD-89-25. Investigation of interstate child support enforcement examined case loads and collections, state processes, and barriers to interstate enforcement. State processes reviewed include paternity determination, establishment of support orders, and collections. Information on state demonstration projects is also furnished.

2375. U.S. Internal Revenue Service. *Child Support Enforcement Handbook.* IRS Publication 1105. Washington, DC: GPO, 1989. 40p. T22.44/2:1105/989. Handbook provides procedural details on IRS collection of delinquent child support payments through tax refund offsets.

2376. U.S. Office of Child Support Enforcement. *Handbook on Child Support Enforcement.* Washington, DC: The Office, 1989. 47p. HE25.8:C43/2. Handbook for families on the Child Support Enforcement Program reviews costs to custodial parents, absent parent locator services, paternity establishment, establishing support orders, and child support enforcement procedures and options. Questions about interstate enforcement under the

Uniform Reciprocal Enforcement of Support Act are also addressed. A glossary of child support enforcement terms are included in the appendix.

2377. U.S. Congress. House. Committee on Ways and Means. *Technical and Miscellaneous Social Security Act Amendments of 1990, Report to Accompany H.R. 5828.* H. Rept. 101-899, part 1, 101st Cong., 2d sess., 18 Oct. 1990. 152p. Report details miscellaneous changes in SSA programs including extension of IRS intercepts of child support for non-AFDC families, extending the Commission on Interstate Child Support, administrative changes in AFDC, amendment of the Minnesota Family Investment Plan Demonstration, and spousal benefits under Social Security.

2378. U.S. Congress. House. Committee on Ways and Means. Subcommittee on Human Resources. *Written Comments on Possible Amendments to H.R. 4229, Miscellaneous Human Resources Amendments of 1990.* 101st Cong., 2d sess., 1990. Committee print. 78p. Y4.W36:WMCP101-31. Written comments on proposed amendments to a social programs bill focus on the issue of child support enforcement and disability payments. Submitted materials on child support enforcement focus on rules governing state handling of child support collection, specifically, requirements for timeliness of payment to the child of collected support.

2379. U.S. General Accounting Office. *Interstate Child Support: Better Information Needed on Absent Parents for Case Pursuit.* Washington, DC: The Office, 1990. 36p. GA1.13:HRD-90-41. The problem of missing or inaccurate information as a barrier to effective interstate enforcement of child support orders is explored. The extent of the problem and recommendation for improving the situation are presented.

SERIALS

2380. U.S. Bureau of the Census. *Child Support and Alimony [Year].* Current Population Reports Series P-23, nos. 124, 140, 148, 152, 154. Washington, DC: GPO, 1981-1985. biennial. C3.186:P-23/no. Report on child support and alimony awards and payments provides statistics on award and amount of child support and alimony by marital status, race, age of woman, educational attainment and number of children. The same data is also reported for women with incomes below the poverty level. Provides additional data on percentage of child support and alimony payments actually made and property settlements following divorce.

2381. U.S. Bureau of the Census. *Marriage and Divorce.* Washington, DC: GPO, 1916-1932. irreg. C3.46:year. Mostly annual report on marriage and divorce furnishes state statistics on divorces by cause, party to which granted, place of marriage, granting of alimony, and presence of children. Also provides data on number of marriages and divorces by county with some statistics from earlier years presented for comparison.

2382. U.S. National Center for Health Statistics. [agency varies] *Vital Statistics of the United States, Vol. 3, Marriage and Divorce.* Washington, DC: GPO, 1966-. annual. HE20.6210:date; HE20.2212:date; FS2.112:date.

2383. U.S. National Child Support Enforcement Reference Center. *Abstracts of Child Support Techniques.* Rockville, MD: The Center, 1982-. irreg. HE24.11:year-no. One page overviews profile successful techniques for collecting child support.

2384. U.S. National Child Support Enforcement Reference Center. *Information Sharing Index.* Washington, DC: GPO, 1979-. annual. HE24.12:year. Index to the collection of published and unpublished materials in the National Child Support Enforcement Reference

Center's collection covers laws, regulations, programs, and administrative procedures in child support.

2385.   U.S. Office of Child Support Enforcement. *Action Transmittals.* Rockville, MD: The Office, 1985-. irreg. HE24.14:year-no. Information for state agencies administering child support enforcement plans under Title IV-D of the Social Security Act consists primarily of instructions, clarifications and reprints of regulations.

2386.   U.S. Office of Child Support Enforcement. *Child Support Enforcement: Annual Report to the Congress.* Washington, DC: GPO, 1979-1985, 4th - 10th. annual. HE24.1:year. Annual report reviews the activities and accomplishments of the Child Support Enforcement Program at the state and federal level. Describes the problems experienced and presents statistics on collections and program costs for AFDC and non-AFDC child support enforcement under IV-D plans, establishment of paternity cases, and establishment of obligation cases. The tenth annual report was issued in two volumes with the first volume presenting a review of child support enforcement from 1975 to 1985.

2387.   U.S. Office of Child Support Enforcement. *Child Support Report.* Rockville, MD: National Child Support Enforcement Reference Center, 1979-. monthly. HE24.9:vol./no. Newsletter reports on legislation, programs, conferences and personnel related to the Child Support Enforcement Program.

16

Public Assistance and Poverty

Over the years government programs and publications on poverty generally only considered women as mothers of young children. Prior to the passage of the Social Security Act most of the documents on women and public assistance were Children's Bureau publications describing state and foreign laws governing mothers' pensions. A historical perspective on public assistance through 1930 is found in *Perspectives in Public Welfare, a History* (2454). The minor role of Aid to Dependent Children at the time the Social Security Act was passed is reflected in the 1937 speech by Mary Mewson, *What Social Security Act Means to Women* (2402), which describes benefits to women as wives of covered workers with only a passing reference to ADC. The majority of the documents on ADC for the next two decades are primarily statistical reports on recipients and expenditures. By the mid-1950s, concern over the poverty rate in the U.S. began to appear in government documents. The 1956 hearings on revision of the public assistance portions of the Social Security Act featured significant discussion of illegitimacy and ADC (2412), and in 1961 and 1962 public assistance was the focus of numerous hearings (2419-2421). At these hearings some discussion of work programs and day care for ADC families is found, although the main topic of debate was the extension of benefits to two-parent families with unemployed fathers.

The first report to specifically focus on women and poverty is a 1964 Women's Bureau report which highlights the problems of low wages and intermittent employment (2426). Possibly the most significant aspect of the "war on poverty" for women was their exclusion. With the exception of family planning programs, the congressional hearings and reports of the 1960's paid little attention to the problems of female-headed households. In most cases the discussion of women was so insignificant that the documents were not included in this bibliography. Even when AFDC employment and training programs were discussed, the particular problems of women were rarely considered (2436-2439). One of the few documents of this time period which does specifically address women and the Work Incentive Program is the 1969 Manpower Administration report, *The Potential for Work among Welfare Parents* (2450).

The emphasis on work programs in AFDC was more pronounced in the documents beginning in the 1970s, and the availability and provision of day care services was a major theme (2456, 2458-2460). The effectiveness of the WIN program was questioned in 1972 Senate hearings on poverty programs which highlighted the problems of single mothers (2476-2477). In 1973 the General Accounting Office issued its report. *Social Services, Do They Help Welfare Recipients Achieve Self-Support or Reduce Dependency?* (2488), which examined the effectiveness of child care and jobs programs. The overwhelming themes of welfare reform from the early 1970s on are work requirements, training programs, work disincentives, and child support. Welfare fraud was also a common theme, however, those documents were generally excluded from this bibliography as were documents dealing with purely administrative issues. Over the years the characteristics of AFDC recipients were described in a number of documents, but of particular note is a series of reports on studies of AFDC families. These studies, conducted every two years between 1967 and 1979, provide detailed data on family characteristics, employment, child care, and family finances to create a statistical profile of AFDC households (2464, 2471-2472, 2482, 2492, 2612).

The contributing factors to women's poverty status are explored in a number of reports including the Commission on Civil Rights' 1974 report *Women and Poverty* (2489), its 1979 followup report, *Women Still in Poverty* (2519), and the 1983 report *Disadvantaged Women and Their Children: A Growing Crisis* (2538). Also in 1983, two House committee hearings focused on poverty among female-headed households (2540, 2514). By the 1980s the congressional hearings clearly reflect the preponderance of female-headed households in the poverty population, and focus attention on the problem of long-term dependency. A series of reports, *Up from Dependency*, by the Interagency Low Income Opportunity Advisory Board, describe existing public assistance programs and alternatives (2554-2555, 2572-2573, 2576, 2587), and serve as a the basis for congressional hearings on approaches to the problem on long term dependency (2571).

The economic problems of older women are examined in the documents in Chapters 17 and 18. Other documents on public assistance programs are located in Chapter 13, Birth Control and Abortion, Chapter 14, Illegitimacy and Adolescent Pregnancy, and Chapter 15, Divorce and Child Support. Documents on public assistance which focused primarily on employment and job training or on day care services are found in Volume Two.

2388.   U.S. Children's Bureau. *Laws Relating to "Mothers' Pensions" in the United States, Denmark and New Zealand.* Publication no. 7. Washington, DC: GPO, 1914. 102p. L5.20:7. Prints the texts of state laws and the laws of Denmark and New Zealand providing for the care of dependent children in their own homes

2389.   U.S. Children's Bureau. *Governmental Provisions in the United States and Foreign Countries for Members of the Military Forces and Their Dependents.* Publication no. 28. Washington, DC: GPO, 1917. 236p. L5.20:28. Detailed report describes allowances and dependents' pensions in the U.S., Austria, France, Germany, Great Britain, Austria, New Zealand, South Africa, Italy, Netherlands, Russia, and Switzerland.

2390.   U.S. Children's Bureau. *Laws Relating to "Mothers' Pensions" in the United States, Canada, Denmark, and New Zealand.* Publication no. 63. Washington, DC: GPO, 1919. 316p. L5.20:63. Revisions of an earlier document (2388) with the addition of laws for Canada.

2391.   U.S. Women's Bureau. *Mothers' Pension Laws in the United States.* Chart no. 10. Washington, DC: The Bureau, 1920. 4 sections, each 1p. L13.5:10/sec.1-4.

2392.   U.S. Children's Bureau. *The Administration of the Aid-to-Mothers Laws in Illinois.* by Edith Abbott and Sophonisba P. Breckinridge. Publication no. 82. Washington, DC: GPO, 1921. 176p. L5.20:82. Description of the aid-to-mothers law in Cook County and outside of Cook County in Illinois. Areas covered include methods of determining pension grants, adequacy of amounts, and histories of families made ineligible by changes in the law. Accompanying statistics describe family characteristics and income data.

2393.   U.S. Women's Bureau. *Mothers' Pensions Laws.* Baltimore, MD: A. Hoen & Co., 1921. 1p. map. L13.6:6.

2394.   U.S. Children's Bureau. *Proceedings of a Conference on Mothers' Pensions, Providence, R.I., June 28, 1922.* Publication no. 109. Washington, DC: GPO, 1922. 31p. L5.20:109. Reports the results of a survey of state methods of compiling budget schedules for mothers' pensions and discusses general standards of aid.

2395. U.S. Children's Bureau. *Standards of Public Aid to Children in Their Own Homes.* by Florence Nesbitt. Publication no. 118. Washington, DC: GPO, 1923. 145p. L5.20:118. Study of the standard-of-living of families receiving public aid to children, primarily mothers' pensions, serves as a base for states administering such programs. Areas covered include living standards, determining aid, work of mothers, and services other than relief.

2396. U.S. Children's Bureau. *Laws Relating to Mothers' Pensions in the United States Passed during the Years 1920 to 1923, Inclusive.* Washington, DC: GPO, 1924. 99p. L5.2:M85/2. Provides texts of relevant state laws governing mothers' pensions for widowed or abandoned mothers.

2397. U.S. Children's Bureau. *Public Aid to Mothers with Dependent Children, Extent and Fundamental Principles.* Publication no. 162. Washington, DC: GPO, 1926. 18p. L5.20:162. Reviews the concept of mothers' aid and the standards and provisions of existing laws. Revised edition issued in 1928.

2398. U.S. Congress. Senate. Committee on the District of Columbia. Subcommittee on S. 120 and S. 1929. *Mothers' Aid in the District of Columbia, Hearings on S. 102 and S. 1929.* 69th Cong., 1st sess., 11, 21 Jan. 1926. 92p. Y4.D63/2:M85. Testimony favors the establishment of a board of mothers' assistance in aid of destitute mothers in the District of Columbia. Expert testimony from a New York mothers' aid administrator discusses the administration and benefits of mothers' aid legislation. The witness for the National Women's Party urges that a non-sex specific approach be taken.

2399. U.S. Children's Bureau. *Administration of Mothers' Aid in Ten Localities with Special Reference to Health, Housing, Education, and Recreation.* by Mary F. Bogue. Publication no. 184. Washington, DC: GPO, 1928. 206p. L5.20:184. Review of mothers' allowances discusses legal provisions, administration, physical and mental health programs, housing, educational activities, and recreation programs in the U.S. and in Manitoba, Canada.

2400. U.S. Children's Bureau. *Mothers' Aid, 1931.* Publication no. 220. Washington, DC: GPO, 1933. 39p. L5.20:220. Survey of mothers' aid in the states describes eligibility and amount of aid, characteristics of families aided, and expenditures for mothers' aid by state.

2401. U.S. Works Progress Administration. Legal Research Section. *Digest of State and Territorial Laws Granting Aid to Dependent Children in Their Own Homes as of Sept. 1, 1936.* Washington, DC: The Administration, 1936. 29p. Y3.W89/2:5C43. Charts summarize the provisions of state aid to dependent children laws in the U.S. describing provisions regarding age of child, residence requirement, social conditions under which aid is granted, maximum allowance, administration, and source of funds.

2402. U.S. Social Security Board. *What Social Security Act Means to Women, Speech Made by Miss Mary Mewson, Member, Social Security Board, before National Radio Forum, Sponsored Jointly by Washington Evening Star and National Broadcasting Company, NBC Coast-to-Coast Network, Washington, D.C., October 11, 1937.* Washington, DC: The Board, 1937. 10p. SS1.8:D51. Discussion of the Social Security program as it relates to women mostly speaks of the impact on the family, the older worker maintaining the family relationship, the unemployed worker supporting his family, and, finally, ADC and a mother's ability to preserve the family.

2403. U.S. Social Security Board. *Estimated Composition of Beneficiaries under Modified Title II Coverage as Set Forth in Various AC Plans with Particular Reference to Wives, Widows and Dependent Children.* Actuarial Study no. 7. Washington, DC: The Board, 1938. 12p. SS1.34:7.

2404. U.S. Congress. House. Committee on Ways and Means. *Social Security, Hearings Relative to the Social Security Act Amendments of 1939.* 76th Cong., 1st sess., 1 Feb. - 7 Apr. 1939. 2612p. 3 vol. Y4.W36:So1/v.1-3. Extensive hearing on revision of the Social Security Act focuses primarily on old age pensions and unemployment insurance, but briefly discusses the ADC program. The proposed amendments to ADC would raise the federal contribution to fifty percent, the same as other Social Security Act programs. Most testimony centers on taxes and financing and on the effect of Social Security on the economy.

2405. U.S. Social Security Board. Bureau of Research and Statistics. *Trends in Public Assistance, 1933-1939.* Bureau Report no. 8. Washington, DC: GPO, 1940. 98p. FS3.9:8. Along with data on old-age assistance and aid to the blind, the report details ADC payments by state, 1936-1939, and by county for December 1939.

2406. U.S. Bureau of Public Assistance. *Aid to Dependent Children: A Study in Six States.* Public Assistance Report no. 2. Washington, DC: The Bureau, 1941. 87p. FS3.13:2. Study of ADC in six states examines policies for determining eligibility, meeting the financial need of the family, and the employment and child care arrangements of the supervising adult.

2407. U.S. Bureau of Public Assistance. Division of Program Statistics and Research. *Distribution of Assistance Payments to Recipients, Old-Age Assistance, Aid to Dependent Children, Aid to the Blind.* Research Memorandum no. 2. Washington, DC: GPO, 1941. 19p. FS3.12:2. State data for November 1940 details the amount of assistance payments received by size of family and the distribution of families by payment received. Updated to May 1941 by Research Memorandum no. 4, FS3.12:4.

2408. U.S. Children's Bureau. *List of References on Homemaker Service.* Washington, DC: The Bureau, 1942. 11p. L5.40:H75/2. Annotated list of books, articles, and government documents on homemakers services in public welfare.

2409. U.S. Bureau of Public Assistance. *Families Receiving Aid to Dependent Children, October 1942.* Public Assistance Report no. 7. Washington, DC: GPO, 1945. 2 vol. FS3.13:7/pt.1-2. Part one describes race, size, and composition of ADC families and reasons for dependency, while part two details family income by source for eight states.

2410. U.S. Bureau of Public Assistance. *Characteristics of State Plans for Old-Age Assistance, Aid to the Blind and Aid to Dependent Children.* Information Service Circular no. 62. Washington, DC: GPO, 1946. 103p. FS3.4:62. State charts provide information on administration and regulation of state public assistance programs.

2411. U.S. Bureau of Public Assistance. *Aid to Dependent Children in a Postwar Year: Characteristics of Families Receiving Aid to Dependent Children.* Public Assistance Report no. 17. Washington, DC: GPO, 1950. 34p. FS3.13:17. Report on state ADC program recipients examines race and status of the father.

2412. U.S. Congress. House. Committee on Ways and Means. *Public Assistance Title of the Social Security Act, Hearings on H.R. 9120 and H.R. 9091 and H.R. 10283 and H.R. 10284.* 84th Cong., 2d sess., 12 - 20 Apr. 1956. 358p. Y4.W36:So1/13. Witnesses examine the need for public assistance programs such as OASI and ADC in the context of proposed revisions. Illegitimate children and ADC is discussed at length.

2413. U.S. Bureau of Public Assistance. *Homemaker Service in Public Assistance.* by Elizabeth Long. Public Assistance Report no. 31. Washington, DC: The Bureau, 1957. 29p. FS3.13:31. Homemaker services are generally set up to provide care of children and households during the incapacitation of the mother. Methods of recruiting women for positions as homemakers and qualifications are discussed.

2414.   U.S. Public Health Service. Division of Public Health Methods. *Homemaker Services in the United States, 1958, a Nationwide Study.* by William H. Stewart, Maryland Y. Pennell, and Lucille M. Smith. Washington, DC: GPO, 1958. 106p. FS2.2:H75/2. Results of a nationwide survey of homemaker services describe the types of services offered, the families that receive such services, and the screening process for hiring women for the homemaker programs. Provides statistics on salaries or wage scales of homemaker service employees by region; homemakers by age, race, marital status and educational level; and previous paid employment of homemakers by occupation.

2415.   U.S. Public Health Service. Division of Public Health Methods. *Homemaker Services in the United States, 1958, Twelve Statements Describing Different Types of Homemaker Services.* Washington, DC: GPO, 1958. 99p. FS2.2:H75/3. Describes homemaker services provided by twelve local agencies and the administration of each program. The case histories included with these descriptions are particularly interesting for the insight they provide into the lives of the women who sought out the help of this service.

2416.   U.S. Bureau of Public Assistance. *Services in Aid to Dependent Children Program, Implications for Federal and State Administration.* Washington, DC: GPO, 1959? 63p. FS3.2:C43/3. Describes needed ADC programs from the state's point of view.

2417.   U.S. Bureau of Public Assistance. *Homemaker Service in Public Welfare, North Carolina Experience.* Washington, DC: GPO, 1961. 46p. FS3.2:H75. Description of the development and administration of a statewide homemaker service to provide assistance to North Carolina low-income families and to the elderly includes case studies of services provided.

2418.   U.S. Bureau of Public Assistance. *State Methods for Determining Need in the Aid to Dependent Children Program.* Public Assistance Report no. 43. Washington, DC: GPO, 1961. 35p. FS3.13:43. Discusses state methods of calculating need for families in the ADC program.

2419.   U.S. Congress. House. Committee on Ways and Means. *Temporary Unemployment Compensation and Aid to Dependent Children of Unemployed Parents, Hearings.* 87th Cong., 1st sess., 15-17 Feb. 1961. 423p. Y4.W36:Un2/8. Lengthy hearing deals primarily with unemployment insurance but also discusses ADC and unemployed fathers in relation to family abandonment.

2420.   U.S. Congress. House. Committee on Ways and Means. *Public Welfare Amendments of 1962, Hearings on H.R. 10032.* 87th Cong., 2d sess., 7 - 13 Feb. 1962. 697p. Y4.W36:P96/2. General hearing on extending and improving public assistance programs under the SSA covers everything from day care to services for the blind with an emphasis on the role of social work and the structure of ADC. Day care services are discussed both from the working mother and child development perspective. State residency requirements for ADC is also a common topic.

2421.   U.S. Congress. Senate. Committee on Finance. *Public Assistance Act of 1962, Hearings on H.R. 10606.* 87th Cong., 2d sess., 14-17 May 1962. 603p. Y4.F49:P96/8. Hearing on public assistance and child welfare services under the Social Security Act examines the ADC program and the federal matching funds formula. Proposed changes include extending a temporary program to provide ADC to two parent families where the husband is unemployed. Testimony centers on work programs and retraining for ADC parents with some discussion of provisions for day care. Also presented are views on the role of social workers in public assistance. Included in the testimony is an analysis of ADC problems in Cook County, Illinois, and a discussion of the problem of migration and public assistance on residency requirements.

2422. U.S. Bureau of Family Services. *Dependent Children and Their Families.* Washington, DC: GPO, 1963. 31p. FS14.202:C43/3. Summary of characteristics of AFDC families covers education and job training of AFDC mothers, length of time on AFDC, parentage of illegitimate children receiving AFDC, size of AFDC families, and race of AFDC children.

2423. U.S. Children's Bureau. *Homemaker Service, History and Bibliography.* Publication no. 410. Washington, DC: GPO, 1964. 116p. FS14.111:410. Brief history of homemakers services from 1903 to the 1960s highlights the major goals of such services. The greater part of the publication is an annotated bibliography on all aspects of homemaker services.

2424. U.S. Congress. House. Committee on Education and Labor. *Poverty in the United States.* 88th Cong., 2d sess., 1964. Committee print. 252p. Y4.Ed8/1:P86. Report on the characteristics of families and individuals in poverty emphasizes the predominance of minority and female-headed households and widows among those below the poverty line. The role of social legislation past and present in addressing poverty issues is reviewed. Factors of age, education, race, residence and marital status are all examined in relation to poverty, and numerous tables and diagrams support the analysis. Includes a selected reference list and an appendix with charts.

2425. U.S. Welfare Administration. *Homemakers, a National Need.* by Ellen Winston. Washington, DC: GPO, 1964. 12p. FS14.11:W73/12. Paper delivered at National Conference on Homemaker Services, Washington, D.C., April 29, 1964, describes the need for homemaker services.

2426. U.S. Women's Bureau. *Women in Poverty.* Washington, DC: The Bureau, 1964. 7p. L13.2:P86. Report on women in poverty pulls together data on the number of women living in poverty, their employment status, marital and family status, and race. The case of working women whose wages or opportunity for continuous employment keep them below poverty and the educational attainment of low-income women are examined.

2427. U.S. Bureau of Family Services. *Characteristics of State Public Assistance Plans under the Social Security Act: Provisions for Medical and Remedial Care.* Public Assistance Report no. 49. Washington, DC: GPO, 1965. 192p. FS14.213:49. Chart for each state describes provisions of medical and remedial care to recipients of OAA, AB, APTD, and AFDC. Includes information on services provided, eligibility, state and local advisory groups, state-local financing and methods of payment.

2428. U.S. Bureau of Family Services. *Homemaker Service in Public Welfare, the North Carolina Experience.* by North Carolina Department of Public Welfare. Washington, DC: The Bureau, 1965. 48p. FS14.202:H75. Description of the homemaker program in North Carolina outlines the development of the service and its operating structure. The duties and training of homemakers and coordination with other agencies is detailed. Case studies illustrate the nature of the service.

2429. U.S. Dept. of Health, Education, and Welfare and U.S. Housing and Home Finance Agency. *New Programs in Health, Education and Welfare for Persons and Families of Low Income.* Washington, DC: GPO, 1965. 14p. FS1.2:F21. Brief description of HEW programs covers AFDC, prenatal care, and job training.

2430. U.S. Welfare Administration. *Homemaker Service and Social Welfare.* by Ellen Winston. Washington, DC: GPO, 1965. 19p. FS14.11:W73/14. Paper delivered at the International Congress of Homehelp Services, at Koenigstein/Taunis, Federal Republic of Germany, September 8, 1965, illustrates the role of the homemaker service in helping families learn to function on their own. The qualifications of women recruited for homemaker services and the need to provide status, salary, and benefits in order to recruit quality applicants is stressed. Also noted is the growth of the homemaker service and the need for more federal and state support to expand the service to marginally poor families.

2431. U.S. Welfare Administration. *Proceedings of the International Congress on Home Help Services, Held in Paris, France, September 1962.* Washington, DC: GPO, 1965. 71p. FS14.2:H75/2. Presentations provide an international perspective on the utilization and training for homemaker services. Papers also review the changing structure of the family and the need for homemaker services, and the medical aspects of home help work. Brief descriptions of home help services by country are furnished.

2432. U.S. Women's Bureau. *Women's Earnings in Low-Income Families.* Washington, DC: The Bureau, 1965. 2p. L13.2:Ea7/2. Summary information on earnings of women in low income families examines sex of family head, race and work experience.

2433. U.S. Bureau of Family Services. *Characteristics of State Public Assistance Plans under the Social Security Act: Provisions for Social Services.* Public Assistance Report no. 53. Washington, DC: GPO, 1966. 133p. FS14.213:53. State charts describe services provided to OAA, AB, APTD, and AFDC recipients. Briefly summarizes special services to target groups such as unwed mothers and families disrupted by desertion.

2434. U.S. Commission on Civil Rights. Indiana State Advisory Committee. *Gary Midtown West Families on AFDC, Report of Public Meeting Concerning the Aid to Families with Dependent Children Program in Gary, Indiana.* Washington, DC: The Commission, 1966. 39p. CR1.2:G19. Speakers at a public meeting on assistance levels for AFDC in Indiana examine the problems of black mothers on AFDC in the Gary Midtown West area. Problems of housing, education, employment, police protection, and community organizations are review as they effect black AFDC families.

2435. U.S. Welfare Administration. *Proceedings of the International Congress of Koenigstein on Home Help Services Held in Koenigstein, Germany, September 1965.* Washington, DC: GPO, 1966. 102p. FS14.2:H75/2/965. Papers presented at an international conference on homemaker services cover topics of the role of homemaker services in social welfare, the type of work performed, training standards, working conditions, and organization of services.

2436. U.S. Congress. House. Committee on Ways and Means. *President's Proposals for Revision in the Social Security System, Hearings on H.R. 5710.* 90th Cong., 1st sess., 1 - 3 Mar. 1967. 445p. Y4.W36:So1/25/pt.1. Hearing on revision of the Social Security Act presents Administration witnesses discussing primarily retirement benefits but also changes to expand state participation in AFDC, raise benefits, and require employment training programs. The case of working women under the Social Security system is also briefly discussed, particularly that of widows who return to work.

2437. U.S. Congress. Senate. Committee on Finance. *Social Security Amendment of 1967, Hearings on H.R. 12080.* 90th Cong., 1st sess., 22 - 24 Aug. 1967. 736p. Y4.F49:So1/8/967/pt.1. Administration witnesses discuss the need for and probable outcome of proposed changes in Social Security. Retirement pensions, unemployment, and AFDC are reviewed. The AFDC discussion centers on proposed work training requirements and on which agency should operate the program. Definitions of poverty and the Medicare and Medicaid programs are also debated.

2438. U.S. Congress. Senate. Committee on Labor and Public Welfare. Subcommittee on Employment, Manpower, and Poverty. *Examination of the War on Poverty, Hearings, Part 7.* 90th Cong., 1st sess., 8 June 1967. 2047-2371pp. Y4.L11/2:P86/4/pt.7. Hearing on S. 1545 focuses on crime and welfare and on family planning services as they relate to Economic Opportunity Act programs. Effectiveness of community action and job training programs are also reviewed. Provides a summary of AFDC cases by mother's age and educational attainment and parents' health problems, ethnic origin, employment status by sex, and usual occupation.

2439. U.S. Congress. Senate. Committee on Labor and Public Welfare. Subcommittee on Employment, Manpower, and Poverty. *Examination of the War on Poverty, Hearings, Part 12.* 90th Cong., 1st sess., 12 May 1967. 3743-4005pp. Y4.L11/2:P86/4/pt.12. Review of Economic Opportunity Act programs in Los Angeles covers job training, family planning, Headstart, and community action programs. Includes data for poverty areas on marital status by sex, female headed families, labor force status by sex, occupation by sex, and family income by sex of head.

2440. U.S. Office of Economic Opportunity. *Conference Proceedings, Women in War on Poverty, May 8, 1967.* Washington, DC: GPO, 1967. 68p. PrEx10.2:W84. Panel discussion on poverty and women highlights the extent and problems of women in poverty noting the problems of female headed households, older women, and low paying female-dominated professions. Other topics touched on are day care, Mexican-American women, education, and training programs for women. The federal response to poverty, particularly the Job Corps and the role of volunteer organizations such as the Women in Community Service are examined. The participation of girls in the Neighborhood Youth Corps is also reviewed along with the involvement of the Council of Negro Women and the YWCA in the war on poverty.

2441. U.S. Welfare Administration. *Welfare Programs and Services.* Washington, DC: GPO, 1967. 40p. FS14.2:W45/3. Collection of one to two page descriptions of major welfare programs includes the Maternal and Child Health Service Programs, Special Project Grants for Maternity and Infant Care, International Maternal and Child Health Programs, Aid to Families with Dependent Children, and the Work Experience Program.

2442. U.S. Women's Bureau. *Fact Sheet on Women's Earnings in Poor Families.* Washington, DC: The Bureau, 1967. 3p. L13.2:P79. Summarizes facts on the poor families including employment of women in poor families, sex of the family head, family income by race, and occupation and labor force status.

2443. U.S. Congress. Joint Economic Committee. Subcommittee on Fiscal Policy. *Income Maintenance Programs, Hearings.* 90th Cong., 2d sess., 11 - 27 June 1968. 720p. 2 vol. Y4.Ec7:In2/3. Hearing on the concept of a guaranteed income discusses problems with AFDC, focusing on the millions of ineligible families below the poverty line. The adequacy of current benefits and the situation of the working poor are examined. The welfare bureaucracy and the difficulty of establishing eligibility are also discussed. Work disincentives in the current system is a recurring theme. The concept of a negative income tax is discussed at length. The appendix in volume two provides a wealth of material on poverty and public assistance in the United States.

2444. U.S. Women's Bureau. *Fact Sheet on the American Family in Poverty.* Washington, DC: The Bureau, 1968. 3p. L13.2:P86/2/968. Summary profile of families below the poverty line provides data on number and types of families in poverty, the extent of poverty by sex of head and number of children, and the number of children living in poverty by race and sex of family head. Earlier editions published in 1965 and 1966.

2445. U.S. Children's Bureau. *Social Services for Children and Families in Your State.* Publication no. 464. Washington, DC: GPO, 1969. 31p. FS17.210:464. Summary of state provided services connected with AFDC emphasizes child care for working mothers, family planning, and services to unwed pregnant girls.

2446. U.S. Congress. House. *Aid to Families with Dependent Children, Conference Report to Accompany H.R. 8644.* H. Rept. 330, 91st Cong., 1st sess., 1969. 2p. Serial 12837-2. Point of disagreement between the House and Senate on a bill suspending the duty on crude chicory root was a Senate amendment repealing a section of the Social Security Act limiting the number of dependent children under 18 who may receive AFDC with federal financial participation.

2447. U.S. Congress. House. Committee on Ways and Means. *The President's Proposal for Welfare Reform and Social Security Amendments, 1969, Including Draft Bills, Summaries, and Other Material Transmitted by the Department of Health, Education, and Welfare.* 91st Cong., 1st sess., 1969. Committee print. 106p. Y4.W36:W45. Changes in Social Security proposed include an increase in the widow's benefit to 100 percent of husband's benefit for widows who began receiving benefits at age 65 or older and the equalization of the treatment of male and female workers in the calculation of average monthly earnings. Changes in the AFDC program were also proposed relating to job training and child care. The preferential treatment of female-headed families under AFDC is discussed.

2448. U.S. Congress. House. Committee on Ways and Means. *Report on Monitoring of Special Review of Aid to Families with Dependent Children in New York City Conducted by the Department of Health, Education and Welfare and the New York State Department of Social Services by the Comptroller General of the United States.* 91st Cong., 1st sess., 1969. Committee print. 59p. Y4.W36:M74/2. Reprint of the GAO report on the HEW review of AFDC in New York focused on eligibility determinants and the progress in moving AFDC recipients to self-sufficiency. The impact of a state policy limiting a single mother's eligibility for work and the lack of sufficient day care facilities are highlighted.

2449. U.S. Congress. House. Committee on Ways and Means. *Social Security and Welfare Proposals, Hearings.* 91st Cong., 1st sess., 15 Oct.- 13 Nov. 1969. 2757p. 7 vol. Y4.W36:So1/27/pt.1-7/970. Extensive hearings consider proposed changes to Social Security and family assistance programs which would raise widows' benefits, change work requirements under AFDC, and expand training and day care opportunities. Examines current problem areas in Social Security and AFDC benefits and administration. Part four in particular focuses on child care issues.

2450. U.S. Manpower Administration. *The Potential for Work among Welfare Parents.* by Leonard J. Hausman. Research Monograph no. 12. Washington, DC: GPO, 1969. 32p. L1.39/3:12. Summary of a dissertation analyzes the potential for moving AFDC families into jobs and off of public assistance. The primary focus is on whether AFDC recipients can earn enough per month at their former occupation to exceed the amount received through AFDC. The provisions of the 1967 Public Assistance Amendments are examined in light of potential earnings and the WIN program's likelihood of helping AFDC mothers attain financial independence.

2451. U.S. National Center for Social Statistics. *1967 AFDC Study, Preliminary Report of Findings from Mail Questionnaire.* Washington, DC: The Center, 1969. 18p. FS17.602:Ai2/967/prelim. Survey of AFDC mothers looks at the adequacy of their access to medical services, their ability to pay for necessities, and their attitudes toward the welfare system.

2452.   U.S. National Center for Social Statistics. *Social Services for Families and Children.* Washington, DC: The Center, 1969. 10p. HE17.618:969. Describes the information provided by the states on the number of recipients of family related social services, particularly day care, homemaker, and foster care services.

2453.   U.S. Office of Economic Opportunity. *Women in War on Poverty.* OEO Pamphlet 1405-5. Washington, DC: GPO, 1969. 12p. PrEx10.23:1405-5. The role of women in the war on poverty as volunteers, as Job Corps and Upward Bound participants, as executives in OEO programs, and as members of women's organizations is discussed.

2454.   U.S. Social and Rehabilitation Service. Office of Research, Demonstration, and Training. *Perspectives in Public Welfare, a History.* Washington, DC: GPO, 1969. 107p. FS17.2:P96/3. History of public welfare from Medieval poor laws to the reform movement of the 1920's describes both attitudes toward the poor and methods of providing necessities. Provides statistics on relief aid of wages for men, women and widows in England and Wales, 1840, 1843, 1846; gainfully employed women workers 10 years old and over by occupations, 1900-1930; and mothers' aid maximum monthly grants and annual income by state, 1926.

2455.   U.S. Social and Rehabilitation Service. Office of Research, Demonstration and Training. Division of Intramural Research. *Welfare Policy and Its Consequences for the Recipient Population, a Study of the AFDC Program.* by Samuel M. Meyers and Jennie McIntyre. Washington, DC: GPO, 1969. 217p. HE17.2:W45. Study of randomly selected urban and rural counties in 10 states reports on the effect of state differences in welfare policy on AFDC clients' lives and attitudes. In addition, the effect of the Work Experience and Training Program is assessed.

2456.   U.S. Congress. House. Committee on Rules. *Family Assistance Act of 1970, Hearings on H.R. 16311.* 91th Cong., 2d sess., 7 - 14 Apr. 1970. 253p. Y4.R86/1:F21. Hearing on a welfare reform proposal with strong work registration requirements mostly discusses the welfare family with an unemployed father, rather that the female-headed welfare family.

2457.   U.S. Congress. House. Committee on Ways and Means. *Brief Summary of Principal Provisions of H.R. 16311, "The Family Assistance Act of 1970."* 91st Cong., 2d sess., 5 1970. Committee print. 8p. Y4.W36:F21. Summarizes the provisions of the Family Assistance Act of 1970 in the areas of eligibility, registration, state contribution, work and training, and child care.

2458.   U.S. Congress. House. Committee on Ways and Means. *Family Assistance Act of 1970, Report on H.R. 16311.* H. Rept. 91-904, 91st Cong., 2d sess., 1970. 85p. Serial 12884-1. Report with additional and dissenting views on changing the welfare system to include the working poor and to require job registration focuses on work incentives for AFDC recipients. Child care assistance is a recurring topic.

2459.   U.S. Congress. House. Committee on Ways and Means. *Service to AFDC Families: First Annual Report of the Department of Health, Education, and Welfare on Services to Families Receiving Aid to Families with Dependent Children under Title IV of the Social Security Act.* 91st Cong., 2d sess., 21 July 1970. 64p. Y4.W36:Ai2/3. Annual Report on AFDC highlights the WIN program and family planning services. In relation to WIN, the problems of day care access and transportation are addressed. Significant progress is reported in family planning areas but access to medical care was noted as a problem. Services to reduce illegitimacy are also highlighted.

2460. U.S. Congress. Senate. Committee on Finance. *Family Assistance Act of 1970, Hearings on H.R. 16311.* 91st Cong., 2d sess., 29 Apr. - 10 Sept. 1970. 2343p. 3 vol. Y4.F49:F21/pt.1-3. Parts one and two of hearings on the Family Assistance Act of 1970 present administration witnesses on AFDC and WIN. Major issues are work disincentives and the child care issue. The focus of the second part is on costs and operating procedures and on income tested programs and female-headed households. Part three contains public witnesses and written testimony on benefit levels, minimum wage, work disincentives, work requirements and mothers, day care facilities, and bias against two parent households. Health care and utilization of the food stamp program are also discussed.

2461. U.S. Congress. Senate. Committee on Finance. *H.R. 16311, the Family Assistance Act of 1970, June Revision.* 91st Cong., 2d sess., 1970. 322p. Y4.F49:F21/2/970-2. Analysis of June and October revisions of the Family Assistance Act of 1970 reprints revisions. Major areas affected are state supplemental payments, child care, obligation of deserting parents, and work disincentives. Estimates of eligibility by family characteristics is given.

2462. U.S. Congress. Senate. Committee on Finance. *H.R. 16311, the Family Assistance Act of 1970, Revised.* 91st Cong., 2d sess., 1970. 308p. Y4.F49:F21/2. Results of an administrative review of H.R. 16311, conducted in response to hearings on the bill, addresses issues of work disincentives, improvement of the WIN program, child care, subsidized housing, family health insurance plan, and social services such as foster care and adoption assistance. Cost data and estimates of families eligible are provided by sex of family head and family size, education of family head, occupation of family head, race and region.

2463. U.S. Congress. Senate. Committee on Finance. *Material Related to H.R. 16311.* 91st Cong., 2d sess., 1970. 51p. Y4.F49:F21/4. Material summarizes federal costs for AFDC, WIN, and Aid to the Aged, Blind and Disabled in relation to the Family Assistance Act of 1970. Chart compares present law and H.R. 16311 in the areas of eligibility and benefits, work incentive, administration, and federal financial participation.

2464. U.S. National Center for Social Statistics. *Findings of the 1967 AFDC Study: Data by State and Census Division.* Washington, DC: GPO, 1970. 2 vol. HE17.639/3:967. Part one of a nationwide study of AFDC families provides data, by state, on characteristics of families including number and ages of children; absence of father; incapacity of mother or father; age, place of birth, and previous residence in another state; education, occupation, and employability of father and mother; parentage of children; and child care arrangements of working mothers. Part two reports on family finances including income of mother, father and children. For later studies see 2471, 2482, 2492, and 2612.

2465. U.S. Congress. House. Committee on Education and Labor. *Economic Opportunity Amendments of 1971, Part 1, Hearings.* 92d Cong., 1st sess., 22 Mar. - 19 April 1971. 769p. Y4.Ed8/1:Ec7/971/pt.1. Part one of extensive hearings on amendments to the Economic Opportunity Act of 1964 discusses family planning, maternal health, and the Headstart program as well as job training programs such as the Job Corps.

2466. U.S. Congress. House. Committee on Ways and Means. *Social Security Amendments of 1971, Report on H.R. 1.* H. Rept. 92-231, 92d Cong., 1st sess., 1971. 386p. Serial 12934-3. Topics of child care, family planning and child support collection are touched on in this report on a welfare bill which emphasizes a work incentive approach. Also affected are eligibility requirements for divorced women under Social Security.

2467. U.S. Congress. House. Committee on Ways and Means. *Statistical Information Related to Family Assistance Provisions of H.R. 1.* 92d Cong., 1st sess., 1971. Committee print. 35p. Y4.W36:F21/2. Most of the statistics presented are on the cost of the welfare reform proposal, however, some are on social characteristics of families eligible for benefits including age, work experience, number of earners in family, race, and number of children by sex of head of household.

2468. U.S. Congress. Senate. Committee on Finance. *Material Related to H.R. 1, Welfare Programs for Families.* 92d Cong., 1st sess., 1971. Committee print. 77p. Y4.F49:W45/2. Overview of the welfare program contained in H.R. 1 focuses on AFDC. Provides data on welfare eligibility by state and projected eligibility by sex of family head. Also presents data on children receiving AFDC by status of father, 1940-1970, and summarizes data from the 1969 study of Aid to Dependent Children (2471).

2469. U.S. Dept. of Health, Education and Welfare and Dept. of Labor. *Welfare Reform Charts.* Washington, DC: GPO, 1971. 41p. HE1.2:W45. Charts illustrate problems with the welfare system and highlight reform proposals.

2470. U.S. National Center for Social Statistics. *AFDC: Selected Statistical Data on Families Aided and Program Operations.* Washington, DC: GPO, 1971. 60p. HE17.640:F21. Report provides statistics on AFDC families such as characteristics of mother, child care arrangements, enrollment in WIN, and family income.

2471. U.S. National Center for Social Statistics. *Findings of the 1969 AFDC Study: Data by Census Division and Selected States.* Washington, DC: GPO, 1971. 2 vol. HE17.639/3:969/pt.1-2. See the 1967 report (2464) for abstract; for later reports see 2482, 2492, and 2612.

2472. U.S. National Center for Social Statistics. *National Cross-Tabulations from the 1967 and 1969 AFDC Studies.* Washington, DC: The Center, 1971. 59p. HE17.602:Ai2/2. Analysis of data from the 1967 and 1969 AFDC studies allows comparison of characteristics of AFDC families in the areas of employment and educational status of mother, status of father, size of household, age of mother, place of residence, and length of residence in state where receiving benefits.

2473. U.S. National Center for Social Statistics. *Trends in AFDC: 1965-1970 and Selected Annual Periods.* Washington, DC: The Center, 1971? 23p. HE17.640:4. Report looks at national and state level factors effecting the increase in recipients of AFDC between 1965 and 1970.

2474. U.S. Women's Bureau. *Fact Sheet on the American Family in Poverty.* Washington, DC: The Bureau, 1971. 3p. L13.2:Am4. Basic statistics presented on the characteristics of families living in poverty include race, medium income deficit, and children under 18 in poverty by sex of family head.

2475. U.S. Congress. House. Committee on Education and Labor. *Economic Opportunity Amendments of 1972, Hearings on H.R. 12350.* 92d Cong., 2d sess., 25,26 Jan. 1972. 122p. Y4.Ed8/1:Ec7/972. Witnesses testifying on reauthorization of the Economic Opportunity Amendments of 1972 discuss Job Corps, Legal Services Corporation, and Headstart. Brief discussion of day care covers standards, fee schedules and the role of the Office of Economic Opportunity.

2476. U.S. Congress. Senate. Committee on Finance. *Establishing Priorities among Programs Aiding the Poor, Hearing.* 92d Cong., 2d sess., 15 Feb. 1972. 201p. Y4.F49:P79/2. Included in testimony on antipoverty programs is a discussion of issues involving welfare mothers, workfare, and child care. In particular the effectiveness of the WIN program is brought into question. The appendix includes a summary of programs aiding the poor and data on related costs and number of beneficiaries per program. Appendix C presents HEW comments on public testimony on H.R. 1, welfare reform, and in particular addresses day care, "man-in-the-house" rules, and child support issues.

2477. U.S. Congress. Senate. Committee on Finance. *Social Security Amendments of 1971, Hearings on H.R. 1.* 92d Cong., 1st and 2d sess., 27 July 1971 - 9 Feb. 1972. 3464p. 6 vol. Y4.F49:So1/8/971/pt.1-6. Testimony on welfare reform proposals discusses work requirements, family abandonment, child care, and the effectiveness of the WIN program. The primary discussion of the proposal and AFDC is in part one of the hearings, however, part four also includes testimony on child care and the WIN program. Part one compares benefits available to female-headed families under 1970 and 1971 laws and under H.R. 1 and H.R. 16311, the welfare reform bill of the 91st Congress. Tables and charts detail the characteristics of persons and families below the poverty level and compare costs for alternative reform plans. The WIN program comes in for heavy criticism. Part three focuses on fraud, work requirements, and state versus federal control. Child care facilities, work requirements and the problem of illegitimacy are briefly explored. Much of the discussion focuses on the job skills of welfare recipients and effective approaches to work incentives.

2478. U.S. Congress. Senate. Committee on Finance. *Social Security Amendments of 1972, Report to Accompany H.R. 1 Together with Additional Views.* S. Rept. 92-1230, 92d Cong., 2d sess., 1972. 1285p. Serial 12973-4. Lengthy report on revision of the Social Security Act highlights the establishment of a Bureau of Child Care within the Work Administration and changes in eligibility and administration of AFDC and child support enforcement. The additional views discuss work requirements and welfare mothers.

2479. U.S. Congress. Senate. Committee on Finance. *Social Security and Welfare Reform, Summary of the Principal Provisions of H.R. 1 as Determined by the Committee on Finance.* 92d Cong., 2d sess., 13 June 1972. 129p. Y4.F49:So1/30. Major areas addressed by H.R. 1 are Social Security cash benefits; Medicare-Medicaid provisions; financing Social Security, Aid to the Aged, Blind and Disabled; guaranteed job opportunities for families; child welfare; and social services including family planning, child care, AFDC, and child support.

2480. U.S. Congress. Senate. Committee on Finance. *Welfare Reform and the Family Assistance Plan, Statement of Roger A. Freeman.* 92d Cong., 2d sess., 27 Jan. 1972. 104p. Y4.F49:W45/8. Statement before the Committee on Finance analyzes the current welfare system, in particular AFDC. Issues of child support by absent fathers and work requirements for AFDC mothers are addressed relative to the potential of H.R. 1 to address these problems.

2481. U.S. Congress. Senate. Committee on Finance. *Welfare Reform, Guaranteed Job Opportunity, Explanation of Committee Decisions.* 92d Cong., 2d sess., 28 Apr. 1972. 9p. Y4.F49:W45/7. Summarizes the reasoning behind the Committee on Finance's recommendation on H.R.1, the administrations welfare reform proposal for AFDC and workfare.

2482. U.S. National Center for Social Statistics. *Findings of the 1971 AFDC Study.* Washington, DC: The Center, 1971-1972. 4 vol. HE17.639/3:971/pt. Parts one and two provide 1971 data on characteristics of AFDC families by state including number and ages of children; absence of father; incapacity of mother or father; age, place of birth, previous residence in another state; education, occupation, and employability of father and mother; parentage of children; and child care arrangements of working mothers. Part two reports on family finances including income of mother, father and children. A supplement to part two provides a summary of financial circumstances. Part three, National Cross Tabulations, pulls together the state data from parts one and two to provide a national statistical profile of AFDC families. For earlier studies see 2471 and 2463; later see 2492 and 2612.

2483. U.S. Social Security Administration. Office of Research and Statistics. *Disabled Widows.* by Donald T. Ferron. Social Security of the Disabled, 1966, Report no. 22. Washington, DC: GPO, 1972. 21p. HE3.54/2:22. Data from the Social Security for the Disabled survey on disabled widows is analyzed in the areas of participation in the labor force and receipt of public income maintenance payments by severity of disability. Comparisons are made to nondisabled widows and all disabled women.

2484. U.S. Congress. Joint Economic Committee. Subcommittee on Fiscal Policy. *The Family, Poverty, and Welfare Programs: Factors Influencing Family Instability.* Studies in Public Welfare, Paper no. 12, part 1. 93d Cong., 1st sess., 1973. Committee print. 180p. Y4.Ec7:W45/paper 12/pt.1. Collection of papers provides detailed analysis of trends in illegitimacy, female-headed households, martial instability and welfare families. Papers also explore the relationship between public assistance programs and the functioning of low income families.

2485. U.S. Congress. Joint Economic Committee. Subcommittee on Fiscal Policy. *The Family, Poverty, and Welfare Programs: Household Patterns and Government Policies.* Studies in Public Welfare, Paper no. 12, part 2. 93d Cong., 1st sess., 3 Dec. 1973. 181-350pp. Y4.Ec7:W45/paper 12/pt.2. Volume two of papers on welfare programs and family structure provides a focus on the black community along with analysis of family welfare under public assistance programs.

2486. U.S. Congress. Senate. Committee on Finance. *Social Services Regulations, Hearings, Part 2, Public Witnesses and Written Testimony.* 93d Cong., 1st sess., 15-17 May 1973. 173-611pp. Y4.F49:So1/35/pt.2. Hearing on HEW regulations for social services under the SSA focuses primarily on AFDC. Eligibility requirements and day care are at the center of debate while family planning programs are also covered. Day care discussion deals primarily with issues of eligibility and quality.

2487. U.S. Congress. Senate. Committee on Finance. *Staff Data and Materials on Social Service Regulations.* 93d Cong., 1st sess., 1973. Committee print. 79p. Y4.F49:So1/34. Overview of regulations established by HEW for social services under the SSA summarize former and new regulations for mandatory and optional services. Also provides excerpts of a study of fiscal year 1972 social services. Regulations for AFDC eligibility, family planning services, and day care provision are included.

2488. U.S. General Accounting Office. *Social Services, Do They Help Welfare Recipients Achieve Self-Support or Reduce Dependency? Social and Rehabilitation Services, Department of Health, Education, and Welfare.* Washington, DC: The Office, 1973. 123p. GA1.13:So1/2. Study of the relationship between social services provided to AFDC recipients and the movement of families off AFDC questions the effectiveness of current services. Problems of job availability and child care are noted.

2489. U.S. Commission on Civil Rights. *Women and Poverty.* Washington, DC: GPO, 1974. 81p. CR1.2:W84. The basics on federal programs to assist women in poverty, notably AFDC, WIN, and CETA, and the problems and prospects for change are presented. Child care is briefly discussed and elderly women, Social Security and private pension plans are also covered.

2490. U.S. Congress. House. Committee on Education and Labor. Subcommittee on Equal Opportunities. *Equal Opportunity and Full Employment Act of 1976, Hearing on H.R. 15476.* 93d Cong., 2d sess., 8 Oct. 1974. 97p. Y4.Ed8/1:Em7/13. Hearing considers an act to combat unemployment by creating a Job Guarantee Office and a standby Job Corps. Testimony highlights the disparate effects of recession on women, minorities, teenagers, and the aged.

2491. U.S. Congress. Joint Economic Committee. Subcommittee on Fiscal Policy. *Public Welfare and Work Incentives: Theory and Practice.* Studies in Public Welfare Paper no. 14. 93d Cong., 2d sess., 15 Apr. 1974. 55p. Y4.Ec7:W45/paper 14. Chart book summarizes in non-technical language the relationship between welfare benefits and existing work incentive provisions. Specifically addresses work incentives and welfare mothers.

2492. U.S. National Center for Social Statistics. *Findings of the 1973 AFDC Study.* Washington, DC: GPO, 1974. 5 vol. HE17.639/3:973/pt.1, 2A & B, 3-4. Statistics previously found in part one of the 1969-1971 (2471, 2482) studies have been split into two parts for 1973. Part one now describes the number and ages of children; age, education, and employment status of mother and father; and participation in the WIN program. Services to families are covered in part three where child care arrangements, family planning services, educational services, non-WIN employment services, and use of alcohol or addictive drugs by family members are detailed. Part two, financial circumstances, provides data on AFDC family sources of income and expenses. Detailed statistics on assistance discontinued by characteristics of the family are given in part four. For later studies see 2612.

2493. U.S. Congress. Senate. Committee on Finance. *Staff Data and Materials on Social Service Proposals.* 94th Cong., 2d sess., 6 May 1976. 37p. Y4.F49:So1/34/976. Compilation of background information on social service programs reviews legislation and regulations from 1972 to 1974. Proposals dealing with eligibility and child care standards are examined. A chart allows comparison of present law, the 1974 Senate bill, and the administration proposal. Tables provide state data on expenditures, income limits on eligibility, and additional federal funding for children. State staffing requirements for day care are also presented in tabular form.

2494. U.S. Dept. of Health, Education, and Welfare. *Income Supplement Program: 1974 HEW Welfare Replacement Proposal.* Technical Analysis Paper no. 11. Washington, DC: The Department, 1976. 111p. HE1.52:11. Analysis of a proposed replacement for federal assistance programs such as AFDC, food stamps, WIN, and SSI examines the proposed changes and briefly reviews the 1960's and 1970's welfare reform proposals.

2495. U.S. Bureau of Community Health Services. *Studies on Institutions and Planning: Research to Improve Health Services for Mothers and Children.* Washington, DC: GPO, 1977. 24p. HE20.5114/2:In7. Summary report of research describes developing community-wide health information systems to support maternal and child health program planning and profiles mothers and children receiving public assistance from the Midway District Office.

2496. U.S. Congress. House. Committee on Agriculture, U.S. Congress. House. Committee on Education and Labor, and U.S. Congress, House. Committee on Ways and Means. Welfare Reform Subcommittee. *Administration's Welfare Reform Proposal: Joint Hearings on H.R. 9030.* 95th Cong., 1st. sess., 19 Sept. - 4 Nov. 1977. 3010p. 4 vol. Y4.Ag8/1:W45/pt.1-4. First four parts of extensive hearings on the administration's welfare proposal, which would consolidate AFDC, SSI and the Food Stamp Program into a single cash benefit program, focuses on job programs. The first part presents the testimony of administration witnesses, the second part presents the views of members of Congress and public witnesses, and public witnesses also comprise parts three and four. Public witnesses in particular address the issues of workfare, wages and child day care.

2497. U.S. Congress. House. Committee on Agriculture, U.S. Congress. House. Committee on Education and Labor, and U.S. Congress. House. Committee on Ways and Means. Welfare Reform Subcommittee. *Administration's Welfare Reform Proposal: Joint Hearings on H.R. 9030, Part VI, Public Witnesses.* 95th Cong., 1st. sess., 9,14 Nov. 1977. 450p. Y4.Ag8/1:W45/pt.6. Public testimony at hearings held in Salem, Oregon, and Oakland, California, focuses on the administration's workfare proposals. Minimum wage and waiting periods for benefits are the primary topics of discussion.

2498. U.S. Congress. House. Committee on Government Operations. Subcommittee on Intergovernmental Relations and Human Resources. *Administration of the AFDC Program, Hearing.* 95th Cong., 1st sess., 19 July - 5 Oct. 1977. 676p. Y4.G74/7:Ai2/2. Hearing on the effectiveness of the current AFDC program focuses on issues of welfare and work and on welfare abuse. The situation of welfare mothers and the philosophy of work requirements for welfare mothers are specifically discussed although most testimony does not specifically take female-headed households into account. Includes data on work experiences of low income women with children.

2499. U.S. Congress. House. Committee on the Budget. Task Force on Distributive Impacts of Budget and Economic Policies. *President Carter's Welfare Proposals, Hearing.* 95th Cong., 1st sess., 13 - 21 Oct. 1977. 206p. Y4.B85/3:C24/2. Hearing on the effect of the Carter welfare reform proposals on the various segments of the welfare population includes testimony from the Women's Lobby discussing the effect of the proposals on female-headed households receiving AFDC.

2500. U.S. Congress. House. Committee on Ways and Means. *Public Assistance Amendments of 1977, Report Together with Supplemental Views to Accompany H.R. 7200.* H. Rept. 95-394, 94th Cong., 1st sess., 1977. 106p. Serial 13172-7. Among the provisions of this bill is an increase in Title XX day care funding, extension of provisions for incentives to hire welfare recipients as child care workers, and suspension of federal day care staffing requirements. Also authorized are federal matching funds for child support collection and paternity establishment services for certain non-AFDC individuals. A chart compares the provisions of H.R. 7200 with existing public assistance programs.

2501. U.S. Congress. House. Committee on Ways and Means. Subcommittee on Public Assistance and Unemployment Compensation. *Information on Public Assistance Legislative Recommendations for FY78 Considered During May 2-6, 1977 Hearings.* 95th Cong., 1st sess., 1977. 37p. Committee print. Y4.W36:WMCP95-18. Presents a concise tabular summary of pending administration budget requests and basic background information on current expenditures and program requirements for public assistance programs. Issues within the budget requests are summarized, and include expiration of federal reimbursement for non-AFDC child support enforcement.

2502. U.S. Congress. House. Committee on Ways and Means. Subcommittee on Public Assistance and Unemployment Compensation. *Public Assistance Legislative Recommendations, Hearings.* 95th Cong., 1st sess., 2-5 May 1977. 395p. Y4.W36:95-14. Witnesses addressing legislative recommendations on AFDC, Title XX and Title IV-B programs discuss their impact on child welfare. A concise summary of the program goals and services is provided. Among the provisions discussed are earnings disregards and dependent care allowances in the AFDC program, non-AFDC reimbursement for child support enforcement, and food stamp eligibility. Public assistance in the territories and U.S. possessions and eligibility of aliens are primary topics. Child protection services, day care, and work incentives are also discussed.

2503. U.S. Congress. Joint Economic Committee. *Work, Welfare, and the Program for Better Jobs and Income, a Study.* by Barry L. Friedman and Leonard J. Hausman. 95th Cong.,

1st sess., 1977. Committee print. 114p. Y4.Ec7:W89. Study analyses the Carter administration welfare reform proposal, the Program for Better Jobs and Income, specifically addressing the effect of the program on female-headed households. The report also examines the effectiveness of the entire workfare approach.

2504. U.S. Congress. Senate. Committee on Finance. *Public Assistance Amendments of 1977, Report on H.R. 7200.* S. Rept. 95-573, 95th Cong., 1st sess., 1 Nov. 1977. 245p. Serial 13168-11. Among the major provisions of this bill are child care funding, child support enforcement and a work incentive program. The bill primarily makes administrative changes in public assistance programs. The moratorium on day care staffing requirements is also extended. The report summarizes the provisions of existing laws and the changes proposed.

2505. U.S. Congress. Senate. Committee on Finance. Subcommittee on Public Assistance. *Principles of Welfare Reform, Hearings.* 95th Cong., 1st sess., 5,12 May 1977. 87p. Y4.F49:W45/10. Joseph A. Califono, Jr., Secretary of HEW and Ray Marshall, Secretary of Labor, testify on the elements of President Carter's welfare reform approach. Work incentive programs are a major topic.

2506. U.S. Congress. Senate. Committee on Finance. Subcommittee on Public Assistance. *Public Assistance Amendments.* 95th Cong., 1st sess., 1977. Committee print. 78p. Y4.F49:P96/13. Provides basic data and materials concerning the programs affected by H.R. 7200, a bill to amend the Social Security Act, and describes its effect on SSI, social services and child care, child welfare services, and AFDC. Background data on recipients of SSI and AFDC, child center staffing, WIN registrations and outcomes, and child support enforcement by state is furnished.

2507. U.S. Congress. Senate. Committee on Finance. Subcommittee on Public Assistance. *Public Assistance Amendments of 1977, Hearings on H.R. 7200.* 95th Cong., 1st sess., 12 - 20 July 1977. 581p. Y4.F49:P96/14. Extensive hearings on proposed changes in SSI, AFDC, Child Welfare Services, and social services programs are characterized by recurring discussion of single parent families, job programs, work incentives, foster care, federal versus state and local funding, and administrative structure of programs.

2508. U.S. Congressional Budget Office. *Welfare Reform: Issues, Objectives, and Approaches.* Washington, DC: GPO, 1977. 175p. Y10.9:W45. Report analyzes welfare objectives and the impact of various reform approaches on subsets of the welfare population, e.g. female headed households, the aged, and the disabled. Detailed tables illustrate the effect of reform options on the welfare population.

2509. U.S. Women's Bureau. *Women with Low Incomes.* Washington, DC: GPO, 1977. 10p. L36.102:W84/5. Statistical profile of low-income women includes data on persons living in poverty by sex and age; occupational groups of low-income wage and salary workers by sex; median years of school completed by low-income persons by age, sex and race; educational attainment of low-income persons by sex; low income families by race and sex of household head; and percentage of female-headed families with low incomes by age, race, and Spanish origin.

2510. U.S. Congress. Senate. Committee on Finance. *Social Services, Child Care, and Child Support, Report to Accompany H.R. 12973.* S. Rept. 95-1306, 95th Cong., 2d sess., 1978. 62p. Serial 13197-13. Reports a bill making administrative changes in social services programs, extending provision of Title XX authorizing incentives to hire welfare recipients as child care workers, and continuing the suspension of Title XX day care staffing standards. The bill also increases the level of matching funds provided to states for implementation of computerized information systems for child support enforcement. Also related to child support enforcement are provisions for determining a parents' wage and extending the IRS collection responsibilities to non-AFDC cases. Provides data by state on expenditures for day care programs, AFDC parent located and paternity established cases, and child support payments collected.

2511. U.S. Congress. Senate. Committee on Finance. Subcommittee on Public Assistance. *Welfare Reform Proposals, Hearings.* 95th Cong., 2d sess., 7 Feb. - 4 May 1978. 5 parts. Y4.F49:W45/12/pt.1-5. Administration witnesses present testimony in part one of hearings focusing on program costs, Medicaid eligibility, "family-splitting" incentives, and child support. Provides detailed statistics on characteristics of families in poverty with an emphasis on characteristics of female-headed families. In part two supporting materials are provided including a comparison of bills S. 2777 and H.R. 10711 and data on eligibility, state expenditures for public assistance, characteristics of WIN participants, employment of AFDC mothers, and child support enforcement cases and collections. Also provides answers to questions directed at HEW Secretary Califano on AFDC and family stability, the rise in the welfare roles, and work disincentives. Parts three through five present oral testimony which continues to center on issues of work incentives and family stability.

2512. U.S. Congress. Senate. Committee on Finance. Subcommittee on Public Assistance. *Welfare Research and Experimentation, Hearings.* 95th Cong., 2d sess., 15-17 Nov. 1978. 426p. Y4.F49:W45/15. Review of research and experimental programs in AFDC describes benefit levels and types of payments, work programs, the effect of welfare on family stability, and the negative income tax concept.

2513. U.S. Congress. Senate. Committee on Human Resources. *Better Jobs and Income Act, 1978, Hearings on S. 2084.* 94th Cong., 2d sess., 22-23 Mar. 1978. 286p. Y4.H88:B46/978. Hearing on a welfare reform jobs program fails to discuss the special needs of female-headed household but does use them in scenarios illustrating how the Program for Better Jobs and Income would operate.

2514. U.S. Congressional Budget Office. *The Administration's Welfare Reform Proposal: An Analysis of the Program for Better Jobs and Income.* Washington, DC: GPO, 1978. 171p. Y10.12:W45. Analyzes a welfare reform proposal to restructure public assistance programs to include incentives to work. The proposed Program for Better Jobs and Income would replace AFDC, SSI, Medicaid, Food Stamps, and other assistance programs with a single cash assistance program. The effect of the program on various family types is examined.

2515. U.S. General Accounting Office. *Wisconsin's Aid to Families with Dependent Children and Child Support Enforcement Programs Could Be Improved.* Washington, DC: GPO, 1978. 86p. GA1.13:HRD-78-130. The high growth rate of AFDC cases in Wisconsin between 1966 and 1976 prompted this study of ways the state could improve its management of the AFDC program and of areas of needed improvement in the Milwaukee County Child Support Enforcement Program.

2516. U.S. Social Security Administration. Office of Research and Statistics. *Aid to Families with Dependent Children: A Chartbook.* Washington, DC: GPO, 1978. 29p. HE3.2:C43/5. Bar graphs profile the characteristics of AFDC families.

2517. U.S. Women's Bureau. *Employment and Economic Issues of Low Income Women: Report of a Project.* Washington, DC: GPO, 1978. 31p. L36.102:Em7/2. Describes a project sponsored by the Women's Bureau to bring together low-income women, community service organization representatives, and the staff of social service agencies to discuss the problems of low-income women.

2518. U.S. Administration for Public Services. Division of Program Management. State Administration and Management Branch. *Title XX National Comprehensive Annual Services Program Plan (CASP) Information.* Washington, DC: GPO, 1979. 132p. HE23.1002:C73. Planned expenditures and the expected number of recipients for Title XX programs administered at the state level are detailed in tables showing type of service to be offered, federal and state funding levels, and category of recipients.

2519. U.S. Commission on Civil Rights. *Women Still in Poverty.* Clearinghouse Publication no. 60. Washington, DC: GPO, 1979. 50p. CR1.10:60. The problems of the AFDC and WIN programs are illustrated by testimony at hearings held in Chicago in 1974. Job segregation and lack of child care options are identified as factors in the high number of women living in poverty.

2520. U.S. Congress. House. Committee on Ways and Means. *Social Welfare Reform Amendments of 1979, Report Together with Dissenting and Additional Views to Accompany H.R. 4904.* H. Rept. 96-451, 96th Cong., 1st sess., 1979. 281p. Serial 13301. Substantial background information on AFDC recipients and child support enforcement is included in this report on a bill making numerous change in the AFDC and SSI programs. The bill changes eligibility requirements, benefits standards, and administrative provisions.

2521. U.S. Congress. House. Committee on Ways and Means. Subcommittee on Public Assistance and Unemployment Compensation. *Welfare Reform Legislation, Hearings on H.R. 4122, H.R. 4321, and H.R. 4460.* 96th Cong., 1st sess., 15 - 27 June 1979. 654p. Y4.W36:96-37. Hearing on a welfare reform proposal to increase employment and training, improve adequacy of cash benefits, and eliminate error and fraud presents testimony concentrating on benefits for the working poor, unemployed fathers, food stamps, child care expenses, and the WIN and CETA programs.

2522. U.S. Congress. House. *Adoption Assistance, Child Welfare, and Social Services, Conference Report to Accompany H.R. 3434.* H. Rept. 96-900, 96th Cong., 2d sess., 1980. 70p. Serial 13363. Report on a bill dealing primarily with adoption and foster care programs also settles House and Senate differences on the level of funding for Title XX services, continuation of employer reimbursement for hiring welfare recipients as child care workers, and federal matching funds for AFDC child support enforcement services.

2523. U.S. Congress. Senate. Committee on Finance. Subcommittee on Public Assistance. *How to Think about Welfare Reform for the 1980's, Hearings.* 96th Cong., 2d sess., 6,7 Feb. 1980. 449p. Y4.F49:W45/16. Welfare reform hearing centers on approaches and costs with minimal discussion of the recipients themselves. The testimony briefly examines breaking the cycle of poverty for AFDC mothers through subsidized work.

2524. U.S. Congress. Senate. Committee on Finance. Subcommittee on Public Assistance. *Statistical Data Related to Public Assistance Programs.* 96th Cong., 2d sess., 1980. Committee print. 119p. Y4.F49:P96/20. Statistical tables illustrate characteristics of AFDC families with data on benefits paid and administrative expenditure by state, unemployed AFDC mothers by age and number of children, employment status of AFDC mothers by usual occupation, and child support enforcement collections and expenditures. Also presents statistics on the food stamp program, Medicaid, and Title XX services.

2525. U.S. Dept. of Agriculture. Food and Nutrition Service. *Characteristics of Food Stamp Households, February 1978.* Washington, DC: GPO, 1980. 119p. A98.9:204. Extensive statistical analysis of food stamp recipients provides detailed information on the employment and public assistance status of the female-headed households which make up 68.8 percent of the food stamp population.

2526. U.S. Dept. of Housing and Urban Development. Office of Policy Development and Research. *Families and Housing Markets: Obstacles to Locating Suitable Housing.* by Margaret C. Sims. Washington, DC: GPO, 1980. 64p. HH1.2:F21/4. Study of access to adequate housing for families focuses on the obstacles faced by minority and female-headed families. Some of the discussion is on discrimination by mortgage lenders and real estate agents, but the primary focus is on the problem of low incomes and affordable housing. Provides statistics by race and female-headed household for renting and homeownership, adequacy of housing, affordability of housing and poverty status of families.

2527. U.S. Congress. House. Committee on Ways and Means. Subcommittee on Public Assistance and Unemployment Compensation. *Administration's Proposed Savings in Unemployment Compensation, Public Assistance, and Social Services Programs, Hearings.* 97th Cong., 1st sess., 11,12 March 1981. 363p. Y4.W36:97-7. Extensive hearings on proposed reductions in public assistance and social service programs describes administration proposals to eliminate waste and fraud. Witnesses debate the issues of welfare fraud, the extent of recipients' willingness to work, and the barriers to AFDC recipient employment. The effect of Title XX cuts on services such as teenage pregnancy prevention programs and child abuse programs are discussed, and the effect of the cuts on poor, female-headed households is stressed.

2528. U.S. Congress. House. Committee on Ways and Means. Subcommittee on Public Assistance and Unemployment Compensation and Subcommittee on Oversight and U.S. Congress. House. Committee on Energy and Commerce. Subcommittee on Health and the Environment. *Impact of Program Changes and Budget Cuts in AFDC, Medicaid, and Social Services Programs, Joint Hearing.* 97th Cong., 1st sess., 9 Nov. 1981. 117p. Y4.W36:97-41. Hearing held in Memphis, Tennessee on the impact of changes and reductions in AFDC, Medicaid, and Title XX programs in Tennessee, Arkansas and Mississippi debates the fiscal responsibility of the federal government versus the state for helping the poor. Funding cuts and the issue of day care services are addressed.

2529. U.S. Congress. Senate. Committee on Labor and Human Resources. Subcommittee on Aging, Family and Human Services. *Fighting Poverty, Private Initiatives and Public Assistance, Hearing.* 97th Cong., 1st sess., 25 Aug. 1981. 124p. Y4.L11/4:P86. Hearing held in Alabama on federal funding for poverty programs highlights the good and the bad in the AFDC program. Also briefly covers the foster grandparent and senior aide programs and Headstart.

2530. U.S. Social Security Administration. Office of Research and Statistics. *AFDC Standards of Need, an Evaluation of Current Practices, Alternative Approaches, and Policy Options.* Washington, DC: GPO, 1981. 2 vol. HE3.2:St24/v.1-2. Detailed examination of state policies and practices for determining eligibility and need of AFDC families describes current practices and evaluates alternative models.

2531. U.S. Social Security Administration. Office of Research and Statistics. *AFDC Standards of Need, an Evaluation of Current Practices, Alternative Approaches, and Policy Options, Appendix A: Catalogue of Current State Practices.* Washington, DC: GPO, 1981. 179p. HE3.2:Ev1/2/app. Describes through charts and tables current state AFDC need determination practices and payment amounts.

2532. U.S. Social Security Administration. Office of Research and Statistics. *Evaluation Design Assessment of Work-Welfare Projects Phase I: Final Report.* Washington, DC: GPO, 1981. 150p. HE3.2:Ev1. Presents a design for a generic method of assessing the success of workfare programs for welfare recipients. Existing research on work-welfare programs is reviewed.

2533. U.S. Congress. House. Committee on Ways and Means. *Explanation of H.R. 6878, The Medicare, Unemployment Compensation, and Public Assistance Amendments of 1982, Including Summary, Explanation and Cost Estimates of the Congressional Budget Office.* 97th Cong., 2d sess., 2 Aug. 1982. Committee print. 95p. Y4.W36:WMCP 97-35. Committee description of H.R. 6878, a bill revising Medicare, unemployment compensation, and public assistance programs, reviews problems under AFDC, mostly due to the 1981 Budget Reconciliation Act. The particular problems of female-headed households and their earnings potential are related to proposed AFDC changes. Tables illustrating AFDC benefits under current and proposed legislation are included.

2534. U.S. Congress. House. Committee on Ways and Means. *Extension of Unemployment Benefits and AFDC Work Incentives Amendments, Report Together with Dissenting Views to Accompany H.R. 97-587.* H. Rept. 97-587, 97th Cong., 2d sess., 1982. 42p. Serial 13484. Reports a bill changing unemployment benefits and AFDC earned income disregards. The bill requires states to disregard CETA earnings of children in AFDC families and makes other changes affecting AFDC eligibility and benefit levels.

2535. U.S. Congress. House. Committee on Ways and Means. Subcommittee on Public Assistance and Unemployment Compensation. *Administration's FY83 Legislative Proposals for Unemployment Compensation and Public Assistance, Hearings.* 97th Cong., 2d sess., 25 Mar. - 22 Apr. 1982. 1148p. Y4.W36:97-62. The impact of reductions in AFDC and Title XX social services are discussed in depth along with proposals for changing AFDC and unemployment compensation programs. Work proposals and the high unemployment rate are examined, and strong support for federal child support enforcement programs is expressed. The importance of child care services is a recurring theme in testimony which recognizes the predominance of single mothers among the poor.

2536. U.S. Congress. House. Committee on Ways and Means. Subcommittee on Public Assistance and Unemployment Compensation. *Effect of Fiscal Year 1983 Budget Resolutions on Public Assistance Programs, Hearing.* 97th Cong., 2d sess., 23 June 1982. 129p. Y4.W36:97-76. Hearing dramatizes the effect on AFDC recipients of 1982 public assistance budget cuts and makes a case for exempting AFDC from further cuts. The approach of requiring AFDC mothers to accept employment or community projects work is briefly discussed in light of cuts in Title XX day care funding. Operating costs and federal funding levels are debated.

2537. U.S. Social Security Administration. Office of Research and Statistics. *Family Demography and Transfer Payments during the 1970's.* by Dorothy S. Projector and Mary P. Roen. Studies in Income Distribution no. 12. Washington, DC: GPO, 1982. 194p. HE3.67/2:12. Examines demographic changes during the 1970's as they relate to income support programs noting trends in age and sex of the family head and the presence of the spouse in the family.

2538. U.S. Commission on Civil Rights. *Disadvantaged Women and Their Children: A Growing Crisis.* Clearinghouse Publication no. 78. Washington, DC: GPO, 1983. 66p. CR1.10:78. Study found that female-headed families made up a disproportionate number of persons living in poverty and that the situation was worse for black and Hispanic women. Trends in marital status, employment and education that effect women's ability to rise above the poverty level are examined. Statistics illustrate family income by race and type of family, female and male poverty rates by race and household type, births to unmarried women, 1950-1979, women and men maintaining families below the poverty level by employment status, employment and disposable income of AFDC families, education level and poverty in female-headed households, and occupations and educational level by gender.

2539. U.S. Congress. House. Committee on the Budget. Task Force on Entitlements, Uncontrollables, and Indexing. *Overview of the Administration's Entitlement Policies, Hearing.* 98th Cong., 1st sess., 10 March 1983. 176p. Y4.B85/3:En8/3. The focus of this hearing is on the effect of the Reagan administration's public assistance policies on the ability of the poor to meet basic needs for food, clothing, and shelter. Witnesses document the erosion of AFDC benefits.

2540. U.S. Congress. House. Committee on the Budget. Task Force on Entitlements, Uncontrollables, and Indexing. *Women and Children in Poverty, Hearing.* 98th Cong., 1st sess., 27 Oct. 1983. 110p. Y4.B85/3:W84. Hearing testimony highlights the growing number of women and children living in poverty and the effect of AFDC reductions on female-headed households. Several AFDC mothers describe the problems of trying to become self-sufficient and the deficiencies in existing welfare coverage. Problems of enforcing child support, cuts in food stamps, and loss of Medicaid coverage if employment is secured are revealed. A report of a study of women raising families alone provides insight into the characteristics of single mothers who are self-sufficient. The particular problems of black female-headed households are also stressed.

2541. U.S. Congress. House. Committee on Ways and Means. Subcommittee on Oversight and Subcommittee on Public Assistance and Unemployment Compensation. *Poverty Rate Increase, Hearings.* 98th Cong., 1st sess., 3 Nov. 1983. 397p. Y4.W36:98-55. Hearing explores the increased poverty rate in the U.S. and the role of the Reagan administration budget cuts and the recession in the increase. The demographics of poverty, particularly the representation of the elderly and female-headed households among the poor, is explored. Witnesses express their views on the anti-poverty effect of the AFDC program. Economic principles and the relationship between the economy and poverty rates are discussed.

2542. U.S. Congress. House. Committee on Ways and Means. Subcommittee on Public Assistance and Unemployment Compensation. *AFDC and Social Service Bills and Related Oversight Issues, Hearing.* 98th Cong., 1st sess., 18 July 1983. 252p. Y4.W36:98-37. Hearing explores issues relating to the 1981 cuts in AFDC to the working poor and cuts in Title XX funds affecting provision of day care and other social services. Primary issues of work incentives and reporting requirements for AFDC are highlighted by testimony on the experience in the States under OBRA.

2543. U.S. Congress. Senate. Committee on Finance. *Administration's Fiscal Year 1984 Budget Proposals - II, Part 1, Hearings.* 98th Cong., 1st sess., 15,16 June 1983, 226p. Y4.F49:S.hrg.98-332/pt.1. Hearing to review administration proposals to reduce public assistance programs includes discussion of the government role in funding child support enforcement for AFDC families. Medicare and Medicaid programs and maternal and child health block grant programs are also discussed. Witnesses argue for continued funding of child welfare programs at existing levels citing supporting data on AFDC recipients. The question of the AFDC recipient's desire to work and the structure of the work requirement are discussed.

2544. U.S. Congress. Senate. Committee on Finance. *Nomination of Margaret M. Heckler and John A. Svahn, Hearing.* 98th Cong., 1st sess., 25 Feb. 1983. 79p. Y4.F49:S.hrg.98-59. Hearing on the nomination of Margaret M. Heckler to be Secretary of Health and Human Services includes close questioning on day care, AFDC funding, and the abortion issue.

2545. U.S. Congress. House. Committee on Ways and Means. Subcommittee on Public Assistance and Unemployment Compensation. *GAO Analysis of the 1981 AFDC Reductions, Hearing.* 98th Cong., 2d sess., 2 May 1984. 96p. Y4.W36:98-101. Witnesses describe the effect of the AFDC program cuts under the Omnibus Budget

Reconciliation Act of 1981 as revealed by a GAO study of families cut from the AFDC program (2546). The study focused on work histories after being cut, earned income and total income before and following OBRA, and the effect on the general circumstances of the family. Problems related to the of types of jobs held by low income women and the lack of health insurance coverage are examined.

2546. U.S. General Accounting Office. *An Evaluation of the 1981 AFDC Changes: Initial Analysis.* Washington, DC: GPO, 1984. 56p. GA1.13:PEMD-84-6. An analysis of the effect of the Omnibus Budget Reconciliation Act of 1981 on working AFDC recipients found that many lost their AFDC and food stamp benefits and were without health insurance coverage since losing Medicaid. Most AFDC families experienced a significant loss of income as a result of OBRA.

2547. U.S. Congress. House. Committee on Government Operations. *Opportunities for Self-Sufficiency for Women in Poverty, Twenty-Fifth Report Together with Dissenting Views.* H. Rept. 99-459, 99th Cong., 1st sess., 1985. 51p. Serial 13662. Report explores the barriers female-headed AFDC families face in achieving self-sufficiency and examines experimental programs aimed at elevating women from the welfare rolls. Child care, education and training, and employment opportunities are among the barriers discussed. The problems encountered by states establishing work-welfare programs and the problem of federal workfare approaches and program funding are reviewed.

2548. U.S. Congress. House. Select Committee on Hunger. Domestic Task Force. *Appalachia: Rural Women and the Economics of Hunger.* 99th Cong., 1st sess., 22 Oct. 1985. 159p. Y4.H89:99-8. The Food Stamp Program and Women, Infants and Children program are the focus of this hearing which discusses poverty among women and children in Appalachia.

2549. U.S. Congressional Budget Office. *Reducing Poverty among Children.* by Robert G. Williams, et al. Washington, DC: GPO, 1985. 173p. Y10.2:P86. Report on government policies and programs to reduce poverty among children provides a concise summary of the objectives and structure of the AFDC program. The bulk of the report analyzes policy alternatives in the areas of tax credits, food assistance, health care, housing assistance, adolescent pregnancy, employment and training, and child care. Approaches to measuring poverty are also reviewed.

2550. U.S. General Accounting Office. *An Evaluation of the 1981 AFDC Changes: Final Report.* Washington, DC: GPO, 1985. 168p. GA1.13:PEMD-85-4. The effect of AFDC changes under OBRA 1981 on the economic well-being of those AFDC families who lost benefits is examined. Employment and income before and after losing AFDC benefits is examined by recipient characteristics, and the problem of health insurance once Medicaid eligibility runs out is also stressed. The question of employment disincentives both before and after OBRA is considered.

2551. U.S. Social Security Administration. Office of Family Assistance. Office of Policy and Evaluation. *Aid to Families with Dependent Children: Findings of the May 1981 -May 1982 Aid to Families with Dependent Children Study, Recipient Characteristics, Financial Circumstances, the Effect of the Omnibus Budget Reconciliation Act of 1981.* Washington, DC: The Office, 1985. 21p. HE3.2:Ai2. Report examines the status of AFDC families in 1981 and 1982 with particular attention to the effects of cuts to the program under OBRA. Demographic characteristics and financial circumstances of families are highlighted, and the effect of OBRA in the area of gross income limitation, earnings disregards, work expense disregards, dependent care expenses, and stepparents in the household are examined.

2552. U.S. Congress. House. Select Committee on Hunger. *Self-Help Programs, Hearing.* 99th Cong., 2d sess., 15 May 1986. 30p. Y4.H89:99-17. Former AFDC recipients, mostly single mothers, describe the education, training, and job placement programs that helped them become self-sufficient.

2553. U.S. Congress. Senate. Committee on Labor and Human Resources. Subcommittee on Employment and Productivity and U.S. Congress. Senate. Committee on Finance. Subcommittee on Social Security and Income Maintenance. *Work and Welfare.* 99th Cong., 2d sess., 1986. Committee print. 162p. Y4.L11/4:S.prt.99-177. Historical background on the issue of AFDC and work requirements chronicles the work philosophy of AFDC from its inception. Special jobs programs under AFDC, such as the creation of WIN and the role of JTPA and CETA, are reviewed. Concerns over the purpose of AFDC and the structure of work requirements for mothers of young children are explored. Statistics describing current AFDC recipient characteristics are provided.

2554. U.S. Executive Office of the President. Office of Policy Development. *Up from Dependency, A New National Public Assistance Strategy. Supplement 1: The National Public Assistance System, Volume 1: An Overview of the Current System.* Washington, DC: GPO, 1986. 105p. PrEx15.2:D44/supp.1/v.1. Documents the operation of the current public assistance system, its eligibility levels, and its efficiency and effectiveness. Includes data for 1960 to 1985 on female headed families below the poverty level and the number of families receiving aid by type of assistance.

2555. U.S. Executive Office of the President. Office of Policy Development. *Up from Dependency: A New National Public Assistance Strategy. Supplement 3: A Self-Help Catalog.* Washington, DC: GPO, 1986. various pagings. PrEx15.2:D44/supp.3. Profiles low-income assistance programs which are not dependent on state or federal funds and which involve the low-income persons or families in a "self-help" program.

2556. U.S. Congress. House. *Omnibus Budget Reconciliation Act of 1987, Conference Report to Accompany H.R. 3545.* H. Rept. 100-495, 100th Cong., 1st sess., 1987. 1033p. Serial 13843. Conference report on the Omnibus Budget Reconciliation Act of 1987 settles differences between House and Senate bills relating to child support enforcement, Medicaid services to pregnant women and children, and AFDC fraud programs. Minor changes affecting survivor benefits are also mentioned in the bill.

2557. U.S. Congress. House. *The Trade, Employment, and Productivity Act of 1987, Message from the President of the United States Transmitting a Draft of Proposed Legislation, Pursuant to 19 U.S.C. 2112(e)(2), 2212(a).* H. Doc. 100-33, 100th Cong., 1st sess., 19 Feb. 1987. 499p. Serial 13782. Message from President Reagan summarizes the goals of the proposed Trade, Employment, and Productivity Act of 1987, whose draft comprises the bulk of this report. Title I of the bill proposes an employment and training program for AFDC recipients with special emphasis on high school diplomas for teenage parents under Subtitle E, the Greater Opportunities Through Work Act of 1987. Other provisions of the act deal with U.S. competition in the world market.

2558. U.S. Congress. House. Committee on Agriculture. *The Food Stamp Family Welfare Reform Act of 1987, Report Together with Minority Views to Accompany H.R. 3337.* H. Rept. 100-396, 100th Cong., 1st sess., 1987. 109p. Serial 13809. Report recommends changes in the Food Stamp Program including work incentives and higher child care deductions. The bill also provides for better coordination between AFDC and the Food Stamp Program.

2559. U.S. Congress. House. Committee on Education and Labor. *Family Welfare Reform Act of 1987, Report Together with Minority and Additional Views to Accompany H.R. 1720.*

H. Rept. 100-159, part 2, 100th Cong., 1st sess., 1987. 113p. Serial 13802. Reports a measure for the replacement of AFDC with a Family Support Program combining child support, need-based family support supplementals, and work while encouraging education and training. At the center of the bill is the Fair Work Opportunities Program. Background on past work and training programs is provided and mandatory participation and support services requirements are described. The importance of child care to the program is noted repeatedly.

2560. U.S. Congress. House. Committee on Education and Labor. *Hearing on Welfare Reform: H.R. 30, Fair Work Opportunities Act of 1987 and H.R. 1720, Family Welfare Reform Act of 1987.* 100th Cong., 1st sess., 29 Apr.- 5 May 1987. 467p. Y4.Ed8/1:100-30. Alternatives to the WIN program are explored with witnesses describing innovative state welfare transition programs. The educational needs of AFDC recipients are stressed and the lack of available, affordable child care is noted. In addition to discussing remedial education, the need to sanction participation in postsecondary degree programs is supported. Witnesses also review the concept of workfare or unpaid jobs for welfare recipients. Other topics addressed include community and business support and job development programs. Reprinted in the hearing is "Changing Welfare: An Investment in Women and Children in Poverty," a proposal of the National Coalition on Women, Work, and Welfare Reform.

2561. U.S. Congress. House. Committee on Energy and Commerce. *Family Welfare Reform Act of 1987, Report Together with Additional and Dissenting Views to Accompany H.R. 1720.* H. Rept. 100-159, part 3, 100th Cong., 1st sess., 1987. 46p. Serial 13802. Reports a bill to replace AFDC with a Family Support Program. The transition from AFDC to employment and the need in many cases for continued Medicaid coverage is highlighted through background information on the medical insurance status of female-headed families.

2562. U.S. Congress. House. Committee on Energy and Commerce. Subcommittee on Health and the Environment. *Medicaid Issues in Family Welfare and Nursing Home Reform, Hearings.* 100th Cong., 1st sess., 24 Apr., 12 May 1987. 592p. Y4.En2/3:100-73. First day of hearings on Medicaid and nursing home reform focuses on Medicaid coverage during the transition from AFDC to paid employment. Starting from the premise that many women will enter low paying jobs with no health insurance benefits, the witnesses explore ways to continue Medicaid coverage. The extent to which loss of health insurance is an employment disincentive for welfare mothers is discussed.

2563. U.S. Congress. House. Committee on the Budget. *Omnibus Budget Reconciliation Act of 1987, Report to Accompany H.R. 3545, a Bill to Provide for Reconciliation Pursuant to Section 4 of the First Concurrent Resolution on the Budget for Fiscal Year 1988 Together with Supplemental, Additional and Minority Views.* H. Rept. 100-391, 100th Cong., 1st sess., 1987. 1747p. Serial 13808. Part one of this report covers the welfare section of the Omnibus Budget Reconciliation Act incorporating Title I of H.R. 1720, the Family Welfare Act of 1987. A summary of hearings on welfare reform and job and training programs stresses the need for child care services. The bill authorizes the Fair Work Opportunities Program, which requires the participation of most AFDC recipients and includes a child care assistance requirement. Part two discusses Title IX of the proposed budget act, replacement of AFDC with the Family Support Program made up of job training and support services. Also included are "workfare" and job search programs, child care reimbursements for recipients in school, training or work, and a child support enforcement program.

2564. U.S. Congress. House. Committee on Ways and Means. *Family Welfare Reform Act of 1987, Report Together with Additional and Dissenting Views to Accompany H.R. 1720.* H. Rept. 100-159, part 1, 100th Cong., 1st sess., 1987. 182p. Serial 13802. Child support enforcement improvements, day care expenses, and work incentives are highlighted in this report with amendments on legislation to replace AFDC with a Family Support Program. The report describes the National Education, Training and Work (NETWORK) program designed to help welfare families attain self-sufficiency. The report summarizes components of current law and the provisions of the bill. Dissenting views express the opinion that the program operates as a disincentive to work.

2565. U.S. Congress. House. Committee on Ways and Means. Subcommittee on Public Assistance and Unemployment Compensation. *Family Welfare Reform Act, Hearings on H.R. 1720.* 100th Cong., 1st sess., 30 Mar., 1 Apr. 1987. 435p. Y4.W36:100-38. Hearing explores a welfare reform plan to replace AFDC with a new program utilizing child support and education and training to end long-term dependency. Testimony reflects the needs of the existing welfare population's female-headed households and stresses actively seeking out non-supporting fathers. Work disincentives in the current system are examined. Reprints a report of the National League of Cities, *Poverty in America: New Data, New Perspectives*, which provides a concise overview of the welfare population and its distribution.

2566. U.S. Congress. House. Committee on Ways and Means. Subcommittee on Public Assistance and Unemployment Compensation. *Family Welfare Reform Act of 1987: H.R. 1720.* 100th Cong., 1st sess., 1987. Committee print. 26p. Y4.W36:WMCP100-8. Report describes the features of the subcommittee version of H.R. 1720, a plan to replace AFDC with the Family Support Program. Features of the plan include employment and training programs, child care reimbursement, revised state child support enforcement requirements, and unemployed parent benefits in certain two-parent families.

2567. U.S. Congress. House. Committee on Ways and Means. Subcommittee on Public Assistance and Unemployment Compensation. *Welfare Reform, Hearings.* 100th Cong., 1st sess., 28 Jan. - 13 Mar. 1987. 690p. Y4.W36:100-14. Hearings on welfare reform reflects theories on breaking the cycle of poverty and provides testimony describing state level education, training, and work programs for AFDC recipients. The form in which welfare payments should be made and the management of welfare systems are also considered. The situation of both two-parent families and female headed households living below the poverty line are discussed.

2568. U.S. Congress. Senate. Committee on Finance. *Data and Materials Related to Welfare Programs for Families with Children.* 100th Cong., 1st sess., 1987. 340p. Y4.F49:S.prt.100-20. Background information on the AFDC program reviews the regulation and operation of the program in the States. Data is provided by state on eligibility requirements, funding, recipient characteristics, work program participation, child support collections and establishment of paternity, and Medicaid coverage. Other data provided includes health insurance status of employed, unmarried women with children by wage rate and federal tax amounts by family size and poverty level. A comparison of the recommendations of public and private welfare reform study panels is also furnished.

2569. U.S. Congress. Senate. Committee on Finance. *Welfare Reform, Part 2, Hearings on S. 869, S. 1001, S. 1511.* 100th Cong., 1st sess., 14,28 Oct. 1987. 316p. Y4.F49:S.hrg.100-450/pt.2. Hearing on the Family Security Act of 1987 explores a proposal to replace AFDC with a Child Support Supplement Program. Witnesses discuss the merits of the proposal which emphasizes child support enforcement and education and training programs for welfare recipients. The issues of women with very young children and child care availability are repeatedly raised.

2570. U.S. Congress. Senate. Committee on Finance. Subcommittee on Social Security and Family Policy. *Welfare Reform Hearings in New York City, Hearings.* 100th Cong., 1st sess., 27 Apr., 15 June 1987. New York, N.Y. 441p. Y4.F49:S.hrg.100-299. General discussion of welfare reform and specific information on welfare programs and problems in New York City characterize this hearing. Day care cost and availability is discussed at length as is effective child support enforcement. A teen pregnancy prevention program is described. Also examined is the need to sanction enrollment in postsecondary degree programs under the WIN work requirements.

2571. U.S. Congress. Senate. Committee on Finance. Subcommittee on Social Security and Family Policy. *Welfare: Reform or Replacement? (Short-Term v. Long-Term Dependency), Hearing.* 100th Cong., 1st sess., 2 Mar. 1987. 164p. Y4.F49:S.hrg.100-484. The primary focus of this hearing is on the fundamental problems of the welfare system and current theory on how to eliminate long-term dependency. The *Up from Dependency* report is a basis for the Administration's program and the need to improve the system, not just programs, is stressed. The place of training, work programs, and child support in past and current welfare reform proposals are discussed. The issue of cash benefits is raised and the cost of working for single mothers is also highlighted.

2572. U.S. Executive Office of the President. Interagency Low Income Opportunity Advisory Board. *Up from Dependency: A New National Public Assistance Strategy. Supplement 1: The National Public Assistance System, Volume 2: A Compendium of Public Assistance Program, Major Federal Cash, Food and Housing Programs.* Washington, DC: GPO, 1987. 554p. PrEx15.2:D44/supp.1/v.2. Describes spending, persons served and administrative characteristics of federal and state assistance programs.

2573. U.S. Executive Office of the President. Interagency Low Income Opportunity Advisory Board. *Up from Dependency: A New National Public Assistance Strategy. Supplement 1: The National Public Assistance System, Volume 3: A Compendium of Public Assistance Programs, Major Federal Health, Service, Employment, and Education Programs, Other Federal and State Programs.* Washington, DC: GPO, 1987. 451p. PrEx15.2:D44/supp.1/v.3. Describes eligibility, participation and costs of non-cash or commodity assistance programs, mostly in health, employment and education. Program summary includes administrative structure of programs, objectives, and program spending by state.

2574. U.S. General Accounting Office. *Welfare: Issues to Consider in Assessing Proposals for Reform: Briefing Report to the Honorable William V. Roth, Jr., United States Senate.* Washington, DC: The Office, 1987. 43p. GA1.13:HRD-87-51-BR. Concise overview of AFDC and related welfare issues touches on topics of recipient populations, type of benefits, work disincentives, and the effect on family stability. Whether such programs are effective in reducing poverty and how benefits should be delivered are also reviewed noting conflicting research findings.

2575. U.S. National Center for Health Services Research and Health Care Technology Assessment. *The Feminization of Poverty and Older Women: An Update.* by Robyn Stone. Washington, DC: GPO, 1987. 26p. HE20.6514/2:P86. Review of the health and financial circumstances of elderly women highlights the financial gap between men and women over age 65 and particularly notes the percentage of unmarried elderly black or Hispanic women in poverty.

2576. U.S. White House Domestic Policy Council. Low Income Opportunity Working Group. *Up from Dependency: A New National Public Assistance Strategy.* Washington, DC: GPO, 1987. 70p. PrEx15.2:D44. Study report examines the problems of the current welfare system and explores ways to change the system to help those in poverty achieve self-sufficiency. Successful community and state programs are highlighted and statistics on federal and state spending for public assistance programs, number of families and persons in poverty, and length of time spent on welfare are provided.

2577. U.S. Congress. House. *Family Support Act of 1988, Conference Report to Accompany H.R. 1720.* H. Rept. 100-998, 100th Cong., 2d sess., 1988. 227p. Serial 13904. Reports the conference committee agreements on the differing versions of the proposed Family Support Act of 1988, a replacement for the AFDC program. Provisions of the bill address work and training incentives, child support, and technical requirements. Provisions of existing law, House and Senate versions of the bill, and the conference committee action are clearly set out.

2578. U.S. Congress. House. Committee on Ways and Means. Subcommittee on Public Assistance and Unemployment Compensation and U.S. Congress. Senate. Committee on Finance. Subcommittee on Social Security and Family Policy. *Using AFDC Funds for Homeless Families, Joint Hearing.* 100th Cong., 2d sess., 28 Mar. 1988. Brooklyn, NY. 250p. Y4.W36:100-65. Hearing on the problem of homelessness and families focuses on rules governing the use of AFDC Emergency Assistance funds. The cost of providing temporary housing for AFDC recipients in welfare hotels and the need for flexibility to support permanent housing options are stressed. The dramatic increase in female-headed families is noted by several witnesses. In addition to AFDC, the issue of federal funding for low income housing and its relation to family homelessness is debated.

2579. U.S. Congress. House. Select Committee on Children, Youth, and Families. *A Domestic Priority: Overcoming Family Poverty in America, Hearing.* 100th Cong., 2d sess., 22 Sept. 1988. 133p. Y4.C43/2:P86/3. Examination of family poverty in the U.S. examines the problems of welfare and the working poor with considerable discussion of the problems of single parents. Family instability and low wages are a common topic of testimony. Intervention possibilities are also explored, and the inter-relation between wages, work effort and employment opportunity is examined.

2580. U.S. Congress. Senate. Committee on Agriculture, Nutrition, and Forestry. *Hunger Prevention Act of 1988, Report Together with Additional Views.* S. Rept. 100-397, 100th Cong., 2d sess., 1988. 142p. Serial 13862. Changes in government food programs made by this bill include an increased reimbursement for child care under the Employment and Training Program in order to encourage employment among food stamp households. The bill also would prohibit denial of WIC benefits to women and children on the basis of homelessness.

2581. U.S. Congress. Senate. Committee on Finance. *Data and Materials Related to Welfare Programs for Families with Children.* 100th Cong., 2d sess., 1988. Committee print. 331p. Y4.F49:S.prt.100-101. Detailed information by state on AFDC provides statistics and summaries of benefit levels, number and characteristics of recipients, child support enforcement and paternity establishment, employment and training, and health programs. Tax treatment and social services for low-income families are also reviewed and welfare reform proposals are compared.

2582. U.S. Congress. Senate. Committee on Finance. *Family Security Act of 1988, Report on S. 1511 Together with Additional Views.* S. Rept. 100-377, 100th Cong., 2d sess., 1988. 190p. Serial 13861. Reports the Family Security Act of 1988, a proposed replacement for AFDC. The need for strengthening child support and work training program is presented along with arguments supporting extension of child care and medical benefits for a transitional period after employment is secured.

2583. U.S. Congress. Senate. Committee on Finance. *Welfare Reform, Hearing, Part 3.* 100th Cong., 2d sess., 4 Feb. 1988. 291p. Y4.F49:S.hrg.100-450/pt.3. Welfare reform hearing provides testimony focussing primarily on long term dependent AFDC recipients. Work programs and child care are two of the topics discussed in detail as approaches to moving single mothers off public assistance are examined. The value of the work done by homemakers is discussed in support of the argument that forcing AFDC mother to work in fact forces them to take a second job. Enforcement of child support orders is also viewed as vital to welfare reform.

2584. U.S. Congress. Senate. Committee on Labor and Human Resources. *Social Services for the Homeless Reauthorization Act of 1988, Report to Accompany S. 2742.* S. Rept. 100-482, 100th Cong., 2d sess., 1988. 72p. Serial 13865. Reports a social service bill which includes the "Job for Employable Dependent Individuals Act", a program to encourage states, through business incentives, to improve the inclusion of long-term AFDC beneficiaries in training and employment programs resulting in non-subsidized employment. The fact that most long-term AFDC beneficiaries are young single mothers is noted.

2585. U.S. Dept. of Housing and Urban Development. Office of Policy Development and Research. *Partners in Self-Sufficiency.* Washington, DC: The Department, 1988. [8]p. HH1.2:Se4/7. Glossy brochure highlights the accomplishments of Project Self-Sufficiency, a project linking housing and employment assistance for very low-income single parents.

2586. U.S. Dept. of Housing and Urban Development. Office of Policy Development and Research. *Partners in Self-Sufficiency Guidebook.* Washington, DC: GPO, 1988. 94p. HH1.6/3:P25. Guidebook describes successful community Partners in Self-Sufficiency programs. The programs, designed to help single parents on welfare achieve self-sufficiency, combines counseling, training, job development, child care, housing, and other support services. Strategies for involving the community, particularly local businesses, in the program are detailed.

2587. U.S. Executive Office of the President. Interagency Low Income Opportunity Advisory Board. *Up From Dependency: A New National Public Assistance Strategy. Supplement 4: Research Studies and Bibliography.* Washington, DC: GPO, 1988. 187p. PrEx15.2:D44/supp.4. Reviews the research literature on welfare and furnishes a 62 page bibliography of books, articles, and government publications on public assistance.

2588. U.S. General Accounting Office. *Welfare: Expert Panels' Insights on Major Reform Proposals.* Washington, DC: The Office, 1988. 70p. GA1.13:HRD-88-59. Report of two panel discussions on welfare reform proposals highlights issues of case management, "contracts" between agency and recipients and sanctions for failure to comply, coordination of services, and targeting services to specific populations. Panels looked at the issues from both a national and local perspective.

2589. U.S. Bureau of the Census. *Characteristics of Persons Receiving Benefits from Major Assistance Programs.* by John M. McNeil. Current Population Reports Series P-70, no. 14. Washington, DC: GPO, 1989. 27p. C3.186:P-70/2/no.14. Statistical profile of persons receiving public assistance reports recipient characteristics including sex, race, Hispanic origin, age, educational attainment, place of residence, household type, and work experience.

2590. U.S. Congress. House. Committee on Agriculture. Subcommittee on Domestic Marketing, Consumer Relations, and Nutrition. *Hunger in Rural America, Hearing.* 101st Cong., 1st sess., 17 May 1989. 223p. Y4.Ag8/1:101-15. Hearing on the Food Stamp Program and other federal nutrition programs focuses on hunger in rural America. The nutritional status of women and children is emphasized.

2591. U.S. Congress. House. Committee on Agriculture. Subcommittee on Domestic Marketing, Consumer Relations, and Nutrition. *Minnesota Family Investment Plan, Hearing.* 101st Cong., 1st sess., 11 July 1989. 88p. Y4.Ag8/1:101-25. Hearing examines the proposed Minnesota Family Investment Plan demonstration project, a cash benefit public assistance program combining Food Stamps, AFDC, and state-run assistance programs. The hearing provides discussion of the problem of long-term dependency and stresses the benefits of a coordinated programs combining cash assistance, job training, child support, and child care.

2592. U.S. Congress. House. Committee on Ways and Means. *General Explanation of the Family Support Act of 1988.* 101st Cong., 1st sess., 10 Feb. 1989. Committee print. 46p. Y4.W36:WMCP101-3. Concise explanation of the Family Support Act of 1988 provides an overview of the major provisions of the act including child support and paternity establishment, Job Opportunities and Basic Skills Training (JOBS), and transitional assistance for families leaving AFDC. Information on effective dates is provided in chart form by title and effective date. Cost estimates for the programs are furnished.

2593. U.S. Congress. Joint Economic Committee. *The Underclass, Hearing.* 101st Cong., 1st sess., 25 May 1989. 77p. Y4.Ec7:Un2/17. Expert witnesses discuss theories of long-term dependency and public policy options to address poverty. The place of female-headed households in the cycle of poverty and educational issues predominate as witnesses discuss work force conditions and work incentives among the poor.

2594. U.S. Congress. Senate. Committee on Finance. Subcommittee on Social Security and Family Policy. *Implementation of the Family Support Act of 1988, Hearing.* 101st Cong., 1st sess., 15 May 1989. 146p. Y4.F49:S.hrg.101-323. Witnesses discuss the provisions of the Family Support Act of 1988 and note actions taken to date to implement the act. Areas which should be stressed to make the law effective are outlined with emphasis on building state-federal partnerships and fostering innovation at the state level. The implementation of the JOBS component is the major focus as witnesses discuss how the program can work and how it can be abused.

2595. U.S. Congressional Budget Office. *Staff Working Papers: Work and Welfare, The Family Support Act of 1988.* Washington, DC: The Office, 1989. 73p. CIS89-J932-6. Examination of the employment and training aspects of the Family Support Act of 1988 primarily analyzes the cost of the program and its potential for reducing the number of welfare recipients. Although the focus is on cost, the report also provides insight into the expected experience of states with work programs and with transitional child care and Medicaid programs.

2596. U.S. Congress. House. Committee on Education and Labor. Subcommittee on Human Resources. *Hearing on the Reauthorization of the Community Services Block Grant Program.* 101st Cong., 2d sess., 1 Mar. 1990. 169p. Y4.Ed8/1:101-87. Witnesses describe the importance of the Community Services Block Grant Program to the ability of local service agencies to provide assistance to needy persons. Some of the programs highlighted include day care, teenage pregnancy programs, self-help for AFDC recipients, and food assistance.

2597. U.S. Congress. House. Committee on Ways and Means. Subcommittee on Human Resources. *Implementation of the Family Support Act of 1988, Hearings.* 101st Cong., 2d sess., 26 Mar., 30 Apr. 1990. San Diego, CA; Little Rock, AK. 179p. Y4.W36:101-

82. Field hearings on implementation of the Family Support Act of 1988 focus mainly on the JOBS program. The San Diego hearing explores the success of the GAIN (Greater Avenues for Independence) program in California, highlighting program components which contribute to its success. Child care and work expenses under the act are examined in both the California and Arkansas hearings. A lengthy review of the child support enforcement provisions of the act is also furnished, and support for basic education programs as a part of job readiness is stressed. Problems particular to Louisiana and other southern states in implementing the provisions of the act are highlighted in the Arkansas hearing.

2598. U.S. Congress. Senate. Committee on Finance. Subcommittee on Social Security and Family Policy. *Wisconsin Learnfare Program, Hearing.* 101st Cong., 2d sess., 18 June 1990. 97p. Y4.F49:S.hrg.101-1194. The Learnfare program in Wisconsin, an AFDC demonstration project which withholds AFDC payments for teenagers who do not attend school, is examined. Debate over Learnfare centers on concerns that the program places too much power in the hands of children and places unfair financial pressure on already dysfunctional families.

SERIALS

2599. U.S. Assistance Payments Administration. *Characteristics of State Public Assistance Plans: General Provisions, Eligibility, Assistance, Administration.* [title varies] Public Assistance Report no. 50. Washington, DC: GPO, 1964-1973. irreg. FS14.213:50, HE17.19:50/no. Charts for each state shows eligibility requirements and administrative characteristics of public assistance programs under the Social Security Act including old-age assistance and AFDC. Earlier see 2600.

2600. U.S. Bureau of Family Services. *Characteristics of State Public Assistance Plans under Social Security Act, Old-Age Assistance, Aid to the Blind, Aid to Dependent Children, Aid to the Permanently and Totally Blind: General Provisions, Eligibility, Assistance Administration.* Public Assistance Report no. 50. Washington, DC: GPO, 1962. 107p. FS3.13:50. See 2602 for earlier editions, and 2599 for later editions.

2601. U.S. Bureau of Public Assistance. *Characteristics of State Plans for Aid to Dependent Children.* Information Service Circular no. 18. Washington, DC: GPO, 1937-1940. irreg. FS3.4:18/no. Occasionally revised chart provides information on eligibility requirements, administration and procedures for state ADC plans.

2602. U.S. Bureau of Public Assistance. *Characteristics of State Public Assistance Plans.* Public Assistance Report nos. 18, 21, 27, 33. Washington, DC: GPO, 1950-1957. irregular. FS3.13:nos. See 2599 for abstract.

2603. U.S. Bureau of Public Assistance. *Public Assistance [Year].* Public Assistance Reports nos. 1 and 4. Washington, DC: GPO, 1940-1941. annual. FS3.13:nos. Describes changes in public assistance programs and eligibility requirements and provides monthly statistics by state on number of recipients and expenditures by program.

2604. U.S. Bureau of Public Assistance. *Social Data on Recipients of Public Assistance Accepted in [year], Part 2: Aid to Dependent Children, Tables.* Research Memorandum Nos.1 and 39. Washington, DC: The Bureau, 1937/38-. annual. FS3.11:42/pt.2, FS3.12:1/pt.2, SS1.27:39/pt.2. Provides data on amount of grant, previous assistance, reasons for dependency, composition of families, age, race, sex, nativity and residence of children, and cases closed by reason. Most data is given by state or region.

2605. U.S. Children's Bureau. *Tabular Summary of State Laws Relating to Public Aid to Children in Their Own Homes, in Effect [date], and Text of Laws of Certain States.* [title varies]. Chart no. 3. Washington, DC: GPO, 1922-1934. irreg. L5.21:3/year.

2606. U.S. Community Services Administration. *Services to AFDC Families.* Washington, DC: The Administration, 1970-1972. annual. HE17.709:year. Annual report to the Congress on programs administered under AFDC describes activities, accomplishments, and problems. Provides some basic statistics on characteristics of recipients and programs by state.

2607. U.S. Congress. House. Committee on Ways and Means. *Background Material and Data on Programs Within the Jurisdiction of the Committee on Ways and Means.* Washington, DC: GPO, 1981-. annual. Y4.W36:10-4/year (1987-); SuDoc number varies prior to 1987. Compilation of information on social service programs reviews legislation and provides background statistics on OASI, Disability, Medicare, Unemployment Compensation, AFDC, child support enforcement, SSI, and Title XX programs. Eligibility requirements, recipient data, and federal/state outlays are reviewed. Detailed information on AFDC work programs, child support collections, and trends in illegitimacy are provided. Some brief analysis of the effect of government programs on the "poverty gap" is furnished.

2608. U.S. Dept. of Health and Human Services. Office of Human Development Services. *Annual Report to the Congress on Title XX of the Social Security Act.* Washington, DC: GPO, 1977-1980. annual. HE23.2009:year. Annual report details programs, expenditures, and number of recipients of Title XX services. Major programs relating to women are AFDC, Child Day Care Services, and family planning services.

2609. U.S. Dept. of Health, Education and Welfare. Office of the Assistant Secretary for Planning and Evaluation. *Summaries and Characteristics of States' Title XX Social Services Plans for Fiscal Year.* Washington, DC: The Office, 1977-1980. annual. HE1.2:So1/3/year. Detailed report describes state social service programs and expenditures under Title XX of the Social Security Act including day care services and family planning. Tables provide data on services and expenditures by state.

2610. U.S. National Center for Social Statistics. *Aid to Families with Dependent Children: Standards for Basic Needs.* [title varies] Washington, DC: The Center, 1969-1977. annual. HE17.625:year. Summary outlines basic need standards, payment standards, and largest amount paid under AFDC by state and family size. Later see *AFDC Standards for Basic Needs* (2613).

2611. U.S. Social and Rehabilitation Service. *Welfare in Review.* Washington, DC: GPO, July 1963-May/June 1972. vol. 1 - vol. 10. bimonthly. FS14.10:vol/no.; HE17.9:vol/no. Journal includes articles, research notes and book reviews on public assistance programs and service delivery methods.

2612. U.S. Social Security Administration. Office of Policy. Office of Research and Statistics. *Aid to Families with Dependent Children, Recipient Characteristics Study.* Washington, DC: GPO, 1975-1979. biennial. HE3.65:year/part. Part 1 presents statistics on AFDC households by state and number of children, relationship of persons in household, occupation and money status of AFDC mothers, and residence and employment status of father. Data on sources of income of AFDC families, including child support payments, nonassistance income, and food stamps, is furnished in part two. The 1975 edition was issued in four parts: Part 1, Demographic and Program Statistics; part 2, Child Support Enforcement; part 3, Financial Circumstances, and part 4, Social services. Continues *Findings of the AFDC Study*, (2464, 2471, 2482, 2492)

2613. U.S. Social Security Administration. Office of Research and Statistics. *AFDC Standards for Basic Needs*. Washington, DC: The Office, 1979-1980. annual. HE3.64:year. Earlier see *Aid to Families with Dependent Children: Standards for Basic Needs* (2610).

17
Retirement and Survivor Benefits

Documents on women's retirement income published prior to 1963 are mostly House and Senate reports on survivor benefits to various groups of government workers. A few reports detail the status of women's coverage under Social Security (2649, 2651, 2667), and reports in 1962 and 1966 describe how widowed mothers get by on their Social Security benefits (2659, 2672).

The first major report on women under Social Security was the 1963 report of the Committee on Social Insurance and Taxes of the President's Commission on the Status of Women (2662). A more detailed examination of the topic was issued in 1968 by the Task Force on Social Insurance and Taxes of the Citizen's Advisory Council on the Status of Women (2678). The retirement income problems of women received significant congressional scrutiny in 1975 when eight hearings and reports focusing on women under pension plans and Social Security were published. Since that time women's retirement income has been a recurring theme of congressional hearings. Between 1979 and 1981 the House Select Committee on Aging held extensive hearings on the *Treatment of Women under Social Security* (2712-2713, 2731-2732), and HEW issued its report, *Social Security and the Changing Roles of Men and Women* (2715), which analyzed the past assumptions and current conditions affecting Social Security and women. An excellent review of the gender-based distinctions in Social Security at that time is found in the report of HEW's Advisory Council on Social Security (2722).

Although the initial focus was on Social Security, by 1979 the private pension system was also receiving scrutiny in the Justice Department report, *The Pension Game: The American Pension System from the Viewpoint of the Average Woman* (2716). The move to reform the Employee Retirement Income Security Act of 1974 (ERISA) to remove the inequities against women as survivors, former spouses, and working women began in earnest at 1982 hearings (2735), and peaked in 1983 and 1984 with hearings and reports on the Retirement Equity Act (2740-2741, 2744, 2748-2750, 2754). The effect of the Retirement Equity Act of 1984 is outlined in a 1986 publication of the Women's Bureau (2770).

While reform of ERISA was taking place, Congress and the Social Security Administration continued to examine the problem of old age and survivor benefits under Social Security. Most of the documents since 1980 focus on earnings-sharing proposals, such as those outlined in the 1986 Congressional Budget Office report, *Earnings Sharing Options for the Social Security System* (2769). The failure to resolve the issues of women's retirement income is evident from the testimony presented at a 1990 House Select Committee on Aging hearing, *Women in Retirement: Are They Losing Out?* (2784). The evolution of survivor benefit rules in the Civil Service Retirement System, particularly in the areas of divorce and waiver of benefits, are also detailed in the documents in this chapter. The treatment of women as survivors of military personnel is covered in Chapter 18.

2614. U.S. Congress. House. *Eight Memorials from Mrs. Chief Justice Waite, and the Officers of the Women's National Relief Association and Citizens of the United States, Praying for a Pension to Those Who Became Disabled or Who Die while in the Life-Saving Service.* H. Misc. Doc. 166, 50th Cong., 1st sess., 1888. 7p. Serial 2565.

2615. U.S. Congress. House. Committee on the District of Columbia. *The Edes Home, Report to Accompany S. 4046.* H. Rept. 2475, 59th Cong., 1st sess., 1906. 4p. Serial 4906. See 2615 for abstract.

2616. U.S. Congress. Senate. Committee on the District of Columbia. *The Edes Home, Report to Accompany S. 4046.* S. Rept. 998, 59th Cong., 1st sess., 1906. 2p. Serial 4904. Committee reports favorably on a bill to aid in establishing a home for aged and indigent widows in the District's Georgetown area using funds bequeathed for that purpose by Margaret Edes.

2617. U.S. Congress. House. Committee on Accounts. *To Pay One Year's Salary and Funeral Expenses to Widows of Deceased Employees of the House of Representative, Report to Accompany H. Res. 293.* H. Rept. 866, 68th Cong., 1st sess., 1924. 1p. Serial 8232.

2618. U.S. Congress. House. Committee on Foreign Affairs. *For the Relief of the Widows and Wife of Certain Foreign Service Officers, Report to Accompany H.R. 1113.* H. Rept. 1008, 71st Cong., 2d sess., 1930. 3p. Serial 9195. Report on survivor benefits for wives of foreign service officers summarizes the careers of the deceased husbands but does not describe the situation of the widows or the amounts granted.

2619. U.S. Congress. House. Committee on the District of Columbia. *Relief of Certain Widows of Members of Police and Fire Departments of District of Columbia Who Were Killed or Died from Injuries Received in the Line of Duty, Report to Accompany H.R. 9792.* H. Rept. 1635, 71st Cong., 2d sess., 1930. 3p. Serial 9196. Private bill authorizes a payment of $5,000 to certain widows of members of the D.C. police and fire departments.

2620. U.S. Congress. House. Committee on Claims. *Relief of Widows of an Inspector and Certain Special Agents of the Division of Investigation, Department of Justice, and Operative in Secret Service Division, Department of the Treasury, Killed in Line of Duty, Report to Accompany S. 2488.* H. Rept. 1427, 74th Cong., 1st sess., 1935. 7p. Serial 9893. See 2621 for abstract.

2621. U.S. Congress. Senate. Committee on Claims. *Relief of Widows of an Inspector General and Certain Special Agents of the Division of Investigation, Department of Justice, Killed in the Line of Duty, Report to Accompany S. 2488.* S. Rept. 884, 74th Cong., 1st sess., 1935. 5p. Serial 9884. Provides for the payment of $5,000 to the widows named as special recognition of the hazardous nature of their deceased husband's work.

2622. U.S. Congress. House. Committee on Merchant Marine and Fisheries. *Amending the Act of May 29, 1944, so as to Provide Annuities for Certain Remarried Widows, Report to Accompany H.R. 1896.* H. Rept. 1810, 80th Cong., 2d sess., 1948. 4p. Serial 11211. Reports a bill amending the act granting lifetime annuities to widows of Panama Canal construction workers who lived with their husbands in the Canal Zone to include remarried widows.

2623. U.S. Congress. House. Committee on the District of Columbia. *Providing Increased Pensions for Widows and Children of Deceased Members and Retired Members of the Police Department and of the Fire Department of the District of Columbia, Report to Accompany H.R. 6295.* H. Rept. 2217, 80th Cong., 2d sess., 1948. 7p. Serial 11212.

2624. U.S. Congress. Senate. Committee on the District of Columbia. *Providing Increased Pensions for Widows and Children of Deceased Members and Retired Members of the Police Department and the Fire Department of the District of Columbia, Report to Accompany H.R. 6295.* S. Rept. 1672, 80th Cong., 2d sess., 1948. 7p. Serial 11208.

2625. U.S. Congress. House. *Increased Pensions for Widows and Children of Deceased Members of the Police Department and Fire Department of the District of Columbia, Conference Report to Accompany H.R. 2021.* H. Rept. 1107, 81st Cong., 1st sess., 1949. 2p. Serial 11300.

2626. U.S. Congress. House. Committee on the District of Columbia. *Increased Pensions for Widows and Children of Deceased and Retired Police and Fireman of the District of Columbia, Report to Accompany H.R. 2021.* H. Rept. 753, 81st Cong., 1st sess., 1949. 3p. Serial 11299.

2627. U.S. Congress. Senate. Committee on Post Office and Civil Service. *Providing Survivorship Annuities to Widows of Retiring Employees at a Reduced Cost to Such Employees, Report to Accompany S. 1440.* S. Rept. 506, 81st Cong., 1st sess., 1949. 2p. Serial 11292. The bill reported changed the formula used to pay retirement annuities when the Civil Service employee elected to provide a survivor benefit.

2628. U.S. Congress. Senate. Committee on the District of Columbia. *Providing Increased Pensions for Widows and Children of Deceased Members and Retired Members of the Police Department and the Fire Department of the District of Columbia, Report to Accompany H.R. 2021.* S. Rept. 558, 81st Cong., 1st sess., 1949. 2p. Serial 11293.

2629. U.S. Congress. House. Committee on Merchant Marine and Fisheries. *Providing Benefits for the Widows of Certain Persons Who Were Retired or Are Eligible for Retirement under Section 6 of the Act Entitled "An Act to authorize aids to navigation and for other workers in the lighthouse service and other Purposes," Approved June 20, 1918, as Amended, Report to Accompany H.R. 7192.* H. Rept. 2328, 81st Cong., 2d sess., 1950. 2p. Serial 11381. Reports a bill setting the provisions for pensions to widows of Lighthouse Service employees.

2630. U.S. Congress. Senate. Committee on Interstate and Foreign Commerce. *Providing Benefits for the Widows of Lighthouse Service Personnel, Report to Accompany H.R. 7192.* S. Rept. 2218, 81st Cong., 2d sess., 1950. 2p. Serial 11371. See 2629 for abstract.

2631. U.S. Congress. Senate. Committee on the Judiciary. *Provision for Annuity for Widows and Children of Federal Judges, Report to Accompany S. 3108.* S. Rept. 2216, 81st Cong., 2d sess., 1950. 7p. Serial 11371.

2632. U.S. Congress. Senate. Committee of the Judiciary. *Provision for Annuity for Widows of Federal Judges, Report to Accompany S. 16.* S. Rept. 716, 82d Cong., 1st sess., 1951. 6p. Serial 11489. Favorable report on a bill to provide survivor pensions to widows of federal judges explains the need for the pensions to ensure that judges do not have to worry about earning money while serving on the bench.

2633. U.S. Congress. Senate. Committee on Foreign Relations. *Grants of Loans to Needy Widows of Foreign Service Officers, Report to Accompany S. 3413.* S. Rept. 1986, 82d Cong., 2d sess., 1952. 2p. Serial 11569. Reports a bill that basically grants pensions of up to $100 a month to needy widows of foreign service officers who died prior to the effective date of the Foreign Service Act of 1946.

2634. U.S. Bureau of Old-Age and Survivors Insurance. *Benefits for Women under 1956 Amendments to Social Security Law.* Washington, DC: GPO, 1956. [8]p. leaflet. FS3.25/2:956/2.

2635. U.S. Congress. House. *Annuities for Widows of Judges, Conference Report to Accompany H.R. 11124.* H. Rept. 2934, 84th Cong., 2d sess., 1956. 10p. Serial 11901.

2636. U.S. Congress. House. Committee on Merchant Marine and Fisheries. *Increasing from $50 to $75 per Month the Amount of Benefits Payable to Widows of Certain Former Employers of the Lighthouse Service, Report to Accompany S. 2937.* H. Rept. 2300, 84th Cong., 2d sess., 1956. 4p. Serial 11899. Report recommends raising survivor pensions to widows of former Lighthouse Service employees citing the rising cost of living and increases in widows benefits under other retirement laws.

2637. U.S. Congress. House. Committee of the Judiciary. *Annuities for Widows and Dependent Children of Federal Judges, Report to Accompany H.R. 11124.* H. Rept. 2170, 84th Cong., 2d sess., 1956. 15p. Serial 11898. Report on a bill providing survivor benefits to widows of federal judges reviews the arguments for a program of financial security for judges' widows stressing the desire to relieve judges of the pressure to provide such financial security by supplementing their salary. Also reviews the status of survivor benefits for other federal employees.

2638. U.S. Congress. House. Committee on the Judiciary. Subcommittee No. 5. *Annuities for Widows and Dependent Children of Federal Judges, Hearings on H.R. 75, H.R. 678, H.R. 3764, and H.R. 6974.* 84th Cong., 2d sess., 6 Feb. 1956. 49p. Y4.J89/1:84/17. Hearing discusses a proposed voluntary survivor benefit program for federal judges.

2639. U.S. Congress. Senate. Committee on Interstate and Foreign Commerce. *Increasing Benefits to Widows of Former Lighthouse Service Employees, Report to Accompany S. 2937.* S. Rept. 1968, 84th Cong., 2d sess., 1956. 6p. Serial 11888. Justification for the increased pensions to widows of Lighthouse Service employees cites the rising cost of living and the fact that the wife of the employee was required to take over her husband's duties in his absences or illness.

2640. U.S. Congress. Senate. Committee of the Judiciary. *Annuities to Widows and Dependent Children of Judges, Report to Accompany S. 3410.* S. Rept. 1983, 84th Cong., 2d sess., 1956. 24p. Serial 11888. Favorable report on a bill to provide survivor benefits to widows and dependent children of federal judges provides a good overview of survivorship provisions of other civil service retirement programs.

2641. U.S. Congress. House. Committee on Merchant Marine and Fisheries. *Increasing from $50 to $75 per Month the Amount of Benefits Payable to Widows of Certain Former Employers of the Lighthouse Service, Report to Accompany S. 235.* H. Rept. 787, 85th Cong., 1st sess., 1957. 5p. Serial 11986. Reports a bill increasing pensions to widows of former Lighthouse Service employees. The rising cost of living and increases in annuities to other civil service employees are cited as justification for the measure.

2642. U.S. Congress. Senate. Committee on Interstate and Foreign Commerce. *Increasing Benefits to Widows of Former Lighthouse Service Employees, Report to Accompany S. 235.* S. Rept. 133, 85th Cong., 1st sess., 1957. 4p. Serial 11976. Favorable report discusses the proposed pension increase for Lighthouse Service employees' widows in relation to other civil service retirement rates.

2643. U.S. Women's Bureau. *What Social Security Means to Women.* Washington, DC: GPO, 1957. 26p. L13.19:3. Reviews the benefits of OASI for working women and for women as spouses of insured workers.

2644. U.S. Congress. House. Committee on Ways and Means. *Mother's Insurance Benefits, Report to Accompany H.R. 5411.* H. Rept. 1344, 85th Cong., 2d sess., 1958. 3p. Serial 12072. Reports a bill amending Title II of the Social Security Act so as to allow a woman who loses mothers' insurance benefits through remarriage to regain her entitlement based on her former husbands earning record should her second husband die within one year of marriage. The existing law created a one year gap in protection since the right to the benefit terminated upon remarriage but the woman did not become entitled to benefits under the second marriage unless she stayed married more than one year.

2645. U.S. Congress. Senate. Committee on Finance. *Mother's Insurance Benefits, Report to Accompany H.R. 5411.* S. Rept. 2167, 85th Cong., 2d sess., 1958. 6p. Serial 12064. See 2644 for abstract.

2646. U.S. Congress. Senate. Committee on the District of Columbia. *Making the Policemen and Firemen's Retirement and Disability Act Amendments of 1957 Applicable to Widows, and Children of Former Members of the Metropolitan Police Force, the Fire Department of the District of Columbia, the United States Park Police Force, and the United States Secret Service Division, Who Were Retired or Whose Death Occurred Prior to the Effective Date of Such Amendments of 1957, Report to Accompany H.R. 740.* S. Rept. 2332, 85th Cong., 2d sess., 1958. 5p. Serial 12065.

2647. U.S. Congress. House. Committee on Government Operations. *Annuities for Widows and Dependent Children of Comptroller General and Retired Comptroller General, Report to Accompany H.R. 7062.* H. Rept. 540, 86th Cong., 1st sess., 1959. 22p. Serial 12160.

2648. U.S. Congress. Senate. Committee on Government Operations. *Annuities for Widows and Dependent Children of Comptroller General and Retired Comptroller General, Report to Accompany H.R. 7062.* S. Rept. 403, 86th Cong., 1st sess., 1959. 22p. Serial 12150.

2649. U.S. Bureau of Old Age and Survivors Insurance. *Employment of Women under Old-Age, Survivors, and Disability Insurance Program.* by Ella J. Polinksy. Washington, D.C: The Bureau, 1960. 19p. FS3.47:114. Review of the status of women covered by Social Security from 1949 to 1959 presents statistics and brief analysis of men and women covered, and of employment by industry, division and age.

2650. U.S. Congress. House. Committee on Ways and Means. *Annuities to Widows and Dependent Children of Tax Court Judges, Report to Accompany H.R. 8732.* H. Rept. 1958, 86th Cong., 2d sess., 1960. 18p. Serial 12247. The problems inherent in providing survivor benefits for tax court judges through the Civil Service Retirement system are outlined in this favorable report on creating a survivor benefit plan within the retirement system for tax court judges.

2651. U.S. Bureau of Old-Age Survivors Insurance. *Earnings of Retired-Worker, Aged-Widow, and Widowed-Mother Beneficiaries during Survey Year.* Beneficiary Studies Note E-5. Washington, D.C: GPO, 1961. 5p. FS3.46:E5. Reports data on beneficiary earnings of retired male workers by marital status, of retired female workers by marital status, of aged widows, and of widowed-mothers for employed beneficiaries and all beneficiaries.

2652. U.S. Congress. House. *Annuities to Widows and Dependent Children of Tax Court Judges, Conference Report to Accompany H.R. 4317.* H. Rept. 1199, 87th Cong., 1st sess., 1961. 4p. Serial 12343. See 2653 for abstract.

2653. U.S. Congress. House. Committee on Ways and Means. *Annuities to Widows and Dependent Children of Tax Court Judges, Report to Accompany H.R. 4317.* H. Rept. 361, 87th Cong., 1st sess., 1961. 18p. Serial 12339. The bill reported establishes survivor annuities for widows and dependent children of Tax Court judges similar to the provisions for other judges in the federal courts. The need for the bill and the provisions for calculating annuity rates are described.

2654. U.S. Congress. Senate. Committee on Finance. *Annuities to Widows and Dependent Children of Tax Court Judges, Report Together with Minority Views, to Accompany H.R. 4317.* S. Rept. 730, 87th Cong., 1st sess., 1961. 27p. Serial 12325. Favorable report on legislation to provide a survivor benefit plan for tax court judges describes the inadequacy of the Civil Service Retirement System for survivor benefits in this case.

2655. U.S. Congress. Senate. Committee on Foreign Relations. *Providing Annuities for the Widows of Certain Foreign Service Officers, Report to Accompany S. 1067.* S. Rept. 129, 87th Cong., 1st sess., 1961. 3p. Serial 12322. Report recommends providing annuities to widows of Foreign Service officers who retired prior to the effective date of the Federal Employees Group Life Insurance Act of 1954.

2656. U.S. Congress. Senate. Committee on the District of Columbia. *Extending Benefits of the Policemen and Firemen's Retirement and Disability Act Amendments of 1957 to Widows and Surviving Children of Former Members of the Metropolitan Police Force, the Fire Department of the District of Columbia, the U.S. Park Police Force, the White House Police Force, and the U.S. Secret Service Division, Who Were Retired or Who Died in the Service of Any Such Organization Prior to the Effective Date of Such Amendments, Report to Accompany S. 1918.* S. Rept. 859, 87th Cong., 1st sess., 1961. 2p. Serial 12326.

2657. U.S. Congress. Senate. Committee on the District of Columbia. *Relating to Retirement Compensation Payable to Each Officer or Member of the Metropolitan Police Force, the Fire Department of the District of Columbia, the U.S. Park Police Force, the White House Police Force, and the U.S. Secret Service, and to Their Widows, Widowers, and Children, Report to Accompany S. 1528.* S. Rept. 858, 87th Cong., 1st sess., 1961. 5p. Serial 12325. Among other things, the bill reported raises pension rates for widows and dependent children of deceased member of the various District of Columbia services.

2658. U.S. Bureau of Labor Statistics. *Pension Plans under Collective Bargaining: Benefits for Survivors, Winter 1960-61.* Bulletin no. 1334. Washington, DC: GPO, 1962. 26p. L2.3:1334. Provides information on characteristics of survivor benefit plans and distribution of plans by selected characteristics.

2659. U.S. Bureau of Old-Age and Survivors Insurance. Division of Program Analysis. *Relatives in Household of Mother-Child Beneficiary Groups under Old-Age and Survivors Insurance.* National Survey of Old-Age and Survivors Insurance Beneficiaries, 1957, Highlights Report no. 7. Washington, D.C: The Bureau, 1962. 19p. FS3.48:7. Report on living arrangements of mother-child beneficiary groups receiving Social Security summarizes living arrangements. Brief case histories of families headed by widows and details of how they get by on OASI benefits are provided. Includes data on age of mother, age of children, and household composition.

2660. U.S. Social Security Administration. Division of the Actuary. *Remarriage Tables Based on Experience under OASDI and US Employee Compensation Systems.* Actuarial Study no. 55. Washington, DC: The Division, 1962. 38p. FS3.19:55.

2661. U.S. Congress. Senate. Committee on the Judiciary. *Annuities of Widows of Supreme Court Justices, Report to Accompany S. 1686.* S. Rept. 623, 88th Cong., 1st sess., 1963.

4p. Serial 12535. Recommends increasing annuities to widows of Supreme Court Justices to $10,000 per annum, the amount paid to the widow of a President.

2662.   U.S. President's Commission on the Status of Women. *Report of the Committee on Social Insurance and Taxes to President's Commission on Status of Women.* Washington, DC: GPO, 1963. 81p. Pr35.8:W84/So1. Detailed report examines women's sources of income and eligibility for benefits under Social Security. Maternity benefits and the effect of federal tax laws on working women are also discussed, and the recommendations of the committee regarding unemployment benefits, retirement programs, benefits to divorced women, maternal benefits, and child care deductions for federal taxes are presented. Provides statistics on women 65 and over with income from employment or public programs; social security benefits payable by class of beneficiary; number and average monthly social security benefit by type of claim and sex of beneficiary; and average monthly payment by type of benefit.

2663.   U.S. Congress. House. Committee on Foreign Affairs. Subcommittee on State Department Organization and Foreign Operations. *Foreign Services Annuity Adjustment Act of 1964, Hearings on S. 745 and H.R. 10485.* 88th Cong., 2d sess., 9 - 18 Mar. 1964. 45p. Y4.F76/1:F76/23/964. Hearing on expanding benefits for certain windows of Foreign Service officers who retired prior to 1960 and on providing cost-of-living adjustments discusses the cost of contributions to survivor annuities.

2664.   U.S. Congress. House. Committee on the Judiciary. *Annuities of Widows of Supreme Court Justices, Report to Accompany S. 1686.* H. Rept. 1615, 88th Cong., 2d sess., 1964. 13p. Serial 12619-3. Reports with amendments a bill increasing the pension rate for widows of Supreme Court Justice to $10,000 per annum, the same rate granted to widows of Presidents.

2665.   U.S. Congress. Senate. Committees on Labor and Public Welfare. Subcommittee on Railroad Retirement. *To Eliminate Restrictions on Spouse's Benefits under the Railroad Retirement Act of 1937, Hearing on H.R 12362.* 88th Cong., 2d sess., 25 Sept. 1964. 22p. Y4.L11/2:R13/10. Hearing discusses a bill which would eliminate the required reduction in a souses's benefit under Railroad Retirement when the spouse is also receiving Social Security benefits based on her earnings.

2666.   U.S. Social Security Administration. *Answer to Women's Questions about Social Security.* Washington, DC: GPO, 1964. 32p. FS3.35:27/2.

2667.   U.S. Social Security Administration. *Old Age, Survivors, and Disability Insurance, Number and Average Monthly Amount of Widow's or Widower's Benefits in Current-Payment Status and Distribution by Amount of Benefit, by State, at End of Dec. 1963.* Washington, DC: The Administration, 1964. 1p. FS3.2:Ol1/19/963.

2668.   U.S. Social Security Administration. *Answer to Women's Questions about Social Security.* Washington, DC: GPO, 1965. 32p. FS3.35:27/3.

2669.   U.S. Social Security Administration. *A Brief Explanation, Benefits for Widows at Age 60 under Social Security.* Washington, DC: GPO, 1965. leaflet. FS3.25/2:965/5/rev.

2670.   U.S. Congress. House. Committee on Ways and Means. *Qualification for Social Security Benefits as Widow, Widower, or Stepchild, Report to Accompany H.R. 18085.* H. Rept. 2296, 89th Cong., 2d sess., 1966. 4p. Serial 12713-7. Reports an amended version of a bill changing the Social Security eligibility requirement for benefits as a widow or stepchild by requiring that the wife or stepchild shall have occupied that status for a 6 month period rather than the one year previously stipulated.

2671. U.S. Congress. Senate. Committee on Commerce. *Increased Annuities for Widows of Former Lighthouse Service Employees, Report to Accompany S. 2980.* S. Rept. 1742. 89th Cong., 2d sess., 1966. 7p. Serial 12710-6.

2672. U.S. Social Security Administration. Office of Research and Statistics. *Widows with Children under Social Security.* by Gertrude L. Stanley and Robert H. Cormier. Research Report no. 16. Washington, DC: GPO, 1966. 96p. FS3.49:16. A 1963 national survey of the socioeconomic status of women with children receiving survivor benefits under OASDHI found that the larger, usually younger, families were more likely to be below poverty level then smaller families headed by widows. Widow-headed families are compared with fatherless families and with families where the father is present. Data on age of mother and children, by race and educational attainment of mother, and income, assets and expenditure, by race and age of children, is furnished.

2673. U.S. Congress. House. Committee on Merchant Marine and Fisheries. *Increasing Amount of Benefits Payable to Widows of Certain Former Employees of the Lighthouse Service, Report to Accompany H.R. 169.* H. Rept. 344, 90th Cong., 1st sess., 1967. 6p. Serial 12753-3. The bill reported increases pensions for Lighthouse Service widows to the same level as civil service survivor benefits and ties future increases to cost-of-living increases in civil service pensions.

2674. U.S. Congress. House. Committee on Merchant Marine and Fisheries. *Providing Annuity Benefits to Widows of Employees of the Lighthouse Service, Report to Accompany H.R. 3351.* H. Rept. 345, 90th Cong., 1st sess., 1967. 4p. Serial 12753-3. The bill reported extends survivor benefits to widows of ex-professional employees of the Lighthouse Service who were originally excluded from claiming pensions on the basis that they did not render any service or face any hardship in connection with the service of their husband.

2675. U.S. Congress. House. Committee on the District of Columbia. *Pensions for Widows of Retired D.C. Policemen and Firemen, Report to Accompany H.R. 2824.* H. Rept. 200, 90th Cong., 1st sess., 1967. 4p. Serial 12753-2. Reports a bill qualifying widows of retired D.C. policemen and firemen, who married the officer or member after his retirement, for survivor benefits. The bill requires that the widow be married to the officer for at least 2 years immediately preceding his death.

2676. U.S. Congress. Senate. Committee on Commerce. *Increasing Amount of Benefits Payable to Widows of Certain Former Employees of the Lighthouse Service, Report to Accompany H.R. 169.* S. Rept. 791, 90th Cong., 1st sess., 1967. 6p. Serial 1270-5. See 2673 for abstract.

2677. U.S. Congress. Senate. Committee on Commerce. *Providing Annuity Benefits to Widows of Employees of the Lighthouse Service, Report to Accompany H.R. 3351.* S. Rept. 789, 90th Cong., 1st sess., 1967. 6p. Serial 12750-5. See 2674 for abstract.

2678. U.S. Citizens' Advisory Council on the Status of Women. *Report of the Task Force on Social Insurance and Taxes.* Washington, DC: GPO, 1968. 139p. Y3.In8/21:2So1. Study of three aspects of working women under social insurance and taxes analyzes problems and makes recommendations regarding unemployment, temporary disability, social security, workmen's compensation, medical insurance, and federal income tax. Provides data on working mothers and child care arrangements.

2679. U.S. Congress. Senate. Committee on Labor and Public Welfare. Subcommittee on Railroad Retirement. *Widow's Pensions under Railroad Retirement, Hearing on S. 2838.* 90th Cong., 2d sess., 1 May 1968. 42p. Y4.L11/2:W63. Hearing examines a bill increasing the amount paid to widows and widowers under Railroad Retirement. Debate focuses more on the extent and cost of the increase than on the need which is generally recognized.

2680. U.S. General Accounting Office. *Report to Congress: Need to Strengthen Procedures for Determining Continued Eligibility of Widows for Federal Benefits, Department of Health, Education, and Welfare, Veterans' Administration, Civil Service Commission, Railroad Retirement Board, Department of Labor.* Washington, D.C: The Office, 1968. 44p. GA1.13:W63. Report of an investigation into the extent of unreported remarriages of widows receiving survivor benefits recommends a study of the feasibility of using state marriage records to identify ineligible widows.

2681. U.S. Congress. House. Committee on the District of Columbia. *Pensions for Widows of Retired D.C. Policemen and Firemen, Report to Accompany H.R. 4183.* H. Rept. 91-363, 91st Cong., 1st sess., 1969. 4p. Serial 12837-2. The bill reported grants survivor benefits to the widow of a former D.C. policemen and firemen who married after the officer or member's retirement, provided that she was married to the officer at least two years prior to his death or is the mother of his children.

2682. U.S. Congress. Senate. Committee on the District of Columbia. *Pensions for Widows of Retired District of Columbia Policemen and Firemen, Report to Accompany H.R. 4183.* S. Rept. 91-1299, 91st Cong., 2d sess., 1970. 2p. Serial 12881-6. Reports a bill changing existing laws governing D.C. policemen and firemen survivor benefits to allow a widow to collect a pension although she married the officer or member after his retirement. The history of the legislation discusses the comparability of the years of marriage requirement with similar provisions in veterans' survivor pensions laws.

2683. U.S. Congress. House. Committee on the Judiciary. *Annuities of Widows of Supreme Court Justices, Report to Accompany H.R. 12101.* H. Rept. 92-1148, 92d Cong., 2d sess., 1972. 14p. Serial 12974-3. Legislation favorably reported would raise current pensions to widows of Supreme Court justices and give presiding Supreme Court justices the option of participating in the existing annuity system for federal judges.

2684. U.S. Congress. Senate. Committee on the Judiciary. Subcommittee on Improvement in Judicial Machinery. *Annuities of Widows of Justices of the Supreme Court, Hearing on S. 2854 and S. 1480.* 92d Cong., 2d sess., 2 Feb. 1972. 26p. Y4.J89/2:W63. Hearing examines bills extending the Judicial Survivors Annuity System to the Supreme Court and phasing out the flat rate annuity of $5,000 for widows of Supreme Court justices. Statements include a concise history of annuities for widows of justices and judges. Charts show retirement and pension provisions of state appellate court and trial court judges.

2685. U.S. Congress. House. *Texts of International Labor Organization Convention No. 128 and ILO Recommendation No. 131 Concerning Invalidity, Old-Age, and Survivors' Benefits; Communication from Acting Assistant Secretary of State for Congressional Relations.* H. Doc. 93-107, 93rd Cong., 1st sess., 1973. 52p. Serial 13020-2. Transmits texts of ILO Convention no. 128 and Recommendation no. 131 concerning minimum standards for invalid, old-age, and survivors' benefits, with survivor in this context defined as the wife and children deprived of the support of the family breadwinner.

2686. U.S. Congress. Senate. Committee on Post Office and Civil Service. *Civil Service Survivors Benefits, Report to Accompany S. 2174.* S. Rept. 93-395, 93rd Cong., 1st sess., 1973. 3p. Serial 13017-6. Recommends a bill changing the marriage requirement for survivor benefits under the civil service retirement system by reducing the length of time the surviving spouse was married to the employee from two years preceding death to one year. Length of marriage requirements in other systems are briefly reviewed.

2687. U.S. Social Security Administration. Office of Research and Statistics. *Women and Social Security: Law and Policy in Five Countries.* Research Report no. 42. Washington, DC: GPO, 1973. 95p. HE3.49:42. The treatment of women under the social security systems of Belgium, Federal Republic of Germany, France, Great Britain, and the United States are reviewed, and the status of proposed policy changes in each country are discussed.

2688. U.S. Congress. House. *Surviving Spouse Annuities, Conference Report to Accompany S. 628.* H. Rept. 93-1431, 93rd Cong., 2d sess., 1974. 5p. Serial 13061-9. Conference report on the disagreement between the House and Senate on a House amendment to S. 628 eliminates the reduction of the principle annuity in order to provide a survivor annuity.

2689. U.S. Congress. House. Committee on Post Office and Civil Service. *Changes in Definitions of Widow and Widower under Civil Service Retirement System, Report to Accompany S. 2174.* H. Rept. 93-882, 93rd Cong., 2d sess., 1974. 6p. Serial 13061-2. Reports a bill reducing the duration of marriage required for survivor annuity eligibility from two years to one year under the Civil Service Retirement System. Such requirements under other federal retirement system are summarized in comparison.

2690. U.S. Congress. House. Committee on Post Office and Civil Service. *Surviving Spouse Civil Service Retirement Annuities without Reduction in Principal Annuities, Report to Accompany S. 628.* H. Rept. 915, 93rd Cong., 2d sess., 1974. 21p. Serial 13061-2. Report on a bill to change regulations governing survivor benefits in the Civil Service Retirement System explains the provisions of the bill in the areas of automatic coverage of the spouse and the proposed elimination of the reduction of the annuity of the employee in order to provide a survivor benefit.

2691. U.S. Congress. House. Committee on Merchant Marine and Fisheries. *Lighthouse Service Widows Benefits, Report to Accompany H.R. 1535.* H. Rept. 94-661, 94th Cong., 1st sess., 1975. 6p. Serial 13099-9. Report on raising annuities for Lighthouse Service widows repeats the argument that these women often performed the duties of the husband during his illness or absence, and that they deserved a pension that will keep them above the poverty level. Objections to the measure point out that the Lighthouse widows would receive much higher annuities than their nearest counterpart, the pre-1948 civil service widows.

2692. U.S. Congress. House. Committee on Post Office and Civil Service. *Elimination of Automatic Restoration of Annuity Reduction upon Remarriage, Report to Accompany H.R. 8550.* H. Rept. 94-448, 94th Cong., 1st sess., 1975. 9p. Serial 13099-7. Recommends a bill allowing remarried retired annuitants one year to elect whether their new spouse will receive survivor benefits. Under existing laws the survivor annuity was automatic upon the remarriage of a civil service annuitant, widowed or divorced, who had elected to accept a lower benefit in order to provide survivor benefits at the time of retirement.

2693. U.S. Congress. House. Select Committee on Aging. Subcommittee on Retirement Income and Employment. *Age and Sex Discrimination in Employment and Review of Federal Response to Employment Needs of the Elderly.* 94th Cong., 1st sess., 10 Dec. 1975. 66p. Y4.Ag4/2:Em7. Discussion of sex discrimination in Social Security focuses on the situation of the full-time homemaker, sex discrimination in survivor benefits, and the inequities to dually entitled women. Also addressed is the issue of age discrimination in employment, and background data on employment seeking and labor force participation by age is furnished.

2694. U.S. Congress. House. Select Committee on Aging. Subcommittee on Retirement Income and Employment. *Income Security of Older Women: Path to Equity.* 94th Cong., 1st sess., Dec. 1975. Committee Print. 43p. Y4.Ag4/2:In2/2. Report provides information on the problems of older women under Social Security and Supplemental Security Income, under private and federal pension plans, and with employment discrimination. The situation of minority women is examined in relation to poverty, education, and cultural barriers. Background data is included on employment status by sex, employment status and work experience of women 55 and over by age, and occupational characteristics of women by age.

2695. U.S. Congress. House. Select Committee on Aging. Subcommittee on Retirement Income and Employment. *Pension Problems of Older Women, Hearing.* 94th Cong., 1st sess., 21 Oct. 1975. 78p. Y4.Ag4/2:P38. Hearing is highlighted by the statement of staff from the National Senior Citizens Law Center on the condition of older women under current pension systems. In particular, testimony looks at survivor's benefits and at earning limitations and social security payments. A reprint of the study "Legal Issues Affecting the Older Woman in America Today" is included.

2696. U.S. Congress. House. Select Committee on Aging. Subcommittee on Retirement Income and Employment. *Social Security Inequities against Women, Hearings.* 94th Cong., 1st sess., 1, 29 Sept. 1975. 37p. Y4.Ag4/2:So1/2. Brief examination of women under Social Security highlights the problems of low paying jobs, displaced homemakers, and the "widow's gap" between the time the children reach 18 and the age when retirement benefits begin.

2697. U.S. Congress. House. Select Committee on Aging. Subcommittee on Retirement Income and Employment. *Women and Railroad Retirement, Hearing.* 94th Cong., 1st sess., 19 Nov. 1975. 26p. Y4.Ag4/2:R13. Hearing examines the treatment of widows and divorcees under the Railroad Retirement Act. The primary focus is on the situation of older divorced women who lose any claim to their ex-husband's railroad pension and are left with inadequate income.

2698. U.S. Congress. Senate. Special Committee on Aging. *Future Directions in Social Security, Part 18: Women and Social Security, Hearing.* 94th Cong., 1st sess., 22 Oct. 1975. 1665-1730pp. Y4.Ag4:So1/2/pt.18. Witnesses react to the working paper *Women and Social Security: Adapting to a New Era* (2700), discussing topics such as the number of years of marriage required for a divorced spouse to receive benefits and the benefits provided to widows. Changing work patterns for women are discussed along with the very low incomes of elderly women. Recommendations relating to displaced homemakers are criticized. The appendix includes correspondence detailing discrimination against women under Social Security.

2699. U.S. Congress. Senate. Special Committee on Aging. *Future Directions in Social Security, Part 19: Women and Social Security, Hearings.* 94th Cong., 1st sess., 23 Oct. 1975. 1731-1786pp. Y4.Ag4:So1/2/pt.19. Continued hearings on the recommendations of the Task Force on Women and Social Security, *Women and Social Security: Adapting to a New Era* (2700) explore approaches to making Social Security work for women. The gender-based distinctions in Social Security are reviewed and ways to eliminate them are discussed. The question of dependency, the treatment of working wives, and the long term effect of sex discrimination in employment on retirement income are examined. The particular problems of black women and retirement income are noted.

2700. U.S. Congress. Senate. Special Committee on Aging. Task Force on Women and Social Security. *Women and Social Security: Adapting to a New Era.* 94th Cong., 1st sess., 1975. Committee print. 87p. Y4.Ag4:W84. Examination of sex discrimination in Social Security looks at the changing role of women in the labor force and its relationship to the Social Security system. The pros and cons of legislative proposals to establish sex equity in Social Security are detailed. Statistics are furnished on marital status by age index,

1940 and 1970; years of school completed by sex, 1940 and 1970; participation in labor force by age and sex, 1940 and 1970; occupational group by sex, 1940 and 1970; earnings in 1939 of the experienced labor force by sex; median earning in 1969 of the experienced labor force, by occupational group and sex; and number and percentage distribution of benefits in current payment state, by sex and for dually entitled women.

2701. U.S. Social Security Administration. Office of Research and Statistics. *Demographic and Economic Characteristics of the Aged, 1968 Social Security Survey.* Research Report no. 45. Washington, DC: GPO, 1975. 186p. HE3.49:45. Presents data on income size and sources, benefits, beneficiary characteristics, pensions, employment and earning, financial assets, and living arrangements of the aged. Most of the data is broken down by sex and marital status.

2702. U.S. Congress. House. Committee on Post Office and Civil Service. *Payments to Former Spouses, Report to Accompany H.R. 8771.* H. Rept. 95-713, 95th Cong., 1st sess., 1977. 12p. Serial 13172-13. The history of committee action on the question of a divorced spouse's right to a portion of a civil service employee's retirement annuity is included in this favorable report on a bill authorizing the Civil Service Commission to comply with court ordered property settlements in the case of divorce, annulment or legal separation. The Civil Service Commission's response to a proposal to make former spouses automatically eligible for a portion of the annuity, if the former spouse had been married to the annuitant at least 20 years, is also included in the report.

2703. U.S. Congress. House. Committee on Post Office and Civil Service. *Survivor Annuities, Report to Accompany H.R. 3447.* H. Rept. 95-283, 95th Cong., 1st sess., 1977. 15p. Serial 13172-4. Reports a bill to change the civil service survivor benefit provisions by allowing a civil service annuitant the right to elect whether a new spouse will receive a survivor annuity. The bill also eliminates the reduction from an annuitant's benefit to provide for a surviving spouse.

2704. U.S. Congress. House. Committee on Post Office and Civil Service. Subcommittee on Compensation and Employment Benefits. *Annuity Provisions for Former Spouses, Hearings on H.R. 3951.* 95th Cong., 1st sess., 19 Apr. - 30 July 1977. 139p. Y4.P84/10:95-17. Hearing presents testimony both for and against a bill to provide older divorced spouses of federal employees a portion of the employee's annuity. Supporting testimony discusses the plight of older displaced homemakers and argues for the homemakers claim to part of the former husband's pension. A report by the Congressional Research Service included in the hearing record reviews divorce law reform in Canada, France, Britain and Germany.

2705. U.S. Congress. House. Committee on Ways and Means. Subcommittee on Social Security. *Brief Summary of Testimony Presented to the Subcommittee on Social Security during Public Hearings Held July 18-22 and July 26-27, 1977, on H.R. 8218, the "Social security financing, benefit indexing and equal rights amendments of 1977," and Other Social Security Issues.* 95th Cong., 1st sess., 8 Sept. 1977. 37p. Y4.W36:WMCP 95-49. Summarizes statements of support and recommendations from testimony on the Social Security Amendments. One provision of the amendments provides for equal treatment of men and women under Social Security.

2706. U.S. Congress. House. Committee on Ways and Means. Subcommittee on Social Security. *President Carter's Social Security Proposals, Part 2, Hearings.* 95th Cong., 1st sess., 21-27 July 1977. 565-1123pp. Y4.W36:95-27. First day of hearings on Social Security proposals presents witnesses discussing the problems of women under Social Security due to gender-based distinctions. The need to protect homemakers under Social Security is particularly stressed. The complex nature of the Social Security eligibility rules is illustrated as it relates to various scenarios involving women as homemakers and as wives in paid employment.

2707.   U.S. Congress. Senate. Committee on Governmental Affairs. *Correction of Survivor Annuity Inequities, Report to Accompany H.R. 3447.* S. Rept. 95-904, 95th Cong., 2d sess., 1978. 15p. Serial 13197-6. Report supports changing the civil service retirement annuity rules in regard to the annuitant whose spouse dies during the payment of the annuity. The first section of the bill gives the annuitant up to one year after remarriage to decide if a new spouse will collect a survivor annuity, and the second section deals with restoring the full annuity to a retiree upon the death of the survivor beneficiary.

2708.   U.S. Congress. Senate. Committee on Governmental Affairs. *Restoration of Survivor Annuities for Certain Widows and Widowers, Report to Accompany H.R. 3755.* S. Rept. 95-905, 95th Cong., 2d sess., 1978. 8p. Serial 13197-6. Favorable report on restoring benefits to surviving spouses of civil service annuitants who lost their survivor benefits because of remarriage prior to July 18, 1966, provides background on civil service survivor annuities.

2709.   U.S. Social Security Administration. Office of Research and Statistics. *Simulation Model of Woman under Social Security: Initial Model File.* Staff Paper no. 31. Washington, DC: GPO, 1978. 25p. HE3.56:31.

2710.   U.S. Congress. House. Committee on Ways and Means. Subcommittee on Social Security. *Treatment of Men and Women under the Social Security Program, Hearings.* 96th Cong., 1st sess., 1-2 Nov. 1979. 268p. Y4.W36:96-60. Hearing explores options for reducing or eliminating inequities in Social Security which affect women. In particular the proposed "earnings sharing" approach is explored as a way to address the earnings of couples who both contribute to Social Security. The problem of displaced homemakers in the areas of retirement, disability, and dependent child benefits is also brought forward. Opponents of the bill portray it as anti-homemaker and anti-family.

2711.   U.S. Congress. House. Select Committee on Aging. Subcommittee on Retirement Income and Employment. *Women and Retirement Income Programs: Current Issues of Equity and Adequacy.* by the Congressional Research Service. 96th Cong., 1st sess., 1979. Committee print. 119p. Y4.Ag4/2:R31/9. Report examines how women have fared under Social Security and under public and private pension plans. The issue of women's work patterns and their effect on pensions is examined. The report also analyzes the main issues facing women as dependents and survivors, such as loss of pension rights in the event of a spouse's pre-retirement death, decisions on survivor options, and the status of retirement benefits in a divorce. Provides statistics on labor force participation rates by sex, age, and marital status; median years on current job for women by marital status, age, and full-time/part-time status; and median earnings by industry, occupation and sex.

2712.   U.S. Congress. House. Select Committee on Aging. Subcommittee on Retirement Income and Employment. Task Force of Social Security and Women. *Treatment of Women under Social Security, Hearings, Volume 1.* 96th Cong., 1st sess., 16 May - 13 Sept. 1979. 331p. Y4.Ag4/2:W84/6/v.1. Examination of bias against women in the Social Security system explores the treatment of employed married women, workers not covered by Social Security, and housewives. Inequities under Unemployment Insurance are also reviewed. The position of homemakers in the Canadian Peninsula is presented for purposes of comparison. The concept of earnings sharing as one method of calculating benefits is examined.

2713.   U.S. Congress. House. Select Committee on Aging. Subcommittee on Retirement Income and Employment. Task Force of Social Security and Women. *Treatment of Women under*

Social Security, Hearings, Volume 2. 96th Cong., 1st sess., 16 May - 13 Sept. 1979. 494p. Y4.Ag4/2:W84/6/v.2. Appendices to Volume 1 include an illustrative earnings sharing plan, a report of the HEW Task Force on the Treatment of Women under Social Security, and a report from the Department of Justice on the treatment of men and women under Social Security. Background statistics from the Bureau of Labor Statistics include women in the labor force, 1900-78; changes in the civilian labor force by sex and marital status, 1970, 1977, 1978; occupational distribution of employed women 1950, 1960, 1970, 1978; unemployment rates by sex, selected years 1930-1979; and median weekly earnings of full-time workers by sex and occupation, 1979.

2714. U.S. Congress. Senate. Special Committee on Aging. *Adapting Social Security to a Changing Work Force, Hearing.* 96th Cong., 1st sess., 28 Nov. 1979. 102p. Y4.Ag4:So1/5. Hearing on changes in women's labor force participation and the Social Security system focuses on proposals to establish an earnings sharing structure. Testimony centers on the current inequities to two earner families and divorced women and on the pluses and minuses of the earnings sharing approach. The current retirement test for benefits is also discussed in relation to older women.

2715. U.S. Dept. of Health, Education and Welfare. *Social Security and the Changing Roles of Men and Women.* Washington, DC: The Department, 1979. 323p. HE1.2:W84/5. Report analyzes the original philosophy of social security and the way social security relates to the status of men and women in society. The conflict between the assumptions of Social Security system and current thought is highlighted, and options for changing the system are analyzed. Earnings sharing and double-decker benefit structures are examined in detail with projections of benefits by type of recipient. Provides statistics on retirement income and poverty rates by sex and marital status; earnings of people aged 55 to 64 by sex; sources of income for married couples, unmarried women and unmarried men; and lifetime earnings and benefits for widowed, divorced and never married persons by sex.

2716. U.S. Dept. of Justice. Task Force on Sex Discrimination. *The Pension Game: The American Pension System from the Viewpoint of the Average Woman.* Washington, DC: GPO, 1979. 78p. J1.2:P38. Provides a detailed description of the principles on which the American pension system is based and how this system affects women.

2717. U.S. Social Security Administration. *Women and Social Security.* Washington, DC: The Administration, 1979. leaflet. HE3.2:W84. Briefly describes the problems of the Social Security system as it relates to women.

2718. U.S. Social Security Administration. Office of Research and Statistics. *Simulation Model of Women under Social Security: Estimation of Labor Supply Relationships.* by Russell Roberts. Staff Paper no. 32. Washington, DC: GPO, 1979. 48p. HE3.56:32. Presents the labor supply relationships to be incorporated into a microanalytic simulation model. The purpose of the model is to predict labor market behavior with a primary emphasis on married women over age 30. Although the work focuses on the wages and labor supply of married women, behavioral relationships for men and for single women are also estimated.

2719. U.S. Congress. House. Committee on Foreign Affairs. *Foreign Service Act of 1980, Report to Accompany H.R. 6790 Which on March 12, 1980, Was Referred Jointly to the Committee on Foreign Affairs and the Committee on Post Office and Civil Service.* H. Rept. 96-992, part 1, 96th Cong., 2d sess., 1980. 258p. Serial 13367. Among the major changes proposed by the Foreign Service Act of 1980 are sections mandating the establishment of recruitment programs for women and minorities and providing for spousal consent to waive survivor annuities for both currently married and certain divorced officers. The report also discusses the career hardship experienced by Foreign Service spouses whose employment opportunities while abroad are limited.

2720. U.S. Congress. House. Committee on Post Office and Civil Service. *Foreign Service Act of 1980, Report on H.R. 6790.* H. Rept. 96-992, part 2, 96th Cong., 2d sess., 1980. 293p. Serial 13367. Summary explanation of the motivating factors behind Foreign Service retirement changes recognizes the spousal claim on a portion of the officers' retirement annuity in the case of divorce. The problem of family members, particularly the wife, in finding employment at an oversees posting is noted.

2721. U.S. Congress. House. Committee on Post Office and Civil Service. *Notification of Loss of or Reduction in Civil Service Survivor Benefits for Spouses, Report to Accompany H.R. 5410.* H. Rept. 96-850, 96th Cong., 2d sess., 1980. 8p. Serial 13361. Recommends a requirement that a civil service system annuitant notify his or her spouse before electing not to provide survivor benefits.

2722. U.S. Congress. House. Committee on Ways and Means. *Report of the 1979 Advisory Council on Social Security Transmitted by the Secretary of Health, Education and Welfare on December 7, 1979.* 96th Cong., 2d sess., 1980. Committee print. 402p. Y4.W36:WMCP96-45. Detailed report of the Advisory Council study of the Social Security system includes an excellent review of issues relating to women under Social Security and descriptions of possible remedies. The appendix provides a list of gender-based distinctions under Social Security law and an illustrative earnings-sharing plan.

2723. U.S. Congress. House. Committee on Ways and Means. Subcommittee on Social Security. *Demographic Trends and the Social Security System, Briefing.* 96th Cong., 2d sess., 2 Dec. 1980. 37p. Y4.W36:96-129. Examination of demographic trends in the U.S. as they will affect the Social Security system focuses on trends in women's labor force participation both as it affects fertility rates and women's contribution to and benefits from the system.

2724. U.S. Congress. House. Committee on Ways and Means. Subcommittee on Social Security. *Social Security Dependents' Benefits, Field Hearing.* 96th Cong., 2d sess., 28 July 1980. Falls Church, VA. 73p. Y4.W36:96-111. Hearing explores the problems with Social Security as it relates to two-earner couples and divorced women. The inequities in the current system and the proposed earnings sharing approach are examined.

2725. U.S. Congress. Senate. Committee on Foreign Relations. *Foreign Service Act of 1980, Report together with Additional Views to Accompany S. 3058.* S. Rept. 96-913, 96th Cong., 2d sess., 1980. 269p. Serial 13328. Favorable report on an act to make improvements in the Foreign Service addresses the problem of the Foreign Service spouse living overseas. Proposed changes would establish the claim of a former spouse to pension and survivor benefits and make it possible to collect such funds under court order or collect 50 to 55% of the annuity creditable to the period of the marriage.

2726. U.S. Congress. Senate. Committee on Governmental Affairs. *Notification of Loss of or Reduction in Civil Service Survivor Benefits for Spouses, Report to Accompany H.R. 5410.* S. Rept. 96-903, 96th Cong., 2d sess., 1980. 7p. Serial 13328. Reports a bill requiring a retiring civil service employee to notify his or her spouse if electing not to provide a survivor benefit or to provide a reduced survivor benefit.

2727. U.S. Labor-Management Services Administration. Pensions and Welfare Benefit Programs. *Women and Private Pension Plans.* by Helene A. Benson. Washington, DC: GPO, 1980. 13p. L1.2:W84/2. Text of a speech briefly covers the main issues of women as wage earners and as spouses under pension plans. Some of the issues described include vesting, breaks in service, portability, divorce, and IRA's. Presents a concise overview of the particular problems of old age income for women.

2728. U.S. Social Security Administration. Office of Research and Statistics. *Women Social Security Beneficiaries Age 62 and Older, 1960-79.* Research and Statistics Note 1980, no. 8. Washington, DC: The Office, 1980. 7p. HE3.28/2:980/8. Presents statistics which illustrate the major changes in Social Security entitlements for women due to the increased participation of women in the labor force.

2729. U.S. Congress. House. Committee on Ways and Means. Subcommittee on Social Security. *Social Security Financing Issues, Hearings.* 97th Cong., 1st sess., 17 Feb. - 23 Mar. 1981. 1019p. Y4.W36:97-3. Along with discussion of survivor benefits for students and eligibility criteria for disability is discussion of measures to improve the Social Security system's treatment of women. Witnesses support continued benefits for dependent wives and widows and support the role of the full-time homemaker.

2730. U.S. Congress. House. Select Committee on Aging. Subcommittee on Retirement Income and Employment. *Preparing for Widowhood: A Guidebook.* 97th Cong., 1st sess., 1981. Committee print. 38p. Y4.Ag4/2:W63. Presents information on financial planning for widowhood and on education and reentry employment geared toward wives in an attempt to prevent the problems of older women in poverty.

2731. U.S. Congress. House. Select Committee on Aging. Subcommittee on Retirement Income and Employment. Task Force of Social Security and Women. *Treatment of Women under Social Security, Hearings, Volume 3.* 97th Cong., 1st sess., 4 Feb., 20 July 1981. Washington, D.C., Cleveland, OH. 206p. Y4.Ag4/2:W84/6/v.3. Testimony highlights the dire financial conditions of many elderly women and their experiences under Social Security. Questions concerning treatment of two-wage earner families and the concept of income sharing are discussed. Also noted by witnesses is the plight of widows too young to draw on their spouse' Social Security but with no work history or job skills. Proposed cuts in Social Security are discussed with an emphasis on the effect on women.

2732. U.S. Congress. House. Select Committee on Aging. Subcommittee on Retirement Income and Employment. Task Force of Social Security and Women. *Treatment of Women under Social Security, Hearings, Volume 4.* 97th Cong., 1st sess., 3 June 1981. 196p. Y4.Ag4/2:W84/6/v.4. Three separate panels discuss administrative proposals to change Social Security. The first panel presents the administration views, the second the views of policy study and legal organizations, and the third the view of women's and senior citizen's organizations. Testimony cites individual cases of women under Social Security and notes how changes in eligibility, especially in the area of disability, will affect women. The problems of divorced women under Social Security are also explored. The impact of the earnings sharing approach to husband and wife incomes is examined. Provides data on pension income and total income of persons over 65 for couples, unmarried women and unmarried men.

2733. U.S. Congress. Senate. Special Committee on Aging. *Impact of Federal Estate Tax Policies on Rural Women, Hearing.* 97th Cong., 1st sess., 4 Feb. 1981. 57p. Y4.Ag4:T19/4. Witnesses describe the inequities in the estate tax laws which fail to recognize the contribution of the farm woman to the business and her resulting precarious economic status upon the death of her husband. Reform of the tax laws to recognize the economic contribution of wives to family enterprise is supported. A number of statements and letters from women involved in agricultural enterprise are included in the hearing record.

2734.   U.S. Congress. House. *Intelligence Authorization Act for Fiscal Year 1983, Conference Report to Accompany H.R. 6068.* H. Rept. 97-779, 97th Cong., 2d sess., 1982. 24p. Serial 13488. Conference report resolves House and Senate differences on a bill relating to retirement benefits for former spouses of CIA officers. Both House and Senate versions were designed to provide CIA spouses with the same retirement benefits as those accorded to Foreign Service spouses by the Foreign Service Act of 1980. The bill recognizes the investment of a CIA officer's spouse in the officer's career while assigned outside of the U.S. by providing a statutory entitlement to a share of the retirement annuity of the officer in cases of divorce.

2735.   U.S. Congress. House. Committee on Education and Labor. Subcommittee on Labor-Management Relations. *Legislative Hearing on Pensions Issues, Hearing on H.R. 1641, H.R. 3632, H.R. 6462.* 97th Cong., 2d sess., 14 Oct. 1982. San Francisco, CA. 293p. Y4.Ed8/1:P38/5. Testimony on the Private Pension Reform Act of 1981 describes the economic situation of older women and the need to make ERISA more equitable for women. The inequities under the current private pension laws for women are described highlighting denial of survivor benefits to widows when the husband dies prior to retirement. The economics of divorce for women, particularly as it relates to the pension issue, are also discussed. Options for correcting the inequities through legislation are described.

2736.   U.S. Congress. Senate. Select Committee on Intelligence. *Central Intelligence Agency Spouses' Retirement Equity Act of 1982, Report to Accompany S. 2422.* S. Rept. 97-484, 97th Cong., 2d sess., 1982. 15p. Serial 13450. Report recognizes the personal and professional sacrifices of spouses of CIA officers working overseas and recommends a bill guaranteeing the spouse's right to a portion of the officer's retirement annuity in the case of divorce. The existing problems related to divorce and CIA Retirement and Disability System benefits are described in support of this legislation.

2737.   U.S. Administration on Aging. *Income Maintenance Concerns of Older Women.* by Marilyn R. Block. National Policy Center On Women and Aging Working Paper no. 3. College Park, MD: The Center, 1983. 46p. HE23.3002:W84/2/wk. paper 3. Study examines the economic status of older women and the policy options for addressing their income maintenance needs. Data on number of weeks worked and median income by occupation and sex; median income by type of family; older women below poverty level; income level and sources of income for older persons by sex; pension plan coverage by sex; and social security benefits by sex is reported and analyzed.

2738.   U.S. Congress. House. *Communication from the President of the United States Transmitting a Legislative Proposal Entitled the "Pension equity act of 1983."* H. Doc. 98-114, 98th Cong., 1st sess., 1983. 24p. Serial 13529. Statement of support from President Reagan accompanies the draft of the "Pension Equity Act of 1983," a measure to amend ERISA and the Internal Revenue Code to provide an greater chance for working women to earn their own pensions and for widowed and divorced women to secure a retirement income. Age of participation, breaks in service, and survivor annuity requirements are among the areas addressed. The bill also addresses the issue of administration of court ordered divorce settlements in the area of pensions.

2739.   U.S. Congress. House. Committee on Education and Labor. *Survivor Benefits for Federal Law Enforcement Officers and Firefighters, Report Together with Minority Views to Accompany H.R. 622.* H. Rept. 98-309, 98th Cong., 1st sess., 1983. 26p. Serial 13541. Recommends a bill providing a lump-sum payment of $50,000 to the family of federal law enforcement officers or firefighters killed in the line of duty. A lengthy minority view rejects the proposed legislation as providing an unnecessary special benefit.

2740. U.S. Congress. House. Committee on Education and Labor. Subcommittee on Labor-Management Relations. *Legislative Hearings on Pension Equity for Women, Hearings on H.R. 2100.* 98th Cong., 1st sess., 1 Nov. 1983. 63p. Y4.Ed8/1:P38/6. Continued hearings on the proposed Private Pension Reform Act of 1983 presents the views of labor union and pension plan representatives on the provisions of the bill. The portions covering divorced spouses receive the most attention with employers expressing concern over administrative costs.

2741. U.S. Congress. House. Committee on Education and Labor. Subcommittee on Labor-Management Relations. *Pension Equity for Women, Hearing on H.R. 2100.* 98th Cong., 1st sess., 29 Sept. 1983. 230p. Y4.Ed8/1:P38/7. Examination of proposed changes in ERISA to provide better pension coverage for women provides support for the idea of change, but also includes testimony opposing provisions relating to maternity/paternity leaves and expressing concern over the administrative costs of other aspects. Provisions for divorced spouses, notification of the wife before dropping survivor options, and minimum age of pension plan participation are examined.

2742. U.S. Congress. House. Committee on Post Office and Civil Service. Subcommittee on Compensation and Employee Benefits. *Civil Service Spouse Retirement Equity Act, Hearing on H.R. 2300.* 98th Cong., 1st sess., 20 Oct. 1983. 68p. Y4.P84/10:98-13. The often destitute state of divorced wives of civil service employees is described in relation to a bill guaranteeing a spouse's ability to collect retirement and survivor benefits in the case of divorce from an employee covered under civil service retirement.

2743. U.S. Congress. House. Committee on Ways and Means. *Economic Equity Act and Related Tax and Pension Reform, Hearing.* 98th Cong., 1st sess., 25 Oct. 1983. 212p. Y4.W36:98-51. The economic problems of women as wage earners and as homemakers under pension systems are explored in hearing testimony. Along with survivor benefits, assignment of pension benefits in divorce cases, and pension plan participation rates is discussion of a targeted job credit program for displaced homemakers and a dependent care tax credit. Retirement and child care issues predominate.

2744. U.S. Congress. House. Select Committee on Aging. *Women's Pension Equity, Hearing.* 98th Cong., 1st sess., 14 June 1983. 369p. Y4.Ag4/2:W84/9. Hearing explores the problems faced by women under existing private pension plans and examines provisions of proposed legislation to remove discrimination toward women. Some of the issues discussed are notification of spouse when waiving survivor benefits, survivor benefits for divorced spouses, vesting requirements, and maternity and paternity leaves. Three panels, women who have personally experienced the inequities faced by women in cases of divorce, representatives of women's organizations, and experts on pensions plans, document the issues under consideration.

2745. U.S. Congress. House. Select Committee on Aging. Subcommittee on Retirement Income and Employment. Task Force of Social Security and Women. *Inequities toward Women in the Social Security System, Hearings.* 98th Cong., 1st sess., 22 Sept. 1983. 171p. Y4.Ag4/2:In3. Testimony highlights the financial status of older women in America and the factors which contribute to the large number of elderly women living in poverty. The effect of possible changes in the Social Security system are explored emphasizing earnings sharing approaches and discussing private pension plan coverage.

2746. U.S. Congress. Joint Committee on Taxation. *Description of S. 19 ("Retirement Equity Act of 1983") and S. 888("Economic Equity Act of 1983"), Scheduled for Hearings before the Committee on Finance.* 98th Cong., 1st sess., 16 June 1983. Committee print. 37p. Y4.T19/4:D45/14. The purpose and effect of two bills aimed at improving the economic status of women are detailed. The Retirement Equity Act of 1983, S.19, would change

ERISA rules governing participation, vesting, breaks in service, and survivor annuities. The Economic Equity Act of 1983, S. 888, also includes provisions relating to former spouses of retired federal employees, child care tax credit, gender-based discrimination in insurance, gender-based distinctions in federal agency rules, and child support enforcement. Provisions in present laws and the proposed changes are reviewed.

2747.   U.S. Congress. Senate. Committee on Finance. *Potential Inequities Affecting Women, Hearings on S. 19 and S. 888.* 98th Cong., 1st sess., 20 June - 2 Aug. 1983. 3 vol. Y4.F49:S.hrg.98-313/pt.1-3. Hearings examine two bills addressing the provisions of pensions plans and tax laws which adversely affect women. Testimony highlights current pension plan practices focusing on issues of age of participation, handling of maternity leave, notification of spouse before waiving survivor benefits, and benefits in cases of divorce. Tax provisions proposed add displaced homemakers to targeted jobs tax credit, increase the zero bracket amount for heads of household, and increase child and dependent care credit. Bill S. 888 also provides for stronger child support enforcement. Part one of hearings focus on the pensions plan issue while part two examines child support and income tax proposals in the context of female-headed families living in poverty. Some pension plan proposals are also covered in part two statements. Part three presents the administration views on the bills.

2748.   U.S. Congress. Senate. Committee on Finance. *Retirement Equity Act of 1983, Report to Accompany H. R. 2769.* S. Rept. 98-285, 98th Cong., 1st sess., 1983. 27p. Serial 13513. The bill reported makes a number of changes to pension plan rules in an effort to make the system more equitable to women. The proposed Retirement Equity Act of 1983 lowers the maximum pension plan participation age to 21 and the maximum vesting age to 18, and provides an exception to the ERISA prohibition against the alienation or assignment of benefit to permit the enforcement of court ordered child support. Other divorce settlement survivor benefits, break in service, and maternity/paternity leave rules are also affected.

2749.   U.S. Congress. Senate. Committee on Labor and Human Resources. Subcommittee on Labor. *Retirement Equity Act of 1983, Hearing on S. 19.* 98th Cong., 1st sess., 4 Oct. 1983. 253p. Y4.L11/4:S.hrg.98-417. Hearing on amendment of ERISA examines proposals to remove inequities and provide greater security to the widow whose husband dies before reaching retirement age, to women workers whose job patterns reduce their pension eligibility, and to former spouses of covered workers. In addition to discussing the cases mentioned previously, the hearing also examines the use of sex-based insurance and pension rates and the Supreme Court decision in *Arizona Governing Committee v. Norris* relating to calculation of retirement benefits without regard to sex.

2750.   U.S. Congress. House. Committee on Education and Labor. *Retirement Equity Act of 1984, Report Together with an Individual View to Accompany H.R. 4280 which on November 2, 1983, Was Referred Jointly to the Committee on Education and Labor and the Committee on Ways and Means.* H. Rept. 98-655, part 1, 98th Cong., 2d sess., 1984. 87p. Serial 13588. Reports a bill to amend the Employee Retirement Income Security Act of 1974 and the Internal Revenue Code of 1954 in order to enhance women's retirement pension coverage by recognizing the work pattern of women and by adjusting the ERISA rules to recognize these patterns. Changes in the areas of age of participation and vesting, breaks in service and maternity leave all address the situation of working women. The bill also addresses the pension problems of homemakers by changing the rules on provision of survivor benefits and waiver of such benefits, and clarifying the payment of such benefits to divorced spouses under court order and when the divorce occurs after retirement. The situations addressed by each of these provisions is clearly presented.

2751.   U.S. Congress. House. Committee on Post Office and Civil Service. *Civil Service Retirement Spouse Equity Act of 1984, Report to Accompany H.R. 2300.* H. Rept. 98-

1054, 98th Cong., 2d sess., 1984. 49p. Serial 13600. Recommends that certain former spouses, married to a federal employee for ten years or more, be automatically entitled to a portion of the employee's annuity and any surviving spouse's annuity. Other major changes in civil service survivor benefits for former spouses include spousal consent to waiver of survivor benefit and eligibility of former spouses for the federal employees health benefits program. Discussion of the subtleties of a former spouse's claim on retirement annuities makes up the bulk of the report.

2752. U.S. Congress. House. Committee on Post Office and Civil Service. Subcommittee on Compensation and Employee Benefits. *Revisions to H.R. 2300, the Civil Service Spouse Retirement Equity Act, Hearing.* 98th Cong., 2d sess., 20 June 1984. 65p. Y4.P84/10:98-42. Hearing on changing civil service retirement to address the problems of divorced spouses explores the implications of proposed changes in retirement and survivor benefits rules.

2753. U.S. Congress. House. Committee on Ways and Means. *Explanation of Proposed Amendments to H.R. 4280, the Retirement Equity Act of 1984, as Marked Up by the Committee on Ways and Means on Mar. 27, 1984.* 98th Cong., 2d sess., 16 May 1984. 3p. CIS84-H782-24.

2754. U.S. Congress. House. Committee on Ways and Means. *Retirement Equity Act of 1984, Report Together with Additional Views to Accompany H.R. 4280.* H. Rept. 98-655, part 2, 98th Cong., 2d sess., 1984. 88p. Serial 13588. The bill reported was designed to provide women with improved pension coverage by amending ERISA in relation to age of participation and vesting, breaks in service, maternity/paternity leave, survivor benefits, spousal consent to waiver, and preretirement survivor annuities. The bill also clarifies the ability to include retirement annuities in divorce settlements. The report does not provide background material on the reasons for the changes in most cases.

2755. U.S. Congress. House. Committee on Ways and Means. *Summary Description of H.R. 4280 (Retirement Equity Act), Scheduled for Markup.* 98th Cong., 2d sess., 26 Mar. 1984. 8p. CIS84-H782-14.

2756. U.S. Congress. House. Select Committee on Aging. Subcommittee on Retirement Income and Employment. Task Force of Social Security and Women. *Earnings Sharing Implementation Plan, Hearing.* 98th Cong., 2d sess., 12 Apr. 1984. 51p. Y4.Ag4/2:Ea7. The focus of this hearing is on the progress made by the Department of Health and Human Services in conducting a study of the earnings sharing approach to computing Social Security benefits.

2757. U.S. Congress. Joint Committee on Taxation. *Comparison of H.R. 4280 and H.R. 2769 (Retirement Equity Act of 1984).* 98th Cong., 2d sess., 31 July 1984. 16p. CIS84-J862-41. Comparison of two versions of the Retirement Equity Act of 1984 summarizes provisions relating to age of participation, credit for paternal leave, survivor annuity procedures, and assignment or alienation of benefits in divorce.

2758. U.S. Congress. Senate. Committee on Finance. *Retirement Equity Act of 1984, Report to Accompany H.R. 4280.* S. Rept. 98-575, 98th Cong., 2d sess., 1984. 37p. Serial 13562. See 2754 for abstract.

2759. U.S. Congress. Senate. Committee on Government Affairs. Subcommittee on Civil Service, Post Office, and General Services. *Civil Service Former Spouses Benefits Act of 1984, Hearing on S. 2821.* 98th Cong., 2d sess., 1 Aug. 1984. 85p. Y4.G74/9:S.hrg.98-1014. Testimony explores the issues of retirement, health insurance, and survivor benefits for divorced wives under the Civil Service Retirement System and the Federal Employee

Health Benefits Program. The implications of proposed changes designed to ensure a divorced spouses' ability to claim pensions are examined.

2760. U.S. Congress. House. Committee on Post Office and Civil Service. *Federal Employees Benefits Improvement Act of 1985, Report to Accompany H.R. 3384.* H. Rept. 99-292, 99th Cong., 1st sess., 1985. 18p. Serial 13655. Reports a bill making technical changes to the Civil Service Spouse Equity Act of 1984 relative to survivor benefits for former spouses and for surviving spouses who remarry after age 55.

2761. U.S. Congress. House. Committee on Ways and Means. *Technical Corrections Act of 1985; and Technical Corrections to the Retirement Equity Act of 1984, Hearing on H.R. 1800 and H.R. 2110.* 99th Cong., 1st sess., 16 May 1985. 877p. Y4.W36:99-29. Hearing on two bills making technical corrections includes only brief discussion of provisions of H.R. 2110, a bill amending the Retirement Equity Act of 1984.

2762. U.S. Congress. House. Committee on Ways and Means. Subcommittee on Social Security. *Report on Earnings Sharing Implementation Study.* 99th Cong., 1st sess., 14 Feb. 1985. 632p. Y4.W36:WMCP 99-4. Study explores options for implementing an earnings sharing approach to Social Security and discusses options that would improve Social Security protection for women retiring in the near future. As a preface to discussion of earnings sharing the report analyzes how women fare under Social Security and the issues raised by concerned groups.

2763. U.S. Congress. Joint Committee on Taxation. *Description of Amendments by Chairman Rostenkowski and Mr. Duncan to H.R. 1800 (The Technical Corrections Act of 1985) and H.R. 2110 (Technical Changes to the Retirement Equity Act of 1984).* 99th Cong., 1st sess., 1985. Committee print. 18p. CIS85-J862-62.

2764. U.S. Congress. Joint Committee on Taxation. *Description of H.R. 2110 Relating to Technical Changes to the Retirement Equity Act of 1984, Scheduled for a Hearing before the Committee on Ways and Means.* 99th Cong., 1st sess., 1985. Committee print. 12p. Y4.T19/4:D45/34. Review of the provisions of the Retirement Equity Act of 1984, P.L. 98-397, describes proposed technical changes in break-in-service rules, minimum age requirements, survivor benefit requirements, transfer plan rules, spousal consent, and tax treatment of divorce distributions.

2765. U. S. Congress. House. Committee on Education and Labor. *Retirement Equity Technical Correction Act of 1986, Report Together with Additional Views to Accompany H.R. 2110.* H. Rept. 99-526, part 2, 99th Cong., 2d sess., 1986. 58p. Serial 13699. Reports a bill making technical corrections to the Retirement Equity Act of 1984 by clarifying language which created problems in the operation of the act. Effected areas include break-in-service rules, mandatory employee contributions, maximum age requirement, coordination between qualified joint and survivor annuity and qualified preretirement survivor annuity, spousal consent requirements, tax treatment of divorce distributions, and coordination of domestic relations provisions with federal garnishment restrictions.

2766. U.S. Congress. House. Committee on Post Office and Civil Service. Subcommittee on Compensation and Employee Benefits. *Legislation to Extend Civil Service Retirement Credit, Hearing on H.R. 680, H.R. 702, H.R. 1169, H.R. 1838, H.R. 2663, H.R. 3006, H.R. 3638.* 99th Cong., 2d sess., 12 Mar. 1986. 92p. Y4.P84/10:99-45. Hearing examines bills to extend civil service retirement benefits to several special groups, including members of the WWII Cadet Nurse Corps. The bill would only affect former members of the Cadet Nurse Corps already eligible for civil service retirement by allowing credit for the time in the Corps. Administration witnesses oppose the bills based on the decision that most of the group, including the Cadet Nurse Corps, were not in an employer/employee relationship with the Government.

2767. U.S. Congress. House. Committee on Ways and Means. *Retirement Equity Technical Correction Act of 1986, Report to Accompany H.R. 2110.* H. Rept. 99-526, part 1, 99th Cong., 2d sess., 1986. 53p. Serial 13699. Reports a bill making technical changes to clarify the application of the Retirement Equity Act of 1984 in the areas of break-in-service, mandatory employee contributions, maximum age requirements, coordination between qualified joint and survivor annuity and qualified preretirement survivor annuity, transfer plan rules, spousal consent requirements, notice requirements for individuals hired after age 35, tax treatment of divorce distributions, application of domestic relations provisions to plans not subject to assignment or alienation restrictions, and coordination of domestic relations provisions with federal garnishment restrictions.

2768. U.S. Congress. Joint Committee on Taxation. *Additional Technical Corrections to the Retirement Equity Act of 1984.* 99th Cong., 2d sess., 20 Mar. 1986. 2p. CIS86-J862-10.

2769. U.S. Congressional Budget Office. *Earnings Sharing Options for the Social Security System.* by Ralph E. Smith, et al. Washington, DC: GPO, 1986. 137p. Y10.2:Ea7. Report provides background on earnings sharing proposals which would calculate Social Security benefits by combining the earnings of husbands and wives, then dividing them equally. The effect of the proposals by marital status and work status is reviewed.

2770. U.S. Women's Bureau. *Retirement Equity Act of 1984: Its Impact on Women.* Washington, DC: GPO, 1986. 13p. L36.102:R31. The benefits for women in the Retirement Equity Act of 1984 are outlined within the context of the Employee Retirement Income Security Act of 1974. Particular areas noted as affecting women are new rules for age of participation, vesting, breaks in service, maternity and paternity absence, survivor benefits, and benefits for divorces spouses.

2771. U.S. Social Security Administration. Office of Research and Statistics. *SSA's Retirement History Study.* Washington, DC: GPO, 1987. 398p. HE3.2:R31/14/v.1. Reprints research articles from *Social Security Bulletin* based on the longitudinal study of aging and retirement, the Retirement History Study. Many of the articles examine the status of women and retirement income.

2772. U.S. Congress. House. *Retirement and Survivors' Annuities for Bankruptcy Judges and Magistrates Act of 1988, Conference Report to Accompany S. 1630.* H. Rept. 100-1072, 100th Cong., 2d sess., 1988. 18p.

2773. U.S. General Accounting Office. *Retirement Income: 1984 Pension Law Will Help Some Widows But Not the Poorest.* Washington, DC: The Office, 1988. 43p. GA1.13:HRD-88-77. Report analyzes the ability of the Retirement Equity Act of 1984 to address the income needs of widows. The focus of the report is the spousal consent requirement to waive survivor benefits. By examining new beneficiaries, GAO analyzed the probable effect of more pension survivor benefits on the poverty level of elderly widows. The report indicates that widows most at risk of poverty were married to husbands who lacked a pension. The continued importance of Social Security benefits to widows is stressed.

2774. U.S. Congress. House. Committee on Veteran's Affairs. *Court of Veterans Appeals Judges Retirement Act, Report to Accompany H.R. 2727.* H. Rept. 101-189, 101st Cong., 1st sess., 1989. 31p.

2775. U.S. Congress. House. Committee on Ways and Means. Subcommittee on Social Security. *The Oldest and Poorest Social Security Beneficiaries, Hearing.* 101st Cong., 1st sess., 23

May 1989. 67p. Y4.W36:101-16. Hearing considers the situation of women under Social Security revealing data which shows that widowed and single women beneficiaries are likely to live in extreme poverty. Proposals to increase benefits and the cost of those proposals are discussed. Testimony focuses on the economic status of the 85 and older population, but also discusses other Social Security issues such as the treatment of disabled widows.

2776. U.S. Congress. Senate. Committee on Veterans' Affairs. *Court of Veterans Appeals Judges Retirement Act, Report to Accompany S. 1243.* S. Rept. 101-86, 101st Cong., 1st sess., 1989. 75p. See 2777 for abstract.

2777. U.S. Congress. Senate. Committee on Veterans' Affairs. *Court of Veterans Appeals Judges Retirement Act, Report to Accompany S. 1243.* S. Rept. 101-171, 101st Cong., 1st sess., 1989. 75p. Report provides details of a retirement and survivor annuity plan for Court of Veterans Appeals judges. The survivor annuity plan presented is modeled on the Tax Court plan. The bill does not address the case of former spouses.

2778. U.S. Office of Personnel Management. *Survivor Benefits under the Civil Service Retirement System.* Retirement Facts 5. Washington, DC: GPO, 1989. leaflet. PM1.10:RI83-5. Non-technical summary describes survivor benefit rules under the Civil Service Retirement System.

2779. U.S. Social Security Administration. *Survivors.* Washington, DC: GPO, 1989. 10p. He3.2:Su7/5/989. Details the provisions of the Social Security survivor benefit system.

2780. U.S. Congress. House. Committee on Ways and Means. Subcommittee on Social Security. *Social Security Benefits for Widows and Spouses, Hearing.* 101st Cong., 2d sess., 5 Apr. 1990. 120p. Y4.W36:101-91. Recognizing the continuing impoverished status of older widowed and divorced women, this hearing explores the Social Security regulations which contribute to the situation by reducing widows' or former spouses' benefits. Two specific areas of concern are eligibility rules governing benefits to disabled wives and widows and the two-year waiting period for a divorced spouse to be eligible for benefits.

2781. U.S. Congress. House. Permanent Select Committee on Intelligence. *Intelligence Authorization Act for Fiscal Year 1990, Report Together with Minority Views to Accompany H.R. 5422.* H. Rept. 101-725, part 1, 101st Cong., 2d sess., 1990. 40p. Report on an authorization bill for intelligence-related activities includes changes in retirement annuity regulations for former spouses and surviving spouses who remarry.

2782. U.S. Congress. House. Select Committee on Aging. Subcommittee on Retirement Income and Employment. *Retirement Income for Women, Hearing.* 101st Cong., 2d sess., 2 July 1990. Cedar Rapids, IA. 105p. Y4.Ag4/2:R31.24. The effect on women's Social Security benefits of "dropping out" of the labor force to care for children and elderly parents is explored in hearing testimony. A study of women's experience under Social Security conducted by the Older Women's League is the focus of much of the testimony. Other factors which effect women's retirement income, such as employment patterns, divorce, and ERISA rules, are also reviewed.

2783. U.S. Congress. House. Select Committee on Aging. Subcommittee on Retirement Income and Employment. *Women, Caregiving, and Poverty: Options to Improve Social Security, Hearing.* 101st Cong., 2d sess., 3 Oct. 1990. 122p. Y4.Ag4/2:W84/12. Noting that by 2020 most of the elderly living in poverty will be women, the hearing focuses on ways that Social Security's method of calculating benefits could be adjusted to lessen the negative impact of women's caregiving years. Also discussed is the problem of full-time homemakers widowed in their 50s and their difficulty in finding employment until they are eligible for survivor benefits at age 62. A common theme is dually entitled women, particularly those who are in and out of the work force. Details of the Canada Pension Plan are reviewed as a possible reform model.

2784. U.S. Congress. House. Select Committee on Aging. Subcommittee on Retirement Income and Employment. *Women in Retirement: Are They Losing Out? Hearing.* 101st Cong., 2d sess., 22 May 1990. 172p. Y4.Ag4/2:W84/11. Testimony highlights the vulnerability of women to poverty in old age and describes in detail the negative impact on women's retirement income of the Social Security laws and the ERISA rules for private pensions. Women's employment patterns, the situation of full-time homemakers, and the treatment of dual career families are highlighted.

2785. U.S. Office of Personnel Management. Civil Service Retirement System. *Information for Survivor Annuitants.* Washington, DC: The Office, 1990. 27p. PM1.10:RI25-26/990. Booklet answers questions about survivor annuities in the Civil Service Retirement System covering eligibility, divorce, remarriage, and taxation of benefits.

2786. U.S. Railroad Retirement Board. *Widow(er)'s Annuity.* Washington, DC: GPO, 1990. 28p. RR1.2:An7/2. Review of rules for survivor annuities under the Railroad Retirement Board programs covers eligibility requirements, marriage requirements, former spouse eligibility, and basic procedures.

SERIALS

2787. U.S. Social Security Administration. *A Woman's Guide to Social Security.* Washington, DC: GPO, 1981-. irreg. HE3.6/3:W84/year. Information booklet issued periodically provides a concise summary of Social Security rules and benefits of interest to women.

2788. U.S. Social Security Board. Office of the Actuary. *Estimated Amount of Life Insurance Value in Force under Survivors Benefits of the Old-Age and Survivors Insurance System.* Actuarial Studies. Washington, DC: The Office, 1941-1958. irregular. FS3.19:no. Title varies. Actuarial Studies nos.16 (1941), 31 (1951), 37 (1953), 43 (1955), 47 (1958).

18

Military Survivor Benefits

The payment of pensions to widows of military personnel and of veterans is among the oldest topics of congressional debate directly related to women. Depending on the state of the budget, pensions were either granted or not, but a unifying theme of almost all of the pension bills from the Revolutionary War to the present is the delimiting marriage date. In report after report, committees debated and set either a specific marriage date or a number of years married to define eligibility for pensions. The congressional obsession with preventing young women from marrying old veterans for their pension is discussed in historical perspective in a 1922 hearing on Civil War and Mexican War pensions (2905).

The hearings and reports also reflect changing concepts of dependency and government obligations to widows. While an 1880 report firmly rejected a bill to continue pensions to remarried widows based on the theory that they were no longer dependent (2851), the question of remarriage was still a topic of debate in 1989 (3094). The issue of dependency is raised in numerous documents, usually in relation to income limitations and eligibility requirements. While early pensions laws often granted pensions if the widow was dependent on her own labor for support, by 1931 the "modern tendency of women to enter the business world" was used as justification for excluding World War I widows without children from pension benefits (2937). By the time World War II ended, the idea of widows' employment was firmly established, as reflected in a 1948 request to help widows by providing educational benefits (3008, 3010). The potential of educational benefits to help widows support themselves was again discussed in 1968 in relation to the Vietnam War (3046).

The reports on the late 1930s and early 1940s are characterized by combined reports covering large numbers of private bills requesting pensions or increased pensions. The interesting aspect of these reports is the information they provide of the medical and financial conditions of hundreds of individual widows.

During the 1970s and 1980s, when reform of Social Security and private pension laws was under discussion, the treatment of widows under military retirement and survivor benefit plans was also reviewed. The most controversial topic was the awarding of pension and survivor benefits to former spouses. Hearings held between 1980 and 1982 describe the sacrifices of military spouses and consider the claim of the divorced spouse to a portion of the serviceman's military retirement pay (3079-3081, 3083-3084). A good review of the treatment of women under military pension and annuity systems is provided in the 1988 hearing, *Military Widows' Issues* (3091). The evolution of retirement benefits for servicewomen, particularly for armed forces nurses, is detailed in Volume Two.

2789. U.S. Congress. House. Committee on Naval Affairs. *Ellen Dix, Harriet J. Kissam, Gratia Ray, Penelope Denny, Elizabeth Whitehead, Eleanor Wills, Charlotte M. Thorn, Susanna Lippencot, and Louisa Booth, Widows, and Joseph Sillcock, Guardian of the Infant Children of Caleb Crew, Claiming to be Placed on the Role of Navy Pensioners.* H. Rept. 103, 20th Cong., 2d sess., 1829. 2p. Serial 190. Report rejects these and future pension cases where the pension claim is based on death by disease or injury incurred during "the last war," and reviews the laws passed and then repealed governing such cases without discussing individual claims.

2790. U.S. Congress. House. Committee on Naval Affairs. *Pensions to Widows, &c., Letter from the Secretary of the Navy, upon the Subject of Pensions to Widows, Chargeable upon the Privateer Pension Fund.* H. Doc. 135, 22d Cong., 1st sess., 1832. 1p. Serial 219. Letter from the Secretary of the Navy indicates that, should Congress revive pensions to widows under the privateer pension fund, an appropriation would have to be made for relief of the fund.

2791. U.S. Congress. House. *Army Officers - Fort Monroe, Memorial [against a Bill to Provide for the Support of Widows and Orphans of Officers of the Army.]* H. Doc. 130, 23rd Cong., 1st sess., 1834. 3p. Serial 256. Petition against a bill to provide for a compulsory deduction from the pay of officers and cadets of the Army to create a survivor benefit fund argues that the proposal is unfair and unfeasible.

2792. U.S. Congress. House. *Army-Officers of the United States, Remonstrance [against a Bill to Provide for the Support of the Widows and Orphans of Such Officers of the Army as May Die while in the Service of the United States]* H. Doc. 96, 23rd Cong., 1st sess., 1834. 2p. Serial 256. Officers state objections to a proposed plan to deduct a small percentage of the pay of officers and cadets in order to create a fund from which survivor benefits would be paid.

2793. U.S. Congress. House. *Officers, Fort Dearborn, Illinois; Petition against Bill to Provide for Widows of Officers, &c.* H. Doc. 205, 23rd Cong., 1st sess., 1834. 1p. Serial 257. Petition argues against the imposition of a tax on Army officers to be used for the creation of a widows' pension fund.

2794. U.S. Congress. Senate. *Memorial of Sundry Officers of the Army and Military Academy, Remonstrating against the Passage of the "Bill to provide for the support of the widows and orphans of such officers of the Army as die while in the service of the United States."* S. Doc. 74, 23rd Cong., 1st sess., 1834. 12p. Serial 239. Argument against a plan to impose a tax on Army officers to create an annuity fund for widows and orphans and retirement fund for officers is based on demonstrations that the fund plan is impracticable and that the concept of compulsory contributions is unacceptable.

2795. U.S. Congress. House. Committee on Naval Affairs. *Arrears of Naval Pensions, Report.* H. Rept. 129, 23rd Cong., 2d sess., 1835. 2p. Serial 276. History of the Navy pension fund and of its extension to widows of those killed in the line of duty is included in this report. The report suggests that the primary purpose of the fund is for officers and seamen disabled in the line of duty and that extension of the fund to other classes, i.e. widows, would endanger the fund.

2796. U.S. Congress. House. Committee of Claims. *Major Dade, et al. Pensions to Widows and Children, Report to Accompany H.R. 426.* H. Rept. 415, 34th Cong., 1st sess., 1836. 4p. Serial 294. Report reviews past legislation granting survivor benefits to widows and children of officers killed in the line of duty and recommends that the policy of survivor benefits be extended on a equal basis to all military units.

2797. U.S. Congress. House. Committee on Revolutionary Pensions. *Amend Acts Allowing Pensions to Widows, to Accompany Bill H.R. No. 133.* H. Rept. 123, 26th Cong., 1st sess., 1840. 1p. Serial 370. An act to amend the pension act of 7 July 1838 allowing the widow of an officer to receive a pension, even if she later remarried, as long as she was a widow at the time she applied for the pension is favorably reported.

2798. U.S. Congress. House. *Resolutions of the Legislature of the State of Vermont for Continuing for Five Years the Pensions to Widows.* H. Doc. 34, 27th Cong., 3rd sess., 1842. 1p. Serial 420. Resolution requests Vermont's congressmen to use their influence to pass legislation continuing pensions to widows of Revolutionary War soldiers married prior to January 1794.

2799. U.S. Congress. House. Committee on Revolutionary Pensions. *Amend Acts Allowing Pensions to Widows, Report to Accompany Bill H.R. No. 132.* H. Rept. 86, 27th Cong., 2d sess., 1842. 1p. Serial 407. Reports a bill extending the provision of the act of July 7, 1838 granting Revolutionary War widows' pensions and inserting a clause removing a restriction barring pensions to remarried widows.

2800. U.S. Congress. Senate. Committee on Pensions. *[Petitions of "The Widow of William Davis," "Elizabeth Norwood," and "Jane Burgress," Sundry Widows of Revolutionary Soldiers - "the Widow of John Phillips," "Ester Town," and "the Widow of Buckminster White" - All Praying for Renewal of the Pensions Granted by the July 7, 1838...]* S. Doc. 354, 27th Cong., 2d sess., 1842. 1p. Serial 399. Committee expresses the opinion that the act of July 7, 1832, granting a pension for five years to "all widows of Revolutionary soldiers who were married before the year 1794, when the soldier, if alive, would have been entitled to a pension under previous law", went too far and that, given the current state of the Treasury, there was no cause to revive it.

2801. U.S. Congress. House. *Pensions to Widows of Revolutionary Officers and Soldiers; Resolution of the Legislature of Pennsylvania, in Relation to the Widows of Revolutionary Officers and Soldiers.* H. Doc. 164, 27th Cong., 3rd sess., 1843. 1p. Serial 422. Resolution of the Pennsylvania legislature instructs the State's congressmen to work for the extension of the law of 1838 granting Revolutionary War widows' pensions.

2802. U.S. Congress. House. Committee on Revolutionary Pensions. *Pensions to Widows of Revolutionary Soldiers, to Accompany Bill H.R. No. 655.* H. Rept. 32, 27th Cong., 3rd sess., 1843. 3p. Serial 426. Explains the situation of the widow married to a solder at the time of the Revolutionary War and of the widow married to the soldier after the war in relation to the pension laws. Equalization of benefits is recommended.

2803. U.S. Congress. Senate. *Petition of Citizens of Baltimore, Maryland, for a Renewal of the Act Granting Pensions to the Widows and Children of Deceased Naval Officers and Seamen.* S. Doc. 32, 28th Cong., 1st sess., 1844. 2p. Serial 432. Protest over changes in the Navy pension laws, which the memorialist claim struck widows and orphans from the pension rolls while high ranking officers collected disability pensions, criticizes the granting of back pensions as endangering the fund.

2804. U.S. Congress. Senate. *Resolution of the General Assembly of Pennsylvania, on the Subject of Granting Pensions to the Widows of Revolutionary Soldiers.* S. Doc. 195, 28th Cong., 1st sess., 1844. 1p. Serial 434. Resolution of the General Assembly of Pennsylvania directs the congressmen of that state to work toward the amendment and extension of legislation granting half-pay pensions to widows of Revolutionary War soldiers.

2805. U.S. Congress. Senate. Committee on Naval Affairs. *Report to Accompany Bill S. 109 [Petitions of Sundry Widows.]* S. Doc. 184, 28th Cong., 1st sess., 1844. 3p. Serial 434. Report on a bill extending widows' pension programs discusses the classes of military widows brought under pension laws since 1813 and the effect of these changes on the pension fund. Recommends continued pensions to widows of officers and seamen who died in the line of duty or from service-related disease or injury and the exclusion of widows of men who died while in the service but whose death was non-service connected.

2806. U. S. Congress. Senate. *Petition of Officers of the United State Army in Mexico, Praying an Amendment of the Pension Law for Widows and Orphans of Officers and Soldiers of the Army.* S. Misc. Doc. 12, 30th Cong., 1st sess., 1847. 6p. Serial 511. Petition of Army officers serving in Mexico requests Congress to pass legislation granting lifetime pensions to widows of soldiers killed in the line of duty.

2807. U. S. Congress. House. *Widows and Orphans of Soldiers Who Have Been Killed, &c., in the Mexican War.* H. Rept. 796, 30th Cong., 1st sess., 1848. 4p. Serial 527. Report on a bill to provide full pay to widows, orphans, and dependent parents of soldiers killed in the war with Mexico describes the bill as small repayment for the service rendered.

2808. U. S. Congress. House. *Widows of Revolutionary Officers and Soldiers; Resolutions of the Legislature of New York, in Relation to Extending the Pension Laws by Which Widows of Revolutionary Officers and Soldiers Are Entitled to Pensions.* H. Misc. Doc. 46, 30th Cong., 1st sess., 1848. 1p. Serial 523.

2809. U. S. Congress. House. *Widows, Orphans, &c., of Persons Who Have Served in the Mexico War, Memorial of the Legislature of Alabama, Relative to the Reversion of the Bounty Land and Pay for Services of Deceased Soldiers of the Mexican War.* H. Misc. Doc. 62, 30th Cong., 1st sess., 1848. 2p. Serial 523. Memorial asks that the widows and orphans of Mexican War soldiers be able to claim money or lands due them from the government without administration on their estates.

2810. U.S. Congress. House. Committee on Naval Affairs. *Widows and Orphans of Officers and Seamen of the United States Navy, to Accompany H.R. No. 375.* H. Rept. 444, 30th Cong., 1st sess., 1848. 2p. Serial 525. Report recommends continuing widow and orphan pensions for survivors of naval personnel.

2811. U.S. Congress. House. Committee on Revolutionary Pensions. *Widows of the Officers and Soldiers of the Revolutionary War Who Were Married Subsequent to January 1, 1794.* H. Rept. 295, 30th Cong., 1st sess., 1848. 9p. Serial 525. Unfavorable report with accompanying minority report discusses the justification for the delimiting marriage date of January 1, 1794. Provides summary statistics by state on the number of pensions by authorizing act.

2812. U.S. Congress. Senate. *Resolution of the Legislature of New York, in Relation to the Pensions of Widows and Orphans Who Fall in Battle or Die of Wounds Received.* S. Misc. Doc. 119, 30th Cong., 1st sess., 1848. 1p. Serial 511. Resolution of the legislature of New York instructs the state's congressmen use their influence to gain passage of legislation granting pensions to widows and orphans of officers and soldiers who died in the line of duty equal to the full pay of the officer or soldier.

2813. U.S. Congress. House. Committee on Revolutionary Pensions. *Citizens of Essex County, Massachusetts, Report.* H. Rept. 33, 30th Cong., 2d sess., 1849. 1p. Serial 545. Committee report rejects the memorial of the citizens of Essex County, Mass. requesting congress to amend the Revolutionary War widows' pensions laws relative to marriage limitations. The report does not reprint the memorial, however, it appears that the subject was the delimiting marriage date.

2814. U.S. Congress. House. Committee on Revolutionary Pensions. *Pensions - Widows' and Orphans', Report.* H. Rept. 265, 31st Cong., 1st sess., 1850. 2p. Serial 584. The committee rejects a resolution granting two years of pension to certain widows for the period for March 4, 1841 to March 4, 1843. The history of widows' pensions which created the gap in payments which the resolution sought to fill is presented.

2815. U. S. Congress. Senate. *Report of the Secretary of the Interior, Communicating the Report of the Commission of Pensions, with Lists Required by the Provisions of the Act of July 10, 1832, for the Regulation of the Navy and Privateer and Navy Hospital Funds.* S. Ex. Doc. 3, 31st Cong., 2d sess., 1850. 27p. Serial 588. List of persons on the Navy pension rolls includes name of widow, husbands' name and rank, monthly allowance, and date pension commenced.

2816. U. S. Congress. Senate. *Report of the Secretary of the Interior with a Letter from the Commissioner of Pensions, Transmitting an Alphabetical List of Navy Invalid Pensions, Complete to November 4, 1851.* S. Ex. Doc. 2, 32rd Cong., 1st sess., 1851. 30p. Serial 614. List of Navy pensioners and widows receiving pensions details rank, date of commencement of pension, and monthly pension granted.

2817. U. S. Congress. Senate. Committee on Pensions. *Report to Accompany Bill S. No. 158 [for the Relief of Certain Surviving Widows of Officers and Soldiers of the Revolutionary War].* S. Rept. 290, 31st Cong., 2d sess., 1851. 1p. Serial 593. Rejects a bill to provide pensions to widows of Revolutionary War officers and soldier regardless of marriage date.

2818. U.S. Congress. House. *Resolutions of the Legislature of Massachusetts in Favor of Extending the Bounty of Land and Pensions Laws to the Widows of All Officers, Soldiers, and Sailors, Who Served in the War of 1812.* H. Misc. Doc. 75, 33rd Cong., 1st sess., 1854. 1p. Serial 741.

2819. U.S. Congress. House. Committee on Invalid Pensions. *Widows' Pensions, Report to Accompany Bill H.R. No. 167.* H. Rept. 101, 33rd Cong., 1st sess., 1854. 1p. Serial 742. Favorable report on a bill relating to the starting date of pensions to certain widows.

2820. U. S. Congress. Senate. *Report of the Secretary of the Interior Communicating a List of Rejected Applications for Pensions and Recommending that the Act of February 3, 1853, to Continue Half-Pay to Widows and Orphans, be Amended.* S. Ex. Doc. 21, 33rd Cong., 1st sess., 1854. 3p. Serial 694. Lists widows of Revolutionary War naval officers who should be granted pensions, but who are not provided for under existing law. Report is also reprinted in Senate Report 285 (2822).

2821. U. S. Congress. Senate. Committee on Pensions. *[Petitions of Widows of Officers of the Army Who Have Died in the Service Since the War with Mexico, Praying to Be Allowed Half-Pay for Five Years].* S. Rept. 320, 33rd Cong., 1st sess., 1854. 3p. Serial 707. Reports a bill equalizing benefits to widows of men in the Army and Navy, specifically providing survivor benefits in the case of death while in the service during peacetime.

2822. U. S. Congress. Senate. Committee on Pensions. *[Recommending That the Act of February 3, 1853, "To continue half-pay to certain widows and Orphans," Be Amended] Report to Accompany Bill S. 383.* S. Rept. 285, 33rd Cong., 1st sess., 1854. 3p. Serial 707. Favorable report on amending the Act of February 3, 1853, "To continue half-pay to certain widows and Orphans," in order to provide for survivors of Revolutionary War

Naval officers includes a list of widows whose applications have been rejected due to an oversight in the original legislation.

2823. U.S. Congress. House. *Pensions to Soldiers and Widows, Resolutions of the Legislature of New York, in Relation to Granting Pensions to Soldiers of the Indian Wars of 1791-2-4 and 5, and to the Widows of the Deceased Soldiers of Those Wars.* H. Misc. Doc. 24, 33rd Cong., 2d sess, 1855. 1p. Serial 807.

2824. U.S. Congress. Senate. Committee on Pensions. *[Pensions of Mrs. J. Josephine McClelland, Mrs. Mary A. M. Jones, Mrs. Irene G. Searritt, and Mrs. Francis M. Webster, Widows of Officers of the Army, Praying to Be Allowed Pensions].* S. Rept. 453, 33rd Cong., 2d sess., 1855. 3p. Serial 775. Report reiterates views stated in S. Rept. 320 regarding granting of pensions to widows of Army officers who die in the service although not during wartime. Reprints S. Rept. 320 (2821) and urges the speedy passage of that bill.

2825. U.S. Congress. House. Committee on Private Land Claims. *Widows and Children of Soldiers Who Have Received Bounty Lands, Report to Accompany H.R. No. 351.* H. Rept. 121, 34th Cong., 1st sess., 1856. 1p. Serial 868. Reports a bill extending to widows and children the same privileges as granted to soldiers in relation to bounty lands.

2826. U.S. Congress. Senate. *Report of the Secretary of the Interior, in Compliance with a Resolution of the Senate of August 30, 1856, Calling for Information Respecting the Amount Necessary to Pay the Allowances Proposed to be Made by the Bill for the Settlement of Claims of Officers of the Revolution, and the Widows and Orphans of Those who Died in Service.* S. Ex. Doc. 2, 34th Cong., 3rd sess., 1856. 7p. Serial 874.

2827. U.S. Congress. Senate. Committee on Pensions. *[Petitions of Catherine Warner, Martha Morris, and Jane Stanbrough, Widows of Soldiers of the Revolution, Praying that the Act of February 3, 1853, may be so Amended as to Make Pensions Paid to Widows of Revolutionary Soldiers under it Date Back, as Provided in the Act of July 29, 1848].* S. Rept. 68, 34th Cong., 1st sess., 1856. 1p. Serial 836. Committee recommends that the petition be denied stating that it would set a precedent "for entire change in the policy of the legislation in regard to widows of Revolutionary soldiers."

2828. U.S. Congress. Senate. Committee on Revolutionary Claims. *Report to Accompany Bill S. 109 [for the Relief of the Officers of the Revolutionary Army, Their Widows and Orphans].* S. Rept. 7, 34th Cong., 1st sess., 1856. 4p. Serial 836. Reports a bill granting half-pay for life to Revolutionary Army officers, widows, and lineal descendants and the payment of seven years half-pay to the widows of officers who died in the service during the war.

2829. U.S. Congress. Senate. *Report of the Secretary of the Interior, Communicating, in Compliance with a Resolution of the 18th Instant, Information Respecting the Widows Pensions, under the Second Section of the Act of February 3, 1853.* S. Ex. Doc. 63, 34th Cong., 3rd sess., 1857. 7p. Serial 881. Report provides some background on widows' pension legislation provisions in addition to an accounting of the number of widows on the pension rolls and the cost of such pensions.

2830. U.S. Congress. House. *Resolutions of the Legislature of the State of New York, in Relation to the Claims of Officers of the Revolutionary Army, Their Widows and Orphans.* H. Misc. Doc. 111, 35th Cong., 1st sess., 1858. 2p. Serial 963.

2831.   U.S. Congress. House. Committee on Invalid Pensions. *Pensions for Certain Widows and Orphans, to Accompany H.R. No. 517.* H.Rept. 312, 35th Cong., 1st sess., 1858. 1p. Serial 965.

2832.   U.S. Congress. House. Committee on Revolutionary Pensions. *Pensions to Be Paid in Certain Cases to Widows and Children, Report to Accompany J.R. No. 23.* H. Rept. 241, 35th Cong., 1st sess., 1858. 4p. Serial 965. Report on the question of the ability of surviving widows or children to claim pensions amounts due but not paid at the time of the pensioners death reviews administrative practice and laws relating to the claiming of pensions.

2833.   U.S. Congress. Senate. *Resolution of the Legislature of the State of New York, Instructing the Senators and Requesting the Representatives of That State in Congress to Use Their Influence to Procure the Enactment of a Law Granting a Pension to the Surviving Soldiers of the Indian Wars from 1791 to 1795, and the Widows of the those Deceased.* S. Misc. Doc. 199, 35th Cong., 1st sess., 1858. 1p. Serial 936.

2834.   U. S. Congress. House. Committee on Claims. *Construction of Second Section of Act of February 3, 1853, "to Continue Half-Pay to Certain Widows and Orphans, to Accompany J.R. No. 33.* H. Rept. 399. 36th Cong., 1st sess., 1860. 2p. Serial 1069. Report supports the interpretation of the Act of February 3, 1853 as granting pensions to widows of Revolutionary War soldiers commencing on March 4, 1848, as is the case with other Revolutionary War widows.

2835.   U.S. Congress. House. Committee on Revolutionary Pensions. *Construction of Second Section of Act Continuing Half-Pay to Certain Widows and Orphans, to Accompany J.R. No. 18.* H. Rept. 127, 36th Cong., 1st sess., 1860. 1p. Serial 1067. Report recommends granting Revolutionary War widows married after 1800 arrears of pensions due them under the act of February 3, 1853.

2836.   U.S. Congress. House. Committee on Revolutionary Pensions. *Explanation of Act to Continue Half Pay to Certain Widows and Orphans, to Accompany Joint Resolution No. 14.* H. Rept. 486, 36th Cong., 1st sess., 1860. 1p. Serial 1069. Recommends a resolution affirming the Court of Claims construction of the Act of February 3, 1853, such that pension are granted from the 4th day of March 1848.

2837.   U.S. Congress. House. Committee on Revolutionary Pensions. *Revolutionary Soldiers-Widows and Children of, to Accompany Joint Resolution No. 38.* H. Rept. 485, 36th Cong., 1st sess., 1860. 5p. Serial 1069. Discussion of the right of the widow, children, or legal representative of a soldier who dies while in the process of making a claim for pension, to collect any amounts due at the time of the entitled person's death.

2838.   U.S. Congress. House. *Resolutions of the Legislature of Iowa, Relative to Pensions to Widows of Deceased Army Chaplains and Surgeons.* H. Misc. Doc. 34, 38th Cong., 1st sess., 1864. 1p. Serial 1200.

2839.   U.S. Congress. House. Committee on Invalid Pensions. *Widows of Persons in the Revenue Service.* H. Rept. 87, 38th Cong., 1st sess., 1864. 1p. Serial 1206. Negative report on extending pensions privileges to the Revenue Service.

2840.   U.S. Congress. Senate. *Resolutions of the Legislature of Iowa in Favor of an Amendment to the Pension Laws Allowing Pensions to Widows of Chaplains and Surgeons in the Army, Who Die or May Be Killed while in the Service of the United States.* S. Misc. Doc. 32, 38th Cong., 1st sess., 1864. 1p. Serial 1177.

2841. U.S. Congress. House. *Resolutions of the Legislature of Michigan in Favor of a Pension of Eight Dollars per Month to the Survivors of Soldiers in the War of 1812, and the Widows of Those Who are Dead, from April 1, 1865.* H. Misc. Doc. 35, 40th Cong., 1st sess., 1867. 1p. Serial 1312.

2842. U.S. Congress. House. *Pensions to Widows of Soldiers of the War of 1812: Resolutions of the Legislature of Tennessee in Favor of an Act Granting Pensions to the Widows of Soldiers of the War of 1812.* H. Misc. Doc. 17, 42d Cong., 2d sess., 1871. 1p. Serial 1524.

2843. U.S. Congress. Senate. *Resolution of the Legislature of Rhode Island in Favor of the Passage of an Act Granting Pensions to the Soldiers and Sailors, and Widows of Those Who Served in the War of 1812.* S. Misc. Doc. 50, 41st Cong., 3rd sess., 1871. 1p. Serial 1442.

2844. U.S. Congress. Senate. *Resolution of the Legislature of Indiana, in Favor of the Bill to Enable Honorably Discharged Soldiers and Sailors, Their Widows and Orphan Children, to Acquire Homesteads.* S. Misc. Doc. 23, 42d Cong., 3rd sess., 1873. 1p. Serial 1546.

2845. U.S. Congress. House. Committee on Invalid Pensions. *Continuation of Certain Pensions [to Widows and Children of Invalid Pensioners Pensioned for Total Disability, without Reference to Cause of Death].* H. Rept. 179, 43rd Cong., 2d sess., 1875. 1p. Serial 1659. Report rejects H.R. 1612, a bill which provides for the continuation of pensions to widows of invalid pensioners regardless of the relationship of the pensionable condition to cause of death.

2846. U.S. Congress. House. Committee on Military Affairs. *Protection of Army Officers' Widows, Orphans, and Heirs at Law, Report to Accompany Bill H.R. 4308.* H. Rept. 56, 43rd Cong., 2d sess., 1875. 1p. Serial 1656. Report on an annuity plan for Army officers to provide survivor benefits recommends passage.

2847. U.S. Congress. Senate. *Resolution of the Legislature of Michigan in Favor of Pensions to Soldiers (and the Widows of Soldiers) of the War of 1812 Who Were Honorably Discharged after Five Days' Service.* S. Misc. Doc. 8, 44th Cong., 1st sess., 1875. 1p. Serial 1665.

2848. U.S. Congress. Senate. Committee on Pensions. *Report to Accompany Bills S. 17 and S. 198 [Amending the Laws Granting Pensions to the Soldiers and Sailors of the War of 1812 and Their Widows].* S. Rept. 50, 45th Cong., 2d sess., 1878. 2p. Serial 1789. Reports bills lowering the length of service required for soldiers of the War of 1812 to collect a pension and granting pensions to widows married to the soldier after the war and who have remained unmarried after the death of the spouse.

2849. U.S. Congress. House. Committee on Revolutionary Pensions. *Pensions to Teamsters and Indians Who Were in the Service of the United States in the War of 1812, and to Widows Who Remarried, Report to Accompany Bill H.R. 4312.* H. Rept. 264, 45th Cong., 2d sess., 1879. 2p. Serial 1867. Reports a bill which would, among other things, restore pensions to widows who remarried but then were widowed a second time.

2850. U.S. Congress. House. Committee on Invalid Pensions. *Arrears of Pensions to Widows and Heirs, Report to Accompany Bill H.R. 2949.* H. Rept. 488, 46th Cong., 2d sess., 1880. 1p. Serial 1935. Report on a bill to allow widows and heirs of disabled soldiers to collect pensions not paid to the disabled soldier during his lifetime is reported.

2851.   U.S. Congress. House. Committee on Pensions. *Pensions for Certain Soldiers' Widows, Report to Accompany H. Res 39.* H. Rept. 477, 46th Cong., 2d sess., 1880. 2p. Serial 1935. Report expresses the opinion that remarried widows can not be considered as deprived of support and therefore the government is not obligated to provide a pension.

2852.   U.S. Congress. House. Committee on Invalid Pensions. *Section 4706 of the Revised Statutes of the United States, Report to Accompany Bill H.R. 7055.* H. Rept. 174, 46th Cong., 3rd sess., 1881. 1p. Serial 1982. Favorable report on a bill to allow payment of pensions to the children of a soldier in cases where the widow is ineligible, i.e. the children's stepmother.

2853.   U.S. Congress. House. Committee on Invalid Pensions. *Pensions to Widows and Children, Report to Accompany Bill H.R. 6229.* H. Rept. 1342, 47th Cong., 1st sess., 1882. 1p. See 2852 for abstract.

2854.   U.S. Congress. House. Committee on Pensions, Bounty, and Back Pay. *Amendment of Section 4702, Title 57, Revised Statutes, Report to Accompany Bill H. R. 3919.* H. Rept. 1780, 47th Cong., 1st sess., 1882. 1p. Serial 2070. Favorable report on a bill allowing children to draw the pension on the remarriage of an eligible widow also comments on pensions to widows in notorious adulterous cohabitation.

2855.   U.S. Congress. House. Select Committee on the Payment of Pensions, Bounty, and Back Pay. *To Amend Section 4702 of the Revised Statutes in Relation to Pensions, Report to Accompany Bill H. R. 1739.* H. Rept. 1111, 47th Cong., 1st sess., 1882. 1p. Serial 2068. Unfavorable report on a bill making minor changes in the date of pension payment to eligible children upon the remarriage of the widow.

2856.   U.S. Congress. Senate. *Letter from the Second Auditor of the Treasury Relative to Changes Needed in Existing Laws to Enable the Widows and Heirs of Deceased Soldiers to Receive the Benefits of Bounties Due to Said Soldiers while Living, and Remaining Unpaid at the Time of Decease.* S. Misc. Doc. 51, 47th Cong., 1st sess., 1882. 2p. Serial 1993. The point at issue was the payment of enlistment bounties to the widows and heirs of deceased black soldiers who were initially deprived bounty and whose claims could not be reopened unless the law was changed.

2857.   U.S. Congress. House. Committee on Invalid Pensions. *Increase of Pensions of Widows and Dependent Relatives of Deceased Soldiers and Sailors, Report to Accompany Bill H.R. 4009.* H. Rept. 605, 48th Cong., 1st sess., 1884. 3p. Serial 2254.

2858.   U.S. Congress. House. Committee on Invalid Pensions. *Pensions for Disabled Soldiers and Widows of Soldiers, Report to Accompany Bill H.R. 6866.* H. Rept. 1438, part 1, 48th Cong., 1st sess., 1884. 3p. Serial 2257. Reports a bill providing disability pensions and widows' pensions to soldiers held prisoner at Andersonville and other Confederate military prisons.

2859.   U.S. Congress. Senate. *Letter from the Commissioner of Pensions Transmitting a List of All Widows of Officers of High Rank, Army or Navy, Whose Pensions Have Been Fixed, or Increased by Special Acts of Congress.* S. Misc. Doc. 42, 48th Cong., 1st sess., 1884. 7p. Serial 2171.

2860.   U.S. Congress. Senate. *[Statement, by Hon. W.W. Dudley, Commissioner of Pensions, Showing the Names of the Widows of Officers in the Army and Navy Who Have Been Pensioned at the Rate of $50 per Month and Over.]* S. Misc. Doc. 93, 48th Cong., 1st sess., 1884. 3p. Serial 2171.

2861. U.S. Congress. House. Committee on Invalid Pensions. *Increase of Pensions of Widows and Dependent Relatives, Report to Accompany Bill H.R. 545.* H. Rept. 48, 49th Cong., 1st sess., 1886. 3p. Serial 2435.

2862. U.S. Congress. Senate. Committee on Pensions. *Report to Accompany Bill H.R. 545 [to Increase the Pensions to Widows and Dependent Relatives of Deceased Soldiers and Sailors].* S. Rept. 170, 49th Cong., 1st sess., 1886. 1p. Serial 2358.

2863. U.S. Congress. Senate. Committee on Military Affairs. *Report to Accompany Bill S. 2116 [to Provide Aid to State Homes for the Support of Soldiers and Sailors of the United States and Their Widows and Orphans].* S. Rept. 754, 50th Cong., 1st sess., 1888. 13p. Serial 2523. The number of soldiers and sailors in homes and requesting entrance into homes in the U.S. along with some basic data on the number of dependents cared for is given in this report which recommends dropping widows and orphans from the bill.

2864. U.S. Congress. Senate. Committee on Pensions. *Report to Accompany Bill S. 389 [Granting Pensions to Soldiers, and Sailors Incapacitated for Labor, and Providing Pensions to Widows, Minor Children, and Dependent Parents].* S. Rept. 90, 51st Cong., 1st sess., 1890. 2p. Serial 2703.

2865. U.S. Congress. Senate. Committee on Pensions. *Report to Accompany S. 389, with the Amendments of the House of Representatives [Granting Pensions to Soldiers and Sailors Who Are Incapacitated for the Performance of Labor, and Providing for Pension to Their Widows, Minor Children, and Dependent Parents].* S. Rept. 989, 51st Cong., 1st sess., 1890. 40p. Serial 2709. Detailed analysis of the differences between the Senate and House versions of a Civil War disability pension bill (S. 389 and H.R. 8297) reprints H. Rept. 1160, S. 389 and the amended House bill. Major differences exist in eligibility requirements between the bills.

2866. U.S. Congress. House. Committee on Invalid Pensions. *Widows of Union Soldiers and Sailors, Report to Accompany H.R. 7217.* H. Rept. 2068, 52d Cong., 1st sess., 1892. 1p. Serial 3051. Reports a bill permitting formerly eligible widows who remarried to resume their pensions if again widowed, provided that they are dependent on their own labor for support.

2867. U.S. Congress. House. Committee on Pensions. *Amendment to Pensions Law, Report to Accompany H.R. 5951 [to Amend Laws Relative to Widows and Children of Soldiers Who Died in Service].* H. Rept. 500, 52d Cong., 1st sess., 1892. 1p. Serial 3043. The bill reported corrects wording in the original pension laws which effectively excluded widows of soldiers who died before being discharged.

2868. U.S. Congress. House. Committee on Invalid Pensions. *Pensions to Widows in Certain Cases, Report to Accompany H.R. 7440.* H. Rept. 1114, 53rd Cong., 2d sess., 1894. 2p. Serial 3271. Reports a bill providing pensions to formerly eligible widows upon the death or divorce from a second husband. The report succinctly states the condition a widow must meet to receive a pension in such instances.

2869. U.S. Congress. House. Committee on Invalid Pensions. *To Restore the Pensions of Widows in Certain Cases, Report to Accompany H.R. 4175.* H. Rept. 1771, 54th Cong., 1st sess., 1896. 1p. Serial 3463. The amended bill reported restores a pension to the remarried widow of a soldier if she married the soldier during his wartime service.

2870. U.S. Congress. House. Committee on Invalid Pensions. *Widows of Soldiers and Sailors, Report to Accompany H.R. 5287.* H. Rept. 2125, 54th Cong., 1st sess., 1896. 1p. Serial

3464. Reports a bill allowing the widow of a Civil War soldier married to the soldier during his service, to collect the pension without supplying proof of service-related death.

2871.   U.S. Congress. Senate. *Letter from the Commissioner of Pensions, Transmitting a List, Compiled from the Statutes at Large of the United States, Showing the Names of Widows of Colonels, Brevet Brigadier-Generals, and Brigadier-Generals of the Volunteers Who are in Receipt of Pensions under Special Acts.* S. Doc. 110, 54th Cong., 1st sess., 1896. 3p. Serial 3350. List of widows of high-ranking officers receiving pensions lists name of widow, name and rank of soldier, date of act, and rate of pension in chart form.

2872.   U.S. Congress. Senate. Committee on Pensions. *Report to Accompany S. 2647 [to Prohibit Pensioning of Widows Married after Date of Pension Act].* S. Rept. 453, 55th Cong., 2d sess., 1898. 1p. Serial 3620. Reports a bill aimed at curbing the payment of pensions to widows who married a solder long after the close of the war.

2873.   U.S. Congress. Senate. *Pensions to Commissioned Officers, etc.: Statement Showing Special Acts of Congress Passed Since March 4, 1861, Granting Pensions to Commissioned Officers, and Widows of Commissioned Officers, of the United States Army, Navy, and Marine Corps.* S. Doc. 108, 56th Cong., 1st sess., 1899. 28p. Serial 3851. List of commissioned officers and widows of commissioned officers drawing pensions gives information on the officer's rank, date of pension, and pension rate under special act of Congress and under general law.

2874.   U.S. Congress. House. Committee on Invalid Pensions. *Amendments to the Pension Laws, Report to Accompany S. 1477.* H. Rept. 1193, 56th Cong., 1st sess., 1900. 8p. Serial 4025. Favorable report on a bill to amend the Civil War pension laws includes a separate section on widows' income which discusses raising the amount of income a widow may have before she is denied a pension. The basic functioning of the current law for widows' pensions is reviewed.

2875.   U.S. Congress. House. Committee on Invalid Pensions. *Restoring Certain Widows to the Pension Roll, Report to Accompany H.R. 9886.* H. Rept. 1087, 56th Cong., 1st sess., 1900. 2p. Serial 4025. Committee report recommending passage of a bill to restore to the pension rolls widows who remarried upon the death of or divorce from the second husband includes a little poem on the soldier's wife.

2876.   U.S. Congress. Senate. Committee on Pensions. *Restoration of Pensions to Widows in Certain Cases, Report to Accompany S. 2345.* S. Rept. 436, 56th Cong., 1st sess., 1900. 1p. Serial 3887. Reports favorably on a bill to restore pensions to certain widows who lost their pension due to remarriage but who have since been widowed again and who are dependent on their own labor for support.

2877.   U.S. Congress. House. Committee on Invalid Pensions. *Pensions to Remarried Widows, to Accompany H.R. 12141.* H. Rept. 1526, 57th Cong., 1st sess., 1902. 3p. Serial 4404. Recommendation of the committee expands the coverage of the law providing for the restoration of pensions to remarried widows upon the death or divorce from their second husband to include widows of militiamen and other non-enlisted personnel serving with a military unit.

2878.   U.S. Congress. Senate. Committee on Pensions. *Pensions to Remarried Widows, Report to Accompany H.R. 12141.* S. Rept. 2579, 57th Cong., 2d sess., 1903. 2p. Serial 4411. See 2877 for abstract.

2879.   U.S. Congress. House. *To Increase Pension of Widows of Soldiers and Sailors of Civil War, War with Mexico, and Various Indian Wars, etc., Conference Report to Accompany*

H.R. 15653. H. Rept. 1436, 60th Cong., 1st sess., 1908. 2p. Serial 5226. Conference report works out the difference between the House bill and the Senate amendments relative to eligibility of Spanish War widows and widows of the regular establishment as to date of marriage.

2880. U.S. Congress. House. Committee on Invalid Pensions. *To Increase Pensions to Widows, etc., of Soldiers and Sailors of Civil War, War with Mexico, Indian Wars, etc., Report to Accompany H.R. 15653.* H. Rept. 531, 60th Cong., 1st sess., 1908. 3p. Serial 5225. Favorable report on a bill increasing widows' pensions and removing the dependency requirement for widows summarizes the cost of the bill.

2881. U.S. Congress. Senate. Committee on Pensions. *To Increase Pensions of Widows of Soldiers and Sailors of Civil War, War with Mexico, and Various Indian Wars, etc., Report to Accompany H.R. 15653.* S. Rept. 322, 60th Cong., 1st sess., 1908. 3p. Serial 5218. Report examines the provisions of a bill to increase widows' pensions with specific emphasis on issues such as limiting marriage date, the payment of pensions to widows who are relatively young women, and the increased cost of the various provisions.

2882. U.S. Congress. Senate. Committee on Pensions. *Increase of Pensions of Widows and Minor Children of Deceased Soldiers and Sailors of Civil War, Report to Accompany S. 7960.* S. Rept. 847, 60th Cong., 2d sess., 1909. 2p. Serial 5380. Favorable report examines the date of marriage issue for widows' pension eligibility and recommends that the arbitrary marriage date of June 27, 1890 be eliminated.

2883. U.S. Congress. Senate. Committee on Pensions. *Pensions to Widows of Soldiers and Sailors of the Late Civil War Married Subsequent to June 27, 1890, etc., Report to Accompany S. 6058.* S. Rept. 225, 61st Cong., 2d sess., 1910. 2p. Serial 5582. Report on a bill to broaden the eligibility for Civil War widows' pensions describes the June 27, 1890 marriage date limitation as arbitrary and recommends pensions to all Civil War soldiers' widows as long as they were married for three years prior to the soldier's death.

2884. U.S. Congress. House. Committee on Pensions. *Pensions to Widows and Minor Children of Officers and Enlisted Men Who Served in the War with Spain and Philippine Insurrection, Report to Accompany H.R. 17470.* H. Rept. 838, 62d Cong., 2d sess., 1912. 3p. Serial 6132. Reports a bill providing pensions to widows and dependent children of veterans of the War with Spain and the Philippine Insurrection provided that such widows are without means of support.

2885. U.S. Congress. House. Committee on Pensions. *Proceedings Hearing under Consideration H.R. 17470, Introduced by Mr. Thomas S. Crages, Entitled "A Bill to Pension Widow and Minor Children of Any Officer or Enlisted Man Who Served in the War with Spain or Philippine Insurrection."* 62d Cong., 2d sess., 4 Apr. 1912. 25p. Y4.P38/1:Sp2. Issues of property qualifications and dependency, determination of service-related cause of death, date of marriage, and the case of second or third wives are explored as they relate to survivor benefits.

2886. U.S. Congress. Senate. Committee on Pensions. *Increasing Pensions of Widows of the Civil War, Report to Accompany S. 6400.* S. Rept. 1337, 62d Cong., 3rd sess., 1913. 2p. Serial 6330. Recommends passage of a bill granting higher pensions to widows of Civil War veterans who were married to the soldier during his enlistment.

2887. U.S. Congress. Senate. Committee on Pensions. *Pensions to Widows and Minor Children of Officers and Enlisted Men Who Served in the War with Spain and Philippine Insurrection, Report to Accompany H.R. 17470.* S. Rept. 1325, 62d Cong., 3rd sess., 1913. 4p. Serial 6330. See 2884 for abstract.

2888.   U.S. Congress. Senate. Committee on Pensions. *Widows of Solders of War with Spain, Hearing on H.R. 17470.* 62d Cong., 3rd sess., 20 Jan. 1913. 35p. Y4.P38/2:W63. Hearing on a bill to provide pensions to widows and minor children of veterans of the War with Spain or the Philippine Insurrection discusses property qualifications and the date of marriage to the veteran. Discouraging young women from marrying old veterans for their pensions is a common theme.

2889.   U.S. Congress. House. Committee on Pensions. *Pensions to Widows and Minor Children of Officers and Enlisted Men, War with Spain, Report to Accompany H.R. 13044.* H. Rept. 282, 63rd Cong., 2d sess., 1914. 6p. Serial 6558. Favorable report on providing pensions to destitute widows and children of veterans of the War with Spain and the Philippine Insurrection discusses the number of potential beneficiaries and the costs.

2890.   U.S. Congress. Senate. Committee on Pensions. *Pensions to Widows and Helpless Children of Officers and Enlisted Men, War with Spain, Report to Accompany H.R. 13044.* S. Rept. 551, 63rd Cong., 2d sess., 1914. 3p. Serial 6553. Report with amendments recommends passage of a bill pensioning widows and minor children of veterans of the War with Spain and the Philippine Insurrection and changing the marriage date provision relating to Civil War widows.

2891.   U.S. Congress. House. Committee on Invalid Pensions. *Increase of Pensions for Widows of Soldiers of the Civil War, Report to Accompany H.R. 11707.* H. Rept. 283, 64th Cong., 1st sess., 1916. 3p. Serial 6903. Reports a bill raising the pensions of Civil War widows married at the time of the war to $20 a month and increasing the pension of all Civil War widows to $20 upon attaining the age of 70. Provisions of the pension laws relating to remarriage and date of marriage are also changed.

2892.   U.S. Congress. House. Committee on Pensions. *Pensions to Widows and Minor Children of Officers and Enlisted Men Who Served during the War with Spain, Philippine Insurrection, or in China, Report to Accompany H.R. 54.* H. Rept. 59, 64th Cong., 1st sess., 1916. 8p. Serial 6903. Pension bill focuses on the equal treatment of veterans' widows regardless of the war. Reprinted in S. Rept. 285 (2894).

2893.   U.S. Congress. Senate. Committee on Pensions. *Pensions to Widows and Minor Children, Civil and Other Wars, Report to Accompany H.R. 11707.* S. Rept. 586, 64th Cong., 1st sess., 1916. 4p. Serial 6899. See 2891 for abstract.

2894.   U.S. Congress. Senate. Committee on Pensions. *Pensions to Widows and Minor Children of Officers and Enlisted Men Who Served during the War with Spain, Philippine Insurrection, or in China, Report to Accompany H.R. 54.* S. Rept. 285, 64th Cong., 1st sess., 1916. 6p. Serial 6897. Senate report recommends passage and reprints the House Report 59 (2892).

2895.   U.S. Congress. House. Committee on Invalid Pensions. *Proof of Widowhood in Pension Claims, Report to Accompany H.R. 20353.* H. Rept. 1333, 64th Cong., 2d sess., 1917. 1p. Serial 7110. Recommends passage of a bill to accept as proof of marriage for the purpose of widow's pension evidence that the woman cohabited with the soldier and was recognized as his wife for 20 years or more preceding his death. The bill was necessitated by inadequacies of early record keeping of marriages and divorces.

2896.   U.S. Congress. Senate. *Pensions to Commissioned Officers, etc., Army: Statement Showing Special Acts of Congress Passed Since Mar. 4, 1861, Granting Pensions to Commissioned Officers and Widows of Commissioned Officers, of Army, Navy and Marine Corps.* S. Doc. 702, 64th Cong., 2d sess., 1917. 34p. Serial 7126 List of pensions granted to officers and officers' widows by special act of Congress gives widow's name, officer's name and rank, monthly pension granted by special act, and the amount of the pension due under general laws.

2897. U.S. Congress. House. Committee on Invalid Pensions. *To Amend Chapter 470, Statutes at Large, Relating to Pensions, Report to Accompany H.R. 9093.* H. Rept. 254, 65th Cong., 2d sess., 1918. 2p. Serial 7307. The bill reported corrects inequities in pensions to Civil War widows married more than once since the death of her soldier husband.

2898. U.S. Congress. House. Committee on Pensions. *Pensions to Widows and Minor Children of Officers and Enlisted Men Who Served during the War with Spain, Philippine Insurrection, or in China, Report to Accompany S. 4444.* H. Rept. 675, 65th Cong., 2d sess., 1918. 7p. Serial 7308. Most of this report on a widow's pension bill is a reprint of S. Rept. 285, 64th Congress (2894) with the addition of correspondence from the National Headquarters United Spanish War Veterans on the number of needy widows who might benefit from the bill.

2899. U.S. Congress. Senate. Committee on Pensions. *Pensions to Widows and Minor Children of Officers and Enlisted Men Who Served during the War with Spain, Philippine Insurrection, or in China, Report to Accompany S. 4444.* S. Rept. 479, 65th Cong., 2d sess., 1918. 8p. Serial 7304. Favorable report on a pension bill for widows of veterans of the War with Spain, Philippine Insurrection, and Boxer Rebellion focuses on the number of widows eligible. Reprints S. Rept. 285, 64th Congress (2894).

2900. U.S. Congress. House. Committee on Invalid Pensions. *Widows' Pension Bill, Report to Accompany H.R. 6376.* H. Rept. 56, 66th Cong., 1st sess., 1919. 2p. Serial 7592. Recommends passage of a bill providing for the pensioning of Civil War veterans' widows remarried more than once since the soldier's death.

2901. U.S. Congress. House. Committee on the Public Lands. *Homestead Credit to Widows, Report to Accompany H.R. 5000.* H. Rept. 243, 66th Cong., 1st sess., 1919. 2p. Serial 7593. Reports a bill placing WWI veterans' widows on an equal basis with widows of the Civil War and the Spanish-American War in regard to application of the length of the husband's military service toward the homestead residence requirement.

2902. U.S. Congress. House. Committee on Invalid Pensions. *Proof of Widowhood in Claims for Pensions, Report to Accompany H.R. 11489.* H. Rept. 538, 66th Cong., 2d sess., 1920. 2p. Serial 7652. Favorable report on a bill to accept proof of cohabitation for at least seven years prior to the veteran's death as proof of marriage for the purpose of pensions discusses the burden of proof of legal marriage placed upon the widow under the existing rules.

2903. U.S. Congress. Senate. Committee on Pensions. *Revisions and Equalization of Rates of Pensions, Hearing on H.R. 9369.* 66th Cong., 2d sess., 10 Feb. 1920. 25p. Y4.P38/2:C49. Hearing on a bill to adjust pensions to veterans, widows and civilian nurses discusses widows briefly in relation to the question of remarriage after the veterans' death and the equalization of survivor benefit rates for the Spanish and Civil War veterans.

2904. U.S. Congress. House. Committee on Pensions. *Relief of the Widows of Certain Officers and Enlisted Men of the United States Navy, Hearings on H.R. 11335.* 67th Cong., 2d sess., 8 June 1922. 18p. Y4.P38/1:N22. Hearing considers the granting of pensions to widows and dependents of Navy men killed while testing the airship ZR-2 in England.

2905. U.S. Congress. Senate. Committee on Pensions. *Increase of Pensions for Soldiers and Sailors of the Civil and Mexican Wars, Hearing on S. 3275.* 67th Cong., 2d sess., 24 Mar. 1922. 18p. Y4.P38/2:C49/2. The main issue in this hearing on raising pensions of veterans and their widows is the extent of the practice of young women marrying veterans for their pensions. Evidence is presented refuting this contention. Testimony from Isabel Worrel Ball of the Women's Relief Corps presents one view of how the congressional obsession with young woman/elderly veteran marriages came about in the 1880's. The inclusion of a qualifying marriage date in the bill is portrayed as unfair but necessary for passage.

2906. U.S. Congress. Senate. Committee on the Public Lands. *Credit for Husbands' Military Service in Case of Homestead Entries by Widows, Report to Accompany H.R. 70.* S. Rept. 646, 67th Cong., 2d sess., 1922. 2p. Serial 7951.

2907. U.S. Congress. House. Committee on Military Affairs. *Authorizing Mothers of Deceased World War Veterans to Visit Graves in Europe, Report to Accompany H.R. 9538.* H. Rept. 909, 68th Cong., 1st sess., 1924. 12p. Serial 8229. Favorable report recommends providing mothers of WWI soldiers buried in Europe the opportunity to visit the graves, and details logistics and expenses.

2908. U.S. Congress. House. Committee on Military Affairs. *To Authorize Mothers of Deceased World War Veterans Buried in Europe to Visit the Graves, Hearings.* 68th Cong., 1st sess., 19 Feb. 1924. 26p. Y4.M59/1:M85. Hearing on a bill to organize and pay for trips to Europe for mothers of World War One casualties buried there presents patriotic and sentimental appeals and reviews costs and logistics of the proposed trips.

2909. U.S. Congress. House. Committee on Military Affairs. *To Authorize Mothers of Deceased World War Veterans Buried in Europe to Visit the Graves, Hearing, Supplemental Containing War Department Study of Proposed Legislation.* 68th Cong., 1st sess., 3 May 1924. 27-37pp. Y4.M59/1:M85/supp.

2910. U.S. Congress. House. Committee on Pensions. *War with Spain: Pensions to Certain Soldiers and Sailors, Widows, Minor Children, and Helpless Children of Soldiers and Sailors, Hearing on H.R. 98.* 69th Cong., 1st sess., 12 Jan. 1926. 33p. Y4.P38/1:Sp2/3. Points of discussion relating to widows' pensions include rates, proof of dependency and cost to a widow prosecuting a claim. Also, the date of marriage issue and discrepancies in this area between Civil War and Spanish War widow's eligibility is examined.

2911. U.S. Congress. House. Committee on Invalid Pensions. *Increase of Civil War Widows' Pensions, Report to Accompany H.R. 13450.* H. Rept. 1667, 69th Cong., 2d sess., 1927. 2p. Serial 8688. Report on a bill to increase the pensions of widows of Civil War veterans notes that the average age of the widows is 76. With the women dying at a rate of 2,000 a month the measure is viewed as a relatively short-term drain on the Treasury.

2912. U.S. Congress. Senate. Committee on Pensions. *Granting Increase of Pensions to Widows and Former Widows of Certain Soldiers, Sailors, and Marines of the Civil War, Report to Accompany S. 5443.* S. Rept. 1513, 69th Cong., 2d sess., 1927. 3p. Serial 8685.

2913. U.S. Congress. Senate. Committee on Pensions. *Granting Pensions and Increase of Pensions to Widows and Former Widows of Certain Soldiers, Sailors, and Marines of the Civil War, Report to Accompany H.R. 13450.* S. Rept. 1614, 69th Cong., 2d sess., 1927. 2p. Serial 8685. Committee reports favorably on a bill to raise the pensions of Civil War veteran's widows to $40 a month regardless of age.

2914. U.S. Congress. House. Committee on Invalid Pensions. *Increase of Civil War Widows' Pensions, Report to Accompany H.R. 10159.* H. Rept. 698, 70th Cong., 1st sess., 1928. 4p. Serial 8836. Favorable report on a bill raising the pensions of Civil War widows married to the veteran subsequent to his discharge is a response to some 3,400 private bills seeking such increase. The bill sets the age of 75 as a requirement for the increase. The minority report argues that the pensions rate should be raised to $50 a month instead of the $40 a month granted in the bill.

2915. U.S. Congress. House. Committee on Invalid Pensions. *Pensions and Increase of Pensions to Widows and Former Widows of Certain Soldiers, Sailors, and Marines of the Civil War, Conference Report to Accompany H.R. 10159.* H. Rept. 1661, 70th Cong., 1st sess., 1928. 1p. Serial 8838.

2916. U.S. Congress. House. Committee on Military Affairs. *Enabling Mothers and Unmarried Widows of Deceased Soldiers, Sailors, and Marines to Visit European Cemeteries, Report to Accompany H.R. 5494.* H. Rept. 543, 70th Cong., 1st sess., 1928. 4p. Serial 8835. Reports legislation to organize and fund pilgrimages of mothers and unmarried widows of personnel killed in WWI to the European cemeteries in which they were buried.

2917. U.S. Congress. House. Committee on Military Affairs. *To Authorize Mothers and Unmarried Widows of Deceased World War Veterans Buried in Europe to Visit the Graves, Hearing.* 70th Cong., 1st sess., 27 Jan. 1928. 30p. Y4.M59/1:M85/2. Hearing looks primarily at the organization and cost of government financed trips to Europe for mothers and unmarried widows of World War One casualties buried there. The role the National Red Cross would play in organizing the trips is discussed.

2918. U.S. Congress. Senate. Committee on Military Affairs. *To Authorize Mothers and Unremarried Widows of Deceased World War Veterans Buried in Europe to Visit Their Graves, Hearing on H.R. 5494.* 70th Cong., 1st sess., 14 May 1928. 29p. Y4.M59/2:M85/pt.1. Statements of several mothers of men killed in WWI support legislation to organize visits to graves of sons buried in Europe.

2919. U.S. Congress. Senate. Committee on Pensions. *Granting Pensions and Increase of Pensions to Widows and Former Widows of Certain Soldiers, Sailors, and Marines of the Civil War, and for Other Purposes, Report to Accompany S. 1939.* S. Rept. 139, 70th Cong., 1st sess., 1928. 1p. Serial 8829. Report recommends a bill to increase the pensions of Civil War widows who married the veteran after his discharge but prior to June 27, 1905 regardless of age.

2920. U.S. Congress. Senate. Committee on Pensions. *Granting Pensions and Increase of Pensions to Widows and Former Widows of Certain Soldiers, Sailors, and Marines of the Civil War, Report to Accompany H.R. 10159.* S. Rept. 832, 70th Cong., 1st sess., 1928. 1p. Serial 8830.

2921. U.S. Congress. Senate. Committee on Pensions and U.S. Congress. House. Committee on Invalid Pensions. *Increase of Pensions to Widows and Former Widows of Certain Soldiers, Sailors, and Marines of the Civil War, Joint Hearing on S. 1939.* 70th Cong., 1st sess., 18 Jan. 1928. 22p. Y4.P38/2:C49/3. Discussion on raising widows' pensions and on granting pensions to women who married a veteran after the Civil War argues the need to fix an eligibility date for marriages to prevent women from marrying elderly veterans for their pensions.

2922. U.S. Congress. House. Committee on Military Affairs. *To Authorize Mothers of Deceased World War Veterans Buried in Europe to Visit the Graves (Proposed Amendments to Law), Hearings.* 71st Cong., 2d sess., 17 Dec. 1929. 30p. Y4.M59/1:M85/3. Hearing examines proposed amendments to the act providing for mothers of veterans buried in Europe to visit the graves at government expense. Amendments eliminate the clause barring mothers who had already visited the graves, include mothers of those missing and presumed dead, and change the definition for women who stood in loco parentis to the veteran.

2923.   U.S. Congress. House. Committee on Printing. *Reprinting of House Document No. 140, Report to Accompany H. Con. Res. 15.* H. Rept. 87, 71st Cong., 2d sess., 1929. 1p. Serial 9194. Reports a resolution to reprint H. Doc 140 (2926), a list of the mothers and widows of WWI soldiers buried in Europe who were eligible for a government paid pilgrimage to visit the graves.

2924.   U.S. Congress. Senate. Subcommittee of the Committee on Military Affairs. *To Authorize Mothers and Unremarried Widows of Deceased World War Veterans Buried in Europe to Visit the Graves, Hearing on H.R. 5494.* 70th Cong., 2d sess., 12 Feb. 1929. 34p. Y4.M59/2:M85/pt.2. Continued hearing on financing visits of mothers and unremarried widows of servicemen killed in Europe to visit the graves focuses on cost and logistics of the trips.

2925.   U.S. Congress. House. *Mothers and Widows of Deceased Soldiers, Sailors, etc., to Visit Cemeteries in Europe, Conference Report to Accompany H.R. 4138.* H. Rept. 1337, 71st Cong., 2d sess., 1930. 3p. Serial 9192. Conference report on a bill redefining the eligibility of mothers and widows of deceased WWI servicemen who were buried in Europe to visit Europe at government expenses settles the question of whether relatives of those buries at sea or in unknown graves are eligible.

2926.   U.S. Congress. House. *Pilgrimage for the Mothers and Widows of Soldiers, Sailors, and Marines of the American Forces Now Interned in the Cemeteries of Europe as Provided by the Act of Congress of March 2, 1929: Letter from the Acting Secretary of War, Transmitting to Congress a Report of the Number of Mothers and Widows of the Deceased Soldiers, Sailors, and Marines of the American Forces Now Interned in the Cemeteries of Europe Who Desire to Make the Pilgrimage to These Cemeteries during the Year 1930 or Later, a List of Their Names and Addresses, and the Probable Cost.* H. Doc. 140, 71st Cong., 2d sess., 1930. 339p. Serial 9225. Lists by state women eligible for the pilgrimage giving names and addresses, relationship to the deceased, name, rank, and organization of the deceased, cemetery, and whether or not she desires the pilgrimage.

2927.   U.S. Congress. House. Committee on Invalid Pensions. *Increase of Pensions of Civil War Survivors and Widows, Report to Accompany H.R. 12013.* H. Rept. 1353, 71th Cong., 2d sess., 1930. 3p. Serial 9192. Reports a bill making changes in pension rates and eligibility of Civil War veterans and their widows. Under the bill the age for a widow to receive the $40 monthly allowance was lowered from 75 years to 70 years.

2928.   U.S. Congress. House. Committee on Invalid Pensions. *Original and Increase Pensions to Widows and Former Widows of Certain Soldiers, Sailors, and Marines of the Civil War, Also Increase to Certain Soldiers, Sailors, and Marines Now on the Pension Roll under the Provisions of the Maimed Veterans' Act of February 11, 1927, Hearing on H.R. 3239, H.R. 8765 and H.R. 9106 and Companion Bills.* 71st Cong., 2d sess., 11 Feb. 1930. 24p. Y4.In8/5:In2/4. Hearing on bills granting a pension of $50 a month to widows married to eligible veterans prior to enactment of this legislation, and whose marriage was not for the purpose of securing the pension, focuses on cost and savings as veterans and their widows die. The average age of veterans was 86 and the average age of widows was 75 at the time of the hearing.

2929.   U.S. Congress. House. Committee on Military Affairs. *Pilgrimage of Mother and Widows of Deceased Soldiers, Sailors, and Marines to Cemeteries in Europe, Report to Accompany H.R. 8527.* H. Rept. 538, 71st Cong., 2d sess., 1930. 6p. Serial 9191. Reports on a bill amending the act providing for a pilgrimage to Europe for mothers and widows of servicemen buried there. Explains the need to add coverage of expenses should a woman become ill or die while in Europe and addresses the administration of the trips.

2930. U.S. Congress. House. Committee on Military Affairs. *Pilgrimage of Mothers and Widows of Soldiers and Sailors in European Cemeteries, Report to Accompany H.R. 4138.* H. Rept. 571, 71st Cong., 2d sess., 1930. 5p. Serial 9191. The bill reported amends the act providing for a pilgrimage of mothers and widows of deceased servicemen buried in Europe to visit the graves at government expense. The report offers an amendment defining "mother" to include stepmother and women who stood in loco parentis for at least five years prior to the soldier's 18th birthday.

2931. U.S. Congress. House. Committee on Pensions. *Increase of Pensions to Widows, etc., of Soldiers and Sailors of the Regular Army and Navy, Report to Accompany S. 958.* H. Rept. 1586, 71st Cong., 2d sess., 1930. 8p. Serial 9193. Favorable report on a bill setting the eligibility requirements and rates for peace-time pensions in the case of service-related death or disability recommends widows' pension rates which are lower than those for war veterans' widows.

2932. U.S. Congress. Senate. Committee on Military Affairs. *Amend the Act Approved March 2, 1929, Authorizing Mothers and Widows of Deceased Soldier, Sailors, and Marines of American Forces Now Interned in Those Cemeteries of Europe to Make a Pilgrimage to Those Cemeteries, Report to Accompany S. 3062.* S. Rept. 95, 71st Cong., 2d sess., 1930. 2p. Serial 9185. Amendment to the law authorizing the pilgrimage of WWI widows and mothers of deceased Army personnel buried in Europe extends the length of time the women will be supported at government expenses while in Europe.

2933. U.S. Congress. Senate. Committee on Military Affairs. *Pilgrimage of Mothers and Widows of Deceased Soldiers, Sailors, and Marines to Cemeteries in Europe, Report to Accompany H.R. 8527.* S. Rept. 201, 71st Cong., 2d sess., 1930. 6p. Serial 9185. See 2929 for abstract.

2934. U.S. Congress. Senate. Committee on Military Affairs. *Pilgrimage of Mother and Widows of Soldiers and Sailors in European Cemeteries, Report to Accompany H.R. 4138.* S. Rept. 387, 71st Cong., 2d sess., 1930. 5p. Serial 9185. See 2930 for abstract.

2935. U.S. Department of State. Passport Division. *To Clerks of Courts Who Take Passport Applications, Applications for Special Pilgrimage Passports and Pilgrimage Travel Documents for Aliens Issued under Act of Mar. 2, 1929.* Washington, D.C: The Department, 1930. 4p. S1.2:P26/20. Transmits instructions regarding the pilgrimage of mothers and widows of deceased soldiers, sailors, and marines buried in Europe.

2936. U.S. War Department. *Pilgrimage Regulation [For Mothers and Widows of Deceased Soldiers, Sailors, and Marines of American Forces Now Interred in Cemeteries in Europe].* Washington, D.C: The Department, 1930. 8p. W1.12:P64. Change sheet issued Mach 8, 1930.

2937. U.S. Congress. House. Committee on World War Veterans' Legislation. *Amend the World War Veterans' Act, 1924, as Amended, Report to Accompany H.R. 17116.* H. Rept. 2721, 71st Cong., 3rd sess., 1931. 4p. Serial 9327. Reports a pension bill for widows with children and dependent parents of ex-servicemen of WWI who died of non-service connected disability. Widows with no child are not included due to "the comparatively young age of widows of World War veterans and the modern tendency of women to enter the business world."

2938. U.S. Congress. House. Committee on Pensions. *Granting Uniform Pensions to Widows and Children of Certain Pensions Who Served the United States in Time of War, and for Other Purposes, Report to Accompany H.R. 7230.* H. Rept. 492, 72d Cong., 1st sess., 1932. 3p. Serial 9491. Committee approves a uniform widows' pension bill which eliminates rate differentials based on war-time widows versus widows married after the war and removes conditions requiring proof of service-related death.

2939. U.S. Congress. House. Committee on Pensions. *Uniform Pensions to Widows and Children and Dependent Parents of Certain Persons Who Served the United States in Time of War, and for Other Purposes, Hearing on H.R. 7230.* 72d Cong., 1st sess., 4 Feb. 1932. 42p. Y4.P38/1:W63. Hearing examines a bill which would grant pensions to widows of veterans of any U.S. war based on age of widow with rates increasing at age 50 and age 70. The cost of the bill is a major point of debate and ways of cutting the cost through rules on age for payments to dependent children and eliminating remarried widows are discussed. A legal chart provides comparison of existing and proposed laws.

2940. U.S. Congress. House. Committee on World War Veterans' Legislation. *Amend the World War Veterans' Act, 1924, as Amended, Report to Accompany H.R. 8578.* H. Rept. 312, 72d Cong., 1st sess., 1932. 5p. Serial 9491. Report on a bill setting pension rates for the widows, children, and dependent parents of ex-servicemen of WWI who died of non-service connected disability briefly discusses a provision setting an income limit for widows and children.

2941. U.S. Congress. House. Committee on the Public Lands. *Homestead Entries to Widows of Pensioners Who Served in Indian Wars, Report to Accompany S. 2654.* H. Rept. 2097, 72d Cong., 2d sess., 1933. 2p. Serial 9649. The bill reported allows widows of men who served in the Indian Wars to credit the length of the husbands' military service toward the homestead residence requirement. Similar provisions were previously made for Civil War, Spanish-American War, and WWI widows.

2942. U.S. Congress. Senate. Committee on Finance. *To Maintain the Credit of the United States Government, Hearing.* 73rd Cong., 1st sess., 10 Mar. 1933. 44p. Y4.F49:C86/2. Originally confidential executive session on ways to cut the amount of money expended on pensions includes a provision to cut remarried widows and briefly discusses an income limitation for widows receiving military survivor pensions.

2943. U.S. General Land Office. *Widows of Persons Who Served in Certain Indian Wars Allowed Credit for Deceased Husbands' Military Service in Such Wars by Act of Mar. 3, 1933 (Public 414).* Circular no. 1296. Washington, D.C: GPO, 1933. 2p. I21.4:1296.

2944. U.S. Congress. House. Committee in Invalid Pensions. *Increase of Pensions to Certain Former Widows of Soldiers and Sailors of the Civil War, Report to Accompany H.R. 8423.* H. Rept. 1143, 74th Cong., 1st sess., 1935. 11p. Serial 9892. Favorable report on increases of pensions to 29 remarried widows of Civil War veterans whose medical condition requires a higher pension presents some background on each case.

2945. U.S. Congress. House. Committee in Invalid Pensions. *Increase of Pensions to Certain Widows and Former Widows of Soldiers of the Civil War, Report to Accompany H.R. 8937.* H. Rept. 1624, 74th Cong., 1st sess., 1935. 12p. Serial 9894. Combined report gives brief case histories on 31 private bills increasing Civil War widow's pensions.

2946. U.S. Congress. House. Committee on Invalid Pensions. *Increase of Pensions to Certain Widows of Soldiers and Sailors of the Civil War, Report to Accompany H.R. 8424.* H. Rept. 1144, 74th Cong., 1st sess., 1935. 161p. Serial 9892. Report summarizes the pension cases presented in 478 private bills, most of which seek an increased pension for medical reasons.

2947. U.S. Congress. House. Committee on Invalid Pensions. *Pensions to Certain Former Widows of Soldiers and Sailors of the Civil War, Report to Accompany H.R. 8422.* H. Rept. 1142, 74th Cong., 1st sess., 1935. 12p. Serial 9892. Report recommends pensions for 25 widows of Civil War veterans ineligible under existing law, usually due to the delimiting marriage date. The usual background information is provided.

2948. U.S. Congress. House. Committee on Invalid Pensions. *Pensions to Certain Widows and Former Widows of Soldiers of the Civil War, Report to Accompany H.R. 8938.* H. Rept. 1625, 74th Cong., 1st sess., 1935. 20p. Serial 9894. Report combines 43 private bills relating to Civil War widows' pensions provides basic background information in support of each case.

2949. U.S. Congress. House. Committee on Invalid Pensions. *Pensions to Certain Widows of Soldiers and Sailors of the Civil War, Report to Accompany H.R. 8421.* H. Rept. 1141, 74th Cong., 1st sess., 1935. 165p. Serial 9892. Reports on 374 private bills relating to pensions for Civil War veterans' widows, many of whom are widows who married the soldier after the delimiting marriage date. Background information is provided in each case.

2950. U.S. Congress. House. Committee on Pensions. *War with Spain: Pensions to Veterans of the Spanish-American War, Including the Boxer Rebellion and the Philippine Insurrection, Their Widows and Dependents, and for Other Purposes, Hearing on H.R. 6995.* 74th Cong., 1st sess., 6,8 May 1935. 59p. Y4.P38/1:Sp2/4. Committee hearing on pensions for veterans and their dependents gives the basic amounts and regulations of pensions including a provision for women who served as nurses. Focus is on restoring benefits reduced by the Economy Act of 1933.

2951. U.S. Congress. Senate. Committee on Pensions. *Granting Increase of Pensions to Certain Former Widows of Soldiers and Sailors of the Civil War, Report to Accompany H.R. 8423.* S. Rept. 1247, 74th Cong., 1st sess., 1935. 3p. Serial 9885. Brief case histories describe four widows of Civil War veterans seeking increases in pension rates.

2952. U.S. Congress. Senate. Committee on Pensions. *Granting Increase of Pensions to Certain Widows of Soldiers and Sailors of the Civil War, Report to Accompany H.R. 8424.* S. Rept. 1248, 74th Cong., 1st sess., 1935. 20p. Serial 9885. Favorable report provides case summaries for about 40 widows seeking increased pensions.

2953. U.S. Congress. Senate. Committee on Pensions. *Granting Pensions to Certain Former Widows of Soldiers and Sailors of the Civil War, Report to Accompany H.R. 8422.* S. Rept. 1246, 74th Cong., 1st sess., 1935. 4p. Serial 9885. Presents case histories of seven women seeking pensions as widows of Civil War veterans but who were ineligible under existing pension laws.

2954. U.S. Congress. Senate. Committee on Pensions. *Granting Pensions to Certain Widows of Soldiers and Sailors of the Civil War, Report to Accompany H.R. 8421.* S. Rept. 1244, 74th Cong., 1st sess., 1935. 35p. Serial 9885. Combined report on pensions to selected Civil War widows summarizes age and financial status of the petitioners and in most cases recommends a pension of $30 per month.

2955. U.S. Congress. House. Committee in Invalid Pensions. *Increase of Pensions to Certain Widows and Former Widows of Soldiers and Sailors of the Civil War, Report to Accompany H.R. 12702.* H. Rept. 2649, 74th Cong., 2d sess., 1936. 166p. Serial 9997. Favorable report on adjustment of 486 widow's pensions gives the usual age, address, relationship to veteran, financial and medical background information.

2956. U.S. Congress. House. Committee in Invalid Pensions. *Pensions and Increase of Pensions to Certain Widows, Former Widows, and Helpless and Dependent Children of Soldiers of the Civil War, Report to Accompany H.R. 12908.* H. Rept. 2889, 74th Cong., 2d sess., 1936. 19p. Serial 9998. Report on 51 widow's pension cases brought before Congress as private bill give basic age, address, relationship to soldier, financial and medical background information.

2957. U.S. Congress. House. Committee in Invalid Pensions. *Pensions to Certain Widows and Former Widows of Soldiers, Sailors, and Marines of the Civil War, Report to Accompany H.R. 12703.* H. Rept. 2650, 74th Cong., 2d sess., 1936. 166p. Serial 9997. Favorable report on pensions for 375 widows and former widows of Civil War veterans gives age, address, relationship to deceased veteran, financial and medical status information.

2958. U.S. Congress. Senate. Committee on Pensions. *Increase of Pensions to Certain Widows and Former Widows of Soldiers and Sailors of the Civil War, Report to Accompany H.R. 12702.* S. Rept. 2351, 74th Cong., 2d sess., 1936. 15p. Serial 9991. An additional 43 Senate private bills for widow's pensions were added to the House bill combining 478 private bills. The background information on the widows under the Senate bill is provided.

2959. U.S. Congress. Senate. Committee on Pensions. *Increase of Pensions to Certain Widows and Former Widows of Soldiers of the Civil War, Report to Accompany H.R. 8937.* S. Rept. 2346, 74th Cong., 2d sess., 1936. 6p. Serial 9991. Presents sixteen widows' pension claims with standard background information.

2960. U.S. Congress. Senate. Committee on Pensions. *Pensions to Certain Widows and Former Widows of Soldiers and Sailors of the Civil War, Report to Accompany H.R. 12703.* S. Rept. 2352, 74th Cong., 2d sess., 1936. 7p. Serial 9991. Substitute for 15 private bills granting Civil War widows' pensions is favorably reported with brief background on the age and condition of the widow in each case.

2961. U.S. Congress. Senate. Committee on Pensions. *Pensions to Certain Widows and Former Widows of Soldiers of the Civil War, Report to Accompany H.R. 8938.* S. Rept. 2347, 74th Cong., 2d sess., 1936. 22p. Serial 9991. Fifty-five Senate bills were added to the House bill carrying 43 bills to make this combined widows' pension bill for Civil War widows. The usual basic background information is provided on each case.

2962. U.S. Congress. House. Committee on Invalid Pensions. *Increase of Pensions to Certain Widows and Former Widows of Soldiers and Sailors of the Civil War, Report to Accompany H.R. 7897.* H. Rept. 1255, 75th Cong., 1st sess., 1937. 176p. Serial 10089. Individual pension claims are summarized in this combined bill on Civil War widows' pensions. The usual information on age, relationship to soldier, financial and medical condition is given.

2963. U.S. Congress. House. Committee on Invalid Pensions. *Pension to a Soldier, and Pensions and Increase of Pensions to Certain Widows, Former Widows, and Helpless and Dependent Children of Soldiers and Sailors of the Civil War, Report to Accompany H.R. 8280.* H. Rept. 1593, 75th Cong., 1st sess., 1937. 15p. Serial 10089. Reports a combined bill on various pension requests, primarily of widows, giving a background summary on each pension case.

2964. U.S. Congress. House. Committee on Invalid Pensions. *Pensions and Increase of Pensions to Certain Widows, Former Widows and Dependent Children of Soldiers of the*

Civil War, Report to Accompany H.R. 7905. H. Rept. 7905, 75th Cong., 1st sess., 1937. 10p. Serial 10089. Report provides background on 22 private widow's pension bills.

2965. U.S. Congress. House. Committee on Invalid Pensions. *Pensions to Certain Widows and Former Widows of Soldiers, Sailors, and Marines of the Civil War, Report to Accompany H.R. 7808.* H. Rept. 1256, 75th Cong., 1st sess., 1937. 187p. Serial 10089. Report on a combined widows' pension bill summarizes each case with background on each widow's health and financial situation.

2966. U.S. Congress. House. Committee on Pensions. *Granting Pensions and Increases of Pensions to Certain Soldiers, Sailors and Nurses of the War with Spain, the Philippine Insurrection, or the China Relief Expedition, and for Other Purposes, Report to Accompany H.R. 5030.* H. Rept. 319, 75th Cong., 1st sess., 1937. 1p. Serial 10083.

2967. U.S. Congress. Senate. Committee on Pensions. *Pensions for Certain Widows of Civil War Veterans, Hearing on S. 2219.* 75th Cong., 1st sess., 8 June 1937. 14p. Y4.P38/2:C49/4. Hearing on a bill extending pension benefits to widows of Civil War veterans married 10 years or more prior to the veteran's death includes testimony opposing granting more liberal benefits to Civil War widows than are granted to widows of veterans serving in other wars. Background statistics are provided on length of marriage of Civil War widows on the pension roles.

2968. U.S. Congress. House. Committee on Invalid Pensions. *Pension and Increase of Pensions to Certain Widows, Former Widows, and Helpless and Dependent Children of Soldiers, Sailors, and Marines of the Civil War, Report to Accompany H.R. 10332.* H. Rept. 2164, 75th Cong., 3rd sess., 1938. 51p. Serial 10236. Combined bill recommends pensions and increased pensions to aged widows of Civil War veterans. The report briefly describes the age, basis for pension claim, economic status, and health status of each widow.

2969. U.S. Congress. House. Committee on Pensions. *Granting a Pension to Widows and Dependent Children of World War Veterans, Report to Accompany H.R. 9285.* H. Rept. 1757, 75th Cong., 3rd sess., 1938. 7p. Serial 10233. Favorable report on legislation to provide pensions to widows and minor children of deceased WWI veterans includes supporting Veterans Administration correspondence.

2970. U.S. Congress. House. Committee on Pensions. *Pensions - World War Widows, Pensions to Widows and Children of World War Veterans, Hearings on H.R. 8690 (Now Known as H.R. 9285).* 75th Cong., 3rd sess., 25,28 Jan. 1938. 53p. Y4.P38/1:W89. Hearing on granting survivor benefits to widows and dependents of WWI veterans provides a good overview of military widows' pensions. Arguments for the bill are based on the theory that the women and children would be on relief without the pension benefits so the government pays them either way. Women from the VFW Ladies' Auxiliaries describe cases of widows and their children living in poverty because they could not prove service-connected disability. Background statistics are provided on the number of active pensions and compensation claims by war and type of claim.

2971. U.S. Congress. House. Committee on World War Veterans' Legislation. *Liberalizing the Provisions of Existing Laws Governing Death Compensation Benefits for Widows and Children of World War Veterans, Report to Accompany H.R. 9725.* H. Rept. 1905, 75th Cong., 3rd sess., 1938. 3p. Serial 10233. Report recommends amendment of laws governing death compensation benefits for widows and children of WWI veterans by reducing the percent of disability required and defining the term "widow of a World War veteran."

2972.   U.S. Congress. Senate. Committee on Finance. *Liberalizing the Provisions of Existing Laws Governing Death-Compensation Benefits for Widows and Children of World War Veterans, Report to Accompany H.R. 9725.* S. Rept. 1570, 75th Cong., 3rd sess., 1938. 3p. Serial 10229. See 2971 for abstract.

2973.   U.S. Congress. House. Committee on Invalid Pensions. *Increase of Pensions to Certain Former Widows of Civil War Veterans, Report to Accompany H.R. 6902.* H. Rept. 862, 76th Cong., 1st sess., 1939. 8p. Serial 10299. Report on private bills increasing pensions for 18 remarried widows of Civil War veterans outlines the facts of each case.

2974.   U.S. Congress. House. Committee on Invalid Pensions. *Increase of Pensions to Certain Widows of Veterans of the Civil War, Report to Accompany H.R. 6901.* H. Rept. 861, 76th Cong., 1st sess., 1939. 115p. Serial 10299. Report on a combined bill increasing pensions to 341 widows of Civil War veterans outlines each case briefly.

2975.   U.S. Congress. House. Committee on Invalid Pensions. *Increase of Pensions to Certain Widows of Veterans of the Civil War, Report to Accompany H.R. 7039.* H. Rept. 1001, 76th Cong., 1st sess., 1939. 5p. Serial 10300. Recommends granting increased pensions to ten Civil War widows whose cases are outlined.

2976.   U.S. Congress. House. Committee on Invalid Pensions. *Pensions to Certain Former Widows of Veterans of the Civil War, Report to Accompany H.R. 6900.* H. Rept. 860, 76th Cong., 1st sess., 1939. 10p. Serial 10299. Report supports the increase or grant of pensions to 21 remarried widows of Civil War veterans whose cases are summarized.

2977.   U.S. Congress. House. Committee on Invalid Pensions. *Pensions to Certain Widows of Veterans of the Civil War, Report to Accompany H.R. 6897.* H. Rept. 857, 76th Cong., 1st sess., 1939. 139p. Serial 10299. Favorable report on a bill to increase the pensions of 310 widows of Civil War veterans outlines each case.

2978.   U.S. Congress. House. Committee on Invalid Pensions. *Pensions to Certain Widows of Veterans of the Civil War, Report to Accompany H.R. 7038.* H. Rept. 1000, 76th Cong., 1st sess., 1939. 6p. Serial 10300. Report of a bill granting pensions to eleven Civil War widows and increasing the pension of one widow includes basic details of each case.

2979.   U.S. Congress. House. Committee on Pensions. *Granting Pensions and Increase of Pensions to Certain Soldiers and Sailors, etc., Report to Accompany H.R. 2301.* H. Rept. 310, 76th Cong., 1st sess., 1939. 4p. Serial 10297. Favorable report on a bill changing the restricting date of marriage for Spanish War widows' pension eligibility reviews the widows' rights under the existing law and the cost of the change.

2980.   U.S. Congress. House. Committee on Pensions. *Pensions for Widows of Spanish-American War Veterans, Hearings on H.R. 2301, H.R. 2874, H.R. 2875.* 76th Cong., 1st sess., 8 Feb 1939. 25p. Y4.P38/1:Sp2/6. Discusses a bill to change the eligible marriage date for widows of Spanish War veterans to receive benefits from Sept. 1, 1922 to January 1, 1938. Topics of testimony include the added cost of including these women and whether they are already adequately covered by Social Security.

2981.   U.S. Congress. House. Committee on Pensions. *Pensions to Widows and Orphans of Deceased Veterans of the Spanish-American War, Boxer Rebellion, or Philippine Insurrection, Report to Accompany H.R. 2875.* H. Rept. 448, 76th Cong., 1st sess., 1939. 2p. Serial 10297. Report recommends amending the pension laws for widows of deceased veterans of the Spanish-American War, the Boxer Rebellion, and the Philippine Insurrection by making the pension effective as of the date of the veterans' death.

2982. U.S. Congress. Senate. Committee on Pensions. *Increase of Pensions to Certain Widows of Veterans of the Civil War, Report to Accompany H.R. 6901.* S. Rept. 996, 76th Cong., 1st sess., 1939. 12p. Serial 10295. The cases of 31 Civil War veterans' widows are outlined in this favorable report on a bill increasing widows' pensions in 372 cases.

2983. U.S. Congress. Senate. Committee on Pensions. *Pensions to Widows and Orphans of Deceased Veterans of the Spanish-American War, Boxer Rebellion, or Philippine Insurrection, Report to Accompany H.R. 2875.* S. Rept. 997, 76th Cong., 1st sess., 1939. 3p. Serial 10295. See 2981 for abstract.

2984. U.S. Congress. House. *Certain Widows of Veterans of the Civil War: Message from the President of the United States Returning Without Approval the Bill (H.R. 6901) Entitled "An Act granting increase of pensions to certain widows of veterans of the Civil War."* H. Doc. 710, 76th Cong., 3rd sess., 1940. 19p. Serial 10502. Veto message of Roosevelt on the bill increasing pensions of 362 widows of Civil War veterans is based on the principle that they represent but a small group of the 50,017 Civil War widows, many of whom are just as needy.

2985. U.S. Congress. House. Committee on Invalid Pensions. *Increase of Pensions to Sundry Widows, Report to Accompany H.R. 7831.* H. Rept. 1481, 76th Cong., 3rd sess., 1940. 85p. Serial 10440. Favorable report on a bill granting increased pensions to 13 widows of high ranking offices of the Army, Navy, and Coast Guard summarizes the case of each widow.

2986. U.S. Congress. House. Committee on Invalid Pensions. *Pensions and Increase of Pensions to Certain Widows, Former Widows, and Dependent Children of Veterans of the Civil War, Report to Accompany H.R. 8015.* H. Rept. 8015, 76th Cong., 3rd sess., 1940. 28p. Serial 10440. Report on a bill to increase pensions of 63 widows and former widows of Civil War veterans provides a brief summary of each case.

2987. U.S. Congress. House. Committee on Invalid Pensions. *Pensions and Increase of Pensions to Certain Widows, Former Widows, and Dependent Children of Veterans of the Civil War, Report to Accompany H.R. 9390.* H. Rept. 1960, 76th Cong., 3rd sess., 1940. 28p. Serial 10441. Report on combined private bills covering 65 cases where a pension or increase of pension was sought for a Civil War veteran's widow or dependent children provides a brief summary of each case.

2988. U.S. Congress. House. Committee on Invalid Pensions. *Pensions to Certain Unremarried Dependent Widows of Civil War Veterans, Report to Accompany H.R. 7981.* H. Rept. 1780, 76th Cong., 3rd sess., 1940. 5p. Serial 10441. The committee recommends granting pensions to unremarried widows of Civil War veterans who married the veteran after the June 26, 1905 eligibility data.

2989. U.S. Congress. Senate. Committee on Pensions. *Pensions to Certain Unmarried Dependent Widows of Civil War Veterans, Report to Accompany H.R. 7981.* S. Rept. 1543, 76th Cong., 3rd sess., 1940. 4p. Serial 10429. See 2988 for abstract.

2990. U.S. Congress. House. Committee on Invalid Pensions. *Pensions and Increase of Pensions to Certain Dependents of Veterans of the Civil War, Report to Accompany H.R. 4256.* H. Rept. 357, 77th Cong., 1st sess., 1941. 149p. Serial 10553. Report on a substitute bill granting pensions or increase in pension for 377 widows or dependent children of Civil War veterans briefly details each case.

2991. U.S. Congress. House. Committee on Invalid Pensions. *Pensions to Certain Unmarried Dependent Widows of Civil War Veterans, Report to Accompany H.R. 1091.* H. Rept.

396, 77th Cong., 1st sess., 1941. 6p. Serial 10553. Report recommends granting pensions to widows of Civil War veterans married after June 26, 1905 provided the widow was married to the veteran for the 10 years preceding his death, was over 60, was in dependent circumstances, and had not remarried. The fairness of the delimiting marriage date is discussed in a letter from the Administrator of Veteran's Affairs.

2992. U.S. Congress. House. Committee on Pensions. *Granting Increases in Pensions to Certain Widows and Dependents of Persons Who Served in the Military or Naval Forces of the United States during the War with Spain, the Boxer Rebellion, or the Philippine Insurrection, Report to Accompany H.R. 5339.* H. Rept. 968, 77th Cong., 1st sess., 1941. 5p. Serial 10556. Report supports a bill increasing pensions to widows of veterans of the Spanish-American War, the Boxer Rebellion, and the Philippine Insurrection to equal pension rates granted WWI widows.

2993. U.S. Congress. House. Committee on Pensions. *Granting Pensions and Increase of Pensions to Certain Soldiers and Sailors, etc., Report to Accompany H.R. 2310.* H. Rept. 970, 77th Cong., 1st sess., 1941. 4p. Serial 10556. Favorable report on a bill advancing the restricting date of marriage for Spanish War widows for the purpose of pension eligibility provides a brief overview of widow's rights under existing laws.

2994. U.S. Congress. Senate. Committee on Pensions. *Granting Increases in Pensions to Certain Widows and Dependents of Persons Who Served in the Military or Naval Forces of the United States during the War with Spain, the Boxer Rebellion, or the Philippine Insurrection, Report to Accompany S. 876.* S. Rept. 542, 77th Cong., 1st sess., 1941. 4p. Serial 10545. A bill equalizing widows' pension rates between Spanish-American War, Boxer Rebellion, Philippine Insurrection, and WWI veterans' widows is recommended.

2995. U.S. Congress. Senate. Committee on Pensions. *Granting Pensions and Increase of Pensions to Certain Soldiers and Sailors, etc., Report to Accompany H.R. 2310.* S. Rept. 686, 77th Cong., 1st sess., 1941. 2p. Serial 10546. See 2993 for abstract.

2996. U.S. Congress. Senate. Committee on Pensions. *Pensions to Certain Unmarried Dependent Widows of Civil War Veterans, Report to Accompany H.R. 1091.* S. Rept. 678, 77th Cong., 1st sess., 1941. 6p. Serial 10546. See 2991 for abstract.

2997. U.S. Congress. House. Committee on Naval Affairs. *To Amend the Provisions of the Act Authorizing Payment of 6 Months' Death Gratuity to Widow, Child, or Dependent Relative of Officers, Enlisted Men, or Nurses of the Navy or Marine Corps, and for Other Purposes (H.R. 3502).* Sundry Legislation Affecting the Naval Establishment, 1943, Hearings no. 145. 78th Cong., 1st sess., 8 Oct. 1943. 1111-1112pp. Y4.N22/1a:943-44/145. Report transmits a draft of a proposed bill which would ensure that military death gratuities are paid to the widow or dependents and are not considered part of the deceased's estate.

2998. U.S. Congress. House. Committee on Pensions. *Increase of Pensions for Veterans, and Pensions and Increase of Pensions for Widows Spanish-American War, Hearings on H.R. 2350, H.R. 2784.* 78th Cong., 1st sess., 12 Oct. 1943. 22p. Y4.P38/1:Sp2/7. Hearing examines a bill to bring pensions and widows' pensions for the Spanish-American War up to the amount granted Civil War veterans and their widows and to change the delimiting marriage date from September 1, 1922 to January 1, 1938. One point of contention is defining eligibility of widows by using date of marriage, number of years married, etc.

2999. U. S. Congress. House. Committee on World War Veterans' Legislation. *Providing Government Protection to Widows and Children of Deceased World War Veterans, Report to Accompany H.R. 1744.* H. Rept. 114, 78th Cong., 1st sess., 1943. 2p. Serial 10760. Favorable report on legislation to provide pensions to dependent widows of WWI veterans briefly describes the committee's views on a limiting marriage date and on proof of service connected disability.

3000. U.S. Congress. House. Committee on Invalid Pensions. *Pensions to Certain Unremarried Dependent Widows of Civil War Veterans Who Were Married to the Veteran Subsequent to June 26, 1905, Report to Accompany H.R. 86.* H. Rept. 1288, 78th Cong., 2d sess., 1944. 7p. Serial 10845. History of attempts to include unremarried widows of Civil War veterans married after June 26, 1905 under service pension laws is reviewed.

3001. U.S. Congress. House. Committee on Naval Affairs. *Hearing on S. 1428 to Amend the Provisions of the Act Authorizing Payment of 6 Months' Death Gratuity to Widow, Child and Dependent Relative of Officers, Enlisted Men, or Nurses of the Navy or Marine Corps, and for Other Purposes.* Sundry Legislation Affecting the Naval Establishment 1944, Hearings no. 198. 78th Cong., 2d sess., 25 Feb. 1944. p.1357. [1p.] Y4.N22/1a:943-44/198. Very brief hearing discusses a bill to ensure that death gratuities are paid to beneficiaries and not to the estate where it would be subject to creditors' claims.

3002. U.S. Congress. Senate. Committee on Finance. *Increasing the Service-Connected Disability Rate of Compensation or Pension Payable to Veterans of World War I and World War II and Veterans Entitled to Wartime Rates Based on Service on or after September 16, 1940, for Service-Connected Disabilities; Increasing the Rates for Widows and Children under Public Law 484, Seventy-Third Congress, as Amended, and Including Widows and Children of World War II Veterans for Benefits under the Latter Act, Report to Accompany H.R. 3356.* S. Rept. 854, 78th Cong., 2d sess., 1944. 3p. Serial 10841. The general pension bill reported increases pension rates for WWI veterans' widows and extends widow's pension benefits to widows of WWII veterans.

3003. U.S. Congress. Senate. Committee on Finance. *Providing Government Protection for Widows and Children of Deceased World War I Veterans, Report to Accompany H.R. 1744.* S. Rept. 1297, 78th Cong., 2d sess., 1944. 11p. Serial 10843. Favorable report on a bill setting the eligibility requirements for World War I widows' pensions focuses on service-connected disability.

3004. U.S. Congress. Senate. Committee on Pensions. *Pensions to Certain Unremarried Dependent Widows of Civil War Veterans Who Were Married to the Veteran Subsequent to June 26, 1905, Report to Accompany H.R. 86.* S. Rept. 1148, 78th Cong., 2d sess., 1944. 3p. Serial 10843. Report on legislation extending pension privileges to widows of Civil War veterans married after June 26, 1905 explains the eligibility requirements relating to age, length of marriage, dependency status and remarriage.

3005. U. S. Congress. House. Committee on World War Veterans' Legislation. *Removing the Limitations on the Amount of Death Compensation or Pension Payable to Widows and Children of Certain Deceased Veterans, Report to Accompany S. 2100.* H. Rept. 2699, 79th Cong., 2d sess., 1946. 6p. Serial 11026. Recommends a bill removing the maximum amount payable as war widows' pensions, allowing the widow to collect for each child regardless of the number of children. The report of the Veterans' Administration comprises the bulk of the report.

3006. U.S. Congress. Senate. Committee on Finance. *Removing the Limitations on the Amount of Death Compensation or Pension Payable to Widows and Children of Certain Deceased Veterans, Report to Accompany S. 2100.* S. Rept. 1409, 79th Cong., 2d sess., 1946. 4p. Serial 11016. See 3005 for abstract.

3007. U.S. Congress. House. Committee on Veterans' Affairs. *Providing Additional Compensation to Widows and Other Dependents of Certain Veterans, Report to Accompany*

H.R. 3748. H. Rept. 1068, 80th Cong., 1st sess., 1947. 3p. Serial 11122. Reports a bill raising pension rates for widows, children, and dependent parents of deceased veterans of WWI or WWII when death was related to service in the war.

3008. U.S. Congress. House. Committee on Veterans' Affairs. Subcommittee on Education, Training, and Rehabilitation. *Educational and Loan Benefits for Widows and Children of World War II Veterans, Hearings on H.R. 1385, H.R. 2106, H.R. 2172.* 80th Cong., 1st sess., 25 Apr.- 5 June 1947. 41p. Y4.V64/3:Ed8/3. Hearing on bills providing education and loan benefits to widows and children of WWII veterans highlights the economic plight of young war widows and the inadequacy of widows' pensions. In terms of educational benefits for widows, it is pointed out repeatedly that those testifying did not expect many women to complete four years of college, but assumed that they might want secretarial courses. The loan portion of the bill addresses surveys results which indicated that war widows had acute problems securing housing.

3009. U.S. Congress. House. Committee on Interstate and Foreign Commerce. *Amending Section 326(B) of the Public Health Service Act, with Respect to Widows of Certain Deceased Coast Guard Personnel, Report to Accompany H.R. 6868.* H. Rept. 2318, 80th Cong., 2d sess., 1948. 2p. Serial 11213. Recommends providing medical services to widows of deceased Coast Guard personnel who died during active duty while under Navy jurisdiction.

3010. U.S. Congress. House. Committee on Veterans' Affairs. *Education and Training Benefits for Widows and Children of Deceased Veterans of World War II, Hearings on H.R. 5301.* 80th Cong., 2d sess., 20 May 1948. 15p. Y4.V64/3:Ed8/5. Statements by representatives of Gold Star Wives of America, Inc. support legislation to provide educational benefits to widows and children of decreased veterans of WWII with a focus on increasing the ability of the widow to support herself and her family. The question of remarriage of widows and the effect of education and training benefits on remarriage decisions are briefly discussed.

3011. U.S. Congress. House. Committee on Veterans' Affairs. *Providing Additional Compensation to Widows and Other Dependents of Certain Veterans, Supplemental Report to Accompany H.R. 3748.* H. Rept. 1068, part 2, 80th Cong., 2d sess., 1948. 2p. Serial 11209. Supplemental report corrects cost estimates for the changes in pension rates and eligibility.

3012. U.S. Congress. House. Committee on Veterans' Affairs. *Providing Pensions for Certain Widows of Spanish-American War Veterans, Report to Accompany H.R. 4962.* H. Rept. 2316, 80th Cong., 2d sess., 1948. 5p. Serial 11213. Report describes a bill altering the marriage delimiting date for Spanish-American War, Boxer Rebellion, and Philippine Insurrection widows' pensions by providing pensions to all unremarried widows who had been married to the veteran for at least ten years prior to the veterans' death.

3013. U.S. Congress. House. Committee on Veterans' Affairs. Subcommittee on Spanish War Veterans. *Pensions for Widows and Hospitalization for Veterans in Certain Spanish-American War Cases, Hearings on H.R. 4962 and H.R. 5464.* 80th Cong., 2d sess., 4 June 1948. 22p. Y4.V64/3:Sp2/2. The bill reported raises the pensions of Spanish-American War, Boxer Rebellion, and Philippine Insurrection veterans, widows and dependents and changes the marriage date requirements for widows' pension eligibility.

3014. U.S. Congress. Senate. Committee of Finance. *Increasing the Rates of Service-Connected Death Compensation Payable to Certain Widows, Children, and Dependent Parents of Persons Who Served in the Active Military or Naval Service, Report to Accompany S. 2825.* S. Rept. 1584, 80th Cong., 2d sess., 1948. 7p. Serial 11208. Report on a bill increasing pension payments to widows, children, and dependent parents of deceased persons who served in the Regular Army discusses the general tendency to request increases in pensions and the philosophy of survivor benefits.

3015. U.S. Congress. Senate. Committee of Finance. *Providing Pensions for Certain Widows of Veterans of the Spanish-American War, Including the Boxer Rebellion and the Philippine Insurrection, Report to Accompany H.R. 4962.* S. Rept. 1747, 80th Cong., 2d sess., 1948. 4p. Serial 11208. Report briefly examines a bill increasing widows' pensions and changing rules relating to the delimiting marriage date.

3016. U.S. Congress. Senate. Committee on Post Office and Civil Service. *Amending the Veteran's Preference Act of 1944 to Extend the Benefits of Such Act to Certain Mothers of Veterans, Report to Accompany H.R. 5508.* S. Rept. 1561, 80th Cong., 2d sess., 1948. 2p. Serial 11208. The bill reported clarifies language in the Veterans' Preference Act of 1944 relating to eligibility of widowed mothers.

3017. U.S. Congress. House. Committee on Veterans' Affairs. *Pensions for Veterans, Increasing Income Limitations for Veterans and Dependents Reviewing Pensions, and Making Widows of World War II Veterans Eligible for Pensions in Same Manner as Widows of World War I, Hearings on H.R. 3821.* 81st Cong., 1st sess., 29 Mar. - 28 Apr. 1949. 187-548pp. Y4.V64/3:P38/3. Lengthy hearing on WWII veterans pensions includes scattered discussion on tying widows' eligibility to the service connected disability of the husband. Also discusses Social Security coverage as a substitute for pensions in some instances.

3018. U.S. Congress. House. Committee on Veterans Affairs. *Extending Certain Veterans' Benefits to or on Behalf of Dependents Husbands and Widowers of Females Veterans, Report to Accompany H.R. 6561.* H. Rept. 1537, 81st Cong., 2d sess., 1950. 4p. Serial 11378. Reports a bill providing equal veterans' benefits to dependent husbands and widowers of female veterans as are provided to wives and widows of male veterans. Correspondence from the Veterans' Administration reviews past legislation and practice relating to payment of benefits to husbands and widowers of veterans.

3019. U.S. Congress. House. *Message from the President of the United States Transmitting without Approval, the Bill (H.R. 3549) to Modify Eligibility Requirements for Payment of Pensions to Certain Widows of Veterans of the Civil War, Indian Wars, and Spanish-American War, Including the Boxer Rebellion, and the Philippine Insurrection.* H. Doc. 221, 82d Cong., 1st sess., 1951. 3p. Serial 11525. Veto message from President Truman rejects the bill to remove the dependency requirement for pre-WWI widows' pensions on the grounds that it would set a precedent for such pensions for WWI and WWII veterans' widows.

3020. U.S. Congress. House. Committee on Veterans Affairs. *Extending Certain Veterans' Benefits to or on Behalf of Dependent Husbands and Widowers of Female Veterans, Report to Accompany H.R. 301.* H. Rept. 555, 82d Cong., 1st sess., 1951. 4p. Serial 11497. Favorable report on a bill to extend veterans' benefits relates primarily to pension, retirement, and compensation payments to the dependent husband or widower of a female veteran.

3021. U.S. Congress. House. Committee on Veterans Affairs. *Liberalizing Eligibility to Pensions for Widows of Civil War, Indian Wars, and Spanish-American War.* 82d Cong., 1st sess., 5 Apr. 1951. 16p. Y4.V64/3:P38/6. Witnesses discuss changing the regulations governing eligibility for widows' pensions from a determination of dependency to a straight income limitation.

3022.   U.S. Congress. House. Committee on Veteran's Affairs. *Removal of the Dependency Requirement in Connection with Certain Widows' Pensions, Report to Accompany H.R. 3549.* H. Rept. 562, 82d Cong., 1st sess., 1951. 5p. Serial 11497. Reports a bill removing the dependency requirement for pensions to widows of Civil War, Indian Wars, Spanish-American War, Boxer Rebellion, and Philippine Insurrection veterans. The administrative implications of changing from a dependency requirement to an income limitation for widows' pensions are explored in correspondence from the Veteran's Administration.

3023.   U.S. Congress. Senate. Committee on Finance. *Removal of the Dependency Requirement in Connection with Certain Widows' Pensions, Report to Accompany H.R. 3549.* S. Rept. 562, 82d Cong., 1st sess., 1951. 5p. Serial 11488. See 3022 for abstract.

3024.   U.S. Congress. House. Committee on Veterans Affairs. *Pensions for Widows of World War II Veterans of Service on or after June 27, 1950, on Same Basis as Pensions for World War I Widows, Hearing on H.R. 298, 299, 300, 357, 5894, and 5899.* 82d Cong., 2d sess., 22 Jan. 1952. 787-814pp. Y4.V64/3:P38/10. Hearing examines legislation changing the requirement that a WWII veteran be suffering from a service-connected injury at the time of death for a widow to collect a non-service-connected pension. Such a requirement did not exist for WWI widows.

3025.   U.S. Congress. House. Committee on Veteran's Affairs. *Income Limits First Year of Non-Service Connected Death Pensions, Report to Accompany H.R. 9841.* H. Rept. 2035, 84th Cong., 2d sess., 1956. 5p. Serial 11898. Favorable report on a bill to increase the income limit for widows and children collecting a death pension in the first year after the veteran's death by $600 justifies the greater allowance by noting the cost of burial expenses and remaining medical costs.

3026.   U.S. Congress. House. Committee on Veteran's Affairs. *Increasing Pensions for Spanish-American War Widows, Report to Accompany H.R. 2867.* H. Rept. 2739, 84th Cong., 2d sess., 1956. 6p. Serial 11900. Reports a bill increasing pension rates to widows and former widows of Spanish-American War, Boxer Rebellion, and Philippine Insurrection veterans. Correspondence from the Veterans' Administration reviews the history of pension rates and eligibility requirements for Spanish-American War widows.

3027.   U.S. Congress. House. Committee on Veteran's Affairs. *Marriage Delimiting Date of Widows of Spanish-American War Veterans Who are Entitled to Receive Compensation, Report to Accompany H.R. 8458.* H. Rept. 2033, 84th Cong., 2d sess., 1956. 7p. Serial 11898. Report recommends liberalizing the delimiting marriage date for survivor pensions for widows of Spanish-American War veterans.

3028.   U.S. Congress. House. Committee on Veteran's Affairs. *Widow Eligibility for Veterans' Administration Benefits, Report to Accompany H.R. 10542.* H. Rept. 2032, 84th Cong., 2d sess., 1956. 7p. Serial 11898. Favorably reports a bill changing pension or death compensation eligibility requirements for widows of veterans. The bill provides a uniform alternative to the date of marriage limitation by making a widow eligible if she was married to the veterans five or more years or if she had a child by the veteran. Veterans' Administration correspondence provides background on the philosophy and provision of widows' pensions for previous wars.

3029.   U.S. Veterans Administration. *Survivors Benefits Information for Widows, Children and Parents of Veterans Who Died Prior to January 1, 1957 as a Result of Military or Naval Service.* Washington, DC: GPO, 1956. 12p. leaflet. VA1.19:8-2.

3030. U.S. Congress. House. Committee on Veteran's Affairs. *Increasing Pension for Spanish-American War Widows, Report to Accompany H.R. 358.* H. Rept. 282, 85th Cong., 1st sess., 1957. 6p. Serial 11984. Reports a bill raising the pension for Spanish-American War, Boxer Rebellion, and Philippine Insurrection widows and equalizing pensions between widows married to the veteran at the time of his service and those married later. Correspondence from the Veterans' Administration criticizes various plans to raise widows' pensions.

3031. U.S. Congress. House. Committee on Veteran's Affairs. *Widow Eligibility for Veterans' Administration Benefits, Report to Accompany H.R. 3658.* H. Rept. 284, 85th Cong., 1st sess., 1957. 5p. Serial 11984. Report recommends passage of a bill eliminating the disparity in marriage eligibility dates for the widows of veterans of various wars relative to eligibility for VA benefits. The bill liberalizes the requirements and removes certain restrictions. The report summarizes the various requirements for widows' pensions by war or conflict.

3032. U.S. Congress. Senate. Committee on Finance. *Widow Eligibility for Veterans' Administration Benefits, Report to Accompany H.R. 3658.* S. Rept. 849, 85th Cong., 1st sess., 1957. 5p. Serial 11978. Reports a bill establishing uniform eligibility requirements for widows' pensions to replace existing delimiting marriage dates for the various wars.

3033. U.S. Congress. House. Committee on Veterans' Affairs. *Extending Certain Veterans' Benefits to or in Behalf of Dependent Husbands and Widowers of Female Veterans, Report to Accompany H.R. 5322.* H. Rept. 2020, 85th Cong., 2d sess., 1958. 5p. Serial 12074. Recommends expanding the definition of "wife" and "widow" to include dependent husbands and widowers of female veterans for the purposes of laws administered by the Veterans' Administration.

3034. U.S. Congress. Senate. Committee on Finance. *Extending Certain Veterans' Benefits to or on Behalf of Dependent Husband and Widowers of Female Veterans, Report to Accompany H.R. 5322.* S. Rept. 2058, 85th Cong., 2d sess., 1958. 5p. Serial 12064. See 3033 for abstract.

3035. U.S. Congress. Senate. Committee on Finance. *Increasing the Monthly Rates of Pensions Payable to Widows and Former Widows of Deceased Veterans of the Spanish-American War, Civil War, Indian Wars, and Mexican War, and Providing Pensions to Widows of Veterans Who Served in the Military or Naval Forces of the Confederate States of America during the Civil War, Report to Accompany H.R. 358.* S. Rept. 1489, 85th Cong., 2d sess., 1958. 7p. Serial 12062. Reports a bill setting a uniform pension for pre-WWI military widows at $75 a month.

3036. U.S. Congress. House. Committee on Veterans' Affairs. *Non-Service-Connected Pensions for Veterans of World War I, II, and Korean Conflict and Their Widows and Children, Report to Accompany H.R. 7650.* H. Rept. 537, 86th Cong., 1st sess., 1959. 39p. Serial 12160. Legislation favorably reported here proposes standardized eligibility requirements for pensions to widows of veterans of WWI, WWII, and the Korean Conflict and the creation of a sliding scale of income limitations and pension rates. Views of various veterans groups are expressed. The explanation of the bill illustrates payments at various income levels under the proposed legislation and the current system. Data is also provided by war, starting with Revolutionary War, on number of participants, deaths in service, number of living veterans and number of veterans and dependents on the pensions rolls.

3037. U.S. Congress. House. Committee on Post Office and Civil Service. *Definition of Mothers for Purposes of the Veterans' Preference Act of 1944, Report to Accompany H.R. 1907.* H. Rept. 1489, 86th Cong., 2d sess., 1960. 8p. Serial 12244. The bill reported would include adoptive mothers and women who stood in loco parentis to a deceased or disable veteran under laws granting preference to mothers of service men and women for Civil Service positions.

3038.   U.S. Veterans Administration. *The New Pension Law for Widows and Children.* VA Pamphlet 21-3. Washington, DC: GPO, 1960. 20p. VA1.19:21-3. Describes the new pension laws and instructions for filing claims.

3039.   U.S. Congress. House. Committee on Veterans' Affairs. *Increased Dependency and Indemnity Compensation for Certain Veterans' Widows, Report to Accompany H.R. 6969.* H. Rept. 877, 87th Cong., 1st sess., 1961. 9p. Serial 12341. Reports on a bill correcting the situation where a widow collecting a non-service-connected death pension could receive a higher monthly amount than a similarly situated widow collecting dependency and indemnity compensation for a service-connected death.

3040.   U.S. Congress. Senate. Committee on Finance. *Increased Dependency and Indemnity Compensation for Certain Veterans' Widow, Report to Accompany H.R. 6969.* S. Rept. 850, 87th Cong., 1st sess., 1961. 2p. Serial 12325. See 3039 for abstract.

3041.   U.S. Congress. Senate. Committee on Finance. *Restoration of Widow's Benefits, Report to Accompany H.R. 5234.* S. Rept. 1842, 87th Cong., 2d sess., 1962. 7p. Serial 12419. The bill reported provides uniformity in rules determining when a remarriage is considered "void" for the purpose of reestablished veterans benefits to widows. The bill also establishes when a "remarriage" is deemed to exist in the case of a widow who does not remarry but who is openly living with another man and presenting herself as his wife while continuing to collect a pension. A report from the Veterans' Administration supports the bill and notes the need for legislation on the points addressed.

3042.   U.S. Congress. House. Committee on Veterans' Affairs. *Increased Payments for Widows of Veterans Dying from Service-Connected Disabilities, Report to Accompany H.R. 5250.* H. Rept. 678, 88th Cong., 1st sess., 1963. 3p. Serial 12543.

3043.   U.S. Congress. Senate. Committee on Finance. *Increased Payments for Widows of Veterans Dying from Service-Connected Disabilities, Report to Accompany H.R. 5250.* S. Rept. 494, 88th Cong., 1st sess., 1963. 3p. Serial 12534.

3044.   U.S. Congress. House. Committee on Veterans' Affairs. *Increasing Dependency and Indemnity Compensation for Certain Widows, Report to Accompany H.R. 3177.* H. Rept. 1500, 89th Cong., 2d sess., 1966. 4p. Serial 12713-2. Reports a bill allowing widows with children whose husband died of a service-connected cause to collect dependency and indemnity compensation equal to non-service connected death pensions paid to widows with children. The bill only affected widows with eight or more children.

3045.   U.S. Congress. Senate. Committee on Finance. *Increasing Dependency and Indemnity Compensation for Certain Widows, Report to Accompany H.R. 3177.* S. Rept. 1218, 89th Cong., 2d sess., 1966. 5p. Serial 12710-2. See 3044 for abstract.

3046.   U.S. Congress. House. Committee on Veterans' Affairs. *Educational Assistance to Widows, Report to Accompany H.R. 16025.* H. Rept. 1379, 90th Cong., 2d sess., 1968. 22p. Serial 12795-2. Favorable report with amendments on a bill to establish an educational assistance program for widows receiving Dependency and Indemnity Compensation emphasizes the need for such a program in light of the youth of Vietnam War widows. Report from the Veteran's Administration states its position on the bill.

3047. U.S. Congress. Senate. Committee on the Labor and Public Welfare. *Improving Educational and Training Programs for Veterans and Providing Educational Assistance for Certain Widows, Report to Accompany H.R. 16025.* S. Rept. 1394, 90th Cong., 2d sess., 1968. 34p. Serial 12792-4. Among the topics discussed in this report is the need to provide educational loans to widows of veterans dying from service-connected disabilities so that they can supplement their income and return to the mainstream.

3048. U.S. Congress. House. Committee on Armed Services. Special Subcommittee on Survivor Benefits. *Inquiry into Survivor Benefits.* 91th Cong., 2d sess., 7-23 July 1970. 9559-9910pp. Y4Ar5/2a:969-70/69. Testimony of Defense Department personnel and of widows of military men examines the adequacy of survivor benefits to dependents of personnel killed during active duty and benefits to survivors of retired personnel. At the time of the hearing there were no survivor benefits for widows of retired personnel. Statistics on survivor benefit rates are furnished.

3049. U.S. Congress. House. Committee on Armed Services. Special Subcommittee on Survivor Benefits. *Inquiry into Survivor Benefits, Report.* 91st Cong., 2d sess., 10 Oct. 1970. 9503-9557pp. Y4.Aar5/2a:969-70/68. Summary of information gathered at hearings on the gaps in survivor benefit coverage for widows of military personnel recommends a course of action to provide better coverage for widows. Military retirement coverage of survivors and survivor benefits in the Civil Service system are compared.

3050. U.S. Congress. Senate. Committee on Labor and Public Welfare. *GI Bill Benefits for Families of Servicemen Missing, Captured or Interned, Report to Accompany S. 3785.* S. Rept. 1232, 91st Cong., 2d sess., 1970. 26p. Serial 12881-5. Agency views and supporting correspondence from national organizations are included in this favorable report on amending Title 38 of the *U.S. Code,* to authorize educational assistance and home loan benefits to the wives of servicemen who are missing in action or prisoners of wars.

3051. U.S. Congress. House. Committee on Armed Services. *Establishing a Survivor Benefit Plan for Members of the Armed Forces in Retirement and for Other Purposes, Report to Accompany H.R. 10670.* H. Rept. 92-481, 92d Cong., 1st sess., 1971. 54p. Serial 12932-4. Report supports the establishment of a military survivor benefit plan to supplement Social Security benefits. The plan includes provisions for a minimum income guarantee for present military widows and attachment of retirement or retainer pay to comply with court orders in favor of a spouse, former spouse, or children. Eligibility, marriage subsequent to retirement and income of widow are discussed.

3052. U.S. Congress. Senate. Committee on Armed Services. *Equality of Treatment of Military Personnel in the Application of Dependency Criteria, Report to Accompany S. 2738.* S. Rept. 92-1218, 92d Cong., 2d sess., 1972. 7p. Serial 12971-7. The bill reported changes the definition of a military dependent to automatically include the spouse of a female member of the armed forces, thereby giving the husband the same rights and benefits as the wife of a serviceman.

3053. U.S. Congress. Senate. Committee on Armed Services. *Report to Accompany S. 3905 on Establishing a Survivor Benefit Plan for Members of the Armed Forces in Retirement and for Other Purposes.* S. Rept. 92-1089, 92d Cong., 2d sess., 1972. 87p. Serial 12971-6. Details of the survivor benefit plan for military personnel includes discussion of annuity rates to widows under Dependency and Indemnity Compensation and under Social Security. Compares the provisions of Social Security, DIC, the Retired Servicemen's Family Protection Plan, and S. 3905. A foldout chart compares the military and civil service retirement and survivor benefit systems in a concise form.

3054. U.S. Congress. Senate. Committee on Armed Services. Special Subcommittee on Survivor Benefits. *Survivor Benefit Plan, Hearing on H.R. 10670.* 92d Cong., 2d sess., 8 Aug. 1972. 120p. Y4.Ar5/3:Su7. Review of plans to shape a new military survivor benefit plan discusses existing plans, particularly noting gaps in coverage under Dependency and Indemnity Compensation and the Retired Serviceman's Family Protection Plan. Comparisons with the Civil Service Retirement System are made and detailed charts show the potential number of widows receiving payment and costs. The deduction of Social Security from the widow's payment is also discussed.

3055. U.S. Congress. House. Committee on Veterans' Affairs. *Increases in Rates of Disability and Death Pension, and for Other Purposes, Report to Accompany H.R. 9474.* H. Rept. 93-398, 93rd Cong., 1st sess., 1973. 19p. Serial 13020-4. Reports a bill increasing pensions rates to veterans and their widows.

3056. U.S. Congress. House. Committee on Veterans' Affairs. *Veterans and Survivors Pension Adjustment Act of 1974, Report to Accompany S. 4040.* H. Rept. 93-1499, 93rd Cong., 2d sess., 1974. 33p. Serial 13061-10. Favorable report with amendments describes a bill liberalizing veterans' pension regulations.

3057. U.S. Congress. House. Committee on Veterans' Affairs. *Veterans' and Survivors' Compensation Increases, Report to Accompany H.R. 14117.* H. Rept. 93-991, 93rd Cong., 2d sess., 1974. 20p. Serial 13061-3.

3058. U.S. Congress. Senate. Committee on Veterans' Affairs. *Veterans and Survivor Pension Adjustment Act of 1974, Report to Accompany S. 4040.* S. Rept. 93-1226, 93rd Cong., 2d sess., 1974. 36p. Serial 13057-9. Reports a bill liberalizing death and disability pensions and Dependency and Indemnity Compensation and increasing income limitations. The report provides some historical background on veterans' pension legislation.

3059. U.S. Congress. Senate. Committee on Veterans' Affairs. *Veterans Disability Compensation and Survivor Benefits Act of 1974, Report to Accompany S. 3072.* S. Rept. 93-798, 93rd Cong., 2d sess., 1974. 53p. Serial 13057-2. Favorable report provides background information on S. 3072, a bill providing cost-of-living increases for widows receiving DIC and equalizing survivor benefits in case of peacetime and wartime service.

3060. U.S. Congress. House. Committee on Veterans Affairs. *Veterans' Administration Study of Needs of Veterans and Widows 72 Years of Age or Older, a Report...by the Administrator of Veteran's Affairs.* 94th Cong., 1st sess., 24 July 1975. 70p. Y4.V64/3:V64/14. Report on veterans and widows 72 years old and over reviews pension legislation and presents results of a study of the problems of veterans and widows. Veterans and widows are compared in areas such as income, distribution of income, net worth, expenses, expenditures on necessities, and problems meeting basic needs for food, shelter, and medical care.

3061. U.S. Congress. Senate. Committee on Veterans Affairs. *Needs of Veterans and Widows 72 Years of Age or Older, a Study Prepared by the Veterans' Administration.* 94th Cong., 1st sess., 28 July 1975. 121p. Y4.V64/4:V64/5. See 3060 for abstract.

3062. U.S. Congress. Senate. Committee on Veterans' Affairs. *Veterans and Survivor Pension Interim Adjustment Act of 1975, Report to Accompany H.R. 10355.* S. Rept. 94-568, 94th Cong., 1st sess., 1975. 52p. Serial 13096-9. Background on the number and amount of need-based veterans and survivor pensions currently paid is included in this report on a bill raising the income limitation for such pensions. The bill is presented as a interim measure pending a total restructuring of the veterans' pension program.

3063. U.S. Congress. Senate. Committee on Veterans' Affairs. *Veterans and Survivors Pension Reform Act, Report to Accompany S. 2635.* S. Rept. 94-532, 94th Cong., 1st sess., 1975. 177p. Serial 13096-8. Report on revision of Veterans' Administration need-based pension programs discusses survivor benefits and income limitations and provides supporting data on widows on the pension rolls by available income and age.

3064. U.S. Congress. Senate. Committee on Veterans Affairs. Subcommittee on Compensation and Pensions. *Veterans and Survivor Pension Reform Act, Hearing.* 94th Cong., 1st sess., 18 Nov., 2 Dec. 1975. 1079p. Y4.V64/4:V64/8. Extensive hearing discusses a bill to reorganize the pension payment structure for veterans and widows so as to assure an income above the poverty level. One provision of the measure is to treat veterans and widows equally with regard to income and benefit amounts. Data on veterans and widows on the pension roles and their income is provided.

3065. U.S. Congress. House. Committee on Appropriations. *Making Certain Annuity Entitlement Provisions for Survivors of Non-Regular Retired Personnel, Retroactive to November 1, 1953, Report to Accompany S. 2090.* H. Rept. 94-1436, part 2, 94th Cong., 2d sess., 1976. 2p. Serial 13134-10.

3066. U.S. Congress. House. Committee on Appropriations. *Making Improvements in the Survivor-Benefit Program for Retired Military Personnel, Report to Accompany H.R. 14773.* H. Rept. 94-1458, part 2, 94th Cong., 2d sess., 1976. 4 p. Serial 13134-11.

3067. U.S. Congress. House. Committee on Armed Services. *Authorizing Benefits under the Retired Serviceman's Family Protection Plan to Widows of Certain Deceased Reservists, Report to Accompany S. 2090.* H. Rept. 94-1436, part 1, 94th Cong., 2d sess., 1976. 8p. Serial 13134-10. Minor change in the regulations for survivor benefits under the Retired Serviceman's Family Protection Plan affects eligibility in the case where a serviceman dies after attaining the age of sixty but before the first day of the month after turning sixty.

3068. U.S. Congress. House. Committee on Armed Services. *Making Improvements in the Survivor-Benefit Program for Retired Military Personnel, Report Including Congressional Budget Office Cost Estimate to Accompany H.R. 14773.* H. Rept. 94-1458, part 1, 94th Cong., 2d sess., 1976. 38p. Serial 13134-11. See 3069 for abstract.

3069. U.S. Congress. Senate. Committee on Armed Services. *Making Improvements in the Survivor-Benefit Program for Retired Military Personnel, Report to Accompany H.R. 14773.* S. Rept. 94-1328, 94th Cong., 2d sess., 1976. 13p. Serial 13130-11. Changes made in the Retired Serviceman's Family Protection Plan and the Survivor Benefit Plan include shortening the marriage eligibility requirement from two years to one year, clarifying the law to permit a retiree to leave benefits to children even though there is a surviving spouse, and increasing the minimum income payment to certain widows of retired members.

3070. U.S. Congress. Senate. Committee on Veterans' Affairs. *Veterans Disability Compensation and Survivor Benefits Act of 1976, Report to Accompany H.R. 14299.* S. Rept. 94-1226, 94th Cong., 2d sess., 1976. 68p. Serial 13130-10. Among the provisions of the bill reported is an increase in survivors' Dependency and Indemnity Compensation and a directive to the Veterans' Administration to carry out a study of the adequacy of the survivor benefit program.

3071. U.S. Congress. Senate. Committee on Veterans Affairs. Subcommittee on Compensation and Pensions. *Veterans Disability Compensation and Survivor Benefits Act of 1976, Hearing on S. 3596 and Related Bills.* 94th Cong., 2d sess., 23 July 1976. 513p. Y4.V64/4:V64/7. Hearing examines a bill to increase compensation for disabled veterans, dependents, and survivors and to increase payments and eligibility for selected special allowances.

3072. U.S. Congress. House. Committee on Armed Services. *Making Improvements in the Survivor Benefit Program for Retired Military Personnel, Report to Accompany H.R. 3702.* H. Rept. 95-72, 95th Cong., 1st sess., 1977. 24p. Serial 13172-1. The bill reported makes several changes in the Retired Serviceman's Family Protection Plan and the Survivor Benefit Plan including cost-of-living increases, payment of benefits to a spouse who remarries after age 60 in certain circumstances, and reduction of the Social Security offset.

3073. U.S. Congress. House. Committee on Armed Services. Military Compensation Subcommittee. *Hearings on Survivor Benefits for Reservists.* 95th Cong., 1st sess., 15, 20 Sept. 1977. 80p. Y4.Ar5/2a:977-78/45. Hearing addresses the survivor benefit situation in the National Guard and Armed Forces Reserves, where no survivor benefits exist if a Guard or Reservist dies before age sixty.

3074. U.S. Congress. House. Committee on Veterans' Affairs. *Veterans' Disability Compensation and Survivor Benefits Act of 1977, Report to Accompany H.R. 1862.* H. Rept. 95-356, 95th Cong., 1st sess., 1977. 24p. Serial 13172-6. Reports legislation which would increase the rates of Dependency and Indemnity Compensation for widows and children of veterans. Charts compares DIC increases and the Consumer Price Index by pay grade since 1957 and illustrates widows' compensation rates under existing law and H.R. 1862.

3075. U.S. Congress. House. Committee on Veterans' Affairs. Subcommittee on Compensation, Pension, and Insurance. *Increased Rates of Pension, Hearings [on] H.R. 1863, H.R. 1865.* 95th Cong., 1st sess., 17,18 May 1977. 45p. Y4.V64/3:P38/25. Cost of living increases in pension benefits for non-service connected disabled veterans and their dependents are discussed. A provision to raise pension rates for widows over age 78 is also examined. Testimony focuses on the inadequacy of the pension rates and the desirability of a needs-based system.

3076. U.S. Congress. House. Committee on Armed Services. *Reserve Survivors' Benefits Act of 1978, Report to Accompany H.R. 11797.* H. Rept. 95-1077, 95th Cong., 2d sess., 1978. 23p. Serial 13201-4. Reports on a plan to provide survivor benefits for Reserve and National Guard personnel who complete twenty years of service but who die before attaining the age of sixty.

3077. U.S. Congress. Senate. Committee on Armed Services. Subcommittee on Manpower and Personnel. *Benefits for Survivors of Military Personnel, Hearing on S. 520, S. 623, S. 724, S. 1996, H.R. 3702, H.R. 11707.* 95th Cong., 2d sess., 17 Aug. 1978. 139p. Y4.Ar5/3:B43/3. Hearing on changes in survivor benefit rules for military personnel discusses extension of survivor benefits to families of personnel who die before retirement, cost-of-living increases, remarriage after age sixty, and the Social Security offset for widows.

3078. U.S. Congress. House. Committee on Armed Services. *Uniformed Services Survivor Benefits Amendments of 1980, Report to Accompany S. 91.* H. Rept. 96-1315, 96th Cong., 2d sess., 1980. 23p. Serial 13376. Changes proposed to the Survivor Benefit Plan include changes in the Social Security offset and in the calculation of contribution to the plan from the annuitants benefit.

3079. U.S. Congress. House. Committee on Armed Services. Military Compensation Subcommittee. *Hearing on H.R. 2817, H.R. 3677, and H.R. 6270, Legislation Related to Benefits for Former Spouse of a Military Retiree.* 96th Cong., 2d sess., 28 May 1980. 126p. Y4.Ar5/2a:979-80/65. Hearing on various bills to ensure the ability of former military wives to collect a portion of their ex-husband's military retirement pay includes testimony from former wives and experts on the situation of divorced military spouses. The main point of discussion is the difference between one plan which would establish a right to a portion of the military pay and another that would merely allow compliance with court settlements. Whether these women could have worked as military wives is debated along with discussion of the expected role of the military wife.

3080. U.S. Congress. House. Committee on Armed Services. Subcommittee on Military Personnel and Compensation. *Benefits for Former Spouses of Military Members, Hearing.* 97th Cong., 1st sess., 5 Nov. 1981. 62p. Y4.Ar5/2a:981-82/70/pt.1. Several bills addressing the claims of former spouses to a portion of the military retirement pay of their ex-husbands are reviewed. The bills follow in the wake of the Supreme Court's decision in *McCarty v. McCarty*, in which the court ruled that military retirement pay was not community property. Most of the bills provide for direct payment of court-ordered child support, alimony, or other property settlements from military retirement pay. The contribution of the military wife to her husband's career and the hardships faced by them are cited in support of the bills. Opponents stress that military retired pay is different from a pension or annuity.

3081. U.S. Congress. House. Committee on Armed Services. Subcommittee on Military Personnel and Compensation. *Benefits for Former Spouses of Military Members, Hearing, Part 2.* 97th Cong., 1st sess., 8 Dec. 1981. 59p. Y4.Ar5/2a:981-82/70/pt.2. Hearing examines the situation where divorced wives of military personnel were deemed to have no claim to the military pension of their former spouse. Testimony highlights the retirement problems of divorced women with a particular emphasis on former military spouses and on the courts handling of pension issues.

3082. U.S. Congress. House. Committee on Veteran's Affairs. *Veterans' Disability Compensation and Survivors' Benefits Amendments of 1982, Report to Accompany H.R. 6782.* H. Rept. 97-660, 97th Cong., 2d sess., 1982. 94p. Serial 13486. Amendments to veterans' disability compensation and DIC laws raise rates and make other administrative changes. Some basic background on DIC recipients and compensation rates is included. Departmental correspondence appended relates primarily to eligibility and cost.

3083. U.S. Congress. Senate. Committee on Armed Services. *Uniformed Services Former Spouse Protection Act, Report to Act, Report to Accompany S. 1814.* S. Rept. 97-502, 97th Cong., 2d sess., 1982. 57p. Serial 13451. The bill reported provides for the inclusion of military retirement pay in divorce settlements. The *McCarty v. McCarty* decision's effect on the courts ability to divide military retired pay in divorce settlements and the past legislative action on the issues is reviewed. Summary of testimony at committee hearings reviews the issues of divorce and the military spouse.

3084. U.S. Congress. Senate. Committee on Armed Services. Subcommittee on Manpower and Personnel. *Uniformed Services Former Spouses Protection Act, Hearings on S. 1453, S. 1648, S. 1814.* 97th Cong., 1st and 2d sess., 22 Sept. 1981 - 29 Apr. 1982. 234p. Y4.Ar5/3:Un3/4. Hearing explores the rationale behind several measures designed to ensure the ability of a former spouse to claim part of a military pension in a divorce settlement. Proponents describe the contributions and sacrifices of military wives while opponents describe military retirement pay as fundamentally different from retirement pensions and annuities. Testimony refers repeatedly to the *McCarty* decision, which established military retirement pay as outside community property.

3085.   U.S. Army. *Help Your Widow while She's Still Your Wife.* Army Pamphlet 608-22. Washington, DC: GPO, 1983. 29p. D101.22:608-22. Reviews planning survivor benefits for widows of retired Army personnel and other aspects of estate planning as it relates to widow's income.

3086.   U.S. Air Force. *Benefits for Dependents and Survivors of Active Duty Air Force Casualties.* Air Force Pamphlet 211-15. Washington, DC: GPO, 1985. 17p. D301.35:211-15/985. Pamphlet briefly outlines monetary and in-kind benefits for survivors and dependents of active duty Air Force personnel.

3087.   U.S. Congress. House. *Department of Defense Authorization Act, 1986, Conference Report to Accompany S. 1160.* H. Rept. 99-235, 99th Cong., 1st sess., 1985. 520p. Serial 13651. Conference committee report discusses 1986 Department of Defense authorization for procurement, research, and personnel. Personnel provisions include VA medical care for survivors of reservists who die of illness or disease during inactive duty training and major changes in the Survivor Benefit Plan. Spousal consent to waive survivor benefits, authorization of former spouse coverage, and notification of a spouse in the case of remarriage and survivor benefit elections are among the areas covered. Also provided in the committee bill is a provision for hiring preferences for spouses at overseas locations. A requirement for child care facilities on military bases was not adopted, but a directive to the Secretary of Defense to conduct a study of the need for such services was included.

3088.   U.S. Congress. House. Committee on Veterans' Affairs. *Veterans' Compensation and Health Care Amendments of 1985, Report Together with Supplement View to Accompany H.R. 1538.* H. Rept. 99-337, part 1, 99th Cong., 1st sess., 1985. 109p. Serial 13656. Reports a bill increasing DIC compensation rates and directing the VA to conduct a gender-specific study of adverse health effects of herbicides containing dioxin (Agent Orange) on female veterans who served in Vietnam.

3089.   U.S. Congress. Senate. *Department of Defense Authorization Act, 1986, Conference Report to Accompany S. 1160.* S. Rept. 99-118, 90th Cong., 1st sess., 1985. 520p. Serial 13651. Same as H. Rept. 99-235 (3087).

3090.   U.S. Congress. Senate. Committee on Veterans' Affairs. *Veterans' Compensation and Benefits Improvements Act of 1985, Report to Accompany S. 1887.* S. Rept. 99-200, 99th Cong., 1st sess., 1985. 188p. Serial 13625. Provisions affecting women in this bill on VA compensation and benefit programs are an increase in DIC rates, more flexible time limitations on educational assistance to survivors, and a requirement that the VA arrange for a epidemiological study of the health of women Vietnam veterans. The last provision stems from the fact that women were excluded from the Center of Disease Control study of the effect of Agent Orange on veterans.

3091.   U.S. Congress. House. Committee on Armed Services. Military Personnel and Compensation Subcommittee. *Military Widows' Issues, Hearing.* 100th Cong., 2d sess., 8 Sept. 1988. 162p. Y4.Ar5/2a:987-88/118. Hearing considers the provision of survivor benefits to widows of retired servicemen who died prior to the creation of the Survivor Benefit Plan in 1972 and to the widows of reservists who died before reaching age sixty and before 1978. The poverty status of the "forgotten widows" is described through correspondence and testimony. Background on the treatment of widows under military pension and annuity systems is provided.

3092.   U.S. Congress. House. Committee on Veterans' Affairs. *To Remove a Limitation on the Payment of Pension to Veterans Furnished Long-Term Hospital Care by the Department of Veterans Affairs and to Reduce the Period of Marriage of Certain Surviving Spouses Required for Dependency and Indemnity Compensation, Report to Accompany H.R. 1334.*

H. Rept. 101-105, 101st Cong., 1st sess., 22 June 1989. 11p. Brief report details a bill allowing a widow who had only been married one year to a disabled veteran to collect death benefits at the DIC rate.

3093. U.S. Congress. House. Committee on Veterans' Affairs. *Veterans' Compensation Amendments of 1989, Report to Accompany H.R. 1335.* H. Rept. 101-262, 101st Cong., 1st sess., 1989. 34p. The bill reported changes the benefit structure for surviving spouses under DIC. A concise summary of DIC compensation rates and rules is provided along with data on the number of DIC beneficiaries by armed action, e.g. Civil War, WWII, Korean Conflict, etc.

3094. U.S. Congress. House. Committee on Veterans' Affairs. Subcommittee on Compensation, Pension and Insurance. *Compensation and DIC COLA, H.R. 1335; DIC Eligibility Criteria, H.R. 1336; and Pension for Hospitalized Veterans, H.R. 1334, Hearing.* 101st Cong., 1st sess., 5 Apr. 1989. 89p. Y4.V64/3:101-4. Hearing considers bills to change DIC benefits including a cost of living adjustment and a change in eligibility criteria. The most controversial aspect is the reduction to one year of the required length of marriage for a widow of a veteran who died of a service connected cause to be eligible for DIC benefits. Witnesses also discuss allowing widows to remarry after age 55 without losing benefits.

3095. U.S. Dept. of Veterans Affairs. *An Evaluation of the Department of Veterans Affairs' Restored Entitlement Program for Survivors.* Washington, DC: GPO, 1989. 51p. VA1.2:Ev1/3. Review of the Restored Entitlement Program for Survivors (REPS) looks at the history of the program and its operation. The program restored benefits lost in the 1981 amendments to the Social Security Act to children and surviving spouses of military personnel who died while on active duty of a service-connected disability.

3096. U.S. Congress. House. Committee on Armed Services. Military Personnel and Compensation Subcommittee. *Uniformed Services Former Spouses Protection Act (FSPA), Hearing.* 101st Cong., 2d sess., 4 Apr. 1990. 450p. Y4.Ar5/2a:989-90/76. Witnesses present diverse views on the 1982 Uniformed Services Former Spouses' Protection Act and on the need to amend the act. At the heart of the debate is the role the federal government should play in proscribing the treatment of military retirement pay in divorce settlements. Allowing states' to apply state law verses a federally set formula for dividing pay is debated from the viewpoint of the military, the former spouse, and the second family.

3097. U.S. Congress. House. Committee on Veterans' Affairs. *Veterans' Compensation Amendments of 1990, Report to Accompany H.R. 5326.* H. Rept. 101-857, 101st Cong., 2d sess., 1990. 52p. Background on DIC rates for surviving spouses is provided in a report on a bill raising DIC rates and making other changes in veterans' benefit programs.

3098. U.S. Congress. House. Committee on Veterans' Affairs. Subcommittee on Compensation, Pension and Insurance. *H.R. 4418 - Cost-of-Living Adjustment for Service-Connected Disabled Veterans and Heir Dependents, Hearing.* 101st Cong., 2d sess., 19 Apr. 1990. 96p. Y4.V64/3:101-45. Witnesses support a cost-of-living increase in DIC but debate how benefit rates should be determined. Also discussed is the inability of military widows to remarry after age 55 and retain their benefits, even though other federal pension plans allow remarriage.

3099. U.S. Dept. of Defense. American Forces Information Service. *Survivor Benefit Plan for the Uniformed Services Made Easy.* Washington, DC: The Service, 1990. 32p. D2.14:PA-11G. Details of the Survivor Benefit Plan described include contributions, spousal consent, remarriage, former spouses, tax aspects, and the Social Security offset.

SERIALS

3100.	U.S. Dept. of Defense. American Forces Information Service. *Survivor Benefit Plan for the Uniformed Services.* DoD pamphlet 11. Washington, DC: GPO, 1974-. rev. irreg. D2.14:PA-11(letter). Describes rules governing the Survivor Benefit Plan for spouses and children of military personnel.

19

Violence against Women

The documents on violence against women deal with the two distinct topics of sexual assault and domestic violence. The earliest documents identified were House and Senate reports, from 1888 and 1889 respectively, reporting bills to define statutory rape in the Revised Statutes of the District of Columbia (3101-3102). The next significant report on rape does not appear until 1975, when the National Institute of Law Enforcement and Criminal Justice released *Rape and Its Victims*, a survey-based report on the handling of rape by the police, the courts, and victim services providers (3112). Numerous significant reports followed. Among the most notable are a 1977 report of the National Institute of Mental Health on the social and psychological effects of rape (3123), a 1978 congressional hearing, *Research into Violent Behavior: Overview and Sexual Assaults* (3130), and a series of reports covering all aspects of forcible rape issued between and 1977 and 1978 by the National Institute of Law Enforcement and Criminal Justice (3133-3137).

A number of documents describe model community services programs for victims of sexual assault. The most detailed of these is the 1980 report, *Rape, Guidelines for a Community Response* (3173). The reform of rape laws is discussed in a number of documents, but the clearest discussion is possibly that of the House hearings in 1984 on *Federal Rape Law Reform* (3198) and in 1986 on the Sexual Abuse Act of 1986 (3214), both of which discuss shifting the focus to the accused and the issue of spousal immunity. While acquaintance rape is briefly mentioned in earlier documents, the only lengthy discussion is found in a 1990 Senate hearing on women and violence (3236).

Domestic violence, like sexual assault, first appears in government documents in respect to the laws of the District of Columbia. The 1906 House report on a bill providing for corporal punishment of men convicted of wife abuse presents statistics on arrests for wife abuse in the District of Columbia (3105). Domestic violence does not figure prominently in documents again until the mid-1970s, when the Commission on Civil Rights focused attention on the problem. Dozens of significant documents since that time explore the problem of wife abuse, among them the 1978 report of the Commission on Civil Rights, *Battered Women: Issues of Public Policy* (3124), and a hearing held by the House Committee on Education and Labor (3126). Also in 1978, the House Committee on Science and Technology held extensive hearings on *Research into Violence Behavior* which examined the incidence, causes, and effect of domestic violence in-depth (3128-3129).

Both Congress and the Civil Rights Commission held hearings and issued substantial reports in the years that followed. Some of the more noteworthy are *Prosecution of Spouse Abuse: Innovations in Criminal Justice Response* (3179), the Commission on Civil Right's report, *Under the Rule of Thumb: Battered Women and the Administration of Justice* (3193), and the final report of the Attorney General's Task Force on Family Violence (3197). Congress dealt with the issue of domestic violence on a regular basis in conjunction with federal family violence programs. In 1987 the House Select Committee on Children, Youth, and Families held a hearing, *Women, Violence and the Law* (3219), which specifically addressed the criminal justice system's response to domestic violence. In 1990 Congress was still exploring the problem of domestic violence, this time in relation to the proposed Violence against Women Act of 1990 (3234, 3236).

3101.   U.S. Congress. House. Committee on the District of Columbia. *Protection of Girls and Punishment of the Crime of Rape.* H. Rept. 92, 50th Cong., 1st sess., 1888. 1p. Serial 2598. Reports bills H.R. 1496 and H.R. 5870 amending the Revised Statutes of the District of Columbia to clarify the law on statutory rape.

3102.   U.S. Congress. Senate. *Disagreeing Votes of the Two Houses on the Amendment of the Senate to the Bill (H.R. 5870) to Amend the Revised Statutes of the District of Columbia, for the Protection of Girls for the Punishment of the Crime of Rape.* S. Misc. Doc. 44, 50th Cong., 2d sess., 1889. 1p. Serial 2615. Conference committee report approves the wording of a bill defining the crime of statutory rape in the District of Columbia and setting the punishment for the crime.

3103.   U.S. Congress. Senate. Committee on the District of Columbia. *Age of Protection for Girls in the District of Columbia, Report to Accompany S. 1498.* H. Rept. 1500, 54th Cong., 2d sess., 1897. 2p. Serial 3476. Reports a bill raising the age of statutory rape to eighteen in the District of Columbia.

3104.   U.S. Congress. Senate. *Convictions for Wife Beating in the District of Columbia since 1900.* S. Doc. 129, 58th Cong., 3d sess., 1905. 2p. Serial 4765. In response to a Senate resolution the Board of Commissioners sent this brief report on the number of convictions for wife abuse in the District of Columbia for the years 1900 to 1904. The numbers are estimates and do not include cases where the wife withdrew the charge before trial.

3105.   U.S. Congress. House. Committee on the District of Columbia. *Punishment for Wife Beating, Report to Accompany H.R. 8133.* H. Rept. 1057, 59th Cong., 1st sess., 1906. 2p. Serial 4906. Reports, without recommendation, a bill providing for the infliction of corporal punishment upon all male persons convicted of wilfully beating their wives. Attached correspondence supporting the bill includes a letter from the Major and Superintendent of the Metropolitan Police Department giving data on arrests on the charge of wife assault in the previous two years. The Superintendent also recommends extending the law to cover "common law wives or other females, as numerous instances of the kind have been recorded."

3106.   U.S. Congress. House. Committee on the District of Columbia. *Amending Section 808, Code of Law for the District of Columbia, Report to Accompany H.R. 21712.* H. Rept. 552, 62d Cong., 2d sess., 1912. 1p. Serial 6131. Report supports an amendment of the code of the District of Columbia by changing the age for statutory rape to twelve years old and by adding a lesser crime of "carnal knowledge and abuse of a female" between the ages of twelve and sixteen.

3107.   U.S. Commission on Obscenity and Pornography. *Technical Report of the Commission on Obscenity and Pornography.* Washington, DC: GPO, 1971-1972. 9 vol. Y3.Ob7:10/vol. no. In-depth report on obscenity and pornography reviews the literature, the laws, and the pornography industry. Volumes 7 discusses pornography and possible links to sexual offenses.

3108.   U.S. National Institute of Law Enforcement and Criminal Justice. *Family Crisis Intervention: From Concept to Implementation.* by Morton Bard. Washington, D.C. GPO,

1973. 13p. J1.44/2:F21. Discussion of the concepts of family crisis intervention by law enforcement personnel accompanies a summary of results of studies on crisis intervention by the Law Enforcement Assistance Administration. Organizational and operational considerations in implementing a program of family crisis intervention are briefly reviewed.

3109. U.S. National Institute of Mental Health. *Violence at Home: an Annotated Bibliography.* by Mary Lystad. Washington, DC: GPO, 1974. 102p. HE20.8113:V81. Annotated bibliography lists English and foreign language references on theories and incidence of family violence and on services to families with violent members.

3110. U.S. Congress. House. *Health Services and Nurse Training, Conference Report to Accompany S. 66.* H. Rept. 94-348, 94th Cong., 1st sess., 1975. 84p. Serial 13099-6. Conference report on S. 66, a bill to amend the nurse training assistance and health revenue sharing programs, details the House amendments which were at odds with the Senate version. Included in the bill under revenue sharing programs are Title X family planning services and a newly instituted rape prevention and control program. Provisions relating to coercive abortions and sterilizations and natural family planning methods were points of difference between the two versions.

3111. U.S. Congress. Senate. *Message from the President of the United States Returning without My Approval S. 66, a Bill to Amend the Public Health Service Act to Provide Support for Health Services, Nurse Training, and the National Health Service Corps Programs.* S. Doc. 94-92, 94th Cong., 1st sess., 1975. 70p. Serial 13102-2. Veto message on S. 66 cites "excessive appropriations levels" as a major objection but also rejects new programs, such as the rape prevention and control segment of the bill, as potentially costly and duplicating existing programs. The message also rejects the nurse training provisions as unnecessary on the ground that the nurse shortage is disapproved and that nurse training programs should be integrated into other health professions education measures, not treated separately.

3112. U.S. National Institute of Law Enforcement and Criminal Justice. *Rape and Its Victims: A Report for Citizens, Health Facilities, and Criminal Justice Agencies.* by Lisa Brodyaga, et al. Washington, DC: GPO, 1975. 361p. J1.8/3:R18. Survey results describe procedures of police departments, medical facilities, prosecutors' offices, and citizens' action groups in dealing with the crime of forcible rape and provides guidelines based on the survey findings. Coordination of all agencies involved is stressed. Some model programs are described, and selected articles on the social and psychological consequences of rape are included.

3113. U.S. Air Force. *Project Concern.* Washington, D.C. The Department, 1976. 17p. D301.2:P94/2. Outlines programs Air Force wives clubs can develop to combat the effects of alcoholism on the family.

3114. U.S. Congress. House. Committee on the Judiciary. Subcommittee on Criminal Justice. *Privacy of Rape Victims, Hearing on H.R. 14666 and Other Bills.* 94th Cong., 2d sess., 29 July 1976. 106p. Y4.J89/1:94-58. Hearing on bills making a rape victim's past sexual behavior inadmissible evidence explores issues of the victim's right to privacy and the accused's right to a fair trial. Examines in detail the intricacies of determining guilt in rape trials and the treatment of rape victims in the courts.

3115. U.S. National Institute of Law Enforcement and Criminal Justice. *An Exemplary Project, a Community Response to Rape, Polk County Rape/Sexual Assault Care Center.* Washington, DC: GPO, 1976. 12p. leaflet. J1.10:R18/desc. Summarizes a report (3120) on a sexual assault victim assistance program in Des Moines, Iowa.

3116. U.S. Army. *Victims of Sexual Assault.* Training Circular 19-14. Washington, DC: The Department, 1977. 28p. D101.24:19-14. Handbook for MPs handling reports of sexual assault defines rape and other forms of sexual assault and discusses procedures and victim treatment. The pamphlet shows a good deal of sensitivity toward the victim and discusses the special handling of cases involving children and the elderly.

3117. U.S. Commission on Civil Rights. Colorado Advisory Committee. *The Silent Victims: Denver's Battered Women.* Washington, DC: GPO, 1977. 22p. CR1.2:W84/2. After an overview of the problem of battered women, the report assesses the incidence of domestic violence against women and the effectiveness of police efforts in the Denver area. The need for improved social service support for battered women is stressed.

3118. U.S. National Commission on the Observance of International Women's Year. *Rape.* Washington, DC: GPO, 1977. 66p. Y3.W84:10/15. Guidelines and materials for conducting a workshop on rape includes fact sheets, a bibliography, a list of speakers and resource people, and a list of films.

3119. U.S. National Commission on the Observance of International Women's Year. *Wife Abuse: a Workshop Guide.* Washington, DC: GPO, 1977. 22p. Y3.W84:10/17. Workshop guide includes fact sheets on wife abuse and resource lists covering refuges, speakers, films, and publications.

3120. U.S. National Institute of Law Enforcement and Criminal Justice. *An Exemplary Project, a Community Response to Rape, Polk County Rape/Sexual Assault Care Center.* by Gerald Bryant and Paul Cirel. Washington, DC: GPO, 1977. 200p. J1.10:R18. Describes a rape/sexual assault victim program in Des Moines, Iowa designed to deal with the physical, psychological, and criminal aspects of rape and sexual assault. The Center coordinates victim services and community education programs and works closely with the criminal justice system.

3121. U.S. National Institute of Law Enforcement and Criminal Justice. *Forcible Rape: Medical and Legal Information.* Washington, DC: GPO, 1977. 18p. J1.2:R18/3. Booklet written for rape victims discusses the medical and legal aspects of rape in layman's terms.

3122. U.S. National Institute of Mental Health. *Rape Prevention and Control, a New National Center.* Washington, DC: GPO, 1977. 5p. HE20.8102:R18.

3123. U.S. National Institute of Mental Health. *Victims of Rape.* Washington, DC: GPO, 1977. 30p. HE20.8102:R18/2. Report of the Philadelphia Assault Victim Study focuses on the social and psychological effects of rape on female victims and on the events and their effect as the victim passes through the criminal justice system. The background, characteristics of the rape, and reaction to the rape are examined separately for children, adolescent and adult victims.

3124. U.S. Commission on Civil Rights. *Battered Women: Issues of Public Policy, a Consultation Sponsored by the United States Commission on Civil Rights, Washington, D.C., January 30-31, 1978.* Washington, DC: The Commission, 1978? 706p. CR1.2:W84/3. Expert witnesses present their views on the effectiveness of police and judicial policies and practices for dealing with wife abuse. The services provided by shelters and the funding problems they face are also described. Theories on the societal basis of wife abuse are presented.

3125. U.S. Congress. House. Committee on Education and Labor. *Domestic Violence Assistance Act of 1978, Report to Accompany H.R. 1127.* 95th Cong., 2d sess., 1978. 9p. Serial 13201-5. Reports a bill authorizing federal grants to communities for domestic violence services, establishing an Office of Domestic Violence to disseminate information and coordinate programs, and creating a Council on Domestic Violence to oversee the grants. The report focuses primarily on the administrative aspects of the bill.

3126. U.S. Congress. House. Committee on Education and Labor. Subcommittee on Select Education. *Domestic Violence, Hearings on H.R. 7927 and H.R. 8948.* 95th Cong., 2d sess., 16-17 Mar. 1978. 753p. Y4.Ed8/1:D71. Representatives from the legal community, public service agencies, women's groups and battered women's shelters testify on the extent of domestic violence in America and the need for services to aid its victims.

3127. U.S. Congress. House. Committee on Education and Labor. Subcommittee on Select Education. *Domestic Violence in Vermont, Hearing.* 95th Cong., 2d sess., 22 July 1978. Montpelier, VT. 71p. Y4.Ed8/1:D71/3. Hearing on the problem of domestic violence in Vermont presents testimony on the services offered to victims and on the ways government can respond to the needs of battered women and their children.

3128. U.S. Congress. House. Committee on Science and Technology. Subcommittee on Domestic and International Scientific Planning, Analysis and Cooperation. *Research into Violent Behavior: Domestic Violence.* 95th Cong., 2d sess., 1978. Committee print. 47p. Y4.Sci2:95/YY. Summary of information gathered during hearings on research into family violence reviews the causes of violence between family members, the legal and criminal justice responses to household violence, alternative prevention and treatment strategies, and federal agency activities.

3129. U.S. Congress. House. Committee on Science and Technology. Subcommittee on Domestic and International Scientific Planning, Analysis and Cooperation. *Research into Violent Behavior: Domestic Violence, Hearings.* 95th Cong., 2d sess., 14-16 Feb. 1978. 1041p. Y4.Sci2:95/60. Hearing reviews federal support for research on domestic violence and the results of selected projects. Research reported covers the incidence of family violence, profiles of battered women and the psycho-social climate of domestic violence. Additional material submitted for the record includes an annotated bibliography on child abuse and family violence.

3130. U.S. Congress. House. Committee on Science and Technology. Subcommittee on Domestic and International Scientific Planning, Analysis and Cooperation. *Research into Violent Behavior: Overview and Sexual Assaults, Hearings.* 95th Cong., 2d sess., 10-12 Jan. 1978. 934p. Y4.Sci2:95/64. Hearing testimony reviews research findings on violent behavior and examines the relationship between research and criminal justice. The incidence of violent behavior in general and sexual assault in particular and at what is known regarding psychological and sociological factors related to this behavior is reviewed. Areas of potential focus for additional research are noted.

3131. U.S. Congress. Senate. Committee on Human Resources. *Domestic Violence Prevention and Services Act, Report to Accompany S. 2759.* S. Rept. 95-824, 95th Cong., 2d sess., 1978. 64p. Serial 13197-3. Comprehensive legislation to provide for domestic violence services and research is reported with numerous committee amendments. The bill authorized federal grants to state and local agencies with a focus on providing shelter services, and established the National Center on Domestic Violence and an interagency coordinating council. Research money authorized by the bill was mostly earmarked for the Alcohol, Drug Abuse and Mental Health Administration. Background on the need for the bill is provided in a summary of information presented at the committee hearings which examined domestic violence from the criminal justice viewpoint and looked at its socioeconomic impact on families.

3132. U.S. Congress. Senate. Committee on Human Resources. Subcommittee on Child and Human Development. *Domestic Violence, 1978, Hearings.* 95th Cong., 2d sess., 4, 8 Mar. 1978. Los Angeles, CA; Washington, DC. 708p. Y4.H88:D71. Testimony from a wide array of witnesses representing victims of spouse abuse, women's organizations, social service agencies, and providers of shelter services explores the problem of domestic violence. Topics covered include background information on the causes, extent, and psychological impact of domestic violence and on the response of local, state, and federal government to the problem of domestic violence.

3133. U.S. National Institute of Law Enforcement and Criminal Justice. *Forcible Rape, a Literature Review and Annotated Bibliography.* by Duncan Chappell and Faith Fogarty. Washington, DC: GPO, 1978. 84p. J1.20/2:R18. Ten page literature review on forcible rape accompanies 153 annotated citations on socio-cultural aspects of rape, victimization, offenders, police procedures, legal issues, and rape in foreign countries and cultures.

3134. U.S. National Institute of Law Enforcement and Criminal Justice. *Forcible Rape, an Analysis of Legal Issues.* Washington, DC: GPO, 1978. 97p. J1.2:R18/5. Overview of the legal issues of rape describes attitudes past and present, problems of enforcement, and movements towards legal reform. Compares alternative statutory approaches to rape and discusses some of the problems of adjudication of rape cases. Summarizes current and proposed state legislation.

3135. U.S. National Institute of Law Enforcement and Criminal Justice. *Forcible Rape, Final Project Report.* Washington, DC: GPO, 1978. 80p. J1.2:R18/4. Final report on the LEAA study of forcible rape summarizes the project findings collected from police and prosecutor surveys, rape victims, offenders, and law enforcement records.

3136. U.S. National Institute of Law Enforcement and Criminal Justice. *Forcible Rape, Police.* Washington, DC: GPO, 1977-1978. 4 vol. J1.2:R18/2/v.1-4. Volume one reports the results of a national survey of police response to rape with statistics on police handling of rape cases, factors frequently observed in rape cases such as characteristics of victims and offenders, victim services, and prosecution. Volume 2 is a manual on handling rape cases for patrol officers and volume 3 is a manual for sex crime investigators. Volume 4 discusses administrative and policy issues including selection and training of personnel and interactions with non-police agencies.

3137. U.S. National Institute of Law Enforcement and Criminal Justice. *Forcible Rape, Prosecutors' Volume.* Washington, DC: GPO, 1977-1978. 3 vol. J1.2:R18/v.1-3. The first volume reports results of a national survey of the response of prosecutors to rape with information on factors in rapes and factors affecting decision to press charges. Interaction with victim and victim services is also examined. Volume 2 is a manual on the responsibilities of filing and trial prosecutors. Policy change to encourage reporting of rape and more sensitive treatment of victims are discussed in Volume 3.

3138. U.S. National Institute of Law Enforcement and Criminal Justice. *Forcible Rape, the Criminal Justice System Response.* Washington, DC: The Institute, 1978. 6p. J26.2:R18. Describes LEAA publications on rape and the criminal justice system.

3139. U.S. Army. Criminal Investigation Command. *Rape: What Every Woman Should Know.* Washington, DC: The Department, 1979. [6]p. leaflet. D101.2:R18.

3140. U.S. Commission on Civil Rights. Colorado Advisory Committee, et al. *Energy Resource Development: Implications for Women and Minorities in the Intermountain West.* Washington, DC: GPO, 1979. 221p. CR1.2:En2/5. Energy boomtowns can have serious effects on women in the communities. Increases in alcoholism, family violence, and suicide are common in boomtowns. Study by the advisory committees of six western states looks at the problems and possibilities boomtowns present to women and at the Indian rights issues involved.

3141. U.S. Commission on Civil Rights. Connecticut Advisory Committee. *Battered Women in Hartford, Connecticut.* Washington, DC: GPO, 1979. 28p. CR1.2:W84/5. An investigation into legal and social services to support abused wives in Hartford found that police were inadequately trained to handle domestic violence and often discouraged the wife from pursuing charges. In the opinion of the advisory committee, the judicial system in Hartford did not adequately protect the rights of battered women and public assistance regulations failed to meet their needs.

3142. U.S. Congress. House. Committee on Education and Labor. *Domestic Violence Prevention and Services Act, Report Together with Dissenting Views, to Accompany H.R. 2977.* H. Rept. 96-613, 96th Cong., 1st sess., 1979. 26p. Serial 13303. Report on a bill authorizing a federal grant program for domestic violence prevention and services provides some background on the extent of domestic violence in the U.S. and on the need for more shelter services. Dissenting views express the opinion that sufficient federal programs already exist to address the problem of domestic violence.

3143. U.S. Congress. House. Committee on Education and Labor. Subcommittee on Select Education. *Domestic Violence: Prevention and Services, Hearings.* 96th Cong., 1st sess., 10-11 July 1979. 550p. Y4.Ed8/1:D71/4. Extensive hearing on the problem of domestic violence focuses on service needs, such as shelters and hot lines, and on the criminal justice response to domestic violence. Current programs both public and private are described including the LEAA family violence program. A report of a national survey of domestic violence assistance organizations is included.

3144. U.S. National Center for the Prevention and Control of Rape. *Materials Available from the National Rape Information Clearinghouse.* Washington, DC: GPO, 1979. 3p. HE20.8113:R18.

3145. U.S. National Center for the Prevention and Control of Rape. *Printout of Literature Search on Rape.* Washington, DC: GPO, 1979. 284p. HE20.8113:R18/2. Results of a literature search of the National Rape Information Clearinghouse database on the topic of sexual assault includes journal articles, books, conference papers, and government documents primarily published between 1976 and 1978.

3146. U.S. National Clearinghouse on Domestic Violence. *Funding Family Violence Programs: Sources and Potential Sources for Federal Monies.* by Susan Cohen. Rockville, MD: The Clearinghouse, 1979. 19p. HE23.1002:F21/2. Guide provides brief program summaries of major federal grant programs whose money could be used to fund family violence programs and other federal monies available at the local level through state agencies.

3147. U.S. National Criminal Justice Information and Statistics Service. *Rape Victimization in 26 American Cities.* by M. Joan McDermott. Applications of the National Crime Survey Victimization and Attitude Data Analytic Report SD-VAD-6. Washington, DC: GPO, 1979. 80p. J26.10:SD-VAD-6. Report analyzes data on rapes profiling victims by age, race, martial status, major activity, and income, and characteristics of offenders by characteristics of victim. Elements of victimization and some of the consequences are also studied.

3148. U.S. National Institute of Law Enforcement and Criminal Justice. *Spouse Abuse: A Selected Bibliography.* by Carolyn Johnson, et al. Washington, DC: GPO, 1979. 61p.

J26.9:Sp6. Citations from the National Criminal Justice Reference Service on spouse abuse look at the nature of the problem and the role of law enforcement intervention.

3149.   U.S. National Institute of Law Enforcement and Criminal Justice. Office of Development, Testing and Dissemination. *Stop Rape Crisis Center, Baton Rouge, Louisiana, an Exemplary Project.* Washington, DC: GPO, 1979. 10p. J26.22:R18. Describes a rape crisis center where law enforcement and support personnel work together to encourage reporting of rapes and prosecution.

3150.   U.S. National Institute of Mental Health. *Rape and Older Women, a Guide to Prevention and Protection.* Rockville, MD: The Institute, 1979. 171p. HE20.8108:R18. Guide to prevention of sexual assaults on elderly women looks at the psychological and social characteristics of women which put them at risk as victims. Prevention programs described feature avoidance behavior, community organization, and physical design of the residential environment. Education and training programs are also discussed. Includes statistics on crime rate and victimization by sex and a bibliography.

3151.   U.S. National Institute of Mental Health. *Rape, Prevention and Control...the Federal Focal Point.* Rockville, MD: The Institute, 1979. folder and cards. HE20.8102:R18/3. Packet describes the National Center for the Prevention and Control of Rape and its grant program, and the National Rape Information Clearinghouse.

3152.   U.S. Administration for Children, Youth and Families. Office on Domestic Violence. *Violence against Women: Causes and Prevention, a Literature Search and Annotated Bibliography.* by Caroline F. Wilson, University of Wisconsin-Extension, Women's Education Resources. Domestic Violence Monograph Series no. 3. Rockville, MD: National Clearinghouse of Domestic Violence, 1980. 37p. HE23.1015/2:3. Review of the literature on violence against women examines social and psychological factors and the response of law enforcement, government, and the women's movement. Also provides a brief history of violence directed at women and a selective annotated bibliography covering the topic from multiple perspectives.

3153.   U.S. Commission on Civil Rights. *Domestic Violence, Hearing Held in Harrisburg, Pennsylvania, June 17-18, 1980.* Washington, DC: The Commission, 1980. 267p. CR1.8:H24. Shelters, treatment in the court system and by police, and public assistance in domestic violence cases are explored in this hearing focusing on the Harrisburg area.

3154.   U.S. Commission on Civil Rights. New Hampshire Advisory Committee. *Battered Women and the New Hampshire Justice System.* Washington, DC: GPO, 1980. 34p. CR1.2:W84/7. The incidence of wife abuse in Hew Hampshire and the attitudes which account for much of the inaction in the judicial system are recounted. The consultation outlines the specific problems of the police and court response to battering in New Hampshire. The strengths and weaknesses of a 1979 domestic violence reform law are assessed.

3155.   U.S. Congress. House. *Domestic Violence Prevention and Services Act, Conference Report to Accompany H.R. 2977.* H. Rept. 96-1401, 96th Cong., 2d sess., 1980. 43p. Serial 13379. Conference committee report spells out the differences between House and Senate versions of the Domestic Violence Prevention and Services Act, most of which relate to administrative aspects of the domestic violence grant program.

3156.   U.S. Congress. House. Committee on Interstate and Foreign Commerce. *Mental Health Systems Act, Report Together with Dissenting Views to Accompany H.R. 7299.* H. Rept. 96-977, 96th Cong., 2d sess., 1980. 47p. Serial 13366. Among the programs authorized by the bill reported here is a rape prevention program under the authority of the Community Mental Health Centers Act.

3157. U.S. Congress. Senate. Committee on Labor and Human Resources. *Domestic Violence Prevention and Services Act and National Service Commission Act, Report Together with Supplemental and Minority Views to Accompany S.1843*. S. Rept. 96-685, 96th Cong., 2d sess., 1980. 78p. Serial 13323. The incidence and social consequences of domestic violence in the United States and the need for programs aimed at prevention and services to victims are described in this favorable report on the establishment of a federal domestic violence grant program. Excerpts from hearing testimony highlight the economic, social, and law enforcement aspects of domestic violence and the effectiveness of various treatment approaches.

3158. U.S. Congress. Senate. Committee on Labor and Human Resources. *The Mental Health Systems Act, Report to Accompany S. 1177*. S. Rept. 96-712, 96th Cong., 2d sess., 1980. 150p. Serial 13324. Reports a bill continuing the authorization of the rape prevention and control program at the National Institute of Mental Health. Provides minimal background on the committee's support of this program with only summary information on the incidence and psychological impact of rape.

3159. U.S. Congress. Senate. Committee on Labor and Human Resources. Subcommittee on Child and Human Development. *Domestic Violence Prevention and Services Act, 1980, Hearing on S. 1843*. 96th Cong., 2d sess., 6 Feb. 1980. 584p. Y4.L11/4:D71/3/980. Hearing on a bill to provide assistance for state and local activities to prevent domestic violence and to assist its victims focuses on the nature and extent of the problem and on the need for federal assistance to provide adequate services. Also discusses the various local agencies both public and private involved in providing services to battered women. Testimony explores the problem of domestic violence from the police department's view and describes the LEAA's Police Crisis Intervention Program.

3160. U.S. Dept. of Health and Human Services. Office of Human Development Services. *A Monograph on Services to Battered Women*. Washington, DC: GPO, 1980. 146p. HE23.2:W84. Results of a survey of all known programs in the U.S. focusing on services to battered women is presented together with addition information gathered from site visits.

3161. U.S. Dept. of Health and Human Services. Office of the Assistant Secretary for Planning and Evaluation. Project Share. *Issues in Domestic Violence*. Washington, DC: GPO, 1980. 25p. HE 1.18/4:D71. Selective annotated bibliography focuses on wife abuse and psychosocial theories of family violence. Books and journal articles predominate with some state agency reports and ERIC documents included.

3162. U.S. Interdepartmental Committee on Domestic Violence. *Handbook of Federal Resources on Domestic Violence*. Rockville, MD: National Clearinghouse on Domestic Violence, 1980. 261p. Pr39.8:In8/D71 or HE23.1008:D71/2. Describes in detail federal agency programs, mostly demonstration or research programs, which may have relevance for domestic violence research or victim assistance. Includes public assistance, health, education, housing, human development, labor, and law enforcement programs.

3163. U.S. Law Enforcement Assistant Administration. *Prosecutor's Responsibility in Spouse Abuse Cases*. Washington, DC: GPO, 1980. 55p. J26.2:P94/7. Information on the nature and extent of spouse abuse explores the responsibility of the prosecutor in assault cases. A reading list on spouse assault and the legal system is furnished.

3164. U.S. Law Enforcement Assistance Administration. *A Survey of Spousal Violence against Women in Kentucky*. by Mark A. Schulman. Washington, DC: GPO, 1980. 82p.

J26.2:Sp6. Surveys of spousal violence in Kentucky found that 10% of female partners experienced some form of spousal violence. The characteristics of couples in relation to spousal violence and the response of the wives are examined.

3165.   U.S. National Center on Child Abuse and Neglect. *Family Violence: Intervention Strategies.* Washington, DC: GPO, 1980. 104p. HE23.1210/4:V81. Manual is designed to make case workers more aware of the nature of wife abuse and to help them identify violent families. Intervention strategies and the legal issues involved are explored.

3166.   U.S. National Clearinghouse on Domestic Violence. *The Effective Coordination of Volunteers.* Domestic Violence Monograph Series no. 1. Washington, DC: GPO, 1980. 133p. HE 23.1015/2:1. Guide to the administration, recruitment, screening, and training of domestic violence project volunteers provides samples of management and training materials including job descriptions, orientation exercises, goal statements, and work forms.

3167.   U.S. National Clearinghouse on Domestic Violence. *Federally Funded Projects on Domestic Violence.* Rockville, MD: The Clearinghouse, 1980. 15p. HE23.1002:F21/3. Describes research and demonstration projects on domestic violence receiving funds directly from the federal government.

3168.   U.S. National Clearinghouse on Domestic Violence. *Funding Family Violence Programs: State, Local, and Private Sources of Funds.* Rockville, MD: The Clearinghouse, 1980. 43p. HE23.1002:F21. Guide for persons setting up local domestic violence services explains the system for distributing federal funds to state and local government and notes state and local funds which may be available for domestic violence programs.

3169.   U.S. National Clearinghouse on Domestic Violence. *Programs Providing Services to Battered Women.* by Center for Women Policy Studies. 3d ed. Washington, DC: GPO, 1980. 214p. H23.1015:1. Directory lists shelters and related service providers for battered women at the state and local level. Each entry provides directory information and a short summary of services provided and funding source.

3170.   U.S. National Clearinghouse on Domestic Violence. *The Shelter Experience: a Guide to Shelter Organization and Management for Groups Working against Domestic Violence.* Washington, DC: GPO, 1980. 124p. HE23.1015/2:4. Guide to the management of shelter services comes complete with sample forms and hints on housekeeping, zoning, and staffing.

3171.   U.S. National Clearinghouse on Domestic Violence. *State Domestic Violence Laws and How to Pass Them: a Manual for Lobbyists.* by Julie E. Hamos. Washington, DC: GPO, 1980. 170p. HE23.1015/2:2. Detailed guide to constructing state level domestic violence laws suggests funding possibilities and lobbying strategies. Includes a chart summary of state legislation and texts of the codes on domestic violence of Arkansas, California, Massachusetts, Minnesota, Pennsylvania, Texas, Washington, and Wisconsin.

3172.   U.S. National Clearinghouse on Domestic Violence. *Violence against Women: Causes and Prevention, a Literature Search and Annotated Bibliography.* by Carolyn F. Wilson and Kathryn F. Clarembach. 2d ed. Washington, DC: GPO, 1980. 37p. HE23.1015/2:3. Excellent review of the literature on violence against women provides background on historical and sociological aspects as well as on the legal system and federal government responses. The selective bibliography covers legal, anthropological, medical, sociological, and cross-cultural perspectives.

3173. U.S. National Institute of Law Enforcement and Criminal Justice. *Rape, Guidelines for a Community Response.* by Deborah M. Carrow. Washington, DC: GPO, 1980. 296p. J26.16:R18. Information from research and existing programs is synthesized to create program models for community handling of rape victims in the areas of victim services, legal system treatment, medical treatment, and public education. Includes sample forms and letters.

3174. U.S. Office of Justice Assistance, Research and Statistics. *Take a Bite Out of Crime: How to Protect Yourself against Sexual Assault.* Washington, DC: GPO, 1980? 17p. J26.2:C86/12/sexual.

3175. U.S. Commission on Civil Rights. *Domestic Violence, Hearing Held in Phoenix, Arizona, February 12-13, 1980.* Washington, DC: GPO, 1981. 639p. CR1.8:D71. Issues in domestic violence, such as the double standard in handling cases, victim/witness programs, shelters, and the availability of social and legal services, are examined. The situation in Arizona and the city of Phoenix are described with illustrative statistics provided.

3176. U.S. Commission on Civil Rights. New Jersey Advisory Committee. *Battered Women in New Jersey.* Washington, DC: GPO, 1981. 33p. CR1.2:W84/8. Primary focus of this report is the extent to which police attitudes and court procedures fail to meet the needs of battered women. Difficulties in obtaining support payments, child custody, and emergency financial assistance and with the availability of shelter and support services are also covered.

3177. U.S. Congress. House. Committee on the District of Columbia. *Sexual Assault Reform Act of 1981 (Council Act No. 4-69), Hearing and Disposition on H. Res. 208.* 97th Cong., 1st sess., 24 Sept. 1981. 141p. Y4.D63/1:97-6. Hearing considers a resolution to veto the District of Columbia Sexual Assault Reform Act of 1981 which consolidated and updated the District sexual assault laws. Hearing includes an analysis of the provisions of the old and new laws and a discussion of the issues of homosexuality, age and consent, adultery, and fornication as related to the law.

3178. U.S. Congress. Senate. Committee on Government Affairs. Subcommittee on Governmental Efficiency of the District of Columbia. *District of Columbia Sexual Assault Laws, Hearing on S. Res. 207.* 97th Cong., 1st sess., 30 Sept. 1981. 207p. Y4.G74/9:D63/17. Hearing discusses a resolution to disprove District of Columbia Act 4-69, a revision of the sexual assault laws of the District. The act decriminalizes sexual relations between unmarried consenting adults and lowers the penalty for first degree sexual assault to 20 years. Most of the discussion centers on whether fornication, adultery, and sodomy between consenting adults should be defined as criminal and on the moral decay in the District.

3179. U.S. Law Enforcement Assistance Administration and U.S. Administration for Children, Youth and Families. *Prosecution of Spouse Abuse: Innovations in Criminal Justice Response.* by Center for Women Policy Studies. Washington, DC: GPO, 1981. 206p. J26.2:Ab9. Report synthesizes information from a number of sources to present methods for prosecutors responding to spouse abuse. The focus is on improving the criminal justice system response through more effective prosecution, alternative dispositions, and police intervention. Appendix provides statistical information and supporting material from successful domestic violence programs.

3180. U.S. National Center for the Prevention and Control of Rape. *Grants Awarded by the National Center for the Prevention and Control of Rape, Short Summaries.* Washington, DC: GPO, 1981. 16p. HE20.8102:G76/4. Describes grant projects funded between 1976 and 1980 by the National Center for the Prevention and Control of Rape.

3181.   U.S. National Center for the Prevention and Control of Rape. *National Directory: Rape Prevention and Treatment Resources.* Washington, DC: GPO, 1981. 151p. HE20.8102:R18/4. Directory lists 700 rape crisis centers, mental health centers, women's centers, and state and local government agencies and commissions that provide assistance to rape victims or have expertise in the problems resulting from sexual assault.

3182.   U.S. National Center for the Prevention and Control of Rape. *Public and Private Sources of Funding for Sexual Assault Treatment Programs.* Washington, DC: GPO, 1981. 35p. HE20.8102:Se9/3. Describes federal and private funding programs, agencies, and organizations likely to provide funds for sexual assault treatment programs. Includes a bibliography of resources on grantsmanship and fund raising.

3183.   U.S. National Clearinghouse on Domestic Violence. *Family Violence, a Workshop Manual for Clergy and Other Providers.* by Marie M. Fortune and Denise Hormann. Washington, DC: GPO, 1981. 121p. HE23.1015.2:6. Information packet for service providers, particularly the religious community, describe educational and outreach efforts to reach victims of domestic violence in rural areas. Includes a model educational program and sample presentations.

3184.   U.S. National Clearinghouse on Domestic Violence. *Liability and Unauthorized Practice.* by National Public Law Training Center. Rockville, MD: The Clearinghouse, 1981. 49p. HE23.1002:L61. Examination of the legal issues involved in operating a shelter for victims of domestic violence discusses liability concerns and suggests strategies to recommend to abused women when timely legal advice is not available.

3185.   U.S. National Clearinghouse on Domestic Violence. *National Clearinghouse on Domestic Violence.* Rockville, MD: The Clearinghouse, 1981? leaflet. HE1.2:D71.

3186.   U.S. National Clearinghouse on Domestic Violence. *Overview of Public Benefits.* by National Public Law Training Center. Rockville, MD: The Clearinghouse, 1981. 49p. HE23.1002:P96. Brief descriptions of assistance programs such as WIN, food stamps, AFDC, SSI, Social Security, Medicare, Medicaid, and other specialized programs are accompanied by examples of barriers clients may face in their efforts to get public assistance. The clients' legal rights and preventative measures that counselors can take are reviewed.

3187.   U.S. National Clearinghouse on Domestic Violence. *Programs Providing Services to Battered Women.* by Center for Women Policy Studies. 4th ed. Washington, DC: GPO, 1981. 248p. HE23.1015:2. Directory lists local programs and services for battered women.

3188.   U.S. National Clearinghouse on Domestic Violence. *Title XX Social Services.* Rockville, MD: The Clearinghouse, 1981. 34p. HE23.1008:D71. Guide reviews the provisions of Title XX of the Social Security Act for persons providing services to victims of domestic violence.

3189.   U.S. National Clearinghouse on Domestic Violence. *Wife Abuse in the Medical Setting: An Introduction for Health Personnel.* Washington, DC: GPO, 1981. 54p. HE23.1015/2:7. Overview describes the psychological and sociological perspectives of wife abuse and the battering syndrome. Special considerations in identifying women who are victims of battering and in treating battered women are reviewed. A brief annotated bibliography is included.

3190.   U.S. Women's Bureau. *CASA: New Directions, a Program Model for Battered Women.* Pamphlet no. 22. Washington, DC: GPO, 1981. 32p. L36.112:22. Describes a CETA-funded battered women's program called Citizens Assisting and Sheltering the Abused/ New Directions for Women (CASA) located in Hagerstown, MD. Information on planning, funding and community support, and the monitoring/evaluation process is furnished.

3191. U.S. Centers for Disease Control. *Rape Prevention and Services Bibliography.* Washington, DC: The Centers, 1982. 89p. HE20.7019:R18. Annotated bibliography of printed resources and program descriptions on rape drawn from the National Criminal Justice Reference Service, ERIC, and other national databases covers the topics of community prevention approaches, victim services, legislation, and offender treatment.

3192. U.S. Commission on Civil Rights. *The Federal Response to Domestic Violence.* Washington, DC: GPO, 1982. 173p. CR1.2:D71. The needs of abused wives are examined drawing on interviews and the research literature. Areas specifically addressed are housing, social services, financial assistance, legal services, mental health, and employment and training. Federal agencies whose programs could address some of these needs are noted.

3193. U.S. Commission on Civil Rights. *Under the Rule of Thumb: Battered Women and the Administration of Justice.* Washington, DC: The Commission, 1982. 100p. CR1.2:W84/10. Information gained from commission hearings on wife abuse is pulled together for this review of the shortcomings of the criminal justice system in meeting the needs of abused wives. Examines each level of the criminal justice process and provides information on support services such as shelters and public assistance.

3194. U.S. Congress. House. Committee on Education and Labor. Subcommittee on Select Education. *Hearing on Domestic Violence.* 98th Cong., 1st sess., 23 June 1983. 268p. Y4.Ed8/1:D71/5. The incidence, psychology and sociology of domestic violence is explored through testimony of victims, abusers and service providers. Key issues explored are the government response to domestic violence and the training of law enforcement personnel to provide supportive action in domestic violence cases. State legislative responses to the problem are highlighted and witnesses suggest ways government can help encourage shelters and other services. Provides ample documentation of state approaches.

3195. U.S. Congress. House. Committee on Ways and Means. Subcommittee on Public Assistance and Unemployment Compensation. *Welfare, Social Services, and Unemployment Issues: Impact of Federal Budget Cuts, Hearing.* 98th Cong., 1st sess., 18 Nov. 1983. 560p. Y4.W36:98-58. The ability of private sector sources to pick up the provision of social services when the federal funding is cut is the focus of testimony by representatives of local social service providers. Programs supported by government grants, such as food and shelter services, domestic violence programs and foster child care agencies, and the effect of budget cuts are described by witnesses.

3196. U.S. National Institute of Mental Health. *Plain Talk about...Wife Abuse.* Rockville, MD: The Institute, 1983. [3]p. HE20.8128:W63. Brief summary of wife abuse defines the problem and the psychological factors influencing both the victim and the abuser. Actions that the battered woman can take are outlined.

3197. U.S. Attorney General. Task Force on Family Violence. *Attorney General's Task Force on Family Violence: Final Report.* Washington, DC: The Task Force, 1984. 157p. J1.2:F21/2. Recommendations and supporting discussion of the Task Force on Family Violence reviews family violence and the criminal justice system, victim assistance, prevention and awareness, educational training, data collection and reporting, research, and legislative action. Also briefly looks at the topics of violence in the media, pornography, and the military.

3198.   U.S. Congress. House. Committee on the Judiciary. Subcommittee on Criminal Justice. *Federal Rape Law Reform, Hearings.* 98th Cong., 2d sess., 31 Aug., 12 Sept. 1984. 115p. Y4.J89/1:98-162. Hearing on the Sexual Assault Act of 1984 explores the experience in Michigan under a reformed rape law. The issue of rape within marriage is discussed in relation to the proposed removal of spousal immunity from prosecution for rape. The primary focus of the bill is to improve the conviction rate for sexual assaults by shifting the focus to the actions of the accused rather than the non-consent of the victim.

3199.   U.S. Congress. House. Committee on the Judiciary. Subcommittee on Criminal Justice. *Legislation to Help Crime Victims, Hearings on H.R. 2661, H.R. 2978, H.R. 3498, and H.R. 5124.* 98th Cong., 2d sess., 2 Feb. - 2 Aug. 1984. 470p. Y4.J89/1:98/161. Hearing on bills to compensate victims of crime and to provide funding for victim support and crisis intervention services describes existing services. Witnesses note that the majority of users of victim services are female victims of rape or domestic violence. The gun control controversy is also examined.

3200.   U.S. Congress. House. Select Committee on Children, Youth and Families. *Violence and Abuse in American Families, Hearing.* 98th Cong., 2d sess., 14 June 1984. 146p. Y4.C43/2:V81. Examination of the patterns of family violence stresses the importance of social services and of legal system support for victims. The primary focus is child abuse but spouse abuse is also discussed. A moving account from a woman with a history of abusive relations is given.

3201.   U.S. Congress. Senate. Committee on the Judiciary. Subcommittee on Criminal Law. *Impact of Media Coverage of Rape Trials, Hearing.* 98th Cong., 2d sess., 24 Apr. 1984. 99p. Y4.J89/2:S.hrg.98-1246. Examination of the controversy surrounding media coverage of rape trails includes constant reference to the televised coverage of the New Bedford, Massachusetts rape trial. The rights of the victim, rights of the press, and rights of the accused are examined, particularly in reference to revealing the name of the victim.

3202.   U.S. Congress. Senate. Committee on the Judiciary. Subcommittee on Juvenile Justice. *Effect of Pornography on Women and Children, Hearing on Oversight on Pornography, Magazines of a Variety of Courses, Inquiring into the Subject of Their Impact on Child Abuse, Child Molestation, and Problems of Conduct against Women.* 98th Cong., 2d sess., 8 Aug. - 30 Oct. 1984. 346p. Y4.J89/2:S.Hrg.98-1267. Hearing focuses on the relationship between television sex and pornography and child sexual abuse. One of the arguments explored is that pornography should be considered sex discrimination in that it "fosters the second-class status" of women in society. The tendency for soft pornography magazines to portray women as young girls is also discussed. Use of pornography by men while sexually abusing their daughters is also described by victims.

3203.   U.S. Office of Justice Assistance, Research, and Statistics. *How to Protect Yourself against Sexual Assault.* Washington, DC: The Office, 1984? 17p. J26.2:P94/13. Suggestions on preventing sexual assault recommends actions victims should take.

3204.   U.S. Congress. Senate. Committee on Labor and Human Resources. Subcommittee on Children, Family, Drugs and Alcoholism. *Domestic Violence and Public Health, Hearing.* 99th Cong., 1st sess., 30 Oct 1985. 98p. Y4.L11/4:S.hrg.99-443. Hearing examines ways to address the problems of spouse abuse, child sexual abuse, and abuse of the elderly through education of health care professionals and community support programs.

3205.   U.S. Congress. Senate. Committee on the Judiciary. Subcommittee on Juvenile Justice. *Juvenile Rape Victims, Hearing.* 99th Cong., 1st sess., 24 Apr. 1985. 39p. Y4.J89/2:S.hrg.99-91. Hearing on the handling of juvenile victims in sexual assault cases focuses on testimony of Cathleen Crowell Webb, who made headlines by recanting testimony which had put a man in prison for rape six years earlier. The treatment of juvenile rape victims in the court system is examined as is research on psychological reactions to rape.

3206. U.S. National Center for the Prevention and Control of Rape. *The Evaluation and Management of Rape and Sexual Abuse: a Physicians Guide.* by Elijah Thomas Sproles, III. Washington, DC: GPO, 1985. 70p. HE20.8108:R18/2. Guide for emergency room physicians treating rape victims emphasizes the relationship between the doctor's role and that of the police, social worker, nurse, and district attorney, and addresses both the physical and mental health needs of the victim.

3207. U.S. National Center for the Prevention and Control of Rape. *Facts about Sexual Assault, a Research Report for Adults Who Work with Teenagers.* by Suzanne S. Ageton. Rockville, MD: The Center, 1985. 17p. HE20.8102:Ad9/2. Teenagers were surveyed on sexual assault to obtain information on victims and offenders. This booklet discusses the results of the survey and the implications of the responses for working with teenagers.

3208. U.S. National Center for the Prevention and Control of Rape. *Facts about Sexual Assault, a Research Report for Teenagers.* by Suzanne S. Ageton. Washington, DC: GPO, 1985. 15p. HE20.8102:T22. Report on results of a national survey on teenagers and sexual assault is designed to help teenagers better understand sexual assault and to prevent it from happening to them.

3209. U.S. National Center for the Prevention and Control of Rape. *The Sexual Victimization of Adolescents.* Washington, DC: GPO, 1985. 48p. HE20.8108:Se9. Describes the incidence of sexual assault among adolescents, the reactions of victims and family members to the assault, the needs of victims and offenders, methods of treatment, and strategies for prevention.

3210. U.S. Bureau of Justice Statistics. *Preventing Domestic Violence against Women.* Washington, DC: GPO, 1986. 8p. J29.13:V81/2. Review of the research literature on the prevention of domestic violence summarizes results of studies on the effectiveness of selected police actions on preventing future assaults. The basic characteristics of domestic violence, including victim/offender relationship, reporting characteristics, and the recurrence of victimization, are reviewed.

3211. U.S. Congress. House. Committee on Government Operations. *The Federal Role in Investigation of Serial Violent Crime.* H. Rept. 99-888, 99th Cong., 2d sess., 1986. 11p. Serial 13709. Problems of identifying serial killers and rapists are highlighted in this report which stresses the need for the Department of Justice and particularly the FBI to play a lead role in coordinating local efforts.

3212. U.S. Congress. House. Committee on Government Operations. Subcommittee on Government Information, Justice, and Agriculture. *Federal Role in Investigation of Serial Violent Crime, Hearings.* 99th Cong., 2d sess., 9 Apr., 21 May 1986. 96p. Y4.G74/7:C86/6. Hearing on the need to provide federal coordination of investigations of serial violent crimes details numerous serial sexual assault and murder cases where the victims were women.

3213. U.S. Congress. House. Committee on the Judiciary. *Sexual Abuse Act of 1986, Report to Accompany H.R. 4745.* H. Rept. 99-594, 99th Cong., 2d sess., 1986. 29p. Serial 13700. Favorable report on a bill to update federal rape statutes provides a brief overview of the historical development of sexual abuse laws and highlights the weaknesses of existing federal laws.

3214. U.S. Congress. House. Committee on the Judiciary. Subcommittee on Criminal Justice. *Sexual Abuse Act of 1986, Hearing on H.R. 596 and H.R. 4745.* 99th Cong., 2d sess., 29 April 1986. 91p. Y4.J89/1:99/77. Brief hearing on a bill to revise federal rape laws notes the tendency of existing laws to favor the accused male rather than to protect women. Changes involve redefining rape to include homosexual rape and eliminating the concept of "utmost resistance", noting its unfortunate effects on victims. Elimination of the marital rape exception and the practice of such exemptions in the states is reviewed.

3215. U.S. Congress. House. Committee on Education and Labor. *Child Abuse Prevention, Adoption, and Family Services Act of 1987, Report to Accompany H.R. 1900.* H. Rept. 100-135, 100th Cong., 1st sess., 1987. 62p. Serial 13802. Reports a bill extending child abuse prevention and services programs including continuation of the Family Violence Prevention and Services Act. The act provides grants for family violence programs and funds demonstration programs for law enforcement training and technical assistance programs.

3216. U.S. Congress. House. Committee on Education and Labor. Subcommittee on Select Education. *Reauthorization of the Child Abuse Prevention and Treatment Act and the Family Violence Prevention and Services Act, Hearing.* 100th Cong., 1st sess., 29 Apr. 1987. 264p. Y4.Ed8/1:100-57. Although the primary focus of this hearing is child abuse intervention, the problem of wife abuse is also detailed. Witnesses described the extent and characteristics of domestic violence and support reauthorization of the Family Violence Prevention and Services Act.

3217. U.S. Congress. House. Committee on Education and Labor. Subcommittee on Select Education. *Reauthorization of the Child Abuse Prevention and Treatment Act, Hearing.* 100th Cong., 1st sess., 3 April 1987. 67p. Y4.Ed8/1:100-29. Hearing on reauthorization of the Child Abuse Prevention and Treatment Act and the Family Violence Prevention and Services Act presents two panel discussions on the programs. Discussion of domestic violence aimed at women is minimal.

3218. U.S. Congress. House. Committee on Education and Labor. Subcommittee on Select Education. *Reauthorization of the Child Abuse Prevention and Treatment Act, Hearing.* 100th Cong., 1st sess., 23 Apr. 1987. 92p. Y4.Ed8/1:100-46. Hearing on reauthorization of the Child Abuse Prevention and Treatment Act and the Family Violence Prevention and Services Act focuses primarily on the growing problem of child abuse but does discuss shelters for battered women. The Administration witness describes programs under the Child Abuse Prevention and Treatment Act and indicates that the Administration did not support reauthorization of the Family Violence Prevention and Services Act.

3219. U.S. Congress. House. Select Committee on Children, Youth and Families. *Women, Violence and the Law.* 100th Cong., 1st sess., 16 Sept. 1987. 187p. Y4.C43/2:W84. Battered women and the response of the criminal justice system is the theme of this hearing which features the personal experiences of several women with abuse and with the police response. The case of abused women who kill their abusers is also examined.

3220. U.S. Congress. Senate. Committee on Labor and Human Resources. *Child Abuse Prevention and Treatment Act Reauthorization of 1987, Report to Accompany S.1663.* S. Rept. 100-210, 100th Cong., 1st sess., 1987. 28p. Serial 13738. Reports a bill reauthorizing the Family Violence Prevention and Services program along with the Child Abuse Prevention and Treatment and Adoption Opportunities programs. Numerous changes are made to the child abuse and adoption programs, but the family violence program is basically unchanged.

3221. U.S. Congress. Senate. Committee on Labor and Human Resources. Subcommittee on Children, Family, Drugs and Alcoholism. *Reauthorization of the Adoption Reform Act of 1978 and the Family Violence Prevention and Services Act of 1984, Hearing.* 100th Cong., 1st sess., 21 May 1987. 175p. Y4.L11/4:S.hrg.100-383. The adoption portion of the hearing focuses on the need for federal assistance in solving the problem of adoption placement of minority children. The family violence program reauthorization portion of the hearings provides testimony on the value of shelters for victims of abuse and on the need for federal assistance to make shelters available nationwide.

3222. U.S. Congress. House. *Child Abuse Prevention, Adoption, and Family Services Act of 1987, Conference Report to Accompany H.R. 1900.* H. Rept. 100-543, 100th Cong., 2d sess., 1988. 38p. Serial 13891. Conference report settles the disagreement over Senate amendments to a bill reauthorizing the Child Abuse Prevention and Treatment Act, the Child Abuse Prevention and Treatment and Adoption Reform Act of 1978, and the Family Violence Prevention and Services Act.

3223. U.S. Congress. Senate. Committee on Labor and Human Resources. *Comprehensive Alcohol Abuse, Drug Abuse, and Mental Health Amendments of 1988, Report Together with Additional Views to Accompany S. 1943.* S. Rept. 100-328, 100th Cong., 2d sess., 1988. 126p. Serial 13860. Among the drug and alcohol abuse and mental health research and demonstration programs authorized by this bill are focus programs on post-legal adoption mental health and counseling, and treatment and prevention related to sex offenses.

3224. U.S. Congress. Senate. Committee on the Judiciary. *Child Protection and Obscenity Enforcement Act and Pornography Victims Protection Act of 1987, Hearing on S. 703 and S. 2033.* 100th Cong., 2d sess., 8 June 1988. 541p. Y4.J89/2:S.hrg.100-1083. The main focus of this hearing on anti-pornography legislation is protection of children from exploitation by pornographers. The legal ambiguity of a bill to allow civil action by adults "coerced" or "intimidated" into posing or acting in pornographic materials is discussed. Some testimony reviews evidence of a link between pornography and sexual abuse of women and children.

3225. U.S. General Accounting Office. *Coast Guard: Information Needed to Assess the Extent of Sexual Assaults on Ships.* Washington, DC: The Office, 1988. 32p. GA1.13:RCED-89-59. Report examines the problem of the sexual assault of women aboard ships in the U.S. merchant marine. The problem of unreported assaults and suggested changes in laws regarding sexual assault aboard ship are reviewed. The conditions on board ship which contribute to unreported sexual assaults are noted.

3226. U.S. Congress. House. Committee on Merchant Marine and Fisheries. Subcommittee on Merchant Marine. *MARAD Authorization, Fiscal Year 1990, Hearing on H.R. 1486.* 101st Cong., 1st sess., 22 Mar. 1989. 215p. Y4.M53:101-48. Hearing to review the Maritime Administration's budget includes brief discussion of the extent of sexual harassment and assault on board ships in the merchant marine. The GAO report *Information Needed to Assess the Extent of Sexual Assaults on Ships* (3225) is reprinted.

3227. U.S. General Services Administration. Public Buildings Service. Federal Protective Service. *What You Should Know about Avoiding Rape and Sexual Assault in the Federal Workplace.* Washington, DC: The Administration, 1989. 14p. GS6.2:R18/989. Using a quiz format this booklet provides advice on avoiding sexual assault when working in federal buildings and while traveling. Earlier edition published in 1988.

3228. U.S. Congress. House. Committee on Education and Labor. Subcommittee on Postsecondary Education. *Hearing on H.R. 3344, the Crime Awareness and Campus*

Security Act of 1989, Hearing. 101st Cong., 2d sess., 14 Mar. 1990. 176p. Y4.Ed8/1:101-75. Hearing on a bill to require postsecondary institutions to publish their crime statistics includes testimony on the incidence and handling of murder, assault, and rape cases on campus. The link between substance abuse and campus crime is a recurring theme. The actions campus security programs can take to reduce sexual and physical assaults are described.

3229. U.S. Congress. House. Committee on the Judiciary. *Sense of Congress Respecting Child Custody Determinations, Report to Accompany H. Con. Res. 172.* H. Rept. 101-737, 101st Cong., 2d sess., 24 Sept. 1990. 4p. Favorable report provides brief background information on a resolution to encourage states to create a statutory presumption that it would be detrimental to grant child custody to a parent when there is evidence that the parent has abused his or her spouse.

3230. U.S. Congress. House. Committee on the Judiciary. Subcommittee on Administrative Law and Governmental Relations. *Sense of Congress - Evidentiary Presumption in Child Custody Cases, Hearing on H. Con. Res. 172.* 101st Cong., 2d sess., 15 May 1990. 162p. Y4.J89/1:101-81. Hearing explores the issues surrounding child custody determination and spousal violence. Evidence that spouse abuse, usually wife abuse, is also detrimental to the child is presented in support of a congressional resolution stating that evidence of spouse abuse should "create a statutory presumption that it is detrimental to the child to be placed in the custody of the abusive parent." The effect of joint custody and visitation decisions on the psychological health of the abused wife is discussed in depth as is the reluctance of abused wives to seek divorce for fear of losing the children.

3231. U.S. Congress. House. Select Committee on Children, Youth, and Families. *Victims of Rape, Hearing.* 101st Cong., 2d sess., 28 June 1990. 201p. Y4.C43/2:R18. The psychological consequences of rape are discussed in this hearing on the incidence of rape and the need for victim support services. The attitudes of victims toward rape and their effect on reporting the crime and seeking support services are discussed. A number of anti-abortion articles related to rape are included in the hearing record.

3232. U.S. Congress. Senate. Committee on Labor and Human Resources. *Mental Health Amendments of 1990, Report to Accompany S. 2628.* S. Rept. 101-389, 101st Cong., 2d sess., 1990. 18p. Reports a bill reauthorizing a number of National Institute of Mental Health grant programs including programs for the prevention of sex offenses and the development of community-based programs for victims of sex offenses and family violence.

3233. U.S. Congress. Senate. Committee on Labor and Human Resources. Subcommittee on Children, Family, Drugs and Alcoholism. *Domestic Violence: Terrorism in the Home, Hearing.* 101st Cong., 2d sess., 19 Apr. 1990. 118p. Y4.L11/4:S.hrg.101-897. The consequences of domestic violence for wives and children and the need for federal funds to support victim services are explored in hearing testimony. Counseling services and criminal justice treatment of the abuser are also discussed.

3234. U.S. Congress. Senate. Committee on the Judiciary. *The Violence against Women Act of 1990, Report to Accompany S. 2754.* S. Rept. 101-545, 101st Cong., 2d sess., 1990. 88p. Report on a grant authorization bill highlights specific types of violence against women and the provisions of the bill to address them. Areas dealt with include rape and assault by strangers, domestic violence, and acquaintance rape on college campuses. The bill also supports education and training of judges and court personnel to recognize gender bias in court proceedings.

3235. U.S. Congress. Senate. Committee on the Judiciary. *Women and Violence, Part 1, Hearing on Legislation to Reduce the Growing Problem of Violent Crime against Women.* 101st Cong., 2d sess., 20 June 1990. 112p. Y4.J89/2:S.hrg.101-939/pt.1. Two victims of violent attacks describe the effect of the assaults on their lives and detail the victimization of women in the courts. The hearing goes on to explore the rising trend in violence against women and the concept of a federal role in stopping gender-based hate crimes. This hearing focuses on random violence against women with only brief mentions of acquaintance rape and domestic violence.

3236. U.S. Congress. Senate. Committee on the Judiciary. *Women and Violence, Part 2, Hearings on Legislation to Reduce the Growing Problem of Violent Crime against Women.* 101st Cong., 2d sess., 29 Aug., 11 Dec. 1990. 306p. Y4.J89/2:S.hrg.101-939/pt.2. Continued hearings on violence against women focuses on acquaintance rape and domestic violence. The trauma of these crimes for the victims and the societal attitudes which cause women to blame themselves are explored. In the case of domestic violence, the economic dependency of battered women is reviewed. Deficiencies in reporting acquaintance rape and the failure of the National Crime Survey to clearly survey the incidence of rape is detailed in research study results.

3237. U.S. Congress. Senate. Select Committee on Indian Affairs. *Indian Child Protective Services and Family Violence Prevention Act, Hearing on S. 2340.* 101st Cong., 2d sess., 7 June 1990. 210p. Y4.In2/11:S.hrg.101-1008. Hearing on a bill to address child abuse on Indian reservations focuses on the child welfare aspects of family violence. Some statements criticize the Bureau of Indian Affairs for ignoring the problem of domestic violence aimed at adult women, and note that to address child abuse legislative measures must also address the total domestic violence problem.

3238. U.S. Congress. Senate. Select Committee on Indian Affairs. *The Indian Child Protective Services and Family Violence Prevention Act, Report to Accompany S. 2340.* S. Rept. 101-403, 101st Cong., 2d sess., 1990. 18p. Information from hearings on problems of child abuse and domestic violence on Indian reservations is summarized in support of a bill to fund Indian Child Protection Services Programs and Indian Family Violence Prevention and Treatment Programs.

3239. U.S. National Institute of Justice. *Civil Protection Orders: Legislation, Current Court Practices, and Enforcement.* by Peter Finn and Sarah Colson. Washington, DC: GPO, 1990. 68p. J28.23:C49/2. The use of civil protection orders to protect victims of domestic violence is examined. Information on the statutory basis for the various types of relief in each state and discussion of case law upholding the statutes is provided. The application of these laws and their strengths and weaknesses for protecting women are noted. Differences in how the remedies are applied and enforced are examined for their effect on the protection of the woman and the "message" sent to the abusive spouse. Eviction of the offender, child custody, mandatory counseling, no-contact provisions, and mutual restraining orders are specifically addresses as are weaknesses in the legal process.

20

Female Offenders

Government reports and documents on female offenders deal primarily with the problem of controlling prostitution up until the 1970s, when more in-depth studies were made of the characteristics, facilities, and rehabilitation programs for female offenders. Some of the earliest documents are on the establishment of a reform school for the youthful female offender in the District of Columbia (3373, 3240, 3243-3244, 3246-3252), and this theme of reforming young women is found in later publications on protective work in the 1910s and 1920s (3272, 3287), during WWII (3320, 3324-3325, 3329), and in recent times (3361, 3368).

During the early 1900s many of the documents addressed the suppression of the traffic in white women, the white-slavery problem, on both a national and international level. The reports generally view the majority of prostitutes as innocent victims of fiendish persons and describe in lurid terms the methods employed to entice pure girls into a life of prostitution and the methods used to control the women in houses. Most of these documents are long on rhetoric and short on facts with the exception of the report of the Immigration Commission (3255), which details the known status of the trade in women. The impression that most women offenders were brought in on morals charges is further supported by Volume XV of the *Report on Condition of Women and Child Wage-Earners in the United States* (3258), which explores the relationship between occupational history and criminal activity among women with particular reference to occasional and professional prostitutes. Also reflecting the nature of crimes committed by female offenders are hearings on the establishment of a Federal Industrial Institution for Women (3290-3295) and hearings on the establishment of a Woman's Bureau within the D.C. Metropolitan Police Department (3296-3297, 3299-3304).

Documents from the WWI and WWII eras reflect a concern for protecting members of the armed forces from venereal disease through suppressing prostitution near military and naval bases. Many of the documents suggesting methods of suppressing prostitution provide insight into the structure of the business of prostitution and approaches to handling "wayward" girls (3311, 3316, 3320-3321, 3324-3325, 3329).

The 1970s focus on civil rights produced numerous documents on the treatment of female offenders in the criminal justice system. The report of the Bureau of Prisons on female offenders in the federal prison system (3356), the report of the Law Enforcement Assistance Administration Task Force on Women (3355), and the *National Study of Women's Correctional Programs* (3359), along with several GAO reports and a congressional hearing (3363), document in detail the characteristics and inequitable treatment of female offenders. Gender discrimination in paroles caused by the lack of prison facilities for women in the District of Columbia are described in a 1990 hearing (3371).

3240. U.S. Congress. House. Committee on the District of Columbia. *Industrial School for Girls in the District of Columbia, Report to Accompany H.R. 5702.* H. Rept. 1010, 46th Cong., 2d sess., 1880. 1p. Serial 1937. Reports on H.R. 5702, a substitute for bills H.R. 2904 and H.R. 4204, establishing an industrial school for homeless or orphan girls which will save the girls from a life of vice and crime through the efforts of "pure-minded, lofty-souled Christian women."

3241. U.S. Congress. Senate. Committee on Epidemic Diseases. *Petitions of Elizabeth R. Post and Other Citizens of Westbury, N.Y.; Francis G. Shaw and Fifty Other Citizens of Richmond County New York; Kate Garnett Wells and Other Members of the Moral Education Association of Massachusetts, and of the New York Committee for the Prevention of State Regulation of Vice, Praying That the Power to Promote or Inaugurate any Scheme of Regulated Prostitution, with the Registration and Compulsory Medical Examination of Women, Not Be Given to the National Board of Health.* S. Rept. 615, 47th Cong., 1st sess., 1882. 1p. Serial 2007. Report on the petition points out that Congress has no authority to regulate local sanitation and that the National Board of Health would only be concerned with the importation of infectious diseases from one state to another.

3242. U.S. Congress. Senate. Committee on the District of Columbia. *Petition of Belva A. Lockwood and Others, That a Woman Deputy Warden be Appointed to the Jail of the District of Columbia.* S. Rept. 169, 48th Cong., 1st sess., 1884. 1p. Serial 2174. The committee reports that such an appointment should be made, but that it falls under the authority of the chief justice of the District and the warden of the jail.

3243. U.S. Congress. House. Committee of the District of Columbia. *Reform School for Girls, District of Columbia, Report to Accompany H.R. 10824.* H. Rept. 4030, 49th Cong., 2d sess., 1887. 1p. Serial 2501. Reports a bill incorporating the Reform School for Girls of the District of Columbia with an amendment stating that the attendants employed and the work and occupation be suitable to girls.

3244. U.S. Congress. House. Committee on the District of Columbia. *Girls' Reform School of the District of Columbia.* H. Rept. 3278, 50th Cong., 1st sess., 1888. 1p. Serial 2607. Favorable report on appropriations for the Girls' Reform School for the District of Columbia.

3245. U.S. Congress. House. Committee on the District of Columbia. *Police Matrons for the District of Columbia, Report to Accompany Bill H.R. 8039.* H. Rept. 2031, 50th Cong., 1st sess., 1888. 1p. Serial 2603. Committee report briefly summarizes the need for the appointment of matrons for the police department of the District of Columbia.

3246. U.S. Congress. House. Committee on the District of Columbia. *Reform School for Girls of the District of Columbia, Report to Accompany H.R. 1361.* H. Rept. 1862, 50th Cong., 1st sess., 1888. 1p. Serial 2603. Report recommends incorporation of Senate amendments to a bill establishing a reform school for girls in the District of Columbia.

3247. U.S. Congress. House. Committee on the District of Columbia. *Reform School for Girls, Report to Accompany H.R. 1361.* H. Rept. 323, 50th Cong., 1st sess., 1888. 1p. Serial 2599. Reports a bill to establish a reform school for girls convicted of small offenses in the District of Columbia.

3248. U.S. Congress. House. Committee on the District of Columbia. *Girls' Reform School, District of Columbia.* H. Rept. 1783, 50th Cong., 1st sess., 1890. 3p. Serial 2812. Report on a bill for the purchase of a site and erection of buildings for the Girls' Reform School of the District of Columbia includes letters from Chief-Justice Bingham of the

Supreme Court of the District of Columbia and from Judge Thomas F. Miller of the police court of the District supporting the urgent need for a girls reform school.

3249. U.S. Congress. Senate. Committee on the District of Columbia. *[To Provide for the Purchase of a Site and the Erection of Buildings for the Girls' Reform School of the District of Columbia.]* S. Rept. 1946, 51st Cong., 2d sess., 1891. 3p. Serial 2826. Report recommends passage of a bill appropriating funds for the purchase of land and erection of a building for the Girls' Reform School of the District of Columbia, and is accompanied by letters of support from the Superintendent of the Metropolitan Police, the Chief-Justice of the Supreme Court of the District of Columbia, and a D.C. police court judge.

3250. U.S. Congress. Senate. Committee on the District of Columbia. *[To Provide for the Purchase of a Site and Erection of Building for the Girls' Reform School of the District of Columbia.]* S. Rept. 92, 52d Cong., 1st sess., 1892. 2p. Serial 2911. Quotes from the President and from Judge Kimball of the District police court highlight the need for appropriations for the construction of a girls' reform school in the District.

3251. U.S. Congress. House. Committee on the District of Columbia. *Reform School for Girls of the District of Columbia.* H. Rept. 2453, 56th Cong., 2d sess., 1901. 15p. Serial 4213. Report on a bill supplementing "An Act to incorporate the Reform School for Girls of the District of Columbia" provides a history of the act and discussed equalization of statutes relating to the Boys, Reform School and the Girls' Reform School, primarily in the matter of age of commitment. Also covers transfer of older girls to the workhouse and reprints related correspondence in support of the bill.

3252. U.S. Congress. Senate. Committee on the District of Columbia. *Reform School for Girls in the District of Columbia, Report to Accompany H.R. 13802.* S. Rept. 2172, 56th Cong., 2d sess., 1901. 3p. Serial 4065. Favorable report on lowering the age at which girls may be committed to the school includes related correspondence of the Attorney General.

3253. U.S. Congress. Senate. Committee on Immigration. *Immigration of Aliens, Report to Accompany S. 7025.* S. Rept. 4210, 58th Cong., 3d sess., 1905. 1p. Serial 4756. Reports a bill relating to the importation of women for immoral purposes.

3254. U.S. Congress. House. Committee on Interstate and Foreign Commerce. *White Slave Traffic, Report to Accompany H.R. 12315.* H. Rept. 47, 61st Cong., 2d sess., 1909. 33p. Serial 5591. Favorable report on a bill to control the interstate traffic in prostitution discusses the provisions of the act and its validity, as well as the history and development of the law. The extent of the traffic in women on an international scale is reviewed. Documents printed with the report include the international agreement on the repression of trade in white women, the Supreme Court opinion in *Keller v. United States,* and other supporting documentation on the repression of prostitution.

3255. U.S. Congress. Senate. *Importing Women for Immoral Purposes: A Partial Report from the Immigration Commission on the Importation and Harboring of Women for Immoral Purposes.* S. Doc. 196, 61st Cong., 2d sess., 1909. 61p. Serial 5662. Report on the importation of women to the U.S. for prostitution describes the extend of the traffic by nationality, recruitment practices used with immoral women and with innocent girls, methods of importation, and the methods used to place and control the girls and women. Also reports on the profits of the trade and the difficulty of suppressing the business. Appendices include letters showing the working of the system and partial court testimony of women lured to the U.S. for prostitution.

3256. U.S. Congress. Senate. *Suppression of the White-Slave Traffic: Message from the President of the United States, Transmitting, with Accompanying Letters, in Response to Senate Resolution No. 86, of December 7, 1909, Information Concerning the Repression of the Trade in White Women.* S. Doc. 214, 61st Cong., 2d sess., 1909. 6p. Serial 5657. Correspondence from the Secretary of State and the Department of Commerce and Labor discusses enforcement of the international agreement regarding the traffic in white women and the legal authority of the government to carry out the agreement.

3257. U.S. Congress. House. Committee on Interstate and Foreign Commerce. *White Slave Traffic: Views of the Minority.* H. Rept. 47, part 2, 61st Cong., 2d sess., 1910. 5p. Serial 5591. Mr. Richardson argues that H.R. 12315 infringes on state police powers.

3258. U.S. Congress. Senate. *Relation between Occupation and Criminality of Women.* by Mary Conyngton. Report on Condition of Woman and Child Wage-Earners in the United States, vol. XV. S. Doc. 645, 61st Cong., 2d sess., 1910. 119p. Serial 5699. Analysis of statistics on female offenders looks at their age, literacy, conjugal condition, nativity, and occupations and at the relationship between occupation, criminality and immorality among women. The relationship between low wages and prostitution is examined as are the occupational histories of the occasional and professional prostitute. Statistics are provided on occupation and offense, nativity and offense, offenders employed in traditional and the "newer" pursuits, and earlier occupation and present occupation of women offenders. The question of whether criminality is on the rise among women is examined.

3259. U.S. Congress. Senate. *Steerage Conditions, Importation and Harboring of Women for Immoral Purposes, Immigrant Homes and Aid Societies, and Immigrant Banks.* Reports of the Immigration Commission v. 37. S. Doc. 753, 61st Cong., 3d sess., 1910. Serial 5877. The report on "Importing and Harboring Women for Immoral Purposes" reviews the extent of the white slavery trade in the early 1900's without the sensationalism or moralistic tone of many publications on the topic. Data on nationality of prostitutes and procurers is provided for 1908 and 1909, and the methods of recruiting foreign women for prostitution in the U.S. are reviewed. Also examined are methods of importation and the difficulties of detection, the prices paid for the girls, and the fate of the girls once they begin their life of prostitution. Finally, recommendations are made on controlling the importation of women for immoral purposes. Appendices include seized letters which reveal the operation of white slave rings. Sections of the report on the investigation of immigrant homes and aid societies provide insight into the treatment women and girls received in these houses and the incidence of employment referrals to "sporting houses."

3260. U.S. Congress. Senate. *Suppression of the White-Slave Traffic: Message from the President of the United States, Transmitting, in Further Response to Senate Resolution No. 86, of December 7, 1909, Information Concerning the Repression of Trade in White Women.* S. Doc. 214, part 2, 61st Cong., 2d sess., 1910. 34p. Serial 5657. Report of the Bureau of Immigration and Naturalization details provisions made to carry out the treaty of March 1, 1905, for the suppression of white-slave traffic. The report reviews the authority of the government to enforce the treaty and the problems of detecting prostitutes at the time of entry into the country. The effect of the Supreme Court decision in *Keller v. United States* on efforts to prosecute is reviewed.

3261. U.S. Congress. Senate. *White Slave Traffic Act of June 25, 1910: Its Passage Through the Senate of the United States - with Views of the Majority and Minority of the Senate Committee on Immigration.* S. Doc. 702, 61st Cong., 3d sess., 1910. 22p. Serial 5943. Provides a brief history of the development of the law and its provisions, summarizes existing laws, and reviews the validity of the act. Also includes the basic rhetoric on the evil of the white-slave trade and its prevalence in the United States. A minority view analyses the act section-by-section and assesses its effects and its ability to regulate as intended.

3262. U.S. Immigration Commission. *Abstract of Report on Importation and Harboring of Women for Immoral Purposes.* Washington, DC: The Commission, 1910. 30p. Y3.Im6:w84/1. Full report issued in S. Doc. 753 (3259).

3263. U.S. Congress. Senate. *Juvenile Delinquency and Its Relation to Employment.* Report on Condition of Woman and Child Wage Earners in the United States, vol. VIII. S. Doc. 645, 61st Cong., 2d Sess., 1911. 177p. Serial 5692. Investigation looks at correlations between employment of juveniles and delinquency with separate consideration of trends for boys and girls. Occupations and offenses are examined with special attention to girls in domestic service. Nightwork, hours of labor, and home conditions are also factors considered. The double standard by which courts judge the actions for boys and girls is noted in several cases, highlighting judges' tendency to consider immoral tendencies in girls rather than the crime committed. Numerous tables showing age, offense, occupation, home conditions, etc., by sex, and a detailed subject index are furnished.

3264. U.S. Congress. House. *Reform School for White Girls: Letter from the President of the Board of Commissioners of the District of Columbia Transmitting Report of the Commissioners on the Necessity of Establishing a Reform School for White Girls Within the District of Columbia, as Required by Act of June 26, 1912.* H. Doc. 1066, 62d Cong., 3d sess., 1912. 3p. Serial 6503. See 3266 for abstract.

3265. U.S. Congress. Senate. *The Iowa Injunction and Abatement Law: A Letter from Hon. George Cosson, Attorney General of Iowa, and a Speech of Senator T.J. Brooks, Delivered in the State of Tennessee, and an Address and Article by Mr. James B. Hammond on the Iowa Injunction and Abatement Law, Together with a Copy of the Law.* S. Doc. 435, 62d Cong., 2d sess., 1912. 28p. Serial 6175. The Iowa Injunction and Abatement Law, Chapter 214, Acts of the Thirty-third General Assembly of Iowa, aimed at the suppression of houses of prostitution, is examined in the letter from Cossons. The speech by Senator Brooks provides typical rhetoric on prostitution, white slavery, and venereal disease with liberal use of quotes from magazines of the day. Finally, an article reprinted from *The Light* (July 19, 1910) discusses the extent to which Iowa has a "real social evil or white slave" problem.

3266. U.S. Congress. Senate. *Letter from the President of the Board of Commissioners of the District of Columbia Transmitting a Memorandum Prepared by the Board of Charities Relating to the Necessity for Existing Facilities and the Cost of Maintenance for a Proposed Reform School for White Girls in the District of Columbia.* S. Doc. 979, 62d Cong., 3d sess., 1912. 3p. Serial 6366. Report of the commissioners describes the need for a training school for wayward white girls, the existing private facilities, and the cost of constructing and maintaining such a school.

3267. U.S. Congress. Senate. *The White Slave Traffic.* by Stanley W. Finch. S. Doc. 982, 62d Cong., 3d sess., 1912. 9p. Serial 6364. Address by Stanley W. Finch, Chief of the Bureau of Investigation of the Department of Justice, delivered before the World's Purity Congress, Louisville, K.Y., May 7, 1912, describes the "downfall and eternal ruin" of innocent girls who are "ravished" then forced into a life of prostitution. The tactics of the procurer and estimates the extent of the trade in white women are reviewed. Approaches to suppressing the white-slave traffic through federal action are outlined.

3268. U.S. Congress. Senate. Committee on the District to Columbia. *Abatement of Houses of Ill Fame, Hearing on S. 5861, Part I.* 62d Cong., 3d sess., 9 Dec. 1912. 15p.

Y4.D63/2:I/6. Testimony discusses the prevalence of houses of prostitution in Washington, D.C. and the effect of an Iowa law on prostitution in that state.

3269. U.S. Congress. House. Committee of the District of Columbia. *Houses of Ill Fame, Report to Accompany S. 5861.* H. Rept. 1517, 62d Cong., 3d sess., 1913. 1p. Serial 6334. Reports a bill to enjoin and abate houses of "lewdness, assignation and prostitution" by declaring them a nuisance and taking action against the proprietor and the building owner.

3270. U.S. Congress. Senate. Committee on the District of Columbia. *Houses of Ill Fame.* S. Rept. 82, 63d Cong., 1st sess., 1913. 2p. Serial 6510. Favorable report on what is essentially the same bill reported in S. Rept. 1102, 62d Congress (3271), which is reprinted here.

3271. U.S. Congress. Senate. Committee on the District of Columbia. *Houses of Ill Fame, Report to Accompany S. 5861.* S. Rept. 1102, 62d Cong., 3d sess., 1913. 1p. Serial 6330. See 3269 for abstract.

3272. U.S. War Department. Commission on Training Camp Activities. *Committee on Protective Work for Girls.* Washington, DC: The Commission, 1917. 16p. W85.2:G44. Report on the problem caused by young girls in the vicinity of military training camps presents the establishment of local girls' protective bureau as a solution. The report covers the training of bureau workers and the establishment of a house of detention.

3273. U.S. War Department. Commission on Training Camp Activities. *Documents Regarding Questions of Alcohol and Prostitution in the Neighborhood of Military Camps.* Washington, DC: The Commission, 1917. 10p. leaflet. W85.2:Al1. Leaflet reprinting correspondence relating to laws and regulations on the availability of alcohol and the repression of prostitution in the vicinity of military camps includes copies of mass mailings from the Secretary of War to governors, mayors, and county sheriffs. Also includes War Dept. Bulletin no. 45, "Regulations issued by the President and the Secretary of War, bearing on Sections 12 and 13 of the Army Law."

3274. U.S. Congress. House. *Intoxicating Liquors and Prostitution Within the Canal Zone: Letter from the Secretary of War.* H. Doc. 1606, 65th Cong., 3d sess., 1918. 2p. Serial 7582. Letter of transmittal and text of a bill detail the prohibition of liquor and prostitution in the Canal Zone.

3275. U.S. Congress. House. *Prohibition in the Canal Zone: Letter from the Secretary of War.* H. Doc. 1840, 65th Cong., 3d sess., 1918. 1p. Serial 7582. Letter from the Secretary of War transmits the gist of a cable from Brig. Gen. Blatchford, commander of the Panama Canal Department, urging the passage of S. 5224, a bill for the control of liquor and prostitution in the Canal Zone.

3276. U.S. War Department. Commission on Training Camp Activities. *Documents Regarding Alcoholic Liquors and Prostitution in the Neighborhood of Military Camps and Naval Stations.* Washington, DC: The Commission, 1918. 15p. No SuDoc number. Update of and earlier publication (3273) includes documents relating to naval stations.

3277. U.S. Commissions on Training Camp Activities of War and Navy Departments. Law Enforcement Division. *Standard Forms of Laws for Repression of Prostitution, Control of Venereal Diseases, Establishment and Management of Reformatories for Women and Girls, and Suggestions for Law Relating to Feeble-minded Persons.* Washington, DC: The Commissions, 1919. 33p. W84.2:L44. Sample laws cover repression of prostitution, fornication, injunction and abatement of houses of prostitution, control of venereal disease, establishment of a reformatory for women and girls, and establishment of institutions for the care of the mentally retarded.

3278. U.S. Congress. House. Committee on the District of Columbia. *Investigation of Salaries of Metropolitan Police Members, Hearing, Part 2, on H.R. 7983.* 66th Cong., 1st.sess., 23,24 Sept. 1919. 23-77pp. Y4.D63/1:P75/2-2. Mrs. Mina C. van Winkle, Chief of the Women's Bureau of the Metropolitan Police Force, testifies on the activities of the bureau. In particular, an attack on the Women's Bureau through the *Washington Post* is noted and the details of the situation are examined. Several of the cases dealing with young women handled by the bureau are described in illustration of the social protection work of the bureau.

3279. U.S. Congress. House. Commission on the District of Columbia. *Investigation of Salaries of Metropolitan Police Members, Hearing, Part 3, on H.R. 7983.* 66th Cong., 1st. sess., 25,30 Sept. 1919. 79-167pp. Y4.D63/1:P75/2-3. Continued examination of charges of improper action made against the Women's Bureau of the Metropolitan Police Department presents Edward McLean, editor and owner of the *Washington Post*, as the primary witness against the bureau.

3280. U.S. Congress. Senate. Committee on the Judiciary. *Amendment to Sections 5549 and 5550 of the Revised Statutes of the United States.* S. Rept. 423, 66th Cong., 2d sess., 1920. 2p. Serial 7649. Report on amendment of the Revised Statutes so as to allow women convicted of prostitution in or around military camps to be remanded to reformatories in selected cases includes a letter from the Assistant Attorney General justifying the changes.

3281. U.S. Interdepartmental Social Hygiene Board. *Manual for the Various Agents of the United States Interdepartmental Social Hygiene Board.* Washington, DC: GPO, 1920. 106p. Y3.In8/2:M31. Report of activities of the Board recounts work with delinquent women and girls. Appendix reports the results of a study of 6,000 case records of delinquent women and girls which details age, nativity, religion, marital status, educational attainment, latest occupation and weekly wage, age of starting work, and average age of first sex offense.

3282. U.S. Congress. House. Committee on the Judiciary. *Amending Sections 5549 and 5550 of the Revised Statutes of the United States, Report to Accompany H.R. 2381.* H. Rept. 34, 67th Cong., 1st sess., 1921. 2p. Serial 7920. Report on a bill allowing judges discretion in the sentencing of women and girls over the age of 16 argues that some women would benefit from a reformatory environment as opposed to jail.

3283. U.S. Congress. Senate. Committee on the District of Columbia. *Repression of Prostitution in the District of Columbia, Hearings on S. 1616.* 67th Cong., 1st. sess., 13,20 Oct. 1921. 48p. Y4.D63/2:P94. Hearing on the control of prostitution makes special reference to Washington, D.C. Issues of race and nationality in relation to prostitution are raised, and the head of the Metropolitan Police Women's Bureau describes the condition of prostitution. Numerous witnesses note the use of taxicabs for prostitution. The question of whether "red light" districts should be allowed to exist as a way to control venereal disease is also discussed.

3284. U.S. Congress. Senate. Committee on the Judiciary. *Amendment to Sections 5549 and 5550 of the Revised Statutes of the United States, Report to Accompany S. 1010.* S. Rept. 122, 67th Cong., 1st sess., 1921. 2p. Serial 7918. Reports with amendments S. 1010, which is essentially the same bill as S. 3875, 66th Congress. Sections of S. Rept. 423, 66th Congress (3280), are reprinted by way of justification of this legislation.

3285. U.S. Public Health Service. *What Representative Citizens Think about Prostitution.* Washington, DC: GPO, 1921. 8p. T27.20:66. Survey results describe attitudes on prostitution, particularly focusing on the need for houses of prostitution, red light districts and mandatory medical examinations of prostitutes and their patrons.

3286. U.S. Congress. House. Committee on the Judiciary. *Amend Sections 5549 and 5550 of the Revised Statutes.* H. Rept. 726, 67th Cong., 2d sess., 1922. 1p. Serial 7955. See 3282 for abstract.

3287. U.S. Interdepartmental Social Hygiene Board. *Detention Houses and Reformatories as Protective Social Agencies in Campaign of Government against Venereal Diseases, Report on Certain Detention Houses and Reformatories That Received Assistance from Government in Caring for Civilian Persons Whose Detention, Isolation, Quarantine of Commitment Was Found Necessary to Protect the Military and Naval Forces of the United States against Venereal Disease.* Washington, DC: GPO, 1922. 227p. Y3.In8/2:V55. Detailed information on the organization and site selection of reformatories and detention houses for women and girls with venereal disease discusses the rules of the houses and the rehabilitation of the women and girls.

3288. U.S. Congress. House. Committee on the Judiciary. *Enlarging the Powers and Duties of the Department of Justice in Relation to the Protection of the Armed Forces of the United States, Report to Accompany H.R. 11490.* H. Rept. 1585, 67th Cong., 4th sess., 1923. 4p. Serial 8158. Reports a bill granting the Justice Department greater power to suppress prostitution in and around military bases and places where ex-soldiers and ex-sailors are stationed.

3289. U.S. Congress. House. Committee on the Judiciary. *Establishment of a United States Industrial Home for Women at Mount Weather, VA, Report to Accompany H.R. 13927.* H. Rept. 1496, 67th Cong., 4th sess., 1923. 3p. Serial 8157. Report states the urgent need for a federal facility for female offenders and articulates the nature of the proposed institution and reasons for the choice of the Mount Weather location.

3290. U.S. Congress. House. Committee on the Judiciary. *Establishment of a United States Industrial Home for Women, Hearing on H.R. 13927.* 67th Cong., 4th sess., 23 Jan. 1923. 18p. Y4.J89/1:W84/12. Hearing explores the proposal to convert the abandoned weather station at Mount Weather, Virginia, to a federal women's prison. The proposal was prompted by a rise in the number of women arrested on narcotics charges and a growing problem of overcrowding at state women's prison facilities making it impossible for them to take any more long-term federal prisoners. The preference for the cottage plan as a way to treat women prisoners and the need for a hospital facility is stressed. Site selection criteria are discussed with particular reference to the problem of women who are drug addicts.

3291. U.S. Congress. Senate. Committee on the Judiciary. *Establishment of a United States Industrial Home for Women at Mount Weather, Va., Hearing on S. 4452.* 67th Cong., 4th sess., 3 Feb. 1923. 25p. Y4.J89/2:W84. Hearing on construction of a federal prison for women sentenced to more than one year describes the problems encountered since state prisons have refused to take any more federal women prisoners. The primary point of discussion is the suitability of the proposed site. Witnesses extol the benefits of outdoor life and agricultural pursuits in reforming urban female offenders.

3292. U.S. Congress. House. Committee on the Judiciary. *Establishment of a United States Industrial Reformatory and a Federal Industrial Farm for Women, Hearing on H.R. 2869, H.R. 685, and H.R. 4125.* 68th Cong., 1st. sess., 9 Jan. 1924. 19p. Y4.J89/1:R25/2.

Discussion highlights the continuing need for a federal prison, or, in this case, an industrial farm for women convicted in federal courts.

3293. U.S. Congress. House. Committee on the Judiciary. *Federal Industrial Institution for Women, Report to Accompany S. 790.* H. Rept. 69, 68th Cong., 1st sess., 1924. Serial 8226. Report reviews the pressing need for a federal institution for female offenders and presents the basic structure and function of the proposed institution.

3294. U.S. Congress. Senate. Committee on the Judiciary. *For the Establishment of a Federal Industrial Farm for Women, and for Other Purposes, Report to Accompany S. 790.* S. Rept. 26, 68th Cong., 1st sess., 1924. 3p. Serial 8220. Report presents amendments to a bill establishing a federal correctional institution for women. Amendments consist primarily of replacing the word "farm" with "institution." The report summarizes the need for the institution and outlines its basic function as an industrial institution rather than a penitentiary.

3295. U.S. Congress. House. *Supplemental Estimate for Federal Industrial Institution for Women: Communication from the President of the United States Transmitting Supplemental Estimates of Appropriation for the Department of Justice for the Fiscal Year Ending June 30, 1925, to Remain Available until June 30, 1926, in the Amount of $909,100.* H. Doc. 604, 68th Cong., 2d sess., 1925. 3p. Serial 8445. Detail of costs for the purchase of land and construction of buildings for the Federal Industrial Institution for Women at Alderson, West Virginia.

3296. U.S. Congress. House. Committee on the District of Columbia. *Establishing a Women's Bureau in the Metropolitan Police Department, Report to Accompany H.R. 12248.* H. Rept. 1588, 68th Cong., 2d sess., 1925. 2p. Serial 8391. Report on a bill to permanently establish a Women's Bureau in the Metropolitan Police Department summarizes the beneficial work of the bureau in preventing the ruin of young girls and in closing immoral dance halls.

3297. U.S. Congress. Joint Subcommittee on the District of Columbia. *Women's Bureau, Police Department, District of Columbia, Joint Hearing on S. 4308.* 68th Cong., 2d sess., 20 Feb. 1925. 41p. Y4.D63/2:W84/2. Hearing testimony clarifies the duties of the present and proposed Women's Bureau of the District of Columbia Metropolitan Police. The work of the bureau, particularly in relation to wayward girls, is highlighted. Dissension surrounds a provision giving the bureau authority to apprehend delinquent women and children, and debate occurs over the definition of children as it pertains to boys.

3298. U.S. Congress. House. *Federal Industrial Institution for Women, Alderson, W. Va.: Communication from the President of the United States Transmitting Supplemental Estimate of Appropriation for the Department of Justice for the Fiscal Year Ending June 30, 1926, to Remain Available Until June 30, 1927, for the Federal Industrial Institute for Women, Alderson, W. VA., $1,734,400.* H. Doc. 277, 69th Cong., 1st sess., 1926. 4p. Serial 8579. Provides details of the budget for land and building construction for the Federal Industrial Institute for Women, Alderson, West Virginia. Correspondence from Attorney General Sergeant justifying the appropriations for the training facilities at the institution is appended.

3299. U.S. Congress. House. Committee on the District of Columbia. *Women's Department in the Metropolitan Police Department of the District of Columbia, Report to Accompany H.R. 7848.* H. Rept. 1501, 69th Cong., 1st sess., 1926. 9p. Serial 8534. Reports a bill permanently establishing a Woman's Bureau in the District of Columbia Police Department. The work of the Women's Bureau in relation to private social agencies and the basic provisions of the bureau in the area of officer qualifications, size of force, and pay are reviewed. The philosophy behind the establishment of the Women's Bureau to perform protective work and a review of typical work of the bureau is given. The report also includes letters of endorsement from various women's organizations.

3300. U.S. Congress. House. Committee on the District of Columbia. Subcommittee on Police and Firemen. *Woman's Bureau, Police Department, Hearings on H.R. 7848.* 69th Cong., 1st. sess., 23 Feb. - 27 Mar. 1926. 204p. Y4.D63/1:W84. Hearing considers a bill to formally establish a Woman's Bureau in the District of Columbia Metropolitan Police Department with authority over matters dealing with women and minors and over sex offenses, performing in many cases a social work function. Testimony discusses the function of the Bureau, particularly repression of prostitution, and the role of policewomen and the attitude of supervisors. The role of policewomen nationwide is described and numerous case studies involving delinquent girls are included in the hearing record as examples of the need for the bureau.

3301. U.S. Congress. Senate. Committee on the District of Columbia. *Woman's Bureau, Police Department, District of Columbia, Hearing on S. 1750.* 69th Cong., 1st. sess., 8 June 1926. 48p. Y4.D63/2:W84/3. Hearing on the legislative establishment of a Woman's Bureau in the District of Columbia Police Department centers on the need for legislative measures to set the number of policewomen and to delineate duties. The work of the police women in ensuring the morality of theater shows and dance halls is described. Opponents argued that the bill gave the Women's Bureau to much power in the apprehension and detention of women and children.

3302. U.S. Congress. Senate. Committee on the District of Columbia. *Woman's Police Bureau of the District of Columbia, Report to Accompany S. 5819.* S. Rept. 1634, 69th Cong., 2d sess., 1927. 2p. Serial 8685. Favorable report on the establish of a permanent Woman's Bureau in the District of Columbia Metropolitan Police Department reviews the current status and work of the bureau in protective work with women and children.

3303. U.S. Congress. House. Committee on the District of Columbia. *To Establish a Woman's Bureau in the Metropolitan Police Department, Report to Accompany H.R. 6665.* H. Rept. 868, 70th Cong., 1st sess., 1928. 8p. Serial 8836. Report on a bill establishing a Woman's Bureau in the District of Columbia Metropolitan Police Department points out that the bill allows lower salaries for female officers. The good work of the bureau is described and endorsements of the bureau are reprinted. Details on the number and type of cases handled by the bureau in Fiscal Year 1926-27 are furnished.

3304. U.S. Congress. Senate. Committee on the District of Columbia. *Woman's Bureau of the Metropolitan Police Department of the District of Columbia, Report to Accompany S. 4174.* S. Rept. 874, 70th Cong., 1st sess., 1928. 3p. Serial 8831. Report on a bill to establish a permanent Woman's Bureau in the District of Columbia Metropolitan Police Department describes how the bill differs from earlier bills, particularly in the areas of powers and personnel of the bureau. The work of the bureau in dealing with runaways and prostitutes is examined with statistics on cases handled by category.

3305. U.S. Congress. House. Special Committee on Federal Penal and Reformatory Institutions. *Federal Panel and Reformatory Institutions, Hearings Pursuant to H.Res. 233.* 70th Cong., 2d sess., 7-15 Jan. 1929. 283p. Y4.F31/3:P93. Although the majority of this hearing is on federal penal institutions for males, information was provided on employment of women prisoners, the National Training School of Girls, and the Alderson Federal Industrial Institution for Women.

3306. U.S. Congress. Senate. Committee on the District of Columbia. *Woman's Bureau of the Police Department of the District of Columbia, Report to Accompany H.R. 6664.* S. Rept.

1827, 70th Cong., 2d sess., 1929. 3p. Serial 8977. Differences between the House and Senate versions of H.R. 6664 are noted and most of S. Rept. 874, 70th Congress (3304), detailing the need for and functions of the bureau, is reprinted.

3307.   U.S. Congress. House. *Suppression of Prostitution in the District of Columbia, Report to Accompany S. 405.* H. Rept. 1740, 74th Cong., 1st sess., 1935. 1p. Serial 9889. Conference committee report recommends acceptance of the House amendments.

3308.   U.S. Congress. House. Committee on the District of Columbia. *Suppression of Prostitution in the District of Columbia, Report to Accompany S. 405.* H. Rept. 1527, 74th Cong., 1st sess., 1935. 2p. Serial 9888. Reports with amendments a bill raising the maximum penalty for solicitation of prostitution. The amendment, which differs from the Senate version, gives the court power to order a medical exam and treatment of offenders.

3309.   U.S. Congress. Senate. Committee on the District of Columbia. *Suppression of Prostitution in the District of Columbia, Report to Accompany S. 405.* S. Rept. 404, 74th Cong., 1st sess., 1935. 1p. Serial 9878. Reports with amendments a bill providing for higher penalties for prostitution convictions.

3310.   U.S. Congress. House. Committee on Military Affairs. *Prohibiting Prostitution near Defense Centers, Report to Accompany H.R. 2475.* H. Rept. 399, 77th Cong., 1st sess., 1941. 5p. Serial 10553. Reports a bill to prohibit prostitution within reasonable distances of military and naval establishments, as determined by the Secretary of War. The need for such a measure to protect the armed forces from venereal disease is reviewed and communications from government officials supporting the bill are reprinted.

3311.   U.S. Congress. House. Committee on Military Affairs. *To Prohibit Prostitution within Reasonable Distance of Military and Naval Establishment, Hearings on H.R. 2475.* 77th Cong., 1st sess., 11 - 18 Mar. 1941. 70p. Y4.M59/1:P94/5. Hearing with testimony from health officials and military groups stresses the need to restrict prostitution and houses of ill fame from operating near military establishments. The focus of testimony is on the spread of venereal disease, moral degeneration, and the descent of local girls from "less protected families" into prostitution.

3312.   U.S. Congress. Senate. Committee on Military Affairs. *Prostitution near Military and Naval Establishments, Report to Accompany H.R. 2475.* S. Rept. 327, 77th Cong., 1st sess., 1941. 5p. Serial 10544. Report without recommendation reprints H. Rept. 399 (3310).

3313.   U.S. Office of Defense Health and Welfare Services. Social Protection Section. *Program of Social Protection Section.* Washington, DC: The Office, 1941. 4p. Pr32.4502:So1. Outline summarizes the objectives of the Social Protection program which are stated as repression of commercialized prostitution, treatment of prostitution, protection of girls in defense areas, and cooperation with other agencies.

3314.   U.S. Congress. House. Committee on Military Affairs. *Making Permanent the Provisions of the Act of July 11, 1941, Prohibiting Prostitution near Defense Centers, Report to Accompany H.R. 6305.* H. Rept. 2004, 79th Cong., 2d sess., 1942. 3p. Serial 11024. The primary objectives of the act to curb the spread of venereal disease among members of the armed forces is reviewed and the changes in existing law made by the proposed bill are presented.

3315.   U.S. Office of Defense Health and Welfare Services. Social Protection Section. *Repression of Prostitution in the Social Protection Program.* by Eliot Ness. Washington, DC: The Office, 1942. 3p. Pr32.4507:N37. Short address before the National Advisory

Police Committee stresses cooperation with local police departments to repress prostitution and the commitment at the national level to controlling the spread of venereal disease. Also briefly mentions prevention through understanding the social and economic causes of prostitution.

3316. U.S. Office of Defense Health and Welfare Services. Social Protection Section. *Social Protection, Excerpts from Paper Prepared and Delivered by Fred R. Kearney, Social Protection Representative, Region 10, before Meeting of Social Workers and Health Workers in Houston, TX.* by Fred R. Kearney. Washington, DC: The Office, 1942. 7p. Pr32.4507:K21. The local responsibility for control of prostitution is the focus of this speech defining the roles of the Social Protection Division, local law enforcement, health officials, and social welfare agencies. The advantage of a repression of prostitution program versus the segregated prostitution approach is examined noting venereal disease rates in areas with a strong program of repression and the ineffectiveness of the medical inspection of prostitutes. The relationship between hotels and "casual" prostitution is reviewed.

3317. U.S. Federal Security Administration. *The Role a Woman's Organization Has Played in Social Protection.* by Mrs. Horace B. Ritchie. Washington, DC: The Administration, 1943? 5p. FS2.30:So1. Address by Mrs. Horace B. Ritchie, Chairman, Department of Public Welfare, General Federation of Women's Clubs, given before the National Social Protection Conference for Women's Organizations, June 9,1943, outlines the role of women in combatting venereal disease through women's organizations.

3318. U.S. Federal Security Administration. *Techniques for Repressing Unorganized Prostitution, Recommendations of Special Committee on Enforcement of National Advisory Police Committee.* Washington, DC: GPO, 1943. 2p. FS1.2:P94. Successful efforts to close down "red light districts" are touted while law enforcement officers are encouraged to prepare a plan of attack on unorganized prostitution.

3319. U.S. Federal Security Agency. Social Protection Division. *How to Curb Prostitution in Hotels.* by Eliot Ness. Washington, DC: The Division, 1943. 4p. FS9.2:P94. Reprint from the February 1943 issue of *Southern Hotel Journal* discusses the responsibility of the hotel manager to discourage prostitution on his premises and presents a case history of a hotel declared off limits to servicemen. The steps taken by the hotel chain's president to address the problem are enumerated. Rules imposed by hotels in one city for accommodating unescorted women are described.

3320. U.S. Office of Community War Services. *Social Protection in Wartime, by Charles P. Taft, Director, Office of Community War Services, Address before the 50th Annual Conference of the International Association of Chiefs of Police, Detroit, Aug. 11, 1943.* by Charles P. Taft. Washington, DC: The Administration, 1943. 7p. FS9.8:So1. Redirecting girls who are just getting into trouble away from prostitution is one of the themes of this speech encouraging law enforcement officers to play an active role in preventing prostitution. Efforts to detour girls from the path to delinquency are described and considerations in handling unattached girls who come to the city are noted.

3321. U.S. Office of Community War Services. Division of Social Protection. *Techniques of Law Enforcement against Prostitution.* Washington, DC: GPO, 1943. 75p. FS9.6:P94. Manual on the control of prostitution describes why and how prostitution should be suppressed. The various types of prostitution are examined, and the problem of teenage girls is discussed. Gives a good overview of the problems of prostitution in wartime.

3322. U.S. Office of Defense Health and Welfare Services. *Venereal Disease, Prostitution, and War, Sound Legislative Program for Control of Venereal Disease and Repression of*

Prostitution Founded upon Experience. by American Bar Association Committee on Courts and Wartime Social Protection. Washington, DC: GPO, 1943. 82p. Pr32.4502:V55. Articulates a general philosophy on the need to control venereal disease as part of the war effort. The bulk of the publication is devoted to state statutes on control of venereal disease and prostitution.

3323. U.S. Office of Defense Health and Welfare Services. National Advisory Police Committee on Social Protection. *Techniques for Repressing Unorganized Prostitution: Recommendations of the Special Committee on Enforcement of the National Advisory Committee.* Washington, DC: GPO, 1943. 4p. FS1.2:P94 General overview of venereal disease and repression of prostitution furnishes specific ideas on dealing with the independent prostitute through investigations of cheap hotels and "B-girls" at saloons.

3324. U.S. Office of Defense Health and Welfare Services. Social Protection Section. *Prostitution Prevention, with Special Reference to Protection of Girls and Women from Involvement in Prostitution and Redirection of Those Who Have Become so Involved, Suggestions for Organizing Services of Local Community Agencies.* Washington, DC: The Office, 1943. 19p. Pr32.4502:P94. Information is provided for communities on effective programs for preventing young women from entering prostitution and on redirecting those already involved. Police activities, medical care, employment assistance, and social work are viewed as the main activities for a successful program. The local agency role in identifying and redirecting prostitutes and sexually promiscuous girls is described.

3325. U.S. Office of Defense Health and Welfare Services. Social Protection Section. *Social Protection through Health and Welfare Services.* by Fred R. Kearney. Washington, DC: The Office, 1943. 15p. Pr32.4502:So1/2. Expands on an earlier speech (3316) addressing the role of social protection in the war effort and the local responsibility for prostitution control. Explains why invoking the May Act is not enough and how prostitution is not just a federal problem. Evidence is presented that repression of prostitution and closing "red light" districts is effective. Also discusses dealing with the problem of sexually promiscuous girls and the increase in "sex delinquency," along with the problem of young women who have been drawn to the defense center for escape or adventure. Action programs focusing on the social issues of prostitution and promiscuous girls are suggested.

3326. U.S. Office of Defense Health and Welfare Services. Social Protection Section. *VDCO and Social Protection.* by Eliot Ness. Washington, DC: The Office, 1943. 6p. Pr32.4507:N37/2. Describes the role of the Social Protection representative, in conjunction with local community officials, in repressing vice, particularly prostitution, which contributes to venereal disease. The idea of "social redirection" is suggested as a component of prostitution prevention activities.

3327. U.S. Congress. House. Committee on Military Affairs. *Extending the Provisions of the Act of July 11, 1941 (Public Law 163, 77th Cong.,) Prohibiting Prostitution near Defense Centers, Report to Accompany H.R. 2992.* H Rept. 512, 79th Cong., 1st sess., 1945. 3p. Serial 10932. Report on the proposed extension of PL 77-163 until the termination of hostilities describes the need for the bill to protect the armed forces from venereal disease.

3328. U.S. Congress. Senate. Committee on Military Affairs. *Prostitution near Military and Naval Establishments, Report to Accompany S. 948.* S. Rept. 261, 79th Cong., 1st sess., 1945. 3p. Serial 10925. See 3327 for abstract.

3329. U.S. Office of Community War Services. Social Protection Division. *Challenge to Community Action.* Washington, DC: GPO, 1945. 76p. FS9.2:C73/2. Community approaches to venereal disease prevention and the problem of moral laxness following the war are the topics of this publication. Includes discussion of the prevalence of prostitution and the problem of "footloose" young women with no home or job. Also covers law enforcement approaches to venereal disease and prostitution repression. The use of police women for work with female delinquents is encouraged.

3330. U.S. Office of Community War Services. Social Protection Division. *Danger Ahead! Statement by Public Health Service, American Social Hygiene Association, Social Protection Division, Office of Community War Services.* Washington, DC: The Office, 1945. 2p. FS9.2:D21. Statement stresses the prevention and repression of prostitution and the control of venereal disease.

3331. U.S. Office of Community War Services. Social Protection Division. *Role of American Hotel Association in Social Protection Program.* By Charles J. Hahn. Washington, DC: The Office, 1945. 5p. FS9.8:Am3. Excepts from an address before the American Hotel Association, Dec. 12, 1944, Chicago, Illinois, encourages hotels to make sure that they do not relax their vigilance in efforts to discourage casual prostitution in their establishments.

3332. U.S. Office of Community War Services. Social Protection Division. *She Looked Clean but...The Prostitute or Good-Time Girl Can Put You Out of Business.* Washington, DC: The Office, 1945. 16p. leaflet. FS9.2:P94/2.

3333. U.S. Office of Community War Services. Social Protection Division. *Social Services in Social Protection Program.* Washington, DC: The Division, 1945. 5p. FS9.2:So1/3. Guidelines detail how voluntary social service agencies can work with local officials to provide services to young men and women who have not been arrested but who have a venereal disease or other delinquency problems. Prostitutes and "extensively promiscuous" women and girls are not viewed as the proper clientele for voluntary social services.

3334. U.S. Office of Community War Services. Social Protection Division. *Techniques of Law Enforcement in the Use of Policewomen with Special Reference to Social Protection.* Washington, DC: GPO, 1945. 93p. FS9.6:P75/945. Manual for new policewomen describes the types of work performed and provides advice on handling children, girls and women in various situations. Specifically discusses dealing with rape and prostitution. Also suggests qualifications for policewomen and department administrative practices.

3335. U.S. Office of Community War Services. Social Protection Division. *Welfare and Community Action.* by Florine J. Ellis. Washington, DC: The Office, 1945. 5p. FS9.8:W45. Address given at the Social Protection Division cooperative regional meeting held in Columbus, South Carolina, March 8, 1945, discusses the social and psychological factors which contribute to a girl becoming a prostitute. Local law enforcement is urged to take steps to prevent prostitution and to "redirect" young women by referring them to social workers before they become professional prostitutes.

3336. U.S. Children's Bureau. *Social Welfare Activities in the League of Nations.* Washington, DC: The Bureau, 1946? 7p. L5.2:So1/4. Activities of the League of Nations to reduce the international traffic of women and children for immoral purposes include the sponsoring of conferences and studies and the ratification of the International Agreements for the Suppression of White Slave Traffic of 1904 and 1910. League activities in the promotion of child welfare are also discussed.

3337. U.S. Congress. House. Committee on the Judiciary. Subcommittee No. 3. *Social Protection, Hearing on H.R. 5234.* 79th Cong., 2d sess., 18 Mar. 1946. 63p. Y4.J89/1:So1. Hearing examines a bill to allow the Federal Security Agency to provide technical assistance to state and local governments on prostitution and "sex delinquency." Within testimony filled with "evils of prostitution" rhetoric lies information on wartime efforts to discourage prostitution and theories of dealing with delinquent girls. The role of local groups, including women's organizations, in combating commercialized prostitution is briefly covered.

3338. U.S. Congress. Senate. Committee on Military Affairs. *Prostitution near Military Establishments, Report to Accompany H.R. 6305.* S. Rept. 1332, 79th Cong., 2d sess., 1946. 2p. Serial 11015. Report on a bill making permanent the provisions of P.L. 77-163 briefly reviews the need to control prostitution near military establishments.

3339. U.S. Public Health Service. *A Message to Women in Technicolor.* Washington, DC: GPO, 1946. 4p. FS2.36:5. Flyer on a film about women and venereal disease is aimed primarily at women's clubs.

3340. U.S. War Dept. *Repression of Prostitution; Apr. 5, 1946.* Special Regulation 600-900. Washington, DC: GPO, 1946. 1p. W1.6:600-900.

3341. U.S. Air Force. *Air Provost Marshal: Apprehension and Confinement of Women in Air Force; July 27, 1949.* Air Force Regulation 125-7. Washington, DC: GPO, 1949. 2p. M301.6:125-7/2. Earlier edition issued November 29, 1948.

3342. U.S. Army. *Personnel: Repression of Prostitution in Areas Adjacent to Military Installations.* Army Special Regulation 600-900-5. Washington, DC: GPO, 1950. 3p. D101.10:600-900-5. Describes proper measures for Army commanders in repressing prostitution which threatens the health and welfare of Army personnel.

3343. U.S. Air Force. *Air Provost Marshal: Repression of Prostitution in Areas Adjacent to Air Force Installation, Dec. 1,1952.* Air Force Regulation 125-43. Washington, DC: GPO, 1952. 2p. D301.6:125-43.

3344. U.S. Air Force. *Provost Marshal Activities, Repression of Prostitution in Overseas Areas; Aug. 16, 1954.* Air Force Regulation 125-45. Washington, DC: The Department, 1954. 1p. D301.6:125-45/2. Earlier regulation issued July 3, 1953.

3345. U.S. Air Force. *Provost Marshal Activities, Suppression of Prostitution near Air Force Installations; Dec. 16, 1955.* Air Force Regulation 125-43. Washington, DC: The Department, 1955. 3p. D301.6:125-43/2. Change sheet issued March 6,1957. 1p.

3346. U.S. National Institute of Mental Health. Center for Studies of Crime and Delinquency. *Not the Law's Business? An Examination of Homosexuality, Abortion, Prostitution, Narcotics and Gambling in the United States.* by Gilbert Geis. Washington, DC: GPO, 1972. 262p. HE20.2420/2:L44. Discussion of the legal issues of homosexuality, abortion, prostitution, narcotics and gambling includes a considerable amount of social philosophy and history relative to these topics.

3347. U.S. Commission on Civil Rights. Arizona Advisory Committee. *Adult Corrections in Arizona.* Washington, DC: GPO, 1974. 189p. CR1.2:C81. Investigation of civil and human rights at Arizona state prisons looks specifically at prison facilities including the Women's Division of the Arizona State Prison. Conditions of housing, recreation, education and training, work opportunities, medical care and disciplinary procedures are examined.

3348. U.S. Commission on Civil Rights. Kansas Advisory Committee. *Inmate Rights and the Kansas State Prison System.* Washington, DC: GPO, 1974. 137p. CR1.2:K13. Although primarily concerned with the civil rights of male inmates, this report also examines the conditions at the Kansas Correctional Institution for Women with particular reference to health care, housing, and educational opportunities. A breakdown of institution staff by race/ethnicity and sex is furnished.

3349. U.S. Congress. House. Committee on the District of Columbia. *Criminal Confinement of Women in the District of Columbia: A Preliminary Analysis.* 93d Cong., 2d sess., 2 Dec. 1974. Committee print. 14p. CIS-75-H302-1. Preliminary report on the problems in the existing system for the confinement of women convicted in the District of Columbia notes inequities in the treatment of female versus male prisoners. Physical facilities and rehabilitation needs are highlighted. The authors suggest alternatives to the existing system.

3350. U.S. Commission on Civil Rights. Nebraska Advisory Committee. *Inmate Rights and Institutional Response: The Nebraska State System.* Washington, DC: The Commission, 1975. CR1.2:P93. Report on the Nebraska state prison system documents treatment of inmates including women incarcerated at the State Reformatory for Women. Issues of housing, medical treatment, discipline, legal services, recreation, and vocational development and education programs are examined.

3351. U.S. Commission on Civil Rights. Oregon Advisory Committee. *Civil and Human Rights in Oregon State Prisons.* Washington, DC: GPO, 1975. 78p. CR1.2:Or3. Study of conditions in Oregon state prisons describes a generally progressive system but also indicates that female prisoners had much more limited educational and vocational training opportunities. The need to place women and minorities in high level, policy making positions is noted.

3352. U.S. National Institute of Mental Health. *The Contemporary Woman and Crime.* by Rita James Simon. Washington, DC: GPO, 1975. 98p. HE20.8114/3:W84. Analysis of crime and criminal justice statistics describes trends in the number and type of crimes committed by women and on the treatment of women in the criminal justice system compared to men. The report provides a review of the research literature on women and crime and theorizes on the effect of the changing social and economic status of women and their criminal activities. Basic socioeconomic statistics on women are presented along with statistics on women as a percentage of all arrests and arrests by type of offense, 1953-73; convictions by sex, 1963-71; percent of females among convictions by offense category; age of offender paroled by sex and type of offense; and ranking of countries by females arrested for various crimes.

3353. U.S. Commission on Civil Rights. Louisiana Advisory Committee. *A Study of Adult Corrections in Louisiana.* Washington, DC: The Commission, 1976. 159p. CR1.2:C81/2. Study of conditions in Louisiana's state correctional facilities includes a separate chapter on the Louisiana Correctional Institute for Women. Areas of investigation include housing, employment and training, health care, disciplinary procedures, and rehabilitation.

3354. U.S. Commission on Civil Rights. North Carolina Advisory Committee. *Prisons in North Carolina.* Washington, DC: GPO, 1976. 65p. CR1.2:P93/2. Study of conditions in North Carolina prisons pays particular attention to the treatment of female prisoners which was found to be below that of male prisoners in terms of treatment and opportunities. The employment of women and minorities in higher level positions in corrections is also examined.

3355. U.S. Law Enforcement Assistance Administration. *The Report of the LEAA Task Force on Women.* Washington, DC: GPO, 1976. 70p. J1.2:W84. Report looks at the treatment of women in the criminal justice system as offenders, victims, and grant recipients, and specifically addresses the employment of women in the LEAA.

3356. U.S. Bureau of Prisons. *Female Offenders in the Federal Prison System.* Lompoc, CA: Federal Prison Industries, 1977. 32p. J16.2:F34. Brief history of the federal prison system and overview of the female prison population examines the living conditions of female prisoners and progress in the federal prison system.

3357. U.S. Library of Congress. Archive of Folk Song. *A Selected List of Songs Dealing with Women in Prison.* Washington, DC: The Library, 1977. 2p. LC1.12/2:W84.

3358. U.S. National Commission on the Observance of International Women's Year. *Female Offenders.* Washington, DC: GPO, 1977. 115p. Y3.W84:10/7. Guide to conducting a workshop on female offenders includes outlines for the workshop, fact sheets, possible films and publications for workshop use, and lists of possible resource people.

3359. U.S. National Institute of Law Enforcement and Criminal Justice. *National Study of Women's Correctional Programs.* Washington, DC: GPO, 1977. 358p. J1.44:W84. National study examines the programs and services provided to women in state prisons, county jails, and community-based correctional programs. Factors studied include location and physical adequacy of institutions, the social environment of institutions, counseling and treatment, health care, education and training programs, work assignments, and recreation. Includes statistics on incarcerated women including age, ethnic group, education, marital status, children, childhood family type, welfare, employment history, offenses, arrests, offense history, and type of incarceration.

3360. U.S. Women's Bureau. *Employment Needs of Women Offenders: A Program Design.* Pamphlet no. 13. Washington, DC: GPO, 1977. 63p. L36.112:13. Description of a Women's Bureau program for International Women's Year focuses on the employment needs to women offenders and ex-offenders and on how communities and government agencies can address these needs. Includes a how-to guide for local organizations wishing to carry out similar programs.

3361. U.S. Office of Juvenile Justice and Delinquency Prevention. *Little Sisters and the Law.* Washington, DC: GPO, 1978. 81p. J1.2:Si8. Detailed look at the treatment of young women in the juvenile justice system summarizes how the system operates and reports on the results of a study of differential treatment of females in state training schools. Includes information on the characteristics of young female offenders in six states. Alternative approaches to programs for young female offenders and resources available are reviewed.

3362. U.S. Commission on Civil Rights. Montana Advisory Committee. *Corrections in Montana: A Consultation.* Washington, DC: GPO, 1979. 59p. CR1.2:C81/3. Consultation examines accusations that the Montana correctional system gives disparate treatment to women and minorities. A major problem identified was the lack of a facility for women inmates causing most long term female offenders to be sent out of state.

3363. U.S. Congress. House. Committee on the Judiciary. Subcommittee on Courts, Civil Liberties and the Administration of Justice. *The Female Offender - 1979-80, Hearings.* 96th Cong., 1st sess., 10,11 Oct. 1979. 1361p. Y4.J89/1:96/59/pt.1-2. Hearing reviews the problems of female offenders and the shortfalls of current practice in handing female offenders. In addition to testimony, the hearing includes reprinted material on female prisoners and health care, GAO reports on the treatment of female offenders, reports on sex role stereotypes in criminal justice and on female offenders as mothers, the U.N. Resolution on Women Offenders, and an annotated bibliography. Provides statistics on female offenders and their criminal records, educational attainment, marital status, age and race, and number of children.

3364. U.S. General Accounting Office. *Female Offenders: Who Are They and What Are the Problems Confronting Them?* Washington, DC: The Office, 1979. 85p. GA1.13:GGD-79-73. Information on the female offender in the criminal justice system was gathered through literature reviews and site visits. Report describes the treatment of women in the system and highlights issues needing further discussion.

3365. U.S. National Institute of Law Enforcement and Criminal Justice. *The Female Offender: A Selected Bibliography.* Washington, DC: GPO, 1979. 50p. J26.9:F34. Annotated bibliography lists current books, research reports, and journal articles on female offenders.

3366. U.S. General Accounting Office. *Women in Prison: Inequitable Treatment Requires Action.* Washington, DC: The Office, 1980. 50p. GA1.13:GGD-81-6. Creative approaches to addressing the inequality of services and facilities for women in correctional systems are described.

3367. U.S. Women's Bureau. *The Women Offender Apprenticeship Program: From Inmate to Skilled Craft Worker.* Pamphlet no. 21. Washington, DC: GPO, 1980. 64p. L36.112:21. Provides information on the Women Offender Apprenticeship Program sponsored by the Federal Prison System, the Bureau of Apprenticeship and Training, and the Women's Bureau. The focus of the program is to provide vocational training for women inmates in order to improve their job prospects after release. A step-by-step guide to developing similar programs and a bibliography of books, pamphlets, and audiovisual materials on women and apprenticeship is provided.

3368. U.S. Office of Juvenile Justice and Delinquency Prevention. *Programs for Young Women in Trouble.* Washington, DC: GPO, 1981. 24p. J26.2:P94/11. Describes programs around the country offering services to young women runaways, delinquents, and drug users.

3369. U.S. Congress. House. Committee on Education and Labor. Subcommittee on Select Education. *Teenage Prostitution and Child Pornography, Hearings.* 97th Cong., 2d sess., 23 Apr., 24 June 1982. 116p. Y4.Ed8/1:T22/7. Hearing testimony explores the problem of teenage prostitution and child pornography in the U.S. and provides case histories of teenage prostitutes. Particularly noted is the problem of young female runaways and prostitution.

3370. U.S. Congress. House. Committee on the District of Columbia. Subcommittee on Judiciary and Education. *District of Columbia Female Offenders in the Federal Prison System, Oversight Hearing.* 97th Cong., 2d sess., 6 May 1982. 71p. Y4.D63/1:97-9. Hearing explores approaches to the problem of the incarceration of District of Columbia female offenders in federal prisons very distant from the D.C. area.

3371. U.S. Congress. House. Committee on the District of Columbia. Subcommittee on Judiciary and Education. *Garnes Decree, Hearing.* 101st Cong., 2d sess., 12 June 1990. 51p. Y4.D63/1:101-11. Brief hearing examines the implementation of the Garnes Decree, an agreement by which female offenders in the District are housed at federal facilities outside the D.C. area. The District of Columbia Department of Corrections' efforts to accommodate the portion of the agreement which provides for the prisoner's transfer back to the D.C. area nine months prior to their parole eligibility date is examined. Also discussed is sex discrimination in the D.C. Good Time Credits Act, an early parole program, as a result of the Garnes Decree. Testimony provides a profile of the District female offender population and an overview of the impact on the women of incarceration at remote federal prisons. Plans for expanded female corrections facilities in the District are examined.

SERIALS

3372. U.S. Bureau of Prisons. Federal Reformatory for Women. *The Eagle.* Alderson, WV: The Reformatory, ?- 1968, v. 1- v. 35. J16.18: vol/no. Newsletter produced by the inmates of the Federal Reformatory for Women at Alderson, West Virginia, includes news items and literary attempts.

3373. U.S. Dept. of Justice. Attorney-General. *Report of Board of the Trustees of National Training School for Girls of District of Columbia.* Washington, DC: The Department, 1894-1919. annual. J9.1:894-919. (Reports for 1894-1991 called *Report of Trustees. Reform School for Girls of District of Columbia.*) The health, deportment, and training of girls assigned to the National Training School for Girls of the District of Columbia are reviewed in the school's annual report. The personal cleanliness, "training for right living", and parole for the young women are also described as is the school's approach to discipline. Farm yields and finances are reported, and commitments, paroles, and paroled girls returned for the year are summarized.

3374. U.S. Interdepartmental Social Hygiene Board. *Report of the United States Interdepartmental Social Hygiene Board for [Year].* Washington, DC: GPO, 1920-1922. annual. Y3.In8/2:R29/year. Annual report describes the activities of the Interdepartmental Social Hygiene Board and of local social hygiene officials. Includes reports on repression of prostitution with case reports and statistical summaries of case work.

21

Women in
Other Countries

Although most U.S. documents focus on women in America, some documents do discuss women in other countries. Most of these documents are on a specific topic and are in the appropriate chapter. The documents listed here are of a general nature, and many focus on U.S. sponsored programs in lesser developed countries (LDCs). The status of women in South American countries was described in documents published between 1943 and 1945 by the Women's Bureau and the Office of the Coordinator of Inter-American Affairs (3375-3379). In 1951 the Women's Bureau issued brief documents on Japan (3380) and the Philippines (3381). Women in West Germany before and after World War II are described in a Department of State report issued in 1952 (3382).

Reports since 1978 are mostly from the Agency for International Development describing the role of women in development in LDCs. Among the topics routinely addressed are food production, education and employment. The general need to include women in development programs is discussed in congressional hearings (3382-3388, 3432, 3439, 3442) and in AID reports (3390, 3405, 3408). Other common themes are the effect of migration on women (3402, 3414, 3416) and the potential role of women's organizations (3412, 3418-3419) in development. Many of the government reports on women in development were issued as technical reports and are not included in this bibliography.

3375. U.S. Women's Bureau. *Women in Brazil Today.* Washington, DC: The Bureau, 1943? 12p. L13.2:W84/7. Describes the expanding opportunities for Brazilian women outside the home as a result of WWI and WWII. The work of the Legias Brasileira de Assestencia in social welfare work and the expanding educational and professional opportunities for women are reviewed. Opportunities for women in government employment are described, and notable positions held by women are noted.

3376. U.S. Office of the Coordinator of Inter-American Affairs. *Status of Women in Argentina.* by Kathleen B. Tappen. Washington, DC: The Office, 1944. 22p. Pr32.4602:W84. Overview of women in Argentina looks at marriage and the family, political and civil rights, labor force participation and protective labor laws, and education. The activities of women's organizations and the social conditions in Argentina are also described. Includes a brief bibliography.

3377. U.S. Office of the Coordinator of Inter-American Affairs. *Status of Women in Brazil.* by Kathleen B. Tappen. Washington, DC: The Office, 1944. 14p. Pr32.4602:W84/2. Overview of the condition of women in Brazil reviews their status in relation to marriage and the family, political and civil rights, education, and employment. Also summarizes the extent of protective labor legislation and social conditions. A short bibliography is provided.

3378.   U.S. Office of the Coordinator of Inter-American Affairs. *Status of Women in Chile.* by Kathleen B. Tappen. Washington, DC: The Office, 1944. 19p. Pr32.4602:W84/3. Background information on the status of women in Chile reviews women's position relative to marriage and the family, political and civil rights, employment and occupations, education, protective labor legislation, and social conditions. Statistics on employed women presented include type of work, salaries, child care arrangements, education, and reasons for working. Includes a short bibliography.

3379.   U.S. Women's Bureau. *Social and Labor Problems of Peru and Uruguay: A Study in Contrasts.* Washington, DC: The Bureau, 1945? 22p. L13.2:So1. Education is the focus of this description of the social and labor problems of Peru and Uruguay. The social situation of the Indians in Peru is described as background. Some of the factors which contributed to improved conditions in Peru were social insurance, low-cost housing, and low-cost restaurants. A general description of the labor problems, labor legislation and labor movement in Peru is provided. The population of Uruguay was mostly European immigrants and the major problems identified were living conditions of farm/ranch workers and housing. Women in Uruguay enjoyed a liberal social status and the country was advanced in social legislation. The primary problem of women workers in Uruguay was low wages.

3380.   U.S. Women's Bureau. *Advance of Women in Japan the Past Six Years.* by Sumiko Tanaka. Washington, DC: The Bureau, 1951? 5p. L13.12:W84/6. Address by Sumiko Tanaka, Chief, Women's Section, Women's and Minors' Bureau, Ministry of Labor, Japan, for the Women's Hour, N.H.K. reviews the changing status of Japanese women since the end of WWII. The election of women to the Diet and the extension of suffrage to women is noted. Changes in family life examined include civil statutes on marriage and inheritance and the plight of war widows with children. The greater opportunities for education and employment of women are noted areas of change since the war. Trade union activity, rural women, and women's organizations are briefly described.

3381.   U.S. Women's Bureau. *Filipino Women: Their Role in the Progress of Their Nation.* by Felina Reyes. Washington, DC: The Bureau, 1951? 9p. L13.2:F47. History of the role of Filipino women in their society and the effect of foreign rule is reviewed. Areas highlighted include educational attainment, women as educators, occupational distribution, women in trade and commerce, women's involvement in social welfare organizations, political participation of women, Filipino women as journalists and authors, and the legal status of women in the Philippines.

3382.   U.S. Dept. of State. Office of the U.S. High Commissioner for Germany. Office of the Executive Secretary. Historical Division. *Women in West Germany.* N.p., 1952. 72p. S1.95:W84. Historical overview and analysis of the position of women in West Germany in the years preceding and following WWII examines women's participation in government and administration programs aimed at women. Employment of women, their occupations, and wages are summarized, and the employment problems of university educated women are specifically addressed. Finally, the report covers the activities of major West German women's organizations and the international contacts of these organizations.

3383.   U.S. Peace Corps. *Women in Peace Corps, You Can't Send a Girl There!* Washington, DC: The Corps, 196? 12p. S19.2:W84. Illustrated overview presents the work of women Peace Corps volunteers.

3384. U.S. Agency for International Development. Bureau for Africa and Europe. *African Women Educators Project Report.* by Verna A. Carley. Washington, DC: The Bureau, 1963. 148p. S18.2:Af8. Reports on the African Women Educators Project, a program which held a series of workshops in Africa and brought a number of African women to the U.S. to study the educational system. Feedback from the participants is liberally incorporated into the report. Provides descriptions of African educational systems with special reference to the education of girls in Ethiopia, Sudan, Tanganyika, Kenya, Uganda, Zanzibar, Northern Rhodesia, Nyasaland, Sierra Leone, Liberia, Ghana, Nigeria, Northern Nigeria, Eastern Nigeria and Western Nigeria.

3385. U.S. Agency for International Development. Office of Women in Development. *Status of Thai Women in Two Rural Areas: Survey Report.* by Nantanee Jayasut. Washington, DC: The Agency, 1977. various paging. S18.2:T32. Report of a survey on rural Thai women examines their economic role and social status. Attitudes toward women and their futures were surveyed of both men and women. Finally, the legal status of Thai women is reviewed in the areas of property rights, marriage, and business and professional rights. Some of the questions asked by the survey include money management roles, education, marital status, birth control, equal pay, ideal family size, and expectations for daughters.

3386. U.S. Agency for International Development. Office of Women in Development. Bureau for Africa. *Sex Roles in Food Production and Food Distribution Systems in the Sahel.* by Kathleen Cloud. Washington, DC: The Agency, 1977. 19p. S18.2:Sal/2. Report of an investigation of the food production and processing role of women in the Sahel notes that modernization and draught have effected traditional food systems, and that development programs are aimed at men and men's crops although women play a significant role in food production.

3387. U.S. Congress. House. Committee on International Relations. *International Development and Food Assistance Act of 1977, Report Together with Supplemental Views on H.R. 6714.* H. Rept. 95-240, 95th Cong., 1st sess., 1977. 87p. Serial 13172-4. Major features of the bill reported are additional funding and policy directives on population planning programs and a policy statement and Presidential reporting requirements relative to the status of women in developing countries. The revised Section 113 of the Foreign Assistance Act requires the President to submit a detailed report on the impact of AID programs on the integration of women into the economic development process.

3388. U.S. Congress. Senate. Committee on Foreign Relations. *International Development Assistance Act of 1977, Report to Accompany S. 1520.* S. Rept. 95-161, 95th Cong., 1st sess., 1977. 73p. Serial 13168-3. Among the programs authorized by the bill are population programs for LDCs and funding for U.S. participation in the U.N. Decade for Women. The report also contains a statement of commitment to the integration of women into development programs.

3389. U.S. Agency for International Development. Office of Women in Development. *Images of Women in the Literatures of Selected Developing Countries; Ghana, Senegal, Haiti, Jamaica.* by Kathleen M. McCaffrey. Washington, DC: The Office, 1978. 230p. S18.2:W84 or S15.55:Im1. Report examines the images and perceptions of women as revealed in the fictional literature of Ghana, Senegal, Haiti and Jamaica, and discusses the use of the information gained to address the problems of integrating women into the development programs for the country.

3390. U.S. Agency for International Development. Office of Women in Development. *Report on Women in Development Submitted to the Committee on Foreign Relations, United States Senate and the Speaker of the House of Representatives.* Washington, DC: The Office, 1978. 229p. S18.2:W84/3. Report on the projects and impact of the Women in

Development (WID) project discusses the need for integrating AID projects with the WID program.

3391.   U.S. Congress. House. Committee on International Relations. Subcommittee on International Organizations and Subcommittee on International Development. *International Women's Issues, Hearing and Briefing.* 95th Cong, 2d sess., 8,22 Mar. 1978. 157p. Y4.In8/16:W84. Hearing on the U.S. contribution to the U.N. Decade for Women centers on the women in development issue and on the related programs of the U.S. Agency for International Development. The work of the U.N. Decade is reviewed, and reports from an informal international meeting held in Paris on the role of women in development is included in the appendix.

3392.   U.S. Consortium for International Development. *Proceedings and Papers of the International Conference on Women and Food, University of Arizona, Tucson, Arizona, January 8-11, 1978.* Washington, DC: The Consortium, 1978. 3 vol. S18.55:F73/v.1-3. Report on the International Conference on Women and Food includes a collection of background papers on the role of women in meeting basic food and water needs in developing countries. Volume II provides session summaries discussing women's involvement in alternative food and nutrition projects, ways women can contribute to the food situation in developing countries, the role of financial institutions in facilitating women's role, and world food conference resolutions on women.

3393.   U.S. Agency for International Development. Office of Women in Development. *Access of Rural Girls to Primary Education in the Third World: State of the Art, Obstacles, and Policy Recommendations.* by Constantina Safilios-Rothschild. Washington, DC: The Office, 1979. 31p. S18.55:G44. Review of the literature on women's education in developing countries looks at literacy rates of urban and rural females and at the barriers in rural areas to the schooling of girls.

3394.   U.S. Agency for International Development. Office of Women in Development. *The Comparative Functionality of Formal and Non-Formal Education for Women: Final Report.* by Vivian Lowery Darryck. Washington, DC: The Office, 1979. 190p. S18.55:Ed8. This discussion of the best possible means of helping women in developing countries through education is presented in five parts reflecting the major areas of study. The final report first looks at the historical aspects of the education of women, particularly in the U.S., and at the current status of women's education in developing countries. Second, the functionality of formal and non-formal education for women in LDC's is examined in the areas of social, economic, demographic, systemic, and structural functionalities. Finally, the report examines the relation of the political environment to progress in female education.

3395.   U.S. Agency for International Development. Office of Women in Development. *Differential Impact of Educational Innovations on Girls and Women: Media-Based Instruction and Curriculum Revision, Phase II: Curriculum Revision as if Women Mattered.* by Vivian Lowery Derryck. Washington, DC: The Office, 1979. 13p. S18.55:M46/2. Report on revising formal education to eliminate sex-bias in developing countries clearly articulates the need for such changes and presents guidelines for curriculum revision.

3396.   U.S. Agency for International Development. Office of Women in Development. *Differential Impact, Women in Media-Based Instruction and the Curriculum Revision Process, Phase I.* by Vivian Lowery Derryck. Washington, DC: The Office, 1979. 18p. S18.55:M46. General discussion explores the effect of changes in media technology and approaches to education in development projects, particularly projects aimed at women. Specific media-based instruction and curriculum revision projects which are related to women are reviewed.

3397. U.S. Agency for International Development. Office of Women in Development. *Jobs for Women in Rural Industry and Services.* by Ruth B. Dixon. Washington, DC: The Office, 1979. 54p. S18.55:J57. Statistical profile of the economic activity of women in developing countries accompanies suggested approaches for increasing women's opportunities for nonagricultural employment in rural areas. Statistics on the percentage of the economically active population which is female by employment status and occupation in 56 countries is furnished. A bibliography is included

3398. U.S. Agency for International Development. Office of Women in Development. *New Technologies for Food Chain Activities: The Imperative of Equity for Women.* by Irene Tinker. Washington, DC: The Office, 1979. 43p. S18.55:T22. Discusses the role of women in food production in LDCs and the impact of policies and new technology on women's work in food production, processing, preservation, and preparation. The author provides a concise overview of the role of women in third world economies and of the gender-bias present in many development programs.

3399. U.S. Agency of International Development. Office of Women in Development. *Women and Economic Development in Cameroon.* Washington, DC: The Office, 1979. 153p. S18.2:C14. Review of research and personal accounts are combined to describe the economic position of women in Cameroon society. Marriage and inheritance customs, education, motherhood and childrearing, and women's role in agricultural production are among the areas stressed. The report is indexed by subject and provides a 191-item annotated bibliography.

3400. U.S. Agency for International Development. Office of Women in Development. *Women in Development: Conference on the Role of Women's Organizations in Development, September 26-28, 1979.* by Pacific Consultants. Washington, DC: The Office, 1979? 75p. S18.55:C76. Report of the Conference on the Role of Women's Organizations in Development focuses on the possible role of women's organizations in developing countries in improving the conditions for poor women. Sessions discuss strategies for receiving governmental and non-governmental support. A bibliography, "Women's Organizations in Development," is included.

3401. U.S. Agency for International Development. Office of Women in Development. *Women in Forestry for Local Community Development: A Programming Guide.* by Marilyn W. Hoskins. Washington, DC: GPO, 1979. 58p. S18.55:F76. Examines the impact of forestry management practices on women in developing countries, and analyzes ways women can be brought into the local community development process in areas relating to forestry.

3402. U.S. Agency for International Development. Office of Women in Development. *Women in Migration: A Third World Focus.* by International Center for Research on Women. Washington, DC: The Office, 1979. 170p. S18.55:M85/3. Analyzes gender differences in migration trends in developing countries, and reviews factors which suggest why women migrate. The characteristics of women migrants are examined as is the impact of migration on family structure. Provides data on sex and age of emigrants and on sex differentials in out-migration from rural areas.

3403. U.S. Agency for International Development. Office of Women in Development. *Women's Organizations and Development: An Assessment of Capacities for Technical Assistance in Sri Lanka and Thailand.* by Lael Swinney Stegall. Washington, DC: The Office, 1979. 49p. S18.55:Or3/3. Profile of formal and informal women's organizations in Sri Lanka and Thailand looks at leadership, networks, interest in development and use of outside assistance.

3404.   U.S. Agency for International Development. Office of Women in Development. Mauritania USAID- Research and Development. *A Study of Female Life in Mauritania.* Washington, DC: The Office, 1979. 51p. S18.2:M44. Overview of the life cycle of Mauritania women from girlhood to old age reviews attitudes and customs towards women's education, marriage, divorce, economic activities, and male-female relations. The views of women on their place in Mauritania society are reflected in quotes from the study. The custom of force feeding girls to make them more attractive is also examined.

3405.   U.S. Agency for International Development. Working Group on World Conference on Agrarian Reform and Rural Development. *Women in Development.* by Elsa Chaney, Emmy Simmons, and Kathleen Standt. Washington, DC: The Agency, 1979. 40p. S18.55:C76/2. Discusses, from a women in development perspective, the items on the U.S. FAO World Conference on Agrarian Reform and Rural Development agenda. Topics on the agenda include access to land and water; agricultural inputs, credit, and services; education, training and extension; nonagricultural employment; and participation. Existing research relating to women's role in these areas is reviewed and a bibliography on women in development is included.

3406.   U.S. Agency for International Development. Office of Women in Development. *Evaluating Small Grants for Women in Development.* by Judith F. Helzner. Washington, DC: The Office, 1980. 36p. S18.55:Ev1. Presents a possible framework for evaluating small grant projects whose purpose is to increase the involvement of women in development activities.

3407.   U.S. Agency for International Development. Office of Women in Development. *Income Generating Activities with Women's Participation: A Re-Examination of Goals and Issues.* by Marilyn W. Hoskins. Washington, DC: The Office, 1980. 45p. S18.55:In2. Overview of development programs focuses on income generating activities which involve women. In particular, the goals, participation, and methods of judging success of these programs are examined. Some case studies of women only and gender-mixed projects are presented.

3408.   U.S. Agency for International Development. Office of Women in Development. *Keeping Women Out: A Structural Analysis of Women's Employment in Developing Countries.* by International Center for Research on Women. Washington, DC: The Office, 1980. 108p. S18.55:Em7. Review of the position of employed women in developing countries discusses poor women's need to work, the importance of women's contribution to a nation's economy, structural forces which restrict the level of demand for women workers, and other factors relating to the employment of low income women. Recommendations for policy interventions are presented. Includes a bibliography and provides statistics on labor force participation rates for women in 1960 and 1978, by country, for Africa, Middle East, Asia, and Latin America; female participation rates in agricultural and non-agricultural activities, 1978, by selected developing country; distribution of female labor force relative to total labor force, 1975, by country; and estimated female contribution to GDP by sector.

3409.   U.S. Agency for International Development. Office of Women in Development. *Limits to Productivity: Improving Women's Access to Technology and Credit.* by Ilsa Schumacher, Jennifer Sebstad and Mayra Buvinic. Washington, DC: The Office, 1980. 65p. S18.55:P94/2. Analyzes the constraints in women's access to technology and to credit in LDCs and presents policy recommendations for improving their access.

3410.   U.S. Agency for International Development. Office of Women in Development. *The Productivity of Women in Developing Countries: Measurement Issues and Recommendations.* by International Center for Research on Women. Washington, DC: The Office, 1980. 46p. S18.55:P94. Analysis of the flaws in current methodology of measuring economic participation of women in LDCs stresses the undervaluation of women's economic contribution. Recommendations for more accurate measures for planning purposes are presented.

3411. U.S. Agency for International Development. Office of Women in Development. *Successful Rural Water Supply Projects and the Concern of Women.* by Paula Roark. Washington, DC: The Office, 1980. 66p. S18.55:W29. An analysis of the stake women have in establishing water supplies based on their traditional roles and the resulting need to include women in development planning for rural water supply is presented. Much of the focus is on community participation and on the local learning process in the success of water supply projects.

3412. U.S. Agency for International Development. Office of Women in Development. *Various Perspectives on Using Women's Organizations in Development Programming.* Washington, DC: The Office, 1980. 48p. S18.55:Or3. Discusses the activities and expectations of groups involved in development projects which use women's organizations to help involve women. Ways in which the use of indigenous and non-indigenous women's groups in development programs can be strengthened are explored.

3413. U.S. Agency for International Development. Office of Women in Development. *Women and Energy: Program Implications.* by Irene Tinker. Washington, DC: The Office, 1980. 12p. S18.55:En2. Review of the energy needs of poor women in developing countries analyzes the implications of development programs for the availability of energy for subsistence level uses.

3414. U.S. Agency for International Development. Office of Women in Development. *Women in International Migration: Issues in Development Planning.* by Elsa M. Chaney. Washington, DC: The Office, 1980. 50p. S18.55:M58. Reviews and analyzes the extent of women's involvement in international migration and the effects of this migration on their lives both as migrants and as family left behind. The focus is on the need to take the migration patterns and the motivation for the migration into consideration in designing development assistance programs. Statistics presented include women as a percentage of all immigrants/emigrants by region. A six page bibliography is provided.

3415. U.S. Agency for International Development. Office of Women in Development. *Women in Mauritania: The Effects of Draught and Migration on Their Economic Status and Implications for Development Programs.* by Melinda Smale, U.S. Dept. of Agriculture, Office of International Cooperation and Development. Washington, DC: The Agency, 1980. 163p. S18.55:D83. Report and accompanying bibliography reviews the way women of various ethnic groups in Mauritania adapted to the extended drought and the related migration of the men. Income earning activities are the primary focus.

3416. U.S. Agency for International Development. Office of Women in Development. *Women, Migration and the Decline of Smallholder Agriculture.* by Elsa M. Chaney and Martha W. Lewis. Washington, DC: The Office, 1980. 56p. S18.55:M58/2. Review of the effects of the decline of smallholder agriculture on the economy and food supply of lesser developed countries focuses on the role of women in smallholder agriculture in LDC's and on the problems of male migration.

3417. U.S. Agency for International Development. Office of Women in Development. *Women's Involvement in High Risk Arable Agriculture: The Botswana Case.* by Louis R. Fortmann. Washington, DC: The Office, 1980. 32p. S18.55:Ag8. Paper prepared for the Ford Foundation Workshop on Women in Agriculture in Eastern and Southern Africa (Nairobi, 9-11 April 1980) reviews the problems of women as farmers in Botswana noting their lack of access to draft animals for plowing and their greater need for hired labor. Cooperative and government subsidized programs to address the problems are suggested. A bibliography of related materials published between 1969 and 1980 is appended.

3418.   U.S. Agency for International Development. Office of Women in Development. *Women's Organizations in Rural Development.* by Kathleen A. Staudt. Washington, DC: The Office, 1980. 71p. S18.55:Or3/4. Argues for the participation of women in politics if they are to be included in the development process. The literature on women's participation in politics and in women's organizations is reviewed, and the constraints on the organizational participation of women are analyzed. Policy implications of the information presented are discussed.

3419.   U.S. Agency for International Development. Office of Women in Development. *Women's Organizations: Resources for Development.* by Katherine Blakeslee Piepmeir. Washington, DC: The Office, 1980. 48p. S18.55:Or3/2. An overview of the role women's organizations can play in channeling development resources to women in LDC's is presented, and possible strategies for increasing the participation of women's organizations are suggested.

3420.   U.S. Bureau of the Census and U.S. Agency for International Development. Office of Women in Development. *Illustrative Statistics on Women in Selected Developing Countries.* Washington, DC: GPO, 1980. 24p. C3.2:W84/2 Indicators of women's status in selected developing countries in Africa, Asia, and Latin America are shown in thirteen charts detailing age of women, residence, longevity, childhood mortality, age at marriage, marital status, fertility, literacy, school enrollment, school completion, labor force participation, sector of employment, and professional occupation.

3421.   U.S. Agency for International Development. *The Role of Haitian Women in Development.* by Jacqueline Nowak Smucker. Port-au-Prince, Haiti: USAID Mission, 1981. 74p. S18.2:H12/2. Examination of the economic role of rural Haitian women explored the threat posed by development to some of women's traditional money-making activities. Constraints on women's employment opportunities, the successful "Food for Work" program, and the traditional values which affect women's role are noted. Recommends development assistance strategies and provides a lengthy list of references.

3422.   U.S. Agency for International Development. Office of Women in Development. *Creating a "Women's Component", A Case Study in Rural Jamaica.* by Elsa M. Chaney and Martha W. Lewis. Washington, DC: The Office, 1981. 36p. S18.55:C73. Describes a component of the Integrated Rural Development Project at Christiana, Jamaica, which focused on helping the women in the area by teaching nutrition and by encouraging vegetable gardening.

3423.   U.S. Agency for International Development. Office of Women in Development. *The Role of Women in Modernizing Agricultural Systems.* by Constantina Safilios-Rothschild. Washington, DC: The Office, 1981. 31p. S18.55:Ag8/2. Review of the literature on the involvement of women in agricultural production in developing countries emphasizes the need to consider women's role when developing modernization programs.

3424.   U.S. Agency for International Development. Office of Women in Development. *Women and Food: An Annotated Bibliography on Family Food Production, Preservation and Improved Nutrition.* by Martha Wells Lewis. Washington, DC: The Office, 1981? 47p. S18.55:F73/2. Bibliography of books and documents on food production and preservation and on improved nutrition focuses on family level production rather than industry production. Although the focus is on developing countries, USDA materials are included.

3425.   U.S. Agency for International Development. Office of Women in Development. *Women in Development: 1980 Report to the Committee on Foreign Relations, United States Senate, and the Committee on Foreign Affairs, United States House of Representatives.* Washington, DC: The Office, 1981. 399p. S18.55:W84. Detailed report of AID's participation in the activities leading up to the U.N. Decade for Women conference in Copenhagen describes small workshops and background papers and the recommendations of the conference. Other activities of AID offices and bureaus are detailed. The report also summarizes women's components of AID activities by country and the dollars allocated for women in development. Appendix includes a reprint of the *Programme of Action for the Second Half of the United Nations Decade for Women: Equality, Development and Peace* (U.N. document A/CONF.94/34) and a report on the nongovernmental organizations forum held in conjunction with the conference.

3426.   U.S. Congress. House. Committee on Foreign Affairs. *Foreign Assistance Legislation for Fiscal Year 1982, Part 1, Hearings.* 97th Cong., 1st sess., 13-23 Mar. 1981. 373p. Y4.F76/1:F76/57/982/pt.1. A portion of the hearing on the administration's authorization request for fiscal year 1982 foreign assistance programs discusses the need to fully consider women's role in development assistance programs, particularly in relations to their traditional role in agriculture. Population planning and health programs are also discussed in relation to women.

3427.   U.S. Peace Corps. Office of Programming and Training Coordination. *Third World Women, Understanding Their Role in Development, a Training Resource Manual.* Washington, DC: GPO, 1981. various paging. PE1.11:W89/2. Curriculum guide for training Peace Corps volunteers stresses understanding of the role women play in development outside of the U.S. cultural assumptions. The purpose is to effectively train volunteers to integrate women into development plans and projects.

3428.   U.S. Bureau of the Census. *Women of the World: Latin America and the Caribbean.* by Elsa M. Chaney. Washington, DC: GPO, 1984. 173p. C3.2:W84/4. Charts and tables provide a statistical profile of women in Latin American and Caribbean countries. Includes data on population by sex and place of residence; sex ratios by age group; literacy and school enrollment by sex and residence; labor force participation by age, sex, and place of residence; marital status by sex and age; fertility rates by place of residence and age of mother; and mortality rates and life expectancy by sex.

3429.   U.S. Bureau of the Census and U.S. Agency of International Development. Office of Women in Development. *Women of the World: Sub-Sahara Africa.* Washington, DC: The Bureau, 1984. 200p. C3.2:W84/5. Statistical compilation on women in Sub-Sahara Africa includes data on population distribution and change, literacy and education, women in economic activity, marital status and living arrangements, fertility, and mortality.

3430.   U.S. Congress. House. Committee on Foreign Affairs. Subcommittee on Human Rights and International Organizations. *U.S. Contribution to the U.N. Decade for Women, Hearing.* 98th Cong., 2d sess., 18 Sept. 1984. 281p. Y4.F76/1:C76/17. Hearing provides an overview of the role of the Agency for International Development in planning the Nairobi Conference of the U.N. Decade for Women and discusses changes in the inclusion of women in LDC development projects. AID projects which benefit women in LDCs are reviewed. In relation to U.S. participation in the U.N. Decade for Women, testimony reviews the progress of women in the U.S. during the decade with a particular focus on educational equity. Also discussed are possible attempts to politicize the Nairobi Conference.

3431.   U.S. Congress. Senate. Committee on Foreign Relations. *Addendum to Women in Development: Looking to the Future, Hearing.* 98th Cong., 2d sess., 7 June 1984. 4p.

Y4.F76/2:S.hrg.98-919/pt.2. Additional statement of Irene Tinker of the Equity Policy Center, Washington, D.C., critiques the structure of existing approaches to women in development and reviews the forces which come into play in deciding approaches to WID programs.

3432. U.S. Congress. Senate. Committee on Foreign Relations. *Women in Development: Looking to the Future, Hearing.* 98th Cong., 2d sess., 7 June 1984. 159p. Y4.F76/2:S.hrg.98-919. Review of AID initiatives to integrate women into the development process emphasizes policy and project support. Also discusses the United Nations role in women in development issues and the role of the U.S. in the Nairobi Conference of the U.N. Decade for Women. Agency and private organization witnesses provide a good overview of the needs of women in developing countries and of the efforts of agencies and of the women themselves to improve conditions in LDCs. Education and training, and private sector contributions to WID projects, are specifically discussed.

3433. U.S. Bureau of the Census and U.S. Agency for International Development. Office of Women in Development. *Women of the World: A Chartbook for Developing Regions.* Washington, DC: GPO, 1985. 70p. C3.2:W84/7 or S18.55:W84/3. Chartbook provides summary information on women in Latin America and the Caribbean, Sub-Sahara Africa, Near East and North Africa, and Asia. Topics illustrated include population, women in urban areas, sex ratios, literacy, school enrollment, labor force participation, single women 20 to 24 years, widowed women over age 50, female-headed households, fertility, infant mortality and life expectancy at birth.

3434. U.S. Bureau of the Census and U.S. Agency for International Development. Office of Women in Development. *Women of the World: Asia and the Pacific.* by Nasra M. Shah. Washington, DC: GPO, 1985. 141p. 63p. C3.2:W84/8. Provides data through tables and charts on the population, fertility, mortality, education, labor force participation, marital status, and living arrangements of women in Asia and the Pacific.

3435. U.S. Bureau of the Census and U.S. Agency for International Development. Office of Women in Development. *Women of the World: Near East and North Africa.* by Mary Chamie. Washington, DC: The Bureau, 1985. 195p. C3.2:W84/6. Statistical profile of the status of women in the Near East and North Africa includes data on population distribution and change, literacy and education, economic activity, marital status and living arrangements, fertility, and mortality.

3436. U.S. Congress. House. Committee on Science and Technology. *Prospects for Sustainable Development in Sub-Saharan Africa.* H. Rept. 99-1009, 99th Cong., 2d sess., 1986. 88p. Serial 13712. Report on sustainable development in Sub-Saharan Africa stress the need to include women in food production projects. Lower maternal and infant mortality rates and a continued high (7.5 children) desired family size are also discussed along with the unavailability of family planning services, particularly in rural regions. Recommendations for AID policies to address the food/population equations in Africa are presented.

3437. U.S. Congress. House. Committee on Science and Technology. *Prospects for Sustainable Development in Sub-Saharan Africa.* 100th Cong., 1st sess., 1987. Committee print. 88p. Y4.Sci2:100/B. Reprints H. Rept. 99-1009, 99th Congress (3437).

3438. U.S. Congress. House. Select Committee on Hunger. *Alleviating World Hunger: Literacy and School Feeding Programs.* 100th Cong., 1st sess., 1987. Committee print. 28p. Y4.H89:H89/3. First part of the report, entitled "Female Education and the Alleviation of World Hunger," reviews current knowledge of the implications for nutrition, health, fertility and agricultural productivity of women's educational level.

3439. U.S. Congress. House. Select Committee on Hunger. *Development with Women: Mainstreamed or Marginal?* 100th Cong., 1st sess., 8 Apr. 1987. 54p. Y4.H89:100-6. Expert witnesses discuss the role of women in third world economics and its implications for Agency for International Development projects. Adverse effects of past AID policies on poor women in LDCs are highlighted. The focus of the questions directed at the AID representative is on efforts to diminish the role of the Women in Development Office.

3440. U.S. Congress. Senate. Committee on Foreign Relations. *International Security and Development Cooperation Act of 1987, Report Together with Additional Views to Accompany S. 1274.* S. Rept. 100-60, 100th Cong., 1st sess., 1987. 183p. Serial 13733. Favorable report on a bill authorizing foreign assistance programs includes family planning programs, assistance to Africa, and instructions to better integrate women into development programs in Sub-Saharan Africa.

3441. U.S. Congress. House. Committee on Foreign Affairs. *Women's Perspective on U.S. Foreign Policy: A Compilation of Views; Report of a Women's Foreign Policy Council Informal Congressional Hearing at National Women's Conference, Washington, D.C., November 19, 1987.* 100th Cong., 1st sess., 1988. Committee print. 46p. Y4.F76/1:W84. Informal hearing begins by noting the almost complete exclusion of women from high level policy making positions in the area of foreign policy. Speakers discuss progress made in women's involvement in international affairs in the ten years since the Houston National Women's Conference. The status of women in the U.N. and in the U.S. Department of State is reviewed. The impact of the debt crisis in Latin America on women is explored. Witnesses also highlight the impact of women as a political force at the grassroots level. International family planning programs are also a topic of discussion with a focus on the health consequences of early childbirth and short birth intervals.

3442. U.S. Congress. House. Select Committee on Hunger. *A.I.D. and Third World Women, the Unmet Potential.* 100th Cong., 2d sess., 11 May 1988. 155p. Y4.H89:100-26. Hearing focuses on AID policy on the integration of women into development programs. Witnesses discuss the effectiveness of current policy and ways to improve programs to reach women in LDCs. Specific AID sponsored programs targeting women are described.

3443. U.S. Congress. House. Select Committee on Hunger. *Humanitarian Needs in Afghanistan, Hearing.* 101st Cong., 1st sess., 27 July 1989. 133p. Y4.H89:101-12. Hearing on U.S. assistance to Afghanistan includes discussion of the role of women in rebuilding the country. Within that discussion is debate over imposing Western ideas of the role of women on other cultures. Most of the discussion deals more generally with the rebuilding of the country and the role of foreign assistance.

Personal Author Index

Crouch, Richard E., 713
Cunningham, Sarah Jane, 695
Cutler, Sidney J., 1335

Daily, Edwin F., 1663
Dale, Deborah, 2339, 2359
Darryck, Vivian Lowery, 3394-3396
Dart, Helen M., 1604
Dawson, Deborah A., 1572
Defeis, Elizabeth F., 697
Del Pesco, Susan C., 679
Delfico, Joseph F., 2369
Dixon, Ruth B., 3397
Dodson, Diane, 2333
Donahue, A. Madorah, 2152, 2155
Dorn, Harold, F., 1335
Dorr, F. Andrew, 1578
Dresselhuis, Ellen, 693

Eaker, Elaine D., 1488
Eccles, Marriner S., 412
Edel, Leon, 258
Eillenchild, Margaret T., 1189
Elkstrom, Ruth B., 1181
Ellis, Florine J., 3335
Eslinger, Victoria L., 707
Evans, Anne M., 356
Ewing, Ellen B., 688

Ferguson, Patricia, 1721
Ferron, Donald T., 2483
Fessenden, Jewell G., 1688
Finch, Stanley, W., 3267
Finn, Peter, 3239
Fogarty, Faith, 3133
Foresta, Merry A., 300
Fortmann, Louis R., 3417
Fortune, Marie M., 3183
Fox, Lynn H., 1177
Frank, Josette, 1147
Franklin, Barbara Hackman, 1111
Freund, Ernst, 2254
Friedman, Barry L., 2503
Friedman, Kathleen O'Farrell, 690
Frysinger, Grace E., 1028, 1036, 1046, 1070

Gallagher, Ursula M., 2178
Gallup, Gladys G., 1069, 1089
Gappa, Judith M., 1243
Garfinkel, Joseph, 1722
Gaud, William S., 1924
Geis, Gilbert, 3346
Gelfand, Donald E., 1419
Gifford, Chloe, 61
Gillispie, Beth J., 1379, 1380

Gladstone, Leslie W., 765
Glassman, Caroline, 689
Glynn, Thomas J., 1424
Goldwaite, Vere, 853
Goodman, Janice, 699
Gordy, Amelia S., 1089, 1098
Grabil, Wilson H., 1719
Greenblatt, Milton, 1338

Hahn, Charles J., 3331
Hahn, Lorena B., 592
Hale, Annie Riley, 890
Hall, Florence L., 1044, 1049, 1056, 1063,
    1069, 1072, 1074
Hamilton, John, 1007
Hamm, Alice C., 1440
Hamos, Julie E., 3171
Harear, Mary V., 697
Harley, Marcia L., 687
Hausman, Leonard J., 2450, 2503
Heckman, John H., 439
Hellman, Forence S., 214, 219, 237-238
Helzner, Judith F., 3406
Henry, Michael R., 2367
Henslee, Tish, 1245
Hersh, Blanche Glassman, 1191
Herzog, Elizabeth, 2174
Hewell, Grace L., 469
Hill, Ann C., 678
Hill, Joseph A., 1587
Hoffman, Ann, 690
Hogan, Mena, 1084
Holden, Martha, 712
Holms, Emma G., 1108
Hormann, Denise, 3183
Horowitz, Robert, 2333
Hoskins, Marilyn W., 3401, 3407
Howard, Jean Ross, 281
Howard, Marion, 2180
Howe, Florence, 1175, 1190
Hunt, Eleanor P., 1679, 1686-1687
Hunt, Vilma R., 1727
Hutchinson, Louise Daniel 299

Irving, Holly Berry, 1782

Jayasut, Nantanee, 3385
Jelliffe, Derrick B., 1693
Johnson, Carolyn, 3148
Johoda, Marie, 44
Jones, Peg, 1245

Kackley, George L., 914
Kahn, Laura Jane, 696
Kaplan, Saul, 2272

Subject Index

Contraception and family planning
(continued)
  cancer risk, 1454, 1921, 1934, 2094-
    2095
  efficacy, 1921, 1934
  failure, 1945
  and heart disease, 1489
  labeling, 1366, 2025
  postmenopausal use, 1356
  research, 1945, 2062
  and smoking, 1366
  user health, 2062
  utilization, 1921, 1934
Contractual powers. *See under* Married
  women
Cooper, Anna J., 299
Coronary heart disease, 1488-1489, 1516,
  1553, 1576
  and oral contraceptives, 1489
  research, 1553
Corporation for Public Broadcasting, 648
Cosmetic surgery, 1522. *See also* Silicone
  breast implants
Cosmetics, adverse effects, 1409, 1499
  bibliography, 1409
Council on Domestic Violence, 3125
Courtship:
  radio script, 17
Cox-McCormack, Nancy:
  works, 212
Credit:
  lesser developed countries, 3409
Credit discrimination, 92, 125, 131-132,
  630, 634-636, 645-646, 650, 654-660,
  667, 673-717, 726-727, 734, 782. *See
  also* Mortgages
  federal enforcement, 734
  federal laws, 630, 650, 654
  Kansas, 645
  state laws, 634-636, 655-660-,673-717,
    727
  Utah, 646
  workshop guide, 667
Crime victims, 105, 168, 3355. *See also*
  Domestic Violence; Sexual Assault
  and the criminal justice system, 3355
  midlife women, 168
  statistics, 105
Criminal justice, 78, 149. *See also under*
  more specific topic
  sex discrimination, 78
  Texas, 149
Criminals. *See* Female offenders

Dalkon Shield, 1993

Dancers:
  radio script, 236
Daughters of the American Revolution, 336,
  343-344, 346-347, 351, 415, 485, 508
  annual report, 508
  insignia, 351
  memorial hall, 336, 343-344
  property taxes, 346-347
  racial discrimination, 415
Daughters of the Union Veterans of the Civil
  War 1861-65, 497, 502-503
Day care. *See* Adult day care, Child care
Defense Fuel Supply Center, 788
Department. *See* other subject
Depo-Provera, 1917, 2016-2017, 2022,
  2054, 2112
  export, 2054
  FDA decision, 2016-2017
  health risks, 2016, 2112
  Indian Health Service, 2112
  lesser developed countries, 2016, 2022,
    2054
  unapproved use, 1972
Depression, mental, 140, 143
  midlife women, 140
  research projects, 143
Diabetes, 1748, 1784
  bibliography, 1748
  pregnancy, 1748, 1784
Dickinson, Emily:
  stamp poster, 271
Diet, 1330, 1336, 1417, 1446, 1465-1466,
  1477-1478, 1506
  college women, 1330, 1336
  low income women, 1465, 1477, 1506
  metabolic response, 1336
Diethylstilbestrol (DES), 1341, 1350-1351,
  1357, 1369, 1392-1393, 1397, 1425,
  1440, 1455, 1486, 1972, 2001
  bibliography, 1369
  breast cancer, 1440, 1486
  cancer in offspring, 1341, 1350-1351,
    1357, 1392-1393, 1397, 1425,
    1455, 1486
  contraceptive use, 1350-1351, 1972
  FDA advisory committee, 2001
  regulation, 1341, 1350-1351, 1972
Disability insurance, 718, 732, 739, 749,
  752, 2678
  sex discrimination, 718, 732, 749, 752
  pregnancy, 739
Disabled, 40, 47, 184, 464-465, 470, 2060,
  2483, 2775, 2780
  family planning, 2060
  rehabilitation, 40, 47

About the Author

MARY ELLEN HULS is assistant professor and head of the Information Services Department at the College of St. Catherine Library. She is the author of *Food Additives and Their Impact on Health: A Bibliography* (1988).

DATE DUE

MAY 02 2001	